DATE DUE

DEMCO 38-296

CONTEMPORARY MUSICIANS

Explore your options!
Gale databases offered in
a variety of formats

DISKETTE/MAGNETIC TAPE

Many Gale databases are available on diskette or magnetic tape, allowing systemwide access to your most-used information sources through existing computer systems. Data can be delivered on a variety of mediums (DOS formatted diskette, 9-track tape, 8mm data tape) and in industry-standard formats (comma-delimited, tagged, fixed-field). Retrieval software is also available with many of Gale's databases that allows you to search, display, print and download the data

ONLINE

For your convenience, many Gale databases are available through popular online services, including DIALOG, NEXIS (Mead Data Central), Data-Star, Orbit, Questel, OCLC, I/Plus and HRIN.

CD-ROM

A variety of Gale titles is available on CD-ROM, offering maximum flexibility and powerful search software.

The information in this Gale publication is also available in some or all of the formats described here. Your Customer Service Representative will be happy to fill you in.

For information, call

GALE

 Gale Research Inc.
1 - 8 0 0 - 8 7 7 - G A L E

ISSN 1044-2197

CONTEMPORARY MUSICIANS

PROFILES OF THE PEOPLE IN MUSIC

SUZANNE M. BOURGOIN,
Editor

VOLUME 13
Includes Cumulative Indexes

 *Gale Research Inc.*

An International Thomson Publishing Company

I(T)P

NEW YORK • LONDON • BONN • BOSTON • DETROIT • MADRID
MELBOURNE • MEXICO CITY • PARIS • SINGAPORE • TOKYO
TORONTO • WASHINGTON • ALBANY NY • BELMONT CA • CINCINNATI OH

STAFF

Suzanne M. Bourgoin, *Editor*

Geri J. Speace, *Associate Editor*

Paul E. Anderson, Robin Armstrong, Barbara Carlisle Bigelow, Matthew Brown, Susan Windisch Brown, John Cohassey, Tim Connor, Ed Decker, Robert Dupuis, Stewart Francke, Simon Glickman, Joyce Harrison, Gina Hausknecht, Charlie Katagiri, Ondine E. Le Blanc, Jeanne Lesinski, Emily McMurray, Sarah Messer, Diane Moroff, Michael E. Mueller, Daniel Passamaneck, Nicholas Patti, Joseph M. Reiner, Joanna Rubiner, Julia M. Rubiner, Pamela L. Shelton, Sonya Shelton, Sandy J. Stiefer, B. Kimberly Taylor, Jordan Wankoff, Thad Wawro, Gillian Wolf, Megan Rubiner Zinn, *Contributing Editors*

Neil E. Walker, *Managing Editor*

Marlene Lasky, *Permissions Manager*
Margaret A. Chamberlain, *Permissions Specialist*
Susan Brohman, H. Diane Cooper, Pamela A. Hayes, Arlene M. Johnson, Barbara A. Wallace, *Permissions Associates*

Mary Beth Trimper, *Production Director*
Shanna Philpott Heilveil, *Production Assistant*
Cynthia Baldwin, *Production Design Manager*
Barbara J. Yarrow, *Graphic Services Supervisor*
Michael L. LaBlanc, *Desktop Publisher*

Cover illustration by John Kleber

⊗™ This book is printed on acid-free paper that meets the minimum requirements of American National Standard for Information Sciences—Permanence Paper for Printed Library Materials, ANSI Z39.48-1984.

♻ This book is printed on recycled paper that meets Environmental Protection Agency Standards.

ISBN 0-8103-5737-2
ISSN 1044-2197

10 9 8 7 6 5 4 3 2 1

ITP™ Gale Research Inc., an International Thomson Publishing Company.
ITP logo is a trademark under license.

Contents

Introduction   ix

Cumulative Subject Index   283

Cumulative Musicians Index   301

Introduction

Fills the Information Gap on Today's Musicians

Contemporary Musicians profiles the colorful personalities in the music industry who create or influence the music we hear today. Prior to *Contemporary Musicians,* no quality reference series provided comprehensive information on such a wide range of artists despite keen and ongoing public interest. To find biographical and critical coverage, an information seeker had little choice but to wade through the offerings of the popular press, scan television "infotainment" programs, and search for the occasional published biography or exposé. *Contemporary Musicians* is designed to serve that information seeker, providing in one ongoing source in-depth coverage of the important names on the modern music scene in a format that is both informative and entertaining. Students, researchers, and casual browsers alike can use *Contemporary Musicians* to meet their needs for personal information about music figures; find a selected discography of a musician's recordings; and uncover an insightful essay offering biographical and critical information.

Provides Broad Coverage

Single-volume biographical sources on musicians are limited in scope, often focusing on a handful of performers from a specific musical genre or era. In contrast, *Contemporary Musicians* offers researchers and music devotees a comprehensive, informative, and entertaining alternative. *Contemporary Musicians* is published twice yearly, with each volume providing information on more than 80 musical artists and record-industry luminaries from all the genres that form the broad spectrum of contemporary music—pop, rock, jazz, blues, country, New Age, folk, rhythm and blues, gospel, bluegrass, rap, and reggae, to name a few—as well as selected classical artists who have achieved "crossover" success with the general public. *Contemporary Musicians* will also occasionally include profiles of influential nonperforming members of the music community, including producers, promoters, and record company executives. Additionally, beginning with *Contemporary Musicians 11,* each volume features new profiles of a selection of previous *Contemporary Musicians* listees who remain of interest to today's readers and who have been active enough to require completely revised entries.

Includes Popular Features

In *Contemporary Musicians* you'll find popular features that users value:

- **Easy-to-locate data sections:** Vital personal statistics, chronological career summaries, listings of major awards, and mailing addresses, when available, are prominently displayed in a clearly marked box on the second page of each entry.

- **Biographical/critical essays:** Colorful and informative essays trace each subject's personal and professional life, offer representative examples of critical response to the artist's work, and provide entertaining personal sidelights.

- **Selected discographies:** Each entry provides a comprehensive listing of the artist's major recorded works.

- **Photographs:** Most entries include portraits of the subject profiled.

- **Sources for additional information:** This invaluable feature directs the user to selected books, magazines, and newspapers where more information can be obtained.

Helpful Indexes Make It Easy to Find the Information You Need

Each volume of *Contemporary Musicians* features a cumulative Musicians Index, listing names of individual performers and musical groups, and a cumulative Subject Index, which provides the user with a breakdown by primary musical instruments played and by musical genre.

Available in Electronic Formats

Diskette/Magnetic Tape. *Contemporary Musicians* is available for licensing on magnetic tape or diskette in a fielded format. Either the complete database or a custom selection of entries may be ordered. The database is available for internal data processing and nonpublishing purposes only. For more information, call (800) 877-GALE.

Online. *Contemporary Musicians* is available online through Mead Data Central's NEXIS Service in the NEXIS, PEOPLE and SPORTS Libraries in the GALBIO file.

We Welcome Your Suggestions

The editors welcome your comments and suggestions for enhancing and improving *Contemporary Musicians*. If you would like to suggest subjects for inclusion, please submit these names to the editors. Mail comments or suggestions to:

The Editor
Contemporary Musicians
Gale Research Inc.
835 Penobscot Bldg.
Detroit, MI 48226-4094
Phone: (800) 347-4253
Fax: (313) 961-6599

CONTEMPORARY MUSICIANS

Adam Ant

Singer

UPI / Bettmann

From his cult punk rock beginnings with his band Adam and the Ants to his solo fame, Adam Ant has been considered a vanguard in the music industry. He has been known for his outlandish stage wear, including feathered headdresses and face paint, and for paving the way for bands that followed him by changing the pop music business from the inside while he was on top. He initiated the now infamous photographers' clause that prevents the unauthorized use of his pictures, and his publishing company charged magazines twice the going rate to reprint his lyrics. Because of this, some have accused him of being a pompous rock star, while others have considered him a hero.

Adam Ant was born Stuart Leslie Goddard on November 3, 1954, in London, England. He had been an art student at the Hornsey School of Art in London before he placed a classified ad in the weekly British music paper *Melody Maker* in June of 1976 that read: "Beat On A Bass With The B-Sides." A few days later he met with Andy Warren and they formed the group the B-Sides. For about a year they rehearsed, then recorded a punk version of "These Boots Are Made for Walkin'" and promptly disbanded. The Ants made their debut not too long after that at the Roxy Club in London. Members came and went while the band made various appearances supporting other groups as well as headlining their own shows.

Antmusic Broadcast

Things started to happen for the Ants when they appeared in the Derek Jarman movie *Jubilee* and were featured on the soundtrack. In January of 1978 the band made their radio debut on BBC Radio 1's *The John Peel Session,* where they performed "Deutscher Girls," "Lou," "It Doesn't Matter," and "Puerto Rican." The group signed a two-single deal with Decca Records in July after recording "Physical," "Zerox," and "Friends & Cleopatra" in their second performance on *The John Peel Session.*

They went on a short European tour in September and October, then returned to record a demo of "Kick" in mid-November. The Decca single of "Young Parisians" floundered, and the band signed to Do It Records in the beginning of 1979, just before their first major U.K. tour. The Ants made a third *John Peel Session* performing "Ligotage," "Tabletalk," "Animals & Men," and "Never Trust a Man With Egg on His Face." In July they released the Do It Recordings "Zerox" and "Whip in My Valise" before embarking on the "Zerox Tour."

For the Record . . .

Born Stuart Leslie Goddard, November 3, 1954, in London, England. *Education:* Attended Hornsey School of Art, London.

Formed group the B-sides with Andy Warren, 1976; formed Adam and the Ants, 1977; performed radio debut on *The John Peel Session,* BBC Radio 1, 1978; signed with Decca Records, 1978; recorded debut album, *Dirk Wears White Sox,* 1979; embarked on solo career and released first album, *Friend or Foe,* 1982; performed at Live Aid concert, 1985; appeared as the first celebrity V.J. on MTV; developed and appeared in Honda Scooter television ad; appeared in films *Nomads, Slam Dance,* and *Trust Me,* and various TV shows, including *The Equalizer* and *Tales From the Crypt.*

Addresses: *Home*—Los Angeles, CA.

In August of 1979 Adam and the Ants recorded their debut album, *Dirk Wears White Sox.* In October of that year former Sex Pistols creator-manager Malcolm McLaren became the group's manager. He introduced the band to the Burundi drums of Africa, inspiring in Adam Ant a whole new musical concept. In January of 1980 *Dirk Wears White Sox* hit the U.K. independent labels chart at Number One. Shortly thereafter, McLaren coaxed the Ants away from Adam's artistic dictatorship so they could become "more autonomous" and paired them up with Anabella Lwin to form Bow Wow Wow.

Although he was left without a band, Adam Ant would not be defeated. He contacted Marco Pirroni, a guitarist whose work with the Models and Siouxsie & the Banshees he had admired. "We met in a cake shop in Covent Garden," Adam Ant told Paul Gambaccini of *Rolling Stone* magazine. "By the end of the day we realized we wanted to form some kind of Rodgers and Hammerstein writing thing." They teamed up with producer Falcon Stewart and bassist Kevin Mooney. Adam Ant, still hearing the pounding of tribal drums in his head, listened to ethnic recordings of tribal drumming and decided to recruit two percussionists, Merrick (Chris Hughes) and Terry Lee Miall, instead of one. "We couldn't achieve the cross-rhythms we wanted with just one drummer," Adam Ant explained to Gambaccini.

With the addition of the two drummers, the 14-date "Ants Invasion" tour began with a sold-out show. By July of 1980, the new Adam and the Ants were signed to CBS Records, and by August the CBS release *Kings of the Wild Frontier* broke into the U.K. charts. By the end of January of 1981, *Kings of the Wild Frontier* had climbed to the top of the chart. Decca reissued the "Young Parisians" single, and Do It reissued the singles "Zerox" and "Cartrouble," all of which promptly broke into the U.K. charts.

Went Solo

In 1981, with the release of the *Prince Charming* album, Adam and the Ants embarked on their sold-out "Prince Charming Revue Tour," which featured an Indian motif, war paint, and pirate costumes. "It's all part of presentation," Adam Ant explained to Gambaccini. "I just hope show biz never becomes a dirty word. I love it. I hope Americans will come [to the show] expecting entertainment, and not a heavy political message." In January of 1982 Adam disbanded the Ants, kept Pirroni as his writing partner, and decided to go solo. Still trying to capitalize on the wondrous success of Adam and the Ants, Polydor reissued the old track "Deutscher Girls" from the *Jubilee* soundtrack, and Do It issued the *Antmusic* EP, a collection of old Do It tracks.

His first solo effort as Adam Ant, "Goody Two-Shoes," was well received and became his first U.S. breakthrough hit reaching Number 12 on the U.S. chart. The album *Friend or Foe* was followed up by *Strip,* and a minor controversy surrounded the title track single. When Adam Ant refused to tone down the lyrics and the accompanying video for "Strip" at the request of BBC-TV, they blacklisted it.

Disappointed with the way things were progressing after the release of *Strip,* Adam Ant began to find other ways to present himself as a performer. During the hiatus, he formed an interest in acting. He played a small role in the film *Nomads* and then appeared in the title role in a stage production of *Entertaining Mr. Sloane* in Manchester, England. "That was probably the most dangerous thing I've ever done," he told Ethlie Ann Vare of *Billboard* magazine. "I wasn't about to get any quarter—not from the critics, not from the other actors. But I went in and rehearsed for four weeks, did a six week run, and got a favorable review."

Acting Career Blossomed

On July 13, 1985, Adam Ant was given the distinction of opening the U.K. segment of the worldwide Live Aid concert at Wembley Stadium. He released *Vive le Rock* in the same month, and the reception it received was disappointing. Later that year he decided to move to the United States to pursue a career in film and TV acting. Shortly thereafter, he appeared in the motion picture *Slam Dance* and in an episode of the television series *The Equalizer*. It was then, in 1986, that CBS decided to release a compilation album called *HITS*, which failed to chart. The only other recording he did that year was a collaboration with Stewart Copeland on the theme song for a movie, *Out of Bounds*. Adam Ant stayed on his musical hiatus until 1989 when he released *Manners and Physique*.

Always proud of the fact that his successes have come from hard work, and ever mindful of being exploited, Adam Ant related to Caroline Sullivan of *Melody Maker* magazine his attitude toward alcohol and drugs, both of which he completely avoids. "When people are around me, they think I will go nuts if they drink or light up a cigarette. I don't care. Drink your liver to a pulp, I don't care. But if it's drugs, if someone takes drugs around me. Why don't they just go jump out of a window?... I've *never* done a show under the influence of anything, and so I know every show I've done has been a result of my labours straight. It'd be horrifying to be only as good as your drugs." His work ethic has paid off for him in the entertainment industries. He continues to be a respected musician and songwriter, in addition to rapidly becoming a reliable "Brit" character actor for television and film.

Selected discography

Friend or Foe, Epic, 1982.
Strip, Epic, 1983.
Vive le Rock, Epic, 1985.

HITS, CBS, 1986.
Manners and Physique, 1989.
Antics in the Forbidden Zone, Epic, 1990.

With Adam and the Ants

Jubilee (soundtrack), Polydor, 1978.
Dirk Wears White Sox, Do It, 1979; reissued, Epic, 1983.
Kings of the Wild Frontier, Epic, 1980; reissued, 1985.
Prince Charming, Epic, 1981.
Antmusic (EP), Do It, 1982.
Peel Sessions, Strange Fruit/Dutch East India, 1991.

Sources

Books

Dickey, Lorraine, *The Ultimate Encyclopedia of Rock,* Carlton Books, 1993.
Rees, Dafydd, and Luke Crampton, *Rock Movers & Shakers,* Billboard Books/ABC CLIO, 1991.
Robbins, Ira A., *Trouser Press Record Guide 4th Edition,* Collier Books, 1991.

Periodicals

Billboard, September 28, 1985.
Creem, March 1983; May 1984.
Melody Maker, December 8, 1979; January 12, 1980; August 30, 1980; November 21, 1982; February 10, 1990.
Rolling Stone, April 30, 1981.
Trouser Press, January 1982; March 1984.

—*Charlie Katagiri*

Mildred Bailey

Singer

Mildred Bailey, the "Rockin' Chair Lady," began her singing profession demonstrating sheet music songs for individual customers in Seattle, Washington, when she was 17 years old. She would then go on to spend her entire career singing in the same intimate, person-to-person manner. Rather than shouting, scatting, or employing gimmicks, Bailey honored a wide variety of lyrics and melodies with her perfect diction and delicate voice, enchanting each listener who came under her spell. Some critics have questioned whether Bailey was truly a jazz singer or simply an exceptional pop singer. Nonetheless, her influence on generations of jazz vocalists who followed is unquestioned. Considered the first female microphone singer, Bailey taught the next generation how to use this new technology.

Born Mildred Rinker on February 27, 1907, Bailey grew up in a musical family. Her Irish father played the violin, and her mother was an accomplished pianist. Bailey's brother Alton would later team up with Bing Crosby and Harry Barris to form the famous Rhythm Boys singing group. When her mother died in 1917, Mildred moved to Seattle to live with an aunt. While she was struggling early in her career, Mildred was married to Ed Bailey, and though the union was short-lived, the name became permanent. As Mildred Bailey, she played piano for silent movies, sang in clubs of various kinds, and moved to Los Angeles, where her brother and Crosby joined her, penniless and jobless. She helped them form a vaudeville act that landed them a job in 1927 with Paul Whiteman, perhaps the hottest name in music.

Became Jazz's First "Girl" Singer

When the Whiteman troupe visited Los Angeles in 1929, Crosby and Al Rinker urged Whiteman to visit Mildred's home for dinner—and an audition. Greatly impressed, Whiteman added Mildred Bailey to his traveling group, and she was soon singing on his popular radio program. In his *Handbook of Jazz,* Barry Ulanov asserted, "Mildred Bailey set the standards for band singing, first with Paul Whiteman and then with the orchestra that she and Red Norvo led; she was generously gifted with preciseness of intonation and tenderness of phrase; she could sing with lilt or a larruping good humor, as the song required; she had rhythmic and tonal instincts that could do justice to every one of the able lyrics and better tunes with which a few song writers were providing jazz singers."

Thus Bailey became the first jazz singer—indeed, the first "girl" singer—to perform regularly with a band. In succeeding years, and throughout the swing and big band era, virtually every band would have a female

For the Record . . .

Born Mildred Rinker, February 27, 1907, in Teoka, WA; died December 12, 1951, in Poughkeepsie, NY; father was an amateur violinist; mother was a pianist; married Ed Bailey (divorced); married Red Norvo, c. 1931 (divorced, c. 1943).

Began career singing sheet music songs in a Seattle music store, 1924; played piano for silent movies; sang in Los Angeles clubs, 1925-28; joined Paul Whiteman Orchestra and began recording career, 1929; recorded first LPs under her own name, 1931; sang in Red Norvo's band, 1936-39; star of *The Mildred Bailey Radio Show*, 1944-45; performed intermittently as health permitted until 1951.

Awards: Silver Award, 1944, and Gold awards, 1945-46, *Esquire*.

vocalist; many of those singers were influenced by or would try to pattern themselves after the original.

Emulating Bailey was not an easy task. She brought a unique blend of qualities to her singing, beginning with a gossamer soprano voice, which darkened slightly in its later years, and an ever-present, almost–too-fast vibrato. Bailey sang simply, without pretense or adornment. Rarely substituting notes for the written melody, she relied on sure pitch and perfect diction throughout her career. The vocalist's sense of time—without which a jazz musician sinks—was elegant.

To her exquisite phrasing of even the most common lyric, she brought a feeling, an accent that imparted new light and meaning to the words. She would often sing slightly ahead of the beat, creating an urgency; at other times she employed a slight pause, a dragging of the beat, a stretching of a word, a shaded intonation, or a glissando to deliver the message. All of this seemed effortless and natural for Bailey.

Throughout her recording career, which stretched from October 5, 1929, with guitarist Eddie Lang, to an April 25, 1950, session accompanied by Vic Schoen's orchestra, Bailey sang the entire range of songs: popular novelty tunes, torch songs, blues, popular love songs, spirituals, and especially the great American classical music of the 1930s and 1940s. Believing that every song deserved her best effort, Bailey never sang down to a tune. In his *In Quest of Music,* Irving Kolodin remarked, "A special wing belongs to the Baileys of

jazz, those of the quieter but no less insinuating persuasion, whose art is in the chamber music category."

While Bailey's exposure to national audiences began with the outsized Whiteman orchestra, and while much of her radio and recorded legacy is with full-sized orchestras, some of her most appealing work was done with smaller, more intimate, "chamber-sized" groups. Even while singing with Whiteman for about five years, Bailey made recordings with other groups, many composed of other Whiteman musicians. Among the noted jazz musicians with whom Bailey recorded were trumpeters Bunny Berigan, Roy Eldridge, and Ziggy Elam; saxophonists Chu Berry, Coleman Hawkins, and Johnny Hodges; the Dorsey Brothers; clarinetist Benny Goodman; drummer Gene Krupa; guitarists Eddie Lang and Dick McDonough; and pianists Mary Lou Williams and Teddy Wilson. Included on any list of the most brilliant Bailey recordings are those with her Alley Cats (Berigan, Hodges, Wilson and bassist Grachan Monchur), those with her Swing Band (Norvo, Berry, Wilson, McDonough, and others), and those made with variations on the Norvo orchestra.

Acclaim and Frustration

One of the musicians Bailey met through Paul Whiteman was Red Norvo, the great xylophonist and vibraharpist. Bailey and Norvo were married for 12 years beginning in 1931, but their musical marriage proved far smoother than their personal relationship, which was marked by monumental and often well-publicized fights and arguments. Between 1936 and 1939 Norvo and Bailey performed and recorded regularly together as "Mr. and Mrs. Swing" with Red's band of various sizes. This group, spiced by the subtle, swinging arrangements of Eddie Sauter, produced what is considered to be some of the most sophisticated jazz of any era.

Bailey and Norvo's home was a regular gathering place for the elite of New York's jazz and show world. During one party the famous Benny Goodman trio was born. Goodman and pianist Teddy Wilson, aided by a guest who was an amateur drummer, spontaneously began playing together. Within months, on July 13, 1935, the first Goodman trio recording surfaced with Gene Krupa on drums. This group, with the later addition of Lionel Hampton on vibraphone, became the nucleus of what was probably the first integrated band to appear in public.

Bailey first recorded the famous song "Rockin' Chair" in 1932 with a Whiteman splinter group led by Matt

Malneck and recut it several times thereafter. The song was written for her by Hoagy Carmichael, and Bailey became permanently associated with it as the "Rockin' Chair Lady." Bailey, with her light, airy voice, was a study in contrasts. Extremely sensitive, Bailey could sometimes explode into temper displays, but her generosity was equally renowned. Friends and audiences enjoyed her ready wit and outgoing, sometimes boisterous manner. Though she never achieved the commercial success she coveted, Bailey was hailed by fellow musicians and singers.

Bailey sought perfection in her performances and expected the same from her accompanists. Toronto trumpeter Paul Grosney, sitting in with a Norvo group in New York in the mid-1940s, received one order from the leader: "Don't step on her lyrics!" Bailey was confident of her ability, but retained a modesty that bordered on self-doubt. She had listened early and often to the great jazz and blues singers who preceded her, especially Bessie Smith. Their styles were vastly different, however: Bessie's was raucous and mesmerizing, while Bailey's was understated and captivating. Smith's only appearance on New York City's 52nd Street, at the Famous Door in February of 1936, caused a sensation and was attended by Bailey. After the "Empress of the Blues" sang, Bailey refused to follow her.

Accolades for a Career

Commenting on Bailey's style, critic Nat Hentoff wrote in the *Progressive*, "Mildred Bailey may have been the first white female singer to understand what black singers and horns were about and to apply that knowledge to her own work without trying to mimic black ways of music.... That is, she used her natural, white, rather small voice.... But what she did with time, with the inner dynamics of phrasing, and with her clear, deep feeling for the stories she sang made her work unfailingly absorbing."

Surprisingly, Bailey's style and basic sound changed little from her earliest to her latest recordings, except for the added self-confidence and sophistication that came with experience. Her radio program of 1944 to 1945 was followed by several years of irregular appearances—often labeled "comebacks"—in clubs and recording studios. When she died in 1951, Bailey left a legacy of recordings for contemporary and succeeding singers. Among those who heard and understood Bailey's message were Irene Daye, Helen Humes, Ella Fitzgerald, Helen Forrest, Peggy Lee, and Kay Starr.

In 1962 John Hammond and Frank Driggs produced a memorial set of Bailey's Columbia recordings spanning from 1929 to 1946; complete with an informative booklet, the collection was re-released in 1981. This and other albums attest to Bailey's vocal strengths and help explain why jazz historian and critic Stanley Dance, writing in his *World of Swing*, called Bailey "one of the greatest jazz singers, a legend in her own time, and a witty woman of taste, temperament, and keen appetites." Bailey's important place in jazz history was recognized in 1994 when, along with other jazz and blues greats, she was featured on her own U.S. Postal Service stamp.

Selected discography

Mildred Bailey: Her Greatest Performances, 1929-1946, Columbia, 1962, reissued, 1981.
Mildred Bailey, a Memorial: The Rockin' Chair Lady, Realm, 1963.
The Mildred Bailey Radio Show—1944-45, Sunbeam, 1975.
Mildred Bailey, Tono, 1984.
Mildred Bailey: All of Me, Monmouth-Evergreen.

Sources

Books

Chilton, John, *Who's Who of Jazz,* Time-Life, 1978.
Dance, Stanley, *The World of Swing,* Scribner's, 1974.
Feather, Leonard, *The New Edition of the Encyclopedia of Jazz,* Bonanza Books, 1965.
Rust, Brian, *Jazz Records 1897-1942,* fifth revised and enlarged edition, Storyville Publications, 1982.
Schuller, Gunther, *The Swing Era: The Development of Jazz, 1930-1945,* Oxford University Press, 1989.
Shaw, Arnold, *The Street That Never Slept: New York's Fabled 52d St.,* Coward, McCann & Geoghegan, 1971.
Ulanov, Barry, *A Handbook of Jazz,* Viking Press, 1957.

Periodicals

Down Beat, September 1982.
National Review, March 12, 1963.
Newsweek, April 9, 1951.
New York Times, December 13, 1951.
Progressive, November 1985.
Saturday Review, January 14, 1967.
Time, June 14, 1948.

—Robert Dupuis

Chet Baker

Trumpeter, singer

MICHAEL OCHS ARCHIVES / Venice, CA

Periodically earning critical acclaim during a career made erratic by drug addiction and other personal problems, Chet Baker was a key force behind the "cool jazz" movement that originated on the West Coast and gained popularity in the 1950s. Baker "produced solos with an introspective beauty that epitomized the sensibilities of the 'cool' school," according to Len Lyons and Don Perlo in *Jazz Portraits.* He established his reputation first as a trumpeter playing with Gerry Mulligan's quartet, then as an instrumentalist and singer with his own combos. His movie-star good looks, similar to those of 1950s screen idol James Dean, helped ensure his popularity and made him a symbol of the cool jazz movement.

Baker played totally by ear and was a master of creating moods with his playing and singing. A sense of foreboding and sadness permeated his performances, and his often tragic life seemed to mirror his style. Avoiding any excess in his playing, Baker performed with what Owen Cordle in *Down Beat* called a "fragile lyricism" with "an undercurrent of melancholy." His soft and mellow singing voice matched the style of his trumpet playing, and he achieved a major hit with his signature version of "My Funny Valentine," which he performed with Mulligan. As Richard Mulligan wrote in *GQ,* "Grace[ful] and understated, [Baker's] voice was both haunted and haunting, imbued with a sexuality that made the issue of gender seem irrelevant by its urgency." Baker's interpretations gave new life to numerous ballads, which he favored, and he put his definitive stamp on many previously unknown songs.

Joined Charlie Parker

The son of a musician who could not break into the professional ranks, Baker came to California from Oklahoma in 1940. He started playing trumpet during his teens and by age 17 was jamming with famed saxophonist Charlie Parker at Billy Berg's club. He further developed his skill as a member of the Army band in Germany after he was drafted into the service in 1946. While playing with the Presidio Army Band back in California in 1950, he began showing up at be-bop jam sessions in San Francisco. Developing his talent rapidly, Baker moved to Los Angeles two years later and worked with Parker once more.

According to an *Interview* writer, Baker was "the maverick jazz trumpeter whom Charlie Parker once told Miles [Davis] and Dizzy [Gillespie] to watch out for." While in Los Angeles, Baker joined up with baritone saxophonist Gerry Mulligan's quartet. Considered somewhat radical at the time for jazz groups, Mulligan's band did not include a pianist. Mulligan's group became famous on the jazz scene, and Baker's reputation rose along with Mulligan's. The pair were part of a group of white musicians who softened the intense sound of be-bop ushered in by black musicians, and the result proved popular with the listening audience.

Referring to the West Coast jazz of the 1950s, Cordle said in *Down Beat* that "Baker's intuitive lyricism curled around Mulligan's thematically playful lines in a complementary counterpoint that practically defined the genre." Baker's restrained style of play, which verged on the classical, was likely influenced in part by Miles Davis's "Birth of the Cool" jazz sessions, and it proved to be highly effective in tandem with Mulligan's. "The harmonic textures created by the interaction of the two horns replaced the traditional background of explicit chords on piano or guitar," according to a writer for *Jazz Portraits.*

Topped Polls; Toured Europe

As his playing began attracting legions of jazz fans, Baker soared to the top of jazz polls conducted by *Metronome* and *Down Beat.* After his recording of "My Funny Valentine" propelled him into major stardom, he left Mulligan to form a quartet with California pianist Russ Freeman, who was known for his freewheeling style. Baker's appeal as a singer nearly equaled his popularity as an instrumentalist; following the release of the album *Chet Baker Sings and Plays* in 1954, he also earned a spot on *Down Beat's* poll of jazz vocalists. Years later, Baker told a *New York Times* interviewer, "I don't know whether I'm a trumpet player who sings or a singer who plays the trumpet."

Baker began a tour of Europe with Freeman's quartet in 1955 that lasted eight months. No other jazz musician from the United States had ever performed for such an extended period on that continent, and for the rest of his career Baker maintained an active presence overseas both as a performer and recording artist. Until late in the decade, the musician maintained his status as a top jazz artist by performing often and releasing a number of widely praised albums.

Drug Problems Hurt Career

By the late 1950s, Baker's reputation began to slide for both personal and other reasons. His addiction to heroin was starting to debilitate him, and a backlash against his similarity to Bix Beiderbecke's style fueled growing criticism. He worked sporadically in Europe from the late 1950s and into the early 1960s, in between dates cancelled for health reasons and due to arrests for drug possession. He spent almost a year and a half in an Italian prison, and at various times was deported from Great Britain, Switzerland, and Germany. Imprisonment also caused him to be replaced by Robert Wagner in the 1960 movie *All the Fine Young Cannibals,* which was based on a jazz musician similar to Baker. By the late 1960s Baker spent most of his time in Europe, because illegal drugs were less difficult to procure there than in the United States.

Just when Baker seemed to be rejuvenating his waning career in 1968, he was severely injured during a beating by thugs in San Francisco. Most of his teeth were knocked out during the fight, and it took nearly two years of recovery before he could perform again. At this point he made an attempt to free himself of addiction, periodically entering methadone treatment programs. During this period he learned a new use of applying his lips and tongue to the trumpet's mouthpiece, and also began playing the flugelhorn to expand his repertoire.

By the late 1970s his playing shifted into an even more expressive and forceful style, as shown on his albums *She Was Too Good to Me* and *Studio Trieste*.

Baker's various attempts at comebacks in his later years were long and difficult, and he often played in pain. He performed with a variety of musicians during the 1970s and 1980s, including in a reunion with Mulligan, but was never able to fully shake the drug problems that limited his ability to work. Baker would often disappear for months at a time, then resurface at a club with a new set of fellow musicians. Critics by this time had basically written him off as not having fulfilled the potential of his youth.

Death a Mystery

Various small combos led by Baker in the 1980s distinguished themselves by their laid-back and wistful style. He often played without a drummer to keep the sound as mellow as possible. In 1987 fashion photographer Bruce Weber made a documentary about Baker called *Let's Get Lost*. Weber followed the artist around for a year to make the film. A few months before the movie was to have its premiere at the Venice Film Festival, Baker died as the result of a fall from a second-floor hotel window in Amsterdam, Holland. Heroin was found in his bloodstream, and it remains unknown whether the fall was accidental or a suicide. At the time of his death, Baker was scheduled for a tour of Holland.

Although plagued throughout his life by his drug dependence, legal problems, and failed marriages, Chet Baker nevertheless made his stamp on the history of jazz both as singer and instrumentalist. His highly introspective style will remain as the ultimate symbol of the "cool" jazz movement.

Selected discography

Chet Baker Sings and Plays, Pacific Jazz, 1954.
Chet, Riverside, 1959.
You Can't Go Home Again, 1977.
This Is Always, 1979.
The Touch of Your Lips, 1979.
Peace, 1982.
Blues for a Reason, 1984.
Candy, Sonet, 1985.
Chet's Choice, Criss Cross, 1985.
Strollin', Enja, 1985.
Trumpet Artistry of Chet Baker '52-'53, Pausa.
It Could Happen to You: Chet Baker Sings, Riverside.

Sources

Books

Lyons, Len, and Don Perlo, *Jazz Portraits: The Lives and Music of the Jazz Masters,* William Morrow, 1989.

Periodicals

American Film, May 1989.
Down Beat, August 1988; August 1989; July 1994.
Esquire, December 1988.
GQ, April 1989.
Interview, February 1989.
New York Times, May 14, 1988.

—*Ed Decker*

Afrika Bambaataa

Rap DJ

© David Corio / MICHAEL OCHS ARCHIVES / Venice, CA

Afrika Bambaataa's personal history parallels the cultural history of hip hop, since he was there in the beginning as one of the first street DJs to achieve recording industry attention as well. Steven Hager, writing for the *Village Voice,* identified Bambaataa as "founder and number one DJ of the mighty Zulu Nation." Ian Pye called him "a cornerstone of black street culture" in *Melody Maker* in 1983.

Furthermore, at a time when rap music has become associated with gang violence and drug use in the minds of its critics, Afrika Bambaataa's voice and history remind audiences that hip-hop culture—of which rap is one facet—started as an effort to pull vulnerable inner-city youths away from the dangers of gang membership. In fact, Bambaataa was at the center of that effort, as the press has extensively documented. "Peacemaker, guidance counselor, spiritual advisor, and purveyor of the music in an adolescent, violence-ridden, and educationally-deprived context, Bam is hiphop's great facilitator," Gary Jardim wrote in the *Village Voice* in 1984. "Stopping bullets with two turntables isn't about sociology, it's about finding the spirit in the music and learning how to flash it."

Bambaataa was born in the Bronx River Projects in New York City in 1958. Describing Bambaataa's home turf, Hager commented that "it looks quiet here but this neighborhood once had a reputation for violence that was unequaled in New York." That environment offered Bambaataa both danger and cultural richness, and, for a time, he became caught up in the danger. In the 1960s the most powerful gang on the streets of New York was the Black Spades; Bambaataa became a member when the gang sprouted a division in the Bronx River Project in 1969, while he was still in junior high school.

Bambaataa admitted to Hager that he was "into the street gang violence. That was all part of growing up in the southeast Bronx." Bambaataa also recalled that the gangs were a part of the community and put a good deal of energy into aid-work. "The Black Spades was also helping out in the community," he told the *Village Voice's* Hager, "raising money for sickle cell anemia and gettin' people to register to vote." A childhood friend of Bambaataa's, however, informed Hager that "anytime there was a conflict, [Bambaataa] would try and straighten it out. He was into communications."

Bambaataa was also interested in politics at this time, bracketing his gang experience in a political consciousness nurtured on the Black Power literature of the Black Panther Information Center, which he was already visiting in the early 1970s.

Bambaataa's influence as a leader in the Bronx River
Project Black Spades grew until 1975, when he decided to leave the gang after two police officers ambushed
and killed one of his best friends. He threw himself into
the music that already supplied a real passion in his life.
"While other gang members were playing basketball
or hanging out on street corners," Hager commented,
"he was scouring record bins for obscure r&b recordings." Bambaataa has credited his mother for nurtur-
ing his early love of music, as well as initiating the
breadth of his musical knowledge. He was, in *Melody
Maker's* Pye's words, "fed on a healthy multicultural
diet, everything from early funk, to Caribbean and
African musics, by a mother with the biggest record
collection on the block."

A Founding Father of Hip-Hop

In particular, Bambaataa was polishing his talents as a
DJ. Bambaataa became an official DJ at a party at the
Bronx River Community Center on November 12, 1976,
spinning his records on a sound system that his mother
gave him as a graduation present the previous year.
"An independent entrepreneur armed with a portable
sound system and extensive record collection, the DJ
emerged as a new cultural hero in the Bronx in 1975,"
Hager wrote in the *Village Voice.*

Bambaataa was among the most prominent of the new
DJs, sharing the spotlight with Kool Herc, Kool Dee,
and Grandmaster Flash. When the *Source* interviewed
Flash, Herc, and Bambaataa for a hip-hop retrospective in 1993, the writer designated these three as "the
founding fathers of hip-hop music," and continued,
"as DJs in the '70s, these three brothers were the
nucleus of hip-hop—finding the records, defining the
trends, and rocking massive crowds at outdoor and
indoor jams in parts of the Bronx and Harlem."

Bambaataa used his reputation as a DJ to form a
largely nonviolent "gang," eventually known as Zulu
Nation. Bambaataa started the Zulus as a social group
at Stevenson High School before he graduated in 1975.
In a 1992 interview with Louis Romain from *The Source,*
Bambaataa explained that part of the purpose of the
crew was safety. "Sometimes," he told Romain, "you
could lose your equipment. Sometimes you might get
rolled on by a crew that didn't like your crew, so you had
to have a powerful organization. That's why I had a lot
of members in the Zulu Nation. But after that it started
branching off into a big social type and awareness
organization." That awareness, however, was something that admirers have credited him with encouraging. "Bam tells them not to drink, smoke, or take drugs,
and to stay in school until they get a diploma," a friend
of Bambaataa's told Hager in the *Village Voice.*

Zulu Nation Grew

A certain political impetus went even into the name of
the group, which originated from a film called *Zulu.* "I
thought *Zulu* was a great movie," Bambaataa told Pye,
"because for once the black man was portrayed as
brave, and sensitive. The Zulus fought like warriors, but
they also spared the British even though they could
have wiped them out." By 1977 the Zulu Nation was
spreading beyond the Bronx, and by the early 1980s
Bambaataa conjectured that the membership had grown
beyond a thousand.

Soon enough, the Zulu Nation even grew beyond New
York. "We even met some 'Zulus' in Cleveland, Ohio,
when we toured there," Bambaataa told Pye. Describing the Zulu Nation as "the single most enduring
institution in hip-hop," *The Source's* 1993 article argued that "while labels and clubs have come and
gone, the Zulu Nation emerged from the Bronx River
Community Center into a collective with adherents
around the world."

As the Zulu Nation flourished, so did Bambaataa's
reputation on the streets and at parties. Bambaataa's
fame as a DJ was shaped by his ability to mix incongru-
ous and unpredictable cuts, all the while keeping a
beat that compelled the crowd to dance. Hager's

description in the *Village Voice* of an early Bambaataa evening typifies his performance: "Bambaataa opened his show with the theme song from the Andy Griffith show, taped off his television set. He mixed the ditty with a rocking drum beat, followed it with the Munster's theme song and quickly changed gears with 'I Got the Feeling,' by James Brown."

"To me a lot of brothers and sisters are losing respect of the 'us syndrome' and getting into the 'I syndrome.' You can't build a nation with an 'I.'"

The *Village Voice*'s Hager reported that Bambaataa's "knack for coming up with unexpected cuts and 'bugging out' the audience earned him the title 'Master of Records.'" His work was further enhanced by the other DJ accessories of the time: breakdance crews and MC groups, or rappers, who would rhyme along freestyle to his mixes. His groups of choice included Soul Sonic Force, the Cosmic Force, and the Jazzy Five.

During Bambaataa's heyday as a street and club DJ in the late 1970s, record producers began slipping into the Bronx and Harlem, looking for talented DJs and rappers who might help the music industry make some money from this phenomenon. "Rapper's Delight," a single by the Sugarhill Gang, proved to be a gold mine for the Sugarhill label in 1979. "It was the single that would transform the grass-roots music movement into an entertainment industry," Eric Berman recalled in *Rolling Stone* in 1993.

But the transformation would take a while, since producers remained wary, not wanting to invest in too many hip-hop groups at a time and only wanting the safest sounds; they expected hip hop to fizzle after a brief fad. Bambaataa's first single, "Zulu Nation Throwdown," came out in 1980 on a small independent label and had nowhere near the success of "Rapper's Delight." After the release, however, Bambaataa discovered that the label's owner, Paul Winley, had added instrumentation to the mix, eradicating the hip-hop beat Bambaataa had laid down.

A year later, Bambaataa had another chance with Tommy Boy—a small label dedicated to marketing hip-hop music. A 1981 contract led to the 1982 release of "Jazzy Sensation" and "Planet Rock." The latter in particular, which Mark Dery described in Keyboard as "an unlikely fusion of bleeping, fizzing techno-rock,

Zulu surrealism, and deep-fried funk," became "the current smash in the streets, clubs, and airwaves of NYC," as Barry Cooper declared in the *Village Voice* in 1982. It not only went on to earn a gold record, but also earned one of the first five 12-inch gold records ever. The single was reportedly moving off the shelves at 650,000 copies a week during its peak.

"Planet Rock" became a milestone in the evolution of pop music culture, winning a broad spectrum of listeners and dancers to its electronic, eclectic brand of hip-hop. "Planet Rock" achieved precisely the goal with which Bambaataa had gone into the recording studio—to make a hip-hop record that would bridge the gap between the Bronx and the then-burgeoning New Wave music. New Music mogul Malcolm McLaren, quoted by Hager in the *Village Voice*, responded to the album with appropriate enthusiasm: "'Planet Rock' is the most rootsy folk music around, the only music coming out of New York City which has tapped and directly related to that guy in the streets with his ghetto blaster.... This music has a magical air about it because it's not trapped by the preconditioning and evaluation of what a pop record has to be."

The *Village Voice*'s Jardim raved over "Planet Rock" and its creator in 1983. He declared that "'Planet Rock' turned rap inside out last year" and argued that "D.J.s like Bambaataa are reprogramming, reprocessing, and twisting the insides of pop music textures to find the soul beat patterns of a pancultural future." An article that appeared *Melody Maker* identified "Planet Rock" as "probably the single most influential record of the Eighties, not only spawning an entire new genre of electronic funk but indirectly leading to a revolution in the way mainstream soul is conceived, recorded and mixed."

A Prophecy for Hip-Hop

By the time "Looking for the Perfect Beat" came out in 1983, Bambaataa was on tour in Europe with other DJs and rappers. He had become central to pop music in the United States and the United Kingdom, as evidenced by mainstream media attention. *Rolling Stone* identified him as "a DJ who perhaps has had more influence on hip hop than anyone else." Furthermore, Bambaataa and Zulu Nation were being hailed as miraculous peacemakers of the inner city. Tim Carr, writing for *Rolling Stone,* described Zulu Nation as "the only inner-city society of its kind ... a tribal-oriented peace-keeping force" and Bambaataa as "a cultural commissar, a former gang leader who has broken through the turf-conscious gang mentality that once terrorized the neighborhoods."

Bambaataa released one more single with Tommy Boy, "Renegades of Funk," just before switching to the French-based Celluloid label in 1984, where he quickly put together his first album, *Shango Funk Theology*. His new work continued to reflect his interest in bridging musical styles, from Jamaican reggae (he recorded with reggae musician Yellowman) to English New Wave. He created two new rap crews in Shango and Time Zone, both of whom were included on the Celluloid release.

Several more adventurous opportunities for Bambaataa came up in 1984, including the chance to record "Unity" with James Brown, recognized as the father of funk. Early in 1985, Bambaataa tried his hand at mixing black American funk with white British punk on the cut called "World Destruction," which he recorded with Public Image Ltd., the outfit headed by former Sex Pistol John Lydon. 1986 marked the end of Bambaataa's association with Soul Sonic Force. He was also experiencing disputes with both Tommy Boy and Celluloid, which held up the marketing for "Bambaataa's Theme," *Beware (The Funk Is Everywhere),* and "World Destruction."

Zulu Crew Turns on *The Light*

Only a year later Bambaataa moved again—this time to the major label security of EMI, where he recorded *The Light* with the Family, his umbrella name for the Zulu Nation crews that still recorded with him, and an eclectic cast of guest artists. Describing Bambaataa as "the founding figure of electro hip hop," *Melody Maker* listed the influences that showed up on the album: "Contributors span [pop singer] Boy George and [funk stalwart] George Clinton, Yellowman and Cabaret Voltaire's Mallinder. Every dance genre—go-go, electro-reggae, Seventies funk, hip hop, disco—tries to occupy the same space." A single from the album, called "Reckless" and recorded with the English reggae band UB40, broke the Top 20 in U.K. charts, demonstrating that Bambaataa's popularity was healthy in England, although it was ailing in the United States.

Bambaataa attempted to account for the way his career stumbled in the mid-1980s when he spoke with Andrew Smith from *Melody Maker* in 1991. "Suddenly I had to change and try to move in new directions," he told Smith. "It was a lot like what happened to [George] Clinton—I had to try to be on a thousand labels, [because] they were afraid of where I was heading. I got really tired of that. I was glad others were having success with stuff they'd got from me, [because] I'm a humble person, but it was frustrating, yeah. Also, I've

never been afraid to speak out against the industry, and that hasn't helped."

Although Bambaataa's recording career slipped during the early 1990s, he was still an active and popular DJ. After cutting *Decade of Darkness: 1990-2000* on EMI in 1991, Bambaataa decided to try a hand at his own label. He created Planet Rock Music, releasing his *Thy Will "B" Funk!* in 1992—just as Tommy Boy re-released the now legendary "Planet Rock" on compact disk. The label appeared to be unsuccessful, since the maxi-single "What's the Name of This Nation?" came out on Profile just a year later.

In the mid-1980s, Bambaataa had sensed the direction in which hip-hop was moving, as he told an interviewer from *Melody Maker*. "I feel that there's a plot to destroy hip hop coming from the record companies and government," he explained, "telling the youth to make crazy records about drugs and disrespecting women and be a clown, be a fool." Almost ten years later, when rap had become the most powerful force in the black music industry, Bambaataa saw his fears coming to life in the lyrics of some young rappers. "Today it gets sickening with the disrespecting of self," he told *The Source* in 1993. "To me a lot of brothers and sisters lost knowledge of self. They're losing respect of the 'us syndrome' and getting into the 'I syndrome.' You can't build a nation with an 'I.'"

Bambaataa located the problem with hip-hop music stemming primarily from the confines of a racist industry within which black artists have to work, explaining that the "white industry owns [hip-hop] now because they control all the record companies. And all our people that make money worry about Benz's and big houses and fly girls instead of being Black entrepreneurs. You need to take the business back."

Selected discography

Singles

"Jazzy Sensation," Tommy Boy, 1982.
"Planet Rock," Tommy Boy, 1982.
"Looking for the Perfect Beat," Tommy Boy, 1983.
"Renegades of Funk," Tommy Boy, 1984.
"World Destruction," Celluloid, 1985.
"Bambaataa's Theme," Tommy Boy, 1987.
"Return to Planet Rock (The Second Coming)," Warlock Records, 1990.
"What's the Name of This Nation?," Profile, 1993.

Albums

Unity, Tommy Boy, 1984.

Shango Funk Theology, Celluloid, 1984.
Planet Rock (includes "Planet Rock," "Looking for the Perfect
   Beat," and "Jazzy Sensation"), Tommy Boy, 1986.
Beware (The Funk Is Everywhere), Tommy Boy, 1987.
The Light, Capitol/EMI, 1988.
Decade of Darkness: 1990-2000, EMI, 1991.
Thy Will "B" Funk!, Planet Rock Music, 1992.

Sources

Books

Rock Movers and Shakers, edited by Dafydd Rees and Luke
   Crampton, Billboard Books, 1991.

Periodicals

Keyboard, November 1988.
Melody Maker, June 11, 1983; April 14, 1984; October 20,
   1984; July 19, 1986; February 27, 1988; November 2, 1991.
New York, May 20, 1985.
Rolling Stone, May 26, 1983; December 23, 1993.
Source, November 1992; November 1993.
Village Voice, May 25, 1982; September 21, 1982; January 25,
   1983; October 2, 1984.

—Ondine E. Le Blanc

Joanie Bartels

Singer, songwriter

Courtesy of Discovery Music

Joanie Bartels, arguably the most popular female performer of children's music of the 1980s and 1990s, engages her fans—roughly toddlers to eight-year-olds—with whimsical lyrics and an energetic style. Her bold-printed dresses and flamboyant hats and bows project an eccentric yet warm persona that does not intimidate her young audience. Praised in *School Library Journal* for her "refreshing way of not talking down to kids," Bartels was also voted favorite female vocalist in a survey of parents by *Child* magazine.

Bartels's appeal to children may have its roots in her own childhood; she was raised among seven siblings and says her parents encouraged musical play. Watching jazz vocalist Rosemary Clooney sing on television was Bartels's first inspiration. She revealed, "I remember watching her and thinking, 'That's what I want to be, a singer!'" Bartels began her musical career as a folksinger, playing the coffeehouse circuit. She sang lead for several jazz and rock groups and supplemented her gigs with jobs doing backup studio vocals. Her recording work included an appearance on pop singer Gino Vanelli's *Pauper in Paradise*.

Bartels entered the field that would bring her fame in 1985 with the release of her recording *Lullaby Magic*. Described by *Parenting* magazine as "a soothing slide into snooze-ville with pretty, lilting classics," the album became a runaway hit in the children's market. *Lullaby Magic* earned gold record certification of over 500,000 units sold, making Bartels the first female children's artist to be awarded the honor.

Bringing Parents and Children Together

Discovery Music, the company that released *Lullaby Magic,* had planned the album as the first in a series of children's recordings. Bartels went on to record a total of eight records in seven years for the *Magic* series. Using a variety of woodwinds, horns, strings, brass, and piano, the recordings feature Bartels's vocals and guitar playing. Ann Reeks, in *Parenting,* cited "her quirky lyrics and sparkling, limber voice" as the reason for her popularity among children. Bartels described the philosophy behind the series to *Billboard* in 1993, stating, "We made the *Magic* series to bring parent and child together. We depict different times of day and interactions and then present them in a fun, entertaining way."

The second *Magic* album, *Morning Magic,* was released in 1986 and included hits from Broadway lyricist Oscar Hammerstein II and the Beatles. The next in the series, *Lullaby Magic II,* followed the format of the first,

For the Record . . .

Born May 21, 1953, in Dorchester, MA.

Began career as folksinger; sang with jazz and rock bands and contributed backup vocals to recordings by other artists, including Gino Vanelli; became children's entertainer and released *Lullaby Magic,* Discovery Music, 1985; released first long-form video for children, *Simply Magic, Episode 1: The Rainy Day Adventure,* Discovery Music, 1993.

Addresses: *Office*—419 N. Larchmont, Ste. 13, Los Angeles, CA 90004. *Record company*—BMG Kidz, 1540 Broadway, Times Square, New York, NY 10036.

with one instrumental-only side and one side with vocals. This second lullaby album reinforced Bartels's position as a leading children's musician, though it did not match the popularity of the first.

As the series progressed, Bartels increasingly included her own compositions. *Travelin' Magic,* released in 1988, depended on many familiar sing-alongs, just as *Lullaby Magic* relied on traditional children's songs. But Bartels's next album, *Sillytime Magic,* highlighted the artist's own brand of silliness. She used sharp images, fun-sounding words, and the incongruities children love in lyrics like those found in her popular "Silly Pie": "You mix some wiggly worms and squiggly squirms and a buzzy bumblebee/ You shake it up and bake it up 'til you have a silly pie." The album received a grade of A+ from *Parenting* magazine.

Incorporated Dance

Christmas Magic was not received as favorably by critics; *Parenting* magazine awarded it only a C+, and *School Library Journal,* after noting its "Lawrence Welk flavor," a reference to the popular but—to some—bland bandleader, warned that it "may appeal more to some adults than to children." However, Bartels's 1991 release, *Dancin' Magic,* once again pleased critics, parents, and children alike. Some of the songs correspond to specific dances, such as the "Hokey Pokey" and the "Loco-Motion," though many are arrangements of dance music from the 1950s and 1960s and even earlier. Bartels also included some original songs, such as her "Dinosaur Rock 'n' Roll."

Bartels and Discovery Music branched out into videos in 1993 with *Simply Magic, Episode 1: The Rainy Day Adventure.* As Discovery Music's premiere video, the project benefited from the experience of writer and director Sydney Bartholomew, known for his award-winning contributions to the television program *Pee-Wee's Playhouse.* The video follows the adventures of three children and their magic babysitter, Bartels, who arrives one stormy afternoon while the children's mother is out. She fixes the electricity, phone, and television and jollies the children out of their fear of the storm and into eating, bathing, and napping. Incorporated into this story are songs from Bartels's records.

According to reviewers, Bartels's transition into the new medium was a smooth one. *Library School Journal,* for one, reported, "Bartels has a good on-stage personality and carries off the magic persona well." *Pulse!* remarked, "Coming off as a [film nanny] Mary Poppins/ [quirky pop singer] Cyndi Lauper hybrid, Bartels is positively vivacious in musical numbers that are a collage of colorful sets."

Bartels followed her successful entry into videos with another in 1994, *The Extra-Special Substitute Teacher.* As with her first such outing, songs from her *Magic* records are interwoven with the storyline. This time appearing as a substitute teacher, Bartels incorporates music into her history, geography, and dancing lessons. The video includes Bartels's own "Dinosaur Rock 'n' Roll," "The Martian Hop," and "Silly Pie," as well as arrangements of "La Bamba" and "Put on a Happy Face."

Broadened Stylistic Range With *Cafe*

In 1993 Bartels began a new series with Discovery: *Joanie's Jukebox Cafe.* The first outing, *Jump for Joy,* primarily includes songs written by Bartels and collaborators. Most of the pieces do not employ her customary background orchestration, relying more on techno-pop and encompassing styles from reggae to country. The recording is aimed at school-age children and focuses on emotions, such as the feelings of anxiety addressed in the song "New Kid on the Block."

Bartels is also a popular live performer, touring from coast to coast. She encourages participation from her audience, many of whom join in by singing and dancing. It's not unusual to see adults and children doing the "Hokey Pokey" or snaking through the aisles in a "Loco-Motion" dance train at Bartels's shows.

Bartels's popularity with children and parents has showed no sign of waning. The *Magic* series continues to prosper, having sold over 2 million units as of mid-1994. In fact, by then Bartels seemed poised to significantly expand her audience with her forays into video and new record series aimed at older children.

Selected discography

On Discovery Music

Lullaby Magic, 1985.
Morning Magic, 1986.
Lullaby Magic II, 1987.
Travelin' Magic, 1988.
Sillytime Magic, 1989.
Bathtime Magic, 1990.
Christmas Magic, 1990.
Dancin' Magic, 1991.
Joanie's Jukebox Cafe, Vol. 1: Jump for Joy (includes "New Kid on the Block"), 1993.

Simply Magic, Episode 1: The Rainy Day Adventure (video), 1993.
The Extra-Special Substitute Teacher (video; includes "Dinosaur Rock 'n' Roll," "The Martian Hop," "Silly Pie," "La Bamba," and "Put on a Happy Face"), 1994.

Sources

Billboard, February 13, 1993.
Parenting, August 1992; October 1993.
Publishers Weekly, October 18, 1991; April 19, 1994.
Pulse!, March 1994.
School Library Journal, March 1991; November 1993; February 1994.

Additional information for this profile was provided by Discovery Music, 1994.

—*Susan Windisch Brown*

The Bellamy Brothers

Country duo

Courtesy of Bellamy Brothers Records

The career of the Bellamy Brothers has traced the course of the Baby Boom generation across the varied and unpredictable terrain of country music. From the time their first single began to scale the peaks of the pop charts in 1979, Howard and David Bellamy have explored the passage of their generation, both musically and through their thought-provoking lyrics. And in a musical genre know for its love of vocal duos, the melodic, acoustic-backed country harmonies of the Bellamy Brothers have been among the most popular and enduring. In a career spanning several decades, the Brothers have had more hit country records than any other duo in the history of country music.

Howard and David Bellamy were born and raised in the west-central Florida town of Darby, the sons of Homer and Frances Bellamy. They resided on a farm that had been in their family for six generations. The boys worked alongside their father tending cattle and helping out in the orange groves of the family's 150-acre spread, while Homer divided his time between the farm and working at nearby ranches to help make ends meet.

Along with hard work, music held an important place in the Bellamy household. The record player would sound the lonesome yodel of Jimmie Rodgers or the recordings by Webb Pierce, Merle Haggard, and Hank Williams, Sr., that made up Homer's record collection. Homer, who played dobro and fiddle in his spare time, often had friends over during the weekend to play and sing bluegrass music, and his two sons quickly got involved "just for the fun of it," as David noted in a Little Horn Communications press biography. "We'd pick with [the migrant Jamaican workers] every year, and when they worked they sang," added Howard. "It was so amazing to hear them sing across the treetops, high on these long wooden ladders. They were like groups of their own, working up parts, doing call and response things with great rhythms. It's funny now; we thought everyone heard beautiful island music as a child." Meanwhile, their older sister introduced Howard and David to the tight vocal harmonies of the Everly Brothers, as well as the sounds of Elvis Presley, Ricky Nelson, and other performers whose music would serve as the roots of the youth culture of the 1960s.

First Gig at Rattlesnake Roundup

Howard learned to play the guitar, while brother David gained expertise on accordion before he discovered keyboards. The brothers made their first public appearance in a performance with Homer at San Antonio, Florida's Rattlesnake Roundup. It was 1958; the brothers would commemorate the event 31 years later by

For the Record . . .

David Bellamy (born September 16, 1950, in Darby, FL; married Susan Bond, 1993), guitar, keyboards, vocals; **Howard Bellamy** (born February 2, 1946, in Darby; wife's name, Ilona), guitar, vocals; sons of Homer (a cattle rancher and amateur musician) and Frances (a businesswoman) Bellamy.

Performed with rock group Jericho, 1968-69; produced jingles for local radio and television stations; signed with Warner Bros., 1975; released debut single, "Let Your Love Flow," 1976; signed with MCA, 1987; signed with Atlantic, 1990; established Bellamy Brothers Records, Nashville, TN, 1991.

Awards: Single of the year, Country Music Association (U.K.), 1979, for "If I Said You Had a Beautiful Body, Would You Hold It Against Me?"; independent video of the year award, Country Music Television, 1992, for "Cowboy Beat"; named duo of the year, German Country Music Federation, 1992; numerous gold albums.

Addresses: *Publicity*—Bridget Dolan Little, Little Horn Communications, 3108 Stoneybrook Rd., Oklahoma City, OK 73120.

our first royalty check, well, for the first time he considered what we were doing legitimate."

Signed With Warner Bros.

When "Spiders and Snakes" shimmied Stafford up the charts, the Bellamys struck out for Los Angeles to seek their fortunes as recording artists. Stafford provided them with a roof over their heads, as well as their first spot on television: an appearance on the Smothers Brothers' summer replacement program, which the veteran entertainer hosted. Stafford's producer, Phil Gernhard, heard some demo tapes that featured the brothers' vocal harmonizing and signed them to a recording contract with Warner Bros. Records. "Nothin' Heavy," the duo's first single, was recorded during some spare minutes of a recording session for pop singer Petula Clark in London; it achieved a good measure of regional recognition.

The year 1976 marked the Bellamys' jump to the top of the pop music charts as a vocal duo. "Let Your Love Flow"—penned by Larry Williams, a roadie for rock musician Neil Young—climbed to the Number One spot on the pop charts in ten countries and has since been counted among the world's biggest pop hits. Three years later, the crossover hit "If I Said You Had a Beautiful Body, Would You Hold It Against Me" became the first of the duo's 12 hits to reach Number One on the country charts, holding that position for three solid weeks before it was eclipsed. "You'll Never Be Sorry," released in 1986, outlasted even that as one of only nine songs on record to hold a position on the country charts for 27 weeks. In addition to doing so in the United States, the Bellamys' albums attained gold status in England, Austria, Germany, Norway, and Sweden; England and Scandinavia were so taken with the group that albums in both countries have gone platinum.

Accepted in Nashville Despite Crossover

Although the twists and turns in the career of the Bellamy Brothers have often moved them along outside the Nashville mainstream, they have not been treated as outsiders within the Nashville-based industry. Numerous awards have been conferred upon the group: they have been the country group most regularly nominated for awards from both the Country Music Association (CMA) and the Association of Country Music (ACM) since they broke ground in 1979.

While considered country artists, the Bellamys' musical influences have remained broad, encompassing not

organizing the first annual Snake, Rattle & Roll Jam. Performing quickly became a pastime, and the boys organized small pop-music groups; later, their love for soul music prompted them to add an African American vocalist, which ensured their popularity at area rhythm and blues clubs.

David joined a soul band, the Accidents, in 1965 and played organ for such artists as Percy Sledge and Little Anthony and the Imperials. In 1968 Howard and David joined musical forces. The brothers moved to Atlanta and formed the rock band Jericho, playing the southeastern club circuit for three years before disbanding to return to Florida and the family farm. They then began their songwriting efforts in earnest, as well as a lucrative sideline producing jingles for area radio and television stations.

During this time, David wrote "Spiders and Snakes," which would sell almost three million copies after it was recorded by pop singer Jim Stafford in 1973. That song was the real start of the Bellamys' musical career, not only in their eyes, but in the eyes of their father. "Our dad used to ask us when we were going to give this up and get real jobs," Howard recalled, "but when he saw only country, but folk, pop, and rock music as well. "We are a conglomeration of so many styles because of the era in which we were raised," noted the duo. "We've been influenced by everyone from the Beatles down to Crosby, Stills & Nash and Joni Mitchell, with a dash of 'island flavor,' since we were raised in Florida." As songwriters, the brothers have been challenged in finding that unique combination of thoughtful subject and clever hook or title that makes their songs stand out. In an effort to retain total creativity over their music, they formed their own record label, Bellamy Brothers Records—in partnership with Intersound Entertainment—in 1991.

The Bellamy Brothers' rock-styled brand of country music continues to stay within earshot of country music listeners in both the United States and Europe. Their Snake, Rattle & Roll Jam has eclipsed the Rattlesnake Roundup, drawing more than 20,000 people to country concerts benefiting regional charities. And Howard and David have continued to draw large audiences as a touring act, with lively stage shows enjoyable for both the band and the audience. "We're doing what we've been doing all along," Howard explained, "and it's taken us all over the world and stayed fun and exciting for us. It's been a really great run. It's become addictive, something we never want to give up."

Selected discography

The Bellamy Brothers (includes "Let Your Love Flow"), Warner Bros., 1976.
Plain & Fancy, Warner Bros., 1977.
Beautiful Friends (includes "If I Said You Had a Beautiful Body, Would You Hold It Against Me"), Warner Bros., 1978.
The Two and Only, Warner Bros., 1979.
When We Were Boys, Elektra, 1982.
Greatest Hits Volume I, Warner Bros., 1982.
Restless, MCA, 1984.
Greatest Hits Volume II, MCA, 1986.
Rebels Without a Clue, MCA, 1988.
Reality Check, MCA, 1990.
Rollin' Thunder, Atlantic, 1991.
Beggars & Heroes, Jupiter/BMG, 1992.
Best of the Best, Bellamy Bros. Records, 1992.
The Latest and the Greatest, Bellamy Bros. Records, 1992.
Rip Off the Knob, Bellamy Bros. Records, 1993.
Let Your Love Flow—20 Years of Hits, Bellamy Brothers Records, 1994.
Nobody's Perfect, Bellamy Bros. Records/Jupiter/BMG, 1994.

Sources

Books

Cackett, Alan, *Harmony Illustrated Encyclopedia of Country Music,* Crown, 1994.
Stambler, Irwin, and Grelun Landon, *Encyclopedia of Folk, Country & Western Music,* St. Martin's, 1983.

Periodicals

Country Song Roundup, June 1993.

Additional information for this profile was provided by Little Horn Communications, 1994.

—*Pamela L. Shelton*

Terence Blanchard

Trumpeter, composer

Terence Blanchard may be most widely known for his work composing music for director Spike Lee's films, but his deepest love remains with his own jazz trumpeting. When Blanchard rearranged his score for Lee's 1992 film, *Malcolm X,* into *The Malcolm X Jazz Suite* for his own quintet in 1993, *Washington Post* reviewer Geoffrey Himes called the album "extraordinary, landmark" and esteemed Blanchard as "[Wynton] Marsalis's only real rival as a modern composer of jazz suites in the Ellington mode." Then in 1994, *Down Beat's* Michael Bourne deemed *In My Solitude: The Billie Holiday Songbook* Blanchard's "most heartfelt album." This flurry of success in the early to mid-1990s followed a steady rise from Blanchard's New Orleans roots to his years starting in 1982 with Art Blakey's Jazz Messengers in New York and through his playing and recording in the late 1980s with fellow Jazz Messenger Donald Harrison.

In 1989 Blanchard's career was well underway, but he met with a nearly critical crisis. The trumpeter had been mistakenly placing his lips over his teeth instead of in front of them in forming his embouchure, his physical connection to his instrument. This caused a lip injury that led to a one-year hiatus from the trumpet. Frustrated in the midst of growing success, Blanchard would have to relearn his fundamental technique in proper form after his lips had a chance to heal.

Gave Dad Credit

Blanchard made it through the ordeal and emerged a leader on the jazz scene. He credited his father with teaching him the patience and wherewithal to overcome deep frustrations in his career—both in retraining himself through his crisis and in maintaining his inspiration during some longer tours on the road. Joseph Oliver Blanchard instilled discipline and determination into his son at a young age. The elder Blanchard was an insurance company manager and part-time opera singer in New Orleans who maintained his passion for music despite a racial stigma that precluded him from singing full time.

When at age five the young Blanchard began picking up TV show themes such as *Batman* on his grandmother's piano, Blanchard's father brought a piano home and hired a teacher for his son. Then he watched him practice. "He would actually sit there while I practiced," Terence recalled for Wayne K. Self in *Down Beat* in 1992. "He'd sit on the couch and listen until I got it straight. If I made a mistake, he would stop me and say, 'Go back; go back. Do it again; you've got to get it right.' I hated it; I hated it with a passion."

Born March 13, 1962, in New Orleans, LA; son of Joseph Oliver Blanchard (insurance company manager and part-time opera singer). *Education:* Studied under Ellis Marsalis at New Orleans Center for the Creative Arts (NOCCA); studied under jazz trumpeter Paul Jeffrey and classical trumpeter Bill Fielder at Rutgers University, 1980-82.

Trumpet player with New Orleans Civic Orchestra, in Dixieland gigs, and with big bands at the Blue Room in New Orleans, late 1970s; with Lionel Hampton's band, 1980-82; with Art Blakey's Jazz Messengers, 1982-86, as musical director, 1983-86; with Donald Harrison in a quintet, 1986-90; founder and leader of Terence Blanchard Quintet, beginning in 1990; performed concerts at Equitable Center, JVC Jazz Festival, New York, 1991; Orpheum Theater, New Orleans, and Jazz Tent, New Orleans Jazz and Heritage Festival, 1992; with Sonny Rollins, Carnegie Hall, 1993; as leader, Jazz at Lincoln Center, 1993; with Terence Blanchard Quintet, Village Vanguard, New York, 1993; and at Jazz Showcase, Chicago, 1994; has also played internationally; performed trumpet music for films; composer of soundtracks and music for films.

Addresses: *Record company*—Columbia Records, 51 West 52nd St., New York, NY 10019.

If his father introduced him to music and taught him aspects of character to stead him well in his art, then Blanchard's experience with legendary teachers of jazz developed his love for the trumpet into a striking ability. First, Blanchard studied with Ellis Marsalis at the New Orleans Center for the Creative Arts (NOCCA). Ellis Marsalis, father of Branford and Wynton Marsalis, introduced the trumpeter to the sounds of Clifford Brown, Miles Davis, Bird, and John Coltrane, all of whom would become influences on Blanchard's playing. Meanwhile, Blanchard continued his classical studies and played around town—in the New Orleans Civic Orchestra, in Sunday afternoon Dixieland gigs, and subbing for a big band at the Blue Room.

Hooked Up With Hamp

In 1980 Blanchard went to New York and studied classical and jazz trumpet at Rutgers University on a scholarship. The head of the jazz program there, Paul Jeffrey, connected Blanchard with the Lionel Hampton band. Blanchard played on the road with Hamp on the weekends while a Rutgers student for two years. Then Wynton Marsalis called Blanchard and fellow NOCCA grad Donald Harrison about taking his place in Art Blakey's band in New York. "We auditioned *in* the band at Fat Tuesday's," Blanchard told Michael Bourne of *Down Beat.* "One night we played a whole set while Wynton and Branford sat in the back. And then Art said, 'You're a Jazz Messenger now.'"

Blakey immediately urged Blanchard to develop his own style. "I used to come in and try to play like Miles Davis or Clifford Brown," Blanchard told Scott Aiges of the New Orleans *Times-Picayune.* "I remember I was playing 'My Funny Valentine' and he said, 'Look, you got to stop doing that, man. You got to pick a ballad that you can make your own and work on your own style and your own sound. Miles did that already. He put his stamp on it.'" With that insistence, Blanchard first imagined himself as a jazz leader. "And when he said that it was like, damn, I wouldn't even put my name in the same breath as Miles Davis or Clifford Brown, but he made me understand that I can have my own identity." One year after joining Blakey's band, Blanchard became musical director and had contributed some tunes of his own to the band's repertoire.

Led Bands, Scored Films

After four years with Blakey's band, Blanchard and Harrison set out in 1986 with their own quintet and recorded five albums, starting with *New York Second Line* in their first year. Blanchard had also worked on the soundtracks for the Spike Lee films *School Daze, Do the Right Thing,* and *Mo' Better Blues* before breaking with Harrison and signing on to Columbia with his own quintet in 1990. Blanchard's first two albums as a leader—*Terence Blanchard,* with Branford Marsalis and others in 1991, and *Simply Stated* in 1992—generated basically positive, although not glowing, reviews. Blanchard attributed that tepid recognition to logistical problems with his Columbia contract and to juggling studio schedules while working on Lee's film *Jungle Fever.*

With his next album, *The Malcolm X Jazz Suite,* culled and translated from the best of his soundtrack for Lee's film *Malcolm X,* Blanchard achieved broad and deep recognition for succeeding in a bold and ambitious project. A *New York Times* review by jazz writer K. Leander Williams included sympathetic comparisons to the legendary Duke Ellington. Both brought heightened force and energy to the extended suite form—a form which in 1943 with Ellington's *Black, Brown and Beige Suite* shifted jazz from a kind of popular music only to an art music as well. "Like the extended compositions of Ellington's later years," Williams wrote, "Mr. Blanchard's suite has succeeded in creating music that, while illuminated by his players, is indelibly shaped by its composer."

In the 1990s Blanchard remained as busy as ever. He continued to score soundtracks for Spike Lee movies, including 1994's *Crooklyn,* and contributed to other film soundtracks, such as *Sugar Hill, Inkwell, Trial by Jury, Housesitter,* and *BackBeat. Entertainment Weekly* considered Blanchard central to a general resurgence of jazz composition for film. Meanwhile, Blanchard recorded another bold album, *In My Solitude: The Billie Holiday Songbook,* for Columbia in 1994. Blanchard's deepest love remained with playing his trumpet, both in recording and especially live. "Writing for film is fun, but nothing can beat being a jazz musician, playing a club, playing a concert," Blanchard was quoted as saying in *Down Beat* in 1994. "When I stood next to Sonny Rollins at Carnegie Hall last fall and listened to him play, that was *it* for me.... You could've shot me and killed me right there, and I would've been happy."

Selected discography

(With Donald Harrison) *New York Second Line,* Concord Jazz, 1983.
(With Art Blakey) *New York Scene,* Concord Jazz, 1984.
(With Harrison) *Discernment,* Concord Jazz, 1986.
(With Harrison) *Nascence,* Columbia, 1986.
(With Blakey) *Live at Kimball's* (recorded 1985), Concord Jazz, 1987.
(With Blakey) *Blue Night* (recorded 1985), Timeless, 1991.
Terence Blanchard, Columbia, 1991.
(With Blakey) *Dr. Jekyle* (recorded 1985), Evidence, 1992.
Simply Stated, Columbia, 1992.
(With Blakey) *Hard Champion* (recorded 1985), Evidence, 1992.
(With Blakey) *New Year's Eve at Sweet Basil* (recorded 1985), Evidence, 1992.

(With Harrison and others) *Fire Waltz* (recorded 1986), Evidence, 1993.
The Malcolm X Jazz Suite, Columbia, 1993.
(With Harrison and others) *Eric Dolphy and Booker Little Remembered Live at Sweet Basil* (recorded 1986), Evidence, 1993.
In My Solitude: The Billie Holiday Songbook, Columbia, 1994.

Film soundtracks; composer

Jungle Fever, Motown, 1991.
Malcolm X, Columbia, 1992.
Crooklyn, 1994.

Film soundtracks; contributor

School Daze, EMI-Manhattan, 1988.
Do the Right Thing, Columbia, 1989.
Mo' Better Blues, Columbia, 1990.
BackBeat.
Housesitter.
Sugar Hill.
Inkwell.
Trial by Jury.

Sources

Billboard, July 13, 1991; June 6, 1992.
Down Beat, August 1983; October 1991; August 1992; May 1994.
Entertainment Weekly, May 13, 1994.
Los Angeles Times, August 15, 1993.
New York Times, June 20, 1993.
Time, May 16, 1994.
Times-Picayune (New Orleans, LA), May 1, 1992.
Washington Post, October 1, 1993.

Additional information for this profile was provided by Columbia Records Media Department publicity materials.

—*Nicholas Patti*

Pat Boone

Singer

During the 1950s Pat Boone was second only to Elvis Presley in rock music popularity; dozens of Boone's songs were hits, songs written and first sung in many cases by black artists such as Chuck Berry, Fats Domino, and Little Richard.

It seems fitting that the singer, born Charles Eugene Boone in Jacksonville, Florida, in 1934, claims direct descent from notable American pioneer Daniel Boone. A genial southerner, Boone lettered in high school varsity sports, was elected student body president, and was voted most popular boy at Nashville's David Lipscomb High School. There he met Shirley Foley, daughter of country and western star Red Foley. In his first year at David Lipscomb College, Boone married Shirley. Later he would transfer to Columbia University, graduating magna cum laude in speech and English in 1958.

In the early 1950s Boone won a talent contest and was selected to appear on the *Ted Mack Amateur Hour*. This exposure led the young baritone to a year-long string of appearances in 1954 on the *Arthur Godfrey Talent Scouts* show and some recording for Nashville's Republic Records. But it was a 1955 Dot recording, a mellow version of Fats Domino's "Ain't That a Shame," that hit Number One and marked the real start of Boone's career.

Recorded Covers of Early Rock Songs

Early rock pianist and singer Little Richard, for one, claimed not to resent Boone's cover versions of his songs. In an April 1990 *Rolling Stone* interview, Richard stated that Boone's versions were "a blessing" and added, "I believe it opened up the highway that would've taken a little longer for acceptance. So I love Pat for that." Nonetheless, decades earlier, after being outsold by Boone on the rocker's own creation "Tutti Frutti," Richard put "so many tricks in 'Long Tall Sally' that [Boone] couldn't get it."

In other interviews, though, Little Richard has taken a harsher view. In the 1987 documentary *Chuck Berry Hail! Hail! Rock 'n' Roll,* the fiery-tempered Richard admitted to "wanting to get" Boone, who he'd felt was stopping his progress. Boone was interviewed in the same issue of *Rolling Stone* and took the opportunity to defend himself. Boone pointed out that in those days, 95 percent of radio stations wouldn't play R&B. Boone remembered, "When I covered his [Little Richard's] music, he was washing dishes in a bus station in Macon, Georgia. His record was out there, but it wasn't going to sell enough for him to quit his dish-washing job until I covered it."

For the Record . . .

Born Charles Eugene Boone, June 1, 1934, in Jacksonville, FL; married Shirley Foley, c. 1952; children: Laury, Lindy, Cherry, Debby. *Education:* Attended David Lipscomb College; graduated magna cum laude with a degree in speech and English, Columbia University, 1958.

Appeared on *Ted Mack Amateur Hour,* early 1950s; appeared on *Arthur Godfrey Talent Scouts,* 1954; recorded for Republic Records, Nashville, TN; recorded for Dot Records, 1955; appeared on weekly television program *The Pat Boone Chevy Showroom;* appeared in films, including *State Fair, Mardi Gras, Journey to the Center of the Earth,* and *April Love;* published *'Twixt Twelve and Twenty,* 1960, *Between You, Me and the Gatepost,* 1960, and *A New Song,* 1970; appeared in *The RV Video Guide,* Paramount Home Video, 1989.

Awards: Israel Cultural Award, 1979; named one of ten "most watchable men in the world," Man Watchers Inc., early 1980s.

Addresses: *Office*—Pat Boone Enterprises, 9200 Sunset Blvd., Ste. 1007, Los Angeles, CA 90069.

Of course a few years later, the pathway paved, radio stations began playing songs by the original black artists. And not long after that, both Little Richard and Pat Boone alike were swept away in the tidal wave of the Beatles. Boone recalled how in the early 1960s his royalties dwindled and he and a painter named Leo Jansen supplemented their income with sales (presumably unauthorized) of Beatles portraits.

Boone always knew that Little Richard touched audiences in a way that he could not. He admitted that it took a dozen listenings for one of Richard's performances to strike Boone as anything other than wild and formless. He did not attempt to imitate this style and watered down the impact of Richard's work further by altering sexually charged lyrics. For example, "Boy, you don't know what you do to me" became "Pretty little Suzie is the girl for me." But sometimes the changes didn't sit well; Boone suggested retitling the Fats Domino number "Ain't That a Shame" to the more grammatical "*Isn't* That a Shame," but the owner of Dot Records rejected this idea.

A "blandly handsome" Pat Boone graced the cover of the August 19, 1957, issue of *Newsweek.* The singer,

hair neatly Brill-creamed, square jawed, dressed in a light plaid shirt and yellow sleeveless sweater, casually fingered an acoustic guitar. The magazine crowed that at 23, Boone had in two years cut a dozen singles selling over 13 million copies. And the singer had signed a three-million-dollar, five-year contract for a weekly TV show, *The Pat Boone Chevy Showroom.* Hollywood was offering the star a million dollars for a multipicture deal. Boone subsequently made some 15 movies, including *State Fair, Mardi Gras,* and *Journey to the Center of the Earth.*

Cultivated a Wholesome Image

Among its breathy pronouncements about Boone's career, *Newsweek* did admit that the star's voice was "quite unspectacular by any standards." Yet even superstar Frank Sinatra was charmed; the Chairman of the Board was quoted as saying that Boone was better than Elvis Presley and would last longer. Noting Boone's membership in the Church of Christ, the article reported that Boone adhered to church rules prohibiting smoking and drinking, though this cost him TV sponsorship by alcohol and tobacco companies. Boone went so far as to refuse to kiss actress Shirley Jones, though the shooting script of *April Love* called for it. Boone's rendition of the film's title song produced yet another hit.

"Even TV columnists, notoriously tough nuts to crack," reported *Newsweek,* "respect him." One such nut was quoted as remarking, "Wiseacres say he's corny but he's a good boy.... Hell, he may even get them [the kids] closer to religion." Rehabilitation of youth was, in fact, on the nation's mind: Boone shared the *Newsweek* cover with a banner headline from an article concerning less successful young men that blared: "Why Boys Kill—Why We Can't Control Them, OUR JUVENILE JUNGLES." Toward the end of the magazine's profile, a critic proclaimed, "The teen-agers are finally revolting against the musical delinquents.... [Boone's] full of charm, extraordinary poise, and ease. Why, this boy is the new [pop crooner] Bing [Crosby]."

By the time of the *Newsweek* article, Boone had already fathered three daughters, and a fourth arrived the following year. Their names were Laury, Lindy, Cherry, and Debby. Debby became famous as a singer in her own right, earning Grammys in 1977 and 1980 (for best inspirational performance). The song "You Light up My Life" made her an overnight sensation.

Boone's status as "the good Elvis," with docile hips, a smile instead of a sneer, and his signature white buck shoes, qualified him to publish a teenage advice book,

'Twixt Twelve and Twenty. All royalties were donated to the Northeastern Institute of Christian Education. The book's Number One best-seller success required a companion volume, which appeared in 1960, discussing romance "from first date to love and marriage." The tome was titled *Between You, Me and the Gatepost*. This book, too, did well. In one passage, "a pretty co-ed" who, lamenting America's materialistic obsession with clothes, cars, and televisions, noted, "It's a terrible thing to discover that we spend more time ... collecting and redeeming Blue Chip stamps than we do in prayer." Boone agreed, though he straddled the fence somewhat by adding that there was nothing really wrong with "a nice TV (especially if you watch the Pat Boone show)."

Faith Tested

Ironically, Boone's own marital life fell prey to difficulty. In his 1970 autobiography, *A New Song,* in a chapter entitled "The Darkest Hour," Boone revealed that though his wife had given up drinking, smoking, and dancing at his insistence, he himself had gradually acquired all these habits as a Las Vegas performer—and had picked up gambling as well. Yet Boone would not give them up when his wife asked. Shirley's love for him and the children began to "slip away," along with her faith in God. So Boone, in an emotional confession before a church congregation, began on a born-again path, and his wife soon found Christ, too.

The couple's born-again faith was immediately tested. On a September day in 1968, Boone was forced to fly to Los Angeles to meet with bankers concerning a $700,000 overdraft related to a disastrous partnership purchase of the Oakland Oaks of the now defunct American Basketball Association. Then, calling home, Boone learned that Shirley's father, Red, had just died.

Also that year, Boone's 13-year contract with Dot Records expired. Poised to sign with comedian and television star Bill Cosby's Tetragrammaton label, at the last minute Boone considered reneging, upset over cover art for the label's other new release: nude pictures of John Lennon and Yoko Ono on the *Two Virgins* album. After much prayer, Boone, ready to opt out of the deal, met with label executives. They were sympathetic to his religious concerns and agreed to a "reverse morals clause"—Boone's contract would lapse if the *record company,* not the performer, did something unseemly. Finally, it was agreed that no formal contract would be drawn up. This was fortunate for Boone, as a few months later the label went bust following Cosby's departure.

Preparing to back out of the contract was a bold move considering the Boones' money problems. The Oakland Oaks debt now amounted to two million dollars. Financial advisors told Boone he would soon have to declare bankruptcy. "It's in God's hands," Boone replied, serene in his newfound faith. Two days later, one Earl Foreman walked into the San Francisco bank handling the singer's affairs and tendered a check for two million dollars for purchase of the Oaks.

In the mid-1970s, often with his family, Boone recorded gospel albums, including *The Pat Boone Family Album,* on the Word label, and on the Lamb & Lion label, *New Songs of the Jesus People,* among others. He made some television appearances in the form of acne cream commercials with his daughters. Toward the end of the decade, he explored country music in albums such as *Country Love* and *The Country Side of Pat Boone.*

Throughout the 1980s, the singer strengthened his ties to the religious right, turning his talents to the anti-abortion movement. In the late 1980s, Boone appeared on *It's Gotta Stop! Artists Against the Abortion Holocaust,* a fundraising effort for the Christian Action Council. The most striking cut, according to a *Christianity Today* reviewer, was Boone's "Let Me Live," sung from a developing fetus's point of view.

The always active Boone has not limited himself to singing. Aside from occasional TV appearances and a regular radio show, Boone and family narrated the 1989 Paramount Home Video production of *The RV Video Guide,* which *Library Journal* deemed "an excellent introduction to the types of vehicles, both motorized and towed."

Selected discography

"Ain't That a Shame," Dot, 1955.
"I Almost Lost My Mind," Dot, 1956.
"Speedy Gonzales," 1962.
The Pat Boone Family, Word, 1974.
Country Love, DJM, 1977.
The Country Side of Pat Boone, Hitsville, 1977.
Pat Boone's Greatest Hits, MCA, 1993.
Pat's Greatest Hits, Curb, 1994.
New Songs of the Jesus People, Lion & Lamb.
It's Gotta Stop! Artists Against the Abortion Holocaust (includes "Let Me Live"), Diadem.

Sources

Books

Boone, Pat, *Between You, Me and the Gatepost,* Dell, 1960.
Boone, Pat, *A New Song,* Creation House, 1970.

Penguin Encyclopedia of Pop Music, edited by Donald
    Clarke, Viking, 1989.

Periodicals

Christianity Today, February 5, 1990.
Library Journal, August 1990.
Newsweek, August 19, 1957.
Rolling Stone, April 19, 1990.

Additional information for this profile was provided by Pat
Boone Enterprises, 1994.

—Joseph M. Reiner

Big Bill Broonzy

Singer, songwriter, guitarist

Frank Driggs Collection / Archive Photos

Big Bill Broonzy was among the finest and most influential of the pre-World War II Chicago blues singers, bringing the blues to new levels of sophistication; in his postwar career as a folk-blues singer, he introduced the music to white audiences, including many young guitarists—Eric Clapton for one—who became rock and blues stars in the 1960s.

Broonzy was born in Mississippi but grew up in Arkansas, one of 17 children of parents born into slavery. Like his father, he became a sharecropper, but in 1903 his uncle, Jerry Belcher, made him a fiddle from a cigar box and taught him how to play. Broonzy and his friend Louis Martin, a guitarist, played country string band music at parties and picnics until 1912, when Broonzy decided to become a preacher and so gave up secular music and abandoned his fiddle. A few years later he was offered $50 and a new violin for a performance; as Sam Charters told it in *The Country Blues,* he would have refused, but his wife accepted for him and spent the money, leaving him no choice but to play. He continued farming as well, but in 1916 drought wiped out his crops, and the next year he was drafted and sent to Europe to fight in World War I.

By the time Broonzy returned from the army, he had lost whatever taste he had for farming, and in 1920 he moved to Chicago to take a job with the Pullman Company. He was making good money, but he was ambitious, and music still appealed to him. Nonetheless, the country fiddle tunes he had learned in Arkansas held no appeal for sophisticated Chicago audiences. Though some sources describe him playing guitar in those early years, he told Studs Turkel in 1958, in an article reprinted in *Guitar Player* 15 years later, "I didn't play guitar until I came to Chicago.... Started in 1921, didn't get good at it until 1923. I must have been around thirty."

Learned to Sing the Blues

Broonzy got Papa Charlie Jackson, a popular blues singer, to teach him guitar, and he began pestering Mayo Williams of Paramount Records for a recording date. Williams was reluctant but finally agreed, and Broonzy's first record, "House Rent Stomp," backed with "Big Bill Blues," was released in 1927. It was not a success. In fact, Charters observed: "Bill's Paramount recordings were probably the most unpromising first records ever made by any blues singer. He was terrible. Arkansas had never had much of a blues tradition; so Bill had to learn to sing by listening to records. He was trying to imitate Blind Lemon [Jefferson], but he didn't have Lemon's voice."

For the Record . . .

Born William Lee Conley Broonzy, June 26, 1898 (some sources say 1893), in Scott, MS; died of lung cancer, August 15, 1958, in Chicago, IL; son of Frank (a farmer) and Mittie (Belcher) Broonzy; married Guitrue Embria, 1916; married Rosie Syphen, 1958; five children.

Worked as farm hand and itinerant preacher, Scott, MS, and Pine Bluff, AR, early 1900s-1917; played violin at local churches and parties; played violin at clubs in Little Rock, AR, 1919-20; worked for the Pullman Company, Chicago, beginning in 1920; accompanied various blues singers at clubs and on record, early 1920s; made first solo recordings, 1927; recorded more than two hundred songs for various labels, including Paramount, American, Banner, Champion, Bluebird, Vocalion, Columbia, Mercury, Chess, Verve, and Folkways; toured the U.S., 1930s and 1940s; worked as a janitor at Iowa State University, c. 1950; toured Europe and performed in South America, Africa, and Australia, 1950s; performed in Chicago area until 1957; appeared in documentary films *Low Light and Blue Smoke*, 1956, and *Big Bill Blues*, 1956. Composer of numerous songs, including "Key to the Highway," "Black, Brown, and White," "Just a Dream," "Hard Hearted Woman," "Romance Without Finance," and "When Will I Get to Be Called a Man." *Military service:* U.S. Army, 1917-19, served in Europe during World War I.

Over the next few years, Broonzy cut more records for Paramount and other labels and experimented with different styles. Many of the early records were "hokum songs," lighthearted, ragtime-based ditties, often with sexually suggestive lyrics; others were straight blues. None sold very well until 1932, when Broonzy made several records for the American Recording Corporation, which for the first time earned him some money.

In 1934 he joined forces with a piano player named Black Bob and began recording on RCA's Bluebird label and scoring real hits. Then, in 1937, he hooked up with another pianist, Joshua Altheimer, and added bass, drums, and sometimes trumpet or clarinet to form Big Bill Broonzy's Memphis Five—though he never seemed to have spent much time in Memphis.

The music, as Bruce Cook wrote in *Listen to the Blues*, "was a kind of good-time style that mixed blues with dance music," and, as *Country Blues* author Charters wrote, "Bill had found his own style.... He had been awkward and stiff as a shouter,... but as a warm, entertaining blues singer he had no equal." It was a polished, danceable, version of the blues, and it went over very well.

Broonzy was soon one of the most popular blues singers in the country, though his popularity was limited to black audiences—few whites had yet been exposed to the blues. Broonzy would soon change that. In 1939 record producer John Hammond was preparing for his second "Spirituals to Swing" concert at New York City's Carnegie Hall. He wanted to emphasize the roots of black music and had chosen Robert Johnson to perform as a representative of "primitive blues." But shortly before the concert, Hammond learned that Johnson had been murdered the year before, and Big Bill Broonzy was tapped as a last-minute replacement. He was, Lawrence Cohn wrote in the liner notes to the CD *Good Time Tonight*, "an unqualified hit, termed 'unforgettable' by some."

Became a Folksinger

The triumph was loaded with irony: Broonzy was by then the Vocalion label's best-selling recording artist with black audiences, playing his modern blues style, but the white urban intellectuals at Carnegie Hall mistrusted commercialism in music—they wanted their blues singers rustic. Accordingly, Broonzy was introduced as an "ex-sharecropper," Charters noted, though he had not been on a farm in over 20 years.

Nor was Broonzy's repertoire based in folk music. He was a prolific songwriter who had learned the blues from records and from the progressive Chicago scene. He was no rustic, but a consummate professional, and in the spirit of professionalism he gave the audience what it wanted: he became a folksinger for the evening, and, as Charters recounted, "when two young enthusiasts cornered him and asked him to sing some sharecroppers' songs, he managed to explain that he didn't want to sing any because he might have to go back to sharecropping."

Broonzy continued to play and record his modern, danceable blues while playing occasional folk-style concerts for white audiences. But by the late 1940s, the new electric-guitar-dominated blues of Muddy Waters—whom Broonzy had introduced to the Chicago blues scene—made Broonzy's sound outdated. He wrote in his autobiography, *Big Bill Blues*, "Some Negroes tell me that the old style of blues is carrying Negroes ... back to slavery—and who wants to be reminded of slavery? And some say this ain't slavery no more, so why don't you learn to play something else?...

I just tell them I can't play nothing else." By 1950 he had given up music almost completely and was working as a janitor at Iowa State University.

It was then that he was "rediscovered" by white folk musicians and audiences in the Chicago area, especially by writer Studs Turkel, who frequently had Broonzy as a guest on his radio show. He changed his style to meet the demands of his revived career: he roughened his voice, simplified his guitar style, used freer rhythmic structures than he had in the dance-oriented blues of his Chicago heyday, and added more spirituals and "folk songs" to his repertoire. His impatience with folk purists, however, gave rise to his most-quoted remark. "I guess all songs is folk songs," *Time* reported him as saying, "I never heard no horse sing 'em."

Took the Blues Overseas

In 1951 Broonzy toured Europe, one of the first bluesmen to do so; he later performed in Africa, South America, and Australia. Audiences were appreciative, especially in England; his records sold well, too, and were heard by many young musicians, including Eric Clapton, who credited Broonzy as one of his first influences and recorded Broonzy's "Key to the Highway" with his band Derek and the Dominoes.

By 1953 Broonzy was able to make a living at music, something that had rarely been possible even at the peak of his early popularity. He enjoyed his role as elder statesman of the blues and appreciated the impact the blues were having on popular music. Of Elvis Presley he said to Turkel: "I like what he's doin'. He's rockin' the blues, that's all he's doin'.... Rock an' roll is here to stay because it comes from natural people. Rock an' roll is a natural steal from the blues an' the blues'll never die. The blues can't die because it's a natural steal from the spirituals." But Broonzy was more ambivalent about Ray Charles's blend of blues and gospel, saying, according to Peter Guralnick in *The Listener's Guide to the Blues,* "He's mixing the blues with the spirituals. He should be singing in church."

In 1957 Broonzy was diagnosed with lung cancer. An operation left him voiceless, but he continued to perform on guitar for the remaining months of his life. He died in an ambulance on the way to a Chicago hospital in August of 1958. He had summed up his life and career in his autobiography a few years earlier: "When you write about me please don't say I'm a jazz musician. Don't say I'm a musician or a guitar player—just write Big Bill was a well-known blues singer and player and has recorded 260 blues songs from 1925 up till 1952; he was a happy man when he was drunk and

playing with women; he was liked by all the blues singers." As Bob Groom wrote in *Blues World* magazine, "He can safely be ranked as one of the blues immortals."

Selected discography

Big Bill Broonzy: His Story, Folkways, 1957.
Big Bill's Blues, Columbia, 1958.
Big Bill Broonzy, Volume 1, Document, 1986.
Big Bill Broonzy, Volume 2, Document, 1986.
Big Bill Broonzy 1934-1947, Story of Blues, 1986.
Black, Brown & White, Storyville, 1986.
(With Washboard Sam) *Big Bill Broonzy and Washboard Sam,* MCA, 1986.
Do That Guitar Rag, Yazoo, 1988.
Big Bill's Blues, Portrait Masters, 1988.
Big Bill Broonzy Sings Folk Songs, Smithsonian Folkways, 1989.
Big Bill Broonzy Sings Country Blues, Smithsonian Folkways, 1989.
Feelin' Low Down, Vogue, 1989.
Good Time Tonight, Columbia, 1990.
In Chicago, EPM Musique, 1990.
(With Memphis Slim and Sonny Boy Williamson) *Blues in the Mississippi Night,* Rykodisc, 1990.
The Young Big Bill Broonzy, 1928-1935, Yazoo, 1991.
Unissued Test Pressings: Le Hot Club de France, Milan, 1992.
Big Bill Broonzy 1935-1947, Best of Blues.
Historic Concert Recordings, Southland.
Big Bill Broonzy (1935-1940), Black and Blue.

Sources

Books

Broonzy, Big Bill, *Big Bill Blues: William Broonzy's Story as Told to Yannick Bruyoghe,* Oak Publications, 1964.
Charters, Sam, *The Country Blues,* Da Capo, 1975.
Cook, Bruce, *Listen to the Blues,* Scribner's, 1973.
Feather, Leonard, *The Encyclopedia of Jazz,* Horizon, 1960.
Guralnick, Peter, *The Listener's Guide to the Blues,* Facts on File, 1982.
Hardy, Phil, *The Faber Companion to 20th Century Popular Music,* Faber & Faber, 1990.
Keil, Charles, *Urban Blues,* University of Chicago Press, 1966.
Stambler, Irwin, *Encyclopedia of Folk, Country, and Western Music,* St. Martin's, 1969.

Periodicals

Blues World, August 1970.
Guitar Player, April 1973.
Time, November 23, 1962.

—*Tim Connor*

Ruth Brown

Ruth Brown's career has spanned five decades, but the 1980s made her the protagonist of a storybook comeback. Beset with such trials as a debilitating car accident that kept her in the hospital a year, she signed her first contract with Atlantic records, and, more devastating, the world's shift of interest from rhythm and blues to rock and roll, Brown's progress has been marked by hills and valleys. The 1980s and early 1990s found her atop a significant peak. Her album *Blues on Broadway* won a Grammy Award for best jazz vocal performance by a female in 1990; her performance in Broadway's *Black and Blue* won her a Tony Award for best actress in a musical, and a Keeping the Blues Alive Award in 1989. On her 65th birthday in 1993 she was inducted into the Rock and Roll Hall of Fame.

These accolades came on the heels, however, of years of financial hardship on Long Island, New York, where she worked as a bus driver, as a teacher for the mentally retarded, and a house cleaner, struggling to raise her two sons, Ronnie and Earl, alone. By this time each of her four marriages had failed. Indeed, as she told Steve Dougherty and Victoria Balfour of *People,* "If I ever write a book, Tina Turner's [life] would look like a fairy tale." Throughout these years she spent far too much of her hard-earned money trying to win back royalties from Atlantic Records—eventually, with the help of her longtime fan and lawyer, Howell Begles, she not only got herself some paychecks but helped to establish the Rhythm and Blues Foundation for other ill-served rhythm and blues stars.

Devil's Music

Born Ruth Weston in Portsmouth, Virginia, in 1928, Ruth grew up the oldest of seven children in a strict church-going household. Her father was a choir director with little patience or appreciation for "the devil's music," as he called the blues. She sang at church functions throughout her childhood, and was first paid to sing at a wedding when she was about seven years old. From then on, she told *Living Blues'* Chip Deffaa, she wanted to be a professional singer.

Ostensibly visiting relatives in New York City, she seized the opportunity to compete at Harlem's Apollo Theater's famed amateur night, where she won first prize for singing "It Could Happen to You." Afraid to tell her parents, she kept her success to herself while she struggled to overcome her own learned prejudice against the blues. But Brown found a way to embrace her calling. She told Deffaa, "Because I have become a woman and experienced life, I know that at one time or the other, the best Christian in the world has had the blues, about something. And it's not until you get the

Born Ruth Weston, January 30, 1928, in Portsmouth, VA; daughter of a choir director and a restaurant employee; married Jimmy Brown (a midshipman and trumpet player; marriage annulled); married Willis Jackson (a saxophonist; marriage ended); married Earl Swanson (a saxophonist; marriage ended); married Bill Blunt (a policeman; divorced); children: (second marriage) Ronnie, (third marriage) Earl.

Began singing career at local Emmanuel AME church; sang in nightclubs in Norfolk, at Langley Field Air Force Base, and Camp Lejeune; won first prize for Amateur Night at Harlem's Apollo Theater; worked briefly for Lucky Milliner; sang in Blanche Calloway's club, Washington, DC; signed contract with Atlantic and released *So Long,* 1949; worked variously as a singer, bus driver, teacher, and house cleaner, 1960s and 1970s; appeared on television in *Sanford and Son,* 1974, *Hello Larry,* 1979-81, and *Checking In,* 1981; appeared onstage as Mahalia Jackson in *Selma* and Off-Broadway in *Amen Corner, Champeen,* and *Stagger Lee,* 1983-87; subject of PBS documentary, *That Rhythm, Those Blues,* 1988; appeared in film *Hairspray,* 1988; played leading role in Broadway production *Black and Blue,* 1989; hosted National Public Radio series *BlueStage,* 1989.

Awards: Bessie Smith Award, *Pittsburgh Courier,* 1953; Grammy Award for best female jazz vocal performance, 1989, for *Blues on Broadway;* Tony Award for best performance by a leading actress in a musical, 1989, Blues Alive Award, 1989, and Outer Critics Circle Award, 1990, all for *Black and Blue;* Image Award from National Association for the Advancement of Colored People (NAACP); Trailblazer Award from One Hundred Black Women; the city of Philadelphia established a Ruth Brown Achievement Award; Portsmouth established a Ruth Brown Scholarship fund for students in the performing arts; inducted into Rock and Roll Hall of Fame, 1993.

Addresses: *Home*—New York City. *Record company*—Fantasy Inc., Tenth and Parker, Berkeley, CA 94710.

blues that you go to Christ for help."

Brown listened attentively to many types of music throughout her career, and various influences can be heard in her own music. Most obviously, Brown owes a debt to Billie Holiday and Ella Fitzgerald, but pop music also had its effect. With the rest of the country, Brown listened to Bing Crosby, the Andrews Sisters, Glenn Miller, and Vaughan Monroe, and she sang their songs effectively, though in later years she voiced a little contempt for pop music.

Though she broke into the industry with the success of "Lucky Lips," by pop songwriting duo Leiber and Stoller, she admitted to Lee Jeske of *Rolling Stone* that she "felt kind of ridiculous singing, 'When I was just a little girl, with long and silky curls.' Never had no long and silky curls in all my life," she announced succinctly. And when Patti Page, Tony Bennet, Georgia Gibbs, and Kay Starr—all white—covered her songs, "it didn't do a damn thing," she made clear to Jeske, "except stop me from getting on the top TV shows. I never got to do *The Ed Sullivan Show.* Patti Page did."

Brown first heard black singers on a radio show called "The Mail Bag," which introduced her to the Ink Spots, the Charioteers, and Sonny Til and the Orioles. She has hosted her own radio shows, "Blues Stages" and "Harlem Hit Parade," which spotlighted black rhythm and blues musicians. Racial issues have been with her from the start. In the 1940s and 1950s, she told *Billboard's* Nelson George, "it was a major decision for a sharecropper whether or not they were going to save that money or go to the show."

Back in the early days of her professional life, Brown explained to Jeske, "the concerts would be—downstairs where the dancers were—jampacked black. Upstairs balcony, all the way around, white spectators.... [Sometimes] they had a dividing line on the floor...; sometimes just a clothesline.... Or there would be some big, burly white cops." Brown sang her way through these obstacles, eventually finding wider and wider audiences through an acting career. Actor Redd Foxx showed off her dramatic talents both on *Sanford and Son* and by giving her the part of Mahalia Jackson in *Selma.* She headlined in two other short-lived sitcoms, *Hello Larry* and *Checking In,* and finally achieved stardom in *Black and Blue.*

Proud of *Black and Blue*

Black and Blue played first in Paris, where nightly, Brown proudly related to George, "we received 12-13 curtain calls." The show was particularly important for its realistic depiction of blacks, according to Brown. She did not need to look like a lithe starlette to play her role; to the contrary, she needed only to look like herself. After the show, she boasted to Stephanie Stein of *Down Beat,* black people would come up and say, "'I am so proud.' That is my paycheck.... I'm really singing my life out here."

The days of sneaking out to clubs in Portsmouth, Virginia; of being discovered first by Lucky Milliner, Blanche Calloway (Cab's sister), and finally by Herb Abramson and Ahmet Ertegun of the just-born Atlantic label; of singing "Mambo Baby" during the 1954 mambo craze; and of thrilling her listeners with "Mama, He Treats Your Daughter Mean," made Brown savvy and wise. Many critics find her work of the 1980s and 1990s her strongest. She remarked to Deffaa, "It took all those years to get to this point."

Brown has concerned herself with quality, and warns against the dangers of too many electronic studios, engineers, and producers. "I'm listening to singers closer than I ever did before," she told Deffaa in 1990. "Because the lyrics are becoming very important. And I think that's the saving grace right now. Otherwise we're going to look up and not have no singers left.... [Unless] we get some people who are sensitive enough to look inside the lyric, we ain't going to have no more [Dinah Shores] and no more [Billie Holidays] and no more [Ella Fitzgeralds] to interpret that lyric."

Queen in Her Own Right

Billie Holiday, Brown told *People,* was smart enough to whip Brown into shape: "If you copy my music, no one will ever copy yours," she berated Brown. So Brown stopped imitating and became, for example, the woman who made *Blues on Broadway,* which Ron Weinstock of *Living Blues* called "simply great stuff and one of the best recordings I've heard in 1989." A writer for *Stereo Review* recounted the experience of listening to *Fine and Mellow:* "Listening to this ... Ruth Brown album is like taking a stroll down memory lane and on into the kind of crowded, smoke-filled club where countless organ-and-vocal combos delighted weekend crowds.... Nobody sings [rhythm and blues] better today."

Rhythm and blues remain Ruth Brown's cause. With great poignancy, she told Deffaa, "If I were ever to really get lucky, really what I would like to do is to take some of that vast farmland back [in Portsmouth] and build a little community for the ... senior citizens from the rhythm and blues business like myself ... who just need a place to pick up their dignity." The disclaimer notwithstanding, Ruth Brown's dignity seems very much intact.

Selected discography

So Long, Atlantic, 1949.
Gospel Time, Lection Records, 1963, reissued, 1989.
Have a Good Time, Fantasy, 1988.
Blues on Broadway, Fantasy, 1989.
Ruth Brown: Miss Rhythm, Atlantic, 1989.
(Contributor) *Black and Blue,* DRG, 1990.
Fine and Mellow, Fantasy, 1992.
The Songs of My Life, Fantasy, 1993.

Sources

Billboard, April 8, 1989; January 25, 1992; August 28, 1993.
Down Beat, March 1990; August 1990; December 1993.
Essence, April 1988.
Jet, February 1, 1993.
Living Blues, May/June 1990; July/August 1990.
People Weekly, March 6, 1989.
Rolling Stone, April 19, 1990; February 4, 1993.
Stereo Review, April 1990; July 1992.

Additional information for this profile was obtained from Fantasy Inc. publicity materials, 1993.

—*Diane Moroff*

Grace Bumbry

Opera singer

Ancient Egypt, Macbeth's Scotland, Spain—singer Grace Bumbry has been transporting opera fans to such exotic worlds for more than 30 years. Initially trained as a mezzo-soprano, she switched to the slightly higher soprano register in 1970. Both repertoires have always shown a voice of silken purity that teams with a vibrant ability to bring operatic characters to life.

Bumbry's schedule is filled a year in advance, but every couple of months between tours she manages to fit in visits with her family. In addition, she finds time to guide young singers and lecture to disadvantaged teenagers about the undisputed benefits of concentration and hard work.

Grace Bumbry was born in 1937 in St. Louis, Missouri, to a freight handler for the Cotton Belt Route railroad and his wife, a Mississippi schoolteacher who had once dreamed of becoming a singer herself. A religious, middle-class couple, Benjamin and Melzia Bumbry taught their three children to count their riches in music. There were always neighborhood kids rehearsing at the house after school; there was singing around the piano in the evenings; and there was warbling around the washtub on Saturdays, when the family did the laundry. Every Thursday night, the parents went off to rehearse with their church choir, while their sons, Benjamin and Charles, sang in the youth chorus. Too young to stay home alone, Grace tagged along with her brothers, who eventually persuaded their choir master to let her join the group, even though she was younger than the other members.

The choir soon became the focus of Bumbry's life. Though unenthusiastic about the piano lessons she took with her mother, she lost no opportunity to practice singing her songs, which were already drawing admiring applause from church audiences when she was 11 years old.

Bumbry entered Sumner High School with her eyes already fixed on the concert stage. Determined to learn as much as she could as fast as possible, she practiced constantly, often storming home from music lessons in tears when dissatisfied with her own performance. The first of several important mentors, no-nonsense voice teacher Kenneth Billups guided her carefully, pacing his lessons to her developing voice and reining her in when she wanted to leap ahead.

Bitter Blessing

In 1954 St. Louis radio station KMOX held a teenage talent contest. Billups encouraged his 17-year-old stu-

For the Record . . .

Born Grace Ann Bumbry, January 4, 1937, in St. Louis, MO; daughter of Benjamin James (a freight handler for a railroad company) and Melzia (a schoolteacher) Bumbry; married Edwin Andreas Jaeckel, 1963 (divorced 1972). *Education:* Studied at Boston University, Northwestern University, and with Lotte Lehmann at the Music Academy of the West, Santa Barbara, California.

Opera singer. Paris Opera debut, March 1960, as Amneris in Verdi's *Aïda;* first black artist to appear at Bayreuth, debuting as Venus in Wagner's *Tannhäuser,* July 1961; Metropolitan Opera debut, 1965; changed to soprano repertoire from mezzo-soprano in 1970; sang title role in Richard Strauss's *Salome,* Covent Garden, 1970; sang role of Abigaille in Verdi's *Nabucco,* 1981, Bess in Gershwin's *Porgy and Bess,* 1985, and Cassandra in Berlioz's *Les Troyens,* 1990.

Awards: John Hay Whitney Award, 1957; Marian Anderson Scholarship, 1957; Metropolitan Opera Auditions of the Air, semifinalist, 1958; Richard Wagner Medal, 1963; honorary degrees from St. Louis University, Rockhurst College, Kansas City, and University of Missouri.

Addresses: Agent—Columbia Artists Management, attention Zemsky-Green, 165 West 57th St., New York, NY 10019.

dent to enter, sharing her pleasure when she won. Grace was now the proud possessor of a $1,000 war bond, a free trip to New York, and a $1,000 scholarship to the St. Louis Institute of Music.

The scholarship proved to be a bitter blessing; it slammed her up against the ugly reality of a prejudiced board of trustees who offered her segregated private lessons at the institute in lieu of admission alongside other students. Rosalyn Story, in her book *And So I Sing,* recalled Melzia Bumbry's parting shot after an acrimonious meeting with institute trustees: "It may be YOUR school, but it's MY daughter," she said, and stalked out.

A crisp revenge came by way of embarrassed KMOX executives, who did their best to neutralize Grace's pain by arranging for her to sing on Arthur Godfrey's nationally televised *Talent Scouts* program. According to a 1962 *Ebony* magazine feature, opera buff Godfrey was moved to tears by her interpretation of the aria "O Don Fatale" from nineteenth-century Italian composer Giuseppe Verdi's *Don Carlos.* "Her name will be one of the most famous names in music one day," he declared. "Beautiful! Just beautiful!"

Godfrey was not alone in his opinion. Soon scholarship offers began to pour in from colleges—several of them known for training far superior to that found at the St. Louis Institute of Music.

Someone to Flatten the Stone

Bumbry was still a high school senior when a second mentor entered her life. Contralto Marian Anderson had been a musical legend for many years. Scheduled to appear in 1955 as the first black member of the Metropolitan Opera Company, Anderson experienced bittersweet triumph over prejudice. Anderson's brush with bigotry had come in 1939, when the Daughters of the American Revolution had barred her appearance in Washington's Constitution Hall. Undaunted, she sang instead for a 75,000-strong Easter Sunday audience on the steps of the Lincoln Memorial, a venue that displayed her magnificent voice and dignified bearing to perfection.

A woman of pragmatic intelligence, Anderson was quick to acknowledge that impresario Sol Hurok had been a wise and steadfast friend on her journey to fame. "My mother taught me you can't do anything by yourself," Anderson told *Ebony* magazine in 1982. "There's always somebody to make the stone flat for you to stand on."

Having reached the pinnacle of her own fame, Marian Anderson gladly made the stone flat for a promising high-school senior when a tour brought her to St. Louis in 1954. She took time out to put a dazzled Bumbry at ease, to listen intently while she sang her good luck aria "O Don Fatale," and to report her opinion of the young singer's "magnificent voice" to Sol Hurok.

A longtime representative of such artists as pianist Arthur Rubenstein and violinist Isaac Stern, Hurok knew that much hard work still lay between Grace Bumbry and any guidance he could provide. At present he simply kept an eye on her, noting that she had picked the Boston University scholarship from the many offers the appearance on Arthur Godfrey's show had brought.

Unfortunately Boston was not a success. Wanting an indefinable "something extra," Bumbry transferred to

Northwestern University in Chicago. She has never been able to explain why Northwestern beckoned so insistently, but she readily admits that the decision to go there transformed her life by introducing her to yet another invaluable mentor.

Enter Madame Lotte Lehmann

Lotte Lehmann had been one of opera's immortals since her debut in 1909. She swiftly matured into the type of singer whose performance becomes a standard for others. Lehmann had retired from the stage in 1951 but continued to contribute to opera by passing her own interpretative techniques on to young singers with promising futures.

Bumbry and Lehmann arrived at Northwestern simultaneously—Bumbry as a student, Lehmann to offer master-classes. Bumbry presented some meticulously prepared operatic scenes and songs for Madame Lehmann's criticism and was thrilled to receive an invitation to spend a summer at her Musical Academy of the West in Santa Barbara, California. Eager to see that nothing stood in the way, Lehmann even arranged a scholarship, which was partly funded by comedian Anna Russell.

Bumbry worked so hard in Santa Barbara that the original summer stretched to three and a half years of study. Still aiming for a career as a concert artist, she studied with a fierce intensity, taking piano lessons; lessons from Lehmann in how to analyze every piece of music down to its skeletal essence; lessons in French, German and Italian, so she could sing the works of the world's best-known composers; and lessons in musical theory.

She also took lessons with voice teacher Armand Tokatyan, who categorized her voice as a dramatic soprano. Lehmann disagreed. Bumbry's voice was a mezzo-soprano, she said, and should be trained as one. It was a significant difference of opinion. A mezzo-soprano's range is lower than that sung by a soprano, and the voice itself, usually darker and more richly textured, covers a different repertoire of roles. Equally qualified to judge, Lehmann and Tokatyan never compromised; their disagreement ended only with Tokatyan's death in 1960.

Lehmann continued to train Grace Bumbry as a mezzo-soprano. Overcoming her student's shyness about acting, she coaxed her into learning songs needing drama to round them out. She tempted her into learning operatic arias and lent her books on the historical periods in which certain operas were set. Then, Leh-

mann persuaded Bumbry to refocus her career goal towards opera itself.

Bumbry was still in California when she began to build a reputation promising enough to merit the Marian Anderson Scholarship and the John Hay Whitney Award for 1957, plus a joint first prize with soprano Martina Arroyo the next year in the Metropolitan Opera Auditions of the Air. Her prize money mounted, allowing her to spend a summer in Europe studying the French art song.

Bayreuth

By 1960 Bumbry's career was clearly on its way. She made her debut at the Paris Opera as Amneris in Verdi's Aïda and signed a two-year contract with the Opera House of Basel, Switzerland. However, these events were but preliminaries to the big break, which came later that year.

Bumbry happened to be in Cologne, Germany, when conductor Wolfgang Sawallisch of Bavaria's Bayreuth Festival was searching for a possible Venus for Richard Wagner's opera Tannhäuser. She sang for him and was invited to audition for Wieland Wagner, director of Bayreuth and grandson of the composer.

Wagner had definite ideas about the ideal Venus. He was planning an avant-garde production, and he wanted a mezzo-soprano who could tempt Tannhäuser the Wanderer into her citadel of love with an elegant mixture of mystery and controlled sexuality. Despite the fact that Venus had previously been sung only by white singers, Wagner offered Bumbry the part.

Immediately, Bayreuth began to buzz with angry letters and unwelcome press coverage. "A cultural disgrace!" blared the neo-Nazi German Reich Party. "If Richard Wagner knew this," wrote another correspondent in a letter quoted in Newsweek, "he'd be turning in his grave! Why does Venus have to be black? We've always known her as pink."

Bayreuth's director kept his head. Wieland Wagner was uncomfortably aware that his composer-grandfather had been such a notorious racist and anti-Semite that black GIs who had liberated the city during World War II had paraded sarcastically through the streets dressed in Wagner opera costumes. He was now determined to erase the Aryan stigma that still hung over Bayreuth. So he answered his critics very carefully, stating, as recounted in Rosalind Story's And So I Sing: "I shall bring in black, brown and yellow artists if I feel them appropriate for productions. When I heard

Grace Bumbry I knew she was the perfect Venus. Grandfather would have been delighted."

Bumbry kept away from the fracas and concentrated on bringing the bewitching temptress to life. Her effort brought its reward on opening night in 1961. Dressed in a spectacular gold costume, she sang the role of Venus with self-assured radiance. It was an unforgettable performance all around. The curtain came down to thunderous applause that rocked the theater for a full 30 minutes and brought the cast back for 42 curtain calls.

> *"When I heard Grace Bumbry I knew she was the perfect Venus."*
> —Wieland Wagner

Bumbry has often remarked that racial prejudice is not a great problem in opera. Far more important are technical perfection and musicality—the ability to interpret the composer's wishes while adding an individual stamp to any role. Yet the question of skin color is one that a black singer must face. For instance, there are certain times when members of an operatic cast play a fictional family, and an opera's realism may be considerably compromised if these family members do not have similar skin tones. The solution, of course, is to use the right makeup.

At Bayreuth, Bumbry's skin color issue had been easily solved with gold body paint to match Venus's golden gown. But the question came up again later in the year, when she had to look Russian for a Basel production of Tchaikovsky's *Evgeny Onegin*. The company makeup artist experimented but came up with a formula that turned the diva's face yellow and did nothing to emphasize her huge doe eyes. Bumbry began to learn the intricacies of personalized stage makeup and came up with a formula so successful that the company adopted it to broaden the color palette for other artists.

This triumphant year was in its full midsummer bloom in August, when impresario Sol Hurok left his watchful place in the shadows to summon Bumbry to London. She signed a five-year, $250,000 contract for recordings, television appearances, and opera and concert engagements. Hurok also outlined plans for an American tour in November of 1962 and made arrangements to bring her back to Washington, D.C. in February, where she sang for President and Mrs. Kennedy and other dignitaries at the White House.

Bumbry's tour at the end of 1962 marked her as one of America's most distinguished artists. Lasting nine exhausting weeks, it consisted of a Carnegie Hall concert debut as well as 25 performances in 21 other cities, including St. Louis, where she sang for a packed 3,000-strong house in the same auditorium in which Marian Anderson had thrilled her eight years earlier. She reveled in the first family Christmas she had enjoyed in years and also visited her alma mater, Sumner High School, where she sat in on one of Mr. Billups's classes. The sight of the mentor who had set her on the road to stardom reportedly moved her to tears.

The Day of the Diva

Since she was now part of the opera company in Basel, Switzerland, Bumbry bought a villa in nearby Lugano. Other new acquisitions included apartments in New York and California, plus a Mercedes Benz, a Jaguar, and a bright-orange Lamborghini that she used for her new hobby—auto-racing.

Nineteen sixty-three was a big year for the singer. Covent Garden audiences were introduced to Bumbry in *Don Carlos,* and Chicago's Lyric Opera featured her in *Tannhäuser.* She was also married that year to Erwin Andreas Jaeckel, a Polish-born tenor she had met in Basel. Jaeckel soon gave up his career to manage hers and was thus able to take care of her 1965 Metropolitan Opera debut.

The 1970s brought several changes. One of the most important was Bumbry's decision to concentrate on soprano roles rather than the mezzo-soprano repertoire. Her first soprano role was that of Salome, which she sang at Covent Garden in 1970. Feeling sure of her ability to handle this new challenge, she gave in to a mischievous urge and "let slip" to the press that the end of the "Dance of the Seven Veils" would show her stripped "to her jewels and her perfume." On opening night, sure enough, the jewels were much in evidence—securely attached to a flesh-colored bikini. *Salome* was an absolute sensation, as she told *Ebony* magazine in 1973. "Covent Garden had never before rented so many opera glasses. When I started dancing everything else on stage stopped and I could see the glasses going up en masse."

Salome became an enduring success, which was soon joined by other dramatic soprano roles in operas such as *Macbeth,* Vincenzo Bellini's notoriously difficult *Norma,* and, in 1975, Paul Dukas's *Ariane and Bluebeard* in a revival staged especially for her. The switch to the soprano range, it seemed, had been a perfect career move.

Jaeckel, however, still thought of his wife as a mezzo-soprano and could not accept that she had reached the decision to change her register independent of his judgment. The disagreement rankled, and along with too much togetherness, was a major factor in the couple's 1972 divorce. With Jaeckel's departure went much of the flamboyant lifestyle, including the orange Lamborghini.

Bumbry in Bloom

As the decade wore on, two other major mentors passed away. Lotte Lehmann died at age 88, and Sol Hurok, reverently eulogized by Marian Anderson, passed away at age 85. Anderson herself, the "stone-flattener" who had given Grace Bumbry her first close-up look at fame, was then still in good health. In February of 1982, then 80 years old, she was honored by Bumbry and African American soprano Shirley Verrett with a Carnegie Hall concert that took a year to arrange.

Not all events were as happy. The previous year, Bumbry had returned to the United States to sing the role of Abigaille in Beverly Sills's New York City Opera production of *Nabucco*, by Verdi. Despite acknowledgement that Abigaille is one of opera's most taxing characters, the production itself met with lukewarm reviews.

The Metropolitan Opera's 1985 production of *Porgy and Bess* was much more successful. Incredibly, this was the 50-year-old opera's first appearance at the Met, since it had previously been regarded as part of the popular, rather than the classical, musical repertoire. American composer George Gershwin had carved this niche for *Porgy and Bess;* adamant that all American productions be played by black artists rather than by white singers in blackface, he chose to unveil it on Broadway, where black singers were more readily available.

At first, feeling that the opera represented a period of history most African Americans preferred to forget, Bumbry was unenthusiastic about the project. But once tempted into accepting it, she threw herself into the work with her usual zest and resurrected Bess in a performance that ended in ten triumphant curtain calls on opening night.

The diva from St. Louis achieved an unshakable artistic maturity with the beginning of the 1990s. Along with the poise that is her longtime trademark, this trait proved invaluable during the 1990 production of French composer Hector Berlioz's *Les Troyens* that opened the brand new Bastille Opera in Paris. The opening night was an ongoing disaster of malfunctioning props, unpopular costumes, and scenery that one critic suspected was unfinished. But Bumbry, along with conductor Myung Whun Chung, was highly praised for heroically holding the performance together. Bumbry matured into an artist capable of "flattening the stone" for less experienced colleagues to stand on.

Selected discography

Verdi, Giuseppe, *Aïda,* RCA, 1971.
Wagner, Richard, *Tannhäuser,* Philips, 1992.

Bumbry's recordings have been released by Deutsche Grammophon, Angel, London, and RCA labels and include Handel's *Messiah,* with Joan Sutherland; *Orfeo; Carmen;* and *Il trovatore,* among others.

Sources

Books

Harries, Meirion, and Susie Harries, *Opera Today,* St. Martin's Press, 1986.
International Dictionary of Opera, St. James Press, 1993.
Rosenthal, Harold, and John Warrack, *The Concise Oxford Dictionary of Opera,* 2nd edition, Oxford University Press, 1979.
Story, Rosalyn, *And So I Sing: African American Divas of Opera and Concert,* Warner Books, 1990.

Periodicals

Ebony, May 1962; December 1973; May 1982.
New York Times, July 22, 1961; July 24, 1961; August 14, 1961; December 10, 1967; June 13, 1970; March 3, 1974; March 7, 1974; August 27, 1976; February 1, 1982; March 20, 1990.
Look, February 26, 1963.
Newsweek, November 19, 1962.
Opera, June 1970.
Opera News, October 1981.
Village Voice, February 26, 1985.
Wall Street Journal, March 20, 1990.

—Gillian Wolf

T Bone Burnett

AP / Wide World Photos

As well known for his production of other artists as for his own pop and folk-inflected albums, T Bone Burnett has been a familiar figure on the rock scene since the late 1960s, when he first left his Texas hometown for Los Angeles. His abilities as producer, singer, songwriter, and studio musician combined with his wide-ranging tastes have brought him into contact with a broad spectrum of musicians. His vast production credits include albums by Elvis Costello, Delbert McClinton, Maria Muldaur, Leo Kottke, Los Lobos, Marshall Crenshaw, Peter Case, Roy Orbison, the BoDeans, Bruce Cockburn, Counting Crows, and his wife, Sam Phillips. Burnett often contributes instrumental and writing support when he produces; he has also performed on many other recordings, including those of Tonio K. and Marti Jones, and has cowritten songs with such artists as Costello and U2's Bono.

Burnett is notable for his intense commitment to making thoughtful, high-quality, socially conscious music. He is outspoken on the subject of politics and frequently critical of the recording industry, and he and his wife—unlike many of his colleagues in the music business—are practicing Christians. Impatient when he finds himself pegged as a "Christian rocker," Burnett insists that labelling him in that way misses the point: in a *Rolling Stone* interview he told Steve Pond, "Morality is a moment-to-moment process of making decisions. It is not a specifically Christian thing. The moral point of view in my songs is something I've always had, not something that comes with my religion."

Burnett has always balanced his own recording career with his work as a producer and band member for other people's acts. Born in St. Louis, Missouri, in 1948, Burnett grew up in Fort Worth, Texas, where he played in local bands, frequented blues bars, and was a member of a performance group called Los Creativos. He picked up the nickname "T Bone" at the age of five. After finishing high school he tried college for a little while, but before long he quit in order to establish a small recording studio. By the end of the 1960s Burnett left Texas and headed for Hollywood. There he began playing with Delaney and Bonnie, produced a record for Delbert and Glen, and, in 1972, released his first solo album, *The B-52 Band & the Fabulous Skylarks*, under the name J. Henry Burnett.

Burnett wasn't ready to tour in order to promote the album. As passionate as he was about making music, live performance did not come naturally to him. Later he explained to George Kalogerakis in *Rolling Stone,* "I never had any ambition to be a famous performer. I started *out* being a record producer.... I've just poked around in this and that a bit." The introspective Burnett concluded, "Probably a lot of that's fear." In 1975,

Born John Henry Burnett in 1948, in St. Louis, MO; raised in Fort Worth, TX; married second wife, Leslie "Sam" Phillips, late 1980s; children: two daughters (first marriage). *Religion:* Episcopalian.

Began playing with and producing bands, 1960s; moved to Los Angeles, early 1970s; made first solo album, *The B-52 Band & the Fabulous Skylarks* (under name J. Henry Burnett), 1972; produced recordings by Delbert and Glen, among others; toured with Delaney and Bonnie and then with Bob Dylan's Rolling Thunder Revue, 1975; formed the Alpha Band with Rolling Thunder veterans Steven Soles and David Mansfield and recorded three albums between 1976 and 1978; appeared in films *Renaldo & Clara,* 1976, and *Heaven's Gate,* 1980; began making solo albums as T Bone Burnett, starting with *Truth Decay,* 1980; toured with Richard Thompson and Elvis Costello, 1984; with Costello, as the Coward Brothers, cut single "The People's Limousine," 1985; produced recordings by numerous artists, including Leo Kottke, Los Lobos, Bruce Cockburn, Roy Orbison, Marshall Crenshaw, Elvis Costello, the BoDeans, Counting Crows, and Sam Phillips.

Awards: Named Songwriter of the Year in *Rolling Stone* Critics Poll, 1983.

Addresses: *Agent*—Addis Wechsler, 955 South Carrillo Dr., 3rd floor, Los Angeles, CA 90048.

however, after he moved to New York City and spent some time on the Greenwich Village club circuit, Burnett joined Bob Dylan's Rolling Thunder Revue. After the tour, Burnett founded the Alpha Band with Revue veterans David Mansfield and Steven Soles. They recorded three albums before disbanding in 1978, and Mansfield and Soles appeared on Burnett's 1980 *Truth Decay.*

Burnett made his film debut in *Renaldo & Clara,* a 1976 documentary by Sam Shepard about the Rolling Thunder experience; in 1980 Burnett appeared in Francis Ford Coppola's colossal flop, *Heaven's Gate.* Around this time Burnett returned to the Episcopalian faith he had left behind in Texas; it was a period when many of his Rolling Thunder bandmates, including Dylan, were discovering Christianity.

Burnett opened for Elvis Costello on tour in 1984, and the two began working together. They briefly per-

formed as the Coward Brothers, sort of a spoof on the 1950s pop vocal duo the Everly Brothers, and even made a single, "The People's Limousine." Burnett went on to produce two albums for Costello, *King of America* and *Spike.*

Became Successful Producer

Burnett worked on Orbison's "comeback" album, the 1989 *Mystery Girl,* along with other Orbison fans such as Elvis Costello, Bono, George Harrison, and Tom Petty, and acted as musical director for an Orbison Cinemax concert special, *A Black and White Night.* Around this time Burnett also produced work by Leo Kottke, Marshall Crenshaw, Peter Case, the debut album of the BoDeans, and three records for Los Lobos that catapulted them onto the charts.

Costello describes Burnett's production style as thoughtful and patient. Discussing the making of *King of America,* Costello told *Musician,* "'Generosity' is a word that flew around a lot. It's something to do with T Bone's influence.... T Bone was saying, 'Remember what the point was. Why did you write it?' People don't often do that. Producers obviously don't do that enough." Sam Llanas of the BoDeans commented in *Billboard,* "[Burnett] can be brutally frank without being brutal; he would make suggestions that clarified the whole thing." Evaluating his own skills in an interview with Dan Ouellette of *Acoustic Guitar,* Burnett reflected on his commitment to the music itself: "My goal as a producer is to try to help the song live and, hopefully, not simply live, but live passionately or defiantly or gloriously or humbly or honestly."

Acclaimed Albums Didn't Sell

Burnett's solo career, meanwhile, was developing more slowly. In a pattern that would characterize his work, his first two releases after the breakup of the Alpha Band, 1980's *Truth Decay* and the 1982 EP *Trap Door,* were received enthusiastically by the critics but did not sell. Burnett's lyrics wrestled with everyday ethics, focusing on personal hypocrisy, daily compromise, and faithless love, but also on the possibility of transcending despair.

In a review in *Rolling Stone,* Ken Tucker wrote that "*Truth Decay* ... suggests that T Bone Burnett is the best singer-songwriter in the country right now. No one this year will make music more forthright, more tender, more scrupulously free of cheap irony and trumped-up passion." Yet despite consistently glowing, appreciative reviews, Burnett never gathered a large following.

Burnett has appeared to take his relative lack of popular success in stride. In concerts, joking about the media's references to his "cult" status, he would ask audiences, "Are you guys a cult?" In *Acoustic Guitar,* Ouellette asked Burnett if he ever doubted his abilities. Burnett answered, "Sure, but it's only been during periods when I've believed in and conformed to the competitive aspect of the music business.... I would think I wasn't very good because I wasn't selling enough records." Despite discouraging sales figures, Burnett continued to make records that were more artistic than commercial and got first-rate studio support on them; Ry Cooder and Richard Thompson played on the 1983 *Proof Through the Night,* for example, and Billy Swan and Los Lobos' David Hidalgo both appeared on *T Bone Burnett.*

Warner dropped Burnett in 1984 after two critically acclaimed but poor-selling records. Burnett, however, went on to release another EP, *Behind the Trap Door,* in England shortly afterward. In 1986 he made the well-received *T Bone Burnett* on Dot, an MCA label. That album, with its country influence and relatively spare sound, is regarded by some critics as Burnett's best. Throughout the 1980s Burnett experimented with a range of sounds, from the rockabilly flavor of *Truth Decay* and simple song-centered *Trap Door* to the more highly produced *Proof Through the Night.* His last album of the decade, 1988's *The Talking Animals,* is among his most ornate and ranks among Burnett's least favorite. A *Billboard* article reported that Burnett considered the album "calculated and pretentious"; the critics tended to agree.

Tired out by a long busy spate of producing and recording, Burnett took some time off after *The Talking Animals.* Around 1986 he had been introduced to a singer and songwriter named Leslie Phillips, who had made several successful records in the early 1980s for the Christian record label Word and wanted to shift out of the Christian rock formula. Burnett produced her 1987 crossover gospel/pop album *The Turning,* after which she took the name Sam Phillips and, with Burnett's help, signed with Virgin. Burnett and Phillips were married in the late 1980s. Burnett did not rush back into the studio to record his own work but with encouragement from Columbia, which had released *The Talking Animals,* he made *The Criminal Under My Own Hat* in 1992.

Returned to a Simpler Sound

In order to make a record he was satisfied with, Burnett had to reevaluate his earlier work. He told *Pulse!,* "I listened to all of my old records and tried to pick out what I do well. I noticed that the more simple stuff, the stuff which comes more naturally to me, is generally the stuff that works best, so I tried to work within that vein." The strategy seemed to work as far as the critics were concerned. The reviews were favorable and the decision to scale back on production was praised: A *Rolling Stone* review commended the album's "broad palate of simple yet subtle instrumental touches," and Detroit's *Metro Times* noted Burnett's use of "simple, straightforward arrangements to deal with the thornier aspects of morals and ethics." Burnett's songs again focused on human treachery and social decay but, as always, dealt as sternly with himself, "the criminal under my own hat," as with uncaring governments or a cruel lover.

It appears likely that Burnett will continue to make thoughtful albums that will be welcomed by his loyal band of listeners and by the critics, and that he will continue to do his best to make his corner of the music business more humane. In *Acoustic Guitar* he discussed problems he had encountered and observed: "There is a sense of camaraderie with many of the people I work with. But there's also that hierarchy of fame that is completely debilitating to everyone.... It puts up too many walls between people to allow for any community." It seems that if anything can create a sense of camaraderie and community within the recording industry, the dedication and diverse talents of T Bone Burnett can.

Selected discography

With the Alpha Band

The Alpha Band, Arista, 1976.
Spark in the Dark, Arista, 1977.
The Statue Makers of Hollywood, Arista, 1978.

With Elvis Costello, as the Coward Brothers

"The People's Limousine," Imp/Demon, 1985.

Solo releases

(As J. Henry Burnett) *The B-52 Band & the Fabulous Skylarks,* UNI, 1972.
Truth Decay, Takoma, 1980.
Trap Door (EP), Warner Bros., 1982.
Proof Through the Night, Warner Bros., 1983.
Behind the Trap Door (EP), Demon, 1984.
T Bone Burnett, Dot/MCA, 1986.
The Talking Animals, Columbia, 1988.
The Criminal Under My Own Hat, Columbia, 1992.

As producer

The Van Dykes, *Sunday Kind of Love,* Bell, 1966.

The Legendary Stardust Cowboy, *Paralyzed,* Psycho-Suabe, 1968.

Delbert and Glen, *Delbert and Glen,* Clean/Atlantic, 1971.

Robert Ealey and His Five Careless Lovers, *Live at the New Bluebird Nightclub,* Hue, 1972.

Maria Muldaur, *There Is a Love,* Myrrh, 1982.

Leo Kottke, *Time Step,* Chrysalis, 1983.

Los Lobos, *... And a Time To Dance,* Slash/Warner Bros., 1984.

Los Lobos, *How Will the Wolf Survive?,* Slash/Warner Bros., 1985.

Marshall Crenshaw, *Downtown,* Warner Bros., 1985.

Peter Case, *Peter Case,* Geffen, 1986.

Elvis Costello, *King of America,* Columbia, 1986.

BoDeans, *Love and Hope and Sex and Dreams,* Slash/Warner Bros., 1986.

Leslie (Sam) Phillips, *The Turning,* Myrrh, 1987.

Los Lobos, *By the Light of the Moon,* Slash/Warner Bros., 1987.

Roy Orbison, *In Dreams: His Greatest Hits,* Virgin, 1987.

Sam Phillips, *The Indescribable Wow,* Virgin, 1988.

Elvis Costello, *Spike,* Warner Bros., 1988.

Joe Henry, *Shuffletown,* A&M, 1990.

Sam Phillips, *Cruel Inventions,* Virgin, 1991.

Bruce Cockburn, *Nothing but a Burning Light,* Columbia, 1991.

BoDeans, *Go Slow Down,* Reprise, 1993.

Counting Crows, *August and Everything After,* DGC, 1993.

Sam Phillips, *Martinis and Bikinis,* Virgin, 1994.

Bruce Cockburn, *Dart to the Heart,* Columbia, 1994.

Sources

Acoustic Guitar, January 1993.

Billboard, August 15, 1992; November 13, 1993.

Creem, July 1988.

Metro Times, September 2, 1992.

Musician, March 1986; July 1992.

Pulse!, August 1992; July 1993.

Record, January 1984.

Rolling Stone, September 30, 1982; November 11, 1982; November 24, 1983; March 24, 1988; September 3, 1992.

Additional information for this profile was obtained from Columbia Records press material, 1994.

—*Gina Hausknecht*

Tevin Campbell

Singer

By the age of four, Tevin Campbell had a passion for singing. Likened to such greats as Stevie Wonder and Michael Jackson, Campbell began by singing gospel, first as a choir member, and then as a soloist at Jacob's Chapel in a small town just south of Dallas, Texas. Apart from his favorite singer, Aretha Franklin, his greatest influence as a child was probably his mother, Rhonda Byrd. Then a postal worker, she was known to the Texas congregation as "little Aretha."

As Campbell told Dennis Hunt of the *Los Angeles Times,* "[My mother] pushed me and made me see trying to be a big solo singer was something I should do. Without her pushing, I'd still be in the background. To some extent, that's what happened to her. She has a good singing voice that she never fully developed. I guess nobody pushed her to get ahead. She didn't want to see me waste my talent too. When I was younger I wasn't sure what I wanted, but she knew what was best for me, and I went along with it." Rhonda went on to become Tevin's co-manager.

In 1988 a friend of Campbell's mother arranged for the budding young singer to audition for jazz flutist Bobbie Humphrey by singing over the phone to her in New York. Humphrey took an immediate interest in Campbell and submitted an audio and videotape to Warner Bros., which led to a meeting with Benny Medina, the label's senior vice president and general sales manager of black music. Humphrey also arranged for Campbell to tryout for the short-lived NBC-TV children's television program "Wally and the Valentines."

Showed Up on Quincy Jones's *Block*

Campbell's first big break came when Quincy Jones was in the process assembling an all-star cast for his *Back on the Block* album. By the ripe old age of 12, Campbell was assigned to Jones's label, Qwest, and spotlighted on two tracks of the 1990 platinum-selling, Grammy-winning album. One of those songs, "Tomorrow (Better You, Better Me)," made it to Number One on the Hot R&B Singles chart.

Later in 1990, Campbell was featured in the musical biopic *Listen Up: The Lives of Quincy Jones* and performed on "Listen Up," a song paying tribute to Jones. Within a year, Campbell was whisked away to Paisley Park Studios in Minneapolis to record "Round and Round" for Prince's movie *Graffiti Bridge,* in which he also snagged a role. "Round and Round" was considered by many critics to be the best single from the soundtrack; it earned Campbell a Grammy nomination for best male R&B vocalist.

Campbell had hopes that Prince (who is now referred to by an unpronounceable symbol) would take the helm of his first solo outing, but co-executive producers Jones and Medina had other ideas. As Jones told Hunt, "Tevin needed to work with some different producers, to explore several directions and maximize his potential." His debut album, *T.E.V.I.N.,* features songs written by Al B. Sure! and Kyle West; Marilyn and Alan Bergman; Narada Michael Walden; and several tracks cowritten by Campbell. The only Prince-influenced song on the release is the soul-mix edit of "Round and Round," which may explain why the album captures less of the much-anticipated funk attitude Campbell displayed in *Graffiti Bridge.*

Made a Name With Solo Album

The 13-track solo album was warmly received upon its release in November of 1991, and the single "Tell Me What You Want Me to Do" became a Top 40 hit. In a review of the album for the *Los Angeles Times,* Connie Johnson gave it three out of four stars and declared the single "positively stunning." Describing the tracks "Just Ask Me To"—previously released as a single

from the Qwest soundtrack to *Boyz N the Hood*—and "She's All That," the reviewer wrote: "He looks like the most talented kid to tackle a pop song since Michael Jackson fronted the Jackson 5." Phyl Garland of *Stereo Review* called it "one of the best debut vocal albums I have heard in many, many years.... [Campbell] sings with an authority of attack, certainty of tone, and maturity of interpretation that immediately command respect. There is a passion in his work that marks the true artist."

"I had no idea we would create a household name with Tevin before the album came out," Benny Medina told Janine McAdams of *Billboard* magazine. "This album was three years in the making, but Tevin has proven he's one of the blessed ones. When you take someone this talented and expose him to great talents like Quincy and Prince, he can only grow."

Between interviews and television appearances following the release of *T.E.V.I.N.,* Campbell found time to contribute to three special projects: *Handel's Messiah,* a Grammy Award-winning album produced by Mervyn Warren of Take 6; a Special Olympics Christmas album, featuring Campbell's rendition of "Oh Holy Night"; and *Barcelona Gold,* the 1992 Olympics album which includes his hit "One Song."

"A More Mature Sound"

Reflecting on the experience of recording his first album, Campbell told Christian Wright of *Vibe:* "It was horrible. I didn't have as much of a relationship with the songs and my voice was changing. I didn't have any control over it. I mean, one day it could be high and the next day it could be gone. And that's why we had to keep going back in and doing songs over."

The singer's second solo effort, the 1993 release *I'm Ready,* was also produced by Jones and Medina. "I wanted to make a more mature-sounding album to reflect my current state of mind," Campbell explained to J. R. Reynolds in *Billboard* magazine. "*I'm Ready* says a lot about who I am as a person because of the things I've been through during the last four years or so. I hope people will see that I'm not the same young kid that I was on my first album."

Part of Campbell's emotional development during this time stemmed from his difficult first meeting with his father, who lived "somewhere in Arkansas." Campbell related the encounter to Christian Wright in a *Vibe* interview: "I wanted to meet him. It's not that I wanted to bond with him or have some sort of relationship, 'cause my mother raised all three of us on her own. I just wanted to meet him 'cause I had never met my father." When *I'm Ready* made its debut at Number Four on the Top R&B Albums chart, Tevin left no doubt he was capable of tackling almost any style of song. A diverse mix of ballads, soul, dance tracks, and a smattering of rap are included on the release, with Prince's influence evident on about a quarter of the tracks.

Despite the ever-growing adulation, Campbell remains surprisingly levelheaded; he has expressed interest in studying computer science at a black university. And though he loves the music industry, he says he can do without the pressures of the business. "Sometimes I think what it might be like if I stayed in the background and was just singing in a choir somewhere," Campbell told Hunt in the *Los Angeles Times*. "That crosses my mind on some of the bad days when I'm overworked. But it's just a fleeting thought. Singing is still the important thing to me. I love singing. I wouldn't be putting myself through all this if I didn't."

Selected discography

Solo albums

T.E.V.I.N., Warner Bros./Qwest, 1991.
I'm Ready, Warner Bros./Qwest, 1993.

With others

Quincy Jones, *Back on the Block*, (includes "Tomorrow [Better You, Better Me]"), Warner Bros./Qwest, 1990.
Prince, *Graffiti Bridge*, (soundtrack; includes "Round and Round"), Warner Bros./Paisley Park, 1990.
Handel's Messiah, Reprise, 1992.
Barcelona Gold, (includes "One Song"), Warner Bros., 1992.

Sources

Billboard, December 15, 1990; February 16, 1991; November 16, 1991; December 4, 1993.
Entertainment Weekly, January 10, 1992.
Los Angeles Times, December 15, 1991.
Musician, March 1992.
People, January 27, 1992.
Rolling Stone, May 17, 1990; April 18, 1991.
Stereo Review, June 1992.
Vibe, November 1993; March 1994.

Additional information for this profile was obtained from Qwest Records press materials, 1991 and 1993.

—*Lazae Laspina*

The Carpenters

Pop duo

Performing songs that some condemned as fluff but millions loved, the Carpenters became an amazing success story after bursting onto the pop music scene in 1970. Karen and Richard Carpenter had 19 Top Ten singles from 1970 to 1981 and released 17 albums during the 1970s that each sold over a million copies. The duo generated sales of 80 million records worldwide with their soft-rock sound, which was "the squeaky-clean antidote to the early-70s brew of antiwar protests and acid rock," according to Tim Purtell in *Entertainment Weekly*.

Richard Carpenter learned to play piano at age 11 while growing up in New Haven, Connecticut, while his younger sister Karen took up the drums. By the time he was 17, Richard was performing with an instrumental trio in various clubs. After the Carpenter family moved to California, Karen was signed to a recording contract with a small local label, Magic Lamp, in 1965. She recorded the single "I'll Be Yours" for the label, with her brother on piano, Wes Jacobs on bass and tuba, and Joe Osborn as session bassist. After this record and a subsequent single went nowhere, the Carpenters formed a jazz instrumental group with Jacobs called

Archive Photos

the Richard Carpenter Trio. The group's talent earned them a victory in a "Battle of the Bands" competition at the Hollywood Bowl in 1966, with first prize a recording contract with RCA Records. However, the two RCA albums they cut never made it to record stores; at the time, the group's sound was considered "too soft."

Concentrated on Harmonies and Arrangements

Jacobs left the group to study music after the connection with RCA was severed, and the Carpenters formed a new band called Spectrum with four students from California State University. Featuring John Bettis on bass and Danny Woodhams as guitarist, the group was short-lived and broke up after a few gigs at Disneyland and Los Angeles clubs such as the Troubadour and the Whisky A-Go-Go. At this point the Carpenters began focusing on vocal harmonies and overdubbing effects, and Richard continued developing what would become his formidable skills as an arranger.

Showcasing Karen's pleasing contralto in both a solo setting and combined with Richard's baritone, they recorded a series of demo tapes in bassist Osborn's garage and began hawking them to record compa-

nies. One of the tapes made its way to Herb Albert, the trumpet player and founder of A&M Records. Albert signed the Carpenters to a contract, and by 1969 the group had recorded *Offering,* their debut album. A cover of the Beatles' "Ticket to Ride" on the album reached Number 54 on the U.S. charts.

Recorded by Dionne Warwick some seven years earlier, "(They Long to Be) Close to You," by Burt Bacharach and Hal David, was transformed in the studio by the Carpenters in 1970. The duo's version became one of pop music's seminal demonstrations of boy/girl harmony and the "easy listening" sound. It featured an understated piano arrangement by Richard, as well as first-rate production by Jack Daugherty. Listener approval for "Close to You" was overwhelming, and the song soared to Number One.

It was soon followed by the hit "We've Only Just Begun," which, according to the *Guinness Encyclopedia of Popular Music,* "highlighted Karen's crystal-clear diction, overladen with intricate harmonies and a faultless production." Thus began the Carpenters' incredible hit parade, which landed 17 of their songs in the Top 40 during the next 11 years.

From 1970 to 1972 alone, the Carpenters generated six Top Five hits—"Close to You," "We've Only Just Begun," "For All We Know," "Rainy Days and Mondays," "Superstar," and "Hurting Each Other." Along with Richard's arranging and musical direction, much of this success was due to the high quality of material the Carpenters were getting from songwriters such as Bacharach, Paul Williams, and Roger Nichols. They also employed the services of top sidemen like virtuoso guitarist Tony Peluso. Richard also wrote some hits for the group in partnership with former Spectrum bassist Bettis. As a result of this output, the group's compilation album, *The Singles 1969-73,* became one of the best-selling albums of all time and was on the LP charts for an amazing 115 weeks.

Worked Relentlessly

One success after another kept the Carpenters working relentlessly in the early 1970s, both in the studio and on the concert circuit. Their fame also won them their own brief television series, *Make Your Own Kind of Music,* in 1971. The show featured trumpet player Al Hirt and Mark Lindsay, former lead singer with Paul Revere and the Raiders. The Carpenters were also asked to perform at the White House in 1974 during a state dinner. While Richard continued to play the piano on their recordings, Karen's drum work became restricted to their stage act.

Inevitably, the performance grind began to take its toll: in 1975 a major tour of Europe was canceled as Karen was reported to be suffering from nervous and physical exhaustion. Reports of her weight having dropped to 90 pounds raised suspicions about crash diets; it was later revealed that she was afflicted with anorexia nervosa. In 1993 Richard Carpenter told *Entertainment Weekly,* "I still have no idea why this disorder struck Karen."

The Carpenters' pop formula began to wear thin in the late 1970s, and their hit production slowed. Cutbacks on touring and Richard's increasing involvement in behind-the-scenes production further reduced their visibility. Karen continued her battle against anorexia, and Richard checked into a drug rehabilitation clinic in 1978 to rid himself of an addiction to prescription drugs. They managed to crack the Top 20 again in 1978 with a cover of Herman's Hermits' "There's a Kind of Hush." Meanwhile, Karen attempted a solo career, but her 1979 album, produced by Phil Ramone, was never released. The siblings reunited and made something of a comeback with their 1981 *Made in America* album, which reached Number 12 in the United Kingdom.

Karen's Death

After her two-year marriage to real estate developer Thomas J. Burris ended in 1982, a distraught Karen entered therapy in New York City. She gained 15 pounds and seemed to have won her eight-year battle with anorexia. But long-term stress on her metabolism had irrevocably affected her heart functioning, resulting in a fatal heart attack in 1983 during a visit to her parents' home in California.

The Carpenters had been planning to tour again and record a new album at the time of Karen's death. Richard put together a few albums using tapes of Karen and in 1987 recorded his *Time* album, which featured performances by Dionne Warwick and Dusty Springfield. In 1993 he was reportedly working on a book about the Carpenters. Karen Carpenter was later immortalized in a song by alternative rock band Sonic Youth, "Tunic—Song for Karen," and in a 1989 television movie about her life.

In her review of 1991's *From the Top,* a retrospective CD package of Carpenter songs, Elizabeth Wurtzel wrote in the *New Yorker* that the collection "documents one of the most undistinguished successful music careers ever." The Carpenters would be remembered "not really as musicians but as cultural icons," she added. Despite this sort of criticism, standards such as

"Close to You" and "We've Only Just Begun" have etched a permanent place for the Carpenters in the pop music pantheon.

Many critics have changed their originally negative views of the group to more favorable ones over the years. As was pointed out in *The Harmony Illustrated Encyclopedia of Rock,* "Although often critically berated for blandness and [their] wholesome, clean-cut image, the Carpenters were praised by musicians and industry insiders for musicianship, excellent choice of sidemen ... and professionalism."

That opinion was confirmed in 1994 with the release of an all-star tribute album, *If I Were a Carpenter.* Leading alternative rock acts including Sonic Youth, Cracker, and the Cranberries recorded the homage to the pop duo whose 1970s hits had influenced so many of the artists of the 1990s. Jeff McDonald of Redd Kross summed up the collective sentiment of the participants: "I'd always been a huge fan of the Carpenters, and an admirer of their songs. The quality of their songs was so wonderful, they were lyrically very sophisticated, not this teenybop fare.... Most bands just want to write perfect pop songs. And these are perfect pop songs."

Selected discography

Singles; on A&M

"(They Long to Be) Close to You," 1970.
"We've Only Just Begun," 1970.
"For All We Know," 1971.
"Rainy Days and Mondays," 1971.
"Top of the World," 1973.
"Please Mr. Postman," 1975.
"Touch Me When We're Dancing," 1979.

Albums; on A&M

Close to You, 1971.
Ticket to Ride, 1972.
Now and Then, 1973.
The Singles 1969-73, 1973.
Horizon, 1975.
A Kind of a Hush, 1976.
Made in America, 1981.
From the Top, 1991.

The group's songs were also featured on the retrospective tribute album *If I Were a Carpenter,* recorded by various artists, including Sonic Youth, Cracker, the Cranberries, Grant Lee Buffalo, Redd Kross, and Michael Sweet, A&M, 1994.

Sources

Books

Coleman, Ray, *The Carpenters: The Untold Story, an Authorized Biography,* HarperCollins, 1994.

The Guinness Encyclopedia of Popular Music, Volume 1, edited by Colin Larkin, Guinness, 1992.

The Harmony Illustrated Encyclopedia of Rock, Sixth Edition, Harmony, 1988.

The Illustrated Encyclopedia of Rock, compiled by Nick Logan and Bob Woffinden, Harmony, 1977.

The Penguin Encyclopedia of Popular Music, edited by Donald Clarke, Viking, 1989.

Rock Movers & Shakers, edited by Dafydd Rees and Luke Crampton, ABC-CLIO, 1991.

Periodicals

Detroit News, September 14, 1994.
Entertainment Weekly, February 5, 1993; September 16, 1994.
Los Angeles Magazine, January 1989.
New Yorker, December 23, 1991.
New York Times, February 5, 1983.
People, October 26, 1987.
TV Guide, December 31, 1988.

—Ed Decker

Peter Case

Singer, songwriter, guitarist

The labels singer, songwriter, and musician are those most often ascribed to Peter Case. But they do not begin to describe the man who has touched so many hearts with songs written from the unconscious. He told Tom Campbell of the *Los Angeles Reader*, "I don't try to come up with just what *my* message will be. I could write a song that had all of my views in it, but it wouldn't resonate or move like a real song. But there are certain songs ... they come from the subconscious or something. I don't know what it is. One song like that was 'A Million Miles Away.' It seemed to express something to a whole lot of people."

Peter Case grew up in western New York State. When he was ten, he got his first guitar. From then on the guitar was his chief interest, though this avocation did not prevent him from getting into trouble. He told Campbell, "I was getting into a wild crowd of people, and we got into some dangerous stuff. I moved out of my parents' when I was fifteen, quit going to school, took a lot of drugs. I destroyed my ego before I even had one." Case was driven from the classroom by, of all things, the poet T. S. Elliot. He explained to Rob Tannenbaum of *Rolling Stone,* "The teacher was up there reading T. S. Elliot's 'The Hollow Men' in this monotone. The poem just really upset me. I broke out in a cold sweat, got up and walked out of class." Being the son of two teachers, though, he eventually earned his high school equivalency diploma and later enrolled in classes at the State University of New York at Buffalo.

Sang on Streets of San Francisco

Then, in the middle of a blizzard, Case packed up his guitar and bought a bus ticket to Chicago. Within a few days he was in San Francisco. "Really, I got in way too deep, way too young," he told Campbell. "When I left Buffalo, I wasn't intending to go to California to be a street musician. I was just heading for California. I had a guitar with me.... I wasn't here (San Francisco) very long when I realized that I could play my guitar on street corners and make enough money to get by." It was a fine living as long as the summer lasted, but the winters were miserable. "I remember being with a bunch of guys. It was raining out, so we—a bunch of street musicians—moved into one hotel room and put all our money together to buy a bag of potato chips." It was a difficult time for Case, who concentrated mainly on getting from one day to the next. His only desire was to play and sing, but he had never thought of music as a career.

In the mid-1970s Case became part of the now legendary San Francisco punk trio the Nerves. He played bass, sang, and wrote songs like "When You Find

For the Record . . .

Born in 1952 in Hamburg, NY; son of teachers; married Victoria Williams (a singer and songwriter), 1985 (divorced); married Dianne Sherry (a writer and actress). *Education:* Attended State University of New York at Buffalo.

Worked as a street musician, San Francisco, CA; member of band the Nerves, 1976-78; worked as housepainter, Los Angeles, CA; member of band the Plimsouls, 1980-84; with band, released single "A Million Miles Away" and album *Everywhere at Once,* Geffen, 1983; signed with Geffen as solo artist and released *Peter Case,* 1986.

Addresses: *Record company*—Vanguard Records, 1299 Ocean Ave., Ste. 800, Santa Monica, CA 90401.

Out," which has since become an impossible-to-find single. In 1978, after touring with punk rabble-rousers the Ramones and such bands as the Germs, Mink De Ville, and the Weirdos, the Nerves broke up and Peter Case moved to Hollywood, where he wrote songs and painted houses for a year.

Formed Plimsouls

In 1980 Case formed the Plimsouls and released an EP that earned the band a major-label record deal. But the record was not adequately promoted and sold poorly; the band and label soon parted company. The Plimsouls subsequently recorded the now-renowned single "A Million Miles Away," which was featured in the popular film *Valley Girl.* The band then signed to Geffen Records, on which they released the 1983 album *Everywhere at Once,* featuring their already famous single. But the group disbanded in the summer of 1984.

Case began traveling as a solo acoustic artist, playing his own songs in bars, coffeehouses, and various other venues from Maine to Montana and Vancouver Island to the Gulf of Mexico. He toured as the opening act for singer-songwriter Jackson Browne. And in 1986 he signed to Geffen Records as a solo artist and released his self-titled debut album. The record received exceedingly favorable reviews, and Case began to touch people with his story-songs about the broken dreams of America.

In 1989 his follow-up album, *The Man With the Blue Postmodern Fragmented Neo-Traditionalist Guitar,* was released to even stronger reviews. Once again Case

was able to connect with his audience, singing about his feelings for "losers in a society built exclusively for winners." It finished the year on a number of Top 10 lists and established him as an important songwriter.

Six Pack of Love

Case's 1992 release, *Six Pack of Love,* was a mix of acoustic and hard-edged material, something of a departure from the more stripped-down and folkish sound he had favored in his solo career to that point. With his first two albums he had wanted to get his listeners' attention, well aware that Plimsouls fans were perhaps more concerned with a rocking soundtrack for their parties than with the perceptiveness of his lyrics. With *Six Pack,* though, he had moved beyond that narrow concern, telling Jon Matsumoto of *Musician,* "It's not really the business of the performer what the people do. Your job (as a performer/musician) is to dig deep and move the place."

His 1994 release, *Peter Case Sings Like Hell,* started out as an outgrowth of his fan club's newsletter, *Travelin' Light.* He recorded the album on a two-track recorder and distributed the primitive result himself on Travelin' Light Records, selling it at his shows. On his way to the Troubadours of Folk Festival in Los Angeles, a representative of folk label Vanguard Records gave him her card. Subsequently, Vanguard called Case to offer him a distribution deal. He was delighted to give the record the opportunity to reach a wider audience.

Peter Case may always be known for his live performances, distinguished as they are by dynamic guitar-playing and his spontaneous spirit. But ultimately, his songwriting will be what best represents him. "Music is my expression, it's my career, and it's what I do for laughs," he told the *Los Angeles Reader's* Campbell. "I'll go see other musicians, and it's a great source of inspiration for me. It makes sense in its own simple way. It's been a whole path for me."

Selected discography

Peter Case, Geffen, 1986.
The Man With the Blue Postmodern Fragmented Neo-Traditionalist Guitar, Geffen, 1989.
Six Pack of Love, Geffen, 1992.
Peter Case Sings Like Hell, Vanguard, 1994.

With the Plimsouls

Zero Hour (EP), Beat, 1980.
The Plimsouls, Planet/Elektra, 1981.

Everywhere at Once, Geffen, 1983.
One Night in America, 1988.

With the Nerves

Nerves (EP), 1976.
The Nerves, 1986.

Sources

Books

DiMartino, Dave, *Singer-Songwriters*, Billboard Books, 1994.
Robbins, Ira A., *Trouser Press Record Guide, 4th Edition*, Collier Books, 1991.

Periodicals

Bakersfield Californian, April 29, 1994.

Billboard, July 15, 1989; April 9, 1994.
Capital Times, May 1994.
Cash Box, June 24, 1989.
Creem, October 1980.
Detroit News, April 23, 1994.
Frets, November 1987.
L.A. Village View, April 15, 1994.
Los Angeles Reader, March 11, 1994.
Musician, April 1992.
Now Magazine, May 5, 1994.
People, June 8, 1992.
Rolling Stone, October 23, 1986; June 2, 1994.
Welcomat, April 27, 1994.

Additional information for this profile was obtained from Vanguard Records press material, 1994.

—*Charlie Katagiri*

The Charlatans

Pop band

The Charlatans timed their entrance into England's music scene impeccably: they formed in North-wich, just 20 miles outside of Manchester, where a new rock and roll sound had developed, in 1989, just as "the Manchester Sound" was about to get a lot of attention. Thus the Charlatans—along with the Stone Roses, Happy Mondays, and Inspiral Carpets—became one of the originators of what was actually the second wave of the Manchester scene, described as a "danceable combination of mind-expanding grooves, sing-along melodies and psychedelia."

Though some accused the Charlatans of planning their strategy specifically to exploit the Manchester scene, they consistently tried to disassociate themselves from it in the press. "Why should we be defined by any city? We've never considered ourselves to be from any scene," singer Tim Burgess told David Wild in *Rolling Stone*. "If we're anything, we're a British band—we're popular all over the country."

Initially, the Charlatans asked Steve Harrison—owner

Photograph by Tom Sheehan, courtesy of Atlantic Records

of Omega Music, a record store in Northwich—to manage the band. Harrison took singer Tim Burgess to one of the Charlatans' club performances; Burgess loved the band, but he thought the singer was "poor." He told Harrison he would like to sing for the band. The band split up for a few months, then reemerged in August of 1989. Burgess had joined bassist Martin Blunt, guitarist Jon Baker, keyboardist Rob Collins, and drummer Jon Brookes in their assault on England's music world.

Independent Single Sold Nearly 20,000 Copies

The Charlatans independently released their first single, "Indian Rope," in early 1990; it sold nearly 20,000 copies. The single and their live performances received favorable responses from their audiences and gained some attention from the U.K. press. Ian McGregor of *Melody Maker* reported his observations of the crowd at one of the Charlatans' early performances, noting, "The audience is seriously baggy—baggy hair, baggy clothes, baggy dancing."

Talent scouts of the British label Beggars Banquet took notice of the band as well and signed them in 1990. They released their debut, *Some Friendly*, that year. Within two days of its release, the record went gold in England and debuted at Number One on the U.K. charts. *Some Friendly* featured the songs "The Only One I Know," "Then," and "Overrising." The Charlatans had made their mark.

When the time came to take their music to the United States, the Charlatans discovered that a San Francisco-based band fronted by one Dan Hicks had played under the same name. So, the Charlatans voluntarily added "UK" to their name to set themselves apart. "Really, it shouldn't be the Charlatans *UK*," Burgess asserted in *Rolling Stone*. "It should be the Charlatans *the World*, shouldn't it?"

The Charlatans did take their tour worldwide from America, performing in Japan, England, and Europe, where they played numerous festival dates. Critics generally received the band with praise but accused them of trying to recreate 1960s music with their psychedelic sound. "We want to be progressive, not retrospective," Burgess insisted in *Rolling Stone*. The singer told Chris Roberts in *Melody Maker*, "We *are* a band of our time, but I think we'll *exceed* the time.... I just think we're the ultimate force. As a unit, we are the ultimate force. I can say that with a lot of confidence."

Plagued by Difficulties

In a thorny twist, the year 1991 threw many obstacles in the path of the Charlatans UK. In August Jon Baker left the band, claiming he had nothing more to offer the project. Then, in October, the group was forced to cancel several concerts in Europe because bassist Martin Blunt had collapsed from a mental breakdown while the band was in the studio. According to a report in *Melody Maker*, Blunt is a diagnosed manic depressive and suffered similar attacks before the Charlatans signed with Beggars Banquet. Blunt kept a doctor in the studio with him after he was discharged from the hospital.

The Charlatans recruited guitarist Mark Collins, formerly of the Waltones, to replace Baker. And in 1992 the band released their second album, *Between 10th & 11th*, and their hit single "Weirdo." Produced by Flood, who had worked with the likes of U2, Depeche Mode, and Nine Inch Nails, the LP nonetheless did not measure up to the success of the group's debut. It spent just two weeks on the *Billboard* 200 and sold less than 100,000 copies in the United States.

Adversity hit the band again in December of 1992, when Rob Collins was arrested with his friend Michael Whitehouse on charges relating to an armed robbery. Collins claimed that he did not think Whitehouse would commit the crime—until he heard a gunshot while he waited for him in his car. When Whitehouse returned, he drove him away from the scene. Collins pleaded guilty to assisting the offender, and the court sentenced him to eight months in jail.

The Charlatans spent 1993 recording their next album, though they did take some time off to play the two-day Daytripper Festival in Brighton, a show in Blackpool, and the alternative-rock Reading Festival. They returned in 1994 with *Up To Our Hips*, which they recorded at Monnow Valley studios in Monmouth, south Wales, with producer Steve Hillage. They released "Can't Get Out of Bed" as the first single from the album and began yet another worldwide jaunt.

The Charlatans had survived the rise and demise of the Manchester music scene. "I think it was really healthy for music at the time," Burgess said in an Atlantic Records press biography. "I'm proud to have grown up in Northwich and lived through it. There were a lot of groups that came and went, but the music's always been more important than where it came from."

The Charlatans had modified their organ-drenched sound to lean more on guitars. "Everyone's always said we're a strong live band," Burgess explained in the band's biography, "and we wanted to sound that good on record. We let ourselves go a bit." With a new approach to their music, the band also decided the time had come to drop the UK from their name. They did not decide to change it to "the Charlatans the World," but no doubt they still plan to conquer it.

Selected discography

Some Friendly, Beggars Banquet/RCA, 1990.
Between 10th & 11th, Beggars Banquet/RCA, 1992.
Up to Our Hips, Beggars Banquet/Atlantic, 1994.

Sources

Billboard, April 20, 1991; May 23, 1992; February 19, 1994.
Melody Maker, January 13, 1990; February 10, 1990; March 3, 1990; March 31, 1990; May 12, 1990; May 19, 1990; June 9, 1990; June 16, 1990; October 13, 1990; November 3, 1990; November 17, 1990; December 22, 1990; March 9, 1991; June 15, 1991; June 22, 1991; October 5, 1991; October 12, 1991; December 21, 1991; February 22, 1992; March 7, 1992; May 22, 1993; August 28, 1993; September 25, 1993.
Musician, June 1992; May 1994.
Raygun, April 1994.
Rolling Stone, April 18, 1991; July 9, 1992.

Additional information for this profile was obtained from Atlantic Records press materials, 1994.

—*Sonya Shelton*

Mark Chesnutt

Singer, guitarist

Photograph by Keith Carter, courtesy of MCA Nashville

Country singer Mark Chesnutt has taken up the reins of traditional honky-tonk for a ride into the future. With his roots in the musical traditions of working-class Texas, Chesnutt can belt out a barnburner, then turn around and tug at a listener's heartstrings with a sentimental ballad. The singer has taken slow, sure steps along the road to success and gained legions of fans that have driven each of his albums to the top of the country charts.

Born in 1963, Chesnutt was raised in Beaumont, Texas, in the thick of the traditional country music milieu. His father, Bob Chesnutt, had recorded several singles on a Nashville label during the 1960s and 1970s before deciding to end his musical career for a more viable way of supporting his family; he was quick to encourage his son's budding musical talent. "There was always a radio going to a country station," Chesnutt told Neil Pond in *Country America,* "and my daddy was always playing records—George Jones, Merle Haggard, Charley Pride, Johnny Cash, Ernest Tubb. Music was everywhere. It was always around." Young Mark practiced by singing to the records in his father's collection, and he still maintains a strong love for the old country classics.

Chesnutt got his first taste of performing in his mid-teens, when he accompanied his parents to local bars. He often sat in with members of the band that his father knew, and was soon singing right along with the other musicians. After a while, he started getting paid for his time and was encouraged to make a commitment to becoming a singer. When he decided to quit high school a year before graduation, his father gave him some strong advice: "My daddy told me if I was gonna quit school that I would have to be damn sure that I was gonna really work hard at music," Chesnutt noted in an MCA Records press release, "because I wouldn't be able to do anything else, which was fine with me because I didn't want to do anything else."

In 1981 at age 17, Chesnutt began recording for independent labels in San Antonio and Houston, while also shopping Nashville for new songs and a deal with a national label. A recording of "Too Cold at Home" that he made for Houston's Cherry label came to the attention of producer Tony Brown and the executives at MCA/Nashville. Once they heard the singer's rich baritone voice, the label was quick in bringing young Chesnutt on board.

Chesnutt hit the national country scene in 1991 with his debut album *Too Cold at Home.* Half the songs from that album became hit singles, including the swinging "Blame It on Texas," the upbeat "Your Love Is a Miracle," and the clever title cut. By the close of that

For the Record . . .

Born September 6, 1963, in Beaumont, TX; son of Bob (a former musician) and Norma Chesnutt; married Tracie Motley, 1992.

Worked for Montgomery Ward department store while attending high school in Texas; sang in nightclubs throughout southern Texas, beginning 1980; signed with MCA/Nashville, 1992.

Awards: Horizon Award, Country Music Association, 1993.

Addresses: *Record company*—MCA/Nashville, 60 Music Sq. E., Nashville, TN 37203. *Publicist*—Sharon Allen, The Brokaw Company, 1106 16th Ave., Nashville, TN 37212.

year, *Too Cold at Home* was certified gold and Chesnutt had received his first nomination for the Country Music Association's (CMA) Horizon Award honoring upcoming talent.

In spite of his youth, Chesnutt had 10 years of solid, on-the-road nightclub performance experience behind him by the time he cut his first album, and when he began touring with the New South Band, audiences sat up and took notice. As a warm-up for more well-known country acts, his show was high-energy honky-tonk and proved to be a hard act to follow. "People who haven't seen us don't realize what kind of show we put on," he modestly explained in an MCA press release. "It's not flashy but a lot of fun, a lot of energy, a lot of movement. It's not choreographed, it's just a bunch of us having a good time."

By the time his second album, *Longnecks and Short Stories,* was released in 1992, Chesnutt was getting top billing on the road. The album earned him four more singles on its way to the gold, including "Old Flames Have New Names," "I'll Think of Something," and the humorous "Bubba Shot the Jukebox." Especially memorable is "Talking to Hank," a duet Chesnutt performs with his musical hero and fellow-Texan George Jones.

As with his first album, *Longnecks* carries the distinctive Chesnutt sound. "There's a certain type of music that comes from southeast Texas," Chesnutt explained to James Hunter in *LA Weekly,* discussing the music that has influenced him since he was a child. "I think it has to do with a fusion of Cajun, zydeco and just pure country. There's a little bit of Texas swing down there, but not much. There's more of a bluesy feel. And hardly any bluegrass."

But Chesnutt's success had a bittersweet side. In 1992 he wed his longtime sweetheart, Tracie Motley, but was still recovering from the death of the man who had served as one of his greatest inspirations: Chesnutt's father died in 1990, just as Mark's career was beginning to take off. "He wanted to be involved in what I'm doin', and that's what I planned on," Chesnutt told *Country Music's* Bob Millard. The singer had hoped that his father would eventually accompany him on the road. "I'd like to think that he's still somewhere around watching and listening," Chesnutt confided to Pond in *Country America.* "A lot of times, when I'm tired or feeling bad, I kind of feel him there, kicking me in the butt and saying, 'Come on, don't start wimping out on me now.'"

Chesnutt was already enjoying a growing reputation as an energetic stage performer and a popular vocalist when his third album, *Almost Goodbye,* hit the charts with a bang in the fall of 1993. "It Sure Is Monday," a country ode to "the day after the big night out," was the first single out of the gate in the race to the top of the charts. "I Just Wanted You to Know" and "Woman, Sensuous Woman" were soon to follow. As singles off *Almost Goodbye* continued to jockey for position at the top of the country music charts, Chesnutt was finally honored by the CMA with the coveted Horizon Award.

"I love to go to a bar now with a jukebox that has all those old songs," Chesnutt told Millard. "That's what I learned to sing on—songs like "She Thinks I Still Care," "Swingin' Doors," and "The Bottle Let Me Down." To me there's a mystique about that. I would rather listen to any old cryin'-in-your-beer George Jones or Merle Haggard song than anything." In fact, Chesnutt probably knows the lyrics to more honky-tonk songs than most people outside Texas have ever heard. As a child, he memorized entire albums of music by his favorite singers, and once he set out to make it in the music business, he worked even harder at expanding his repertoire. "A lot of people can name a singer and an old song, and I probably know it," he admitted.

But the biggest thrill for Chesnutt is when he goes in a honky-tonk back home and the voice from the jukebox is his own. As he told Millard: "After all those years learnin' everybody else's songs, and now somebody else is learnin' mine—even if they're killin' 'em. That's what really tells me something—tells me I'm really here."

Selected discography

Too Cold at Home (includes title track and "Blame It on Texas"), MCA, 1990.
Longnecks and Short Stories (includes "Old Flames Have New Names," "I'll Think of Something," and "Bubba Shot the Jukebox"), MCA, 1992.
Almost Goodbye (includes "I Just Wanted You to Know"), MCA, 1993.

Sources

Billboard, February 13, 1993.
Country America, February 1994.
Country Music, July 1992.
Country Song Roundup, September 1993.
Kansas City Star (Missouri), August 10, 1992.
LA Weekly, April 24, 1992.
Tulsa World, May 4, 1991.

Additional information for this profile was obtained from MCA Records publicity materials, 1994.

—Pamela L. Shelton

Van Cliburn

Pianist

Van Cliburn was transformed from a highly regarded yet relatively unknown artist to musical superstar faster than any other classical musician in history. Through grand playing in the style of great pianists of the past and the luck of timing, he became a worldwide celebrity in the late 1950s. Cliburn was revered as a hero when he won the first Tchaikovsky Competition in the Soviet Union in 1958, idolized both by Soviet fans who respected his immense talent and by Americans who saw him as a symbol of triumph in the Cold War against Communism.

After capitalizing on his new fame by signing a long-term recording contract with RCA after his return from Moscow, Cliburn toured relentlessly over the next two decades. However, over the years his playing lost its freshness, and his performances became more broad and overwrought. Many critics feel that the artist never reached his potential as a concert pianist.

Cliburn was a musical prodigy whose mother was also a gifted pianist and piano teacher. Rildia Bee Cliburn had studied with Arthur Friedheim, who had been a pupil of Franz Liszt in the nineteenth century. Upon hearing the three-year-old Van, who could not yet read music, playing a song she had been teaching one of her pupils, Cliburn's mother began giving her son lessons. She remained his only teacher until he went to New York 14 years later to study at the Juilliard School of Music. Discussing his mother in *Vogue,* Cliburn said, "She watched me like a hawk, even if she wasn't in the same room. She taught me to listen; she taught me everything. And I just loved to play; it seemed like I was born to play the piano."

Progressing rapidly, Cliburn performed at the age of four at Dodd College in Shreveport, Louisiana. He practiced relentlessly, getting up to play for an hour before school, another hour after school, and again after dinner. Family life was subjugated completely to his progress as a musician. His father even had a studio constructed for his son on the back of the garage. In school Cliburn was allowed to avoid physical education classes to prevent hand injury. He continued his studies after the family moved to Killgore, Texas, where he also played clarinet in his in high school band.

Childhood Studies Led to Juilliard

At age 13 Cliburn played his first performance of Tchaikovsky's *Concerto No. 1 in B-flat Minor,* one of the pieces that would later make him famous, with the Houston Symphony Orchestra. One year later he performed for the first time at Carnegie Hall as a result of winning the National Music Award. By this time it was the top students there, winning a number of awards and continuing to appear with major symphony orchestras such as the Dallas Symphony in 1952 and the New York Philharmonic Orchestra at Carnegie Hall in 1954. Cliburn earned his Philharmonic performance by winning the Edgar M. Leventritt Foundation Award that year, an award that had not even been presented for five years before Cliburn was honored. In his review of the concert at Carnegie Hall, Irving Kolodin in the *Saturday Review* called Cliburn the "most talented newcomer of the season," who "literally commands the piano as he plays and in many ways the music too."

After graduating from Juilliard with top honors in 1954, Cliburn began a very active touring schedule. He performed in 30 engagements during the next concert season and continued playing in major U.S. cities over the following two years. Virtually every performance was regarded with critical acclaim. As Michael Sternberg noted in the introduction of *The Van Cliburn Legend,* "In his early career Cliburn was admired for the completeness of his technical command and for his massive, unpercussive tone."

Became Famous for Moscow Victory

Despite the steady stream of accolades for his playing, Cliburn did not break into the top ranks of concert pianists during the mid-1950s. Requests to perform had decreased significantly by late in the decade, and he found himself in debt. Further interrupting his progress was his mother's illness, which necessitated his return home to Killgore to help out with his mother's teaching and physical needs. Although he was ready to stage a European tour in 1958, he was urged by Lhevinne and others to take part in the first International Tchaikovsky piano competition to take place in Moscow that year. In hopes of resuscitating his flagging career, Cliburn practiced up to 11 hours a day for two months while preparing his pieces for the Moscow performance.

Cliburn's work for the Tchaikovsky competition paid off, and almost immediately he took the proceedings by storm. Despite rumors that the Soviet cultural ministers had already ordered the prize to be awarded to a Soviet musician, Cliburn's mastery and his massive popularity with thousands of fervent Soviet fans overruled any favoritism. The judges were unanimous in awarding him the top prize, even though Cliburn had to play with a bandaged index finger and suffered a broken piano string during his final concert.

Many musicians and critics in the Soviet Union compared Cliburn's performing and tour of Russia to that of

clear that Cliburn preferred to play pieces by Romantic composers such as Liszt, Chopin, Rachmaninoff, and Tchaikovsky.

Cliburn attended summer school classes in order to finish high school by age 16 so he could move on to higher musical studies. He entered Juilliard in 1951, where he studied with Rosina Lhevinne, the wife of the late concert pianist Josef Lhevinne. He became one of

Liszt in the previous century. Further publicizing the victory was Americans' eagerness to find an edge over the Soviet Union after the Russians' successful launching of Sputnik, which put a human in space for the first time. By winning the adulation of both Soviet leader Nikita Khrushchev and U.S. President Dwight D. Eisenhower, Cliburn seemed to have single-handedly eased Cold War tensions. He was quoted in *Texas Monthly* as saying, "I think that political events come, and they pass. They have no staying power. But art always remains with us."

Cliburn returned to the United States to a welcome similar to that received by Charles Lindbergh after his epic transatlantic flight in the 1920s. He was the only classical musician in history to be honored by a ticker-tape parade in New York City, and his face appeared on the cover of *Time* magazine as "The Texan Who Conquered Russia." He cashed in on his new fame by signing the most lucrative recording contract ever, with RCA Victor. His debut recording of Tchaikovsky's *B-flat Minor Concerto* for his new label became the first classical record to achieve sales of one million dollars.

Cliburn was besieged by requests to appear on talk shows and to perform upon his return to the United States. After appearing at Carnegie Hall to thunderous acclaim, he moved on to concert engagements in Philadelphia, Chicago, Hollywood, and Denver. Next he went abroad to play in Brussels, London, Amsterdam, and Paris. Cliburn demonstrated his patriotism in every performance of his concerts by leading off with his rendition of "The Star Spangled Banner."

Never Fulfilled Expected Potential

After losing a season due to an infected finger, Cliburn returned to the Soviet Union to stage a triumphant tour in 1960. He began conducting on a limited basis in 1964, but never advanced in that musical realm. Rapid fame and an exhausting schedule of touring, which often had Cliburn playing three days out of four during subsequent years, took their toll on the performer. Partly due to the demands of audiences to hear him play his prize-winning Tchaikovsky piece, he did not broaden his range as critics hoped he would. He was accused of lacking the intellectual curiosity that was necessary to fully develop his talent.

Cliburn became inconsistent in his recitals, and his sound became rougher and trivialized by affectations. He also became somewhat of a prima donna, feeling crippled by expectations and stage fright, and often appearing late or cancelling concerts. Gradually Cliburn reduced his appearances until, after two decades of

performing in almost 100 concerts a year, he withdrew completely from the concert circuit in 1978. At the time he insisted that it was only a temporary respite, although he offered no timetable for returning to public performances.

During the next decade he lived at home with his mother in one of the largest and most famous houses in an exclusive neighborhood of Forth Worth, Texas. In a home with 15 pianos, he spent his time composing both popular and classical music, including a piano sonata that he never performed. Cliburn finally returned to the public as a performer in 1987, when he performed a recital in a concert for U.S. President Ronald Reagan and Soviet General Secretary Mikhail Gorbachev at the White House. Over the ensuing years he made occasional appearances, including as a soloist performing Liszt and Tchaikovsky piano concertos with the Philadelphia Orchestra in 1989. That year he also returned to Moscow to play.

In 1994, at the age of 60, Cliburn began his first national tour since 1978, in accompaniment with the Moscow Philharmonic. Despite his lack of development, Cliburn will always be considered one of the great intuitive musicians, a performer who could channel his emotions into the keyboard to bring out the full intensity of the Romantic composers. As Michael Walsh wrote in *Time,* "Cliburn really is a throwback to the piano's Golden Age of blazing virtuosity and emotional extravagance."

Selected discography

(With Kiril Kondrashin) Tchaikovsky, *Concerto No. 1 in B-flat Minor,* RCA, 1958.

(With Kondrashin and RCA Symphony Orchestra) Rachmaninoff, *Concerto No. 2 in C Minor,* RCA Red Seal, 1958.

(With Kiril Kondrashin and the Symphony of the Air) Rachmaninoff, *Concerto No. 3 in D Minor,* RCA.

Chopin, *Sonata No. 2 in B-flat Minor ('Funeral March')* and *Sonata No. 3 in B Minor,* RCA.

(With Eugene Ormandy and the Philadelphia Orchestra) Grieg, *Concerto in A Minor* and Liszt, *Concerto No. 1 in E Flat,* RCA.

My Favorite Debussy, RCA.

Sources

Books

Chasins, Abram, and Villa Stiles, *The Van Cliburn Legend,* Doubleday, 1959.

Reich, Howard, *Van Cliburn,* Thomas Nelson, 1993.

Periodicals

Musical America, September 1989; March 1991.
New York Post, May 16, 1958.
New York Times, April 12, 1958; April 28, 1991; October 24, 1993; March 3, 1994.
Ovation, September 1989.
Saturday Review, November 27, 1954.
Texas Monthly, May 1987.
Time, April 21, 1958; July 32, 1989; July 25, 1994.
U.S. News, April 25, 1958.
Vogue, October 1990.

—Ed Decker

Curve

Rock band

"I think I'm optimistically paranoid. I don't know the answers; I'm just like everyone else—swimming around with the sharks biting." So Toni Halliday, lead singer of the band Curve, described the mind-set behind their haunting music to Jon Levy of *Strobe* magazine. Halliday and guitarist Dean Garcia, who provides the grating yet ethereal music that entwines the singer's siren vocals, create the dark, menacing sound that is uniquely Curve. Both artists weathered difficult childhood circumstances, experiences that have no doubt inspired the macabre and cynical nature of their music.

When she was four years old, Halliday's father bought a yacht and decided to take the family on a cruise of the Mediterranean. "We had this really idyllic fantastic life, and then it just stopped ... one day," she revealed to Caren Myers of *Details* magazine. The yachtsman abruptly deserted the family in Greece when Halliday was eight, her father simply informing her mother that he didn't love her anymore; the family never saw him again. His sudden departure left a profound impres-

Photograph by Eddie Monsoon, courtesy of Charisma Records

For the Record . . .

Members include **Dean Garcia** (married Julie Fletcher), guitar, bass, keyboards; **Toni Halliday,** vocals; **Alex Mitchell,** guitar; **Steve Monti,** drums; and **Debbie Smith,** guitar.

Garcia and Halliday formed band State of Play, 1984 (disbanded, 1985); formed Curve, c. 1990; recorded EP *Blindfold*, 1991; band expanded to include Mitchell, Monti, and Smith; released album *Doppelgänger*, 1992.

Addresses: *Record company*—Virgin Records, 790 Broadway, 20th Floor, New York, NY 10019; 338 North Foothill Rd., Beverly Hills, CA 90210.

sion on the young girl; she feels that most of her emotional issues stem from an inability to trust, which is perhaps why her sometimes agonizing lyrics fall so naturally unaffected from her lips. "In order for you to be able to do something that is natural and part of you, you have to dig deep inside yourself, which can be quite a dangerous little journey, because you don't know what you're going to find. Often you find things that you f—ing hate." Still, when pressed by Levy, the singer admitted to her belief that "the danger is everything."

Childhood Traumas

Garcia's childhood traumas began before he was born. On learning of the impending pregnancy, his father, a Hawaiian G.I., conveniently disappeared, leaving Garcia's Irish-Catholic mother to face her disapproving family and community alone. Unwed during the socially restrictive 1950s, she was pressured into having an abortion. Although she thought she had successfully terminated the pregnancy, a month later she was still pregnant, discovering that she had been carrying twins. One had been successfully aborted; the other, however, Dean, was born six months later. After his birth, Dean's mother married twice. One husband was abusive; both marriages ended. While he says that he would like to hire a private investigator to track down his father one day, that day has not yet presented itself. From these shattered childhoods emerged the two battered souls that create the abrasive melancholy that is Curve.

When Halliday was 11, she realized that she could sing; at 12 she joined a punk band called Incest. Dave Stewart of Eurythmics discovered her when she was

15. "I met [Dave Stewart] when I was 15 and we both lived in Sunderland [in the northeast of England]. He was still in the Tourists; they were about to do their last record before they split up, and he already had this idea of doing something with Annie [Lennox]. I used to do the B-sides of their singles," she told Paul Sexton of *Billboard*. Stewart urged her to join the Uncles, and she recorded a single with them called "What's the Use of Pretending?" before they split up.

Garcia, meanwhile, had been playing in numerous small bands when he auditioned for Eurythmics in 1983. "It was brilliant: One week I'm on the dole, the next I'm playing for Eurythmics, who'd just got to number one with 'Sweet Dreams.' Dave [Stewart] and Annie [Lennox] got me out of trouble and took me 'round the world," Garcia related to Mat Snow of *Musician*. It was backstage at a 1984 Eurythmics concert that Stewart introduced Halliday and Garcia to each other. Mesmerized by Halliday's "look" and "sound," Garcia recruited her to help him form a techno-pop-funk band called State of Play, which was signed to Virgin Records.

A year and £100,000 in debt later, the band split up. Halliday sued Garcia, and Garcia tried, unsuccessfully, to countersue Halliday. Garcia then married Julie Fletcher and moved to Spain. Halliday signed to Stewart's Anxious label and released a solo album, *Hearts and Handshakes.* In spite of having no commercial success and leaving nothing but debt in its wake, the record is now a collectors item.

Former Adversaries Reunited

In December of 1989, Garcia returned from Spain and found, to his amazement, that Halliday was trying to contact him. Once he was completely convinced that he would be meeting with Halliday, and not a legal representative, he agreed to see her, and they began to heal the old wounds. Amid the drunken bliss of their reunion, they conceived of Curve. They agreed that State of Play's main problems were an "open" budget, an excessive tendency to waste time, and too many outside influences.

Learning from these lessons, when they finally got together to record *Blindfold*, they wrote and recorded all the tracks in one day at a cost of under £300, with producer Alan Moulder on hand, who also played guitar on the EP. Seemingly overnight, the EP became a success in England, which caught Halliday and Garcia off guard. "Everyone immediately expected us to play gigs and be brilliant. But there was only me and Toni. Alan [Moulder] didn't want to know about playing guitar live," Garcia told Alan Di Perna of *Guitar Player*. So they enlisted the help of drummer Steve Monti and additional guitarists Alex Mitchell and Debbie Smith. That May they released the *Frozen* EP, followed in November by the *Cherry* EP.

Toured U.S.

In February of 1992, they unveiled another short disc, *Faît Accompli,* just prior to the release of their much-awaited full-length album *Doppelgänger*. In late 1992 the band toured the United States with the Jesus and Mary Chain and Spiritualized in support of their U.S.-only release *Pubic Fruit,* a compilation of their first three British EPs. They had determined to shoulder the responsibilities of album production largely by themselves.

Garcia explained the process to Di Perna, remarking, "It's a unique situation. Because the co-producer is usually there from the start. But we like to take it to 80% ourselves. Then we transfer and bring someone with us to sprinkle on a little fairy dust." Although it seems like an isolated way to work, this method keeps the band close to the musical core of Curve and prevents anything from adulterating their unique musical chemistry.

Their 1993 follow-up album, *Cuckoo,* was well received by both their fans and the press. When asked about her still melancholy tone in the face of such acceptance, Halliday told Gary Lineker of *Raygun* magazine, "I don't know why, but every time I open my mouth, a minor melody seems to come out." When asked about her goals, the singer told *Strobe's* Levy, "My main wish is to tell great stories, to teach.... It's alright to be terrible, and it's alright to be brilliant, but to be mediocre is the worst thing ever."

Selected discography

Blindfold (EP), Anxious Records, 1991.
Frozen (EP), Anxious Records, 1991.
Cherry (EP), Anxious Records, 1991.
Faît Accompli (EP), Anxious Records, 1991.
Doppelgänger, Anxious Records, 1992.
Pubic Fruit (U.S.) Anxious/Charisma, 1992.
Blackerthreetracker (EP), Anxious/Charisma, 1993.
Cuckoo, Anxious/Charisma, 1993.

Sources

B-Side, December 1993/January 1994.
Billboard, April 18, 1992; October 9, 1993.
Details, August 1992.
Guitar Player, June 1992; August 1992; December 1992.
Melody Maker, February 29, 1992; March 14, 1992; June 20, 1992; July 4, 1992; December 19, 1992; June 5, 1993; August 21, 1993; August 28, 1993; September 11, 1993; September 18, 1993.
Musician, February 1992.
Raygun, November 1993.
Rolling Stone, May 14, 1992.
Spin, April 1992; January 1993.
Strobe, January/February 1994.

Additional information for this profile was obtained from Virgin Records press material, 1994.

—*Charlie Katagiri*

Dick Dale

Guitarist

"The staccato is so fast it heat-treats the strings.... [And] I grind so hard that the guitar picks just melt down," Dick Dale told Jon Pareles of the *New York Times* in 1994. Still playing guitar in the frenzied, powerful style that spawned "surf music" in the late 1950s, Dale was riding a comeback wave in the 1990s.

Dale was born Richard Monsour in Beirut, Lebanon, in the late 1930s. Having immigrated with his family to the United States as a child, he grew up in Boston, Massachusetts, and then moved to Los Angeles in his senior year of high school. The next year, Dale began his musical career by winning a "Rocket to Stardom" contest, but the electric guitar and California surfing had not yet influenced his music: he won as a country singer. The contest victory led to appearances in Los Angeles clubs and on such country television shows as *Spade Cooley* and *Town Hall Party*. His name change dates to this era; a disc jockey suggested Dick Dale, thinking it would make a good name for a country singer.

Courtesy of HighTone Records

For the Record . . .

Born Richard Monsour, c. 1938, in Beirut, Lebanon; immigrated to the United States; married first wife, Jill; married second wife, Jeannie, c. 1967; remarried Jill; children: one son.

Began career as a country singer in California; won a local "Rocket to Stardom" contest, which led to appearances in Los Angeles clubs and on country music television shows; developed new guitar sound, "surf music," in late 1950s; founded band Dick Dale and the Del-Tones and played to capacity crowds at the Rendezvous Ballroom in Balboa, CA, early 1960s; appeared in four Frankie Avalon and Annette Funicello movies; popularity declined in the mid-1960s; took one-year hiatus to recuperate from rectal cancer, then played in clubs until 1976; achieved a small comeback in early 1980s, but retired again soon after; appeared in *Back to the Beach*, 1988; began performing again in early 1990s.

Addresses: *Home*—Twentynine Palms, CA. *Record company*—HighTone Records, 220 4th St., No. 101, Oakland, CA 94607.

Dale grew up a natural musician; he has been known to play piano, drums, trumpet, sax, and harmonica in addition to guitar during his shows. He taught himself the ukulele as a child using a book of chords. However, the left-handed Dale did not realize he was holding the instrument upside down and backwards. As a teenager, he bought his first guitar for eight dollars and proceeded to play it upside down as well. Not knowing what to do with the instrument's extra strings, he began by simply muffling them and playing ukulele chords. Although he later learned to master all of the strings, he continued to play the guitar upside down.

Began Wave of "Surf Music"

Early in his career, Dale was transformed from a country singer who played rhythm guitar to an electric guitarist who favored feverishly picked, instrumental-only music. After Dale learned to surf, he tried to pattern his playing after the rolling and crashing of the waves. By the time he was hired to play at the Rendezvous Ballroom in Balboa, California, in 1957, the majority of his fans were surfers. To insure that all the male members of his audience would meet the club's dress code, on opening night Dale placed a box of ties at the entrance for the surfers who arrived. Despite that modest beginning, Dick Dale and the Del-Tones were soon playing to audiences of 4,000 at the Rendezvous.

Within a few years, Dale had released his first album, *Surfers' Choice*, thanks to financing provided by his father. After the private-label album sold an astonishing 88,000 copies, Capitol Records signed Dale. The contract included a $50,000 advance—an outrageous sum in those days. His first hit, 1961's "Let's Go Trippin'," firmly established the "surf music" sound and helped spread it across the nation. Dale followed with the hits "Surf Beat" and "Miserlou," which combine a mideastern melody and descending sixteenth-note glissandi. His fame swelled quickly in the early 1960s; 21,000 fans attended his performance at the Los Angeles Sports Arena in 1961.

The innovative Dale sound set off a "surf music" craze. Patrick Ganahl described the often-imitated but never duplicated sound in *Guitar Player*: "A heavy, driving beat; an insistent, stomping bass; and, possibly for the first time in popular music, a focus on prolonged, reverb-laden electric guitar solos and instrumentals." Oddly enough, Dale acknowledges no other guitarists as special influences on his sound; instead, he cites jazz drummer Gene Krupa as the inspiration for his style of guitar playing. Dale's own influence, however, goes beyond the indisputable affect he had on surf bands such as the Ventures and the Beach Boys. Strip away the surf label, say some music critics, and Dale's music can be viewed as a precursor to metal.

Dale worked directly with Leo Fender, the famed designer and manufacturer of guitars and amplifiers, to develop the type of equipment he needed to create his now-legendary sound. Fender designed "The Beast" for Dale, a customized Stratocaster guitar that could withstand the abuse Dale piled on his instrument. Sheer volume was an important component of Dale's sound: after blowing up more than 48 amplifiers, Fender and Dale approached Lansing Speaker with specifications for a speaker that would not burn, flex, twist, or break on him.

Surf Craze Washed Up

Although Dale and his Del-Tones had achieved phenomenal popularity in the early 1960s, they faded almost as quickly in the mid-1960s. While partly attributable to Dale's reluctance to tour nationally or to be promoted, the group's decline more probably resulted from the sudden fame of the Beatles and other British-invasion groups. The final blow to the Del-Tones came in 1967 when Dale was diagnosed with rectal cancer. He stopped performing and recording to recuperate in Hawaii for a year.

Although Dale later returned to performing on a small scale, he refused to record further. "I quit recording because they could never capture my guitar the way it should sound. It's so much more powerful and stronger." He parlayed a small investment in real estate into substantial wealth and bought a 40-acre estate and a musical club in California. In 1976 he retired from the musical world completely and turned his attention to his family and his collection of wild animals, among them Siberian tigers and African lions. Dale returned briefly to the music scene in the early 1980s and released one last album before retiring again.

Tides Turned; Comeback a Success

Dale made a reappearance in 1988 with a cameo in the surf spoof *Back to the Beach* starring Annette Funicello and Frankie Avalon. Then in the early 1990s an old friend, Jim Selvin, called to congratulate Dale on the birth of his son and convinced him to travel to San Francisco to perform. Not only was that performance sold out, but so were the next five. Convinced that an enthusiastic audience awaited him, Dale returned whole-heartedly to touring and recording.

Dale used his old Stratocaster, "The Beast," and his old amp, but took his new inspiration from his wild animals rather than the surf. "I'd think about the force of my mountain lion. My African lions, they'd roar at 5:30 and the ground would shake. I would feel that when I played on my guitar, and I would imitate that." Whatever the source, the "Dick Dale sound" had returned. And fans, both old and new, were responding. Dale proved to be popular not only with reminiscing middle-aged listeners, but also with a new college crowd. Fans called the music "Dick-rock" and some sported T-shirts that read "I'm a Dickhead."

HighTone Records released Dale's *Tribal Thunder* in 1993 and *Unknown Territory* in 1994. "If possible,

[Dale's] reverb-soaked sound is better than ever," assessed *Billboard* in a review of *Tribal Thunder*. A *Guitar Player* reviewer noted: "Dick's first new album in nine years brilliantly merges shrill, powerful guitar playing with the thunderous rhythm section of double drummers Prairie Prince and Scott Matthews and bassists Ron Eglit and Rowland Salley." For the first time, Dale toured cross-country and had plans to tour in Europe. He described his pleasure at performing again to *New York Times* writer Pareles: "I just go on sonic, nonchemical rides of sound."

Selected discography

Tribal Thunder, HighTone, 1993.
Unknown Territory, HighTone, 1994.
Surfers' Choice, Deltone.
King of the Surf Guitar, Capitol.
Checkered Flag, Capitol.
Mr. Eliminator, Capitol.
Summer Surf, Capitol.
Rock Out, Live at Ciro's, Capitol.
Greatest Hits, GNP Crescendo.

Also contributed single "Pipeline" to soundtrack *Back to the Beach*, Paramount, 1988.

Sources

Billboard, January 16, 1993; June 12, 1993.
Guitar Player, July 1981; August 1993.
Musician, May 1982; August 1994.
New York Times, May 1, 1994.
Rolling Stone, October 28, 1993.

Additional information for this profile was provided by HighTone Records publicity materials.

—Susan Windisch Brown

Iris DeMent

Singer, songwriter

In the notes to *Infamous Angel,* Iris DeMent's debut album, folk songwriter John Prine recalled listening to "Mama's Opry" while frying up a batch of pork chops. "Being the sentimental fellow I am, I got a lump in my throat and a tear fell from my eyes into the hot oil. Well, the oil popped out and burnt my arm as if the pork chops were trying to say, 'Shut up, or I'll really give you something to cry about.'"

DeMent has a knack for eliciting this sort of reaction. John Grooms of *Creative Loafing* admitted that Prine had good reason to cry: "It's as moving as songwriting can get without becoming maudlin." He pointed out that in the caustic age of the 1990s, the "spellbinding" DeMent puts critics in the precarious position of "sounding sappy." Comparing her to some of the legends of country music, *Guardian* contributor Charlotte Greig explained, "She has the straightforward, pure delivery of a Loretta Lynn or a Hank Williams, a voice that doesn't compromise with the coy mannerisms of pop," while her "songs have a cheerful, bouncy edge, coupled with a lump-in-the-throat emotional directness that stops you in your tracks."

Disregarding the lines between folk, country, bluegrass, and gospel, DeMent writes songs that recall previous generations of performers, especially country music's Carter Family and Jimmie Rodgers. In her "plaintive and imperfect dust bowl storyteller's voice," as Chris Barrett of Knoxville's *Metro Pulse* characterized it, she sings simple, forthright songs of family, love, and loss in a unembellished style, and with a subtle wit, rephrasing age old stories in very contemporary context.

The resulting music sounds very fresh. "Her voice is extraordinary, there's nobody like her," country singer Emmylou Harris effused in the *Chicago Tribune.* "There's such a homogeneous sound on radio today, it's almost a shock to hear something so immediately identifiable and unique."

DeMent was born in Paragould, Arkansas, on January 5, 1961, the youngest of Patric Shaw and Flora Mae DeMent's 14 children. The family had been farmers for generations, but shortly before Iris was born the farm failed and the DeMents moved into town. Three years later, they relocated to California, as did many people from their area. The family settled in Buena Vista, a suburb of Los Angeles, and Patric took a job as gardener and janitor at the Movieland Wax Museum and Palace of Living Art. But the DeMents retained their Arkansas ties, attending a Pentecostal church with the same pastor and much of the same congregation from their church back home.

For the Record . . .

Born January 5, 1961, in Paragould, AR; daughter of Patric Shaw (a farmer, janitor, and gardener) and Flora Mae DeMent; married Elmer McCall (a firefighter and road manager), November 16, 1991.

Began writing songs in 1986; performed at "open mic" nights in Kansas City, MO; moved to Nashville to write and perform; signed with Rounder/Philo, c. 1990; released *Infamous Angel,* 1992; signed with Warner Bros. and reissued *Infamous Angel,* 1993; released *My Life,* 1994.

Addresses: *Home*—P.O. Box 28856, Gladstone, MO 64188. *Record company*—Warner Bros., 3300 Warner Blvd., Burbank, CA 91505. *Management*—Peter Asher Management, 644 North Doheny Dr., Los Angeles, CA 90069.

Church and Music Were Inseparable

Music had always played a key role in the DeMents' lives. Patric was quite a fiddle player before Iris was born, and Flora Mae often dreamed of singing at the Grand Ole Opry—a dream that would later inspire Iris to write "Mama's Opry." The entire family sang at church and home; the children played piano, and Iris's sisters performed gospel for a time as the DeMent Sisters. "My parents wanted the boys to be preachers and the girls to be singers—forget college and all that stuff," DeMent told Greg Kot in the *Chicago Tribune.* "If you could be a preacher or singer, you were really on top."

As a child, DeMent heard mostly gospel music—"kind of old-time gospel, with a lot of harmony," she noted in *Acoustic Guitar*—and the family's favorites were Jimmie Rodgers and the Carter Family. Gospel however, wasn't the only music the budding artist loved. She listened to the folk-inflected music of Joni Mitchell and Bob Dylan, Aretha Franklin's R&B, and Johnny Cash and Tom T. Hall's country sounds. DeMent began making up songs when she was very young but did not have the confidence to pursue songwriting seriously. She recalled in the *Infamous Angel* liner notes, "I was so intimidated by the idea of these people who could really write songs that I could never get one right for me."

Instead of pursuing music, DeMent dropped out of school, left home at the age of 17, and bounced around the country working at a variety of jobs. She also moved away from the church, though its influence remains strong in her songs. By the time she was 25, DeMent was living in Topeka, Kansas, where a college creative writing course rekindled her desire to write music. "The writing and the music, the two things I loved the most, started coming together," she recalled in the *Los Angeles Times.* She began writing songs in her head because she didn't have a piano. Eventually she took up the more affordable guitar and taught herself to play with some help from her brother. The first full-fledged song she wrote was "Our Town," inspired by a drive through a deserted Oklahoma town.

DeMent then moved to Kansas City, Missouri, where she worked on her guitar skills and continued to write. After a year she worked up the courage to perform her songs and started participating in "open mic" nights. "My songs seemed to give me the courage I needed, that I didn't have before, to go out and sing in front of people," she revealed to Steve Dollar in the *Atlanta Journal-Constitution.* During this apprenticeship she saved her money and eventually moved to Nashville.

Took Off in Nashville

In Nashville, DeMent attracted the notice of a number of influential people in the recording industry. Record producer Jim Rooney, instrumental in advancing the career of country-folk musician Nanci Griffith, brought her to the attention of a Rounder/Philo executive, and she was quickly signed to a recording contract. Nashville performers took notice as well. Country singer Emmylou Harris invited DeMent to sing backup on her album *Brand New Dance,* and Griffith included her on the Grammy-winning 1993 album *Other Voices, Other Rooms.*

Rooney assisted DeMent on the production and recruitment of musicians for her first album, *Infamous Angel.* The instrumentation they chose was acoustic and spare—guitar, piano, fiddle, mandolin, dobro, and upright bass. Harris returned DeMent's earlier favor and sang harmony on "Mama's Opry," while on the spiritual "Higher Ground," DeMent gave the lead vocal to her favorite gospel singer—her mother. *Infamous Angel* was released in 1992 complete with John Prine's endorsement in the notes: "So listen to this music, this Iris DeMent. It's good for you."

The music press agreed wholeheartedly. As Steven Rosen wrote in the *Denver Post, Infamous Angel* "astonished those who have heard it." *Los Angeles Times* contributor Mike Boehm marveled at DeMent's "sweet old-time voice," and Mike Joyce, writing in the *Wash-*

ington Post, praised both her "unadorned, often church-inflected balladry" and "stellar" backing musicians.

Infamous Angel was immediately popular on non-commercial radio—public stations, adult album alternatives, and rural country—but mainstream stations showed little interest. Ironically, as a Rounder executive explained to Grooms in a Creative Loafing interview, country radio found her music "too country." Fortunately, many in the industry loved DeMent's music. Singer-songwriter Natalie Merchant took to performing DeMent's songs in concert, and with alternative rocker David Byrne did a rendition of the album's opening tune, "Let the Mystery Be," on MTV's Unplugged. Meanwhile, in early 1993, Warner's London A&R chief Andy Wickham played Infamous Angel for Warner Bros. President Lenny Waronker, who, according to Billboard, knew by the end of "Let the Mystery Be" that he wanted to sign her.

"DeMent's voice is extraordinary, there's nobody like her. There's such a homogeneous sound on radio today, it's almost a shock to hear something so immediately identifiable and unique."
—Emmylou Harris

DeMent agreed to move to Warner Bros. because they promised to let her do her music the way she wanted to do it—without forcing her to fit the glossy mainstream of country music. She told Paul Robicheau in an interview for the Boston Globe that savvy industry people thought she was naive to believe that Warner wouldn't push her into a mold, but she had little to fear. "If it isn't handled that way, I have a pretty loud screaming voice," she reassured him. The label executives held true to their word; that spring, they reissued Infamous Angel without making any changes or recutting any material.

With her album in the stores, DeMent began touring, first in the United States with Griffith, Prine, and country-folk singer Mary-Chapin Carpenter, and then solo in Europe. She even put in an appearance at an inaugural gala for President Bill Clinton in January of 1993. Having made her mark in Nashville, DeMent had by this time moved back to Kansas City to be with her firefighter boyfriend, Elmer McCall. They were married on November 16, 1991; when touring began to take her away from home, Elmer retired and began fighting different fires as DeMent's road manager.

My Life Simple Yet Stunning

DeMent's next album, 1994's My Life, proved she was right to trust Warner Bros. Once again, there was nothing slick about it. The themes of family, love, and loss were similar to her previous work, as was the spare instrumentation. The tone of My Life is darker, however; according to Newsweek's Jeff Giles, the album is "a crushingly sad meditation on love and childhood." Still, the somber lyrics and mood didn't disappoint the majority of music critics, who consistently praised the album. Giles suggested that "in a rational universe ... My Life would win a Grammy." Billboard, which found no track "less than stunning," agreed that the release offers "a more melancholy worldview," but contended that "it's the sweet kind, not the bitter, and it's easy to swallow when the presentation is unadorned acoustic guitar and piano that could be labeled country, bluegrass, or folk."

DeMent continued to receive an unusual amount of attention for such a noncommercial performer, including a feature article in Newsweek and an invitation to perform on The Tonight Show. Warner Bros. looked to this sort of exposure to expand DeMent's following. According to Billboard's Eric Boehlert, the label was anxious for as many people as possible to hear DeMent live, knowing not much of her music would be heard on commercial radio. To that end, she followed the release of My Life with an extensive tour of the United States and Europe. Label President Waronker expressed faith that her audience would grow. "I'll bet on her," he insisted in Billboard.

In "My Life," DeMent sings "My life, it's only a season/ A passing September that no one will recall." Entertainment Weekly contributor Alanna Nash firmly disagreed. "With writing such as this," she concluded, "such a forecast is doubtful." "It's something to watch, how she walks the tightrope of honest emotion without falling over into gushiness," Grooms observed. "Watching her lyrical/emotional highwire act—an act performed without a commercial safety net and one that in the end leaves you face to face with clear insights—can be exhilarating."

Selected discography

Infamous Angel (includes "Let the Mystery Be," "Our Town," "Mama's Opry," and "Higher Ground"), Rounder/Philo, 1992, reissued, Warner Bros., 1993.
My Life, Warner Bros., 1994.

Sources

Acoustic Guitar, July 1994.

Atlanta Journal-Constitution, June 6, 1992 (as reprinted from the *Philadelphia Inquirer*); March 13, 1993; April 23, 1994.

Billboard, March 12, 1994; April 23, 1994.

Boston Globe, June 4, 1993; April 21, 1994.

Chicago Tribune, July 11, 1993; April 21, 1994.

Christian Science Monitor, April 22, 1994.

Country Music, July 1994.

Creative Loafing (Atlanta), April 23, 1994.

Denver Post, October 2, 1992; April 28, 1994.

Detroit News, July 16, 1993.

Entertainment Weekly, September 4, 1992; April 15, 1994.

Guardian (London), May 12, 1993.

Knoxville News-Sentinel (Tennessee), April 24, 1994.

Los Angeles Times, March 6, 1993; April 17, 1994.

Metro Pulse (Knoxville, TN), April 22, 1994.

Metro Times (Detroit), April 27, 1994.

Musician, May 1994.

Nashville Scene, April 28, 1994.

New England Folk Almanac, June 1994.

Newsweek, April 18, 1994.

New York Times, October 31, 1992.

Pulse!, June 1994.

Rolling Stone, May 13, 1993; October 20, 1994.

San Francisco Chronicle, April 10, 1994.

Spin, June 1994.

Stereo Review, September 1992.

Washington Post, June 28, 1992.

Additional information for this profile was obtained from Peter Asher Management, Warner Bros. press materials, and the liner notes to *Infamous Angel* and *My Life.*

—Megan Rubiner Zinn

Devo

Rock band

" **T**hey are *freaked out*," wrote *Rolling Stone's* Michael Goldberg of Devo, the quintessentially 1970s new wave band. Howie Klein in *BAM,* reprinted in the liner notes to Devo's *Greatest Hits,* explained that the group is "a band full of nerds, or, as they call themselves, spuds.... These were the guys who did their homework every single day except the day the teacher decided to check it." Their jerky, mechanized movements, unusual, sci-fi-like stage wear, and heavy electronic keyboard sound underscored their personas as man-machines. Ultimately, Devo was a very political band; their name arose from their de-evolutionist, or "devolutionist" philosophy of life, which holds that the world is in a sorry state of decline, thanks particularly to what Goldberg referred to as "a mechanized, plasticized, programmed and subdued society."

Akron, Ohio, natives and Devo founders Mark Mothersbaugh and Gerald Casale met as art students at Kent State University around the time of the infamous riots during which four students were killed by the National

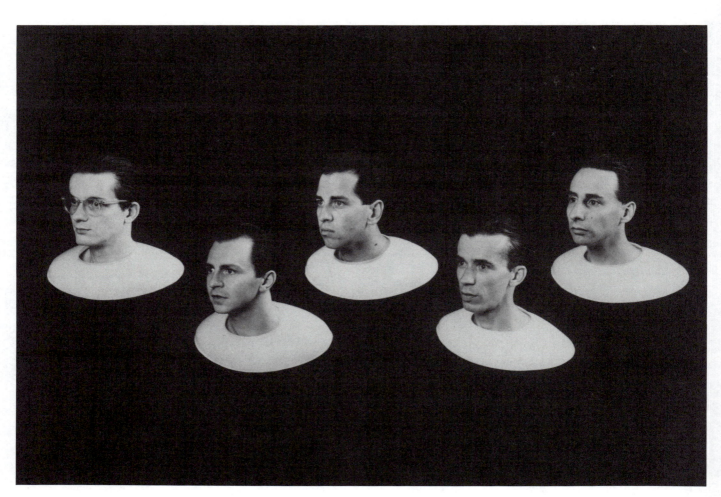

AP / Wide World Photos

Members include **Bob Casale,** guitar, keyboards; **Gerald V. Casale,** bass; **Bob Mothersbaugh,** guitar; **Mark Mothersbaugh,** vocals, synthesizers; **Alan Myers,** drums; **David Kendrick** (replaced Alan Myers in 1988), drums.

Band formed in Akron, Ohio, 1972; released "Jocko Homo/Mongoloid" single, 1976; made films *The Truth About De-evolution* and *In the Beginning Was the End,* late 1970s; released cover of the Rolling Stones' "(I Can't Get No) Satisfaction," 1977; Stiff Records in the United Kingdom licensed Devo's Booji Boy material, 1978; signed with Warner Bros., 1978; appeared in Neil Young's film *Rust Never Sleeps,* 1979, and *Human Highway,* 1981; contributed music to film *Doctor Detroit,* 1983; released *E-Z Listening Disk* (muzak renditions of their hits), 1987; signed with Enigma, 1988.

Gerald Casale has directed videos; Mark Mothersbaugh wrote music for CBS-TV's *Pee-Wee's Playhouse,* for films *It's Pat* and *The New Age,* both 1994, and for MTV's *Liquid Television;* had gallery shows of his silk screens; and wrote *What I Know,* a ten-volume, 3,500-page text.

Addresses: *Office*—Mutato Muzika, 2164 Sunset Plaza Dr., Los Angeles, CA 90069.

Guard; Casale called it "the most devo day of my life." The two were interested in an audio-visual project, with Casale on bass and Mothersbaugh playing progressive-sounding keyboard music and providing vocals. With their brothers, Bob Casale and Bob Mothersbaugh, on guitar, and Alan Meyers on drums, Devo formed, performing for audiences in Ohio, then branching out to New York and Los Angeles.

During live shows, Devo bandmembers dressed identically, often in strange, futuristic-looking garb that included flight suits, plastic toupees, or red tiered headwear resembling inverted flowerpots. Devo's act involved energetic stage antics, images projected on a screen behind the band, and the display of short films and videos. Eventually playing to capacity crowds and making television appearances on shows like *Saturday Night Live,* the band would also begin getting attention from such rock luminaries as Iggy Pop, David Bowie, and Brian Eno.

Devo satirized their views on dehumanization due to industry and technology with their first single, released on their own label, Booji Boy Records. The song, "Jocko Homo," succinctly asserted, "They tell us that/ We lost our tails/ Evolving up/ From little snails/ I say it's all/ Just wind in sails/ Are we not men?/ WE ARE DEVO!/ We're pinheads now/ We are not whole/ We're pinheads all/ Jocko Homo." The tune was a hit in the underground music scene and led to a contract with Warner Bros. in 1978; their first album would be produced by art-rock innovator Brian Eno. A *People* magazine reviewer wrote in 1980, "Devo's debut album (*Q: Are We Not Men? A: We Are Devo!*) no longer seems preposterous. It was obviously seminal."

Bestsellers or Sell-Outs?

Almost ever since, critics have debated whether or not Devo's later work continued the politics on their debut project or sold out to the conditions they were satirizing. Simon Reynolds of *Melody Maker* remembered Devo's music from the 1970s as "a deliberately opaque vision of mass braindeath, in which rock'n'roll, shorn of its rebellious pretensions, would be a prime agent of behaviorist control." With nothing less than pure appreciation, he added, "Disinfecting rock of its dirt, streamlining its all-too-human edges, Devo created perhaps the most repellent rock in history."

Unfortunately, however, Reynolds implied that very innovation is exactly what made the band too quickly dated. Kenneth Korman of *Video* generously suggested that "the larger story ... involves the complex relations among art, commerce and popular culture.... Devo never sold out its original intent—principally to make people stop and think—but eventually sagged under the weight of industry pressures."

Whether or not they "sold out," Devo did experience commercial popularity. Their first album included a clipped-sounding cover version of the Rolling Stones' "(I Can't Get No) Satisfaction," which became a hit, and *Freedom of Choice,* their third album, went gold and contained their hallmark single "Whip It." They also received attention for the 1981 remake of Lee Dorsey's "Working in a Coal Mine," which was included on the soundtrack for the animated film *Heavy Metal.*

Devo's poor man's art struck a nerve in the early eighties despite what *Melody Maker's* Horkins described as an unlikely environment: "Such implorable collisions of art, intellect, insanity and musical experimentation seemed inconceivable, let alone functional, within a corporation so geared up to supplying the world with endless hoards of spandex clad axe heroes and Michael Jackson videos."

But it was precisely the audience alienated by pop music that swarmed to Devo's unconventional side. They were the perfect outcast's band, ignored at best or booed at worst by their hometown audiences who saw them as the high school nerds and awkward rebels they were. They made little effort to combat these perceptions, willing as they were to be "decked out like some Fifties B-movie white supremacist futurists and ... prone to choreographed bouts of spasmodic leaping about," according to *Melody Maker*'s Horkins.

> *Devo was the perfect out-cast's band, ignored at best or booed at worst by their home-town audiences who saw them as the high school nerds and awkward rebels they were.*

Devo's career declined throughout the 1980s, however. True to their analytic spirits, the band seemed to have been cognizant of the shifts both in the world around them and in their music. With genuine sympathy, *Melody Maker*'s Tony Reed reported of 1988's *Total Devo*, "There is a great sadness here, reflected in the titles and the lyrics, and it's the terrifying sense that Devo themselves might know just what an irrelevant anachronism their techno-pop angst strategy has become."

Some critics have come to terms with Devo by labeling them hippies, even folk singers. A *Stereo Review* critic called their 1990 release *Smooth Noodle Maps* "an electrified folk album," and deemed the group "disillusioned idealists whose outlook is more hippie than yuppie." That writer took them quite seriously, however. He concluded that "Devo is and isn't being funny this time. On the precipice of a new age, the band is back from the computerized drawing board with new ideas, banking on a calculated combination of emotion, intellect, wit, and rhythm to point us foolish humans over the hump toward a better future."

Other critics have been less inclined to give Devo the benefit of the doubt: "Depeche Mode for toddlers," reporter Zane termed the group in *Melody Maker*. The release of *Total Devo*, Scott Harrah wrote for *People*, "will make listeners wish that Devo had stayed in its pop-cultural purgatory." Michael Azzerad in *Rolling Stone* aspired for sympathy but ended with contempt. "Maybe the members of Devo are mocking the system that built them up and then knocked them down," he wondered of *Total Devo*, but concluded, "No.... Actually, they're making the kind of vapid music they used to ridicule in countless songs and interviews.... If you listen closely, the bass drum on this record sounds suspiciously like a digital sampling of the sound of a dead horse being beaten."

Azzerad's criticism was particularly painful given that Devo initially achieved fame not only with their ironic lyrics but through their progressive electronic music. "[We] were pioneers in the use of electronics," synthesizer player/singer Mark Mothersbaugh asserted. Their music is really part of a complicated system of noise. Back in the early 1970s, Mothersbaugh elaborated for *Melody Maker*'s Tony Horkins, "I used to take records with a drum solo or something, or just one bass line I liked, and just mutilate the record so that it stuck and skipped back to give you a loop of that one bit. [We'd] use things like windscreen wipers or washing machines as backing tracks." As they progressed, they "went through the whole history of the evolution of sequencers."

To some extent, electronics were an accident of fate for Devo. Mothersbaugh theorized that "perhaps if we had been rich kids, rather than poor factory kids, we would have made a feature film or put on a theatrical play, you know? But what we could afford was guitars and drums and some cheap electronic home built synthesizers and music happened first." Devo's attitude toward their medium, however, was anything but casual. Mothersbaugh claimed that Devo was distinguished from other musicians at the time who "were coming to electronics as keyboards first and approaching them as glorified pianos and organs.... [We] were kind of heading from the opposite direction, coming from electronics first and the keyboard was something for your fist to pound on."

Nice Guys

Apparently shameless, Devo was still very dismayed when they felt misunderstood. In response to various mean-spirited critiques of the group's work, Jerry Casale remarked to *Rolling Stone*'s Goldberg, "Well, obviously, we're Nazis and clowns. They're all right, all those people.... We're assholes. Everything they accuse us of is true. We're subhuman idiots." Casale's bruised ego reveals what the band considers fundamentally true about themselves: that they care, that they want to teach. Their goal is to communicate the message using "information instead of emotions to make decisions. A lot of people make decisions based on paranoia, hatred, selfishness and love." Devo is of the philosophy that it is critics' fear of their difference that makes them reject their music: "[We] threaten them."

Though much of Devo's material was repackaged and reissued in the early 1990s, the band was on hiatus. During this time, Gerald Casale became involved in directing music videos, and Mark Mothersbaugh kept busy in a range of areas. He pursued his interest in fine arts by producing and showing silk screens, wrote a lengthy tome titled *What I Know,* and composed music for the opening and closing credit sequences of television programs, including *Pee-Wee's Playhouse* and *Liquid Television.*

Selected discography

"Jocko Homo" (single), Booji Boy Records, 1976.
Q: Are We Not Men? A: We Are Devo (includes "[I Can't Get No] Satisfaction" and "Praying Hands"), 1978.
Duty Now for the Future, Warner Bros., 1979.
Freedom of Choice (includes "Whip It"), Warner Bros., 1980.
Live (mini-album), Warner Bros., 1981.
New Traditionalists (includes "We're Through Being Cool"), Warner Bros., 1981.
"Working in a Coal Mine" (single included on *New Traditionalists* and on *Heavy Metal* film soundtrack), Warner Bros., 1981.
Oh, No! It's Devo, Warner Bros., 1983.
Shout, Warner Bros., 1984.
Live: Devo, Virgin, 1987.
E-Z Listening Disk, Rykodisc, 1987.
Total Devo, Virgin/Enigma, 1988.
Now It Can Be Told: Devo at the Palace 12/9/88, Enigma, 1989.

Smooth Noodle Maps, Enigma, 1990.
Hardcore Devo, Volume 1, 1974-1977, Rykodisc, 1990.
Hardcore Devo, Volume 2, 1974-1977, Rykodisc, 1991.
Greatest Hits, Warner Bros., 1990.
Greatest Misses, Warner Bros., 1990.
Devo Live: The Mongoloid Years, Rykodisc, 1992.

Also created laserdisc *Devo: The Complete Truth About De-Evolution,* Voyager, 1993.

Sources

Books

Stambler, Irwin, *The Encyclopedia of Pop, Rock, and Soul,* revised edition, St. Martin's, 1989.

Periodicals

Billboard, August 13, 1988; December 3, 1988.
Creem, November 1984.
Melody Maker, August 13, 1988; October 20, 1990; November 3, 1990; December 15, 1990.
People, September 12, 1988.
Rolling Stone, December 10, 1981; February 17, 1983; August 11, 1988.
Spin, December 1990.
Stereo Review, December 1990.
Video, October 1993.

Additional information for this profile was obtained from the liner notes to *Greatest Hits,* 1990.

—*Diane Moroff*

Eazy-E

Rap singer

In a relatively short time, Eric Wright, known to fans and detractors alike as Eazy-E, established himself as an important figure on various fronts: the rise of "gangsta" rap, the debate over free speech, and the music business in general. He hadn't been recording for very long and hadn't released a great deal of music before media attention made him a name in American pop culture. As a rapper with the group N.W.A.— Niggaz with Attitude—Eazy-E was thrust to the forefront of an emerging hip-hop scene in the late 1980s. *Melody Maker* dubbed Eazy-E N.W.A.'s "most notorious hustler" in 1989, while *Rolling Stone's* Alan Light identified the band as "the hardest of the hard core, the group that defined the brutal subgenre known as gangster rap."

Writing for the *Village Voice* in 1989, Gregory Sandow reported on Eazy-E's behind-the-scenes career as the group's "bankroll" through his position as founder and sole owner of Ruthless Records, for which N.W.A recorded. That role and his assumption of the Comptown Records presidency in 1990 would eventually make Eazy-E, in the words of *Vibe's* Kevin Powell, "one of the most successful black businesspeople of the hip hop era."

Like his peers, Eazy-E had preceded his serious effort at a career in music with a "street" career, negotiating the gang scene in Compton, a tough neighborhood just south of Los Angeles, and selling drugs to make his living; "Eazy-E," Sandow reported, "says that without rap he'd be in jail or dead." That kind of background, as is the case for many rappers, gave him the material and credibility to rhyme about inner-city life in a way that won the interest and support of many rap music fans, even in the mid-1980s, before rap had gained a large mainstream following.

That "street" authenticity also characterized N.W.A., comprised of five young men—Eazy-E, Dr. Dre (Andre Young), Ice Cube (O'Shea Jackson), MC Ren (Lorenzo Patterson), and Yella (Antoine Carraby)—who decided to perform as a group in 1986. They quickly became part of a burgeoning rap scene in Los Angeles, where a "hard core" or "gangsta" school of rap to rival that established in New York was gaining momentum.

Solo Debut Hit Market

As N.W.A.'s reputation grew, Eazy-E released a solo record, 1988's *Eazy-Duz-It,* on his Ruthless label, which he had established in 1986. *Eazy-Duz-It* arrived at record stores under the auspices of both Ruthless and Island Records, combining the freedom of an independent label with some major-label distribution security.

"Completely lacking in subtlety and sometimes stability," reported *Melody Maker* in 1989, "'Eazy-Duz-It' is another highly colourful compendium of brutal stories from the war zone, from the darkened streets of Compton." Laden with uncompromising lyrics about the brutality of gangsta life, the album quickly captured listeners' attention and earned platinum status (one million copies sold); it would go on to double-platinum status with time.

N.W.A. made its recording debut with a single, "F— tha Police," that garnered both the praise of an enthusiastic audience and the criticism of conservative politicians. Noting that the "one song N.W.A. seem to care most about is 'F— tha Police,'" Sandow explained that the cut focused on "crime done *against* them, by police whom with bitter sarcasm the group puts on trial for the way they hassle black kinds on the street." Political worry over the implications of the song culminated in a letter to the group from the F.B.I. in 1989.

"F— tha Police" was an accurate preview of the character of and public response to N.W.A.'s first album, *Straight Outta Compton,* also released in 1988 on Ruthless; it was distributed through an independent company, Priority Records, in order to ensure the quintet's freedom of speech. The album would achieve double-platinum status and reach the Number 37 spot on the *Billboard* 200 chart, a remarkable feat for such a record.

Even before the release of "F— tha Police," the band's name had ensured a controversial entrance into the rap scene. "When we first started," Eazy-E explained to *Rolling Stone's* Light, "everybody was black this, black

that, the whole positive black thing. We said f— that— we wanted to come out in everybody's face. Something that would shock people." Light reported that they "got the response they wanted. The group's name set off controversy both inside and outside the rap community."

It was violent imagery, however, that most persistently put the band in the center of ongoing debates about rap and violence. In general, N.W.A. refused to bow down to any demand that they moralize in their music; Light explained that although "N.W.A. have long been accused of glamorizing violence and hatred ... they have always had a defense ready: They're not advocating anything; they're just reporting what they see on the streets around them." Dee Barnes, host of Fox Television's rap video show *Pump It Up,* voiced reservations about this explanation. "Their whole philosophy," she told Light, "has been that they're just telling stories, just reporting how it is on the streets. But they've started believing this whole fantasy, getting caught up in their press, and they think they're invincible. They think they're living their songs."

Caught in Free Speech Debates

When Florida-based right-wing anti-obscenity forces took a selection of musical works to court in 1990, *Eazy-Duz-It* was there, in the company of fellow rappers Ice-T and 2 Live Crew. The complainants intended to test the boundaries of anti-obscenity laws that have always been on the books in the United States, hoping that certain extremes would be deemed unacceptable. The defendants, for their part, argued that freedom of speech, or First Amendment rights, were at stake, insisting that they had the right to say—and record and sell—whatever images they liked, no matter how extreme. The Florida court, however, did not agree and on April 16 ruled *Eazy-Duz-It* obscene. Still, the ruling had no direct effect on the artists, since the statute extended only to what retailers sold.

Eazy-E's status as a controversial figure took an unusual turn when he accepted an invitation to a lunch benefitting the Republican Senatorial Inner Circle hosted by President George Bush in March of 1991, a little less than a year after conservatives had deemed his music obscene in Florida. Since his presence among the right-wing politicians struck the media as somewhat absurd, the event was reported across the country over the next 24 hours.

Not surprisingly, Eazy-E found it necessary to explain in a brief television interview that his invitation was the result of a $2,500 campaign contribution, which he had made to a Republican politician who stood against censorship. Although this made the point that freedom of speech debates cut through party lines, the rapper's appearance among the Republican powers still left many of his fans ill at ease, since Bush's economic policies generally were not seen to be promoting the welfare of inner-city African-Americans. When Eazy-E spoke with Light about the incident that year, he denied any allegiance to the G.O.P. "How the f— can I be a Republican when I got a song called 'F— tha Police'?" he asked. "I ain't shit—ain't a Republican or Democrat. I didn't even vote. My vote ain't going to help! I don't give a f— who's the president."

Eazy-E's "street" background gave him the material and credibility to rhyme about inner-city life in a way that won the support of many rap music fans.

When African-American motorist Rodney King was beaten by police in Los Angeles that April, the beating was caught on videotape and played on television around the country; many viewers came to the conclusion that the beating was not only unnecessary, but also prompted by racism. Eazy-E responded in the same vein, seeing the incident as another example of the police brutality that the N.W.A. single "F— tha Police" had protested in 1988. "We were criticized a lot when we first released that song," he told *Melody Maker* in 1991. "But I guess now after what happened to Rodney King, people might look differently on the situation."

Interest in the song was revitalized, especially when Eazy-E began talking about the possibility of not only rerecording and rereleasing the cut, but of doing so with Rodney King. The controversy also did nothing to harm the popularity and sales of the second full-length N.W.A. release, *Efil4zaggin*. *Rolling Stone* noted that by August of 1991, it had become the best-selling album in the country after claiming the Number One spot on the *Billboard* 200, making it a striking crossover success. *Rolling Stone* also pointed out that the album did so "without a single, a video or even a track suitable for radio play." Within two weeks, a million copies had moved out of record stores.

In 1992 when a largely white jury in conservative Simi Valley, outside of Los Angeles, dismissed charges against the officers who had beaten Rodney King, black communities in the city responded with rage, leading to the largest riots to shake an American metropolis in decades. As had been the case with the beating itself, this marker of the conditions created by racism revived enthusiasm for N.W.A.'s music; *Straight Outta Compton* blasted over the airwaves once again, breaking into the Top 20 on the *Billboard* charts.

Not surprisingly, reporters sought Eazy-E's response to the violence. "I'm not surprised this happened at all," he told *Melody Maker* in 1992. "I knew it was coming. I really think this is just the start of things.... It was stupid to burn down our own neighborhoods though. They shoulda taken their asses to Simi Valley and destroyed stuff there." His position as a representative voice of the black community in Los Angeles was shaken, however, in the spring of 1993, when he appeared to be acting in support of Theodore Briseno, one of the officers charged with beating King. David Thigpen, writing for *Rolling Stone* in 1993, reported that other high-profile rappers were "baffled" by this behavior and even perceived Eazy-E as a "sell-out."

The impact of Ice Cube's departure from N.W.A.—he left to pursue a solo career in 1990—caught up with the group in 1991, when the music press began to focus on increasingly entrenched bad feeling between N.W.A. and Eazy-E, much of it the result of questionable financial dealings on behalf of the latter. When Fox Television ran a segment about the conflict on *Pump It Up* late in 1990, all rappers involved felt that the piece smeared their reputations.

Consequently, when Dr. Dre encountered *Pump It Up* host Dee Barnes at a public event in January, 1991, he attacked his erstwhile friend, kicking and punching her and throwing her against a concrete wall. Barnes charged Dre with assault—to which he plead no contest—and charged Eazy-E, MC Ren, and Yella with libel, allegedly the result of comments they had made to the press asserting that she "deserved it," in Ren's words. The cases would drag on through 1993, exacerbating the group's already shaky reputation with women both inside and outside the black community.

Portrayal of Women Criticized

Like several other all-male rap groups, N.W.A.—and Eazy-E in particular—had come under fire from the beginning for the portrayal of women in their lyrics. Critics pointed out that their lyrics not only portrayed women exclusively as sex objects, but that they often glorified violence against women. Light, for example, argued that "the second half of [*Efil4zaggin*]—which includes such tracks as 'To Kill a Hooker,' 'Findum, F—um and Flee' and 'One Less Bitch'—stands as a graphic, violent suite of misogyny unparalleled in rap."

After Dre's assault on Barnes, it was not hard to see a connection between the lyrics and this incident; Barnes, talking with Light, explained her perspective thus: "Now it's bigger than just me—one individual—getting slapped around. It's a campaign of them with a Number One album calling for violence against women. They've grown up with the mentality that it's okay to hit women, especially black women. Now there's a lot of kids listening and thinking it's okay to hit women."

But by 1993, N.W.A. was a group in name only. Eazy-E and Dre were both leading successful solo careers, though Dre's success was a source of distress for Eazy-E. When Dre embarked on a solo career in 1991, he did so outside the auspices of Eazy-E's Ruthless Records; by late summer, Eazy-E had charged his former friend with breach of contract, claiming that his products and talents were still the property of Ruthless Records. The litigation would drag on for years, rife with suits and countersuits. In the meantime, Ruthless continued to grow: the independent label signed a distribution deal with Sony-Relativity in 1993, harnessing major-label skill and dollars to promote Ruthless artists.

Conflict With Dre Harmed Reputation

Eventually, the conflict with Dre began to effect Eazy-E's reputation as a solo artist. While his 1992 EP, *5150 Home 4 tha Sick,* would do well, a projected full-length project called *Temporary Insanity* appeared to be shelved indefinitely. He became a figure of ridicule when Dre's wildly popular video for the song "Dre Day"—that single a highlight of Dre's multiplatinum release *The Chronic*—lampooned him as "Sleazy-E," complete with a look-alike actor who saw the clip out with a side-of-the-road sign reading "Will rap for food."

When Eazy-E unveiled a disc in October of 1993, it was not the full-length album fans had anticipated. The title, *It's on (Dr. Dre) 187um Killa*—the numbers 187 street slang for a gang-style killing—inspired reviewers to approach it with a grain of salt, despite its debut in *Billboard* at Number Five. It appeared, as Kevin Powell noted, to be "a thinly veiled obsession with the life and career" of Dr. Dre. A reviewer writing for the *Source* in December remarked that Eazy-E "comes up with a trunkload of half-hearted mediocrity. Perhaps realizing that without Dre behind the mixing board and the rest

of the crew leading him along, many people wouldn't be interested in hearing him drop lyrics for a whole record."

Continuing in the same vein, the reviewer sensed that Eazy-E was "having a hard time staying on beat nowadays, and his delivery—which was once passionate, unique and endearing—now sounds like the last gasps of a defeated man just going through the motions." Powell concluded his *Vibe* review similarly, asking, "Is there a more reviled name in hip hop than that of Eazy-E?" He went on to answer his own question: "The breakup of N.W.A. ... and resultant attacks on wax from his former cronies, along with Eazy's ongoing legal battles with Dr. Dre and Dre's own stunning success ..., have made the once infallible Eazy look meek, defeated, even ridiculous." These jibes notwithstanding, few in the record industry, not to mention his fans, believed that Easy-E was down for the count. The rap singer was planning to release a double CD containing 40 tracks in the fall of 1994.

Selected discography

Eazy-Duz-It, Ruthless, 1988.
5150 Home for tha Sick (EP), Ruthless, 1992.
It's on (Dr. Dre) 187um Killa (EP), Ruthless, 1993.

With N.W.A.

N.W.A. and the Posse (EP), Ruthless, 1988.
Straight Outta Compton (includes "F— tha Police"), Ruthless, 1988.
100 Miles and Runnin' (EP), Ruthless, 1990.
Efil4zaggin (includes "To Kill a Hooker," "Findum, F—um and Flee," and "One Less Bitch"), Ruthless, 1991.

Sources

Billboard, April 28, 1990; September 7, 1991; January 25, 1992; October 24, 1992; January 30, 1993; February 13, 1993; August 28, 1993; November 13, 1993.
Daily Variety, July 19, 1993.
Melody Maker, September 23, 1989; March 30, 1991; May 23, 1992; October 31, 1992.
Rolling Stone, August 8, 1991; May 27, 1993.
Source, June 1993; December 1993.
Vibe, December 1993.
Village Voice, April 4, 1989; April 2, 1991.

—*Ondine E. Le Blanc*

Einstürzende Neubauten

Rock band

Since 1980, German rock band Einstürzende Neubauten—in English, "collapsing new buildings"—has been reinventing music by destroying all preconceived ideas of what music is and by redefining the beauty of sound. Their music has the undeniable ability to vibrate every particle of the listener's being, the goal being to make the listener feel absolutely alive. Besides guitars, their musical arsenal includes power drills, shopping carts, oil drums, broken glass, and sheet metal. The sounds Einstürzende Neubauten pioneered became known to a wide audience when the popular British dance band Depeche Mode used them in their 1984 hit "People Are People."

In the 1980s Einstürzende Neubauten's frontman, Blixa Bargeld—a former gravedigger, bartender, and theater manager who appropriated his first name from a brand of German ballpoint pen—predicted that "the entire pop culture would change while we (Einstürzende Neubauten) would remain the same, and the day would come when our 'noise' would sound like their new 'music.'" His prediction was not too far off, evidenced by the popularity in the 1990s of what has come to be known as "industrial" music. By the mid-1990s, in fact, Einstürzende Neubauten's music seemed much tamer, due in part to the "noisification" of mainstream music, and also to the natural growth and change that is part of the band's creative process.

Photograph by Fritz Brinckmann, courtesy of Mute Records

For the Record . . .

Members include **Blixa Bargeld,** vocals; **Mark Chung,** bass; **F. M. "Mufti" Einheit,** percussion; **Alexander Hacke** (born Alexander von Borsig), guitar; and **N. U. Unruh,** percussion. Former members include **Beate Batel** and **Grudrun Gut.**

Original lineup formed in 1980; released *Kollaps,* Zick Zack Records, 1981; released numerous singles and albums on Monogram, Zick Zack, Some Bizzare, and Mute labels, among others; toured Europe and U.S., beginning early 1980s.

Addresses: *Record company*—Mute Records, 140 West 22nd St., Ste. 10A, New York, NY 10011; 345 North Maple Dr., Ste. 123, Beverly Hills, CA 90210.

As Bargeld told Kenneth Laddish of *Mondo 2000:* "When we are at our best, our sounds form sentences as surely as words, which reinforces on another level what we are trying to express. The idea of using sound, stepping away from notes—add to this the quality of what the instrument actually is: this *is* burning oil. Put in a certain context, you compose a sentence dealing with burning oil."

Einstürzende Neubauten started out as a four-piece ensemble comprised of Bargeld, N. U. Unruh, Beate Batel, and Grudrun Gut. For those who missed the quartet's historic first show, Bargeld sold tapes of it in his second-hand store, Eisengrau (Iron Grey). The week after Einstürzende Neubauten formed, the Berlin Kongresshalle collapsed. The band viewed this as a perfect propaganda opportunity and took it as a good omen.

Lineup Evolved

Another German band, Abwärts, of which Bargeld and Unruh were fans, featured F. M. "Mufti" Einheit and Mark Chung, who both eventually became members of Einstürzende Neubauten. As a trio, Bargeld, Unruh, and Einheit released their first LP, 1981's *Kollaps.* This was actually a follow-up to the previous lineup's successful single "Für den Untergang" and the "Kalte Sterne" double-pack 7-inch single. Shortly thereafter, Chung formally joined the group. In 1983 16-year-old Alexander Von Borsig, known as Alexander Hacke, who was involved with many strange musical projects and had performed with Einstürzende Neubauten spo-

radically, began to play with them on a more regular basis.

Soon after the release of *Kollaps,* Einstürzende Neubauten became favorites of the British press and in 1983 released their first album in the United Kingdom, *Drawings of Patient O. T.* Although some felt it lacked the primitive intensity of their first release, most felt *Patient O. T.* had more texture and direction. The sound seemed more stripped down but better structured. The band had torn themselves down and moved on to yet another stage of their evolution.

The following year Einstürzende Neubauten released *Strategies Against Architecture* on the Mute label and *2X4* on ROIR. *Strategies* is a compilation of five tracks from *Kollaps,* two from *Kalte Sterne,* the B-side of the "Für den Untergang" single, and previously unreleased works, some of them live. The cassette-only *2X4,* contains live performances recorded in Europe from 1980-1983.

Apocalypse at Mojave

In 1984 Einstürzende Neubauten began appearing at special-event "site-specific" performances. One of the more notorious of these took place in California's Mojave desert on March 4, 1984. Fans who attended the show were brought to the site on a chartered bus caravan. While refrigerators and other appliances loaded with explosives were detonated for their enjoyment, courtesy of Mark Pauline and Survival Research Laboratories, Einstürzende Neubauten filled the desert air with their music in an unforgettable symphony of apocalyptic sights and sounds.

The band's indoor shows had also become quite notorious. Fire had become a regular part of their program. But at one Los Angeles performance, an onstage fire got out of control and completely burned the props for the second half of the show. The same night, vibrations from the power drill used onstage caused plaster to fall off the ceiling and onto some record company executives who were eating dinner a floor below.

Soon promoters were forced to turn down opportunities to mount Einstürzende Neubauten shows; insurance companies had begun to refuse to cover the venues at which Einstürzende Neubauten was booked. The band rectified this untenable situation by toning down the more "explosive" and uncontrollable elements of their live show. By the mid-1990s, their shows were more restrained; they needed only brandish the drill or empty water out of a gasoline can to raise the tension level and get a strong audience reaction.

Broadened Scope

Displaying their creative compositional techniques by employing grand piano, bizarre dance beats, and their trademark thunder, the band released *Halber Mensch* in 1985. The a cappella title track sounded like part of an avant-garde opera. Then, Einstürzende Neubauten disbanded for a year. In 1987 they reformed and released *Fünf auf der Nach Oben Richterskala,* perhaps their quietest release, one that left many of their fans confused, waiting for the thunder that never emerged from this album. The thunder returned, however, with 1989's *Haus der Lüge* and reappeared again on *Strategien gegen Architektur II* in 1991. And after yet another prolonged hiatus, 1993 saw the release of the highly acclaimed *Tabula Rasa* triptych, which contains the pieces "Blume" and "Wüste," originally composed for the avant-garde Canadian dance troupe La La La Human Steps.

The music of Einstürzende Neubauten has been called everything from "junk rock" to "industrial." The musicians themselves have been labeled "aural terrorists" and "musical mutants," as well as "the Kings of Industrial Rock." Bargeld has termed their efforts "hardcore New Age," while Einheit once classified them as "contemporary German folk music." Bargeld explained the philosophy behind the music to Klaus Maeck in his book *Hör Mit Schmerzen! (Listen With Pain!),* asserting, "Einstürzende Neubauten ... is a positive sound, possibly the most positive sound of all. Old objects, meanings, buildings and music get destroyed, all traces of the past are abandoned: only out of destruction can something really new be created."

Selected discography

"Für den Untergang," Monogram Records, 1980.
"Kalte Sterne," Zick Zack Records, 1981.
Kollaps, Zick Zack Records, 1981.
(With Lydia Lunch and Rowland S. Howard) "Thirsty Animal/ Durstiges Tier," Zick Zack Records, 1981.
Zeichnungen des Patienten O. T. (Drawings of Patient O. T.), Some Bizzare, 1983.
Strategies Against Architecture 80-83, Mute Records, 1984, reissued, Homestead, 1986.
2 X 4, ROIR, 1984.
"Yu Gung," Some Bizzare, 1985.

Halber Mensch, Some Bizzare, 1985.
Fünf auf der Nach Oben Richterskala, Some Bizzare, 1987.
Haus der Lüge, Some Bizzare/Rough Trade, 1989.
Strategien gegen Architektur II, Mute Records, 1991.
Tabula Rasa, Mute Records, 1993.
"Interim," Mute Records, 1993.
"Malediction," Mute Records, 1993.

Sources

Books

Dolgins, Adam, *Rock Names,* Citadel Press Books, 1993.
Maeck, Klaus, *Hör Mit Schmerzen/Listen With Pain,* Max Volume Production/E.M.E., 1989.
Robbins, Ira A., *Trouser Press Record Guide 4th Edition,* Collier Books, 1991.
Thompson, Dave, *Industrial Revolution,* Cleopatra Press, 1993.

Periodicals

Billboard, May 22, 1993.
Chicago Sun Times, April 30, 1993.
Columbia Daily Spectator (SC), April 30, 1993.
Details, April 1993.
Entertainment Weekly, February 19, 1993.
Los Angeles Reader, December 4, 1992.
Los Angeles Times, March 6, 1984.
Melody Maker, March 5, 1983; September 3, 1983; December 3, 1983; September 14, 1985; July 18, 1987; August 3, 1991; February 27, 1993; April 17, 1993.
Mondo 2000, No. 11, 1993.
New Music Express, April 17, 1993.
Option, May/June 1993.
Rockguide, April 1993.
Rockpool, January 15, 1993; February 15, 1993.
San Francisco Weekly, March 17, 1993.
Seattle Rocket, February 1993.
Soundviews, February/March 1993.
Spin, August 1991; March 1993.
Village Noize, No.14 , 1993.
Wall Street Journal, October 3, 1985.

Additional information for this profile was obtained from Mute Records press material, 1994.

—*Charlie Katagiri*

David Foster

Keyboardist, songwriter, composer, producer, arranger, record company executive

David Foster started his music career at the age of five in Victoria, British Columbia, Canada. He began with piano lessons, and his talent quickly distinguished him from the other children his age. When he turned 13, Foster enrolled at the University of Washington to study music. He launched his professional career three years later when he joined the backup band of rock and roll legend Chuck Berry.

Foster moved to Los Angeles in 1971 with his band Skylark. In 1973 Skylark's song "Wildflower" reached Number Nine on the *Billboard* charts. Foster parlayed that milestone into a career as a session keyboard player. When Skylark disbanded and its members decided to return to Canada, Foster remained in Los Angeles. "I had this overwhelming desire to meet all the great musicians and play with them. I was young and hungry, and a very positive thinker," Foster told *Keyboard.*

He played keyboards in the orchestra pit for the Roxy Theatre's production of *The Rocky Horror Picture Show* for a year and eventually became the show's co-director. *Rocky Horror* garnered considerable recognition, and many producers and musicians noticed Foster's talents when they attended performances. The orchestra would play whatever the conductor chose for half an hour before the show. When people in the music industry heard Foster play keyboards, they began calling him to participate in their recording sessions during the day.

Fostered Reputation as Gifted Keyboardist

Foster built a strong reputation as a talented session keyboard player, working with such stars as John Lennon, George Harrison, Barbra Streisand, and Rod Stewart. He added his input to songwriting and arrangement in sessions and eventually worked his way into producing and writing his own songs. His early production clients included Alice Cooper, the Average White Band, Boz Scaggs, and Carole Bayer Sager.

The turning point in Foster's production career came in a conversation with fellow producer Quincy Jones. "We were talking about the Average White Band's album, *Shine,* and I said, 'It's not bad, but it's not a great album. The songs aren't that good.' He said, 'Who produced it?' I said, 'I did.' He said, 'You've just messed up in a big way. Your name's on there. You're responsible for that record. It's got to be absolutely the best you can do.'" Foster realized then that he needed to demand the best from the artists with whom he worked to make the best album he could.

For the Record . . .

Born c. 1950 in Victoria, British Columbia, Canada; immigrated to U.S., 1971. First wife named Rebecca; married Linda Thompson (a songwriter); children: (first marriage) four daughters, (second marriage) two stepsons. *Education:* Studied music at University of Washington.

Began playing piano with singer-guitarist Chuck Berry at 16; member of band Skylark; worked as session keyboard player; became producer, early 1970s; released first solo recording, Sound Design Records, 1982; released album *David Foster,* Atlantic, 1986; established David Foster Foundation, 1986; became senior vice president of A&R, Atlantic Records, 1994. Has produced music for films, including *The Secret of My Success, St. Elmo's Fire, Urban Cowboy, Summer Lovers, One Good Cop, If Looks Could Kill,* and *Karate Kid Part II;* has produced songs and albums for numerous pop artists, including Whitney Houston, All-4-One, Céline Dion, Barbra Streisand, Color Me Badd, and Natalie Cole.

Awards: Grammy awards for (with Jay Graydon and Bill Champlin) best rhythm and blues song, 1979, for "After the Love Has Gone"; producer of the year, 1982, for *Dreamgirls;* producer of the year, for *Chicago 17,* and best instrumental arrangement accompanying vocals, for "Hard Habit to Break," both 1984; producer of the year, for "Somewhere," 1985; and for producer of the year, song of the year, and record of the year, all for *Unforgettable,* 1992; thirty-four Grammy nominations; named top singles producer and top R&B singles producer of 1993 by *Billboard* magazine; order of Canada.

Addresses: *Record company*—Atlantic Records, 75 Rockefeller Plaza, New York, NY 10019.

Foster earned his first big-name producing credit with two albums by Daryl Hall and John Oates, and he continued to take Jones's words to heart. He not only proved he could recognize good songs, he confirmed he could write them as well. In 1979 he won his first Grammy Award, for best rhythm and blues song, for co-writing Earth, Wind and Fire's "After the Love Has Gone" with Jay Graydon and Bill Champlin.

Three years later he received his second Grammy, for producer of the year, for the cast album of the Tony Award-winning Broadway musical *Dreamgirls.* The album climbed to Number 11 on the *Billboard* charts, the highest-charting cast recording since *Hair* in 1969. Foster gained further accolades when Chicago's "Hard to Say I'm Sorry," from *Chicago 16,* which he cowrote and produced, reached Number One on the *Billboard* charts.

Reveled in Variety

Foster released his first solo album, *Best of Me,* on a Japanese label. Then, Sound Design Records released it in the United States in 1982. The following year, Foster produced Lionel Richie's album *Can't Slow Down,* which sold a whopping ten million copies. By that time, he had cemented his place as one of popular music's top producers. Yet he refused to rest on his laurels, relishing the variety his prominence allowed him. "I know I've done a little too much jumping around already in my career," Foster told Paul Green of *Billboard.* "Someone once described me as a person who couldn't keep a job. But I love the fact that I can produce the Tubes and get a big AOR [album-oriented rock] hit and turn around and do a solo album that sounds like 'Love Story '83' and then also work with the R&B acts."

Foster continued producing and writing virtually nonstop. In 1984 he earned his third and fourth Grammy awards: for Chicago's *Chicago 17,* he received another producer of the year award, and for the song "Hard Habit to Break," he was recognized for best instrumental arrangement accompanying vocals.

But his nonstop work pace started to take its toll; after a lifetime of 16-hour days, Foster reached a point of such mental and physical exhaustion that he thought he'd lost his magical musical touch. He decided to return to Canada with his wife Rebecca and take a break. Just as he had settled in, Quincy Jones called and asked him to write and produce the Canadian answer to the English Band-Aid project and the American "We Are the World" efforts to raise money for hunger relief in Africa. He rose to the occasion, composing and producing Northern Lights' "Tears Are Not Enough." When a video about the production hit Canadian TV, Foster gained the recognition that had eluded him in his homeland. Indeed, though many Canadians knew Foster's work, they did not realize that he was Canadian.

Giving up on his hiatus, he went back to Los Angeles. Shortly thereafter, the magic touch clearly still with him, he produced the hit single "Somewhere" for Barbra Streisand's *Broadway Album,* for which he won his fifth Grammy.

Dominated Charts

Beginning on May 5, 1984, when "Stay the Night"—the first single from *Chicago 17*—debuted at Number 49, Foster had at least one single on *Billboard*'s Hot 100 chart every week until April 12, 1986. During most weeks of that two-year period, he had two or more records on the chart simultaneously. And in August of 1985 he had a remarkable five singles on the chart at the same time.

Foster released a self-titled album on Atlantic Records in 1986, which included a duet with Olivia Newton-John. Also that year he established the David Foster Foundation to assist families of children who need organ transplants, and the David Foster Celebrity Softball Game in Victoria, British Columbia, to raise funds for the foundation.

His next solo album, *The Symphony Sessions,* appeared in record stores in 1988. The disc featured Foster performing his compositions with the Vancouver Symphony Orchestra and included "Winter Games," the song he wrote for the 1988 Calgary Winter Olympics. A one-hour TV special, *David Foster: The Symphony Sessions,* aired on CBC-TV in Toronto to promote the album, and the video arm of Atlantic Records released it as a 36-minute home video. Also that year, Foster received the Order of Canada for his humanitarian efforts.

The Symphony Sessions showcased a reworked rendition of Foster's Golden Globe-nominated theme for the movie *The Secret of My Success.* It is just one of the songs Foster has penned for films during his career, among them *St. Elmo's Fire, Urban Cowboy, Summer Lovers, One Good Cop, If Looks Could Kill,* and *Karate Kid Part II.*

1992 an *Unforgettable* Year

Foster released *River of Love* in 1990, which included the single "Grown-Up Christmas," sung by Natalie Cole. Brian Wilson, Bryan Adams, Bruce Hornsby, Mike Reno, and others contributed both songs and performances to the album. The following year, Foster released *Rechordings,* which featured instrumental versions of Foster's best-loved compositions. He also wrote music to second wife Linda Thompson's lyrics for "Voices That Care," the entertainment industry's salute to U.S. troops in the Persian Gulf War. The project raised more than $500,000 for the Red Cross and USO of America.

Foster received three more Grammy awards in 1992 for

Natalie Cole's hit album *Unforgettable:* producer of the year, song of the year, and record of the year. He also co-produced Streisand's album *Back to Broadway,* which entered the *Billboard* charts at Number One on July 17, 1993. As if this weren't enough, at the end of the year he released *The Christmas Album,* which featured some of his favorite vocalists singing their best-loved Christmas songs backed by an 80-piece orchestra. Understandably, *Billboard* named Foster top singles producer and top R&B singles producer in their 1993 year-end wrap-up.

Time reporter Charles P. Alexander noted in 1994, "Over the past two years, Foster productions have held the No. 1 spot on *Billboard* magazine's Hot 100 more than 25% of the time." The pop guru's domination of the charts was secured throughout 1993 and 1994 by Whitney Houstons's "I Will Always Love You," Canadian pop singer Céline Dion's "The Power of Love," and newcomer All-4-One's "I Swear," each of which spent several weeks in the Number One position.

Foster took his career in yet another direction in 1994 when he joined Atlantic Records as senior vice president of A&R (artists and repertoire), with a three-year production contract. Though his contract allowed him to work with artists on other labels, the position gave him an outlet to develop new artists. According to an August 1994 article in *Time,* Foster was also working with pop superstar Michael Jackson, producing tracks for the singer's next album.

With a lifetime of writing, producing, and sometimes performing hit music, the 12-time Grammy-winning Foster summed up the purpose and theory of his career in one sentence of his Atlantic Records press biography, allowing, "I gravitate toward tugging at heartstrings—and I treat every day in the studio as life or death."

Selected discography

Best of Me, Sound Design, 1982.
David Foster, Atlantic, 1986.
The Symphony Sessions, Atlantic, 1988.
River of Love, Atlantic, 1990.
Rechordings, Atlantic, 1991.
David Foster: The Christmas Album, Interscope, 1993.

Sources

Billboard, July 30, 1983; October 26, 1985; May 24, 1986; July 26, 1986; April 23, 1988; October 5, 1991; March 14, 1992; October 9, 1993; December 4, 1993; December 25, 1993.

Keyboard, February 1986; September 1986; March 1988; January 1992.
New York Times, December 10, 1993.
Time, August 29, 1994.
Variety, May 21, 1986; May 11, 1988.

Additional information for this profile was obtained from Atlantic Records press material, 1994.

—Sonya Shelton

Fugazi

Rock band

The Washington, D.C.-based band Fugazi has managed to thrive as a creative unit and as a business organization despite an utter refusal to participate in the mainstream music industry. It is for this reason, they insist, that they've been able to make their volatile, politically charged music without compromise. "While a lot of new music seems manufactured, empty, and devoid of any social consciousness," wrote *Spin's* Daniel Fidler, "Fugazi is an essential change." And though listeners have had mixed reactions to the group's teachings, Fugazi has steadily increased its fan base while working diligently to keep album and ticket prices down. Through relentless touring they have become, in the eyes of critics like *Rolling Stone's* Michael Azerrad, "perhaps America's best live band."

Singer-guitarist Ian MacKaye—often regarded as the band's leader despite Fugazi's insistence that it is a democracy—occupied a pivotal place in D.C.-area punk rock when that form exploded in the early 1980s. Along with Jeff Nelson, he performed with the band Teen Idles in high school; "We had a tape of songs,

Courtesy of John Falls Photography

and we had saved up some money from shows," MacKaye recalled to *Option*. "So we said, 'Let's put out a record. No one else is going to do it for us.'" This decision led to the formation of Dischord Records, which independent music fans—and some envious record industry figures—would later come to regard as a pillar of integrity and non-corporate viability. MacKaye graduated from high school in 1980 and moved into a house in suburban Virginia; this domicile became Dischord House, the fledgling label's nerve center. "We didn't set out to be a record label," the singer explained in a *Melody Maker* interview. "Dischord was set up to document our community, the generation of musicians that came up in Washington with us." MacKaye also played with such bands as the Slinkees and Embrace.

Sound of Dissonance and Tension

MacKaye and Nelson formed the hardcore band Minor Threat, which became one of the most influential punk rock outfits of the decade. Yet some of MacKaye's message slipped by many of his more literal-minded fans; long after Minor Threat's day was done, the song "Straight Edge" would haunt the singer. Written as an attack on complacency and substance abuse, it became a manifesto for a group of kids for whom clean living served as a religion. Much to his chagrin, MacKaye received credit for a movement that turned the non-conformist message of his song into a new, stoic conformity, demonstrating an authority that he never would have imagined.

In 1987 he cofounded Fugazi with singer-guitarist and songwriter Guy Picciotto and drummer Brendan Canty, formerly of the band Rites of Spring, which had rebelled against the negativity and violence that overtook punk. Bassist Joe Lally was a heavy-metal-obsessed fan for whom punk was a revelation; performances by bands like Rites of Spring and San Francisco's Dead Kennedys helped him find his path. "Seeing the shows made me think about what I was doing with my time, being stoned all the time—being bored, depressed ... whatever," he confided to *Option*'s Taehee Kim.

The new band's name came from Vietnam War "slang for a f—ed up situation," as *Melody Maker* noted; the challenge the musicians faced was simply life in America and its capacity to crush the human spirit, not to mention the country's role in exploitation abroad. The group's debut EP appeared in 1988 and was followed by 1989's *Margin Walker*. Fugazi's sound thrived on dissonance and tension, much like England's post-punk political rockers Gang of Four.

Raw and Radical

As Ann Powers of the *Village Voice* opined, "Punk chronology pulses through its songs like a bloodline. [The work of the] Sex Pistols and early PiL, Mission of Burma" and other innovative groups is evident in their style. "But each influence neutralizes the other, with none dominating, so that Fugazi sounds unlike any other band. Its songs are the new language emerging from a Babel that renders all previous differences mute." *Spin*'s Fidler similarly explained, "The band has taken the raw elements of rock, hardcore, funk, heavy metal, and reggae and mixed them together with a radical punk twist." In their songs and in their day to day existence, Fugazi, in the words of *Los Angeles Reader* columnist David Shirley, "have struggled not only to understand how power works in our everyday lives, but to change it."

Fugazi's real power came through most clearly in its performances, which featured what Nisid Najari of the *Village Voice* called a "communal, revivalist atmosphere." Kim noted that "Fugazi's live shows are what really capture the essence of this band—shows that are capable of restoring your faith in the energy and potency of punk rock even a decade after its decline." The band performs at numerous benefits and has a policy of playing exclusively at clubs that charge five dollars or less for admission and admit clubgoers of all ages. As MacKaye told *Spin*, the policy gives the band freedom from high-priced pressure: "For five bucks we could suck. Because we are human and we do suck sometimes." A *Rolling Stone* review of their performance at the Ritz in New York City remarked, "In concert as well as in theory, Fugazi exists to demolish complacency by confounding expectations, so its unpredictable, stop-and-go arrangements are a musical metaphor"; the group's performance, reviewer Azerrad wrote, turned the crowd into "a swarming mass of arms and legs."

Despite the ferocity of Fugazi's music, however, the band—MacKaye particularly—has constantly admonished its audiences not to abuse one another with the ritual of slamdancing or "moshing." "We play loud, electric guitar music, and you'd hope that that doesn't mean you have to act like an asshole," Picciotto groused to Option's Kim. Yet, as Powers asserted, this issue embodies the paradox of the band. "Fugazi chides its fans for going wild," she pointed out, "all the while driving them there."

Indie Heroes

Seeing Fugazi sell 100,000 copies of their album without benefit of major label promotion or distribution drove many record executives wild; the band was continually besieged by offers from industry giants. Of course, if the band were to sign such a pact, it would mean the end of printing a $9.00 price directly on their CDs to avoid retail gouging. "There are some major labels who are suddenly enamored of us because our name is on a list in some trade publication," MacKaye remarked to Spin's Fidler. "Those people I don't really have much time for because they really don't have time for me. We're just not interested. There's nothing the labels can offer us that would be worth the loss of control over our own music."

Likewise, the band has been circumspect about doing interviews in mainstream music magazines; Picciotto scolded Spin for its liquor and cigarette ads, leaving Fidler to cobble together his article from quotes the band gave while explaining why they had collectively declined a formal interview, as well as a few from Kim's Option piece. Fugazi has, however, done many interviews for independent "fanzines," in part, as Picciotto explained, "to support underground music."

The group continued to sell well with albums like 1991's Steady Diet of Nothing, which Melody Maker dubbed "a hard album, a punishing album," adding, "Fugazi trap the embittered, directionless fury of punk inside their own full metal straitjacket." Of 1993's In on the Kill Taker, Matt Diehl of Rolling Stone declared, "As Fugazi grow more diverse, their music only becomes more

powerful"; the album, Diehl claimed, functions "as a virtual encyclopedia of punk-derived musical styles." Spin reviewer Charles Aaron, however, found Kill Taker the band's "most rigid, predictable album yet" and regarded the political anthems contained therein with derision.

To be sure, though, Fugazi has not pursued its uncompromising direction in order to please music critics. As Picciotto told Melody Maker's Joe Dilworth, "We're responsible for the presentation and others are responsible for the interpretation. I hope that people listen to Fugazi and have some kind of understanding of what we're doing, but it comes down to a question of respecting your audience, of letting them figure things out for themselves, rather than ramming it down their throats."

For MacKaye—who, like his bandmates, has on occasion maintained that Fugazi would last only as long as the music stayed fresh—the process of making music has always been about freedom and expression. "There's something incredibly wonderful about having your own thing," he insisted to Kim. "But I'll tell you one thing—if this band was selling [only] 5,000 copies, and we were happy playing, we'd still be together. We'd still be working day jobs and just doing what we want."

Selected discography

On Dischord Records

Fugazi, 1988.
Margin Walker, 1989.
Repeater, 1990.
3 Songs (vinyl 7"), 1991.
Steady Diet of Nothing, 1991.
(Contributors) "In Defense of Humans," State of the Union, 1991.
In on the Kill Taker, 1993.

Sources

Los Angeles Reader, September 24, 1993.
Melody Maker, December 2, 1989; September 7, 1991; October 12, 1991.
Option, November 1991.
Rolling Stone, June 25, 1992; September 30, 1993; November 25, 1993.
Spin, September 1991; September 1993.
Village Voice, September 12, 1989; October 5, 1993.

—Simon Glickman

Gang Starr

Rap duo

Photograph by Daniel Hastings, © 1994 EMI Records Group

A pioneer of jazz-rap fusion, Gang Starr is an innovative hip-hop duo composed of rapper Keith Elam, known as "Guru," and DJ Christopher "Premier" Martin. The group is hailed as one of the most original and forward-looking rap acts around. At a time when most rappers use pre-recorded beats in live performance, Premier does all his cutting and sampling on stage. Guru's slow, sleepy voice produces lyrics that are distinctly hardcore but, while addressing the realities of life on the street, do not glorify violence in the way much "gangsta" rap does.

Gang Starr was formed when Guru, in the studio at Wild Pitch Records recording some singles with a friend, heard a demo tape by Premier. He was impressed by the range of sounds featured on the demo; Premier has an enormous record collection and an encyclopedic knowledge of music. Their early records together incorporated jazz elements, and their career was given a boost by director Spike Lee's commissioning "Jazz Thing" for the soundtrack of his 1990 movie *Mo' Better Blues.* But Gang Starr refuses to be pegged as a pure rap-fusion group. As reported in *Billboard,* Premier insists that "he ventured into using jazz loops out of boredom."

While Premier found himself more and more in demand as a producer—helping out such artists as KRS-One, Arrested Development, Heavy D, and Das EFX—Guru took time away from Gang Starr in 1993 to make the critically acclaimed *Jazzmatazz.* The album brings together a pool of significant jazz talent to provide the accompaniment for his raps. Gang Starr's subsequent group effort, 1994's *Hard to Earn,* foregoes jazz altogether for a stricter hardcore sound; "it's deliberate," Premier told David Thigpen in *Rolling Stone.* "We wanted to show we can go in a different direction."

Determined to Make It Big

A rap career was the last thing Elam's parents expected, or wanted, for their son. Born in the Dorchester neighborhood of Boston, Guru grew up in a comfortable middle-class home, the youngest child of a judge and a librarian. While his siblings followed in their parents' footsteps—one sister is a judge, another is a schoolteacher, and Guru's brother is a professor at Stanford University—Guru was the rebellious one, running around with a tough crowd and aspiring to success as a rapper.

Guru attended Morehouse College in Atlanta, graduating with a degree in business management that has proved useful in music industry negotiations. After

For the Record . . .

Members include **DJ Premier** (born Christopher Martin, c. 1967 in New York City; attended Prairie View University, Houston, TX) and **Guru** (born Keith Elam, c. 1962 in Boston, MA; son of Harry [a judge] and Barbara [a librarian] Elam; children: one son; received degree in business management from Morehouse College; attended Fashion Institute of Technology, New York City).

Group formed in New York City, 1988; signed with Wild Pitch for 1989 debut album, *No More Mister Nice Guy;* signed with Chrysalis; released two albums; in 1993, during a brief hiatus, Guru released *Jazzmatazz* (also on Chrysalis) while Premier produced various rap artists; Gang Starr then released *Hard to Earn* on Chrysalis, 1994.

Addresses: *Record company*—Chrysalis Records, 1290 Avenue of the Americas, New York, NY 10104.

college, he headed for New York City, briefly enrolling in the Fashion Institute of Technology and working while shopping around demo tapes and performing in a variety of hip-hop venues. Having signed with Wild Pitch Records, Guru went into the studio with DJ Mark the 45 King, whom he credits with early jazz-rap experimentation, and released a couple of singles. While at Wild Pitch, Guru heard a demo by a Texas group called the Inner Circle Posse, featuring Chris Martin, a young man from Brooklyn attending Prairie View University near Houston. The two musicians began exchanging tapes through the mail.

Back in Boston, Guru had formed a group called Gang Starr with some friends, one of whom worked with him on the Wild Pitch singles. When Martin left Texas and returned to New York, he hooked up with Guru. They shared an apartment and became the new Gang Starr. Earlier, as a member of the Inner Circle Posse, he was known as Wax Master C, but Stu Fine, the owner of Wild Pitch, didn't like the name. Martin's mother suggested that he call himself "Premier." Martin explained to Michael Gonzales of *Pulse!,* "She said it worked 'cause I wanted to be first at things. Not just music, everything."

Composed for Spike Lee

The ambitious duo was off to a good start with their first album, *No More Mister Nice Guy,* released on Wild Pitch in 1989. One song, "Manifest," was a hit, and another, "Jazz Music," attracted the attention of Spike Lee. Lee asked them to write something for his 1990 film set in the New York City jazz world, *Mo' Better Blues.* The result, "Jazz Thing," pays homage to jazz greats and features saxophonist Branford Marsalis; the cut plays over the film's closing credits and brought Gang Starr further recognition.

Signing with Chrysalis, the company with which the group has made all of their subsequent records, they released *Step in the Arena* in 1991. Though full of standard rap themes, the lyrics do not condone violence but do stress that education is the one sure route out of the ghetto. Discussing the early albums in a conversation with the *Source,* Guru reflected, "I really look at *Step in the Arena* as the first album. I look at *No More Mister Nice Guy* as almost just a demo, an introduction 'cause it was just the beginning and stuff really hadn't evolved."

Operation a Success

The next stage in the evolution was the widely acclaimed *Daily Operation*—of all their albums the one with the most jazz-influenced sound. Premier's increasingly complex montages also demonstrate a taste for '70s funk. Premier, who has wide-ranging musical interests, maintains he simply searches for the best samples for each individual work. "I'll sample anything that fits the atmosphere that we're trying to create. It could be opera, whatever," he told Danyel Smith in *Vibe.*

Although it was Guru who proclaimed that "the Nineties will be the decade of the jazz thing," as *Melody Maker* reported, Gang Starr resists the rap-jazz label. "As much as we respect jazz musicians and recognize that their artform is similar to ours, this is just another era," Guru said in *Billboard.* "Yeah, our music has a jazzy feel to it, but at the same time, it's rugged. It's hardcore rap." Perhaps in reaction to the media's characterization of Gang Starr as a fusion group, the 1994 *Hard to Earn* is a straightforward hip-hop record with no discernable jazz flavoring.

In between Gang Starr albums, both group members worked on independent projects. Guru told Smith, "We know how to give each other creative space. But even on the side projects, we let each other hear what we're doing." Premier, highly in demand as a producer, formed his own company, Works of Mart. He is known for his "old school" use of the turntable, preferring to manipulate the records himself rather than rely on pre-recorded tapes. "I'm one of the few producers who still scratches on his records," he informed Michael Gonzales.

Guru's 1993 release *Jazzmatazz*, meanwhile, features jazz talents such as Branford Marsalis, Lonnie Liston Smith, Donald Byrd, Ronnie Jordan, Courtney Pine, and Roy Ayers. Guru rapped over their live studio performance, an innovative technique for hip-hop. In some quarters hailed as a brilliant experiment, in others as a good but flawed idea, *Jazzmatazz* demonstrated, at the very least, that rappers and jazz musicians have enough in common to make collaboration possible.

Back together for *Hard to Earn,* Gang Starr maintains that they are first and foremost a team: Guru explained to *Billboard,* "The nucleus of everything I do is Gang Starr." The duo's focus returned in the mid-1990s to traditional hip-hop. Guru's lyrics narrate keen-eyed, often autobiographical stories about ghetto life, embracing the hard-edged language of hardcore rap but avoiding many of its cliches. Critics predict that Gang Starr will continue to bring a fresh perspective to rap; however, they are foregoing further experimentation for now. Premier told Gonzales, "Right now, it's all about hard-core. Right now, it's about making real music for the kids in the street."

Selected discography

Singles

"Jazz Thing," Columbia, 1990.

Albums

No More Mister Nice Guy, Wild Pitch, 1989.
Step in the Arena, Chrysalis, 1991
Daily Operation, Chrysalis, 1992.
Hard to Earn, Chrysalis, 1994.

Solo albums by Guru

Jazzmatazz: Volume 1, Chrysalis, 1993.

Sources

Billboard, October 3, 1992; May 8, 1993; June 12, 1993; February 5, 1994.
Boston Globe, October 4, 1992.
Melody Maker, May 18, 1991.
Musician, June 1993; April 1994.
Pulse!, September 1993; May 1994.
Rolling Stone, May 19, 1994.
Source, April 1994.
Spin, January 1991; May 1993.
Vibe, May 1994.

Additional information for this profile was obtained from Chrysalis/ERG press materials, 1994.

—*Gina Hausknecht*

Gwar

Rock band

According to legend, Gwar was created over 100 billion years ago by the Master of All Reality. An ultra-elite group of warriors gathered from the lowest dregs of filth, the group raped and pillaged their way across the universe and finally arrived on Earth. Once on Earth they killed the dinosaurs, created Stonehenge to use as a croquet court, and sunk Atlantis. Displeased by their actions, the Master banished Gwar to Antarctica, where they lay entombed in ice for millions of years, until a hole in the ozone layer (caused by excessive use of hair spray by poofy-haired 1980s rock stars) released them from their icy prison in 1985. Free to roam the Earth once more, Gwar returned to their goal of world domination—this time as a rock band.

So reads the bizarre pseudo-biography of the band called Gwar. The true story of how the band came to be is less outrageous, but the end product lives up to the fantastic saga. The brain-child of vocalist Dave Brockie and film producers Hunter Jackson and Chuck Varga, Gwar lurched into existence in the early days of 1985. By combining a hybrid of heavy metal, punk, and hardcore music styles with outrageous, horror film-inspired costumes and scenery, high-tech special effects, and gory, Grand-Guignol stage antics, Brockie, Jackson, and Varga created a new genre of musical entertainment—part rock and roll, part cartoon, part vaudeville, and part social satire.

Gore and Social Conscience

Brockie first met Varga and Jackson in an old dairy on the outskirts of Richmond, Virginia. Brockie's band, Death Piggy, practiced in the basement, while upstairs, Varga and Jackson's company, Slave Pit Productions, designed costumes and scenery for a horror film called *Scumdogs of the Universe*. After Brockie's band broke up and the film ran out of funds, the trio teamed up and created Gwar using costumes, scenery, and characters from the film.

Gwar's goal was to create not just a band, but a multimedia event that, as Brockie explained to Deidre Pearson in *Underscope*, "would encompass many different forms of communication and expression." But their intent was to do more than just provide a glitzy show. They wanted to create a living form of catharsis. Instead of merely playing songs, the band would act out the lyrics through outrageous fantasy performances that would include decapitations, battles with giant monsters, sodomy, ritual rape, and plenty of blood spewing.

As Brockie told *Contemporary Musicians*, "Gwar was designed to be as obnoxious as the world is obnoxious.

For the Record . . .

Members include **Michael Bishop** (Beefcake the Mighty; left band, 1994), bass; **Dave Brockie** (Oderus Urungus), vocals; **Michael Dirks** (Balsac the Jaws of Death), guitar; **Pete Lee** (Flattus Maximus), guitar; **Casey Orr** (replaced Bishop as Beefcake the Mighty), bass; and **Brad Roberts** (Jizmak da Gusha), drums.

Band formed in Richmond, VA, 1985; self-released debut album, *Hell-o,* 1988; released second album, *Scumdogs of the Universe,* Master Records, 1990; signed with Metal Blade Records, 1992, and released one EP and three LPs, 1992-94; released videos *Live From Antarctica,* 1990, and *Phallus in Wonderland,* 1992; released film *Skulhed ... Face,* 1993.

Addresses: *Record company*—Metal Blade, 2345 Erringer Rd., Suite 108, Simi Valley, CA 93065.

We wanted to give people an escape from the crazy homogenization of the will caused by society by giving people the opportunity to live out their most bizarre fantasies. In a sick way, Gwar teaches people how to deal with reality. Like a paganistic ritual or a mad theme park ride, Gwar gives people a means of purging their pent-up desires and frustrations."

While Varga and Jackson worked on the costumes, scenery, and special effects, Brockie scoured the local Richmond music scene for young musicians to fill the ranks of his fledgling band. He found many performers willing to don the 50-pound latex costumes of Gwar's onstage characters Oderus Urungus, Balsac the Jaws of Death, Flattus Maximus, Jizmak da Gusha, and Beefcake the Mighty, but few stayed with the band long. Most complained that their musical talents were overshadowed by the band's outrageous stage shows. As a result, the band roster changed almost constantly over the next five years.

Another regular stage presence is Slymenstra Hymen, a female dancer whose primal movements, mask-like makeup, and skimpy leather attire lends yet more visual stimulus to the show. Although technically not a band member—she plays no instrument—Slymenstra has been a Gwar staple since their early days and is as integral to the gorefest as the rest of the band. In 1988 Gwar received their first break. After seeing a home-made video of an early Gwar show, Shimmy Disc Records President Mark Kramer invited the band to record in his New York City studio. In a whirlwind, four-day studio session they recorded their debut album, *Hell-o.*

The album and subsequent club performances sparked the interest of British record company Master Records, which gave Gwar a verbal, one-album contract. Gwar recorded and released their second album, *Scumdogs of the Universe,* on the Master label in 1990. They supported the album with a tour of the United States, during which they filmed the concert video *Live From Antarctica.*

Scumdogs of the Universe marked a major turning point for Gwar. The album featured the first solidified Gwar line-up of Dave Brockie as Oderus Urungus on vocals, Pete Lee as Flattus Maximus on guitar, Michael Dirks as Balsac the Jaws of Death on guitar, Brad Roberts as Jizmak da Gusha on drums, and Michael Bishop as Beefcake the Mighty on bass. This line-up would remain intact for the next three years and four Gwar albums. Even though *Scumdogs of the Universe* sold several thousand copies and the tour garnered the band a large underground following, Master Records went bankrupt, leaving Gwar without a recording contract for nearly two years.

Then in 1992, Gwar signed with Brian Slagel's Metal Blade Records and released their third album, *America Must Be Destroyed.* It sold over 100,000 copies in the United States alone and enabled the band to finance their most elaborate stage show to date. The production included the five band members, eight auxiliary onstage characters known as the "Slave Pit," and a technician whose sole responsibility was to control a network of pressurized bottles and tubes that sprayed the audience with fake blood, a signature aspect of Gwar shows for many years.

"Be a Geek for Gwar"

The range and volume of the faux plasma spray steadily increased as the band progressed, and the antics of the Slave Pit became more outrageous. Simulated ejaculation of various body fluids and the catapulting of fake excrement into the audience was to be expected at Gwar concerts. The band "manager," Sleazy P. Martini, would traditionally call a Gwar "fan" on stage at each show for decapitation, causing gallons and gallons of blood to spew out of the neck. During a 1994 tour, Martini did choose five real-life devotees from the venue to display embarrassing or gruesome talents in a "Be a Geek for Gwar" contest, and one fan actually poured lighter fluid on his head and set it afire.

Riding high on the success of *America Must Be Destroyed,* Gwar followed up the album with the five-song

EP *The Road Behind* later in 1992. The band also expanded their realm from the stage to the screen that year with the release of the mini-film *Phallus in Wonderland*. Part movie, part concert performance, *Phallus in Wonderland* tells the story of Oderus Urungus's penis on trial. The story was inspired by Brockie's arrest for obscenity during a show in Charlotte, North Carolina, where police confiscated the two-foot long rubber phallus Brockie wore on stage as part of his costume. The American Civil Liberties Union took up the band's cause and successfully plea bargained for the release of the phallus. It was not the first time, nor would it be the last time, Gwar would have to deal with censorship. Earlier on the same tour, Brockie had been arrested in Athens, Georgia, on similar charges. And the band would again confront censorship with their fourth album.

To the surprise of many, including the band, the film *Phallus in Wonderland* was nominated for a Grammy Award. Ironically, Gwar was asked not to attend the awards ceremony. When they defied the request and showed up in full costume, security guards asked them to leave.

Controversy Continued

In 1993, Gwar once again ventured into the film arena with their 35-millimeter production *Skulhed ... Face*. A science fiction/horror fantasy about the band's battles against the arch-villain Skulhed ... Face (a thinly disguised metaphor for censorship), the film featured band performances, skits, and cameo appearances by producer and ex-Dead Kennedys singer Jello Biafra and Skid Row vocalist Sebastian Bach.

Gwar returned to the studio in 1994 to record their fourth album, *This Toilet Earth,* for Metal Blade. Before its release, Warner Bros., Metal Blade's distributor, requested the band remove a song that contained obscene lyrics from the album. Brockie explained in *Underscope* magazine that the song in question was about "the time-honored tradition of having sex with infants before they're born." The band refused and lost their distribution deal with Warner Bros., only to sign another deal with Priority Records four months later.

Shortly after the release of *This Toilet Earth,* Casey Orr replaced bassist Michael Bishop, who left to form his own band, Kepone. Brockie told *Contemporary Musi-* cians that Bishop left because "he felt musically unsatisfied with the band." So Orr donned the mantel of Beefcake the Mighty and accompanied the band on a brief European tour.

By the end of 1994, Gwar had succeeded in infiltrating virtually every form of the media. In addition to their music and films, they have appeared in their own comic book, were featured on MTV's popular animated series *Beavis and Butt-Head,* and even starred in a computer video game. Although Gwar has been repeatedly dismissed by some critics as nothing more than a gratuitous exploitation band, its creators insist that the group has a much deeper purpose. They acknowledge that that purpose may be lost on some of their fans, but the band is satisfied as long as the fans have a good time. As Hunter Jackson put it in *Melody Maker,* "The images we use are far older than Gwar and make serious artistic and cultural points. If you're intelligent and want an underlying meaning—fine, it's there. And, if you're stupid and just want to have blood splattered over you, that's fine, too."

Selected discography

Hell-o (self-released), 1988.
Scumdogs of the Universe, Master, 1990.
America Must Be Destroyed, Metal Blade, 1992.
The Road Behind, Metal Blade, 1992.
This Toilet Earth, Metal Blade, 1994.

Sources

Axcess, volume 2, issue 2.
Billboard, October 6, 1990; July 4, 1992; November 28, 1992.
Hypno, April 1994.
Los Angeles Times, October 24, 1993.
Melody Maker, February 16, 1991; July 20, 1991; April 4, 1992; October 10, 1992; October 17, 1992.
Pulse!, October 1992; September 1993.
Reflex, issue 29.
Spin, September 9, 1993.
Underscope, March 1994.
Washington Post, February 2, 1993.

Additional information for this profile was obtained from an interview with Dave Brockie, July 28, 1994.

—*Thad Wawro*

Roland Hayes

Classical singer

UPI / Bettmann Newsphotos

Tenor Roland Hayes is acknowledged as a masterful interpreter of both classical songs and black spirituals. In a career that spanned more than 30 years, he performed throughout the United States and Europe. Hayes shattered the color barrier in the world of classical music, becoming one of the highest paid musicians of his time and paving the way for later African American singers. Summing up Hayes's career, Marva Griffen Carter wrote in the *Black Perspective in Music:* "Hayes's life of almost ninety years reveals a remarkable story of a man who went from the plantation to the palace, performing before kings and queens, with the finest international and American orchestras, in segregated communities before blacks and whites alike.... When he sang, art became more than polished excellence. It appealed to something beyond the intellect, something one could call the soul."

One of six children, Roland Hayes was born on June 3, 1887, in Curryville, Georgia. Although neither of his parents were afforded any formal educational opportunities, they recognized the value of good schooling. Hayes's father, William, a former slave turned farmer and carpenter, had an intense appreciation of music; his mother, Fannie, also a former slave, was determined to see that all of her children were educated—and that Roland would pursue a religious vocation.

Music was a natural part of Hayes's life. A timid child, he nevertheless liked to sing while at work on the farm and at the Baptist church the family attended. Hayes learned to read music from a man who conducted a seasonal singing school, and he also played the quills—joints of bamboo tied together like panpipes—to music of African origin.

Determined to Study Music

When Hayes was 11 years old, his father died from injuries suffered several years earlier in a work-related accident. Young Roland and his brother Robert were forced to quit school and work to support the family. In 1900 the Hayes family—then consisting of Fannie, Roland, and his two brothers, Robert and Jesse—moved to Chattanooga, Tennessee. There, Hayes worked at an iron foundry, awaiting his turn to attend school. At age 16, after he had been made a foreman at the foundry, he returned to his studies part-time. Determined to succeed despite the embarrassment of reciting lessons with students much younger than himself, Hayes even hired a tutor. He also started singing lessons with W. Arthur Calhoun, an Oberlin University music student who opened Hayes's ears to classical music. After three months, Hayes knew that regardless of his mother's objections, he had to aspire to a career in music.

In 1905 Hayes entered the preparatory division at Fisk University in Nashville, Tennessee. After three years, during which he received a scholarship and helped support himself through housework and vocal performances with various groups, Hayes reportedly left the university because of a misunderstanding. He worked at a men's club in Louisville for a short time and began to gain notoriety for his singing. After performing a few years at small social functions, he gave a concert in Boston with the Fisk Jubilee Singers in 1911. After that, he stayed in Boston, where he found work as a hotel bellboy, a waiter, and a messenger for an insurance company. He continued his studies with operatic bass Arthur Hubbard and sent for his mother—who finally accepted her son's career choice—to come and live with him in the Northeast.

Early Performances

Hayes performed with American educator Booker T. Washington and singer-composer Harry Burleigh, whose reputations and experience enhanced that of the budding singer. However, early in the twentieth century, no professional manager was willing to sponsor a black performer; thus, in 1915 Hayes gave his first self-managed concert with little success. Two years later the undeterred singer rented Symphony Hall in Boston, then an unprecedented step for an African American. His performance of lieder, or classical songs, by Franz Schubert and arias by Mozart and Tchaikovsky created a sensation.

In early 1918 Hayes began a U.S. tour, which he managed himself, and in 1920 he set sail for London, England. After a year of scraping by with whatever small performances came their way, Hayes and his accompanist, Lawrence Brown, were booked to perform at the prestigious Wigmore Hall. Although he was suffering from pneumonia, Hayes sang masterfully. Two days later he gave a command performance for King George V and Queen Mary. While in London, Hayes also studied lieder singing with Sir George Henschel.

Toured the United States

Upon his return to the United States in 1922, the world famous Hayes performed at Symphony Hall in Boston to rave reviews. Shortly afterward he became the first black singer to appear at Carnegie Hall in New York City. Hayes then began a series of concert tours that took him to nearly every corner of the country. By 1924 he was performing more than 80 concerts per year, many with major orchestras, such as those in Boston, Philadelphia, New York, and Detroit. He was widely praised for his interpretations of German and French songs, as well as his renditions of black folk songs and spirituals, which he later compiled in a single volume titled *My Songs.*

In 1925 Hayes gave a command performance for Queen Mother Maria Christian of Spain. That same year, he was awarded the Spingarn Medal, given annually by the National Association for the Advancement of Colored People for the "most outstanding achievement among colored people." Hayes toured Italy in 1927 and the Soviet Union the following year. He was hailed wherever he went as one of the greatest lieder singers of his era for his silken smooth tone and sensitive lyrical interpretations. Although Hayes often performed concert renditions of arias, he never appeared in an opera because interracial casting was frowned upon during his era.

In a 1947 *Christian Science Monitor* interview, Hayes spoke about the universality of his work. "When I began my career I realized that if I would speak to all men, I must learn the language and the ways of thought of all men," Hayes explained. "What good could I do if I knew only my own ways and the thoughts of my own people? So I learned to sing the songs of all people.... The song I sing is nothing. But what I give through the song is everything. I cannot put into words what I try to do with this instrument that is nearest to me—my voice. If I were to frame it in words, I would lose some of the ability to make it effective."

Remembered as a Master of Song

In addition to his exceptionally long singing career, Hayes taught voice at Boston University beginning in 1950. In 1954 he toured Europe, where he was greatly admired in England, Holland, and Denmark. At age 70 he still garnered rave reviews: "What Mr. Hayes does is live each song he sings," wrote *Boston Herald* music critic Rudolph Elie. "To be sure, there are many others who do the same thing.... The essential difference here, however, is that Mr. Hayes knows what he is living: there is a classic balance between his intellectual comprehension and his emotional concept. The consequence is an atmosphere so intense as to be gripping.... [The listener] is in the presence of a master." In 1962, on his seventy-fifth birthday, Hayes gave his farewell concert at Carnegie Hall.

Although Hayes recorded for a number of labels, including Vocalion, American Columbia, Vanguard, and Veritas, few recordings are available. In 1990, however, the Smithsonian Institution issued *The Art of Roland Hayes,* an audio recording of various performances by Hayes from 1939 to 1965.

Hayes was a groundbreaking figure in the field of music who helped pave the way for classical African American artists such as Marian Anderson, Paul Robeson, Leontyne Price, Simon Estes, William Warfield, and George Shirley. In a television documentary titled *The Musical Legacy of Roland Hayes,* William Warfield recalled a conversation with Hayes, who advised African American singers: "I started all this.... Now, you can't stop where I stopped; you've got to go on."

Selected discography

The Art of Roland Hayes, Smithsonian Collection of Recordings, 1990.

Sources

Books

Hayes, Roland, *My Songs: Aframerican Religious Folk Songs Arranged and Interpreted by Roland Hayes,* Little, Brown, 1948.
Helm, MacKinley, *Angel Mo' and Her Son, Roland Hayes,* Little, Brown, 1942.

Periodicals

Atlanta Journal, November 25, 1990.
Black Perspective in Music, fall 1974; fall 1977.
Boston Globe, June 17, 1990.
Boston Herald, October 21, 1957.
Christian Science Monitor, November 22, 1947.
Record Collector, volume 10, 1955.
Washington Post, February 19, 1990.

Hayes was also the subject of the television documentary *The Musical Legacy of Roland Hayes.*

—Jeanne Lesinski

Tish Hinojosa

Singer, songwriter

Singer and songwriter Tish Hinojosa does not so much cross musical borders as ignore them. Her music combines sounds and styles from American folk music, Nashville's country-western, traditional Mexican genres, and Tejano conjunto music, or Mexican-American music from Texas. She writes everything from love songs to protest songs, ballads to dance tunes. Her exciting and interesting genre-bending style has also delayed her success somewhat, for recording companies like neat classifications, which Hinojosa's music defies. She started singing professionally in the 1970s and began recording albums in the 1980s, but only started receiving regular national attention in the 1990s.

The youngest of 13 children born to immigrant parents, Hinojosa listened to many different kinds of sounds during her childhood. Her older brothers and sisters listened to folk and popular music of the 1960s—by artists like Joan Baez and Judy Collins. Her parents listened to the radio stations playing Mexican music. "I love the music of the traditional aspect of our community," she told *Hispanic* magazine. "Conjunto music, the ballads, and the romantic singer/songwriter songs—the older music from Mexico that my parents like a lot—made a very positive impression."

Hinojosa herself began singing while in high school after her mother bought her a guitar. She explained to the *Dallas Morning News:* "It was just the $20 guitar you get down [in Mexico] at the Mercado. But I was really, really proud, and I still have that guitar."

In music, Hinojosa found something all her own. "Finally," she declared to the *Dallas Morning News,* "I [had] found something I could do myself. I wasn't just tagging along with my sisters somewhere." She also discovered that she had a special gift. She was singing one day at school with her friends, she told the newspaper, "and I started singing one song. They all just sat there kind of quietly, and they said: 'You know that you can sing?'" She did not read musical notation, but taught herself songs by ear from records. Her sister Linda Gonzalez described the process to the *Dallas Morning News:* "She'd sit in her room and play a record over and over again until she could pick the notes out. She never took guitar lessons."

After graduating from high school, Hinojosa started performing around town, recording popular tunes in Spanish for a leading Tejano label, and singing jingles in Spanish for radio commercials. After a few years without moving ahead in her career, she moved first to New Mexico and then to Nashville, seeking new music and new opportunities. She traveled around the coun-

For the Record . . .

Born Letitia Hinojosa, December 6, 1955, in San Antonio, TX; daughter of Felipe and Maria Hinojosa. Married Craig Barker, 1982; children: Adam, Maria Christina (Nina).

Began performing locally and on local radio, 1973; sang for Mel Tillis Production Company, Nashville, TN, 1983-85; recorded first album, *Taos to Tennessee,* 1987; performed at Texas Governor Ann Richard's inauguration, 1991; performed at U.S. President Bill Clinton's inauguration, 1993. Television appearances include *CBS This Morning,* 1993; radio appearances include *Prairie Home Companion* and *All Things Considered,* 1994;

Awards: First Prize for New Folk Songwriter, Kearville Folk Festival, 1979; Folk Album of the Year, National Association of Independent Record Distributors, 1992, for *Culture Swing.*

Addresses: *Management*—Manazo Music Management, P. O. Box 3304, Austin, TX 78764.

try to perform at colleges and coffee houses; she began learning the country-western hits of singers like Emmylou Harris and Roseanne Cash; and she landed a job singing demo tapes for the Mel Tillis Publishing Company. After two years in Nashville without signing a record deal, she moved back home to San Antonio to regroup. In the following years, she began to sing more of her own songs, and in 1987, released a privately-recorded collection entitled *Taos to Tennessee.*

During these years, Hinojosa had trouble landing a major recording label because of her eclectic sound. No one could quite categorize her music. She sang folk music, country-western songs, and conjunto songs; many of her own compositions synthesized traits from all these styles. To critics outside Nashville she was too country, to others inside Nashville, she was not country enough.

That Hinojosa didn't fit any mold gave the record companies a good excuse to ignore her for a few years. "There's so much talk now about artists who have fallen between the cracks," she told the *Los Angeles Times.* "So many of the singer-songwriters just don't fit into niches in Nashville or in pop music anymore. I guess I'm one of those. But I feel like I'm in good company, because I like a lot of people that are in the same crack that I'm in."

Hinojosa's record *Taos to Tennessee* sold well locally, received some notice, and started turning her career around. Two years later, she recorded her first major-label album, *Homeland,* for A&M records. The album contains the sounds and songs typical for Hinojosa—a combination of country-western, folk, and conjunto, presented in both Spanish and English.

While *Homeland* garnered rave reviews, Hinojosa relationship with A&M did not last. Only a week before the company was due to release her second album there was a management shake-up, and they dropped her from their register. "It was one of those hard, fast lessons about what major record labels are about, " she told the *Los Angeles Times.* "It's one of those confusing things. I'm not sure if and who to blame, and why there's people there that I never heard from again and while I was there they acted like they were real good friends. It was kind of a strange little thing."

The end of Hinojosa's association with A&M had a positive side, however, for she recorded the material for the her second album all over again, but this time in Austin rather than in Hollywood. Hinojosa was extremely pleased with the results. "What we got is a lot more personal record," she explained to the *Los Angeles Times.* It's a lot more of me, a lot more of Texas. The sound is a lot more real, my sound.... In L.A. it was a lot less time spent on a lot more frills. And what we did in Texas, a lot more heart went into it, a lot more time and thought." *Culture Swing* was finally released in 1992 by the independent folk-oriented label Rounder Records. The *New York Times* praised the work, calling its typical combination of Spanish and English, folk, country, and conjunto sounds a "panoramic musical landscape."

Hinojosa's fortune seemed to change again after the production of *Culture Swing.* She began writing new material with a new sound. "I was going in all kinds of directions," she explained in *Hispanic* magazine. "Its real personal, but on a different level than *Culture Swing."* This new sound caught the ear of the Warner Brothers label. "Originally, the new album was to have been my second for Rounder Records, the label that released *Culture Swing,"* she continued in *Hispanic.* "But the flavor of the recording took a different direction. It still had some Spanish language in it and a bit of Spanish sensitivity, but lyrically and musically, it stretched out further. I don't want to call it pop, because that's too general a term, but a major label sensed its potential and signed me to a long-term contract."

In the winter of 1994, Warner Brothers released *Destiny's Gate.* After *Destiny's Gate,* Hinojosa began working on several other projects, including a bilingual children's album. Despite the conflicts and problems her unique musical style has engendered for her, Hinojosa has no plans to change her musical approach. As she stated in a 1994 Manazo Music press kit, "When you resist pop formulas for your own artistic vision, the twists are sometimes confusing, but now I'm seeing the wonderful results of not straying from a true road."

Selected discography

Taos to Tennessee, Watermelon, 1987.
Homeland, A&M, 1989.
Aquella Noche, Watermelon, 1991.
Memorabilia Navidena, Watermelon, 1991.
Culture Swing, Rounder, 1992.
Destiny's Gate, Warner Bros., 1994.

Sources

Billboard, December 5, 1992.
Chicago Tribune, February 14, 1993.
Dallas Morning News, May 29, 1994.
Hispanic, January 1994.
Los Angeles Times, November 26, 1992.
New York Times, December 6, 1992.
People, July 11, 1994.
Pulse!, April 1993.
Spin, February 1993.
Stereo Review, May 1993.
Washington Post, November 25, 1992.

Additional information for this profile was provided by Manazo Music Management, 1994.

—*Robin Armstrong*

Lightnin' Hopkins

Guitarist, singer

Photograph by Ed Badeaux, © 1972 Fantasy, Inc.

Bluesman Sam "Lightnin'" Hopkins was a direct link to the rural blues tradition and a key figure in the transition from country to city blues. He recorded for a host of labels and was one of the most prolific blues artists of the twentieth century. In the 1920s, 1930s, and early 1940s Hopkins traveled through Texas playing at beer joints, picnics, and parties. He recorded as a popular artist after World War II and was rediscovered by folklorists in 1959, prompting a resurgence in his popularity and leading him to worldwide fame as a blues guitarist and singer.

Richard C. Walls in *Musician* wrote that Hopkins possessed "a bruised whiskey voice" that had "a clipped but expressive sound" and also noted that Hopkins's delivery was "a singular and affecting mix of private pain and public celebration." The performer rarely emoted on record, Walls remarked, but when he did, it was "hair-raising." "More often he [drew] the listener in, [confiding] or [stating] a plain truth," observed Walls, "letting his virtuosic guitar playing elaborate on the feeling."

As a country blues guitarist, Hopkins was "powerful" and "idiosyncratic," according to *Rolling Stone* reviewer David Fricke. His playing possessed "a dark rhythmic drive" that "in a solo setting, physically charged the rugged poetic beauty of his 'po' Lightnin' laments and the gnarly poignancy of his singing." In a group setting, Hopkins produced some virile blues recordings, though some back-up musicians could not keep up with his improvisational approach.

Taught by a Master

Sam Hopkins was born into the blues life on March 16, 1912, in Centerville, Texas, a small farm town north of Houston. Hopkins's musician father, Abe, was killed over a card game when Sam was only three, and Sam's grandfather had hung himself to escape the indignities of slavery. After his father died, Sam's mother, Francis Sims Hopkins, moved him and his four brothers and one sister to Leona, Texas. When Sam was eight, he made his first guitar out of a cigar box and chicken wire. His brother Joel taught him the basic chords, but it was at the feet of Texas bluesman Blind Lemon Jefferson that Hopkins began his real blues education.

Hopkins met Jefferson around 1920 at a Baptist Church Association meeting in Buffalo, Texas. Jefferson was singing and playing for the crowd; Hopkins, who was only eight, got behind the stage and joined in. At first Jefferson was angered, but when he noticed that Hopkins was just a boy, he softened and showed Hopkins a few licks. It wasn't too much later that

Born Sam Hopkins, March 15, 1912, in Centerville, TX; died of cancer, January 30, 1982; son of Abe Hopkins (a musician) and Frances Sims; married Antoinette Charles, 1943.

Guitarist and singer, 1920-82; played picnics and parties in Houston and eastern Texas, 1920-46; joined with cousin, blues singer Alger "Texas" Alexander, late 1920s; signed with Aladdin Records, 1946; rediscovered by Houston folklorist Mack McCormick, 1959; recorded for a variety of labels and toured the United States and Europe, 1959-82; appeared in films, including *The Blues,* 1962, *The Sun's Gonna Shine,* Flower Films, 1967, *The Blues Accordin' to Lightnin' Hopkins,* Flower Films, 1968, and *A Program of Songs by Lightnin' Sam Hopkins,* University of Washington, 1971.

Awards: New Star award, Male Singer, *Down Beat* magazine International Jazz Critics' Poll, 1962.

Hopkins left home to hobo through Texas playing in the streets, at picnics, parties, and dances—often just for tips. Even at the age of eight he knew he wasn't willing to live the hard life most Texas blacks faced in those days. "Chop that cotton for six bits a day, plow that mule for six bits a day—that wasn't in storage for me," he told Les Blank in the film documentary *The Sun's Gonna Shine.*

Hopkins eventually reconnected with Jefferson and for a time served as his guide. Then in the late 1920s Hopkins formed what was to be a long-running duo with his cousin, blues singer Alger "Texas" Alexander. The two played the Houston bar circuit and toured eastern Texas. During this era Hopkins was chronically short of money. At one point he was sentenced to a chain gang for committing adultery with a white woman. He probably also served time in the Houston County Prison Farm in the late 1930s.

When Hopkins married, he and his first wife hired themselves out to Tom Moore, a farmer whose callousness Hopkins immortalized in the song, "Tom Moore's Blues." "You know," he sang, "I got a telegram this morning/It say your wife is dead/I showed it to Mr. Moore he says/'Go ahead nigger, you know you gotta plow a ridge'/That white man said 'It's been rainin'/Yes sir I'm way behind/I may let you bury that woman/On your dinner time."

In 1943 Hopkins married his third wife, Antoinette Charles, and moved to a large farm north of Dallas, where he worked for a time as a sharecropper. Around 1946, he was given a new guitar by a family friend, "Uncle" Lucian Hopkins. That inspired Sam to move back to Houston where he teamed up with his old partner Tex Alexander to play the local beer joints.

"Thunder and Lightnin'"

As luck would have it, at that time Lola Anne Cullen of Aladdin Records was in Houston scouting for blues artists. She discovered Hopkins and paired him with Wilson "Thunder" Smith, creating the team "Thunder and Lightnin'." Lightnin's pairing with "Thunder" was short lived, but his relationship with Aladdin proved fruitful. "Katie Mae Blues," his first single, was a hit around Houston and its success led to 41 more sides for Aladdin.

After a few years, Hopkins left Aladdin and contracted with Houston's Gold Star Records. Hopkins insisted that record company owner Bill Quinn pay him $100 cash per song at the recording sessions; he was convinced that he would be ripped off otherwise. Looking back, however, historians have commented that this arrangement caused Hopkins to lose large sums in royalties.

Through the early 1950s, Hopkins recorded for small labels and hit *Billboard* magazine's rhythm and blues Top Ten with songs like "T Model Blues" and "Coffee Blues." His uptempo numbers of this era helped to pioneer rock and roll, but rock's teenage audience had little interest in Hopkins himself. To make matters worse, his original black audience also abandoned him for a more teen-oriented sound. Given his declining popularity, record companies lost interest in Hopkins, and he stopped recording as a popular artist in 1956.

Regained Fame

Scarcely three years after his exit from the popular marketplace, Hopkins was "discovered" by Houston folklorist Mack McCormick and introduced to a college-educated audience, which saw the blues as "folk music." That same year folklorist Samuel Charters devoted a chapter of his book *The Country Blues* to Hopkins and recorded a whole album of Hopkins's material for release on Folkways.

When labels realized that Hopkins's sparse acoustic guitar and understated prose appealed to white audiences, they rushed to record him. In 1962 he won *Down*

Beat magazine's International Jazz Critics' Poll in the New Star, Male Singer category. In the years that followed he "became a hero to academia, the young, the educated, and the liberals," according to Greg Drust and Stephen Peeples, who wrote the notes to *Mojo Hand: a Lightnin' Hopkins Anthology*. "Beyond his stature as a bluesman," Drust and Peeples continued, "Lightnin' also functioned as a teacher, philosopher, and shaman of sorts."

Remained True to Roots

Through the 1960s and 1970s, Hopkins continued to record. He became one of the post-World War II blues' most prolific talents. He toured the United States and Europe and completed hundreds of sessions for scores of major and independent labels. But while his fame grew, his attitude toward his career remained much the same as it had when he was roaming around Texas. "He hated to fly, and refused to have a telephone," Les Blank wrote in *Living Blues*. "He turned down tour offers of $2,000 a week yet played in small rough Houston bars for $17 a night." In 1967 Hopkins was featured in Les Blank's short subject documentary, *The Sun's Gonna Shine*. The following year he was featured in another Les Blank documentary, *The Blues According to Lightnin' Hopkins*, which won a Gold Hugo Award at the Chicago Film Festival as the best documentary of 1970.

In 1970 Hopkins was in an auto accident that put his neck in a brace and initiated a steady decline in his health. Nevertheless, he maintained a compulsive work rate during the 1970s, touring the United States, Canada, and Europe. He died of cancer of the esophagus on January 30, 1982. Remembering Hopkins, filmmaker Blank told Drust, "He was a clown and oracle, wit and scoundrel. Like Shakespeare, he had an understanding of all people and all their feelings. He [was] an eloquent spokesman for the human soul which dwells in us all."

Selected discography

Herald Recordings, Collectables, 1954.
Blues in My Bottle, Ace, 1961.
Goin' Away, Fantasy, 1963, reissued, 1988.

Double Blues, Fantasy, 1964.
Lightning Hopkins, With His Brothers & Barbara Dane, Arhoolie, 1964.
Texas Blues Man, Arhoolie, 1968.
Historic Recordings, 1952-1953, Blues Classics, 1986.
Early Recordings, Volumes 1 and 2, Arhoolie, 1990.
Lightnin', Fantasy, 1990, Arhoolie, 1993.
Lightnin' Hopkins, Smithsonian/Folkways, 1990.
The Texas Bluesman, Arhoolie, 1990.
The Complete Aladdin Recordings, EMI, 1991.
The Complete Prestige/Bluesville Recordings, Prestige, 1991.
The Gold Star Sessions, Volumes 1 and 2, Arhoolie, 1991.
The Complete Candid Otis Spann/Lightnin' Hopkins Sessions, Mosaic, 1992. *Forever*, EPM, 1992.
(With Sonny Terry) *Last Night Blues*, Fantasy, 1992.
It's a Sin to Be Rich, Verve, 1993.
Mojo Hand: The Lightnin' Hopkins Anthology, Rhino, 1993.
Sittin' In, Mainstream, 1993.
Shake That Thing, New Rose, 1993.
Swarthmore Concert, Fantasy, 1993.
In Berkeley, Arhoolie.
Golden Classics—Mojo Hand, Collectables.
Hootin' the Blues, Prestige.
How Many More Years I Got, Ace, reissued, Fantasy.
The Lost Texas Tapes, Volumes 1-5, Collectables.

Sources

Books

Blues Who's Who: A Biographical Dictionary of Blues Singers, edited by Sheldon Harris, Arlington House, 1979.
Charters, Samuel Barclay, *The Country Blues*, Rinehart, 1959.
The Guinness Encyclopedia of Popular Music, edited by Colin Larkin, New England, 1992.

Periodicals

Living Blues, summer/autumn 1982.
Musician, August 1992.
Rolling Stone, March 18, 1992; October 1, 1992.

Additional information for this profile was obtained from liner notes to *Mojo Hand: The Lightnin' Hopkins Anthology*, by Greg Drust and Stephen K. Peeples, 1993.

—Jordan Wankoff

Jodeci

Rhythm and blues group

Jodeci have revitalized the traditional rhythm and blues ballad by mixing their sweet harmonies with a streetwise rapper attitude. Rather than adopting the clean-cut look usually associated with balladeers, Jodeci use hip-hop moves on stage and style their appearance after gangsta rappers. DeVante Swing, the primary songwriter and producer; Mr. Dalvin, his brother; and K-Ci and JoJo, a second set of brothers, have "sweet and soulful vocals," according to Albert Watson of *Vibe*. Although Jodeci's sound may be enough to explain their popularity, their bad boy image has also attracted a lot of attention.

The two sets of brothers were raised in strictly religious homes in Charlotte, North Carolina. They were all members of church choirs in their youth and sang gospel music in shows as teenagers. Despite their similar backgrounds, the brothers did not know each other until their late teens, when they became friends and formed an R&B group.

The newly formed group decided to head straight for the top; they took a demo tape to New York City in 1989.

Courtesy of Uptown Enterprises

An appointment at MCA's relatively new label, Uptown Records, began inauspiciously. The group's contact there was not impressed with tape, but rapper Heavy D overheard it and convinced Uptown founder Andre Harrell to audition the group then and there. Impressed with the live performance, Harrell quickly arranged a deal and put Jodeci into development. Before beginning on an album, the group made appearances on other artists' albums, including Father MC's *Treat 'Em Like They Want to Be Treated,* and Jeff Redd's *Quiet Storm.* DeVante helped write and produce songs on Mary J. Blige's *What's the 411?* and Christopher Williams's *Changes.*

Brought Back the Ballad

When Jodeci finally released *Forever My Lady* in 1991, the wait proved to be well worth it. The group's first album was a phenomenal hit, eventually going multi-platinum. *Entertainment Weekly* praised it as "the smoothest soul sound around." The title track rose to Number One on the R&B charts, along with two other songs from the album, "Come Talk to Me" and "Stay." *Forever My Lady* not only garnered the group fame and fortune but also influenced several new, young, black male groups: Boyz II Men, H-Town, Shai, and Silk, to name the most prominent.

Jodeci revived a dying genre with their debut album. Watson commented in *Vibe:* "The Jodeci sound—lush love songs with lots of whispered sweet nothings and declarations of need—is characteristic of the piningly sincere r&b balladry that rap would seem to have all but obliterated. Yet rather than seeming obsolete or old-fashioned, Jodeci have made that sound hip again." A

key component in their ability to make ballads "hip" is their adoption of the outward trappings of rap. The group members wear typical hip-hop gear, including the ever-present boots and hats, and sport a certain "attitude" when not crooning about love.

The Bad Boy Image

Uptown Records not only supports the unusual image for balladeers, but seems to have had an active role in creating it. Uptown founder Harrell settled the boys—fresh from rural North Carolina—in his old Bronx neighborhood to introduce them to the harshness of New York streets. Soon thereafter, rumor has it that Sean "Puffy" Combs, formerly associated with Uptown, tutored Jodeci intensively on tough city style and attitude. Harrell admitted to Watson, "Puffy played a great part in developing the group's visual style as well as its attitude. He put them in the boots and hats and stuff."

Jodeci opened for a Hammer concert in 1992. *Billboard* reported they were a hit with the crowd and described their performance as "energized." *Rolling Stone,* however, criticized their hip-hop moves as excessive: "The group members dropped their pants or humped the stage more frequently than they harmonized. It was a shame, since their voices were strong."

Jodeci's image as bad boys may go deeper than their clothing and hip-hop dance moves. In March of 1993, the group was accused of sexually harassing female participants in one of their video shoots. Jodeci has not commented on these reports. The description of the members' behavior at the shoot came on top of more serious allegations leveled at DeVante and K-Ci the previous year: they were accused of sexually assaulting a woman at gunpoint in April of 1992. In an assessment in *Vibe* of Jodeci's controversial brushes with the law, Watson concluded: "It feels like DeVante'll bend over backwards to prove that he's down, to counter any conclusions you might draw about a Southern choirboy singing sweet love songs—compensating in a way that apparently seems to spill over into Jodeci's lives off-stage."

Crossover to Pop

The accusations apparently did not hurt Jodeci's position in the music world. The group was again at the top of the charts with a rendition of Stevie Wonder's "Lately" in 1993. The track was included on the album *Uptown Unplugged* and went gold. Although the "Lately" track carried the group into the pop sphere, K-Ci claimed the crossover was unintentional: "We would never try and consciously go pop, we're just not a pop group. What's satisfying is that we did what we've always done and the audience came to us."

The group released its second album, *Diary of a Mad Band,* in 1994. Mr. Dalvin produced the album's up-tempo tracks; DeVante did the ballads, which comprise most of the album. Although the ballads feature the same silky, harmonizing style of their earlier album, hip-hop and rap round out the effort. "As far as our music goes," K-Ci commented, "we like those hard core beats. That street attitude is a real part of our style and our performance." *Playboy,* however, found the crooning love songs, including "What About Us" and "Cry for You," the superior part of the album. "Their edgy rap-oriented material may be the direction Jodeci wants to go," a *Playboy* reviewer observed, "but that doesn't matter. What they really are are balladeers."

Selected discography

Forever My Lady, Uptown, 1991.
(With others) *Uptown Unplugged,* 1993.
Diary of a Mad Band, Uptown, 1994.

Sources

Billboard, May 2, 1992.
Entertainment Weekly, December 24, 1993.
Playboy, May 1994.
Rolling Stone, July 9, 1992.
Vibe, December 1993.

Additional information for this profile was obtained from MCA press materials.

—*Susan Windisch Brown*

Jerome Kern

Composer

When Jerome Kern died in 1945, America lost one of its greatest and most beloved composers. Harry Truman, who was the U.S. president at the time of Kern's death, was quoted as saying in David Ewen's book, *Composers for the American Musical Theatre:* "[Kern's] melodies will live in our voices and warm our hearts for many years to come.... The man who gave them to us earned a lasting place in his nation's history." In 1946 Metro-Goldwyn-Mayer released a lavish musical film biography of Kern, *Till the Clouds Roll By,* with appearances by Judy Garland, Frank Sinatra, Lena Horne, and other stars. The centennial of Kern's birth was celebrated in 1985, which saw the issuing of a U.S. postage stamp in his honor, as well as the release of more recordings and performances of his music. *Show Boat,* the most enduring of his works, continues to enjoy Broadway revivals. There is no sign that Kern's legacy is in danger of fading.

Jerome David Kern was born in New York City. He studied piano with his mother and in high school was often asked to play piano and organ and compose music for school theatrical productions. In 1902, at the age of 17, he tried his hand at a business career working for his father, who owned a merchandizing house. But the young Kern's enthusiasm for music led to his ordering 200 pianos from an Italian dealer instead of two—the number he was supposed to purchase. This action almost cost his father his business, and to Kern's relief, it was agreed that he should pursue a career in music.

Kern enrolled in the New York College of Music in 1902 and in 1903 went abroad to study music in Germany. He took up permanent residence in London, where he began writing songs for British musical hall productions. A year later, he returned to New York, taking jobs with music publishers—first the Lyceum Publishing Company and then Shapiro-Remick. At this time, British productions dominated Broadway. Kern was hired in 1904 to adapt one of these shows, *Mr. Wix of Wickham,* for the Broadway stage by "Americanizing" some of the numbers and by writing some additional songs of his own.

A year later, Kern took a job at another music publisher, T. B. Harms & Co.—which eventually became the publisher of his own works—and continued writing musical interpolations for British shows. Ewen noted that "almost a hundred of his songs were heard this way, in approximately thirty musicals.... [This] apprenticeship prepared him for giant tasks and achievements that lay before him."

The 1910s were a productive and noteworthy period for Kern. He married an English woman, Eva Leale, in 1910

Born Jerome David Kern, January 27, 1885, in New York, NY; died of a cerebral hemorrhage, November 11, 1945, in New York, NY; son of Henry Kern and Fannie Seligman Kern; married Eva Leale, 1910; children: Elizabeth (Betty) Kern Miller. *Education:* Attended New York College of Music; further music study in Germany.

Began career by composing adaptations of British musicals, beginning with *Mr. Wix of Wickham,* 1904; first hit, *The Girl from Utah,* produced 1914; wrote numerous stage musicals 1915-39, including *Nobody Home* and *Very Good Eddie,* 1915, *Oh Boy!* and *Leave It to Jane,* 1917, *Oh Lady! Lady!!,* 1918, *Sally,* 1920, *Sunny,* 1925, *Show Boat,* 1927, *The Cat and the Fiddle,* 1931, *Music in the Air,* 1932, *Roberta,* 1933, and *Very Warm for May,* 1939; wrote music for films, including *Swing Time,* 1936, *Lady, Be Good,* 1941, *You Were Never Lovelier,* 1942, *Cover Girl,* 1944, and *Centennial Summer,* 1946. Collaborators included lyricists Guy Bolton, Dorothy Fields, E. Y. "Yip" Harburg. P. G. Wodehouse, Oscar Hammerstein II, and Johnny Mercer. Arrangers included Frank Saddler, until 1921, and Robert Russell Bennett, beginning in 1923.

Awards: Academy awards for best song, 1937, for "The Way You Look Tonight" from *Swing Time,* and 1942, for "The Last Time I Saw Paris," from *Lady, Be Good.*

Kern wrote his most important work, *Show Boat,* in 1927 with lyricist Oscar Hammerstein II. The production, which included the songs "Ol' Man River," "Can't Help Lovin' Dat Man," and "Make Believe," is notable for the richness of its music and its influence on other Broadway composers, who saw it as a model of writing for the musical stage. Today some believe it reflects racist attitudes; protesters tried to ban a 1993 revival in Toronto, Ontario, Canada, but the production went on to great success and re-opened on Broadway in 1994.

A close examination of *Show Boat* reveals that it is actually quite progressive for a show that was written in 1927. The plot, involving a woman who is prohibited from performing on the show boat because she is bi-racial and is married to a white man, is compelling, as is the song "Ol' Man River," which is the complete antithesis of the more upbeat tunes popular at a time when many whites did not wish to acknowledge their injustice to African Americans. *Show Boat* was made into a film musical three times—in 1929, 1936, and 1951. In 1954 it became part of the New York City Opera's standard repertory—the first musical to be adopted by an opera company.

The 1930s saw a string of Kern musicals: *The Cat and the Fiddle; Music in the Air; Roberta,* which was made into a film starring Fred Astaire and Ginger Rogers in 1935 and which included the song "Smoke Gets in Your Eyes"; the Astaire/Rogers film musical *Swing Time,* featuring "A Fine Romance" and the Oscar-winning "The Way You Look Tonight"; and *Very Warm for May,* which was a flop but from which the song "All the Things You Are"—perhaps Kern's best song, if not the best popular song by any composer—survives.

In the 1940s Kern moved to Hollywood and devoted the rest of his career to writing music for films. He contributed the songs "The Last Time I Saw Paris" to *Lady, Be Good,* "Dearly Beloved" to *You Were Never Lovelier,* and "Long Ago and Far Away" to *Cover Girl.* He died in New York in 1945; his last score was for the film *Centennial Summer,* which was released in 1946.

Most of Kern's manuscripts were assumed for decades to be lost. But in 1982 hundreds of manuscripts by Kern and other Broadway composers were found in a warehouse in Secaucus, New Jersey. In an article in the *New York Times* on March 10, 1987, the year that the manuscripts were inventoried after having been moved to Manhattan, Kern scholar John McGlinn was quoted as saying that the discovery was "like opening the tomb of King Tut. There are major works here that had been presumed lost forever; shows that were never revived and were assumed to have vanished off the face of the earth." Included among the findings were

and in 1914 had his first hit, *The Girl from Utah*—another adaptation of a British show. In 1915 Kern began writing musicals for the Princess Theatre in New York. These productions, *Nobody Home, Very Good Eddie, Oh Boy!,* and *Oh Lady! Lady!!,* were distinguished by a new approach to musical theater, developed by Kern in collaboration with librettist Guy Bolton, and, beginning in 1917, the talents of lyricist P. G. Wodehouse.

The musical revue format, with unrelated numbers strung together, was replaced by a more coherent story, more sophisticated songs, and characters that were more believable and realistic. The transformation of the Broadway musical did not happen overnight, however, and Kern also wrote the music for more conventional shows, including *Leave It to Jane, Sally,* which included the popular "Look for the Silver Lining," and *Sunny.*

the complete scores for *Very Good Eddie, Leave It to Jane,* and *Sunny,* and the original manuscripts of "Ol' Man River," "Can't Help Lovin' Dat Man," and music that was cut from *Show Boat* after the 1927 production. This "lost" music was added to a 1988 recording of *Show Boat,* restoring the musical to its original glory.

Selected compositions

Stage musicals

The Girl from Utah, 1914.
Nobody Home, 1915.
Very Good Eddie, 1915.
Oh Boy!, 1917.
Leave It to Jane, 1917.
Oh Lady! Lady!!, 1918.
Sally, 1920; adapted for film, 1929.
Sunny, 1925; adapted for films, 1930 and 1941.
Show Boat (includes "Ol' Man River," "Make Believe," and "Can't Help Lovin' Dat Man"), 1927; adapted for films, 1929, 1936, and 1951.
Sweet Adeline, 1929; adapted for film, 1935.
The Cat and the Fiddle, 1931; adapted for film, 1933.
Music in the Air, 1932; adapted for film, 1934.
Roberta, 1933; adapted for films, 1935 and 1952.

Film musicals

I Dream Too Much, 1935.
Swing Time (includes "The Way You Look Tonight" and "A Fine Romance"), 1936.
High, Wide, and Handsome, 1937.
When You're in Love, 1937.
Joy of Living, 1938.
Very Warm for May (includes "All the Things You Are"), 1939.
One Night in the Tropics, 1940.
"Last Time I Saw Paris," *Lady, Be Good,* 1941.
"Dearly Beloved," *You Were Never Lovelier,* 1942.
"Long Ago and Far Away," *Cover Girl,* 1944.
Can't Help Singing, 1944.
Centennial Summer, 1946.

Instrumental works

Scenario, 1941.
Mark Twain Suite, 1942.

Selected discography

Ella Fitzgerald, *The Jerome Kern Songbook,* 1963, reissued, Verve, 1985.

Show Boat (1988 studio cast—original 1927 Broadway version), Angel, 1988.
Show Boat (reissue of 1951 motion picture soundtrack) Sony, 1990.
A Jerome Kern Showcase (anthology of tunes from musicals and films), Pearl, 1991.
Leave It to Jane (selections from 1959 off-Broadway revival), Stet, 1991.
Till the Clouds Roll By (selections from 1946 motion picture soundtrack), Sony, 1992.
The Heritage of Broadway, Volume 1: Music of Irving Berlin and Jerome Kern, Bainbridge, 1994.
70 Years of Broadway, Volume 1 (selections from *Show Boat* and *Roberta* by various artists), LaserLight, 1994.
The Cat and the Fiddle (1933 motion picture soundtrack), Hollywood Soundstage.
Roberta (1935 motion picture soundtrack), Classic International Filmusicals.
You Were Never Lovelier (1942 motion picture soundtrack), Curtain Calls.
Cover Girl (1944 motion picture soundtrack), Curtain Calls.
Centennial Summer (1946 motion picture soundtrack), Classic International Filmusicals.
Very Good Eddie (soundtrack from 1972 Broadway revival), DRG.

Sources

Books

Bordman, Gerald, *Jerome Kern: His Life and Music,* Oxford University Press, 1980.
Ewen, David, *Composers for the American Musical Theatre,* Dodd, Mead, 1968.
Freedland, Michael, *Jerome Kern: A Biography,* Robson Books, 1978.
Krueger, Miles, *Show Boat: The Story of a Classic American Musical,* Oxford University Press, 1977.
Wilder, Alec, *American Popular Song: The Great Innovators, 1900-1950,* Oxford University Press, 1972.

Periodicals

Musical America, January 1985.
Musical Quarterly, number 4, 1985.
New Yorker, March 25, 1985.
New York Times, November 12, 1945; March 10, 1987.
Time, June 10, 1985.

—*Joyce Harrison*

Nusrat Fateh Ali Khan

Singer

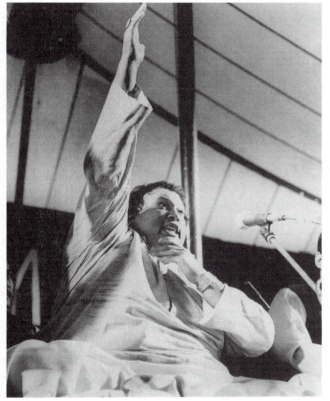

Photograph by Dave Peabody, courtesy of Real World

Nusrat Fateh Ali Khan, internationally recognized for his mastery of a form of Islamic devotional music known as *qawwali* (pronounced kah-*wah*-lee), first gained significant attention in the United States in 1989 when he performed at the Brooklyn Academy of Music's Next Wave Festival. Prior to that, the Sabri Brothers had been the United States' significant import of traditional Pakistani music, appearing in the United States during the mid-1970s. Three years after Khan's first U.S. appearance, the singer would spend a year as artist in residence at the University of Washington's music department.

New York Times music critic Jon Pareles places *qawwali* in an ecstatic musical tradition alongside American gospel, Moroccan *joujouka,* and even techno music, which tends to create emotional highs through simple melodies and driving beats, gathering "intensity through repetition and improvisational flights." *Qawwali* is believed to have originated among the Chisti order of Sufis in the tenth century.

Khan's large, almost Buddha-esque body often moves in rapid motion to his music's emotional peaks; his hands jab outward, brushing, as if carving the images of divine spirit from the air. His rapt audience—at least those of Pakistani background, who comprise the greater portion of his listeners—follows with fevered shouts and dancing, afterwards gathering below the stage to shower their beloved singer with money and flowers. Khan seems to almost goad his listeners into musical intoxication, pleading in fierce cries, imitating the rhythmic insistence of the drums, and calling back and forth with other singers in his "party," the favored term for the other singers (*qawwalis*) and instrumentalists who sit in a group on the stage with the lead *qawwal.*

The World Music Institute, located in New York City, has been a chief promoter of Khan's work in the West, along with many other important nonwestern folk and classical musicians. For example, in 1993 Khan opened and closed a five-hour "Masters of India and Pakistan" concert that featured music of his region, Hindustani, as well as the work of performers from southern Pakistan.

Khan was born in 1948 in the Punjab province of Pakistan, in the town of Lyallpur—during Pakistan's 1979 decolonization, its name was changed to Faisalbad. As a young *qawwal,* Khan learned his art in the traditional manner, through his family. His father, Ustad Fateh Ali Khan, as well as his uncles, were *qawwalis,* and they trained Khan in the family tradition of singing in a high register. Khan also received instruction on the tabla, a small hand drum.

For the Record . . .

Born October 13, 1948, in Lyallpur (now Faisalbad), Pakistan; son of Ustad Fateh Ali Khan (a *qawwal*).

Began performing Islamic devotional music as a *qawwal* in villages and religious shrines; first U.S. tour, 1989.

Addresses: *Record company*—Real World/Caroline, 114 West 26th St., New York, NY 10001.

Khan began performing at shrines and in villages where he would sometimes sing through the whole day or night in religious celebration. "When I had the stamina, I'd sing for 10 hours," he once recalled. But, by age 45, the singer found himself limited to sessions of three or four hours. These shrines, or *dargahs,* are generally the tombs—symbolic or otherwise—of saints where the faithful enter musically induced, trance-like states allowing communion with God. Traditionally, *qawwalis* sat opposite the saint's tomb. In the intervening space would be the audience in a circle formation, and in its center a spiritual leader surrounded by prominent devotees. Such sites are the true home of *qawwali,* although the music has also been performed at important events such as weddings feasts.

Persian Poetry the Basis for Music

In his introduction to the program for Khan's 1993 World Music Institute performance, Robert Browning wrote, "The *qawwal* will dwell on certain words ... creating great depth in the apparently simple language of certain Sufi texts. He will often repeat a phrase or sentence indicating both the obvious and hidden content by emphasizing or ruminating upon particular words and syllables ... [so that, for example] a spinning wheel becomes the wheel of life." *Qawwali* texts are most commonly medieval Persian Sufi poetry, and Khan, like other *qawwalis,* learns each poem by heart. Although the verses are available in books, it is the manner of performing each text that must be learned from another *qawwal.* Thus, the music is basically an oral tradition.

Browning stated that "rarely is a complete poem recited—rather the singer will join segments from different poems or add lines from another text." This free association from memorized poems is done to emphasize a certain meaning, or to try a new direction in the effort to move the audience to spiritual awakening. The *qawwal* must exhibit great sensitivity in noting when a listener is moved to divine ecstasy, and must repeat the same phrase over and over; according to Sufi belief, interruption would threaten the ecstatic with death.

Metaphoric Wine, Women, and Song

Often, *qawwali* poetry's apparent subject is romantic love, or even wine intoxication—though liquor is shunned by Islam. These are symbolic subjects, however: romantic love serves as an allegory and facet of divine love, while intoxication refers to the joyous trance induced by *qawwali.* The oft mentioned "tavern," as in the famous Persian poem "In the Tavern of Ruin," refers to one's spiritual master who houses God's love.

The melodic sources for performing *qawwali* poems are usually set by tradition. The tunes are North Indian in nature, meaning the octave has seven degrees and the various scales come from light classical *ragas.* *Ragas* are a traditional form of Hindu music, calling for improvisation on a theme evoking religious belief, the improvisation generally following prescribed patterns and progressions. Modern *qawwali* represents a spectrum of influences and geographic territories.

Generally associated with the Sufi religion, *qawwali* also has Hindu, Sikh, and Muslim followers. Currently, Urdu is the music's "first language," as Ken Hunt noted in his profile of Khan for *Folk Roots.* However, *qawwalis* also sing in Hindi, Sindhi, Punjabi, and classical Persian, not to mention local tongues. The literary sources of *qawwali* range too, though texts are chiefly medieval Persian Sufi poetry. The program for Khan's 1993 tour included, for example, a thirteenth-century Persian poem by the famed Amir Khusrau.

Temptations of a *Qawwal*

In his article for *Folk Roots,* Hunt described the scowl that comes over Khan's face when discussing the depiction of *qawwali* in films. For several years a debased form of *qawwali* has formed the soundtrack of many movies generated by a prolific Indian film industry. Khan understandably decries this long-standing commercialization of a sacred art form.

Yet, as an artist himself, Khan has embraced nontraditional elements since his 1989 U.S. visit. Western instruments and such big-name musicians as Jan Garbarek and Peter Gabriel have strongly influenced Khan's output in recent years. This Western flavor is evident in the singer's recording *Mustt Mustt* and numerous remixes, including those by Bally Sagoo in *Magic Touch.*

Khan defends such breaks with tradition as "experiments" and seems to feel that attracting an audience is important to make people aware of *qawwali*. The pressures on this revered singer to widen his audience echo those placed on performers of any type of traditional folk music. The artist is pulled in two directions: As a traditionalist, he is entrusted with preserving the music's form, and yet as a musician, he feels the need to discover new forms of self-expression. Noting that many *qawwalis* have abandoned shrine performance for financial reasons, Khan has expressed that he cannot forego his spiritual and personal links to such sites. Each year, he returns to perform at two dargahs, one in Lahore and one in Pak Patan.

Khan has made numerous recordings over the years, with titles now numbering more than 100. While his works of the early 1990s disappoint some fans of the traditional sound who find in the modern output a weakening of musical and spiritual integrity, such early classical recordings as *En Concert a Paris* and *Traditional Sufi Qawwalis Volumes 1 and 2* form a timeless buffer against loss of the past.

Selected discography

Devotional and Love Songs, Real World, 1988.

Traditional Sufi Qawwals—Live in London '89, Navras, 1989.

Shahen-Shah, Real World, 1989.

Day, Night, Dawn, Dusk, Shanachie Records, 1991.

Mustt Mustt, Real World, 1991.

Shahbaaz, Real World, 1991.

Revelation—Ilham, Audiorec, 1993.

The Last Prophet, Real World/Caroline, 1994.

Greatest Hits of Nusrat Fateh Ali Khan, Sirocco/EMI.

Nusrat Fateh Ali Khan & Party Live in New York, Rhythms of the East.

Magic Touch, Oriental Star.

Paris Concert—Live, Ocora.

Jan Garbarek & Nusrat Fateh Ali Khan, ECM.

Nusrat Fateh Ali Khan & His Qawwali Party—Vol. 1, JVC.

Nusrat Fateh Ali Khan—The Ecstatic Qawwal—Vol. 2, JVC.

Sources

Folk Roots, November 1993.

New York Times, October 13, 1992; March 24, 1993; August 17, 1993.

Additional information for this profile was obtained from *The Art of Qawwal, Nusrat Fateh Ali Khan* (concert program), World Music Institute, 1993.

—Joseph M. Reiner

Kool & the Gang

Rhythm and blues/pop band

"In this business, you're always proving yourself," said James "J. T." Taylor, former lead singer of Kool & the Gang in a 1984 interview with *Musician*. "That's why we try not to say we ever made it," he continued, "because you never made nothin'. You can accomplish things to a certain point, but what have you ever made?" In 25 years of recording, the ten-member funk/pop amalgamation has made 34 separate albums that have sold over 40 million copies; won a Grammy award and four American Music awards for Best Soul Group; and released a string of platinum releases. Part of their success is perhaps their continued struggle to prove themselves as some of the top musicians in the fickle trends of American popular music.

According to *Rolling Stone's* Christopher Connelly, "In two decades, Kool & the Gang have run the gamut of black music styles, from hard-edged, James-Brown-like funk to disco to brown-eyed pop." Starting in the early 1970s with their smash singles "Jungle Boogie" and "Hollywood Swinging," and later with disco hits "Emergency" and "Ladies' Night," Kool & the Gang

Courtesy of Buzz Willis, ECI

For the Record . . .

Original members include **Clifford Adams**, trombone; **Robert "Kool" Bell** (born in 1950), bass; **Ronald Bell**, keyboards; **George Brown**, drums; **Robert Mikens**, trumpet; **Charles Smith**, guitar; and **Dennis "D. T." Thomas**, alto sax. Later members include **Robert "Robbie G" Gobel** (played on 1994 release, *Unite*); **Gerard Harris** (played on 1994 release, *Unite*), guitar; **Sennie "Skip" Martin** (joined band 1988), lead vocals, trumpet; **Odeen Mays, Jr.** (joined band 1988), lead vocals, keyboards; **Shawn McQuillar** (played on 1994 release, *Unite*), lead vocals, guitar; **James "J. T." Taylor** (joined band 1977), lead vocals.

Band formed as the Jazziacs, 1964; changed name to Soul Machine review, 1967, and to Kool & the Gang, 1969; released over 25 albums, 1969-94. Debut LP *Kool & the Gang* released on De-Lite, 1970; released *Ladies' Night* with lead singer J. T. Taylor, 1979, and *Celebrate*, 1980; single "Celebration" was played at the 1980 Superbowl and Macy's Thanksgiving Day Parade.

Awards: Received double platinum album for *Emergency*; platinum albums for *Ladies' Night, Celebrate, Something Special,* and *In the Heart*; platinum singles for "Ladies Night," "Too Hot," "Let's Go Dancin'," "Fresh," "Emergency," and "Cherish"; gold albums for *Wild and Peaceful, Light of the Worlds, As One,* and *Forever*; gold singles for "Funky Stuff," "Jungle Boogie," "Hollywood Swingin'," "Too Hot," "Take My Heart," "Big Fun," "Joanna," "Tonight," and "Victory"; Grammy Award for "Open Sesame" from *Saturday Night Fever*; American Music awards for best soul group, 1981, 1983, 1984, and 1987; Tokyo Music Festival award, 1987, for "Cherish."

Addresses: *Management*—Bowen Agency Ltd., 504 W. 168th St., New York, NY 10032. *Record company*—JRS Records, 7758 Sunset Blvd., Hollywood, CA 90046.

established themselves as chart-topping R&B artists. The band's attention to popular music trends has transformed their original horn-driven (two saxophones, two trumpets, and a trombone) dance music through periods of late-1960s "street funk," to 1970s disco, to 1980s pop and synthesized sound.

In 1980 Kool & the Gang's single "Celebration" captured the nation's mood of victory with the increasing prosperity at the beginning of Ronald Reagan's presidency and the return of hostages taken from the American embassy in Tehran, Iran, and held for over a year by radical Moslems in the country. The song was often played over sound systems in packed stadiums, whether for sporting events or their own sold-out concerts. Mark Rowland of *Musician* described Kool & the Gang's concert style as having the "choreographed kineticism of a Busby Berkely movie," containing in its breadth "a series of syncopated gymnastics enough to boggle the Temptations." In one concert, J. T. Taylor performed onstage in a raincoat amid the background rumble of simulated thunder.

The thunder, however, may have foreshadowed the group's need to prove themselves as changeable yet again in the fairweather popular music scene. Although Steve Sutherland of *Melody Maker* once described Kool & the Gang as "damned canny when it comes to translating 'the sayings of the street' into cold, hard cash," reviews of their 1988 release, *Everything Is Kool & the Gang,* were not favorable. *Musician,* which four years earlier lauded the group as a basically unshakable funk institution, described the album as rife with "drab discofield remakes that suck all the funk from the likes of 'Jungle Boogie' and 'Hollywood Swinging.'"

From Jazz to Street Funk

In 1964 Robert Bell, his brother Ronald, and five high school friends formed the instrumental band called the Jazziacs. Their father was a boxer on the upper west side of New York City and ran a gym below the flat of jazz great Thelonius Monk, who became Robert Bell's godfather. Miles Davis, another jazz star who used to work out between gigs, also frequented the gym daily and was friends with Bell's father. Robert adopted the nickname "Kool" (for his mild or "cool" temperament) and was only 14 when he picked up the bass and began leading the Jazziacs at scattered gigs in New Jersey lounges.

Along with the Bell brothers, the band still includes original members Robert Mickens (trumpet), Dennis "D. T." Thomas (alto saxophone), Charles Smith (guitar), Clifford Adams (trombone), and George Brown (drums). Together they began covering contemporary pop and motown, collaborating occasionally with jazz musicians McCoy Tyner, Leon Thomas, and Pharoah Sanders.

In 1967 the Jazziacs changed their name to the Soul Machine Review, and when they finally signed with Red Coach records in 1969, they changed it again to Kool

& the Gang, modifying their originals to combine "street funk," R&B, and pop. According to Connelly, "Kool's bass lines suggested the melodic contours of a song, while horns provided contrapuntal fills, and solos were sculpted around more traditional jazz harmonies." He concluded that "the result was a kind of easy-listening funk," sophisticated for pop, but "propulsive enough to shimmy to." Their early hits, "Let the Music Take Your Mind," "Funky Man," and "Love the Life You Live," made them a street-music sensation, the kings of sweaty dance parties.

Red Coach released Kool & the Gang's first album, *Kool & the Gang,* on the De-Lite label in 1970, but the group didn't reach critical and popular success until the 1973 release of *Wild and Peaceful,* which contained the smash gold singles, "Funky Stuff," "Jungle Boogie," and "Hollywood Swingin'." According to Vernon Gibbs of the *Village Voice,* the Gang's following albums detailed the group's "spiritual phase," driven by some members' growing Muslim convictions and the climate of the country in the mid-1970s.

Although 1974's "Light of the Worlds" achieved gold status, Kool & the Gang's popularity was soon squelched by the country's increasing disco fever. "Ironically," wrote Gibbs, "it was the inclusion of 'Open Sesame' on the *Saturday Night Fever* soundtrack (it had already been a black hit) that gave them another glimpse of life at the top and prompted drastic changes that were long overdue."

Imitator Became Singer

By 1977 Kool & the Gang had reached a self-described "career crossroads," finding themselves to be too progressive for disco and too sugary for funk. "We thought that musically we were there," Kool told *Rolling Stone,* "but we just didn't have the vocals that the Commodores had with Lionel Richie and that Earth Wind and Fire had with Maurice White and Philip Bailey."

The change that the group needed was J. T. Taylor, a schoolteacher and amateur nightclub singer from New Jersey (not to be confused with the folksinger from Martha's Vineyard). Like most of the members of Kool & the Gang, Taylor's familiarity with "the sayings of the street" came from personal experience. "I have eight sisters and two brothers, and when I came here I found that Kool and his brother grew up in a similar situation," Taylor told *Musician* in 1984. "We have a lot in common—poverty, hard times growing up and all."

Taylor was also no stranger to Kool & the Gang's music.

In fact, when he was 13 years old, he and his friends started their *own* band called Kool & the Gang, modeled after the original.

Taylor's drummer named himself "George" after George Brown, and his bass player named himself "Kool." They even made up T-shirts with the original bandmember's names on the back. The only name that was missing was James Taylor's; at the time, Taylor was essentially trying himself out as the absent lead singer in all of the Kool & the Gang songs.

Scored With *Ladies' Night*

Taylor's high school imitations gave way to reality when the Gang was actually looking for a lead singer; he was already a perfect fit. Taylor later told *Musician* that when he returned to his old neighborhood to visit, one of his old bandmates called out across the street, "Remember those T-shirts? Now you're with the *real guys*!" With Taylor on board, the band hit the streets to do some research. They drove around the city and hung out at various clubs and functions. The material that they gathered later became their first platinum album, *Ladies' Night,* which was released in 1979.

"It was like starting all over again," Kool told *Musician.* "We had to tour all the time. New bands like GQ and Instant Funk were getting platinum albums. We had to wonder what they were doing since our music had been danceable since 1969." In a sense, *Ladies' Night* was a comment on the very club scene that the band was trying to break into; in their tours around the city, they found that every Wednesday night was consistently "Ladies' Night" at clubs and discos. "We were trying to capture what was going on," Kool told *Melody Maker.* "Our music became an extension of people's experience." Taylor's melodic voice gave the album instant popularity, the singles "Too Hot" and "Ladies' Night" reaching gold and platinum status.

"We'd always been about change," Kool told *Melody Maker,* citing the band's traverse of musical genres over the decades. "It's the result of a [continued] growth pattern." Yet Kool & the Gang were criticized for this move out of instrumental-based music into pop conformity with the addition of a front man; it was seen by some fans as an abandonment of their black cultural roots and urban street-sound. D. T. Thomas told *Billboard* magazine in a 1988 interview that during this period, the Gang didn't think of their audience in terms of color. "It's true that our material ... has been very heavily crossover. We were doing that purposely, but it was never with the intention of leaving our black base."

"Celebration" Created a Pop Sensation

Besides the inclusion of a new lead singer, the group's change to a pop sound was enhanced by producer Eumir Deodato, who, starting with *Ladies' Night,* produced the group's next four platinum and gold albums, between 1979 and 1982. He made room for Taylor's sweet crooning voice by simplifying the production, moving the keyboards up front, switching the vocal chorus into backup sound, and softening the hard-edged funk horns. The result, according to Gibbs, was that Kool & the Gang sounded "more like a new band in their first great surge than veterans who have seen it all."

With the help of Deodato, the group's next album, *Celebrate,* became one of the biggest hits of their career, the hit single, "Celebration" carving its own niche as a national theme song for the release of the hostages in Iran, as well as scoring the Macy's Thanksgiving Day Parade and the Superbowl. "*Celebrate* is the kind of album that is hard to repeat," Kool told *Melody Maker.* "It happened, the timing was right, the conditions in the world were conducive to what was going on in the song." The lyrics of the title track also seemed to epitomize the group's spiritual values at the time. "Our music is very celebrative," Kool continued in the *Melody Maker* interview. "Life is very celebrative. When you wake up in the morning and the sun is shining, you're thankful that you woke up and that the creator blessed you to live again."

In 1981 Kool & the Gang released the platinum-selling album *Something Special,* which included the gold hit-single "Take My Heart." On a concert tour for the album, the group sold out four shows at Radio City Music Hall in New York, signaling their massive national popularity. Gibbs called *Something Special* "unquestionably the most accomplished album of their career ... every bit as brilliant as the singles 'Ladies' Night' and 'Celebration.'"

Moved Production In-House

Although *As One,* the fourth Deodato-produced album, reached gold in the United States and outsold all of their other albums in Africa and Europe, Kool & the Gang separated amicably from their producer in 1983 and decided to create their own recordings in-house. "After four albums we wanted to make a change and give ourselves a shot at it," Kool told Nelson George of *Billboard* magazine. The 1983 album *In the Heart* credits Ronald Bell, Kool & the Gang, and engineer Jim Bonneford for production, but in all following albums, Ronald Bell became the group's secret production weapon. "We try to stay open to everything, but we don't worry about it 'cause I think basically Kool & the Gang's sound is established," Taylor told *Rolling Stone.*

From the mid-1980s until the early 1990s Ronald Bell kept the sound established, however unconventionally; rock guitars began to replace horns, and their sound was transformed under the power of digital technology. Bell called his production set-up the IBMC, or Itty Bitty MIDI Committee, using MIDI computer synthesizers and mixers. In a 1986 *Musician* article, Jock Baird called the more reclusive Bell brother "a funky jazz mad scientist, Coltrane meets Mr. Wizard, Soul-Train meets micro-chip."

> "*Our music is very celebrative. Life is very celebrative.*"
> —Robert "Kool" Bell

In the 1980s Bell produced the double-platinum *Emergency* and the gold *Forever,* on which he played almost all the instruments. "The Itty Bitty MIDI Committee is basically translating musical ideas into computer language, and bringing it out to sound like what they're really meant to be, instead of sounding like stiff, synthetic computer music," Bell told *Musician.* Through this process, tapes of Kool & the Gang's musicians were taken and translated into MIDI sequencers, and copied and layered, eliminating the need for studio time.

For a band that for over 20 years had experienced as much musical genre change as a band probably could and still stay together, the move to in-house production was just another marker of growth. On the *In the Heart* album, Ronald said that the rest of the band, "wouldn't even let us put a drum machine on because they were against it at that time. It was new to them.... But now they understand technology." The change to in-house production also helped the members increase their outside production; Taylor produced a rap record, and Ronald Bell produced work by Latoya Jackson and Jimmy Cliff.

The biggest change of the 1980s, however, came with the departure of lead singer Taylor. The vocalist, who left in 1988, reportedly departed amicably with plans to make a solo album. "What happened was that he actually had had some physical problems with his voice last year and he was convalescing. We all felt it was a good time to re-evaluate our status together," D. T. Thomas told *Billboard* in 1988. The Gang replaced Taylor with singers/instrumentalists Gary Brown, Odeen Mays, and Skip Martin.

From 1988 until 1994 Kool & the Gang released five more albums, and continued to tour Europe, the United States, and Africa, proving once again the band's tenacity and ability to bounce back in the face of change and the diverse taste of their fans. Even the departed Taylor acknowledged this truth, and in an interview with *Melody Maker*, he summed up the group's credo best by saying, "If you look at our stories, they're very social.... We just write about everyday experiences.... That's our main objective; that's what we're here to do."

Selected discography

On JRS Records

Kool & the Gang, 1970.
Kool & the Gang Live at the Sex Machine, 1971.
The Beat of Kool & the Gang Featuring the Penguin, 1971.
Kool & the Gang Live at P.J.'s Hollywood, 1972.
Music Is the Message, 1972.
Good Times, 1973.
Wild and Peaceful (includes "Funky Stuff," "Jungle Boogie," and "Hollywood Swinging"), 1973.
Kool Jazz, 1974.
Light of the Worlds, 1975.
Greatest Hits, 1975.
Spirit of the Boogie, 1975.
Love and Understanding, 1976.
Open Sesame, 1976.
Hollywood Swinging/Summer Madness/A Kool & the Gang Anthology, 1977.
Jungle Boogie/Funky Stuff/Kool & the Gang Anthology, 1977.
The Force, 1977.
Kool & the Gang Spin Their Top Hits, 1978.

Everybody's Dancin', 1978.
Ladies' Night (includes "Too Hot"), 1979.
Celebrate (includes "Celebration"), 1980.
Something Special (includes "Take My Heart"), 1981.
As One (includes "Big Fun" and "Let's Go Dancin'"), 1982.
In the Heart (includes "Fresh" and "Joanna"), 1983.
Kool & the Gang at Their Best, 1984.
Twice as Kool, 1984.
The Very Best of Kool & the Gang: Let's Go Dancing, 1984.
Emergency (includes "Cherish"), 1984.
Best of Kool & the Gang, 1985.
Forever, 1987.
Everything's Kool & the Gang's Greatest Hits and More, 1988.
The Singles Collection, 1989.
Sweat, 1989.
Kool & the Gang Great & Remixed '91 (released in the United Kingdom and Europe), 1991.
Unite, 1994.

Contributed single "Open Sesame" to *Saturday Night Fever* soundtrack, 1976.

Sources

Billboard, February 13, 1982; December 17, 1983; August 10, 1985; December 6, 1986; November 5, 1988; January 13, 1990.
Entertainment Weekly, May, 28, 1993.
Melody Maker, February 6, 1982; January 1, 1985; January 3, 1987.
Musician, September, 1986; December 1986; October 1998.
Rolling Stone, March 15, 1984.
Variety, August 1, 1984.
Village Voice, March 23, 1982, May 29, 1984.

—*Sarah Messer*

Leo Kottke

Guitarist, singer, composer

Photograph by Dana Wheelock, courtesy of Private Music

Although he once described his voice as the sound of "geese farts on a muggy day," Leo Kottke is best known for his 12-string slide instrumentals and five-finger picking technique, which paved the way for fellow guitarists Michael Hedges and Will Ackerman of the Windham Hill label to combine bluegrass, bottle-neck-blues, and classical rhythms into popular New Age listening music of the 1980s. In 24 years, Kottke has composed scores for film soundtracks, children's shows, and a symphony; he has also released over 21 LPs, some of which (like "Great Big Boy") included his aforementioned craggy baritone, reminiscent of folksinger Tom Waits or a more short-winded radio personality and writer Garrison Keillor.

When his career blossomed with the folk-revival of the late 1960s and 1970s, Kottke earned the early title of "virtuoso"; *Rolling Stone* described him as "so good that he didn't need a band." Folk great Pete Seeger, who (along with John Fahey) was one of Kottke's first influences, called the young guitar player "the best twelve-string guitarist [he has] ever heard."

The inventor of such titles as "When Shrimps Learn to Whistle" and "Burnt Lips," Kottke is known for his self-deprecating, loopy sense of humor and quirky, yet brilliant, stage presence. "What happens in the fretboard appears to mirror the sudden ebbs and flows in his thought process," wrote *Billboard*'s Jim Bessman of Kottke's concert style. "He actually plays guitar like it's a fishing pole, grinning and grimacing as he verges on losing the catch, then reeling it in just when it looks like its gone for good."

Although he has changed his finger-picking technique over the years and switched to six-string guitar, Kottke's mastery of the instrument has remained consistent. "Leo Kottke is one of those rare artists whose latest album never differs radically from its predecessor, yet he never seems to get stuck in a rut," said Randy Lewis of the *Los Angeles Times*. "At any given moment you could close your eyes and imagine three guitarists in the place of Kottke," wrote Ian McFarland of the *Melbourne Review,* describing the speed and complex layering of Kottke's playing in concert. Yet country music eccentric Lyle Lovett, who toured with Kottke in 1989, may have summed up Kottke best when he told *Billboard* magazine in 1989 that "playing acoustic guitar on stage with Leo Kottke is like pitching to Darryl Strawberry."

Trombone Disaster in Early Years

Like his music, Leo Kottke's past is full of rambling and often fragmented stories that may lead the listener down unexpected paths. Kottke blames his idiosyncratic playing on his childhood training in trombone, which he told *Rolling Stone* in 1981,"ruined [him] for studying the classics and theory." Born in Athens, Georgia, Kottke grew up in Oklahoma and Wyoming, and had a brief stint in the Navy before settling in Minnesota. Kottke received his first guitar as a young boy—a gift from his parents to help him recover from the death of his sister.

The abrupt end of Kottke's trombone career was accelerated by a humiliating performance at a state fair in Oklahoma and coincided with the gift of the guitar. "There's an academy form to those things," he told *Musician* in a 1994 interview. "You play the melody in quarter notes, then it repeats in eighth notes, and then ... in 16th notes, then in 64th, cadenza, and you're done." Supposedly Kottke went on stage and said that he was going to play "Down Home on the Farm" (at the suggestion of his teacher), and the audience burst out laughing. "The *judges* laughed, and I knew I was in for it.... It was God awful. And that was really it."

Kottke had less luck in Wyoming, continuing an alienated and angst-filled childhood that he wrote about in "Parade," a song from his 1994 release, *Peculiaroso.*

"I knew I had to get out of that town because I wasn't headed in the right direction. We saw either Roy Rogers or Gene Autry in a parade ... and tried to disturb his horse." Kottke wrote in a 1994 Private Music press release, "We'd walk down to the Capitol building, because somebody had mounted the largest buffalo ever killed in the state of Wyoming on this huge pedestal under the dome, and they'd pointed it directly away from the front door. Existentialism wasn't born in France."

In the meantime, Kottke taught himself how to play guitar and joined the Navy, where he met people who later inspired his work—an odd engineer named "Evil" who drank torpedo fuel (the inspiration for the song "World Made to Order," on *Peculiaroso*) and blues greats Skip James, Son House, and John Hurt—all of whom he saw in Washington, D.C., right before he shipped out.

According to his press release, Kottke recorded his first album, *12 String Blues,* on a small Minneapolis label and by 1969 had tracked down guitar great John Fahey. With Fahey's help, Kottke released the highly acclaimed *6 and 12 String Guitar* on Fahey's Takoma label. Kottke was then signed by Capitol. He released nine albums between 1970 and 1976, including *My Feet Are Smiling, Chewing Pine,* and two compilations.

Kottke attributes his 1970s popularity solely to the changing cycles of American musical taste: "It's a cyclical thing," he told *Billboard* in 1986. "The flurry of interest in Europe a few years ago in the acoustic guitar followed by about eight years of the same surge that was occurring here when I was with Takoma and then Capitol."

Got the Blues

"By 1978, however, something had changed," wrote Charles Young in *Rolling Stone.* Kottke had released *Leo Kottke* for Chrysalis and the 1978 LP *Burnt Lips* (including tracks titled "Endless Sleep," "Cool Water," "Frank Forgets," and "Sonora's Death Row"), which Young described as "a series so depressing that they should be heard only when immobilized by Thorazine." His next LP, *Balance,* released in 1979, featured the equally depressing titles "Losing Everything," "Drowning," and "Whine."

Kottke noted that many of his fans had commented on his music's radical swing into moody blues. "I'd like to deny any autobiographical content but I can't," the musician told Young, illustrating his point with a story about a writer who tried to hang himself, but his necktie broke, and he fell out of the closet laughing hysterically. "I feel better now than I have for twenty years (because) I just don't fight myself anymore," he concluded. His next release, 1981's *Guitar Music*, was more widely received as upbeat and "inspired no thoughts of suicide," according to Young.

Kottke's interview responses and interplay with audiences often took the form of stories, and although he never consciously set out to write "about" anything in particular, stories invariably attached themselves to his sound. "Strange," a song on *Guitar Music*, is a song about a man who has to play music and act happy on stage for a town whose children have all just been killed by a collapsing sag heap. "I've played some rough situations," Kottke told *Rolling Stone*, "but nothing like that."

Because much of Kottke's nonvocal work rambles like a conversation, listeners often create their own narratives, which may not coincide with the artist's vision. In a 1994 interview in *Musician*, singer Rickie Lee Jones—who produced *Peculiaroso*—described the song "Pepe's Hush" as characteristically enforcing Kottke's mystery. "For me that song was about a person about to commit a crime, and he had checked into a motel and was going to get up really early to go commit a crime and the dog kept waking him up. Finally I realized that it was just about [Kottke] sleeping next door to a dog that was barking."

Discontinued Finger-Picks

The late 1970s morbidity that reviewers and fans perceived may have had its roots in Kottke's physical rather than psychological physiognomy. In the early 1980s, after the release of *Time Step* on Chrysalis, Kottke suffered a severe right hand and wrist injury that made him alter his unique finger-picking style. He began a three-and-a-half-year vacation from recording and cut his ties with Chrysalis. In that time period, he began playing the six-string guitar, learned how to read music, and took classical guitar lessons, creating a new way to play with less hand tension.

"I try to avoid that 'dead thumb' steady bass, where the thumb plays on every beat," he related in *Guitar Player*. "I first heard how to break away from that in Pete Seeger's 'Living in the Country.' He often picked a bass note with his thumb and an eighth-note before the down beat." During his hiatus Kottke didn't deliberately try to write anything different. "However, I can see a lot of development in my writing. I've grown harmonically, and I've gotten a better grip on rhythm," he told *Billboard*.

After touring and experimenting for three years, Kottke signed with Private Music and released the voiceless LP *A Shout Towards Noon*, produced by jazz bassist Buell Neidlinger, who also played on the album. Mark Hanson of *Guitar Player* described Kottke's first Private release as "a light-hearted batch of instrumental pieces" in which "he shifted his musical emphasis away from speed and power toward tonal richness and rhythmic intricacy."

> *"I can see a lot of development in my writing. I've grown harmonically, and I've gotten a better grip on rhythm."*

Kottke's third LP for Private, *My Father's Face*—his first vocal recording after an eight-year hiatus—was produced by T Bone Burnett and featured appearances by members of Los Lobos and the Tom Waits Band. While the title track is a tribute to aging, Kottke described the single "Jack Gets Up" in *Billboard* magazine as "a grouchy anthem—about how youthfulness is a curse, until you're old enough to know better." "Jack Gets Up" received quite a bit of radio air-play, becoming a minor FM hit. Hanson described "Jack Gets Up," "My Father's Face," and two songs from his later release *That's What* as perhaps visions of a new pop-song style of "spoken monologues over a finger-picked vamp."

Besides winning seven Grammy awards and composing the score for the animated children's special *Paul Bunyan*, Kottke also created a one-hour PBS special, *Home and Away*. In 1990 he performed his creation "Ice Fields," a suite for guitar and orchestra with composer Steven Paulus and the Fort Wayne Philharmonic, proving, as the *Los Angeles Times* noted, his "uncanny ability to make folk music sound like capital-A art."

Kottke's experiments with vocals continued in *Great Big Boy* and eventually caught the attention of singer/songwriter Rickie Lee Jones. "You don't hear people sing with that Midwestern accent," Jones told *Musician*. "Leo's got a kind of authority that's really intelligent and honest and no-bullshit. I really like hearing his accent and his big booming low voice. I don't know any like it."

Jones was so impressed by *Great Big Boy* that she asked Kottke to play on her next album, *Traffic from Paradise*, which led to Jones's producing Kottke's next album, *Peculiaroso*, released in 1994. *Musician's* Fred Schruers, who conducted an interview with both artists in May of 1994, speculated that Jones found Kottke's sound appealing because he was able "to put a flexible spine in the midst of her comfortably meandering song structures." During the recording of *Traffic from Paradise*, Kottke and Jones became great friends. Kottke told *Musician*, "We wanted to continue the fun. The moment that I always want to mention is when Rickie was on the floor, laughing her head off. And so was I, and I thought, 'God, it would be nice to just keep doing this.'"

Jones was responsible for naming several songs on the album and sang back-up vocals with Syd Straw and Teresa Tudry on "Turning into Randolph Scott (Humid Child)." Yet she described herself otherwise as "the producer who lays on the ground," letting Kottke's own eccentricity seep out. In the label's press release, Kottke described "Peg Leg" as the perfect opening for the album. "The title was changed from Steak Diane, a singer in the '60s who had an album which qualifies with Funkadelics' *Maggot Brain* as the worst album cover I've ever seen. She was covered with raw meat. I decided on 'Peg Leg' because Rickie had a grandfather in vaudeville named Peg Leg Jones, who was a dancer with one leg."

Along with Jones and his mentor John Fahey, Kottke names nonmusicians like sculptor Louise Nevelson and New Zealand author Janet Frame as influences. "[Frame will] write one absolutely staggering paragraph and then you'll wait for a while for the next absolutely staggering paragraph," Kottke commented in *Rolling Stone*. "My staggering paragraphs aren't quite enough to see me through the next few dull ones."

Rickie Lee Jones, however, disagreed with Kottke's sentiment. Closing her interview with *Musician,* she said of Kottke's artistry, "I do feel a kinship with that kind of strange, beautiful painting that is of no *consequence*, doesn't reveal its *intentions*. It's just a little painting with words and beautiful melodies." In the spring of 1994, after he finished recording *Peculiaroso*, Kottke began touring with the "Guitar Summit," a grouping of jazz master Joe Pass, Flamenco great Paco Pena, and classical guitar virtuoso Pepe Romero.

Selected discography

6 and 12 String Guitar, Takoma, 1969.
Mudlark, Capitol, 1970.
Greenhouse, Capitol, 1971.
My Feet Are Smiling, Capitol, 1972.
Ice Water, Capitol, 1972.
Dreams and All That Stuff, Capitol, 1973.
Chewing Pine, Capitol, 1974.
Did You Hear Me?, Capitol, 1975.
Leo Kottke, Chrysalis, 1976.
Burnt Lips, Chrysalis, 1977.
Balance, Chrysalis, 1978.
Guitar Music, Chrysalis, 1981.
A Shout Towards Noon, Private Music, 1986.
Regards From Chuck Pink, Private Music, 1987.
Peculiaroso, Private Music, 1994.
12 String Blues, Oblivion.
Leo Kottke/The Best, Capitol.
Leo Kottke/1971-76, Capitol.
Live in Europe, Chrysalis.
Time Step, Chrysalis.
My Father's Face, Private Music.
That's What, Private Music.
Great Big Boy, Private Music.

Sources

Billboard, February 22, 1986; April 15, 1989; August 19, 1989; June 19, 1993.
Guitar Player, March 1988; January 1991; March 1994.
Los Angeles Times, February 17, 1994.
Melbourne Review (Australia), May 31, 1994.
Musician, May 1994.
People, June 21, 1993.
Rolling Stone, June 11, 1981; October 28, 1993.

Additional information for this profile was obtained from Private Music press materials, 1994.

—*Sarah Messer*

Gene Krupa

Drummer, bandleader

The name Gene Krupa is synonymous with a driving drum style and a dynamic sense of showmanship—qualities that made the Chicago-born drummer one of the musical giants of the Swing Era. Behind his public image—the gum-chewing hipster with the uncontrollable shock of black hair—Krupa was a devoutly serious and self-disciplined musician. As Benny Goodman would recall in his autobiography *Kingdom of Swing,* "No matter how much playing [Krupa] did, he was always working, developing his hands, and getting new ideas." Krupa's technique and explosive attack earned him praise from all quarters of the jazz world, from traditional swing stylists like Buddy Rich to modernist drummer Max Roach.

The youngest of nine children, Eugene Bertram Krupa was born on January 15, 1909, in Chicago, Illinois. After the untimely death of his father when Krupa was young, his mother went to work as a milliner to support her family. At around the age of 11, Krupa got a job running errands and cleaning windows at Brown Music Company, a music store on Chicago's South Side. With the money he earned, Krupa decided to purchase a musical instrument, and he ultimately chose the drums, the "cheapest item" listed in the wholesale catalogue.

Taken with the idea of playing the drums, Krupa searched his South Side neighborhood for the company of young musicians. "There were a few little bands in school that I got to hear at socials and tea dances," the musician recalled in *Drummin' Men.* "I'd watch the drummers and pick up what I could. After a bit, I got to make music with some of these fellows and substitute at the dances and socials."

Soon Krupa's musical activities began to take precedence over his school work. As a result of his late-night musical activities, Krupa often fell asleep during classes. In 1924, in an effort to placate his mother's disappointment over his failing school studies, Krupa enrolled in St. Joseph's College, a seminary prep school in Rensselaer, Indiana. At St. Joseph's, Krupa studied under a classically trained professor of music, Father Ildefonse Rapp.

Although Krupa received first-rate instruction at St. Joseph's, he decided to leave the school in 1925 in order to pursue a career as a professional drummer. He soon played various jobs around Chicago with commercial dance bands such as the Hossier Bellhops, Ed Mulaney's Red Jackets, and the band of Joe Kayser. Living on the South Side, Krupa spent evenings searching for jazz in neighborhood cabarets and nightclubs.

In the spring of 1927 Krupa discovered a talented group of young white jazzmen playing at a South Side

For the Record . . .

Born Eugene Bertram Krupa, January 15, 1909, in Chicago, IL; died of heart failure, October 16, 1973, in Yonkers, NY. *Education:* Studied at St. Joseph's College, 1924-25.

Drummer and swing band leader. Studied drums and performed with local Chicago groups, c. 1920; performed with the Austin High Gang, late 1920s; recorded with Red McKenzie's and Eddie Condon's Chicagoans and performed in jam sessions at the Three Deuces, 1927; worked with commercial groups, such as Red Nicols' Five Pennys, and free-lanced with the bands of Bix Beiderbecke, Benny Goodman, and saxophonist Adrian Rollini, 1930-34; joined Goodman's band and played on NBC-Radio's *Let's Dance,* 1934; left Goodman to form Gene Krupa Orchestra, 1938; drug charge led to disbanding of first group, 1943; briefly rejoined Goodman, 1943; joined Tommy Dorsey, 1944; organized own big band, 1944-51; toured with own trio/quartet, 1950s; played on soundtrack of film *The Gene Krupa Story,* 1959; led big band in Hollywood, 1963; came out of semi-retirement to lead own quartet at Plaza Hotel, 1967; performed at Newport Jazz Festival, 1972; appeared at the last reunion of original Goodman Orchestra, 1973.

Awards: Voted best drummer, *Down Beat* Readers' Poll, 1944.

movie house. Known as the Austin High Gang, this devoted coterie of musicians included banjoist Eddie Condon, saxophonist Bud Freeman, and Dave Tough, the premiere white Chicago drum stylist. Krupa "sat through two shows every night and three on Saturday to hear Tough on drums," remembered Condon in his autobiography *We Called It Music.*

Soon afterward Tough, in an effort to introduce his younger protégé to authentic jazz, took Krupa to see the great New Orleans drummer Baby Dodds. "Baby was the band's central strength," reminisced Krupa in *Drumming Men,* "the way he used the drums, the rims, the cymbals was just marvelous. I kept coming back to dig Baby, always showing my appreciation for the extremely musical things he was doing. He was one of my main inspirations."

Krupa was so impressed by Dodds that he began to immerse himself in the study of black jazz. Austin High Gang member Milton "Mess" Mezzrow recalled in his autobiography, *Really the Blues,* how he and Krupa analyzed the rhythmic patterns of New Orleans drummers: "More than anything, it was the Negroes' time and rhythm that fascinated us. I would sit there with Gene for hours, just beating out rhythms of Zutty Singleton and Johnny Wells until my hands swole double." By 1927 Krupa was attending a regular jazz jam session held at the Three Deuces, located across from the Chicago Theater—legendary sessions that included Austin High Gang clarinetist Frank Teschmaker, trumpeter Bix Beiderbecke, and Krupa's future employer Benny Goodman.

In December of the same year, Red Mckenzie assisted the Austin High Gang in landing a recording session with the Okeh label. Billed as Mckenzie's and Condon's Chicagoans, Krupa, Freeman, Teschmaker, Condon, bassist Jim Lannigan, and pianist Joe Sullivan recorded four sides: "China Boy," "Sugar," "Nobody's Sweetheart," and "Liza." Expecting to use his entire drum set, Krupa became outraged when producer Tommy Rockwell demanded that he play the standard set-up: a snare and cymbals.

Although Krupa argued that the recording equipment could not handle the vibration of the additional drums, Rockwell finally agreed, at Mckenzie's urging, to allow Krupa to use his entire kit. "So they let Gene play the drums, and he beat the heck out of them all the way through the set," described Jimmy McPartland in *Talking Jazz,* "It gave us a good solid beat." Assessing the impact of the session, Condon wrote, "Krupa's drums went through us like triple bourbon."

The Jazz Invasion of the East

The success of the Okeh session didn't just mark the first known recording of the bass drum in jazz music, it defined the Chicago jazz sound. As Richard Hadlock pointed out in *Jazz Masters of the Twenties,* Krupa was the "biggest surprise" of these sessions, "an unknown, whose well-recorded drum work ... rocked the New York Jazz cliques." In 1928 Condon's Chicagoans headed to New York to back singer Bee Palmer. When the job fell through, Krupa and the Chicagoans recorded sessions with trumpeter Red Nichols and trombonist Miff Mole.

After playing with Nichols's band, Krupa performed with the pit band for George and Ira Gershwin's 1930 Broadway production *Strike Up the Band.* "Gershwin was crazy about his playing," explained Max Kaminsky in *My Life in Jazz,* "because Gene was the first white drummer who could swing the beat so that the chorus girls could kick, in time."

While working with commercial groups in the early 1930s, Krupa, determined to become a "legit" drummer, began formal music instruction with "Gus" Moeller. Practicing eight hours a day, he worked on inventing his own rhythmic variations and patterns. "My work with Moeller," related Krupa in *Drummin' Men,* "made possible more graceful playing, better control and freedom to be myself no matter what kind of music I had to interpret."

Played With the King of Swing

In 1934 record producer John Hammond traveled to Chicago to recruit Krupa for Benny Goodman's big band. Although Krupa had reservations about joining, Hammond convinced him that he would be a featured performer of the Goodman band, a noncommercial swing group featuring the arrangements of Fletcher Henderson. "Our drummer was merely adequate," explained Goodman in *Eddie Condon's Treasury of Jazz.* "The man we wanted, Gene Krupa, was in Chicago playing with Buddy Rogers." Through Hammond, Goodman hoped to draw Krupa to New York City, for as he stated in *Kingdom of Swing,* "Gene had some not too favorable recollections of our previous jobs together, but he had the same feeling about real jazz that I did, and the chance to play music the way we felt it was as important in his life as it was mine."

Joining Goodman in New York in December of 1934, Krupa performed on the NBC Saturday broadcast *Let's Dance,* a national radio spot that bolstered the popularity of Goodman's orchestra and brought great attention to Krupa's drumming talent. In 1935 the band's engagement at Los Angeles's Palomar Ballroom extended from four to seven weeks, drawing more than 200,000 listeners who responded wildly to the solos of Goodman, Krupa, and trumpeter Bunny Berigan. Around this time, Goodman formed a trio with Krupa and pianist Teddy Wilson, and a quartet featuring vibraphonist Lionel Hampton. Krupa's brush work with these two groups displayed his musical versatility and refined sense of accompaniment.

By the late 1930s Krupa emerged as a national phenomenon. His work on Goodman's 1936 hit "Sing, Sing, Sing" produced the classic drum anthem of the Swing Era, and his appearance on stage and film catapulted him to superstar status. In 1938 he performed on Goodman's classic live recording *Carnegie Hall Jazz Concert,* which emanates with the intensity of Krupa's near-frantic drum work. Despite the popularity of the Goodman-Krupa combination, however, artistic and personal disputes prompted Krupa to leave the group in 1938. "They had different ideas about how to play music," explained band member Lionel Hampton in his book *Hamp.* "Benny didn't like all the crazy antics and sensationalism that he felt were overshadowing the real music. Gene thought the craziness was just basic showmanship. Although I tended to agree with Gene, I stayed out of it."

The Gene Krupa Orchestra

On April 16, 1938, a crowd of 4,000 listeners gathered in the Marine Ballroom on Atlantic City's Union Pier to hear the newly formed Gene Krupa Orchestra. Following this triumphant debut, Krupa's band recorded several instrumentals, including "Wire Brush Stomp" and "Blue Rhythm Fantasy," for the Brunswick label. Among the Orchestra's talented members were trumpeters Shorty Sherok and Corky Cornelius, saxophonist Sam Donahue, and singer Irene Daye. In 1941 the band enjoyed even greater fame with the addition of trumpeter Roy Eldrige and singer Anita O'Day, who together gave the band its most legendary hit, "Let Me Off Uptown."

In 1943 Krupa was arrested in San Francisco for the possession of marijuana. Out on bail after an 80-day period of incarceration, Krupa returned to New York. Although the case was finally dropped, it caused the break-up of his orchestra. Leaderless, Krupa decided to accept an offer to rejoin Benny Goodman's band. In 1944 he joined Tommy Dorsey, and, despite his condemnation by the media concerning his drug charge, was voted best drummer in the *Down Beat* Readers' Poll.

New Artistic Avenues

In re-forming his orchestra, Krupa made an effort to explore the new modernist trends rooted in the bebop jazz movement. Between 1945 and 1949 his band featured such arrangers as George Williams, Neal Hefti, Eddie Finkel, and saxophonist Gerry Mulligan, who brought the band the instrumental score "Disc Jockey Jump." Krupa's musical line-up featured a number of contemporary jazzmen, including saxophonist Charlie Ventura, clarinetist Buddy DeFranco, trombonist Frank Rosolino, and trumpeter Red Rodney. Describing Krupa's artistic commitment to the new styles of jazz, Rodney explained in *From Swing to Bop,* "Gene was a modern, progressive-type person who, unlike most of the big-name bandleaders of the era, decided change was important, necessary, and right."

With the demise of big bands during the 1950s, Krupa began performing in small combos and toured internationally with Norman Granz's Jazz at the Philharmonic. In 1959 his career was honored with the biographical film *The Gene Krupa Story*, starring Sal Mineo as the famous drummer. After suffering a heart attack in 1960, Krupa became limited to sporadic performances. During 1972 and 1973 he played several reunion concerts with Goodman's band—one of which resulted in the 1972 live album *Jazz at the New School*.

On October 16, 1973, Krupa died at his home in Yonkers, New York. Though he had been under treatment for leukemia for several years, the official cause of death was heart failure. Attending a requiem mass held at St. Dennis Roman Catholic in Yonkers, Goodman, Freeman, McPartland, and Teschmaker gathered to pay their last respects to a man known by millions of listeners as "The Chicago Flash"—the most charismatic and innovative drum legend of the Swing Era.

Selected discography

(With Charlie Ventura) *The Krupa-Ventura Trio*, Commodore, 1950.
Hey! Here's Gene Krupa, Verve, 1951.
Gene Krupa Trio, Clef, 1953.
Gene Krupa Trio at JATP, 1953.
Gene Krupa Sextet #1, Clef, 1954.
Gene Krupa Quartet, Clef, 1955.
Drummin' Man, Columbia, 1955.
Drum Boogie, Clef, 1956.
(With Lionel Hampton and Teddy Wilson) *Selections From "The Benny Goodman Story"*, Clef, 1956.
Krupa's Wail, Clef, 1956.
Sing, Sing, Sing, Verve, 1957.
The Exciting Gene Krupa, Verve, 1957.
Gene Krupa Plays Gerry Mulligan's Arrangements, Verve, 1958.
The Gene Krupa Story (film soundtrack), 1959.
Percussion King, Verve, 1961.
The Original Drum Battle, Verve, 1962.
Drummer Man, Columbia, 1962.
The Great New Gene Krupa Quartet Featuring Charlie Ventura, Verve, 1964.
Let Me off Uptown: The Essential Gene Krupa, Verve, 1964.
Gene Krupa, Metro, 1965.
The Drummer's Band, Verve, 1966.
Compact Jazz: Gene Krupa and Buddy Rich, Verve, 1994.
The Best of the Gene Krupa Orchestra, Columbia, 1993.

With Benny Goodman

Benny Goodman: The Famous 1938 Carnegie Hall Jazz Concert, Columbia.

King of Swing Vol. 1., 1937-1938, Concert No. 2, Columbia.
The Great Benny Goodman: Original Performances of Benny Goodman's Classics in Swing, Columbia.
Benny Goodman's Greatest Hits, Columbia.
Benny Goodman and his Orchestra: The Harry James Years, Vol. 1, Bluebird.

Sources

Books

Condon, Eddie, *We Called It Music: A Generation of Jazz*, Greenwood Press, 1947.
Duruis, Robert, *Bunny Berigan: Elusive Legend of Jazz*, Louisiana State University Press, 1993.
Eddie Condon's Treasury of Jazz, edited by Eddie Condon and Richard Gehman, Dial Press, 1956.
Freeman, Bud, and Robert Wolf, *Crazeology: The Autobiography of a Chicago Jazzman*, University of Illinois Press, 1989.
Gitler, Ira, *Swing to Bop: An Oral History of the Transition of Jazz in the 1940s*, Oxford University Press, 1985.
Goodman, Benny, and Irving Koilodin, *The Kingdom of Swing*, Frederick Unger, 1961.
Hadlock, Richard, *Jazz Masters of the Twenties*, Da Capo Press, 1988.
Hampton, Lionel, and James Haskins, *Hamp: An Autobiography*, Warner Books, 1989.
Jones, Max, *Talking Jazz*, Macmillan, 1987.
Kaminsky, Max, and V. E. Hughes, *My Life in Jazz*, Harper & Row, 1963.
Korall, Burt, *Drummin' Men: The Heartbeat of Jazz, The Swing Years*, Schrimer Books, 1990.
Mezzrow, Milton, and Bernard Wolfe, *Really the Blues*, Signet Books, 1964.
Schuller, Gunther, *The Development of Jazz, 1930-1945*, Oxford University Press, 1989.
Simon, George T., *The Big Bands*, Macmillan, 1967.
Torme, Mel, *Traps: The Drum Wonder, Life of Buddy Rich*, Oxford University Press, 1991.

Periodicals

Down Beat, December 6, 1973.

Additional information for this profile was obtained from the videos *John Hammond: From Bessie Smith to Bruce Springsteen*, CBS Records Inc., 1990, and *Jazz Legend Gene Krupa*, DCI, 1993.

—John Cohassey

Lerner and Loewe

Lyricist and composer

The songs of lyricist Alan Jay Lerner and composer Frederick Loewe are some of the most popular and financially successful ever written. In the short-lived world of Broadway musicals, where shows can close before the end of their first performance, the songwriting team's *My Fair Lady* is not far short of an amazing phenomenon. After the musical opened in 1956, it ran for six years straight. While it cost more to produce than any show had up until that point, it made more money than any other had. Nearly 40 years later, the show still enjoys revivals.

Frederick Loewe seemed destined to write stage musicals. His father, Edmund Loewe, was one of Germany's favorite operetta stars. Fritz, as Frederick was called most of his life, began studying the piano at an early age and almost immediately began to create tunes and songs. He started performing publicly on piano when he was 13, and when he was 15, he published his first song, "Katrina," which sold two million copies.

After Loewe immigrated to the United States in 1924, he spent seven years traveling the country working at a

For the Record . . .

Alan Jay Lerner born August 31, 1918, in New York, NY; died June 14, 1986; son of Joseph and Edith Lerner; married Ruth Boyd, 1940 (divorced 1947); married Marion Bell, 1947 (divorced 1950); married Nancy Olson, 1950 (divorced 1957); married Micheline Muselli Posso de Borgo, 1957 (divorced 1965); married Karen Gundersen, 1966 (divorced 1974); married Sandra Payne, (divorced 1977); married Nina Bushkin, 1977 (divorced 1980); married Liz Robertson, 1981; children: (first marriage) Susan, (third marriage) Jennifer, Lisa, (fourth marriage) Michael. *Education:* Harvard University, B.S., 1940; studied at Juilliard School of Music. **Frederick Loewe** born June 10, 1901, in Vienna, Austria; immigrated to U.S., 1924; died February 14, 1988; son of Edmund and Rose Loewe; married Ernestine Zwerline, 1931 (divorced).

Loewe worked variously as a pianist, boxer, and horseback riding instructor; played piano for Broadway musicals, beginning in 1931; collaborated with Earle T. Crooker on musicals *Salute to Spring* and *Great Lady,* late 1930s; Lerner contributed songs to Hasty Pudding Club shows, 1938 and 1939; worked as an advertising copywriter and radio script writer. Lerner and Loewe collaborated on first musical, *Life of the Party,* 1942; wrote first musical to make it on Broadway, *The Day Before Spring,* 1945; wrote *My Fair Lady,* 1956. Lerner later worked with other composers on several musicals, late 1960s-1980s. Loewe wrote new songs for stage production of *Gigi* and film score for *The Little Prince,* early 1970s.

Selected awards: Lerner, New York Drama Critic's Circle Award, 1947, for *Brigadoon;* Academy Award for best screenplay, 1951, for *An American in Paris;* New York Drama Critic's Circle Award, Donaldson Award, and Tony Award, all 1956, all for *My Fair Lady;* Academy Award for best screenplay and Screenwriters Guild Award, both 1958, both for *Gigi;* Grammy Award, 1965, for "On a Clear Day You Can See Forever"; Loewe, Hollander Medal, Berlin, Germany, 1923; Tony Award, 1957, for *My Fair Lady;* Academy Award for best song, 1958, for a song from *Gigi;* Tony Award, 1974, for *Gigi;* together, inducted into Songwriter's Hall of Fame, 1971; Kennedy Center Honors, 1986.

variety of jobs to earn meal money; he played piano, boxed, and taught horseback riding throughout the midwestern and western states.

In 1931 Loewe arrived in New York City and wound up playing piano in the orchestra pits of Broadway musicals. He also began to write songs, a few of which were included in staged musical revues. In 1938 Loewe met Earle T. Crooker and with him collaborated on two musicals, *Salute to Spring* and *Great Lady,* neither of which was much of a success. While looking for a lyricist for another project in 1942, Loewe stumbled by chance into Alan Lerner at New York's Lambs Club.

Lerner was born more for business than show business, but he fell in love with the theater at an early age. His wealthy father, Joseph Lerner, who owned a chain of clothing stores, took his son to Broadway shows, exposing young Alan to all of the great songs and musicals of giants such as Rodgers and Hart, Kern and Hammerstein, and Cole Porter. Alan started piano lessons as a child and began to write songs as a teenager; he studied music at the Juilliard School of Music during the summers of 1936 and 1937. While he was attending Harvard University, he contributed songs to the Hasty Pudding Club shows of 1938 and 1939. For two years after he graduated from college, he worked as an advertising copywriter and a radio script writer.

Restroom Confusion Led to Meeting

In his autobiography, *The Street Where I Live,* Lerner described how he met Fritz Loewe: "One day late in August of 1942, I was having lunch in the grill [of the Lambs Club] when a short, well built, tightly strung man with a large head and hands and immensely dark circles under his eyes strode to a few feet from my table and stopped short. His destination was the men's room and he had gone the wrong way. He turned to get back on the right road and suddenly saw me. I knew who he was ... a talented, struggling composer.... He came to my table and sat down. 'You're Lerner, aren't you?' he asked. I could not deny it. 'You write Lyrics, don't you?' he continued. 'I try,' I replied. 'Well,' he said, 'would you like to write with me?' I immediately said, 'Yes.' And we went to work."

Lerner and Loewe's first attempts were not very successful. *Life of the Party,* which they wrote in 12 days to meet a deadline, never made it to Broadway and neither did their second effort, *What's Up. The Day Before Spring,* their third work, actually made it on Broadway but closed early. The screen rights, however, were bought by Louis B. Meyer of MGM, and provided both of them with their first financial success.

The pair kept working together and in 1946 began collaborating on *Brigadoon.* At first, they had problems finding producers; they sang through their score for some 58 separate prospective backers before finding enough money. The show opened in 1947 to rave reviews and garnered Lerner a Drama Critics Circle Award. Lerner and Loewe had less trouble finding backers for their next production, *Paint Your Wagon,* which opened in 1951.

Wrote the Fairest One of All

For Lerner and Loewe, putting on a show was much more than simply writing melodies and lyrics for songs. They not only had to find backers, but also all of the other people to make a show work. When they decided to turn George Bernard Shaw's play *Pygmalion* into *My Fair Lady,* they put together more than the score. They hand picked the cast, director, choreographer, music director, and costume and stage designers, all before the writing was finished. After actor Rex Harrison agreed to play the male lead, Lerner and Loewe tailored the songs to fit his inexperienced singing voice; Loewe wrote quick tunes with lots of notes that were to be recited, rather than sung.

When rehearsals began, both Lerner and Loewe worked with the cast and staff, not only revising when necessary but also rehearsing the actors and consulting with the other directors constantly. With a budget of more than $400,000, *My Fair Lady* was the most expensive musical at that time. The most successful musical ever produced, it ran on Broadway for an unprecedented six years and won six Tony awards. The cast album of *My Fair Lady* became the best-selling album in the history of Columbia Records, and the best- selling cast album for any company.

Lerner and Loewe's next project was not for Broadway, but for the movies. *Gigi,* based on a book by the French author Colette, was first written as a film; only later, in 1974, did the pair bring it to stage. While the two would never again repeat the phenomenal success of *My Fair Lady, Gigi* was a hit that went on to win nine Academy awards. Their next work, *Camelot,* based on the Arthurian stories of T. H. White, opened shakily but then fared respectably.

Loewe Retired, Lerner Moved On

After *Camelot,* Lerner and Loewe separated. Fritz Loewe retired to enjoy the money he had worked to so hard to earn, dividing his time between his house in Palm Springs, California, and the Mediterranean coast. He told the *New York Times,* "Too many people have gone in for this senseless chasing of rainbows. How many rainbows does one need?... [I am] having a wonderful time and writing a show is not fun. There is no reason for me to work now. I don't need the glory, I don't need money."

Alan Lerner, on the other hand, kept working. With composer Burton Lane he wrote *On a Clear Day You Can See Forever* (1965) and *Carmelina* (1979), with Andre Previn he wrote *Coco* (1969), with Leonard Bernstein, *1600 Pennsylvania Avenue* (1976), and with Charles Strouse, *Dance a Little Closer* (1983). With the exception of *On a Clear Day,* which won a Grammy Award and was later made into a motion picture, none of the works achieved a considerable measure of success. In the early 1970s Loewe came out of retirement to write a few new songs for a stage production of *Gigi* and a complete score for the film version of *The Little Prince,* neither of which gained much popularity.

Although it is impossible to say exactly what it was, something special imbued the collaboration between Alan Jay Lerner and Frederick Loewe. After Fritz met Alan, he would work with no other lyricist. Lerner tried but was never able to attain the same level of success with other composers that he achieved with Loewe. If they had written nothing else, *My Fair Lady,* which will probably live on in revivals indefinitely, would be achievement enough for both of their lives. As Gene Lees wrote in *Inventing Champagne: The Worlds of Lerner and Loewe:* "Ah, the songs! What a legacy to leave."

Selected scores

Stage

Life of the Party, 1942.
What's Up, 1943.
The Day Before Spring, 1945.
Brigadoon, 1946.
Paint Your Wagon, 1951.
My Fair Lady, 1956.
Camelot, 1960.
Gigi, 1973.

Film

Gigi, 1958.
My Fair Lady, 1964.
Camelot, 1968.
Paint Your Wagon, 1969.

Scores by Alan Lerner

(With Burton Lane) *On a Clear Day You Can See Forever,* 1965.
(With Andre Previn) *Coco,* 1969.

(With Leonard Bernstein) *1600 Pennsylvania Avenue,* 1976.
(With Charles Strouse) *Dance A Little Closer,* 1983.

Film scores by Frederick Loewe

The Little Prince, 1974.

Sources

Books

Ewen, David, *Great Men Of American Popular Song,* Prentice-Hall, 1970.

Lees, Gene, *Inventing Champagne: The Worlds of Lerner and Loewe,* St. Martin's, 1990.

Lerner, Alan Jay, *A Hymn to Him: Lyrics of Alan Jay Lerner,* edited by Benny Green, Pavilion Books, 1987.

Lerner, Alan Jay, *The Musical Theater: A Celebration,* McGraw Hill, 1986.

Lerner, Alan Jay, *The Street Where I Live,* W. W. Norton, 1978.

The New Grove Dictionary of American Music, edited by H. Wiley Hitchcock and Stanley Sadie, Macmillan, 1986.

Periodicals

New York Times, October 1, 1964; July 9, 1993; January 9, 1994.

New Yorker, January 17, 1994.

Newsweek, June 23, 1986; December 20, 1993.

Time, July 21, 1986; January 10, 1994.

Variety, February 17, 1988.

—*Robin Armstrong*

Steve Lillywhite

Producer

When an album creates a sensation with rock audiences and music critics, the band or musician tends to receive the credit. Quite often, however, many people behind the scenes craft the quality of the product. Steve Lillywhite has worked behind a string of great albums by various bands; some reporters have argued that he even shaped a definitive sound of 1980s new wave. In *Trouser Press,* Karen Schlosberg dubbed Lillywhite "a prime mover of punk and post-punk rock."

The producer of some of the most successful albums from such internationally acclaimed artists as U2, the Talking Heads, and the Rolling Stones, and some of the most trend-setting albums by such new wave pioneers as Siouxsie and the Banshees, Ultravox, the Psychedelic Furs, and XTC, Lillywhite shaped several of the musical milestones of the 1980s.

Lillywhite's recognition as a producer ironically conflicts with his view of a producer's function: "Production should be transparent so the band can stand out," he told *Melody Maker's* Paul Colbert in 1981. "I hope I get a different sound each time." In 1984 Lillywhite told

Adam Sweeting of *Melody Maker* that his favorite part of being a producer is having listeners not be able to tell who produced the recording. Despite his desire for invisibility, Lillywhite has developed an identifiable and highly praised sound.

Born in 1955, Lillywhite grew up just outside of London in Egham, England, in a very musical family. Both parents played instruments and encouraged all three of their children to do so as well. Lillywhite became involved in music himself—Schlosberg reported that "he 'fiddled about' with piano, guitar and bass, and played in school bands." His younger brother Adrian would go on to play in a fairly prominent band known as the Members; Lillywhite eventually ended up producing them. His own playing, however, would drop off as he became more and more drawn into the engineering aspect of studio work.

Started Career as "Tea Boy"

Lillywhite started his career in the recording studio at age 16 at the bottom rung of the ladder as a tape operator at Phonogram's Marble Arch studio. In effect, a tape operator was a "tea boy"—someone who ran to get tea and other necessities and indulgences for the musicians and engineers. Soon enough, however, he became an engineer himself.

Summarizing his years with Phonogram, Lillywhite told Schlosberg, "It was a complete cross-section, which was great for me. One morning you'd be working with a 40-piece orchestra with strings; then that same afternoon you'd have a rock band with four blaring guitars. You got to know a lot about your job because it wasn't just one musical style."

While Lillywhite had very little autonomy at Phonogram doing whatever work was required, the studio did offer a perk for its workers: on the weekends, employees could use the studios for their own projects. Lillywhite used them for his first forays into production, helping an unknown band then called Tiger Lily make demo tapes. The enterprise turned out to be a lucrative one.

When Island Records signed a deal with the band—now Ultravox—on the strength of the demos, they also invited Lillywhite to help with the production. Since he was young and unknown, the label insisted that he collaborate with a "name" producer: Brian Eno, one of the most respected alternative musicians and producers of the era. *Ultravox!*, released in 1977, was Lillywhite's first production credit.

Lillywhite continued to work with Island after the Ultravox debut, and was eventually offered a position as a producer with Island Artists. Although the position offered opportunity and credibility, he soon felt cramped by the affiliation; he and the label agreed to terminate the contract. "I was going out to all these punk clubs and meeting the bands," he recalled for Schlosberg. "I started working for these people, who started getting hit records—but none of them were for Island. I suddenly realized, well they're not *really* looking after my career. So ... I decided to branch out on my own."

All in all, Lillywhite had spent two years with the label. He and a friend briefly tried to manage their own label, XS Records, but it never produced anything notable. Lillywhite has worked independently ever since, moving from label to label according to the location of an artist or a band.

"This was just as punk was starting," Lillywhite told Schlosberg. "Punk was the first thing that really made my ears prick up. London in '77 was fantastic." Writing for *Musician,* Jon Pareles traced Lillywhite's "musical awakening" to this period—the height of London's "punk explosion." Lillywhite spent his free time "going to the clubs and seeing all the people," as he told Pareles. "Nobody had any money, and we were all living on floors, things like that. It was fun, but not something to go back to; you've got to grow up sometime." Lillywhite also made connections during these years that would serve him well later, as that "explosion" moved from underground clubs to recording studios.

After Ultravox, Lillywhite's solid reputation in the recording industry came with the 1977 release of the

Siouxsie and the Banshees single "Hong Kong Garden," which became a Top Ten hit. After producing the band's first album, *The Peel Sessions,* Lillywhite worked for his brother's band, the Members. That "got me in with Virgin," he told Sweeting. "Then Virgin offered me XTC."

The Road Paved With Platinum

The solid foundation of Ultravox, Siouxsie, and XTC established Lillywhite as a key player in the postpunk alternative rock sound coalescing at the turn of the new decade. Lillywhite rode that wave into the 1980s, his name value rising as his production credits grew. By 1984, when Lillywhite wasn't yet 30, Sweeting could nonetheless describe his career as "that road paved with platinum."

Lillywhite closed the 1970s with a call from Peter Gabriel, a former member of the art-rock band Genesis who went on to establish an impressive reputation as a solo artist. Gabriel wanted Lillywhite to handle the production of his third solo album. The faith placed in him by such an established artist demonstrated Lillywhite's credibility and desirability as a producer. Furthermore, as Colbert documented, it was "Gabriel's ... album that brought Lillywhite to the attention of a wider public audience." Lillywhite would later concede to Paula Parisi, writing for *Billboard* in 1986, that the album "was thought of as quite a milestone in terms of sound." Colbert, for example, expressed that excitement: "The instruments stood alone and spiky against a backdrop of live reverberant drums, shorn of cymbals. It was an ideal example of a clear production—both in terms of sound and access to the artist and his songs."

Lillywhite further intensified his reputation—and his association with a particular sound—with the smashing success of *Boy,* the debut album released in 1980 by the Irish rock band U2. Lillywhite has characterized the production of this nearly legendary album as especially inspired, rich with energy and experimentation. "Ideas would just flow," Lillywhite told Schlosberg. "I had a bicycle turned upside down; Bono and I would spin the wheels and hit the spokes with a knife. There were also bottles smashing all over the place. We were having a great time—just like little kids."

The combination proved a powerful boon for both producer and band. Parisi asserted that "Lillywhite's spare but textured approach to capturing the group's sound is widely acknowledged as having been a major factor in establishing the band." Schlosberg wrote that the "full yet crisp, clean sound on ... *Boy* was almost an instrument in its own right."

Attempted to Escape Pigeonholing

Since *Boy* entered the market surrounded by work with other alternative rock bands, including the Psychedelic Furs, Big Country, and the Thompson Twins, Lillywhite was becoming known for his sound, which also seemed definitive of new wave at the time. "Lillywhite has established a spacious, spare and crisp production technique all his own," Colbert declared. Pareles went into greater detail documenting Lillywhite's sound: "His records sound big but not bloated, weighty without being ponderous; even on mediocre songs, the sound insists that something important is happening. Lillywhite's trademark, now widely imitated," Pareles concluded, "is a mammoth drum sound." In 1984 Sweeting noted that the "triumvirate of U2, Big Country and Simple Minds has identified him more than he'd like with a certain rock sound."

In an effort to remain true to his belief that a producer should not be what characterizes a band, Lillywhite generally refused to work with bands too regularly. "Until recently I haven't liked doing more than one album with a band.... The best a producer can be is a floating influence," he told Colbert. Lillywhite told Parisi that he didn't think it was "advisable for a producer to form a safe association with any one group. You become identified with a particular sound, and that can be limiting. You get predictable, and I don't think it benefits the band or the producer."

Consequently, Lillywhite pushed himself to take on less typecast projects, the most notable of which were Joan Armatrading's *Walk Under Ladders* in 1981 and the Rolling Stones' *Dirty Work* in 1986. The former challenged him to expand into folk rock; the latter, into hard rock. Jon Pareles described the Armatrading album as Lillywhite's first "curveball." Parisi reported in Billboard that Lillywhite had "gone back to basics" with the Stones, opting for a "no-gimmicks production approach."

In the second half of the decade, Lillywhite's work had evolved such that the sound was less identifiable; he was still, however, putting his name on recordings by highly successful musicians. He had an opportunity to work with the Talking Heads in 1987 and to produce lead singer David Byrne's solo album, *Rei Momo,* in 1988. He enhanced an Irish rock sound markedly different from that of U2 with the Pogues and singer Kirsty MacColl, whom he married in 1984.

The early 1990s brought *Bang!* for World Party, for which Lillywhite received credit for helping Karl Wallinger's career. *Rolling Stone's* David Sprague wrote that "Steve Lillywhite can take credit for reigning in

Wallinger's most glaring excesses. His laid-back production helps siphon off the pretense so that *Bang!*'s innate funkiness can glisten in the spotlight."

The difference also reflected a general shift in Lillywhite's style, as *Billboard*'s Marilyn Gillen noted when she wrote that "Steve Lillywhite doesn't do that drum thing anymore" in 1994. A similar quality would lend itself to *Vauxhall and I*, the 1994 solo release by Morrissey, the former lead singer of British art-rock band the Smiths.

Consequently, although Lillywhite was no longer associated with the trademark Lillywhite sound, he seemed nonetheless to still have an identifiable voice. Possibly in a bid for that ever-evasive transparency, the producer announced in 1994 that he would tackle a wholly fresh challenge: an English country singer named Bo Walton.

Selected discography

As producer

Ultravox, *Ultravox!*, Island, 1977.
Siouxsie and the Banshees, *The Peel Sessions* (includes "Hong Kong Garden"), Dutch East India, 1977.
XTC, *Drums and Wires*, Virgin, 1979.
Peter Gabriel, *Peter Gabriel*, Geffen, 1980.
Psychedelic Furs, *Psychedelic Furs*, Columbia, 1980.

U2, *Boy*, Island, 1980.
XTC, *Black Sea*, Geffen, 1980.
U2, *October*, Island, 1981.
Psychedelic Furs, *Talk Talk Talk*, Columbia, 1981.
Joan Armatrading, *Walk Under Ladders*, A&M, 1981.
Thompson Twins, *Set*, Arista, 1982.
Big Country, *The Crossing*, Mercury, 1983.
Marshall Crenshaw, *Field Day*, Warner Bros., 1983.
U2, *War*, Island, 1983.
Simple Minds, *Sparkle in the Rain*, A&M, 1984.
Rolling Stones, *Dirty Work*, Columbia, 1986.
Talking Heads, *Naked*, Sire, 1987.
David Byrne, *Rei Momo*, Luaka Bop, 1988.
Pogues, *If I Should Fall from Grace with God*, Island, 1988.
Kirsty MacColl, *Kite*, IRS/CEMA, 1989.
Pogues, *Peace and Love*, Island, 1989.
Thompson Twins, *Big Trash*, Warner Bros., 1989.
Red, Hot, + Blue, Chrysalis, 1990.
Pogues, *Essential Pogues*, Island, 1991.
World Party, *Bang!*, Chrysalis, 1993.
Morrissey, *Vauxhall and I*, Sire / Warner Bros., 1994.

Sources

Billboard, February 1, 1986; March 26, 1994.
Melody Maker, January 24, 1981; February 25, 1984.
Musician, March 1982.
Rolling Stone, July 8, 1993.
Trouser Press, April 1982.

—*Ondine E. LeBlanc*

Joe Lovano

Saxophonist, bandleader

Photograph by Guy Aroch, 1994, courtesy of Blue Note Records

Since he emerged as a solo artist with his 1991 album *Landmarks,* tenor saxophone player Joe Lovano has grown increasingly more bold and ambitious in his explorations of modern jazz. Playing with his own Lovano Quartet at such venues as the Village Vanguard in New York City and touring the United States in late 1993, the longtime sideman has stepped out of the background to develop a style of his own. "Lovano's sound on tenor sax, especially—but on alto, soprano, flute, and the clarinet family, too—has quietly become a keynote of the 90s," Howard Mandel wrote in *Down Beat.*

Lovano's sound responds to the history of modern jazz and, drawing on his unique experiences, expands it. He grew up with the music of John Coltrane, Miles Davis, Ornette Coleman, and Art Blakey, and from the 1970s into the 1990s he played with jazz artists Woody Herman, Mel Lewis and the Vanguard Jazz Orchestra, Paul Motian, John Scofield, and Charlie Haden's Liberation Music Orchestra.

Lovano finally left the Vanguard Jazz Orchestra and Scofield's quartet in late 1992 to focus on his own music. "To be an honest musician, you play from your history," Lovano told *Down Beat*'s Mandel. "Of course, we play from the history of the music around us, too. But *your* history, what *you* experience, is what really comes out if you can get deep inside yourself, the music and the personalities of the people you play with."

Born in Cleveland, Ohio, on December 29, 1952, to tenor sax jazzman Anthony "Big T" Lovano, Joe received exposure to modern jazz at an early age. The young Lovano experienced the music of local jazz players as well as some of the pioneers of free jazz, a movement away from the dominant jazz style of the mid-1950s. Jazz artists that Lovano could not hear live could be found in his father's extensive jazz record collection. As a result of this exposure, Lovano gained enough expertise to tour while still a teenager, playing on the local club circuit opposite such leading Cleveland figures as drummer Elvin Jones and saxophonist Stan Getz.

1960s Jazz an Influence

Throughout his career, Lovano would remember the excitement of the 1960s jazz scene and strive to recreate it in his own playing. "That was a beautiful period for creative music, given the interplay among all the players in those different groups," Lovano was quoted as saying in *Down Beat.* "Jazz is a very social music; it's a lot about your contemporaries and how everybody feeds off each other. I know Coltrane played how he did because of how Sonny was playing down the street. I really try to feel that now."

In 1971 Lovano attended Berklee College of Music, where he met future music partners Bill Frisell and John Scofield. Three years later, in 1974, he made his first recording with Lonnie Liston Smith on *Aphrodisiac for a Groove Merchant*. After a brief spell working with Smith and another touring veteran, "Brother" Jack McDuff, Lovano moved to New York City in 1976 and joined the Woody Herman band. In 1980 he joined the big band of Mel Lewis and the following year teamed up with drummer Paul Motian. The late 1980s found Lovano touring Europe, where he recorded *Worlds*, a French album based on his tour de force performance at the 1989 Amiens International Jazz Festival.

Village Voice jazz critic Gary Giddins attributed Lovano's stellar rise during the 1990s to his work with drummer Paul Motian rather than to Lovano's first independent recordings. While Giddins complimented *Village Rhythm*, recorded on the Soul Note label in 1989, he lauded Lovano's work on three previous albums by Motian: "I bet if those records had been released on a major label, not a reader of this page would be unfamiliar with them—they are that good." Motian led tenor saxophonist Lovano, guitarist Bill Frisell, and bassist Charlie Haden for the recordings *Misterioso*, on Soul Note, and *Monk in Motian* and *Paul Motian on Broadway Vol. 1*, on JMT.

Made His Mark at Major Label

With the album *Landmarks*, released by Blue Note in 1991, Lovano debuted as a bandleader, composer, and arranger on a major U.S. label. Zan Stewart of the *Los Angeles Times,* referring to the album' material, called Lovano "one of the major jazz players of the '90s.... Nothing here is mundane." Also reviewing *Landmarks, Rolling Stone*'s Steve Futterman described Lovano as "a dream player for the Nineties who mixes romance with risk."

In the albums following *Landmarks,* Lovano articulated a still sharper style. "He just gets better and better, though he'll have to go some to top this album's 'Body and Soul' and 'Central Park West,'" a critic for *Village Voice* wrote in a review of Lovano's *From the Soul.* Both *From the Soul,* on Blue Note, and *Sounds of Joy,* on Enja, were recorded in 1991 with the participation of the late drum master Ed Blackwell. On these albums, Lovano played tenor, soprano, and alto sax in addition to alto clarinet. "*Sound of Joy* is where I got deeper into who I am," the musician told Bob Blumenthal of the *Boston Globe.*

Released by Blue Note in 1993, *Universal Language* was esteemed as Lovano's "most intensely personal and adventurous undertaking to date" by *Down Beat*'s Bill Milkowski. Incorporating the vocals of soprano Judi Silvano—Lovano's wife—with wordless voice lines circling tightly around his own themes, Lovano achieved "unusual voicings that the session sustains," according to John Fordham of the *Guardian.* "*Universal Language* is by far the saxophonist's boldest sweep idiomatically," Fordham continued. For this album, Lovano played with the seven-piece Wind Ensemble that first appeared on *Worlds.* Milkowski concluded in *Down Beat* that "Lovano makes an evolutionary leap in his career with this remarkable album."

Compared to Legacies After *Legacy*

When *Tenor Legacy* was released in 1994, critics acclaimed Lovano as possibly the most innovative tenor player around. "A sensitive ballad interpreter with a romantic streak, Joe Lovano is also a spirited, free-thinking improviser who loves to work the high wire without a net," Milkowski wrote in *Down Beat.* "He straddles the worlds of bebop and freebop more successfully than any other tenor player around today."

The *Los Angeles Times'* Stewart compared Lovano to jazz saxophone greats Lester Young, Charlie Parker, Sonny Rollins, John Coltrane and Ornette Coleman, observing, "There are many who think that Joe Lovano, with his incantatory blend of unbridled spontaneity and be-bop roots, is the jazz tenor innovator of our day." *Tenor Legacy* also features the young jazz star Joshua Redman, top drummer Lewis Nash, and seasoned percussionist Don Alias, all of whom drew out Lovano's best playing. Lovano's distinct style on *Tenor Legacy* revealed the influence of Thelonious Monk and modern jazz pioneer Ornette Coleman. The musicians who assembled to record *Tenor Legacy* formed a new band, the Joe Lovano Quartet. While Lovano's Wind Ensemble anticipated a five-week tour of Europe in 1993, his new Lovano Quartet began a U.S. tour in the fall of the same year. In the *Boston Globe,* Lovano was quoted as describing the Quartet as "kind of an offshoot of the Wind Ensemble, but more intimate."

Lovano has taken his music to international audiences and hopes to grow from that exposure. "This last year I've played in Chile, I've been in Europe a bunch of times, played all over Japan and Hong Kong. The different flavors of the countries and their people—if you let all that influence you, your music can go anywhere," the jazzman explained in *Down Beat.* "That's what Duke Ellington did, and look at all the beautiful music he gave us. To respect different cultures and let all peoples into your life to influence you is a rich thing—it filters in through *my* music, for sure. I don't ever want to lose that."

Selected discography

Tones, Shapes & Colors, Soul Note, 1986.

Village Rhythm, Soul Note, 1989.
(With Aldo Romano) *Ten Tales,* 1989.
Worlds, Label Bleu, 1990.
Landmarks, Blue Note, 1991.
From the Soul, Blue Note, 1992.
Sounds of Joy, Enja, 1992.
(With Paul Motian and Bill Frisell) *Motian in Tokyo,* JMT, 1992.
Universal Language, Blue Note, 1993.
Tenor Legacy, Blue Note, 1994.
(With John Scofield) *Time on My Hands,* Blue Note.

Sources

Books

Such, David G., *Avant-garde Jazz Musicians: Performing "Out There,"* University of Iowa Press, 1993.

Periodicals

Atlanta Journal & Constitution, February 29, 1992; September 3, 1993.
Boston Globe, September 26, 1993.
Down Beat, March 1993; June 1993; June 1994; July 1994.
Guardian, July 16, 1993.
Los Angeles Times, May 26, 1991; March 27, 1994.
New York Times, March 10, 1994.
People, April 4, 1994.
Rolling Stone, September 5, 1991.
Village Voice, October 1, 1991; November 3, 1992.

—Nicholas Patti

Lush

Rock band

"Lush presents a vision that is sometimes pure stratospheric waltzing, sometimes ethereal thrash-core, and sometimes (as on the band's version of Abba's 'Hey Hey Helen') just plain absurd," remarked David Quantick in *Spin*. Ethereal, moody, and spooky are certainly often-used terms in describing the British group, but vocalist/guitarist Miki Berenyi insisted in *Spin*, "There is rocking out." Enigmatic in interviews, Lush bandmembers usually let the songs speak for themselves and do not mind that they don't get the club play that fellow Brit dance bands command, instead asserting that they just want respect for what Quantick called their "tiny-pearl-dropped-into-the-milky-ocean-of-serenity vibe."

At the age of 14, Berenyi met future bandmate Emma Anderson at Queen's College in England. They found they had a common bond: their parents had bounced them both from school to school depending on family finances at the time. Two years later, the two teenagers wrote and produced a fanzine called *Alphabet Soup*, which only lasted for five issues. In 1988 Berenyi studied English literature at London's Polytechnic University, where she met drummer Christopher Acland, bassist Steve Rippon, and singer Meriel Barham. Along with Anderson, they decided to form their own band. Anderson's friend Kevin Pickering told her he thought Lush would be a perfect name for a band. Anderson agreed, suggested the name to the band, and they started writing and rehearsing. After that conversation, Anderson never saw Pickering again.

Won Critics' Blessings

On March 6, 1988, Lush played their very first performance at Camden Falcon in London. Not long after the band's first show, the U.K. press started to take notice with favorable reviews. But Barham decided he didn't want to stay with the band and later went on to join Lush's 4AD labelmates, the Pale Saints. The remaining members of Lush placed ads in local papers looking for Barham's replacement, but they couldn't find the singer they wanted. Berenyi took over the vocals, and the band continued to perform in clubs around London.

In January of 1989 Chris Roberts in *Melody Maker* wrote a rave review of Lush, describing them as "a delta," "irresistible" and "monstrously wonderful." Once the magazine hit the street, Lush received nonstop phone calls from record companies interested in the band. By the summer, 4AD Records had sent them into the studio with producer John Fryer to record a three-song demo called *Etheriel*. Those three songs became the first side of Lush's debut mini-album, titled *Scar*, which they released that fall.

For the Record . . .

Members include **Christopher Acland** (born September 7, 1966, in Lancaster, England), drums; **Emma Anderson** (born June 10, 1967, in London, England), guitar, backing vocals; **Meriel Barham,** vocals; **Miki Berenyi** (born March 18, 1967, in London, England; replaced Barham, 1988), vocals, guitar; **Philip King** (born April 28, 1960, in London, England; replaced Rippon, c. 1992), bass guitar; **Steve Rippon,** bass guitar.

Band formed in London, England, 1988; signed with 4AD Records in the U.K., 1989; released two EPs before licensing for U.S. distribution with Reprise Records, 1990; released debut LP, *Gala,* 1990; embarked on U.S. tour, 1991; performed on Lollapalooza tour, 1992.

Addresses: *Record company*—4AD, 8533 Melrose Ave., Suite B, Los Angeles, CA 90069; Reprise Records, 75 Rockefeller Plaza, New York, NY 10019.

When Chris Roberts interviewed Lush for *Melody Maker* following his original review, he wrote his impression of the band off the stage: "Lush apologize a lot, whine a lot, fall silent a lot and say, 'I dunno' a lot." The members of the band apologized for any flaws they saw in themselves as a brand-new, still-growing band before any music critic could knock them. But the reviews remained favorable. Lush became their own worst critics. Though their success came relatively quickly, they strived to adapt while continuing to improve their songs and their performances. "I remember when I couldn't play, I wasn't in a band, didn't know anyone else who could play, and now we've got a record out on 4AD. I sometimes find it impossible to come to terms with what's happening," Anderson told Everett True in *Melody Maker.*

Overwhelmed by Success

On February 26, 1990, Lush released their next EP, *Mad Love,* and its first single, "Sweetness and Light." Produced by Cocteau Twins' guitarist Robin Guthrie, *Mad Love* provided another step in their musical growth and got the attention of Warner/Reprise Records, who licensed the band's releases in the United States. Lush didn't set out on a certain plan in their career from this point; they put aside ambition and decided to take things one step at a time.

Anderson and Berenyi continued to write all Lush's material from a "female" rather than "feminist" point of view, and they immediately became the focal point of the band. Annie Liebowitz, the world-famous photographer, saw their picture in a magazine and wanted to set them up as models for the "look of the '90s" in advertising campaigns for companies like the Gap. But the band continued to put all their energy into their music. In December of 1990 4AD/Reprise compiled and released Lush's two preceding EPs as *Gala,* their first release in the United States. The group named the album after Salvador Dali's wife.

Gala also included a version of the Abba song "Hey Hey Helen," which brought an onslaught of comparisons between Lush and the Swedish pop/disco group, which also consisted of two women and two men. Lush received positive initial response in the United States and moved a little further along the success continuum. However, Lush continued to apologize and downplayed their progress. "I don't think we're at all successful ... yet," Anderson told Ted Mico in *Melody Maker.* "Are Lush going to be around in five years? Personally, I don't think so."

Despite their pessimism, the members of Lush proceeded with their musical quest. In April of 1991 they returned to the United States for their second tour co-headlining with Ride. Then, at the end of the year, bassist Steve Rippon left the band to concentrate on writing novels full time. To replace him, Lush approached Philip King, a former *New Musical Express* journalist, who had played bass for many U.K. bands, including Felt and Biff Bang Pow!

Betrayed by the Press

With their new lineup in place, Lush headed back into the studio and released their next EP, *For Love,* in January of 1992. Later in the year, Lush arrived in the record stores once again with their next album—also produced by Robin Guthrie—called *Spooky.* Although it debuted at Number Seven on the U.K. charts, it received a negative reaction from the press. Some critics berated the band for bad songwriting, and others accused Guthrie of subduing the band's talents.

But Lush ignored the press. They toured Great Britain, the United States, and Europe, then returned to the States to join the second annual Lollapalooza tour with Pearl Jam, Ministry, Red Hot Chili Peppers, Soundgarden, the Jesus and Mary Chain, and Ice Cube. At the end of the summer, the band took their tour to Japan and Australia.

Lush spent most of 1993 recording their next album at Rockfield Studios in Wales, but they did take a break to perform at some special events. Lush played in 4AD's "13 Year Itch" celebration at England's Institute of Contemporary Art and joined Rage Against the Machine for a special benefit concert for the Anti-Nazi League at the Brixton Academy.

On June 14, 1994, Lush released *Split,* produced by Mike Hedges. In Great Britain, 4AD simultaneously released two EPs along with the album—*Hypocrite* and *Desire Lines.* Berenyi wrote four of the album's songs, and Anderson wrote the other eight. Chris Gill in *Guitar Player* commented, "*Split* shares moments of hypnotic, resplendent pleasure-punk and hard, lardy angst-pop" and added that the album was "easily the British dream-pop band's most varied, cocksure, and commercial effort."

After six years, Lush elaborated more on the concepts behind their songwriting. "I think the theme on this album is about relationships gone wrong," Anderson said in the band's press biography. "In some way, it's about parental-childhood things that happened when you were small. Some of the things will be really obvious." Berenyi added, "We don't graphically describe everything. They are about specific events, some of them, but we just sort of poeticize them a bit. Thoughts and memories, you know."

Selected discography

Scar, 4AD, 1989.
Mad Love, 4AD, 1990.
Gala, 4AD/Reprise, 1990.
For Love, 4AD, 1992.
Spooky, 4AD/Reprise, 1992.
Split, 4AD/Reprise, 1994.
Hypocrite, 4AD, 1994.
Desire Lines, 4AD, 1994.

Sources

Books

The Trouser Press Record Guide, edited by Ira A. Robbins, Collier Books, 1991.

Periodicals

Billboard, August 29, 1992; May 7, 1994.
Entertainment Weekly, July 15, 1994.
Guitar Player, February 1991; June 1991; September 1994.
Melody Maker, January 28, 1989; March 18, 1989; March 25, 1989; October 14, 1989; October 21, 1989; February 17, 1990; March 3, 1990; March 24, 1990; November 3, 1990; December 1, 1990; December 15, 1990; April 20, 1991; October 5, 1991; October 12, 1991; December 21, 1991; January 11, 1992; January 25, 1992; February 15, 1992; May 23, 1992; February 13, 1993; July 24, 1993.
Musician, June 1992.
New Musical Express, June 4, 1994: June 11, 1994.
Rolling Stone, April 16, 1992.
Spin, April 1992.

Additional information for this profile was obtained from 4AD/Reprise press material, 1994.

—*Sonya Shelton*

Ellis Marsalis

Pianist, composer

Photograph by Ken Nahoum, © 1991 Sony Music

Ellis Marsalis is known as both an accomplished, original jazz pianist and a jazz instructor who has helped shape some of the genre's most important new musicians. A figurehead of the jazz music revival in New Orleans in the late 1950s and early 1960s, Marsalis has enjoyed a career spanning almost four decades. After years of success playing in New Orleans clubs, Marsalis won nationwide recognition in the 1980s and 1990s when appreciation for his teaching skills led to numerous recordings.

Born in New Orleans in 1934, Marsalis began playing the clarinet at age 11 and soon entered classical music studies at Xavier University Junior School. As a teenager, he turned to tenor saxophone, which he played in high school as part of a rhythm and blues band, the Groovy Boys. Although he had dabbled in piano for years, it was not until after majoring in tenor sax at Dillard University that Marsalis chose the piano as his preferred instrument. The decision came after hearing Nat Perrilliat play tenor sax; unsure he could equal such a performance, Marsalis decided he would do better to concentrate on piano.

Marsalis joined the modernist American Jazz Quartet in the mid-1950s, playing with drummer Ed Blackwell, clarinetist Alvin Batiste, and tenor saxophonist Harold Battiste. In 1956 Ellis accompanied Blackwell on a visit to Ornette Coleman, then in the midst of developing his freebop concept of jazz. Marsalis stayed two months, then returned to New Orleans as a temporary band director at Xavier Prep. Soon thereafter, he settled a military conscription by enlisting with the U.S. Marines for two years. Being a Marine, however, did not halt his musical career; Marsalis accepted an assignment to play piano on a Marine Corps-sponsored television program, *Dress Blues,* as part of the show's band. During his stint on the show, Marsalis became adept at providing accompaniment for vocalists.

Small Gigs Better Than No Gigs

When his tour of duty ended, Marsalis returned to New Orleans and created a quartet with Perrilliat and drummer James Black. The group recorded only one album, *Monkey Puzzle,* on AFO. In a review of these tracks *Cadence* remarked, "Marsalis' flowing, linear melodicism was a good foil for Perrilliat's more meticulous exploration of chord and rhythm changes." In 1962 Marsalis, Perrilliat, and Black recorded with Nat and Cannonball Adderley, but the album attracted little notice.

Marsalis continued to play the club scene in New Orleans with moderate success throughout the 1960s.

In 1967, without a gig for the moment, he went to trumpeter Al Hurt's club and, happening to be in the right place at the right time, was asked to join the band. "Although it wasn't about where I wanted to be musically, it turned out to be a very good gig for me," Marsalis revealed in a Columbia Records profile. "It got me back into music on a full time basis, and that's probably the most important thing. Playing is always better than not playing." Although the band's repertoire was small and its style was more rock than Marsalis would have preferred, he gained valuable experience and exposure, playing on the *Today Show,* the *Mike Douglas Show,* and the *Ed Sullivan Show.* He left the band in 1970.

The following year Marsalis began playing with Bob French's Storyville Jazz Band. "That's when I began to learn how to play the traditional literature," Marsalis noted. In 1972 he led the ELM Music Company with drummer Black. The quintet played a steady gig at Lu and Charlie's, a well-known New Orleans jazz club, for approximately a year and a half. Although the Columbia profile extolled those sessions as "[occupying] an almost mythic position in the history of modern jazz in New Orleans," Marsalis downplayed the band's significance in *Down Beat:* "We had some good original stuff, but I'm telling you, it was two or three steps ahead of a rock band."

Marsalis had achieved a fair amount of success in New Orleans, but he was not well known nationally. "I wasn't able to put it together," Ellis told Hank Bordowitz in *Schwann Spectrum.* "When I was growing up, the way that one succeeded in music was to pack up to New York and take a chance. By the time I was really thinking about doing that, we had a lot of kids. It wasn't an easy decision to make to do that, on that kind of gamble." Instead, he continued his musical career in New Orleans and taught music in secondary schools to keep a steady income.

Ushered in New Jazz Generation

In 1967 Marsalis was teaching African American music and jazz improvisation as an adjunct instructor at Xavier University. His influence as a teacher took a significant turn when he was hired to head the music department at New Orleans's new arts magnet school, New Orleans Center for the Creative Arts (NOCCA), in 1974. There he fostered a new generation of jazz artists: Donald Harrison, Kent and Marlon Jordan, Reginald Veal, Nicholas Payton, and Harry Connick, Jr.

In 1986 Marsalis accepted a position as the coordinator of jazz studies at Virginia Commonwealth University in Richmond. Three years later, Marsalis returned to New Orleans as the head of the Jazz Studies Program at the University of New Orleans.

Marsalis's influence did not rest solely with his students; he has also raised several of jazz's most important new artists. Marsalis's two eldest sons, Branford and Wynton, have carved prominent positions for themselves in the jazz world, playing soprano sax and trumpet, respectively; Branford also appears as musical director and co-host of *The Tonight Show with Jay Leno.* Ellis's third son, Delfeayo, plays trombone, but has achieved his greatest success to date as a producer. Delfeayo has produced virtually all of his brothers' and his father's albums since the mid-1980s. At 14, Marsalis's youngest son, Jason, played drums on his father's 1993 album *Heart of Gold.*

Family Affair Led to Success

Marsalis's recording career bloomed late. Having recorded only a few albums in almost 30 years of playing, Marsalis came into his own in the 1980s. *Fathers and Sons,* a 1982 release done with his sons Branford and Wynton, was the first in a series of albums Marsalis would record over the next decade. Brian Case reviewed the album for *Melody Maker,* stating, "Father Ellis has no trouble bedding right down in [the] fast company [of Branford and Wynton], being a fleet boppish piano player of some originality."

His next several albums were well received, particularly *Syndrome* and *Homecoming,* on which Marsalis's experience was evident. Jon Balleras said of Marsalis and *Homecoming* collaborator Eddie Harris, "To say these players are seasoned would be the height of understatement; their playing makes it evident that both men have long since surpassed the point of mastering their instruments and improvisational theory, transcending technique and stylistic limitations to forge a completely transparent, immediate music, music of a broad swirl and swell."

In 1994 Marsalis released *Whistle Stop,* most of whose compositions date from the 1960s; several were written by the late drummer James Black. Although Larry Birnbaum of *Down Beat* praised Marsalis's performance, he felt the pianist was overshadowed by his sidemen: "The subtle artistry of his elegant phrasing and refined touch are best appreciated on the closing ballad ... where he plays unaccompanied." Marsalis, who has said he intends to compose for larger ensem-bles and to explore longer musical forms in the future, told Kalamu ya Salaam that "[*Whistle Stop*] with its emphasis on the small ensemble represents the pinnacle of my work in that format."

Selected discography

The Monkey Puzzle, AFO, 1963.
Gumbo, 1976.
Fathers and Sons, Columbia, 1982.
Syndrome, ELM, 1984.
(With Eddie Harris) *Homecoming,* Spindletop, 1986.
(With Lady BJ) *The New New Orleans Music: Vocal Jazz,* Rounder, 1989
The Vision's Tale, Antilles, 1989.
Piano in E, Rounder, 1991.
Ellis Marsalis Trio, Blue Note, 1991.
The Classic, AFO, 1992.
Heart of Gold, Columbia, 1993.
Whistle Stop, Columbia, 1994.

Sources

Cadence, May 1992.
Down Beat, July 1984; November 1986; April 1992; May 1994.
JazzTimes, December 1990.
Melody Maker, July 31, 1982.

Additional information for this profile was obtained from Columbia Records press materials.

—*Susan Windisch Brown*

The Meat Puppets

Rock band

Usually slotted as part of punk music's "post-punk" development during the 1980s, the Meat Puppets have surfed atop the rise and fall of that movement, riding beyond it into the "grunge" rock boom of the 1990s. Given such a history, it's not surprising that critics have spent a decade arguing over the correct term for the band's music, taking their cues from the mutations occurring from one Meat Puppets album to the next.

"With each of their five albums," Simon Reynolds wrote in *Melody Maker,* "the Meat Puppets have not so much made a giant leap forward as a perplexing step sideways; each time hitting on a totally new, totally original sound that any other band would have milked for 10 albums." While Kurt Loder called them a "thrash band" in *Rolling Stone* in 1984, other critics later commented on their distance from the conventions of hardcore punk. One of the effects of such a resistance to tidy categorization has been the Meat Puppets' reputation for forward-looking music—for anticipating and spearheading changes in musical style.

Photograph by Michael Halsband, © 1993 PolyGram, courtesy of PolyGram Label Group

For the Record . . .

Members include **Derrick Bostrom,** drums, **Cris Kirkwood,** bass; and **Curt Kirkwood,** vocals and lead guitar.

Band formed in Phoenix, AZ, 1979, playing at house parties; cut debut EP, *In a Car,* 1981; signed and recorded with SST Records, 1981-91; released debut album, *Meat Puppets,* 1982; signed with London/PLG, 1991; toured with Nirvana, 1993; appeared in guest spot with Nirvana on *MTV Unplugged,* 1993.

Addresses: *Record company*—London/PLG, 825 Eighth Ave., New York, NY 10019.

As teenagers, Cris and Curt Kirkwood and Derrick Bostrom, who would later create the Meat Puppets in the late 1970s, had grown up in the open spaces surrounding their hometown of Phoenix, Arizona. Brothers Cris and Curt arrived in Phoenix from Wichita Falls, Texas, in 1965, when Cris, the younger sibling, was about five years old. The Kirkwood family's income came from racehorses that they owned. Bored with how little the city had to offer, the two brothers found recreation in using drugs amid Phoenix's desert landscape.

"Punk rock began as an urban phenomenon," Ivan Kreilkamp wrote in *Details,* "a musical response to miles of concrete and industrial noise. The Meat Puppets were the first group to adapt punk to the twisted landscapes and open spaces of the American Southwest." Curt Kirkwood told Kreilkamp, "There's no trees, there's no real society. It's easy to get into drugs there because there's nothing to do." Their hallucinogenic experiences would eventually be credited with shaping the distinctive sound of their music. Kreilkamp, for example, speculated that "The Puppets' music is rooted in the experience of three kids, heads throbbing with LSD-induced visions, riding motorcycles on a canal bed in the Saguaro desert."

Hailed as Visionaries

After a brief effort at the University of Arizona in Tucson in 1977, Curt returned home. Having had some musical training, including classical study, he and his younger brother started playing house parties with area bands. They also played in local cover bands, with Curt on guitar and Cris on bass. After one of the more successful local bands, Eye, broke up in 1979, the Kirkwood

brothers decided it was time to do something on their own. At that point, Derrick Bostrom came on board to play drums.

Bostrom had a practice space in which the Meat Puppets could shape their sound, already heavily influenced by an odd jumble that included the Grateful Dead, the Sex Pistols, Johnny Cash, and Iggy Pop. The group had no particular venue in mind, simply a desire to see what kind of music they could make. "I came to hardcore through experimental music," Curt told David Fricke in a *Melody Maker* interview. "I started getting into Edgar Varese, when he was composing things that sounded like raindrops. I didn't give a shit about composing anything. But I thought if I hooked up a couple of fuzzboxes to my guitar and turned it up real loud, and played faster than anybody could think, what was going to come out was going to be heavily impassioned."

Curt quickly emerged as the band's major force, lending a compelling character on vocals and guitar, as well as his odd skill as a songwriter; Kreilkamp referred to him as the trio's "chief visionary." Jas Obrecht, writing for *Guitar Player* in 1994, described Curt as the "master of the enigmatic lyric and monotone delivery."

While critics have often suggested the dual influences of drugs and the desert landscape on Curt's style, the musician himself also attributes it to a specific childhood experience: "I had encephalitis when I was nine," Curt told Reynolds, "my head swelled up, I was in a coma for a long time. After that I started to daydream an AWFUL lot, I was able to pick and choose what I wanted from my imagination." Reynolds dubbed the three "modern visionaries who liberate the flux of experience from the grids with which we attempt to structure and manage time and reality."

While playing more professional gigs around their hometown in 1980 and 1981, the trio cut their first EP, *In a Car,* on a small label called World Imitation. Michael Azerrad recalled in *Rolling Stone* that "a series of revelatory Los Angeles shows won them a hipster following." In 1981 they also won a contract with a larger independent label, SST, that was just putting together a roster of punk bands—including Black Flag and the Minutemen—that would soon reign over the 1980s punk rock scene.

SST would grow along with its bands to become one of the leading labels of the genre. The company released the Meat Puppets's first album, simply called *Meat Puppets,* in 1982, all 14 songs having been recorded in one day. The band also set out on their first national tour, building their reputation in clubs that catered to an underground music audience. Nonetheless, the band's resistance to pre-established categorization was already apparent.

By the mid-1980s, many critics were claiming the Meat Puppets as the unacknowledged saving grace of music, underground and otherwise.

Mark Coleman revealed in the *Village Voice*, "Assimilating musical ideas from (at least) two rock generations along with cultural by-products of the Southwest—bible-preaching, earth muffin naturalism, the music of hack country-and-Western dance bands—the Meat Puppets spit back a synapse-melting sound that's both lyrical and intense." Furthermore, Coleman sensed the group's ability to challenge the "conventions" of punk. He speculated, "If the Meat Puppets can open up the tightest rock format (and audience) of all to new influences and original sounds, they must have found something pretty universal down in that basement."

By the time their second album, *Meat Puppets II*, was released in 1984, critics were making much of the band's evolution and ascribing diverse values to the role the Meat Puppets had assumed in relation to society: Loder argued that they had "gone beyond head-banging to become what can only be called a kind of cultural trash compacter."

Most notably, the Puppets caused listeners to do a double-take by introducing a country-Western twang into what had appeared, on the first album, to be straightforward thrash. "What we get," Tom Carson wrote in the *Village Voice*, "is country music as it might manifest itself to a young wastrel whose sense of the void is made most immediate by the fact that the springs in the living-room couch have given out."

By the mid-1980s, many critics were claiming the Meat Puppets as the unacknowledged saving grace of music, underground and otherwise. Describing them as "insightful deviant tunesmiths" in his *Melody Maker* review of 1985's *Up on the Sun*, David Fricke claimed that "the Meat Puppets have come to represent in their own anarchic way all that is weird and right about recent American music." Reynolds dubbed *Up on the Sun* "a weird hybrid of warpfunk, country and psych."

Writing for the *Village Voice*, James Nold declared, "Instrumentally, *Up on the Sun* is the most impressive record any hardcore band ... has made. It's frequently beautiful."

The strength of *Up on the Sun* didn't propel the trio from alternative status to mainstream visibility, but it did provide them with a breakthrough of sorts: they made it onto the airwaves of a mainstream rock radio station in their hometown. The promise of the moment, however, was followed by a "mid-'80s dip from their formative grace," as Brian Keizer later recalled in *Spin*. Nisid Hajari described in *Entertainment Weekly* the odd impasse the band had come to by 1985, when "their whimsical desert twang had made them one of the most acclaimed bands on the underground scene, but their anemic sales awarded them the dreaded consolation-prize tag 'critics' darlings.'"

However, the plateau the Puppets stood on still included considerable notice from reviewers. For example, in *Rolling Stone* David Fricke described the band's 1986 effort, *Out My Way*, as "a decisive step in the Meat Puppets's march away from one-dimensional punk to hearty, heartfelt pan-American rock & roll." He concluded, "With sounds and lyrics like these, greatness may only be one more album away." *Huevos* and *Mirage* followed in the late 1980s, precipitating the band's first tour of England in 1988.

Remained Underground

Even as their audience and publicity expanded, the Meat Puppets remained an underground band without major label recording or distribution. When Reynolds asked Curt about that state of affairs, the singer expressed general satisfaction, declaring, "It's a BLAST, man—we put out exactly what we want, we earn enough to get by, we sell a bit more with each album. Plus with SST we just give them a finished record and they put it out. They don't try to direct our development, there's no delay, the songs don't get stale." He also accepted that major labels didn't have a marketing strategy for hardcore; "there's no way they can market us," he told Reynolds.

Ironically, however, just around the time that SST issued a compilation Meat Puppets album called *No Strings Attached* in 1991, the band broke with the label over legal and financial troubles. By the following year, the band was embroiled in a competition of mutual lawsuits with SST that would not come to an end until an out-of-court settlement in June, 1993; SST was left to pursue lawsuits against several other bands from their early roster.

Cult Faves Moved to Major Label

The shift to a major label always leaves a band in danger of either becoming, or being perceived as becoming, "mainstream"—a death knell for a band that has built its reputation on going against the grain. Consequently, 1991's *Forbidden Places,* the Meat Puppets's first release on PolyGram's London subsidiary, came under considerable scrutiny. While Cathi Unsworth insisted in *Melody Maker* that "these three rovers still travel their own path, the fork between acidic psychedelic weirdness and earthy country wildness," Azerrad would later acknowledge that the Puppet's first major-label release had "bombed."

In a sense, however, the Meat Puppets had already become a part of the mainstream; recognition was simply the final piece to fall into place. In particular, their years as underground rock visionaries had greatly shaped the "grunge rock" generation that would capture the market in the 1990s. In 1994 Obrecht described the Meat Puppets as "cult faves for a dozen years," noting specifically their influence on "members of Nirvana, Soul Asylum, Butthole Surfers, and Pearl Jam," the primary forces of grunge rock.

Nirvana and Soul Asylum both made the connection concrete in 1993, when they signed the Puppets on as opening band for their European tours. Although the group sometimes expressed concerns about becoming commercial, Curt was willing to accept the status conferred on him by Nirvana's lead singer, Kurt Cobain; he told Azerrad in *Rolling Stone* that since Cobain was "the guy that made punk rock commercial,... basically we're the inspiration for commercial punk rock."

When the Meat Puppets' second London release, *Too High to Die,* reached record stores in 1994, the attention from Nirvana began to pay off; *Too High to Die* was the first commercial success the Meat Puppets had ever seen. Declaring that the band was "finally getting its due," Carrie Borzillo reported in *Billboard* that the band had, for the first time, broken onto *Billboard's* Top 200 chart; both the album and several single cuts rose into the Top 20 on their respective charts. Furthermore, a guest appearance on Nirvana's *MTV Unplugged* spot "may have guaranteed more sales of the Puppets' latest LP ... than years of good reviews ever could," as Hajari commented.

Of course, not all credit for the Meat Puppets' success was due to Nirvana—critics also noted the strength of the album itself. Chuck Crisafulli, reviewing *Too High to Die* for *Musician,* clearly concurred. Noting the "strong melodies" and "ingenious songwriting," he predicted that the album "should win these pop oddballs some overdue respect."

Regarding their breakthrough, Cris told Azerrad, "I'm way into it, because I haven't had to go out of my way to get to the mainstream. The mainstream veered off course and came over to my little puddle. I've been sitting there for years." Curt mused to Hajari that "It's only recently that punk-rock underground music took on one more eccentric tentacle—that to be a really bitchin' punk-rock band you must also be successful. I don't know how that happened, since the very word *underground* means that your style and substance and art should preempt your actual commercial endeavor." Cris, however, told Borzillo that he found it "neat to see [the band] crawl out of its little art trench and into the mainstream."

Selected discography

In a Car, World Imitation, 1981.
Meat Puppets, SST, 1982.
Meat Puppets II, SST, 1984.
Up on the Sun, SST, 1985.
Out My Way, SST, 1986.
Mirage, SST, 1987.
Huevos, SST, 1987.
Monsters, SST, 1989.
Forbidden Places, London/PLG, 1991.
Too High to Die, London/PLG, 1994.

Sources

Billboard, April 11, 1992; January 22, 1994; May 7, 1994.
Details, April 1994.
Entertainment Weekly, February 11, 1994.
Guitar Player, April 1994.
Melody Maker, May 18, 1985; June 6, 1987; October 3, 1987; December 12, 1987; October 28, 1989; December 16, 1989; January 19, 1991; November 9, 1991; January 11, 1993.
Musician, February 1994.
New York Times, February 15, 1994.
Rolling Stone, April 26, 1984; October 23, 1986; April 15, 1993; June 10, 1993; May 19, 1994; June 2, 1994.
Spin, February 1994.
Village Voice, December 7, 1982; April 24, 1984; July 30, 1985; January 19, 1988.

Additional information for this profile was obtained from London/PLG publicity materials.

—*Ondine E. Le Blanc*

Johnny Mercer

Songwriter, singer, record company executive

Archive Photos

Johnny Mercer wrote lyrics or music for more than 1,000 songs in a career spanning nearly 50 years, making him one of the most successful songwriters of the twentieth century. One of the most versatile lyricists ever, he penned catchy words for everything from bouncy numbers ("Goody Goody") and mysterious mood setters ("That Old Black Magic") to romantic love songs ("Moon River"). During the 1930s and 1940s Mercer was also a popular singer who performed on a number of radio shows with top bands. He was a master at the business of music as well, as evidenced by his co-founding of the highly successful Capitol Records.

Well-turned Mercer phrases for such classics as "Too Marvelous for Words," "Hooray for Hollywood," "Fools Rush In," and scores of other songs have been forever locked into the memories of millions of listeners. Mercer also wrote memorable melodies for such songs as "I'm an Old Cowhand," "Dream," and "Something's Gotta' Give," composing them by using one finger on the piano because he couldn't read a note of music.

Mercer was once quoted as saying that his songwriting success was due to his "feeling for tunes, no matter where they come from." This "feeling" helped him forge effective partnerships with a wide variety of composers over the years, among them Hoagy Carmichael, Jerome Kern, Harold Arlen, Henry Mancini, Rube Bloom, and Michel Legrand. The long and distinguished list of performers who made hit songs of the words and melodies of Johnny Mercer includes Bing Crosby, Frank Sinatra, Billie Holiday, Andy Williams, Peggy Lee, and Tony Bennett.

Gave His Regards to Broadway

An unpublished ditty called "Sister Susie, Strut Your Stuff," written when he was 15, was Mercer's first known attempt at songwriting. His first desire was to be a star on the stage, and he joined a theater group in his hometown of Savannah, Georgia, while still a teenager. After his group won a one-act play competition in the Belasco Cup in New York City, Mercer decided to stay in New York and try to make it on Broadway.

Mercer managed to land a few small parts during the late 1920s in *Volpone, Marco Millions,* and *Houseparty.* During this time, and on into the 1930s, he also worked at a music publishing company and continued his songwriting. After auditioning for the *Garrick Gaieties* in 1929 without landing a part, Mercer offered his and Everett Miller's "Out of Breath and Scared to Death" to the show, and it was sung by Sterling Holloway. The

Born John Herndon Mercer, November 18, 1909, in Savannah, GA; died of a brain tumor, June 25, 1976, in Los Angeles, CA; married Ginger Meehan (a dancer), 1931; children: Amanda, John.

Appeared as bit player on New York City stage, 1927; co-wrote first published song, "Out of Breath and Scared to Death," for *Garrick Gaieties,* 1930; began writing songs for RKO Pictures, 1935; appeared in films *Old Man Rhythm* and *To Beat the Band,* 1935; became emcee and featured vocalist for Paul Whiteman's Orchestra, late 1930s; became vocalist on Benny Goodman's *Camel Caravan* (radio show), c. 1938; co-wrote lyrics for first musical, *Walk With Music,* 1940; hosted own radio show, *Johnny Mercer's Musical Shop,* 1940s; co-founded Capitol Records, 1942.

Collaborated with many popular composers, including Arlen, Hoagy Carmichael, Jerome Kern, Michel Legrand, Henry Mancini, and Jimmy Van Heusen; co-wrote hit songs for Tony Bennett, Bing Crosby, Judy Garland, Billie Holiday, Peggy Lee, Glenn Miller, Andy Williams, and numerous others.

Member: American Society for Composers, Authors and Publishers (ASCAP; director, early 1940s).

Awards: Academy awards for best song, 1946 (with Harold Warren), for "On the Atchison, Topeka, and the Santa Fe," 1951 (with Hoagy Carmichael), for "In the Cool Cool Cool of the Evening," 1961 (with Henry Mancini), for "Moon River," and 1962 (with Mancini), for "Days of Wine and Roses."

song was a minor success but didn't create a demand for Mercer's other songs in the months that followed. He continued working at various jobs to support himself, including as a runner on Wall Street.

Mercer's singing helped him get on the fast track. After winning a contest for unknown singers staged by Paul Whiteman, one of the leading bandleaders of the time, Mercer was hired as a featured vocalist, emcee, and songwriter for Whiteman's orchestra. A key element of Mercer's popularity as a crooner was "a dry Southern drawl that gave his singing a distinctively good-natured character," according to *The Oxford Companion to Popular Music.*

Whiteman put his singer-songwriter in touch with Ho-

agy Carmichael, who at that time was having trouble writing a song. Mercer came to the rescue with his lyrics for "Lazybones," which became his first big hit. According to John S. Wilson in the *New York Times,* this song "drew on his [Mercer's] Southern background in a way that was to prove effective throughout his career." Indeed, many of Mercer's most popular numbers had an easygoing, down-home charm that reflected his early years down South.

By 1934 Mercer was one of the most successful lyricists in the United States. His recorded duets with Jack Teagarden—Whiteman's jazz trombonist—led to an offer from RKO Pictures in 1935 to write songs, as well as sing and act in movies. Mercer's movie star potential, however, proved to be dim, and he would only appear in two films.

However, his songwriting fame soared, thanks to Bing Crosby who sang a number of his songs in the 1936 film *Rhythm on the Range.* Mercer's popularity with movie fans grew throughout the 1930s with tunes such as "You Must Have Been a Beautiful Baby," "Jeepers Creepers," and "Love Is Where You Find It."

After co-writing songs with Richard Whiting for *Hollywood Hotel,* a 1937 film featuring Benny Goodman's orchestra, Mercer became a singer on Goodman's *Camel Caravan* radio show. He also sang on radio with Bob Crosby's orchestra. His steady climb up the musical ladder in the early 1940s led to hosting his own radio show, *Johnny Mercer's Music Shop.* In 1940 Mercer collaborated with Hoagy Carmichael on his first musical, *Walk with Music,* but the show had a very short run on Broadway.

From Writing Songs to Running a Company

Not content to merely add more popular songs to his resume, Mercer teamed up with businessman Glen Wallichs and songwriter-film producer Buddy de Sylva to found Capitol Records in 1942. It was not the best time to start a record company, since the shellac material used to make records was being rationed during World War II. Starting by producing records pressed partly from recycled scrap records, the company's first ventures were Mercer's "Strip Polka," and Freddie Slack and Ella Mae Morse's "Cow-Cow Boogie."

It wasn't long, however, before Capitol Records had signed up budding stars Stan Kenton, Jo Stafford, the King Cole Trio, and Margaret Whiting. In 1946, with Mercer serving as president, the company sold 42 million records, one-sixth of the total record sales in the

United States. Capitol was also the first record company to provide disk jockeys with free promotional records, as well as the first to utilize all three turntable speeds.

Broadway became fertile ground for Mercer in the 1940s. He contributed lyrics to Arlen's score for *St. Louis Woman* in 1946 and Robert Emmett Dolan's *Texas L'il Darlin* in 1949. He also won his first Academy Award, with composer Harry Warren, for "On the Atchison Topeka & Santa Fe," sung by Judy Garland in *The Harvey Girls*. By the end of the 1940s Mercer had logged up over 250 published songs and nearly 60 hits.

Struck Gold With 1950s Musicals

Mercer showed no let-up in giving the public the songs they wanted in the 1950s, and he had his greatest success with musical shows during that period. He earned credits for both music and lyrics for 1951's *Top Banana,* which starred Phil Silvers, and he had major successes in collaborations with Gene DePaul on *Seven Brides for Seven Brothers* in 1954 and *L'il Abner* in 1956. He also penned words to songs in the film *Here's to My Lady,* and two Fred Astaire vehicles, *The Belle of New York* and *Daddy Longlegs.*

A generous spirit was revealed by Mercer in 1959 when he received a song idea from Sadie Vimmerstedt, an Ohio cosmetician who sent him the line, "I want to be around to pick up the pieces when somebody's breaking your heart." After fashioning a song around the contribution, Mercer gave Vimmerstedt a co-author credit that earned her about $3000 a year after the song became a hit for Tony Bennett in 1963.

In the 1960s Henry Mancini proved another valuable songwriting partner for Mercer as the pair earned Academy awards for "Moon River" and "The Days of Wine and Roses." Mancini and Mercer also wrote songs for two other movies, *The Great Race* and *Darling Lili.* Composer Andre Previn became yet another collaborator when Mercer shifted his base of operation to Britain for extended periods in the early 1970s, and the two teamed up for the musical *The Good Companions* in 1974.

Mercer remained active right up to suffering a brain tumor in late 1975. His death marked the end of an incredible stretch of success in a business known for fleeting fame. A precious rarity in the music industry, Johnny Mercer managed to stay in style and continue stirring listeners through four decades of continually evolving musical tastes.

Selected discography

(With Jo Stafford, Paul Weston, and Jack Teagarden) *Johnny Mercer's Music Shop,* Artistic, 1943-44.
(With Bobby Darin) *Two of a Kind,* Atco, 1961.
Audio Scrapbook, Magic/Submarine, 1974.
Two Marvelous for Words: Capitol Sings Johnny Mercer, Capitol, 1992.

Selected songs

As lyricist

"Too Marvelous for Words."
"Ac-Cent-Tu-Ate the Positive."
"You Must Have Been a Beautiful Baby."
"On the Atchison, Topeka, and the Santa Fe."
"In the Cool, Cool, Cool of the Evening."
"Goody Goody."
"Moon River."
"The Days of Wine and Roses."
"Jeepers Creepers."
"That Old Black Magic."
"Fools Rush In."
"Tangerine."

As composer and lyricist

"Dream."
"I'm an Old Cowhand."
"Something's Gotta Give."

Selected musicals

As lyricist

(Co-writer of lyrics) *Walk With Music,* 1940.
(With Harold Arlen) *St. Louis Woman,* 1946.
(With Robert Emmett Dolan) *Texas L'il Darlin,* 1949.
(And composer) *Top Banana,* 1951.
(With Gene DePaul) *Seven Brides for Seven Brothers,* 1954.
(With DePaul) *L'il Abner,* 1956.
(With Robert Emmett Dolan) *Foxy,* 1964.
(With Andre Previn) *The Good Companions,* 1974.

Sources

Books

Guinness Encyclopedia of Popular Music, Volume 2, edited by Colin Larkin, Guinness, 1992.
Halliwell, Leslie, *Halliwell's Film Guide,* seventh edition, Harper & Row, 1990.

Katz, Ephraim, *The Film Encyclopedia,* Harper & Row, 1979.

Oxford Companion to Popular Music, edited by Peter Gammond, Oxford University Press, 1991.

Penguin Encyclopedia of Popular Music, edited by Donald Clarke, Viking, 1989.

Periodicals

Cosmopolitan, April 1946.

New York Times, June 26, 1976.

Newsweek, January 29, 1945.

Los Angeles Magazine, September 1992.

Reader's Digest, June 1991.

Spin, November 1992.

Stereo Review, June 1988.

—*Ed Decker*

Charlie Musselwhite

Harmonica player

Born in Mississippi and raised in Memphis, Tennessee, harmonica stylist Charlie Musselwhite honed his skills under the masters of the post-World War II blues. One of the first white musicians to take up the study of urban folk blues during the blues revival of the 1960s, Musselwhite is a prime exemplar of the art of blues harmonica. After years of personal problems and career setbacks, his current recordings and live performances have brought him both critical acclaim and a new generation of listeners.

The son of a mandolin and guitar maker and the nephew of an itinerant street performer, Charles Douglas Musselwhite was born on January 31, 1944 in Kosciusko, Mississippi. At the age of three, he moved with his family to Memphis—a thriving music center where he heard the sounds of blues, spirituals, and hillbilly bands. As Musselwhite recalled in *Blues Review Quarterly,* "Near my house there was a creek where I would lay in the shade during hot summer afternoons. I could hear people singing in the fields and man, it just took me away. Their singing was exactly the way I felt."

Attracted to African American-inspired music, Musselwhite took up the harmonica at age 13 and began playing with a number of traditional Memphis bluesmen, including Willie Borum, Will Shade, and Furry Lewis, all former members of the Memphis Jug Band. These musicians taught him to play the bottleneck slide guitar. Musselwhite furthered his blues education by watching acts in West Memphis roadhouses. "This was my first real exposure to the blues," commented Musselwhite in *Blues Review Quarterly.* "I was just hanging out absorbing all this great blues music. I never had any intentions of playing for a living. That was the furthest thing from my mind. I just loved it and wanted to play for myself."

Windy City Blues

At the age of 18, Musselwhite moved to Chicago in search of factory work in the industrial North. Unaware of the migration of southern bluesmen to Chicago in the early 1960s, he soon discovered a flourishing blues scene on the city's South Side. Through connections with Bob Koester's Jazz Record Mart, a central hub of the Chicago blues scene, Musselwhite performed with guitarists Robert Nighthawk, Johnny Young, and John Lee Granderson. In South Side clubs, Musselwhite often sat in with blues legend Muddy Waters's band—a band that included pianist Otis Spann and harmonica player James Cotton. But it was Waters's former harmonica sideman, Little Walter Jacobs, who had the

For the Record . . .

Born Charles Douglas Musselwhite, January 31, 1944, in Kosciusko, MS; raised in Memphis, TN; son of Charles Musselwhite II (a mandolin/guitar maker and musician).

Began studying harmonica at age 13; performed with members of the Memphis Jug Band; moved to Chicago, early 1960s, to work outside music; performed with guitarists Robert Nighthawk, Homesick James, J. B. Hutto, and Johnny Young, early to mid-1960s; appeared on blues anthology *Chicago Blues Today!,* 1965; recorded first solo album, *Stand Back!,* 1966; moved to San Francisco in late 1960s and appeared with local blues musicians; performed at blues festivals on the West Coast and in the Midwest throughout the 1970s; toured nationally with various backup bands, 1980s; signed with Alligator Records and released *Ace of Harps,* 1990; recorded *Signature,* 1991, and *In My Time,* 1994.

Awards: W. C. Handy Award for blues instrumentalist of the year, 1990, for *Ace of Harps.*

Addresses: *Record company*—Alligator Records, Box 60234, Chicago, IL 60660.

most profound impact on Musselwhite's musical style. "I really wanted to be around Little Walter because of the way he played," recalled Musselwhite in the liner notes to the album *Goin' Back Down South.* "Walter was playing at a place called Hernando's Hideaway. He would take me down to the bus stop and wait for the bus to come, to see I'd be all right goin' home."

Following his introduction to the South Side blues scene, Musselwhite began to perform on the white folk club circuit on the city's North Side, where he landed a job at the Fickle Pickle with white blues guitarist Michael Bloomfield. At the club, he mingled with pianist Blind John Davis and Tennessee-born acoustic guitarists Sleepy John Estes and Yank Rachell. Later, Musselwhite and Bloomfield played a year-long engagement at Big John's, another North Side folk club.

Although Musselwhite was surrounded by fine talent, his early years on the streets of Chicago were rough. In a promotional release for Alligator Records, he described the poverty he experienced during his apprenticeship in the city: "My feet would be wet from walking in the snow. I had great big holes in my shoes.... Once

you've been there you don't forget." During this time, Musselwhite lived in the basements of Koester's Jazz Record Mart and Old Joe Wells's Record Store with friend and musical companion Big Joe Williams, the famous nine-string guitar blues great. Among other bluesmen to befriend Musselwhite were Otis Rush, J. B. Hutto, Johnny Shines, John Brim, and harmonica legend Big Walter Horton, who often challenged his young harmonica protégé to on-stage harmonica battles.

In 1965 Musselwhite worked on the Vanguard Records release *Chicago Blues Today!* Recording under the name Memphis Charlie, Musselwhite appeared as a guest performer with Big Walter Horton's Blues Harp Band and emerged as the only white performer to be featured on the three volume series—a collection intended to introduce the white folk audience to electric Chicago blues. Musselwhite's first recording as a leader, 1966's *Stand Back! Here Comes Charley Musselwhite's South Side Band,* featured guitarist Harvey Mandel, keyboardist Barry Goldberg, bassist Bob Anderson, and drummer Freddie Below.

Bay Area Blues

After recording three albums for Vanguard, Musselwhite moved to the San Fransico Bay area. His association with West Coast blues guitarist and saxophonist Robben Ford resulted in the 1974 Arhoolie recording *Goin' Back Down South.* A balance between progressive musical ideas and traditional blues, the recording also marked Musselwhite's guitar debut on an acoustic rendition of John Lee Granderson's "Taylor Arkansas."

Over the next two decades Musselwhite appeared on several small labels, including Blue Horizon, Crystal Clear, Charlie, and West Germany's Crosscut. He signed with the Chicago-based Alligator label in 1990 and recorded the album *Ace of Harps,* which won him the W. C. Handy Award for blues instrumentalist of the year. His 1994 release, *In My Time,* features his talents on acoustic guitar and includes two numbers backed by the famous gospel singing group the Five Blind Boys of Alabama. Since the late 1980s, Musselwhite has appeared as a guest artist on numerous recordings such as Bonnie Raitt's *Longing in Their Hearts* and John Lee Hooker's Grammy Award-winning album *The Healer.*

Thirty Years of Blues

In the liner notes to the 1966 album *Stand Back!,* blues writer Pete Welding observed that Musselwhite was "one of the handful of young blues interpreters to have succeeded in penetrating beyond the surface of the music to the development of a thoroughly satisfying, recognizably personal approach to modern blues." Almost three decades later, Musselwhite continues to reaffirm his role as a world-class talent, making music that reflects years of study and a willingness to explore new musical horizons without abandoning the roots of traditional blues.

Selected discography

Stand Back! Here Comes Charley Musselwhite's South Side Band, Vanguard, 1966.
Stone Blues, Vanguard, 1968.
Tennessee Woman, Vanguard, 1969.
Louisiana Fog, Cherry Red, 1970.
Memphis, Tennessee, Vanguard, 1970.
Takin' My Time, Arhoolie, 1971.
Goin' Back Down South, Arhoolie, 1974.
Leave the Blues to Us, Capitol, 1975.
Times Geetin' Tougher Than Tough, Crystal Clear, 1978.
Tell Me Where All the Good Times Have Gone, Blue Rock'it, 1984.
Mellow-Dee, Crosscut, 1985.
Cambridge Blues, Blue Horizon, 1986.
Ace of Harps, Alligator, 1990.
Signature, Alligator, 1991.
In My Time, Alligator, 1994.

With others

Chicago Blues Today!, Volume 3, Vanguard, 1965.
Iver Avenue Reunion, RCA.
Chicago Bluestars, *Coming Home,* Blue Thumb.
William Clarke, *Tip of the Top,* Satch.
Dynatones, *Curtain Call,* Red Lightin'.
Barry Goldberg, *Barry Goldberg Reunion,* Buddah.
Goldberg, *Blast from the Past,* Buddah.
Goldberg, *Blowin' My Mind,* Epic.
Goldberg and Mike Bloomfield, *Two Jews Blues,* Buddah.
John Hammond, *So Many Roads,* Vanguard.
John Lee Hooker, *The Cream,* Tomato.
Hooker, *Never Get Out These Blues Alive,* ABD/Probe.
Hooker, *The Healer,* Cameleon.
INXS, *X,* Atlantic.
Johnny Lewis, *Alabama Slide Guitar,* Arhoolie.
Harvey Mandel, *Christo Redemptor,* Phillips.
Tracy Nelson, *Deep Are the Roots,* Prestige.
Bonnie Raitt, *Longing in Their Hearts,* Capitol.
L.C. "Good Rockin" Robinson, *Ups and Downs,* Arhoolie.
Doc and Merle Watson, *Red Rockin' Chair,* Flying Fish.
Big Joe Williams, *Thinkin' of What They Did to Me,* Arhoolie.
Jimmy Witherspoon, *The Blues Singer,* Bluesaway.

Sources

Books

Blues Who's Who: A Biographical Dictionary of Blues Singers, edited by Sheldon Harris, Da Capo, 1979.

Periodicals

Blues Review Quarterly, summer 1990.
Down Beat, May 1990.
Guitar Player, April 1987.
Rolling Stone, August 25, 1994.

Additional information for this profile was obtained from the promotional biography *Charlie Musselwhite: In My Time,* Alligator Records; from liner notes by Pete Welding to *Stand Back! Here Comes Charley Musselwhite's South Side Band,* Vanguard, 1966; and from liner notes by Dan Forte to *Goin' Back Down South,* Arhoolie Records, 1974.

—*John Cohassey*

The O'Jays

Rhythm and blues group

The O'Jays have enjoyed over 30 years of popularity as R&B vocalists and are still going strong. Adaptability may be the key to their longevity: not just a 1960s and 1970s novelty act, they continue to incorporate contemporary sounds into their signature crooning style and to make it onto the charts. Doo-wop, soul, disco, funk, and rap influences have all found their way into the O'Jays' music. At the core of the O'Jays lineup are two of the original members, Eddie Levert and Walter Williams, who have been singing together since the late 1950s. The tradition is being carried on by Levert's sons Gerald and Sean and their hit-making R&B hip-hop group LeVert.

Several permutations before the O'Jays, Levert and Williams sang together as a gospel duo. Around 1957, McKinley High schoolmates William Powell, Bobby Massey, and Bill Isles joined them to become the Triumphs. Achieving local popularity performing in Canton, Ohio, they changed their name to the Mascots and managed to record a few singles on small labels. Scraping around for work, they did some session singing, including work for Nat King Cole and Phil Spector.

A Cleveland disc jockey, Eddie O'Jay, provided guidance and airplay; in turn, the quintet again renamed themselves, this time after O'Jay. They had tossed around the idea of calling themselves the Almosts because "we almost made it so many times," Levert told *Rolling Stone*'s Mikal Gilmore. Things began to take off, however, when they signed with Imperial in 1963 and achieved their first hit, "Lonely Drifter." This was followed by several other singles that hit the charts and the release of their debut album in 1965, *Comin' Through*.

An Important Collaboration Began

The O'Jays had released one more record, *Soul Sounds*, in 1967 on another independent label, Minit, when they met songwriters and producers Kenny Gamble and Leon Huff. By this time the group was a quartet—Isles had left the O'Jays for family reasons. It was with Gamble and Huff that the O'Jays were destined to achieve stardom, but it didn't happen right away. After some unsuccessful recordings, Gamble and Huff's Neptune label folded and the O'Jays were on their own again.

Talented but lacking any formal training, the O'Jays have often found themselves at a disadvantage. Around 1970, after the Neptune sessions, they tried to produce a record themselves without much luck. In an interview with Jay Grossman in *Rolling Stone* a few years after the experiment, Williams said of the attempt, "It was lousy!"

Original members include **Bill Isles** (born in 1940; left group, 1965); **Eddie Levert** (born June 16, 1942; children: Gerald, Sean); **Bobby Massey** (born early 1940s; left group, 1972); **William Powell** (born c. 1941; left group, 1975; died May 26, 1977); and **Walter Williams** (born August 25, 1942). Later members include **Nathaniel Best** (joined group c. 1992) and **Sammy Strain** (born December 9, 1941; joined group, 1976; left group c. 1992).

Group began as quintet the Triumphs at McKinley High School, Canton, OH, 1957; became the Mascots c. 1960; renamed the O'Jays, c. 1961; released several singles; released debut album, *Comin' Through,* Imperial, 1965; joined forces with producers Kenny Gamble and Leon Huff; recorded as a quartet on Gamble and Huff's Neptune label after Isles's departure in 1967; Massey left group in 1972 and trio reunited with Gamble and Huff on Philadelphia International label; during the 1970s, released 27 Top 100 hits and four Top Five hits; signed with EMI, 1985.

Awards: Grammy Award nominations for "Love Train," 1973, "For the Love of Money," 1974, and "Use Ta Be My Girl," 1978; American Music Award for favorite R&B group or duo, 1990.

Addresses: *Agent*—Star Direction, Inc., 9255 Sunset Blvd., Suite 610, Los Angeles, CA 90069.

In the same interview, the O'Jays reflected on their limited knowledge of musical forms and on the evolution of R&B groups. Powell pointed out that when they were starting out, all they needed to know how to do was sing. "Back then a group of us would just start off singing walkin' home from school, y'know, but now they're taking up the bass or the guitar or something, which is better," Powell remarked, adding, "I've been thinkin' about our bass player givin' me some lessons."

Had Breakthrough With "Back Stabbers"

The O'Jays didn't have long to wait, however, before they were back on track. When they did hit, it was as a trio; Bobby Massey stepped down in 1972 to form his own production company. That same year Gamble and Huff re-emerged with their new record company, the soon-to-be-legendary Philadelphia International, and the O'Jays had a smash with the million-seller "Back Stabbers," which went to the top of the R&B charts and made it to the Number Three spot on the pop charts. The album of the same name was one of the first two albums released on Philadelphia International, and the first of over a dozen that the O'Jays would make for the label.

For the next seven years the O'Jays had a gold or platinum record every year and garnered three Grammy nominations for best R&B vocal group. In 1974 and 1975, respectively, *Live in London* and *Survival* went gold, and 1975's *Family Reunion* went platinum. "Love Train" was Number One on both the pop and R&B charts in 1973; other Number One R&B hits from that period include "Give the People What They Want," "I Love Music," "Use Ta Be My Girl," and "Lovin' You."

Despite the steady stream of hit records, the O'Jays suffered some setbacks. In 1975 William Powell had to leave the group due to illness; he died of cancer two years later. He was replaced by Sammy Strain in 1976. Having been with Little Anthony and the Imperials for some time, Strain had no trouble picking up the O'Jays' music and choreography; he fit right in and stayed in until 1992, when he returned to his former group. The O'Jays continued to rack up hits throughout the decade, including the gold albums *Message in the Music* in 1976 and *Travelin' at the Speed of Thought* in 1977 and two platinum records in the next two years, *So Full of Love* and *Identify Yourself.* Yet the O'Jays were conscious of being received strictly as a black group and thus garnering neither the attention nor sales a crossover act might.

Powell complained to Tom Vickers in a 1976 group interview with *Rolling Stone,* "Why can't I get paid as much as the Rolling Stones?" Levert provided the answer to Powell's rhetorical question: "You can't go out there and try and be a white person." Williams added, "I know we're not a strong white appeal act the way, say, Richie Havens is. We toured with him and we died." Crossing over was, in fact, fairly difficult at the time. In the same article Quentin Perry, a black promoter, named the O'Jays "one of the top three black acts in terms of drawing power" but said that "no act is drawing a crossover audience." He noted that it was a two-way street: "How many blacks go to see Elton John or the Rolling Stones?"

Even within the black community that eagerly, and constantly, bought their records, the O'Jays remained fairly anonymous; few fans could name individual members. The only names that appeared on the album covers were Gamble and Huff's. It is difficult to assess how much of the O'Jays' success can be attributed to the group members and how much to their production team. The O'Jays themselves hadn't written any of their own songs since their early, pre-Gamble and Huff days and did not have any control over production. Speaking to Vickers, Levert insisted the O'Jays brought a key ingredient to the collaboration: "I don't care how good the arrangement or the song is ... if you don't have talent singing it, it won't happen." But Powell maintained, "One thing I hate is the fact that the people don't really respond to *us* but to our records."

Kept Track of Trends

By the late 1970s the O'Jays appeared to be asserting more control over their material. Not always comfortable with the social and religious message-making of Gamble and Huff's songs, they pushed for more up-beat tunes. "There was a time for all that social commentary stuff, but that time's played out now.... We felt like it was time to make happier music," Levert explained to Gilmore in 1978. Keeping abreast of changing musical tastes, the O'Jays released records during this period that reflected a shift from soul to disco. The era of the Philadelphia sound was waning by then and the next few years were relatively fallow as the O'Jays continued to turn out records and draw crowds to their live shows but were not able to score any big hits.

Yet the group stayed in touch with current trends, and their perseverance paid off in 1985 with *Love Fever,* their first record for EMI, which made it on to both the black and pop charts. While retaining the stylistic vocal strengths that made them famous, *Love Fever* was a truly contemporary record, incorporating synthesized rap and funk sounds. In 1987 the O'Jays scored another hit with *Let Me Touch You;* the single "Lovin' You" took the place of a Michael Jackson song at the top of the R&B charts.

After a little time off, the O'Jays were back in 1990 with a new orientation and a new album, *Serious.* Levert explained to *Billboard* how they made the album and how they named it: "It was a serious time in our career because it was the first time we were away from Gamble & Huff, the first time that Walter Williams and myself had a chance to do production and some of the writing, so it was a serious venture." It was a successful venture, too; the single "Have You Had Your Love Today?," with guest voice rapper Jaz, made first place on the R&B charts.

The O'Jays' 1991 release, *Emotionally Yours,* garnered more hits, critical approval, and their first American Music Award. The album features two versions of the title track, which was written by Bob Dylan—one a straightforward R&B version and the other in the gospel tradition. Another song, "Lies," features a rap by Gerald Levert, who also did some of the production on *Serious.* EMI aggressively promoted *Emotionally Yours,* and the O'Jays themselves demonstrated they were eager to get the recognition that they still felt had been lacking, even after all the hits: "It fueled us to the point of saying we're going to go in here and produce one of the greatest albums we've ever done to show people that we are real and that they shouldn't downplay us," Williams told *Billboard.*

"I don't care how good the arrangement or the song is, if you don't have talent singing it, it won't happen."
—Eddie Levert

The O'Jays have certainly proven that they are not to be underestimated. They have managed to evolve for over three decades, maintaining a keen sense of what is working in popular music at any given moment. While the O'Jays' success helped propel LeVert—the R&B group that Eddie Levert's sons formed in the mid-1980s—into the stagelight, it seems to be a mutually beneficial relationship, one which has helped the O'Jays keep current.

The O'Jays experienced one more personnel change in 1992 when Strain left to return to his original group and was replaced by Nathaniel Best. In 1993 the new line-up released *Heartbreaker,* another album that demonstrates the O'Jays' versatility and features gospel, pop, and funk tunes as well as soulful ballads. In press material accompanying the record, Eddie Levert shared the secret of the O'Jays' success: "Good lyrics and good melodies are always the key. It's only the drum and bass sounds that really change with each decade. We're keeping our natural vocal sound—just adapting to those musical changes. That way, we stay in the game."

Selected discography

Comin' Through, Imperial, 1965.
Soul Sounds, Minit, 1967.
O'Jays, Bell, 1967.
Full of Soul, 1968.
Back on Top, 1968.
Back Stabbers, Philadelphia International, 1972.
The O'Jays in Philadelphia, Philadelphia International, 1973.
Ship Ahoy, Philadelphia International, 1973.
Live in London, Philadelphia International, 1974.

Survival, Philadelphia International, 1975, reissued, 1987.

Family Reunion, Philadelphia International, 1975.

Message in the Music, Philadelphia International, 1976, reissued, 1993.

Travelin' at the Speed of Thought, Philadelphia International, 1977.

So Full of Love, Philadelphia International, 1976, reissued, 1993.

Identify Yourself, Philadelphia International, 1979.

Year 2000, Philadelphia International, 1980.

My Favorite Person, Philadelphia International, 1982.

When Will I See You Again, Philadelphia International, 1983.

Love and More, Philadelphia International, 1984.

Love Fever, EMI, 1985.

Close Company, EMI, 1985.

Let Me Touch You, EMI, 1987.

Serious, EMI, 1990.

Emotionally Yours, EMI, 1991.

Home for Christmas, EMI, 1991.

Heartbreaker, EMI, 1993.

Sources

Billboard, March 20, 1976; July 6, 1985; August 26, 1989; March 23, 1991.

Ebony, February 1993.

Essence, September 1992.

Jazz and Blues, December 1972.

Jet, November 16, 1987; August 21, 1989.

Melody Maker, January 12, 1974; February 27, 1988.

Rolling Stone, August 1, 1974; January 15, 1976; September 21, 1978; August 22, 1991.

Soul, July 22, 1974.

St. Louis Post-Dispatch, July 17, 1993.

Village Voice, February 18, 1980.

Washington Post, September 10, 1993.

Additional information for this profile was obtained from EMI Records press materials, 1994.

—Gina Hausknecht

Pantera

Heavy metal band

In the 1980s, four heavy metal cowboys from Texas got together to form a band, creating their niche in the music world as Pantera, the Spanish name for "panther." Singer Philip Anselmo, guitarist Diamond "Dimebag" Darrell, bassist Rex, and drummer Vinnie Paul started out as a cover band in the bars in Texas, playing hits by Motley Crue and Bon Jovi, and went on to become one of the heaviest metal groups of the 1990s.

Brothers Paul and Darrell Abbott developed their interests in music while growing up in Pantego, Texas, where their father owned a recording studio. The boys were encouraged to experiment with the recording equipment and with music in general, which would eventually lead to Paul's influence as Pantera's co-producer. As Darrell recalled in *Guitar World:* "I can remember one birthday of mine where [Dad] said, 'Son, you can either have a BMX bike or you can have this,' and he pointed to a guitar. I ended up taking the bike, but he did plant a seed in my mind."

That seed blossomed into the sound bandmembers categorize as "power groove"; *Village Voice* reviewer Daina Darzin described Pantera as "an angry, cantankerous, ferally aggressive band that channels all the free-floating rage of their environment into a murderous, metallic growl."

Texas Cowboys Begin Their Assault

Pantera released four independent albums before signing with a major label. In 1990, ATCO (now EastWest) released the group's *Cowboys From Hell* LP onto the streets with such vigorous force that it soared to gold status. Featuring metal radio hits like "Cowboys From Hell" and "Cemetery Gates," *Cowboys From Hell* gained most of its exposure from Pantera's live performances. The band kicked off its club tour in April of 1990, and from there moved on to supporting slots on other major metal tours.

"We just tour and tour," Anselmo told *Billboard*. "Our lives are on the bus, in the venue, and on the stage. It's with the kids you get to know along the way. That's what our lives are all about. Every night we play is Saturday night to those kids, and you've got to give it every drop you've got inside."

Pantera played the Monsters of Rock festival tour, where they opened for AC/DC, Metallica and the Black Crowes. Lasting throughout the summer, the 18-date tour reached 1.2 million fans throughout Western and Eastern Europe. And on September 28, 1991, the tour stopped at the Tushino Air Field in Moscow. "We were

Photograph by Michael Miller, courtesy of EastWest Records America

For the Record . . .

Members include **Philip Anselmo**, vocals; **Diamond "Dimebag" Darrell** (born Darrell Abbott), guitar; **Vinnie Paul** (born Vincent Abbott), drums; and **Rex**, bass guitar.

Band formed in Pantego, TX, in the mid-1980s; played cover songs in area nightclubs; self-released four independent albums; signed with ATCO (now EastWest) and released first major-label LP, *Cowboys From Hell,* 1990; released video *Vulgar Video,* 1991.

Awards: Platinum record for *Vulgar Display of Power,* 1990.

Addresses: *Record company*—EastWest Records, 75 Rockefeller Plaza, New York, NY 10019.

the smallest band on the bill," Anselmo told *Metal Edge* about the band's early achievements, "so our personal success could definitely be topped. We're always looking for a little bit more."

Pantera's Success Gains Speed

Pantera got their wish for "a little bit more" when they released their second LP, *Vulgar Display of Power,* in 1992. It reached Number 44 on the *Billboard* charts and sold more than a million copies. The cover of the album, which contained the band's hit singles "Mouth For War" and "This Love," fittingly depicted a fist smashing a face. "'This Love' alternates terrifying lyrics about a kidnapping/rape case with wrecking-ball drumming and an elegiac, poignant twine of melody that points to an infallible songwriting talent," a reviewer noted in *Village Voice.*

Once again, Pantera earned the respect, dedication, and admiration of heavy metal fans across the world with their live shows. They played 285 concerts in 17 months to support *Vulgar Display of Power.* Through their tours, the group established a public image with fans that combined honesty and angst. In celebration of their *Vulgar Display of Power* tour, Pantera released a home movie about their life on the road. Appropriately titled *Vulgar Video,* it featured live footage, candid travel and backstage footage with the band and crew, plus several fan encounters, including one confrontation with Christian fundamentalists in the band's hotel room.

Harry Palmer, president of EastWest, described Pantera's concert appeal to Elianne Halbersberg in *Billboard:* "There is such a passion, a dialogue, between the band and audience. From a musical and lyrical communication viewpoint, they are the real deal. There is credibility; they are totally believable.... With Pantera, it comes totally from the heart."

After recording their first two albums at the Abbott's studio in Pantego, Texas, Pantera moved on to the new recording studio Paul and Darrell's father opened in Nashville, Tennessee, for their third release. Away from their families and friends, with the exception of a two-week interruption to perform in South America, the band put all of their time and effort into *Far Beyond Driven.* As with their other albums, their first Nashville effort was produced by Paul and longtime co-producer Terry Date. Though the band at first considered letting Paul produce the album completely, they had worked so well with Date in the past that they wanted him back at the helm of their latest effort.

Driven to the Top of the Charts

At midnight on March 22, 1994, Pantera launched the release of their third LP with an extensive record store campaign. They travelled to 12 cities in almost five days with MTV documenting their progress. Bandmembers signed autographs, met fans, and promoted *Far Beyond Driven* harder than ever. The band released "I'm Broken" as the album's first single; the LP also contained the first cover song on one of their major-label releases—Black Sabbath's "Planet Caravan." Pantera's hard work paid off; by March the LP had sold over 185,000 copies and had reached Number One on the *Billboard* album charts.

The success of *Far Beyond Driven* didn't come from any musical coercion from EastWest. According to Steve Kleinberg, vice-president of marketing for the record company, EastWest has never attempted to direct Pantera's musical direction. "Given their track record, it would be completely inappropriate for us to try and tell Pantera what to do," Kleinberg told Larry Flick in *Billboard.* "You've got to trust them to know what their fans want. The fact is that they have tremendous credibility and integrity out there. We don't want to get in the way of that.... Their direction is to get musically heavier as time goes on, and they want to be there with the kids who buy their records." As long as heavy metal fans want Pantera around, the band insists they will not let them down. They play the kind of music they would expect from their own favorite band, and release their aggression, honesty, and angst in the hopes that someone will listen.

Selected discography

Cowboys From Hell, ATCO, 1990.
Vulgar Display of Power, ATCO/EastWest, 1992.
Far Beyond Driven, EastWest, 1994.

Sources

BAM, March 25, 1994.
Billboard, October 5, 1991; April 18, 1992; June 20, 1992; February, 12, 1994.
Detroit Free Press, April 15, 1994.
Entertainment Weekly, April 22, 1994.
Guitar Player, May 1994.

Hit Parader, June 1994.
Los Angeles Times, November 18, 1992.
Melody Maker, April 2, 1994.
Metal Edge, June 1994.
Pulse!, May 1994.
RadioActive Magazine, July 23-August 5, 1992.
Request, May 1994.
RIP, July 1994.
Spin, April 1994.
Village Voice, April 28, 1992.

Additional information for this profile was obtained from EastWest Records press material, 1994.

—*Sonya Shelton*

Phish

Rock band

Photograph by Michael Llewellyn, courtesy of Elektra Entertainment

Phish was founded on October 30, 1983, when four college students in Vermont got together to play a distinctive fusion of rock, jazz, funk, bluegrass, boogie, and even vacuum cleaner noises. Although Phish played to a lone fan in a local bar at their first public appearance, within 10 years their popularity and their quirky style mushroomed—independent of media hype—in an unusually obsessive, oddball manner; Phish's longstanding devotees have jealously monitored the band's burgeoning popularity and even begrudge them their new fans. In 1993, a decade after their formation, Phish sold 300,000 concert tickets—even though the band had not sold 300,000 copies of any of their first four albums.

Phish is comprised of bassist Mike Gordon, keyboard player Page McConnell, drummer Jon Fishman—the source of the band's name—and guitarist Trey Anastasio, who is also chief songwriter and lead singer. The band was spawned after Anastasio, with an itch to form a band, distributed some simple flyers on the Burlington campus of the University of Vermont. Gordon, Fishman, and another guitar player responded, and the fledgling group began performing to small crowds at gigs on and around campus. Shortly thereafter, Page McConnell, a student at Goddard College, replaced the original guitarist and introduced keyboards to the band. Anastasio and Fishman soon transferred to Goddard, but Gordon remained at the University of Vermont to study filmmaking. Within ten years, Phish would be earning more than $5 million annually in concert ticket sales.

Since the beginning, Phish's key to success has been the formation of a "secret" band apart from traditional media—one that relies upon word-of-mouth advertising from fans, memorable music, unusual concert antics, and "insider" jokes among fans that can only be appreciated by regularly attending their shows. For example, bandmembers provide certain silent cues for the audience that mean "turn around" or "fall to the floor"; a person who has never seen Phish perform live could conceivably attend a concert and be perplexed when most of the audience drops to the floor or turns to face the other way. This "insider knowledge" is part of the Phish act that longstanding fans seek to preserve.

The History of the Vacuum Cleaner

Since Phish's sound and style are difficult to peg, they have been compared to both the Grateful Dead and the late Frank Zappa, two acts that have faced similar dilemmas. Though not entirely unwarranted, these comparisons rankle many of Phish's most ardent fans, who feel the band is unique. As with followers of the Grateful Dead, Phish's fans willingly travel across the country to see them perform, and many even follow their tour from city to city. In addition, Phish bandmembers incorporate unusual sounds into their music—such as the swoosh of a vacuum cleaner—which is considered reminiscent of Zappa.

But the true inspiration for the band's use of the vacuum cleaner as a musical instrument was drummer Jon Fishman's mother. Putting a new spin on an age-old form of punishment, she once felt compelled to vacuum the profanities right out of her upstart son's mouth. She "sucked all those f-words right down her Hoover," according to *Musician* magazine. "I used to bring up the vacuum cleaner to make her feel guilty," Fishman joked in the same article, "but now she just asks, 'Aren't you glad I did it?'... The first few times you do it, you're going to cut your mouth, so just resign yourself to it. Your cheek will get caught and it will be a nightmare. Bleeding all over the place.... [But] it's the king of flatulence sounds."

Although Phish enthusiasts form an enormous musical tribe at concerts and typically dance for hours, their support extends beyond the realm of live performances: in the 1990s era of computer cyberspace, fans created the Phishnet file on the Internet, which boasted over 40,000 subscribers in the summer of 1994. A Phish hotline was also created for fans who want to know the band's touring itinerary, and the *Phish Update Newsletter,* with a circulation of 50,000, is published regularly in Massachusetts.

A glimpse into the Phishnet file reveals the nature of Phish fans and the struggle between old and new devotees as Phish's popularity continues to grow throughout the 1990s. Esoteric debates as to the significance of particular Phish lyrics or items of clothing are heated and rampant; old fans scorn the "uneducated" newer ones; the pros and cons of drug use at Phish concerts are debated; rides to concerts are offered and requested; copies of live Phish performances are put on the selling block; the merits of general versus reserved tickets are discussed; and fans, for the most part, lament Phish's rising popularity as a threatening prospect.

That Phish Feeling

The mutual admiration society among Phish fans has created a camaraderie and a secret club atmosphere at live shows, which is one reason the fans feel too much media exposure will ruin their fun. With an emphasis on live performances instead of televised videos, Phish has been able to retain their ardent fan base. Phish concerts are also marked by whimsy; often a bandmember will jump on a trampoline while playing, or float a large, helium "earth" ball over the audience; the pitch and tone of the music will then mirror the ball's journey.

"I think a lot of [our popularity] has to do with the feeling at the shows," guitarist Anastasio told *Newsweek* writer Kendall Hamilton. Drummer Fishman added that their live concerts create "that communal spirit." Each step Phish has taken toward greater popularity is accompanied by assurance to longstanding fans that this "communal spirit" will not be compromised— starting with their move from a small bar in Burlington to a larger bar in the same city. But when vocalist Alison Krauss joined Phish on their 1994 record *Hoist,* some original fans were irked—as evidenced on the Phishnet—simply because a guest vocalist was a departure for the band.

After playing in clubs and small theaters for five years, Phish released their first album, *Junta,* in 1988. They signed with the Elektra label in 1992, and the albums *Lawn Boy* and *A Picture of Nectar* soon followed. In 1993 Phish recorded *Rift,* their first record with an outside producer, Barry Beckett; Beckett has also worked with Etta James and Aretha Franklin, and his ear for a soulful tone is evident on *Rift*. The next year, the band released *Hoist,* produced by Paul Fox, who is noted for his work with Robyn Hitchcock and XTC.

Fans Begged, "Say No to Video"

Since the early 1990s, fans have been wondering if Phish would "sell out" and make a video for MTV; many hoped they would remain a safely guarded secret. In the spring 1994 edition of the *Phish Update Newsletter,* a longtime fan wrote: "Is it true that you're coming out with a video? Please don't! Do you know how trendy that will make you? It's great for you, but it sucks for us.... You are so important to me that I feel protective over you."

Phish finally did put out a music video in the spring of 1994 after debating the move for three years. The video may suggest a shift in the band's aspirations, in spite of the fact that Anastasio once told *People* magazine contributor Peter Castro: "What worried us about doing a video was the thought of 'What if we suddenly have this big success?' But we're already successful.... Not everyone needs MTV." One Phish fan, a Brown student, told Hamilton, "Phish couldn't play an empty hall. There needs to be feedback between the crowd and the band."

In spite of their ballooning popularity, the members of Phish remain dedicated to their original personal philosophy. "It all comes down to that instinct for free-dom," Gordon commented in *Musician*. "Those moments of rock 'n' roll, of improvisation at its most intense, celebrate freedom." And as Fishman explained to Castro: "I always believed that if you pursue what you love, all the material things will fall into place. When we start thinking ... 'How do we make this album *big?*' instead of 'How do we make it *good?*,' that's when our decline will begin. I hope that never happens."

Selected discography

Junta, self-released, 1988, reissued, Elektra, 1992.
Lawn Boy, Absolute A Go Go, 1990, reissued, Elektra, 1992.
A Picture of Nectar, Elektra, 1992.
Rift, Elektra, 1993.
Hoist, Elektra, 1994.

Sources

Boston Phoenix, April 8, 1994.
Guitar Player, August 1993, June 1994; September 1994.
Musician, September 1994.
Newsweek, May 2, 1994.
People, June 6, 1994.
Phish Update Newsletter (Lexington, MA), April/May 1994; June/July 1994.

Additional information for this profile was obtained from the Phishnet on-line computer service.

—B. Kimberly Taylor

The Proclaimers

Rock duo

In the spring of 1993, twins Charlie and Craig Reid, also known as the Proclaimers, received a major boost to their musical careers. Actress Mary Stuart Masterson was starring in the motion picture *Benny & Joon,* and the film's director asked her to bring some of her favorite music to the set. Some scenes required her character to paint wild, colorful canvases, and she needed some musical inspiration. When she pulled out her copy of the Proclaimers' *Sunshine on Leith* and played the joyful love song "I'm Gonna Be (500 Miles)," the director knew he had the perfect opening song for the offbeat love story. Soon after *Benny & Joon*'s release, the Proclaimers suddenly had a huge hit in the United States—with a song that was five years old.

Although it took mainstream America years to discover the Proclaimers, American critics had long been fans and the Reids had a huge following around the world, built on what a *Guardian* contributor dubbed their "unique brand of tuneful, old-fashioned pop." They sing with tight harmonies and thick but melodic Scottish accents, and their output sounds like a sampler of

Photograph by Fin Costello, © 1994 ERG

the last several decades of popular music. Jim Sullivan of the *Boston Globe* identified "Scottish-made melodic folk, heartfelt soul, American country, light punk, pop and rock—most all of it imbued with an exuberant, uplifting zeal."

While some critics likened the Proclaimers to early rockers—the Everly Brothers and Buddy Holly—others emphasized their contemporary edge. Sullivan compared them to alternative rocker Elvis Costello, affirming that they share "more than a bit of his songwriting craft, the knack for weaving serious, trenchant lyrics into soothing, gently stinging, songs." They write about adult topics—family, relationships, politics, and spirituality—and as Steve Hochman observed in *Rolling Stone,* "While most of their contemporaries search for the meaning of life, the Reids ... revel in its various manifestations."

"Speccy Eight Eyes"

The comparisons to Costello and Holly are engendered not only by the twins' music but by their striking appearance. Both are over six-feet tall, lanky, and, as writers like to point out, a bit nerdy. In fact, according to the *Guardian,* the British press took to calling them "swotty geeks" and "speccy eight eyes." But when they start playing, the stereotypes and innocence melt away; they sing, in the words of *Rolling Stone's* Peter Galvin, "some of the most muscular folk music you're likely to hear."

The Reids pay little attention to "nerdy" cracks and make it clear that they're hardly naive, remembering the slings and arrows of struggling in the music business. "You've got to remember that we were grown men before we became professional," Charlie reminded *Guardian* writer David Bowker, and as Craig added, "You can't struggle for seven years if you're weak and vulnerable."

The Reids' career began in the small Scottish town of Auchtermuchty in Fife, where they were born in 1962. Their mother was a nurse and their father was a joiner, but more importantly, the Reids' parents loved music. Their father had a large collection of jazz, blues, soul, and country and western, and most of it was American— Merle Haggard, Jerry Lee Lewis, Hank Williams, Ray Charles, Fats Domino, Eddie Cochran, James Brown.

Punk Beginnings

In spite of their penchant for American soul and country and western, the Reid brothers' first foray into music was fronting a punk band in high school. Punk was popular at the time, and in their town it wasn't hip for a teenager to admit to a taste for country and western. "It was quite destructive, in a way," Charlie recalled in the *Chicago Tribune,* "because it 'hijacked' all our ideas for about three years. We wouldn't play anything other than new wave music."

By 1983 the new wave had passed and the Reids formed a duo, calling themselves the Proclaimers. Craig explained the choice in a Chrysalis press bio: "We always wanted a strong name. We wanted something with a gospel feel to it that indicated strength in the vocal delivery, a sort of spiritual element." For three years they played pubs in Edinburgh and Inverness, building a strong following. During that time they gave up their quest for a music career twice, but discovered, as Charlie admitted to Bowker, "we have no other talents whatsoever."

Determined to stay in the business, they wrote to Kevin Rowland of the Scottish pop group Dexy's Midnight Runners. Rowland became a good friend, giving them advice, financial assistance, and help producing a demo. An Inverness fan sent their demo to the British band the Housemartins, who were impressed enough to invite the Proclaimers on their 1986 United Kingdom tour. The exposure of the tour won them another key invitation, this time from British television. In January of 1987, they performed on the BBC show *The Tube*. Two weeks later, they found themselves playing a set for interested Chrysalis Records executives, and they signed a Chrysalis recording contract on March 2. The brothers were in the recording studio the next day and within nine days had finished *This Is the Story*. Six weeks later it hit the record stores.

Scottish Nationalists

This Is the Story is entirely acoustic. Some critics liked this "lean and lively," sound, as Leslie Berman termed it in *High Fidelity*. Others admired the debut album but found the acoustic sound too spare for their tastes: in words of *High Fidelity* contributor Billy Altman, it was "a wee too folky tame." The album's songs were split between songs of family and love, and songs of a more political nature, reflecting the Reids' dedication to Scottish nationalism. "We believe that Scotland would have a lot better standard of living and a lot better society if it would govern itself," Craig insisted in a *Rolling Stone* interview with Shelia Rogers.

The Proclaimers explored this conviction in such cuts as "Throw the 'R' Away," a defense against those who sneer at the distinctive Scottish accent, and "Letter from America," which laments the continued Scottish emigration to the States. British listeners liked the mix of songs on *This Is the Story*, and in eight months it went gold. In November of 1987 a non-acoustic re-recording of "Letter from America" hit Number Three on the singles chart. Throughout the next year, the Reids toured Britain and Europe and generated some interest in the United States.

The Proclaimers' next album, 1988's *Sunshine on Leith*, had an even bigger impact. This time, Charlie and Craig decided to add a band to their duo, in order "to make a fuller sound for what we do," they told Claudia Perry in the *Houston Post*. The band included Dave Mattacks on drums and Jerry Donahue on guitar, both of the seminal folk rock group Fairport Convention, as well as fiddler Steve Shaw of Dexy's Midnight Runners.

Many critics judged the fuller sound on *Sunshine on Leith* a great improvement, and their response to the album was distinctly positive. Altman applauded its "refreshingly joyous music," and in *Rolling Stone*, Hochman declared it "a wonderfully guileless treasure of an album." Again the Proclaimers joined political music with songs about family and love, balancing such cuts as the effusive "I'm Gonna Be (500 Miles)" and "Oh Jean," with the powerfully nationalistic "Cap

in Hand" and "What Do You Do." Playing off the album's title, Ken Capobianco of the *Boston Globe* called this music "potent, Leithal stuff."

"You can't struggle for seven years if you're weak and vulnerable."
—Craig Reid

Again, the Proclaimers followed the album's release with an extensive tour. The touring paid off: *Sunshine on Leith* sold well in Europe, went platinum in the United Kingdom, Canada, and New Zeland, and made it to triple platinum in Australia. "I'm Gonna Be (500 Miles)" was a hit around the world and spent five weeks at the top spot of Australia's singles chart. In the United States, the album had some success on the college charts, but with the exception of some positive reviews in the press, the Proclaimers did not get much attention.

Five-Year Hiatus

After this spurt of activity in the late 1980s, the Proclaimers hit a dry spell and went five years without producing an album. For a time, other parts of their life took precedence—Charlie's marriage broke up and Craig and his wife had a baby girl. Charlie also had trouble with writer's block. "It's not that we'd been sitting doing nothing," Craig emphasized in their Chrysalis press bio in 1994. "We could have had an album out two or three years ago, but it would have been mediocre. Mediocre or bad. And there's no point in doing that."

By the time *Benny & Joon* sent them up the American charts, the Proclaimers hadn't performed in years. After the film came out, "I'm Gonna Be (500 Miles)" spent 28 weeks on the *Billboard* Hot 100, rose to Number Three, and sold almost a million copies. *Sunshine on Leith* sold almost half a million copies, and the Reids returned to the States and toured in 1993.

By this time, the Proclaimers had produced new material, and their smashing success in America gave them the impetus to go ahead with it. They recorded *Hit the Highway* in the fall of 1993 and released it the following spring. Some critics noted that the 1994 effort lacks the political edge of the brothers' earlier work. "There's been really nothing to inspire me in the last four or five years, and that's a terrible thing," Craig acknowledged in the *Boston Globe* interview with Sullivan. "I think our cynicism about government has probably turned not even to despair—just probably resignation."

Taking up the slack were more spiritual songs, including the all-out gospel "I Want to Be a Christian," and "The More I Believe." However, the Reids proved as questioning in religion as they are in politics, penning "The Light," an attack on evangelical organized religion: "But I can't put my faith in / Your words and demands / I believe in God alright / It's folk like you I just can't stand."

Critics enjoyed the album, particularly its harmonies and passion. While *Rolling Stone* contributor Peter Galvin criticized the brothers' occasional vehemence, he found their spirit "infectious," and Scott Schinder, writing in *Pulse!,* delighted that their music "still embodies a proudly untrendy balance of sincerity and playfulness, embracing tradition while effortlessly transcending it."

The Reids probably received their greatest compliment from David Okamoto in *CD Review.* Noting the album's mixture of "vintage Memphis soul," "gospel balladry," "'50s doo-wop," and "percolating New Orleans funk," he concluded: "Even more impressive [than their spirit] is the Proclaimers' expanding grasp of American music." After years of loving and learning American music—and going for so long without an American hit—this estimation must have made the Proclaimers, as they sing in "Don't Turn Out Like Your Mother," "as happy as hell."

Selected discography

This Is the Story (includes "Letter from America" and "Throw the 'R' Away"), Chrysalis/ERG, 1987.

Sunshine on Leith (includes "Cap in Hand," "I'm Gonna Be [500 Miles]," "Oh Jean," and "What Do You Do"), Chrysalis/ERG, 1988.

Hit the Highway (includes "Don't Turn Out Like Your Mother," "I Want to Be a Christian," "The Light," and "The More I Believe"), Chrysalis/ERG, 1994.

Sources

Atlanta Journal-Constitution, May 14, 1989; April 9, 1994.
Boston Globe, March 3, 1989; May 25, 1989.
CD Review, May 1994.
Chicago Tribune, March 9, 1989.
Entertainment Weekly, May 7, 1993.
Guardian, January 18, 1989.
High Fidelity, March 1988; June 1989.
Houston Post, May 16, 1989.
Los Angeles Times, February 12, 1989; April 24, 1994.
Minneapolis Skyway News, July 12, 1994.
New York Times, February 26, 1989.
People, March 27, 1989.
Pulse!, May 1994.
Rolling Stone, April 20, 1989; May 4, 1989; June 30, 1994.
St. Paul Pioneer Press, July 16, 1994 (as reprinted from the *Boston Globe*).
Stereo Review, June 1989.
Twin Cities Reader (Minneapolis/St. Paul), July 13, 1994.

Additional information for this profile was obtained from Chrysalis/ERG publicity materials and staff, and the liner notes to *This Is the Story, Sunshine on Leith,* and *Hit the Highway.*

—*Megan Rubiner Zinn*

Della Reese

Singer, actress, minister

AP / Wide World Photos

Gospel, pop, and blues singer, actress, and talk show host Della Reese admits that her first love is singing. She is well known for her clear, powerful voice, distinctive diction, and emotional delivery. Yet television and movie performances have rounded out her varied career in the entertainment business and proven her to be a talented comedic and dramatic actress. The youngest in a family of six children, she grew up in Detroit, Michigan, where the Baptist church and gospel singing greatly influenced her career. At age six, Deloreese Patricia Early was singing in the church's junior choir.

For the next seven years Deloreese continued her gospel singing in the church. By the time she was 13, the singer had developed such vocal power and talent that she caught the attention of the legendary Mahalia Jackson. Known as the "Queen of Gospel Music," Jackson recruited Deloreese for her Mahalia Jackson Troupe gospel singers. "This opportunity to sing with the world's foremost gospel singer was a thrilling experience," Reese noted in a 1992 press release. "I will never forget the wonderful association which lasted for five consecutive summers, and the lasting things I learned from her ... how to communicate with people through song." The teenaged Reese toured with the gospel group from 1945 through 1949.

Although Reese studied psychology at Wayne State University in Detroit, singing remained very important to her. She formed a women's gospel group called the Meditation Singers during her first year at Wayne State. By the end of that year, Reese's mother had died and her father had become ill. Reese ended her college education to help support her family, working variously as a receptionist and switchboard operator, barber, taxicab driver, and even as a truck driver.

During this time Reese continued to perform with the Meditation Singers. She also had the occasional opportunity to perform with the Clara Ward Singers, the Roberta Martin Singers, and Beatrice Brown's Inspirational Singers. Reese did not consider singing as a career, however. In a December 1957 interview with Don Nelsen for the *New York Sunday News,* she said, "I was interested in singing, but I thought of it as something to do when you didn't have anything else to do."

Launched Performing Career

Since gospel singers made very little money, Reese thought a career in business would be the best way for her to earn a living. Nevertheless, she toyed with the

For the Record . . .

Born Deloreese Patricia Early, July 6, 1931, in Detroit, MI; daughter of Richard (a factory worker) and Nellie (a domestic) Early; married Vermont Adolphus Bon Taliaferro (a factory worker; divorced); married Leroy Basil Gray (an accountant; divorced); married Mercer Ellington, 1961 (annulled 1961); married Franklin Thomas Lett, Jr. (a concert and television producer and businessman), 1978; children: Deloreese Daniels ("Dumpsey"; adopted 1961), James Barger (adopted 1965); stepchildren: Franklin Lett III, Dominique Lett. *Education:* Attended Wayne State University, 1949-50.

Sang with the Mahalia Jackson Troupe, summers, 1945-49; formed gospel group the Meditation Singers, 1949; worked as a receptionist, taxi driver, barber, and truck driver; sang with Clara Ward Singers, Roberta Martin Singers, Beatrice Brown's Inspirational Singers, and the Erskine Hawkins Orchestra; signed with Jubilee Records, 1954; signed with RCA, 1959; performed in nightclubs across the U.S.; made over 300 television guest appearances on popular talk and entertainment shows; guest host of *The Tonight Show;* host of her own variety show, *Della,* 1969-70; guest star in numerous television shows, including *The Mod Squad, Chico and the Man, Designing Women, L.A. Law,* and *Picket Fences;* costar of television situation comedy *The Royal Family,* CBS, 1991-92; actress in films, including *Let's Rock, The Distinguished Gentleman,* and *Harlem Nights;* toured in revue *Some of My Best Friends Are the Blues,* beginning in 1992. Ordained minister, Universal Foundation for Better Living.

Awards: Named Most Promising Girl Singer of 1957; Emmy nomination for best supporting actress, 1977; Grammy nomination for best female soloist—gospel, 1987; approved for star on Hollywood Walk of Fame; numerous gold records.

Addresses: *Agent*—Lett Entertainment, 1910 Bel Air Rd., Los Angeles, CA 90077.

idea of making music her profession. She knew that making a career as a singer would mean performing popular music in nightclubs; this caused her some distress, since the extravagance and excesses she associated with club life clashed with her religious beliefs. Yet when the Reverend E. A. Rundless of Detroit's New Liberty Baptist Church encouraged Reese to pursue a singing career, she put her reservations aside. A short time after Reese became a hostess-singer at a local bowling alley/nightclub, she won a contest in which newspaper readers voted for their favorite local singer. The prize was a week-long engagement at Detroit's famous Flame Showbar.

At the time, Reese was married to Detroit factory worker Vermont Adolphus Bon Taliaferro. Because she could not fit her name on the nightclub marquee, she decided to shorten it to Pat Ferro. By the time her engagement at the Flame Showbar ended 18 weeks later, she had changed her name again. Dividing her first name into Della Reese, she created her professional name, one that would become synonymous with blues, jazz, and gospel music.

During her run at the Flame Showbar, Reese caught the attention of New York agent Lee Magid, who agreed to represent her. In 1953 Reese moved to New York to sing with the Erskine Hawkins Orchestra. In the nine months she was with the orchestra, she further developed her vocal talents and style of delivery, alternating between blues, jump tunes, and Latin music.

In 1954 Reese signed a contract with Jubilee Records. Her first releases included *I've Got My Love to Keep Me Warm, Time After Time,* and *In the Still of the Night,* which sold 500,000 copies. Reese's first big hit, *And That Reminds Me,* sold over a million copies in 1957. She was soon voted "The Most Promising Girl Singer" of the year by *Billboard, Cashbox,* and *Variety* magazines, along with the Disc Jockeys of America and the Jukebox Operators Association.

Broke Into Television

With her recording success in full swing, Reese was in demand for national television appearances. She entertained viewers of the *Perry Como, Jackie Gleason, Joey Bishop,* and *Ed Sullivan* shows during the late 1950s and early 1960s. Appearances on the *Mike Douglas, Merv Griffin, Pat Boone,* and *Hollywood Palace* shows followed, as did radio performances. She toured the nightclub circuit and even landed a singing role in the 1958 Columbia film *Let's Rock.*

In 1959 Della Reese recorded her biggest hit, "Don't You Know?," for RCA Victor. The success of this single, which was adapted from Italian composer Giacomo Puccini's opera *La Bohème,* led to nine years of performing in Las Vegas and more than three decades of recording successes for a variety of labels, including ABC-Paramount and AVCO-Embassy.

Reese became the first woman to stand in for Johnny

Carson when she guest-hosted *The Tonight Show*. In 1969 she made history again, becoming the first black woman to host her own television program, a variety show titled *Della,* which was nationally syndicated by RKO in 1969 and 1970.

When Reese's television contract was not renewed, she resumed her nightclub performing. During her long career, she has entertained in many of the country's top clubs, including such famous night spots as the Cocoanut Grove in Hollywood, the Fontainebleau Hotel in Miami Beach, Los Angeles's Greek Theatre, and the Apollo Theatre and Copacabana, both in New York City. Reese has also toured internationally, performing at venues in Europe, Japan, and South America.

On October 3, 1980, at the age of 48, Reese was taping a segment for *The Tonight Show* when something went terribly wrong. " I hit a horrendous note—the flattest I've ever sung.... My left knee buckled and I fell to the floor," she related in *People* magazine. An aneurysm, or weakened spot on an artery, had broken in her brain. On the brink of death for several days, Reese faced the reality that she might never make a full recovery. But her faith in God and the talents of a Canadian neurosurgeon pulled her through.

Reese's strong religious convictions—evident in the inclusion of spirituals in virtually all of her nightclub performances—prompted her to pursue ordination in the Universal Foundation for Better Living, an organization of 22 churches worldwide. Reese considers this step "a glorious development" in her spiritual life and maintains that without religion, her success in the fields of music and acting would not have been possible.

Expanded Acting Career

Since her television acting debut in 1968 as a disco owner on *The Mod Squad,* Reese has continued appearing on the small screen, singing on many shows, including *The Love Boat, The Great American Gospel Show,* and the *Grand Ole Opry.* Her acting talent is evident in the widely varied guest-starring roles she has landed over the years on such series as *Sanford and Son, Police Story, Chico and the Man, The "A" Team, MacGyver, Night Court, Crazy Like a Fox, Young Riders, Designing Women, L.A. Law,* and *Picket Fences,* in which she played a saucy but ailing blues legend who requires radical, experimental surgery. She even picked up an Emmy nomination for her appearance in *Nightmare in Badham County.* In an interview with *Entertainment Tonight,* Reese lamented the dearth of good "meaty parts for women, especially black women over 60."

Reese credits her success as an actress to her experience as a live singer and nightclub performer. "If you can make people believe your songs of blues and sadness, when you don't feel that way ... well, that takes acting ability I always knew I had," she was quoted as saying in a Lett Entertainment press release. Reese has also appeared on the big screen in *Harlem Nights,* which features a memorable fight scene with Eddie Murphy, and *The Distinguished Gentleman,* another Eddie Murphy production. And during the 1991-92 television season, she costarred in the CBS-TV hit *The Royal Family.* Although the death in 1991 of Redd Foxx—Reese's television husband in the series—cast doubt on the fate of the show, the plot was reworked and the situation comedy continued for the rest of the season.

> *"I was interested in singing, but I thought of it as something to do when you didn't have anything else to do."*

Aside from her fame as an actress, Della Reese continues her first love—singing. Between tapings of television shows she performs in concert halls, in nightclubs, and at music festivals. In 1992 she starred in a new nightclub show created by her husband, Franklin Lett. *Some of My Best Friends Are the Blues* opened at the Cinegrill in Hollywood to rave reviews. Don Heckman commented in the *Los Angeles Times,* "Reese genuinely appeared to be enjoying every minute. Reaching out, pulling her audience into the music, asking them to share both the pleasure and the passion of her experience, she was an irresistible spokeswoman for the joys and tears of the blues."

Selected discography

I've Got My Love to Keep Me Warm, Jubilee, c. 1955.
Time After Time, Jubilee, c. 1955.
In the Still of the Night, Jubilee, c. 1956.
One More Time, ABC-Paramount, 1956.
And That Reminds Me, Jubilee, 1957.
A Date with Della—at Mr. Kelly's, Jubilee, 1958.
Della by Starlight, RCA Victor, 1960.
Della, Della, Cha Cha Cha, RCA Victor, 1960.
I Like It Like Dat, ABC-Paramount, c. 1960.
Special Delivery, Della Reese, RCA Victor, 1961.
Della on Stage, RCA Victor, 1962.
The Classic Della, RCA Victor, 1962.
Waltz With Me, Della, RCA Victor, 1963.

Three Great Girls, RCA Victor, 1963.

Della Reese at Basin Street East, RCA Victor, 1964.

C'mon and Hear, ABC-Paramount, 1965, reissued, Pickwick, 1978.

Moody, Della Reese, RCA Victor, 1965.

On Strings of Blue, ABC-Paramount, 1967.

The Best of Della Reese, RCA Victor, 1972.

Let Me in Your Life, Lee Magid, 1972.

Della Reese, ABC-Paramount, 1976.

One of a Kind, Jazz a la Carte, 1978.

Hush, Somebody's Callin' My Name, CUT, 1979.

Sure Like Lovin' You, Della Reese (Applause), 1983.

Della Reese and Brilliance, AIR Co., 1987.

Black Is Beautiful, AVCO-Embassy.

What Do You Know About Love?, Jubilee.

Amen, Jubilee.

The Story of the Blues, Jubilee.

Sources

Black Elegance, July 1992.

Ebony, May 1989.

Jet, December 9, 1991; July 5, 1993.

Los Angeles Times, July 16, 1992.

Melody Maker, August 29, 1987.

New York Sunday News, December 29, 1957.

People, May 19, 1980.

Variety, November 18, 1981; May 7, 1986.

Village Voice, March 16, 1982.

Additional information for this profile was obtained from a Lett Entertainment press release, 1992, and an interview featured on *Entertainment Tonight,* ABC-TV, April 29, 1993.

—Sandy J. Stiefer and Jeanne M. Lesinski

Trent Reznor

Singer, keyboardist, record company executive

When he was 23 years old, Trent Reznor formed the electronic, machine-driven, industrial music project that would launch his career to superstardom. Nine Inch Nails, the name Reznor attached to his creative endeavor, would also completely change his life in a matter of a few short years. "It's a convenient fiction for me to work under," Reznor told *Musician* when asked why he decided against incorporating his own name with that of the band. Nine Inch Nails—Reznor's "convenient fiction"—would become musical fact by 1989 when it launched the previously underground industrial music genre into mainstream popularity.

Reznor grew up in Mercer, Pennsylvania, where he was raised by his grandparents after his parents divorced. His grandparents forced him to take piano lessons as a child. "I'd get into trouble because the way I played pieces was not the strict way you were meant to play them," Reznor told *RIP*. "I'd add inflections to it, play around with it, and you weren't meant to do that.... I realized that it was a really expressive instrument. There came that moment when I realized how I felt through a musical instrument; I was around 12 or 13 when it struck me."

As a teenager, Reznor joined his first band, the Innocence, where he played mostly covers of songs by Journey and the Fixx. After high school, he moved to Erie, Pennsylvania, where he played for a few months with a new wave band called Urge. He spent a year at Allegheny College studying computer engineering before moving again, this time to Cleveland, Ohio. While working a series of other odd jobs, Reznor got work as an assistant at Cleveland's Right Track recording studios, where he began to work on the foundation of Nine Inch Nails (NIN, which uses a backward second N in its graphic design) during his off hours. Reznor also played in a variety of other bands including the Exotic Birds, Slam Bamboo, Lucky Pierre, and the fictional band Problems, whose only appearance took place at the end of the 1987 movie *Light of Day*.

The Machine Gained Power

Despite his other projects, Reznor continued to develop and promote his own aggressive, industrial music. Nettwerk Records first expressed interest in signing NIN, and sent Reznor and a hired live band on tour with Skinny Puppy. However, Nettwerk couldn't offer Reznor a record contract at the time because of the label's financial position. In the late 1980s, Reznor sent a demo of his music to Tee Vee Toons Records (TVT) in New York. The independent label's greatest success had come from compilations of television theme songs, but

For the Record . . .

Born c. 1965; raised in Mercer, PA. *Education:* Attended Allegheny College.

Joined band the Urge in Erie, PA, following high school; moved to Cleveland, OH; played in bands, including the Exotic Birds, Slam Bamboo, Lucky Pierre, and the Problems; created concept for Nine Inch Nails, c. 1988; signed with TVT Records and released debut album *Pretty Hate Machine,* 1989; performed on Lollapalooza festival tour, 1991; signed with Interscope Records and formed own label, Nothing Records, 1991; mixed soundtrack LP for Oliver Stone's film *Natural Born Killers,* 1994; featured artist at Woodstock II, 1994.

Awards: Grammy Award for best metal performance with vocal, 1993, for *Broken.*

Addresses: *Record company*—Nothing Records, 2337 West 11th St., Suite 7, Cleveland, OH 44113; or TVT/ Interscope Records, 10900 Wilshire Blvd., Suite 1230, Los Angeles, CA 90024. *Management*—Formula Public Relations, 225 Lafayette St., Suite 603, New York, NY 10012.

TVT owner Steve Gottlieb believed in Reznor's music— and in the NIN project—enough to sign him to the label.

In 1989, TVT released NIN's first album, *Pretty Hate Machine,* which Reznor wrote and co-produced, and on which he performed all instrumental and vocal tracks. The album's first singles, "Down in It" and "Head Like a Hole," sparked interest in the band and were huge club hits; they were followed by the release of the single "Sin." As critic Vic Garbarini of *Musician* noted of Reznor, "Though often painted as some bitter, lost soul, his music suggests deeper yearnings toward faith, hope, even charity." After the release of *Pretty Hate Machine,* NIN went on tour, opening for such acts as the Jesus and Mary Chain and Peter Murphy.

Recognition and press attention increased quickly for Reznor and NIN. "I lived a fairly average, anonymous, small-town life till I got the idea to do Nine Inch Nails," he told the *Los Angeles Times.* "Then, I locked myself in a studio for a year, and then got off the tour bus two years after that, and I didn't know who I'd turned into." In 1990 some misplaced footage from the video for "Down in It" landed in the hands of the FBI. The video showed a half-naked man being thrown from a building, and the FBI thought they had stumbled across a

videotape of an actual murder. They quickly launched an investigation, only to discover that the half-naked man was Reznor, whom they found very much alive, on tour with the Jesus and Mary Chain. The FBI ended up with an embarrassing situation, while Reznor gained even more publicity.

NIN Hammered Live Venues

As the success of *Pretty Hate Machine* grew, Reznor and his touring version of NIN were asked to play the first annual Lollapalooza festival tour of alternative music bands. Lollapalooza sent Reznor's debut album soaring to platinum status and he garnered heavy video rotation on MTV with "Head Like a Hole." But once the profits rolled in, Reznor and TVT saw different directions for NIN's next recording. According to Reznor, TVT and Gottlieb tried to force him toward more commercial accessibility. Reznor argued with the label over videos, singles, and tour support and insisted that TVT had not paid him the royalties he had earned. Attempting to sever his contract with the label, he ended up involved in a lawsuit. Several other record labels wanted to purchase Reznor's contract, but TVT wouldn't sell.

Reznor kept NIN touring for two years after the release of *Pretty Hate Machine* just to keep up with legal costs. Finally, he decided to return to the long-missed recording studio to work on a new NIN album. Reznor and his producer checked into recording studios using fake band names such as the Stunt Popes, because if the name NIN appeared on anything, TVT would have legally owned the sessions.

The Next Step to the Becoming

Interscope Records, determined to get NIN on their label, negotiated a joint venture with TVT. Contractually, Reznor would strictly deal with Interscope, but TVT would still get a percentage of the profits. When the ink dried, Reznor presented his next effort to Interscope, a six-song EP with two bonus tracks titled *Broken.* Most of the songs on the EP lyrically express Reznor's anger toward TVT and how the whole situation had affected him. "*Broken* was a hard recording to make," Reznor wrote in his bio for the EP. "*Broken* is an ugly record made during an ugly time in my life. *Broken* marks phase three of Nine Inch Nails: the becoming."

Reznor recorded two cover versions of songs as the unlisted bonus tracks on *Broken,* industrial band Pigface's "Suck" and post-punker Adam Ant's "Physical." Released under his own newly formed Nothing label—in conjunction with Interscope and TVT—the EP reached Number Seven on the *Billboard* charts. In 1993, it earned Reznor a Grammy Award for best metal performance with vocal. That same year, Reznor released a limited-edition CD of various remixes of tracks from *Broken.* The CD, titled *Fixed,* displays the interpretation of the material through the ears of members of bands like Foetus and Coil. Interscope/Nothing/TVT released only 50,000 copies in the United States.

Self-Reflection Led to New Heights

Following the release of *Broken,* Reznor moved to Los Angeles to start work on the 1994 release *The Downward Spiral.* He recorded the album in his own Le Pig studios in the Sharon Tate mansion, where actress Tate and others had been brutally murdered by the Charles Manson family in 1969. Reznor would be the last person to live in the house before its destruction.

Reznor adopted a new musical approach on *The Downward Spiral.* As he described it to *Musician,* "The starting point [on *Broken*] was to make a dense record. We approached the new one from the opposite point of view—a record with holes everywhere." *The Downward Spiral,* which debuted on the *Billboard* charts at Number Two, was written as a concept album about someone who systematically examines himself and everything around him—from comfort to delusion—to discover his own identity and purpose. "I think the very act of wanting to discover and uncover unpleasantries is itself positive," Reznor told Guy Garcia of *Time.* "The act of trying to rid yourself of these demons, to prepare yourself for the worst, is a positive thing."

Together with bass player Lohner, guitarist Robin Finck, keyboardist James Woolley, and longtime friend and drummer Vrenna, Reznor's stage shows—like his heavily censored videos for MTV—reflect the violence and sexual imagery around which he builds his music. "I think Nine Inch Nails are big enough and mainstream enough to gently lead people into the back room a little bit," he told *Rolling Stone*'s Jonathan Gold. "I think that back room could represent anything that an individual might consider taboo yet intriguing, anything we're conditioned to abhor. Why do you watch horror films? Why do you look at an accident when you drive past, secretly hoping that you see some gore?"

Reznor defends the theatricality of his musical persona. "I'm not trying to hide," he explained to Gold. "Or make up for a lack of songs, but essentially Nine Inch Nails are theater. What we do is closer to Alice Cooper than Pearl Jam." Though sometimes accused of "putting on" the trappings of a bizarre personality for his

fan's benefit, Reznor admits to honest bouts of depression. "When I think back as far as I can remember, I've always had an element of melancholy that I should probably have therapy for," Reznor admitted in *Alternative Press.* "But I'm making a career of it. I'm intensely afraid of people, and I don't like to be in social situations. I feel uncomfortable, and I think my shyness and quietness is often misinterpreted as standoffishness.... I'm not trying to be a rock god. I have a multitude of split personalities."

In this assessment, noted film director Oliver Stone would probably agree. Commenting on both Reznor and rap artist Dr. Dre—whose work Stone chose as musical accompaniment to his 1994 film *Natural Born Killers*—the director told Steve Hochman of the *Los Angeles Times:* "I admire both artists very much. They're young and obviously troubled people and their lyrics and music reflect that.... There's something going on in our world.... It's a violent society, violent system, and corrupt—the system, the media, the government." Stone had so much respect for Reznor's musical ideas that he chose him to put together the film's soundtrack album.

"I'm not any more happy or content with my life than I was 10 years ago," Reznor told *Musician* in 1994. "I got everything I wanted in my life ... except I don't really have a life now.... I've turned myself into this music-creation-performance machine." As long as his melancholy and multiple personalities inspire him to continue writing music that breaks the boundaries of commercially successful hits, Reznor will continue to flood the senses of whoever will listen with his industrial brand of aggression known as Nine Inch Nails.

Selected discography

Pretty Hate Machine (includes "Down in It," "Head Like A Hole," "Terrible Lie," and "Sin,") TVT, 1989.
Broken (EP), Nothing/Interscope/TVT, 1992.
Fixed (maxi CD single), Nothing/Interscope/TVT, 1993.
The Downward Spiral, Nothing/Interscope/TVT, 1994.

Sources

Alternative Press, April 1994.
Billboard, March 19, 1994; April 2, 1994.
B-Side, June 1990; February 1994.
Chaos Control, issue 1.
CMJ New Music Report, February 28, 1994.
Creem, May 1994.
Entertainment Weekly, March 18, 1994.
Guitar Player, April 1994.

Guitar World, April 1994.

Keyboard, March 1994.

Los Angeles Times, March 6, 1994; August 14, 1994.

Melody Maker, December 5, 1992; March 12, 1994; March 26, 1994.

Musician, November 1992; January 1993; March 1994.

Request, April 1994.

RIP, April 1993; June 1994.

Rolling Stone, January 21, 1993; March 24, 1994; September 8, 1994.

Spin, March 1992; December 1992; May 1994.

Time, April 25, 1994.

Village Voice, April 5, 1994.

Additional information for this profile was obtained from Formula Public Relations press material, 1992 and 1994.

—Sonya Shelton

Sylvia Rhone

Record company executive

Courtesy of EastWest Records America

Sylvia Rhone has chartered a groundbreaking career in the American recording industry. In 1988, she became the first black woman to serve as vice-president of a major record company—Atlantic Records—and three years later was named co-president and chief executive officer of her own Atlantic label, EastWest Records America. In 1994, she took on the additional responsibility of chairing another Warner Brothers division, Elektra Music. Though she began her career in banking and finance, Rhone has displayed a knack for discovering and developing new music talent as well as salvaging financially struggling record divisions.

The chart-topping acts brought by Rhone to Atlantic—a company that made a major turnaround in the late 1980s—include LeVert, Miki Howard, Gerald Albright, and En Vogue. Rhone's promotion to senior vice-president prompted the following words of praise from Atlantic Chair Ahmet Ertegun, as quoted by Laura B. Randolph in *Ebony:* "Under her expert guidance ... [Atlantic's] commitment to Black music has seen a revitalization marked by innovation, imagination and freshness."

Born in Philadelphia and raised in New York City's Harlem, Rhone received a degree in economics from the prestigious Wharton School of Finance and Commerce at the University of Pennsylvania. After graduating in 1974, she went to work for a major bank in New York City, but after a year decided the atmosphere was too constraining. "I wore pants to work and all eyebrows turned up," she told Randolph. "No one actually said anything but they made it clear that what I'd done was unacceptable." Rhone scrapped her plans for a financial career, took a major pay cut, and started work as a secretary for Buddah Records—at nearly the bottom rung of the music industry ladder. For Rhone, however, the position represented a great opportunity. "I knew I was taking a risk," she told *Black Enterprise,* "but from the moment I sat in my new chair, I knew I was cut out for this business."

Rhone displayed a deftness for work in the recording industry and quickly ran up an impressive resume of promotional work. Shortly after coming on board at Buddah, she was promoted to the position of promotions coordinator and soon thereafter accepted the challenge of heading up national promotions for an independent start-up label. "Suddenly I was responsible for getting my music exposed nationwide," she told Randolph. "I had to jump in the deep water and sink or swim." Her success in the venture, as well as the promotional work she did for several other independent labels, gained her a reputation as a discoverer and shaper of black music talent.

For the Record . . .

Born Sylvia M. Rhone, March 11, 1952, in Philadelphia, PA; daughter of James and Marie (Christmas) Rhone; divorced; children: Quinn (daughter). *Education:* University of Pennsylvania, Wharton School of Business and Commerce, M.A., 1974.

Bankers Trust, international lending, New York City, 1974; Buddah Records, New York City, began as administrative assistant, became promotions coordinator; directed promotional work for several record labels; worked at Atlantic Records, New York City, beginning in 1985, began as director of national black music promotion, became vice-president and general manager of Black Music Operations, named senior vice-president of the company, 1988, appointed chair and CEO of EastWest Records America, 1991; member of board of directors of Alvin Ailey American Dance Theater, Phoenix House Foundation, Rock n' Roll Hall of Fame, and R&B Foundation.

Selected awards: Vice President of the Year, *R&B Report;* Joel Weber Award for Excellence in Music and Business, 1993; Sony Music Excellence Award, 1993.

Addresses: *Home*—21 South End Ave., New York, NY 10280. *Office*—EastWest Records America, 75 Rockefeller Plaza, New York, NY 10019.

Rhone accepted a number of positions in record promotions from the mid-1970s into the 1980s. In 1985 she was hired as director of national black music promotion at struggling Atlantic Records, which in its heyday represented such acts as Aretha Franklin and Otis Redding. Under Rhone's guidance, the black music roster at Atlantic expanded to include such Number One acts as LeVert, Miki Howard, and Gerald Albright. Her work in reaping financial gains for that label resulted in another promotion in 1988—this time to senior vice-president of the entire Atlantic Records company—making her the only black woman to hold as high a position within a major American record company. Chuck Philips in the *Los Angeles Times* declared of Rhone, "She got results. Her company has been on a multimillion-dollar hot streak since the day she took over."

Rhone's success at Atlantic continued. In late 1991, Atlantic formed a new label, Atco/EastWest, to encompass a broader range of musical artists. Atlantic later dropped Atco, and Rhone was named chair and chief executive officer of her own label, EastWest Records America, which features both black and white acts varying in style from rock and pop to R&B to rap. Supervising a staff of more than 40 people, Rhone assumed responsibility for overseeing all facets of the label's recruitment, marketing, and promotion of recording artists.

In an article in *Black Enterprise,* Rhone elaborated on her efforts to make a mark in the music industry, stating: "I'm really excited about this venture because my team will create a distinct personality for the label." Then, in July of 1994, Rhone also took on the responsibility of chairing another Warner division, Elektra Music, along with EastWest. Rhone commented in *Billboard,* "They're two labels with very distinct personalities. I think they complement each other in their diversity."

Much has been written about the sexism and racism prevalent in the entertainment industry, but Rhone has been a vanguard in breaking down barriers. As she remarked in the *Los Angeles Times,* "I think that thanks to my success and the success of others that, eventually, that sexist good ol' boy school of thought will go the way of the dinosaur. It'll take us a few years to accomplish it, but hey, I'm up for the fight. And so are a lot of other women." In addition, Rhone commented in *Black Enterprise* on the impact African-Americans are exerting on the U.S. recording industry: "African-Americans can not only create music, but control it as well. The world is watching us."

Sources

Billboard, April 24, 1993; July 30, 1994.
Black Enterprise, August 1991; December 1991.
Ebony, November 1988; September 1992; March 1993.
Entertainment Weekly, December 6, 1991.
Hollywood Reporter, December 7, 1993.
Los Angeles Times, November 29, 1992; April 18, 1993.

Additional information for this profile was obtained from EastWest publicity materials, 1993.

—*Michael E. Mueller*

Buddy Rich

Drummer

Ask 100 percussionists to name the greatest drummer of all time, and chances are that the majority of them will respond by saying "Buddy Rich." The litany of jazz drummers is long, but Rich was one of a kind, distinguished by his virtuosity, speed, and precision. His long career exposed his talents to countless listeners, and even those whose knowledge of drummers is minimal are likely to have heard of him.

Born in Brooklyn, New York, in 1917, Rich's performing career began before he was two years old. His parents, who had a vaudeville act, showcased their son as "Traps, the Drum Wonder." In his most popular routine, young Rich would tap out the rhythm to "Stars and Stripes Forever" on his drum. His performances as "Traps" continued through the 1920s; he went on an Australian tour in 1924 and appeared in a short film, *Buddy Traps in Sound Effects,* in 1929. His nickname, "Buddy," evolved from "Pal," his parents' pet name for him. By the time Rich was 15, he was earning $1,000 a week and was the highest paid child star next to Jackie Coogan, the actor most famous for his role in Charlie Chaplin's 1920 film *The Kid.*

MICHAEL OCHS ARCHIVES / Venice, CA

For the Record . . .

Born Bernard Rich, September 30, 1917, in New York City; died of heart failure after surgery to remove a brain tumor, April 2, 1987, in Los Angeles, CA; son of Robert and Bess (Skolnik) Rich (both vaudeville performers); married Marie Allison, 1952; children: Cathy.

Performed in parents' vaudeville act, beginning 1919; toured United States and Australia, beginning at age 6; led own stage band, 1932; played drums with several big bands in 1930s and 1940s, including those of Joe Marsala, 1937, Bunny Berigan, 1938, Artie Shaw, 1938, Tommy Dorsey, 1939-42 and 1944-45, and Harry James, on and off from 1953-66; led own big bands, 1946-48, 1950, and 1966-87; performed with Jazz at the Philharmonic, 1950s and 1960s; opened own clubs, Buddy's Place and Buddy's Place II in Manhattan, 1974-75. Appeared with various bands in several motion pictures, including *Buddy Traps in Sound Effects,* 1929, *Dancing Co-ed,* 1938, *Ship Ahoy,* 1941, *DuBarry Was a Lady,* 1942, *Presenting Lily Mars,* 1942, *How's About It?,* 1942, *Thrill of a Romance,* 1944, *Thrills of Music,* 1948, *Harry James and His Music Makers,* 1953, and *Melodies by Martin,* 1955. *Military service:* U.S. Marine Corps, 1942-44.

Rich became interested in jazz drumming while he was still in his teens. For a brief period in 1932, he had his own band, Buddy "Traps" Rich and His Orchestra. He frequented the Crystal Club in Brooklyn, admiring the drumming of Tony Briglia, who played in the Casa Loma Orchestra. In 1937 Artie Shapiro, a bassist who performed at the Crystal Club, suggested that Rich sit in on drums during the Sunday jam sessions that were held at the Hickory House, a club that featured the band of Joe Marsala. Rich waited for his chance for three consecutive Sundays, and on the fourth, finally got an opportunity to play. Marsala was impressed, and asked him to join the band. But Marsala's Dixieland style was not to Rich's taste, and he left after a short time.

Played with Artie Shaw and Tommy Dorsey

Rich had a brief stint in Bunny Berigan's band in mid-1938 but in December of that year joined Artie Shaw's orchestra. By this time, big bands were *the* musical phenomenon in the United States, and Shaw's was one of the best. Rich's playing made the band swing as it never had before. The Shaw orchestra appeared on a

weekly radio show, *Melody and Madness,* and in the feature film *Dancing Co-ed,* with Hollywood star Lana Turner.

Rich was hired by bandleader Tommy Dorsey in 1939. Dorsey's band was phenomenally popular and featured a young singer named Frank Sinatra. Rich and Sinatra roomed together on tours, and because they both had strong personalities, they often clashed with each other. In addition, several critics have suggested that Rich was bored by the inordinate number of ballads the Dorsey band played—ballads often sung by Sinatra—and most likely resented the attention that was heaped on Sinatra by his adoring fans. Regardless of their rocky relationship, they respected each other's musical talents.

In 1942, the year after the United States became involved in World War II, Rich left the Dorsey band and enlisted in the Marines. He never saw active duty and in 1944 was discharged for medical reasons. He rejoined Dorsey in 1944, becoming the highest paid sideman in the business. During the 1940s, motion pictures featuring big bands were the rage, and the Dorsey orchestra performed in several, including *Ship Ahoy* in 1941, Cole Porter's musical *DuBarry Was a Lady* in 1942, *Presenting Lily Mars* with Judy Garland, also in 1942, and *Thrill of a Romance,* starring Esther Williams, released two years later.

Formed Own Band in 1946

Rich started his own band in 1946, receiving $50,000 in backing from Sinatra. "In two years, I was flat broke," Rich told jazz critic Whitney Balliett in a *New Yorker* article that became part of Balliett's book *American Musicians: 56 Portraits in Jazz.* "But [the band] went down swinging and it went down in one piece." He formed another unsuccessful band in 1950, and in between performed with Norman Granz's "Jazz at the Philharmonic" (JATP) tours. The JATP performances were famous for their drum "battles," in which one drummer tried to outshine the other, and Rich took part in many of these, often emerging as the "winner."

Rich's playing displayed an astounding capacity for endurance and velocity, and his ability to get around the drums quickly and with minimal effort was amazing. Rich claimed that he never practiced—apparently believing that practicing squelched spontaneity. "I've never had a lesson in my life, and I never practice," he told Balliett. "That way each night is an expectation, a new experience for me."

In addition to his percussive gifts, Rich was also a

rather good singer who performed ballads and up-tempo numbers in a style similar to Sinatra's. In 1957, he made an album, *Buddy Rich Just Sings,* but never pursued his singing career very doggedly, since his obvious talents lay elsewhere.

Temperamental Personality

Rich's dynamic approach to playing reflected his life-style and personality. He drove himself as hard as he drove his players, and many an alumnus of Rich's bands has a story to tell about Rich's violent temper. A close friend, Mel Tormé, talked to the drummer's surviving siblings while doing research for the biography *Traps, the Drum Wonder.* Tormé discovered that Rich had been beaten as a child by his father; Rich's sisters and brother believed that this "harsh treatment of their brother molded and shaped him into the sometimes difficult man he became later in life," according to Tormé. Rich himself freely admitted to Balliett: "I have the worst temper in the world. When I lose it, oh baby."

Rich married showgirl and dancer Marie Allison in 1952, and the couple had a daughter, Cathy, in 1954. He performed with various ensembles in the 1950s and early 1960s, and in 1966 formed a new big band of his own. From this time on, Rich led his own bands. These groups—which featured young, unknown players—performed largely at colleges and universities, and Rich won over an entirely new generation of jazz listeners. Rich's friend Johnny Carson invited him on the *Tonight Show* frequently, and the drummer became familiar to television audiences not only as a phenomenal musician, but as a witty and engaging personality.

Rich, who suffered from a heart condition for many years, died of heart failure in Los Angeles in 1987 after undergoing surgery for a malignant brain tumor. Sinatra gave the eulogy at his funeral, and many other show business figures, including Johnny Carson, Jerry Lewis, Artie Shaw, and Robert Blake, also paid tribute

to him. In 1988 Rich's daughter, Cathy, established the Buddy Rich Memorial Brain Tumor Research Foundation at the UCLA Medical Center and started a scholarship fund in his name. The Smithsonian Institution in Washington, D.C., acquired Rich's drums in 1989.

Selected discography

Buddy Rich Just Sings, Verve, 1957.
This One's for Basie (recorded 1956), Verve, 1987.
Time Being—The Amazing Buddy Rich, Verve, 1987.
Buddy Rich, Verve, 1988.
(With Gene Krupa) *The Drum Battle* (reissue), Verve, 1988.
No Jive, Novus, 1992.
One Night Stand (recorded live 1946), Bandstand, 1992.
Buddy and Sweets, Verve.
Rich versus Roach, Mercury.

Sources

Books

Balliett, Whitney, *Super Drummer: A Profile of Buddy Rich,* Bobbs-Merrill, 1968.
Balliett, *American Musicians: 56 Portraits in Jazz,* Oxford University Press, 1986.
Korrall, Burt, *Drummin' Men: The Heartbeat of Jazz—The Swing Years,* Schirmer Books, 1990.
Meriwether, Doug, Jr., *We Don't Play Requests: A Musical Biography/Discography of Buddy Rich,* Meriwether, 1984.
Tormé, Mel, *Traps, the Drum Wonder: The Life of Buddy Rich,* Oxford University Press, 1991.

Periodicals

Down Beat, April 11, 1974; February 9, 1978; February 23, 1978; July 1987; February 1994.
Modern Drummer, January 1986; August 1987.
New Yorker, January 21, 1967.
New York Times, April 3, 1987.

—*Joyce Harrison*

Nino Rota

Composer, educator

Italian composer Nino Rota, best known for his prolific composition of film scores, was also an esteemed music teacher and classical composer who worked on operas, ballets, masses, and orchestral and chamber pieces. Although he worked with a variety of motion picture directors, he was best known for providing the musical scores for the most memorable films of Federico Fellini and Francis Ford Coppola. Rota's soundtrack music was uniquely reminiscent of his Italian heritage, often conjuring up a rich, romantic image of pianists and strolling violinists in an Italian piazza. Ranging from graceful and delicate to full-bodied, melodramatic compositions, his scores captured the mood of a film.

Rota's distinctive soundtracks set the dramatic tone of more than 40 films, starting with *His Young Wife* in 1945. In the United States, the films that brought Rota the most exposure were Coppola's *Godfather* and *The Godfather, Part II;* however, Fellini film enthusiasts throughout the world lauded the composer's scores for 1954's *La Strada,* 1960's *La Dolce Vita,* 1963's *8½,* 1965's *Juliet of the Spirits,* and 1974's *Amarcord.* Rota composed dozens of scores for Fellini alone, and critics have noted that his music contributed as much to films as superb directing or acting.

Rota was born and raised in Milan, Italy, and was the grandson of pianist/composer Giovanni Rinaldi. At the age of eight, he began studying the piano and composing. Within three years, he had composed an oratorio for soloists, orchestra, and chorus titled *L'infanzia di San Giovanni Battista,* which was produced in Milan when he was 12. That same year, 1923, Rota entered the Milan Conservatory and benefited greatly as a private pupil of Italy's most distinguished musical teachers, including Casella and Pizzetti.

In 1925, at the age of 14, Rota composed a lyric comedy in three acts to his own text titled *Il Principe porcaro,* as a tribute to nineteenth-century Danish storyteller Hans Christian Andersen. The next year, Rota composed the opera *Il Cappello di paglia di Firenze,* which would finally be performed 20 years later. He left Milan in 1927 to study composition, conducting, and music history in Rome under Casella. From 1931 to 1932, he attended the Curtis Institute in Philadelphia on a special musical scholarship. While in the United States, he studied composition with Rosario Scalero and conducting with Fritz Reiner. During this time, he composed *Serenata* for orchestra in four movements, as well as *Balli,* written for a small orchestra.

Having completed his work in Philadelphia, Rota resumed his studies in Italy and in 1937 received an arts degree in literature from Milan University. He then taught music theory for two years—in 1937 and 1938—at the Liceo Musicale in Taranto. A year later, he became a faculty member at the Liceo Musicale in Bari, where he taught composition and harmony.

Rota maintained a close, longstanding friendship with Russian-born composer Igor Stravinsky throughout his life, yet his style was never influenced by the friendship. Rota preferred a simplicity of style; his melodies were marked by directness and his compositions were often whimsical. He was able to work in many different musical categories without sacrificing technical quality or knowledge, and this adaptability earned him an abiding respect from his musical peers.

After experimenting with various operas, symphonies, and other classical pieces in the late 1930s and early 1940s, Rota composed his first music for film—the score to *His Young Wife*—in 1945. By 1950 he had been named director of the Liceo Musicale in Bari and within three more years had seven additional film scores to his credit. Rota's first project for director Federico Fellini was the soundtrack to the 1954 film *La Strada.* Fellini then decided to use Rota for all of his future works. Rota continued to compose the music for the films of Fellini and other directors in the 1950s and

For the Record . . .

Born Rinaldi Rota, December 3, 1911, in Milan, Italy; died April 10, 1979, in Rome; grandson of composer Giovanni Rinaldi. *Education:* Studied composition at the Milan Conservatory under Casella and Pizzetti, c. 1923-26; received a scholarship to study at the Curtis Institute in Philadelphia, 1931-32; received an arts degree in literature from Milan University.

Composed *L'infanzia di San Giovanni Battista,* an oratorio, at age 12; composed lyric comedy *Il Principe porcaro,* 1925; wrote *Serenata,* 1931, and *Balli,* 1932; studied under Fritz Reiner in the United States; returned to Italy, 1937; taught at the Liceo Musicale in Taranto, 1937-38; became director of the Liceo Musicale in Bari, 1950. Composed first film score, *His Young Wife,* 1945; composed scores until 1979; best known for work on motion pictures by directors Federico Fellini and Francis Ford Coppola. Works include music for *La Strada; La Dolce Vita; 8½; Juliet of the Spirits; Taming of the Shrew; Romeo and Juliet; The Godfather; The Godfather, Part II; Amarcord; Roma;* and *Death on the Nile.*

Awards: Co-recipient of Academy Award for best original dramatic score, 1974, for *The Godfather, Part II.*

1960s, with such international efforts as *The White Sheik, I Vitelloni, Star of India, War and Peace, The Great War, La Dolce Vita, The Innocents,* and *Purple Noon.*

Rota expanded his exposure in America beyond the foreign film audience when he composed the unmistakable soundtrack for director Francis Ford Coppola's tragic Mafia epic *The Godfather* in 1972. *The Godfather* attracted a wide audience in the United States, and the film's popular score was played at that year's Academy Awards ceremony.

In 1974 Rota shared a best original dramatic score Oscar for his work with Carmine Coppola on the music to *The Godfather, Part II.* Around the same time, he composed the soundtrack for director Anthony Harvey's historical drama *The Abdication* and Lina Wertmuller's *Love and Anarchy,* set in 1930s Italy. He continued working on such projects as the score to the British production of Agatha Christie's *Death on the Nile* until shortly before his death in 1979.

Selected discography

The Godfather: Selections, RCA, 1974.
The Godfather, Part II, ABC Records, 1974.
Il Cappello di paglia di Firenze, RCA Red Seal, 1975.
Romeo and Juliet Love Theme, Deutsche Grammophon, 1977.
The Godfather Theme, Vista, 1978.
Nino Rota, RCA, 1978.
The Music of Nino Rota, RCA, 1979.
Fellini/Rota: Music from the Films of Federico Fellini, Silva Screen, 1987.
Romeo and Juliet, Capitol, 1989.
The Godfather Soundtrack, Columbia, 1990.
The Symphonic Fellini/Rota: La Dolce Vita, Silva Screen, 1993.
Rota: Oratoria Mysterium, Claves Records.
Homage to Federico Fellini—Music by Nino Rota, Replay Music.
Casella, Pizzetti, Rota: Chamber Music/Ex Novo Ensemble, Stradivari.

Sources

Books

Osborne, Robert, *60 Years of the Oscar,* Abbeville Press, 1989.

Periodicals

L'espresso, Number 7, 1970.
High Fidelity, November 1975.
Il Messaggero, April 13, 1979.
Records and Recording, June 1979.

—B. Kimberly Taylor

Sawyer Brown

Country band

Sawyer Brown is one of the few bands in country music history to be thrown into the spotlight early in their career as winners of a national award—and then forced for the next decade to try and live it down. However, such obstacles didn't stop the group's energetic members from giving their all for their music. While the Nashville-based country music industry proved to be a tough nut to crack, the band's high-energy compositions have won them legions of fans along the road to Music City acceptance. After over 10 years of constant touring and recording, the members of Sawyer Brown have finally gained a measure of respect from their Nashville peers, as well as critical acclaim as both songwriters and musicians.

The band got its start when Ohio-born singer/songwriter Mark Miller hooked up with Gregg "Hobie" Hubbard while both men were studying at the University of Central Florida in the late 1970s. After moving to Nashville in 1981, Miller and Hubbard formed the band Savannah along with bassist Jim Scholten, guitarist Bobby Randall, and drummer Joe Smyth. The group

Photograph by Beth Horsley, courtesy of Curb Records

Members include **Duncan Cameron** (joined band, 1990), lead guitar, dobro, mandolin, steel guitar, background vocals; **Gregg "Hobie" Hubbard,** keyboards, background vocals; **Mark Miller** (wife's name, Lisa; children: Aden Gunnar Agustus), guitar, vocals, songwriter; **Bobby Randall** (bandmember, 1981-90), lead guitar; **Jim Scholten**, bass; and **Joe Smyth**, drums.

Group formed as Savannah, c. 1981; changed name to Sawyer Brown and worked the club circuit in Nashville, TN; signed with Capitol Records, 1985; released first Number One single "Step That Step," 1985; signed with Curb Records, 1990.

Awards: Winners of *Star Search* competition, 1984; Horizon Award, Country Music Association, 1985; named TNN/*Music City News* vocal band of the year, 1993; video group of the year award, Country Music Television (CMT), 1993.

Addresses: *Record company*—Curb Records, 47 Music Sq. E., Nashville, TN 37203.

soon decided that they needed a more original moniker: they changed their name to the Nashville street where they came to rehearse, and the band Sawyer Brown was born.

Miller's rough-edged vocals provided a perfect instrument for the up-tempo songs about cars and girls that made up much of the group's early material. Their music was a reflection of the bandmembers' own youth and exuberance—which sometimes bordered on too much of a good thing, according to many critics. And while the group was full of confidence after winning the music competition on the syndicated television program *Star Search* in 1984, their award was an honor that didn't mean much to the Nashville music industry. Peter Cronin noted in *Billboard,* "To country music's cognoscenti, Sawyer Brown was a little too uptown and showbizzy to be taken seriously.... [But] in retrospect, the band has done a lot to make country music safe for the bolo-tied slickness of Diamond Rio and the high-energy showmanship of Garth Brooks."

Out of Step With Nashville

In 1985, the year following their *Star Search* award, the band broke their first Number One spot on the country charts with "Step That Step"; the single stayed on the *Billboard* country charts for 21 weeks and earned the band the Country Music Association's Horizon Award for new talent. Unfortunately, gaining a position on the charts turned out to be the exception for Sawyer Brown, rather than the rule. "Musically, what happened to us is that we were always out there on the edge a little bit, and I think radio took a very strong swing toward traditional music for a few years," Miller told Edward Morris in *Billboard.* "We continued to do what we were doing and kind of got into a no-man's land."

Sawyer Brown was determined not to let their lack of radio play affect them; with a rigorous touring schedule of over 220 shows per year, they built a base of loyal fans throughout the United States. "We developed such a cult following that we were able to tour year-round, and we really didn't notice the difference between having a hit song and not having one," Miller asserted in the interview with Morris. Sawyer Brown's energetic performance on stage was one of the reasons their concerts continued to draw large audiences; the group's musicianship and songwriting abilities boosted record sales among their growing following and accounted for their longevity despite lack of mainstream success during the 1980s.

"The Walk" a Runaway Success

The year 1990 marked a turning point for the band. With the departure of Randall, Sawyer Brown welcomed guitarist/songwriter Duncan Cameron on board—and good things began to happen. The group's 1991 album *The Dirt Road*—featuring "The Walk," a single written by Miller—as well as *Cafe on the Corner,* released the following year, each received favorable critical reviews and went on to become gold records.

Sawyer Brown had claimed their position as one of Nashville's top country bands, and the popularity of "The Walk" helped solidify their spot among country music's most respected acts. A poignant look at the growth of a relationship between a father and son, the song garnered several media Top Ten honors and held chart-topping positions for weeks on end.

"That song was kind of an ace in the hole for us," noted Miller in a Curb Records press release. "We believed in it so much that we put our hearts and souls into promoting it. We knew it had the potential to strike some emotional chords with people." The song did just that, with critics as well as fans: "I know my own thinking began to change the day I was riding down the road and first heard 'The Walk,'" admitted *Country Music* contributor Bob Allen. "I remember thinking that day,

'Damn! What a great song! Who the hell is this?' I remember how floored I was to discover it was Sawyer Brown."

"Something More to Say"

Another possible reason for the band's newfound popularity is the emotional maturity reflected in their lyrics in recent years. "I wrote 'Step That Step' when I was 23 years old," explained Miller in the press material. "It's been more than ten years now, and I think we look at life differently. There's a much broader worldview we bring to our writing now. I don't think that means you rock any less. I think we rock as hard as we ever did. It's just that we have something more to say."

Sawyer Brown's wealth of original material, most of it penned by Miller, was supplemented when songwriter Mac McAnally hooked up with the group on their 1992 release, *Cafe on the Corner*. McAnally's "All These Years," a tense portrayal of marital infidelity, was one of the album's three Number One singles and one of the band's biggest hits. The successful songwriting partnership of Miller and McAnally found its way into the recording studio when McAnally signed on as co-producer of both *Cafe on the Corner* and 1993's *Outskirts of Town*. In the studio, McAnally balanced Sawyer Brown's unrestrained enthusiasm with more spare, focused guitar accompaniments than the band had used on past projects, reflecting the group's growing image as chroniclers of the simple lives of working class folks.

The mix of songwriting, studio direction, and maturity seems to have worked, and in the wake of projects like *Cafe on the Corner* and *Outskirts of Town*, Sawyer Brown has been accepted into the Nashville fold: the nominations the group received in 1993 for honors from both the American Music Awards and the Academy of Country Music can attest to that fact. But winning the TNN/*Music City News* award for vocal band of the year

in 1993 had a special significance: as an award generated by the support of the group's fans, it reminded Sawyer Brown of their audience's role in advancing their growth as a group. As Smyth told the *Nashville Banner*, "We got a renewed sense of our direction, musically, and I think that showed.... Over the ten years we've been recording, we've all matured—the songwriting, the performance, us as individuals. The energy is still there, but we've all grown up a bunch."

Selected discography

The Boys Are Back, Curb, 1989.
Greatest Hits, Curb, 1990.
The Dirt Road (includes "Some Girls Do" and "The Walk"), Curb, 1991.
Cafe on the Corner (includes "All These Years"), Curb, 1992.
Outskirts of Town (includes "The Boys and Me" and "Drive Away"), Curb, 1993.
Shakin', Capitol.
Buick, Curb.

Sources

Books

Cackett, Alan, *Harmony Illustrated Encyclopedia of Country Music,* Crown, 1994.

Periodicals

Billboard, May 23, 1992; August 7, 1993.
Country Music, May 1994.
Country Song Roundup, January 1994; April 1994.
Nashville Banner, August 13, 1993.
Stereo Review, November 1993.

Additional information for this profile was obtained from a Curb Records press release.

—Pamela L. Shelton

Gil Scott-Heron

Singer, songwriter, writer, activist

Courtesy of TVT Records

Mixing his unique, highly politicized, and verbally complex poetry with minimal percussion in the early 1970s, and developing a speaking/singing soul-jazz form he christened "bluesology," performer Gil Scott-Heron has been widely credited with helping to invent rap. The title of Scott-Heron's best-known piece, "The Revolution Will Not Be Televised," has become a pop catchphrase, and his evolving activism would influence several highly regarded albums before he took a long hiatus; it was almost a decade before Scott-Heron released a new album to an eager public in 1994. By this time the legacy of his career was apparent; many of the most ambitious young rap and hip-hop artists have laid claim to Scott-Heron as a crucial influence.

Born in Chicago, Illinois, Scott-Heron was raised by his grandmother in Jackson, Tennessee, after his parents divorced. He briefly attended school in his hometown, but as one of a handful of black students in the heart of segregationist America, he was unable to tolerate the abuse ladled out by his white schoolmates. Scott-Heron, now with his mother, moved to New York City. There he discovered his writing talents and a wealth of inspiration provided by black American writers of the "Harlem Renaissance," a literary movement of the early 1900s that included such writers as Langston Hughes. Like Hughes, the precocious Scott-Heron attended Lincoln University in Pennsylvania. Though he left after a year, he made the acquaintance of Brian Jackson, who would figure prominently in his musical endeavors.

Dedicated to Expression

Scott-Heron's literary ambitions were substantial and were backed up by considerable stylistic prowess; he published his first novel, *The Vulture,* at age 19. The story of urban youth, drugs, and death, *The Vulture* indicated an already sophisticated writing voice. Scott-Heron next published the poetry collection *Small Talk at 125th & Lenox.* The title also graced his first album, a spoken-word recording featuring sparse music and percussion tracks released by Flying Dutchman in 1970.

The album *Small Talk at 125th & Lenox* includes an early rendition of "The Revolution Will Not Be Televised," a diatribe against mass media's trivialization of social upheaval and the seeming paralysis of those who watch via television. "A little over 21 years ago I was introduced into what is laughingly referred to as civilization," the young author wrote in the album's liner notes, adding "I am a Black man dedicated to expression; expression of the joy and pride of blackness. I

For the Record . . .

Born April 1, 1949, in Chicago, IL; son of a soccer player and a librarian; raised in Jackson, TN, and New York City. *Education:* Attended Lincoln University, PA.

Writer and recording artist. Signed with Flying Dutchman, 1970-74; recorded debut album *Small Talk at 125th & Lenox* (includes "The Revolution Will Not Be Televised"), 1970; released *The Revolution Will Not Be Televised* (includes "Whitey on the Moon"), Flying Dutchman, 1974; signed with Arista, 1975-85; contributed to all-star benefit projects *No Nukes,* 1980, and *Sun City,* 1985; subject of film *Black Wax,* 1984; participated in MTV Free Your Mind Spoken Word tour, 1994; signed with TVT Records and released album *Spirits,* 1994.

Addresses: *Record company*—TVT Records, 23 East 4th St., New York, NY 10003.

consider myself neither poet, composer or musician. These are merely tools used by sensitive men to carve out a piece of beauty or truth that they hope may lead to peace and salvation."

Scott-Heron recorded two more albums for Flying Dutchman, *Pieces of a Man*—featuring a more developed version of "The Revolution"—and *Free Will. Rolling Stone* deemed the former "an involving, important album," favoring Scott-Heron's singing and "assurance and directness as a songwriter" over what reviewer Vince Aletti considered the heavy-handedness of the poetry. The prolific Scott-Heron also published a new novel, *The Nigger Factory.* After a dispute, Scott-Heron left Flying Dutchman and released *Winter in America* on the Strata-East label in 1974. The mellow, sorrowful jazz of the title track—reflecting black America's melancholy in the midst of conservative retrenchment—and "The Bottle"—a fast-paced, funky sermon on alcoholism—demonstrated their author's increasing breadth as a composer and lyricist.

In 1975 Scott-Heron became the first artist to sign with Clive Davis's new Arista label. "Not only is he an excellent poet, musician and performer—three qualities I look for that are rarely combined—but he's a leader of social thought," Davis proclaimed to *Rolling Stone's* Sheila Weller. Linking up again with Jackson, Scott-Heron developed some of his most acclaimed material. His second Arista release, *From South Africa to South Carolina,* contained the energetic "Johannes-burg," a proclamation of solidarity with blacks in then white-ruled South Africa that reached the Top 40. "Our vibration is based on creative solidarity: trying to influence the black community toward the same kind of dignity and self-respect that we all know is necessary to live," Scott-Heron told Weller. "We're trying to put out survival kits on wax."

Scott-Heron parted company with Jackson in the early 1980s and explored jazzier territory as well as the techno-funk that had begun to dominate black pop. As well as exploring more personal issues, he continued attacking specific political targets. The U.S. presidential election of conservative Republican Ronald Reagan—"Ray-gun," as Scott-Heron was fond of calling him—unleashed a further torrent of musical scorn.

In 1980 Scott-Heron also released his anti-nuclear anthem "Shut 'Em Down" on the all-star *No Nukes* concert album. However, as the decade advanced, Scott-Heron was increasingly isolated in his political militancy. As *Stereo Review's* Phyl Garland observed, "Unlike his peers, he is not afraid to seem a throwback to more outspoken times. Although protest songs are no longer in vogue, Scott-Heron remains a committed wave-maker, sweeping out onto the beach of public awareness such disturbing matters as drug abuse, poverty, police brutality, and international conflict."

Dropped and Rediscovered

In 1984 Arista released *The Best of Gil Scott-Heron,* but would drop the artist the following year. He collaborated with jazz legend Miles Davis on "Let Me See Your I.D." for the anti-apartheid benefit album *Sun City,* but otherwise stopped recording for several years, though he continued to tour and a documentary film was made about him. Unfortunately for fans, most of his albums went out of print. With the exception of the *Best of* collection and the earlier *The Revolution Will Not Be Televised,* much of his work would not be available on CD for many years. The re-release in 1988 of *The Revolution Will Not Be Televised* reintroduced to a new generation the Scott-Heron classic "Whitey on the Moon," a satirical comment on American socioeconomic values. Michael J. Agovino in *Spin* described the piece as having a "right-between-the-eyes punch."

Despite being virtually ignored by the media and suffering from a hereditary disability he identified to Kim Green of *Paper* as "a scoliotic condition," Scott-Heron continued making public appearances with his group, the Amnesia Express, and also as a monologuist. With the dawn of the 1990s and the emergence of hip-hop artists who gravitated both toward jazz and sophisticated political expression, Scott-Heron's legacy came into clearer focus to many who had previously ignored him.

Indeed, such artists as Disposable Heroes of Hiphoprisy, Arrested Development, Digable Planets, KRS-1, and Me'Shell Ndgeocello owed a clear debt to Scott-Heron's articulate messages and the funky lyricism of his music. One of his acolytes—poet Dana Bryant, with whom he shared a stage—was distraught to hear her idol say privately in 1992 that "there ain't no revolution, and there wasn't no revolution, and there will be no revolution." As she told *New York,* "I was devastated." Yet Scott-Heron himself told the *Detroit Free Press* the following year that "The winter [in America] is man-made. So the spring can be man-made too."

Returned with *Spirits*

Ultimately, Scott-Heron insists that what he does is all about feel. He defined "bluesology" to Green: "What bluesology is supposed to say is how it feels. The articulation isn't melodic, exotic or erotic; it ain't none of those things. It's that they all come together and relate what it feels like. I play what it feels like." As far as his influence on younger artists is concerned, he insisted, "I do think that the form of rap has taken more aspects of my particular style than anyone else's in the scope of these kids and their illusions, but I think of myself as the father of black poetry, and I've done far more than anyone would have expected of me."

A record company bio has Scott-Heron musing, "I ain't saying I didn't invent rapping, I just cannot recall the circumstances." In an interview for *Billboard,* he criticized many rap artists, declaring "They need to study music" and "There's not a lot of humor. They use a lot of slang and colloquialisms, and you don't really see inside the person. Instead you just get a lot of posturing." Scott-Heron got a chance to show the rap generation how it's done when he appeared on the MTV Free Your Mind Spoken Word Tour with such younger writers as Reg E. Gaines and Maggie Estep.

At last, in 1993, Scott-Heron signed with TVT Records and recorded a new album, *Spirits,* which was released the following year. The label also announced its intention to acquire a portion of his back catalog on CD. On the song "Message to the Messengers," Scott-Heron spoke directly to young rappers: "I ain't comin' at you with no disrespect / All I'm sayin' is you damn well got to be correct / Because if you're gonna be speaking for a whole generation / And you know enough to handle their education / Be sure you know the real deal about

past situations / And ain't just repeating what you heard on a local TV station."

In the liner notes to *Spirits* Scott-Heron also emphasized the importance of recognizing the "spirits" of black ancestors and the history of the struggle. "In truth I call what I have been granted the opportunity to share 'gifts,'" he wrote. "I would like to personally claim to be the source of the melodies and ideas that have come through me, but that is just the point. Many of the shapes of sound and concepts have come upon me from no place I can trace: Notes and chords I'd never learned, thoughts and pictures I'd never seen. And all as clear as a sky untouched by cloud or smog or smoke or haze. Suddenly. Magically. As if transferred to me without effort."

Such, he seemed to say, was the influence of the artistic and political triumphs of the "spirits"; such, indeed, has been the force of Scott-Heron's own work on a new generation of bluesologists.

Selected writings

The Vulture (novel), World Publishing, 1970.
Small Talk at 125th & Lenox (poetry), World Publishing, 1970.
The Nigger Factory (novel), Dial Press, 1972.
The Mind of Gil Scott-Heron (poetry and lyrics), 1979.
So Far, So Good (lyrics), Third World Press, 1990.

Selected discography

Small Talk at 125th & Lenox, Flying Dutchman, 1970.
Pieces of a Man (includes "The Revolution Will Not Be Televised"), Flying Dutchman, 1971.
Free Will, Flying Dutchman, 1972.
Winter in America (includes "Winter in America" and "The Bottle"), Strata-East, 1974.
The Revolution Will Not Be Televised, Flying Dutchman, 1974; reissued, BMG, 1988.
The First Minute of a New Day, Arista, 1975.
From South Africa to South Carolina (includes "Johannesburg"), Arista, 1975.
It's Your World, Arista, 1976.
Bridges, Arista, 1977.
Secrets, Arista, 1978.
The Mind of Gil Scott-Heron, Arista, 1979.
(Contributor) "Shut 'Em Down," *No Nukes: Musicians for Safe Energy,* Asylum, 1980.
1980, 1980.
Real Eyes, Arista, 1980.
Reflections, Arista, 1981.
Moving Target, 1982.
(Contributor) "Shut 'Em Down," *Sunsplash Live,* Tuff Gong, 1983.

The Best of Gil Scott-Heron, Arista, 1984.
(Contributor) "Let Me See Your I.D.," *Sun City: Artists United Against Apartheid,* Manhattan, 1985.
Tales of Gil Scott-Heron and His Amnesia Express, Peak Top (UK), 1990.
Spirits (includes "Message to the Messengers"), TVT, 1994.

Sources

Books

Faber Companion to Twentieth-Century Popular Music, edited by Phil Hardy and Dave Laing, Faber & Faber, 1990.
Penguin Encyclopedia of Popular Music, Viking, 1989.

Periodicals

Billboard, April 2, 1994.
Detroit Free Press, April 9, 1993.
Down Beat, November 1983.
New York, January 20, 1992.
Paper, June 1993.
Pulse!, November 1993.
Rolling Stone, January 2, 1975.
Spin, August 1984.
Vibe, August 1994.

Additional information was provided by TVT publicity materials and Gil Scott-Heron's liner notes to *Spirits,* 1993-94.

—Simon Glickman

Jon Secada

Singer, songwriter

"I guess you could call my music world pop," cross-cultural crooner Jon Secada told the *New York Times* in a 1994 interview on the eve of his second LP release, *Heart, Soul and a Voice.* The Afro-Cuban Secada has been dubbed a young Julio Iglesias by the press, and his self-titled first album, recorded in both English and Spanish, has sold more than six million copies. In 1993 the Spanish version, *Otro Dia Mas Sin Verte,* won a Grammy Award for best Latin pop album. Its English counterpart crowded the airwaves with Top 40 singles; "Just Another Day," "Do You Believe in Us," and "Angel" went gold and platinum in many countries including Venezuela, Germany, and South Africa.

Secada's largely female audience has embraced the smooth bilingual melodies that play off Secada's smoldering good looks, while record company executives swooned at his instant commercial success. As Jose Behar, president of Secada's label, EMI Latin, told *Billboard,* "In Miami you could have music buyers who would tune into Radio Ritmo (WRTO) and then to Power 96 (WPOW) and would have a hard time not hearing Jon Secada."

In the spring of 1993 Secada wowed teenagers at a Disneyland "Grad Night," singing Spanish and English versions of his hit "Angel." Grad Night is Disneyland's yearly promotional stunt allowing more than 100,000 graduating high school seniors to cavort all night in the park testing rides and listening to the music of hit pop stars. For Latino and Anglo fans alike, Secada's multiethnic swinging equaled twice the cool. "I feel like I'm a perfect example of the American Dream," Secada told *Entertainment Weekly,* happy about his endorsement from the Disney corporation and his newfound fame among the younger set.

Some critics find Secada too perfect, however, comparing him to inflatable pop icons like Vanilla Ice, a rap artist from the same label that turned out to be more show than substance. Even style-minded *People* magazine called Secada's first album "mindless pop." His label may have promoted his sex-symbol image, yet it was manager Emilio Estefan, husband of pop superstar Gloria Estefan, who hired a former fashion model as Secada's full-time image consultant. With her help, Secada honed his appearance; Calvin Klein and Versace silk shirts soon counterbalanced his wobbly cowboy boots and transparent dental braces.

"Yet to dismiss him as another hunk with a heart is unfair," declared Gary Garcia of the *New York Times*. Secada's second album showed much more of his Afro-Cuban roots, echoing rhythm and blues and his

Born in Cuba in 1962; parents' names, Jose and Victoria; immigrated to U.S., 1971, and settled in Miami; married Jo Pat Cafaro (a makeup artist), 1988 (divorced 1993) *Education:* Received bachelor's and master's degrees in voice and jazz theory from University of Miami.

Music instructor at community colleges; hired to sing backup for pop singer Gloria Estefan, early 1980s; co-wrote six songs on Estefan's *Into the Light* album; toured with Estefan, 1990; released self-titled debut album and Spanish version, *Otro Dia Mas Sin Verte,* SBK/EMI Latin, 1992 version; toured extensively in Europe and Asia.

Awards: Grammy Award for best Latin album, 1993, for *Otro Dia Mas Sin Verte;* Premio Lo Nuestro awards for best album for *Jon Secada,* for best male artist, and for best new artist, all 1993; platinum records for *Jon Secada* and *Otro Dia Mas Sin Verte.*

Addresses: *Record company*—SBK/EMI Latin, 810 Avenue of the Americas, New York, NY 10019.

early influence, Earth Wind and Fire. What Garcia noted as unique throughout all the pomp and pop is Secada's consistent yet "unrestrained emotionality." Garcia summarized his review of *Heart, Soul, and a Voice* by emphasizing that "Secada can take a line like 'I promise to love you as if your heart were my own' and deliver it with unabashed conviction."

Raised in Miami's Melting Pot

Secada was born in Cuba in 1962 to a Cuban mother named Victoria and a black father, Jose. When he was eight years old he moved to Miami with his parents who began operating a chain of coffee shops. Secada's parents were always very supportive of his music career. Consequently, Secada grew up immersed in Miami's melting pot of R&B, disco, rock, and Latin, and was influenced by such mainstream stars as Elton John, Billy Joel, and Stevie Wonder. "I might be Hispanic, but I'm also black," Secada told John Lannert of *Billboard,* "and my influences and my roots lie in many places, just because of the diversity of growing up in Miami."

Despite all the cultural distractions, Secada was "the

kid who always got his homework done," according to an interview in *Entertainment Weekly* with high school friend and songwriting partner Miguel Morejon. Secada's good study habits continued all the way through college and graduate school where he earned bachelor's and master's degrees in voice and jazz theory. After graduating from the prestigious jazz program at the University of Miami, Secada taught music at a local community college and was then hired to sing backup for Gloria Estefan.

When they met Secada in the mid 1980s, the Estefans were very much involved with the musical group Miami Sound Machine and the glitz of the Miami scene, which was boosted by television shows like *Miami Vice.* Secada was introduced to Emilio Estefan through mutual friends, and the singer adopted him as his manager and mentor. James Hunter of the *Village Voice* wrote, "The Estefan's were pop, pop, pop, no more worried about bubblegum charges than, say, KC and the Sunshine Band had been banging out their funkier Florida prefabrications during the 70's."

Emilio Estefan hired Secada as a songwriter for his company, and together they produced albums for Pia Zadora, Luis Miguel, and Don Johnson. Secada's big break, however, came in 1990 when Gloria Estefan invited him to tour with her, giving him a solo spot in the show. A recording deal with SBK soon followed.

A Bilingual Release and Worldwide Success

Jon Secada, produced by Emilio Estefan, was released in May of 1992. Hunter described the LP as "recorded and mixed with the high resolution of sound that 80's pop showed with the look of the priciest commercial photography." The hit singles "Otro Dia" and "Angel" were originally released on this English version and topped *Billboard's* Latin charts for months. Six months later, Secada released *Otro Dia Mas Sin Verte,* the Spanish counterpart that remained at the top of the pop album charts for an additional six months.

Secada never actually planned to release the debut album in Spanish and thought of it originally as a fun experiment. "Three singles No. 1 and the first three in Spanish? Never in my wildest dreams," Secada mused in *Billboard* in 1993. "I mean it was an accident, an experiment to do this stuff in Spanish."

Secada's instantaneous success caused some critics to cry wolf, calling him a sell-out to his hits-oriented label. Yet Greg Sandow of *Entertainment Weekly* maintained that Secada "just does his music," the first release recorded with old friends from Miami, including

Morejon, and unglossed by any corporate production from SBK. The *Village Voice's* Hunter captured both Secada's multicultural mutability and his apple-pie profit when he said, "You can hear him as ... a [rock band] Sonic Youth disciple, or a member of a Bulgarian women's choir, if you like you can also hear him while you shop for laundry detergent and blue jeans."

Although Secada's manager/producer Estefan has told some sources that the singer can handle just about any style, in a *Billboard* article he described the first release as a "demo, a way to find out what really was his sound." Despite the record company's dismissal of rumors of creating a personality cult, facts point to massive promotion and image molding.

SBK's distributor EMI spent more than two years marketing the album overseas, encouraging Secada to tour Europe and Asia, and in March of 1993, they held a press junket during which the singer conducted more than 80 interviews with press agents from over 22 countries. In addition, after Secada won the Grammy Award for best Latin album, former Whilhemina model Ingrid Casares was hired to give him a complete makeover. Casares told the *New York Times* that she "was not so much changing Jon's image as creating an image, an image that goes beyond the Cuban-Latino market."

Sought to Recapture the Black Market

Musically and culturally, Secada succeeded in furthering his range beyond the Latin market with his second album, *Heart, Soul and a Voice,* released in 1994. The album has a noticeably more R&B flavor than his first album and draws on Secada's personal musical influences, Earth, Wind and Fire, resulting in a more textured sound. "I'm proud to say that I'm ... Afro-Cuban American. I wanted to make a statement with my Afro-Cuban side."

In contrast to his first two albums, Secada purposely recorded *Heart, Soul and a Voice* to sound different from its Spanish version, *Ti Se Vas* (which means "If You Go"). Stylistically, he added hip-hop rhythm to the English version and strains of soul that counter his signature pop melodies. Writing for the *New York Times,* Garcia commented that "new songs like "Whipped," which hints at racial and economic repression, and "Fat Chance," about a woman who plays hard to get have a noticeably urban edge." The single, "If You Go," became an instant hit, the singer's voice swelling with devotion when he bolts out the song's crescendo, "If you go, say goodbye, there'll be something missing in my life / 'Cause you know that all I really want is you."

For Secada, the move to an R&B sound was a conscious decision to explore the black side of his cultural background. "Integrate, integrate," Secada told the *New York Times,* "its a life philosophy." Yet despite his claims of diversification, Secada's second release was still heartily embraced by the Miami Latin community. Mauricio Zeilic, a Cuban-born reporter for Miami's Spanish-language TV network, commented in *Entertainment Weekly,* "He's one of us ... he's humble. He hasn't forgotten his roots." The singer explained in *Entertainment Weekly,* "My heart hasn't changed, but my life has changed. I didn't know what to expect when I sold all those records.... You touch people's lives. I had no idea how much."

> ## "I feel like I'm a perfect example of the American Dream."

In May of 1994 Secada was planning on touching even more people's lives through the world of music video. His image consultant, Ingrid Casares, hired fashion photographer Matthew Rolston to shoot the glossy MTV video for "If You Go." "The man has sold six million albums and nobody knows who he is," Casares was quoted as saying in the *New York Times.* "After this video and the new album, he'll be huge."

In that same interview, however, Secada responded: "I feel blessed and I don't take anything for granted. The minute you have an ego, that's the moment you start getting into trouble." In several sources, Secada maintains that the most exciting thing that has ever happened to him was to be asked to contribute a song to Frank Sinatra's "Duets II."

In the spring of 1994 Secada was busy moving out of his two-bedroom apartment in Miami beach and into a new ocean-front home. He had plans to explore the possibilities of making a jazz album or a Spanish release with a big band. "And if nothing else happens in my career," Secada announced in *Entertainment Weekly,* "well, I can always go back to teaching."

Selected discography

Jon Secada, SBK/EMI Latin, 1992.
Otro Dia Mas Sin Verte, SBK/EMI Latin, 1992.
Heart, Soul and a Voice, SBK/EMI Latin, 1994.
Si Te Vas, SBK/EMI Latin, 1994.

Also contributed to soundtrack *The Specialist,* Cresent Moon/Epic, 1994.

Sources

Billboard, February 27, 1993; June 5, 1993; July 7, 1993; April 16, 1994.
Entertainment Weekly, June 25, 1993; June 17, 1994.
New York Times, May 29, 1994.
People, May 30, 1994.
Vibe, August 1994.
Village Voice, August 25, 1992.

—Sarah Messer

Paul Shaffer

Keyboardist, bandleader, musical director

Although Paul Shaffer is best known as late-night television guru David Letterman's musical director, quirky sidekick, and bandleader, he is also a definitive role model for aspiring keyboard players, rock repertoire cover bands, and rhythm section leaders. In addition to releasing solo albums with his band—known as the Party Boys of Rock 'n' Roll—he has contributed to the albums of a dazzling array of musicians, including the Blues Brothers, Diana Ross, Nina Hagen, Yoko Ono, Barry Manilow, Paul Rodgers, the Honeydrippers, the Jeff Healey Band, and Joan Armatrading. His trademark approach to covering songs has been to combine a faithfulness to the original material with an infusion of his own enthusiastic, rollicking style.

Shaffer's group was called the World's Most Dangerous Band from 1982 through August of 1993, during their time on NBC-TV's long-running show *Late Night With David Letterman*. When the *Late Show With David Letterman* debuted on CBS-TV on August 30, 1993 (after much political wrangling and network maneuvering), Shaffer changed the name of his band to Paul Shaffer and the CBS Orchestra. On their own albums, however, the ensemble goes by the name the Party Boys of Rock 'n' Roll. Shaffer's band is comprised of drummer Anton Fig, bassist Will Lee, guitarist Sid McGinnis, synthesizer virtuoso and former Funkadelic/Parliament member Bernie Worrell, and rhythm guitarist Felicia Collins.

Shaffer accompanies the musical guests on the *Late Show With David Letterman* and, as a result, has played with an extensive roster of jazz, rock, folk, soul, hip-hop, and reggae musicians since he first became musical director and straight man for Letterman in 1982. Much of his job entails being able to accommodate an array of musical styles—often with less than a half hour's rehearsal—and consequently, he has developed into a laudably flexible musician with a working knowledge of scores of musical forms.

Began With Canadian Teen Parties

An only child, Shaffer was raised in Fort William (later called Thunder Bay), Ontario—then a town of under 100,000 people. He studied classical piano as a child and often performed in piano competitions. However, his interest turned to rock music when he reached his mid-teens. Fellow Canadian Neil Young was an early influence on Shaffer, along with such acts as the Beatles, the Bonnevilles, and the Merseybeats.

Shaffer began his musical career at the age of 16 in a local band called the Fugitives. He played regularly at

Born Paul Allan Shaffer, November 28, 1949, in Toronto, Ontario, Canada; raised in Fort William (now Thunder Bay), Ontario; immigrated to the United States, 1974; only son of a lawyer; married in 1990; children: one daughter. *Education:* Received degree in psychology from the University of Toronto. *Religion:* Jewish.

Began playing the piano at the age of six; played in piano competitions until his mid-teens; joined the band the Fugitives and played throughout Thunder Bay, Ontario, while in high school. Became musical director of Toronto's production of *Godspell,* 1972; moved to New York City, 1974; performed as a pianist in Broadway productions, created commercial jingles, made demo tapes, and worked for *National Lampoon's Radio Hour.* Became writer of special musical material for NBC-TV's *Saturday Night Live,* 1975; toured with the Blues Brothers as their musical director and recorded *Briefcase Full of Blues,* both 1978; worked with Gilda Radner in the Broadway show *Gilda Live;* left *Saturday Night Live* in 1979 to star in television comedy series *A Year at the Top;* returned to *Saturday Night Live* same year. Became David Letterman's musical director, 1982; with band, the Party Boys of Rock 'n' Roll, released *The World's Most Dangerous Party,* 1993.

Addresses: c/o Panacea Entertainment, 2705 Glendower Ave., Los Angeles, CA 90027.

high school dances on Friday nights and at local bars such as the Flamingo and the 4-D, two places where Neil Young used to entertain as well. Since Shaffer couldn't afford a Vox keyboard—and a Hammond organ was too unwieldy to tote—he originally played a Hohner organ with only four octaves, before moving on to a Yamaha single-keyboard organ. One of the highlights of his teen years in Thunder Bay was opening for the Troggs.

Shaffer had anticipated following in his father's professional footsteps. He originally planned to earn a law degree from the University of Toronto and then join the elder Shaffer's law firm. He ceased playing and studying music for his first two years of college and was miserable as a result. A friend urged him to take up his keyboard again; he did, and he then knew he had to follow his heart rather than his family's expectations. Shortly after graduating with a degree in psychology from the University of Toronto, Shaffer auditioned for

the role of musical director for the 1972 Toronto production of *Godspell;* landing the spot was his first big break. *Godspell* ran for 15 months.

During the early 1970s, Shaffer immersed himself in Toronto's cultural scene and created bonds of friendship with several artists who would later dominate American comedy. Fellow *Godspell* cast members included future *Saturday Night Live* performers Martin Short and Gilda Radner; the three remained friends for decades. Canadian-born producer/director Lorne Michaels of *Saturday Night Live,* along with comedians Dan Aykroyd and John Candy, were also influential in Shaffer's early professional life.

Shaffer made his first trip to New York City in 1974 to record the movie album for *Godspell.* He was then hired to play piano in the Broadway musical *The Magic Show,* and soon he was also playing for *National Lampoon's Radio Hour.* Shaffer put in 15-hour days throughout the mid-1970s, jumping from demo taping to commercial jingle gigs to radio show recordings. He never knew with whom he would be playing—everyone from James Brown to Judy Collins would turn up—and he was enthralled with the excitement of his work.

Forays Into Comedy

In addition to being a session musician, Shaffer had a flair for theatrical timing and television presentation. He first began flexing his comedy muscle as writer of special musical material for *Saturday Night Live* in 1975; he also worked on National Lampoon's *Good-Bye Pop* parody album, which was released the next year. In addition, Shaffer collaborated on the Blues Brothers' 1978 album *Briefcase Full of Blues;* it sold over 3 million copies and hit the top of the music charts.

After his stint with the Blues Brothers, Shaffer worked with Gilda Radner on her Broadway show *Gilda Live.* Shortly thereafter, in 1979, he left his post at *Saturday Night Live* to star in a television comedy called *A Year at the Top,* which was produced by Norman Lear and Don Kirshner but, due to disappointing ratings, ran for only six weeks. Shaffer then returned to *Saturday Night Live* and found a comedic niche on the show by impersonating rock emcee Don Kirshner for two seasons in various skits. He also played band manager Artie Fufkin in the comedic mock-documentary *This Is Spinal Tap,* directed by Rob Reiner. By 1982 Shaffer had been offered the position of musical director for late night television personality David Letterman. Due to his witty retorts, hard-driving musical style, and the overall popularity of Letterman's show, Shaffer became a national celebrity.

Music His Top Priority

Even with his late night success, Shaffer shunned the traditional trappings of wealth and fame: the manager, agent, personal trainer, and flashy summer home. He threw all of his energy into his work and music. This commitment took its toll on his personal life: Shaffer he was forced to sever a six-year relationship with a woman who was tired of taking the backseat to his musical career. Shaffer did eventually marry in 1990, and had a daughter soon afterward. And his fervor for music, kitsch, and comedy remain as strong as ever.

In 1991 Shaffer produced an album with Dion, Ben E. King, Bobby Womack, and Wilson Pickett titled *Coast to Coast,* which features standard rock and roll and blues classics such as "Louie Louie," "What Is Soul?," and "Wang Dang Doodle." Shaffer then worked on Blues Traveler's 1993 effort *Save His Soul.* That same year, he released his own band's album, produced by Todd Rundgren and titled *The World's Most Dangerous Party.*

Shaffer told *New York* magazine contributor Michael Stone that the assimilation and appreciation of music is more than just a job or a sound. "I used to listen to rock and roll as a kid," he related. "People were leading such exciting lives. They were going 'under the boardwalk' to make out. Or 'up on the roof' to make love. And I was coming home from school frozen in my long underwear." Music came to represent all that was exciting in life to Shaffer, and over the years he has clearly joined in on the excitement himself.

Selected discography

Godspell, Arista, 1974.
(With Barry Manilow) *This One's for You,* Arista, 1976.
(With National Lampoon) *Good-Bye Pop,* Epic, 1976.
(With the Jeff Healey Band) *Feel This,* Arista, 1977.
(With the Blues Brothers) *Briefcase Full of Blues,* Atlantic, 1978.
(With Joan Armatrading) *Me Myself,* A&M, 1980.
(With Nina Hagen) *Nunsexmonkrock,* Columbia, 1980.
(With Diana Ross) *Silk Electric,* RCA, 1981.
(With the Blues Brothers) *Made in America,* Atlantic, 1982.
(With Yoko Ono) *It's Alright,* Polydor, 1982.
The Honeydrippers, Volume 1, Es Paranza (distributed by Atlantic), 1984.
(With Dion, Ben E. King, Bobby Womack, and Wilson Pickett) *Coast to Coast,* Capitol/EMI Records, 1991.
(With Blues Traveler) *Save His Soul,* A&M, 1993.
(With the Party Boys of Rock 'n' Roll) *The World's Most Dangerous Party* (includes special guest appearances by Richard Belzer, James Coburn, and Harry Shearer), SBK Records, 1993.

Sources

Keyboard, September 1983; October 1986; March 1987; November 1989; October 1993.
New York, June 2, 1986.
New York Post, August 17, 1993.

—B. Kimberly Taylor

Shonen Knife

Rock band

In the landscape of American postpunk music, with its jaded rejection of popular culture, a Japanese "girl band" that sings about candy and cute animals would seem to be an unlikely candidate to become what *Pollstar* has called the "darlings of the underground rock world." Nonetheless, Shonen Knife—three Japanese women enamored of American pop culture and punk music—gradually gained that status, carving a niche for themselves with American underground audiences in the early 1980s by recycling the sounds of 1970s and 1980s punk bands like the Ramones and the Buzzcocks into a format that, as *Musician*'s Chris Rubin quipped, "sometimes suggests a K-Tel Sampler of '70s new wave and punk." Initially treasured by the likes of Nirvana, the lead band of "grunge" rock, Shonen Knife was discovered by mainstream media and major-label record companies in the early 1990s.

Despite Shonen Knife's relentlessly upbeat image, their origins were quietly rebellious in their own culture. The three young women—sisters Naoko and Atsuko Yamano and their friend Michie Nakatani—came from Osaka's middle class, where a young woman's life was expected to follow a strict path. When the three decided to form a band in the early 1980s, they had no intention of pursuing rock and roll fame.

Naoko Yamano told Gary Graff of the *Detroit Free Press* that her parents "used to make us keep our guitars hidden. They thought members of rock bands are bad people; it's a very typical thought of conservative Japanese people." She explained that the financial situation made it difficult for them to pursue their music full time: "If I will be independent from my parents, it is easy [to be in a band]. But I can't get enough money to live alone now. Usually Japanese women live with their parents till get married. If I get married and go out from my family house and my husband [encourages] me, I can play band more."

Band Formed as "Hobby"

Consequently, the Yamanos and Nakatani saw their music as a hobby only, one that would relieve the tedium of their day jobs: Naoko and Atsuko Yamano, who lived with their parents in Osaka, held office jobs with a plastic surgeon and fashion designer, respectively, while Nakatani worked as a word processor. The band's beginnings were appropriately simple, as Naoko described in *Pollstar*. "It was after we finish school," she explained. "Me and Michie were bored so we decide to start a band, but we need drummer. I made a pretty flyer and put it on refrigerator. Soon Atsuko see.... She said she would be drummer." They chose the band's name, like the music that would follow, because its playfulness and incongruity appealed to them. Naoko explained in *Rolling Stone* that a shonen knife is a children's pocket knife; "'Shonen' means boy and is a cute word," she elaborated, "and 'knife' is a sharp word. I like mixing the two."

Taken by the fun of it, the three proceeded to record three albums through the early 1980s with an independent label, Zero Records, based in their home city; Frank Kogan would later dub the EPs "three blasts of gleeful beauty" in the *Village Voice.* Each album sold only approximately 2,000 copies—a negligible number for an ambitious rock band; for Shonen Knife, however, it was a nice extra as they went along with their "hobby."

The group couldn't have anticipated the interest in their music that would surface on the other side of the world after the first imports of their EPs reached the United States in 1983. K, an independent label that Kogan described as "tiny," made a contract with Shonen Knife for their first U.S. release, *Burning Farm,* in 1985. Although the cassette-only recording was restricted to a small audience, it nonetheless began establishing the band with listeners searching out developments in alternative rock.

Chuck Eddy, one of those first listeners, was taken by what he called the group's "surf-gone-funk bass-gurgles" and "shattered-window percussion" in a *Village Voice* review. Critics were particularly intrigued by the band's lyrics—what Rubin described as "guileless songs about the minutiae of daily life [written] with equal enthusiasm and sincerity." *Burning Farm* con-

tained, for example, "Parrot Polynesia," "Elephant Pao Pao," "Banana Fish," and "Twist Barbie"—titles that accurately predict the songs' lyrics.

A slightly more substantial independent label, Subversive Records, brought out a second American album in 1987. The songs on *Pretty Little Baka Guy,* as before, addressed everyday objects and events in playful language, mixing English and Japanese with abandon, and unabashedly displaying their infatuation with American pop culture. The reviews multiplied. Eddy praised the LP in the *Village Voice:* "The surprises come in the tempos thrown awry by spasmodic staccato lisps and adenoidal nonsense scats and histrionic Rob Halford-style screeches, in the trashy farfisa and intercepted shortwave signals and grinding one-chord sludge tattooed onto Ferris wheel samba/blue-beat/exotic-bounce, in the phrasing and pronunciation and grammar that deliberately maul the English language."

A summer vacation in Los Angeles in 1989 brought Shonen Knife the chance to perform one show at the Second Coming club—a slot that friends had arranged for them. Since their musical interests were still too marginal to win them popularity in Japan where they were playing only once a month, the group was astonished to discover the size of their following in the United States. The audience that filled the club demonstrated its enthusiasm in a variety of ways, as promoter Bill Bartell recalled for Kogan: "It was probably the best thing that ever happened to anything ever. People shouted out song names, threw Snickers bars onstage during 'I Wanna Eat Chocobars.'" Kogan recalled that the audience wouldn't let them leave, insisting on a series of encores; local papers, including the *L.A. Weekly* and the *Los Angeles Times,* reviewed the show with approval.

American Following Grew

A year later—almost 10 years after Naoko's note on the refrigerator brought the band into being—Shonen Knife passed from underground oddity to a kind of retro-alternative rock phenomenon. Bartell, who owned the Gasatanka recording label, arranged for them to reissue earlier recordings with Gasatanka and Giant, bringing them one step closer to major-label patronage. The first, *Shonen Knife,* combined cuts from *Burning Farm* and *Yama-no Atchan,* one of the EPs that had been previously released in Japan.

The most unusual event, however, was the tribute album put together by Western bands that had followed the trio for years; some of the most famous indie rock bands in the States, including Sonic Youth, recorded their own versions of the music of this Japanese trio on *Every Band Has a Shonen Knife Who Loves Them.*

After these releases, the Knife's reputation expanded at a remarkable rate, prompting a small tour of the United States in the summer of 1991, where they played at some of the major punk landmarks, including New York City's CBGB. A chance to open for Nirvana on a three-week tour of the United Kingdom brought them under the wing of Kurt Cobain, the leading figure of grunge rock. In the spring of 1994, after Cobain's suicide, Naoko told Graff that Nirvana "took care of us a lot. Shonen Knife and Nirvana were like brothers and sisters. I feel now like I almost lost my good brother."

> *Despite Shonen Knife's relentlessly upbeat image, their origins were quietly rebellious in their own culture.*

In 1991 Shonen Knife released a second album, *712,* and the band had a chart hit in England with "Space Christmas." The momentum from these two years broke them into the major labels in 1992, when Japan's MCA, Creation in Europe, and SBK/ERG in the United States all offered them contracts. Virgin's *Let's Knife* offered re-recordings of songs from earlier releases.

Several critics noted the band's growth with *712:* Steve McClure commented in *Billboard* that "the band has moved from so-bad-it's-good amateurism to a more polished style, without losing its charm or sense of humor"; Scott Schinder remarked in *Pulse!* that the band had "traded the game amateurism of its indie releases for a more driving sound, applying upgraded instrumental chops and studio technique to souped-up reworkings of its indie hits."

The release of *712* anticipated a well-received appearance at New York's 1992 New Music Seminar—the recognized testing ground for alternative rock—and tours throughout 1993 that included a turn through Europe. By the spring of 1993, Shonen Knife's record sales remained comparatively small, but they had attained what McClure called "unprecedented visibility for a Japanese act in the U.S."

As Americans declared their love of Shonen Knife with more frequency, British reviewers began dismembering the band, trying to tear away the Knife's appearance of ingenuousness. Article titles drew on puns demonstrating a simple-minded stereotyping of Japanese culture: "Sushi and the Banshees" and "Toyotas in the Attic," for example.

David Stubbs summed up the debate in *Melody Maker* by asking, "Are the Knife genuine innocents, or are they cynically pandering to a certain racist notion of silly little Nips, scuttling through life happy-snapping at everything uncritically and unselectively?" Stubbs made his position clear when he announced it his "churlish duty ... to indicate that Shonen Knife are bewilderingly, innocuously, irresistibly, cheerfully, naively, exuberantly CRAP." Two weeks later, another *Melody Maker* writer noted, and resisted, the band's quickly rising popularity: "We are supposed to like Shonen Knife. They are the latest pocket-sized Japanese accessory, a funny, throwaway novelty."

Consequently, bandmembers began insisting that there was more substance to their music than writers had previously given them credit for. Explaining their ouevre in *Pollstar,* Naoko commented that "It is like candy. On the outside is sweet, and on the inside is a peanut. Something hard to bite down on." Scott Schinder made an argument for the band's substance in *Pulse!,* insisting that "while their popularity is often attributed to the camp value of the band's innocently skewed take on Western pop culture, Shonen Knife's true appeal lies in the guileless joy of its tunes, and in the more serious subtexts lurking beneath the threesome's infectiously cheerful surface."

Shed Candy Coat on *Rock Animals*

Eddy distinguished Shonen Knife from what he felt were less powerful bands of the same genre, describing how their "cheesy AM-readymade schlocktoons turn gleefully big and brisk and crude before your ears, with a vulnerable nursery school spunk."

"I like Shonen Knife," Frank Kogan explained in the *Village Voice,* "because they've got a sense of joy while being almost matter-of-fact about it. So they sound effortless rather than precious." Eddy agreed in his summary of *Pretty Little Baka Guy,* which struck him "like some Bizarro world teenage utopia, but its giggles and gawkiness affirm life's absurdity without mocking it, and that's a pretty smart thing to do even if everybody else did get too jaded for it a long time ago."

In a *Rolling Stone* review of *Shonen Knife,* Eddy attributed the popularity of the band within America's musical underground to "an innocence that jaded Western postpunks have worked years trying (and failing) to win back."

Released in 1994, *Rock Animals* presented the first slate of new songs from the band in quite a while. The album came at just the right time, challenging the group's candy-coated image with an undeniably hard-rock sound. "Knifers from way back will be pleasantly surprised at the way *Rock Animals* rocks out," Renee Crist claimed in *Spin.* "The Shonen Knife sound is typically spare and a little primitive (and not very sophisticated), but here the band nails its bare-bones style into hard-driving rock 'n' roll guitar solos, killer drumming, feedback, flannel."

Shonen Knife finally went professional in the spring of 1992, when the three women quit their various "office lady" positions in Osaka. Although "still largely viewed as an underground band in its musically conservative homeland," as Schinder noted, their success with Western audiences convinced them to make music as more than a hobby. "Now I'm happy that I can play music all day long," Naoko told Scott Schinder. "To release a CD for a major label isn't our goal. To keep playing music, to keep having fun—that is our goal. If we become rich, we want to make a club in Osaka and invite many American, British and European bands to come and play."

Selected discography

Burning Farm, K, 1985.
Pretty Little Baka Guy, Subversive Records, 1987.
Shonen Knife, Gasatanka/Giant, 1990.
712, Giant/Rockville Records, 1991.
Let's Knife, Virgin, 1992.
Rock Animals, Virgin, 1993.

Sources

Billboard, April 24, 1993.
Detroit Free Press, April 29, 1994.
Guitar Player, June 1993.
Melody Maker, September 19, 1992; November 7, 1992; November 21, 1992.
Musician, March 1993.
Pollstar, March 1, 1993.
Pulse!, August 1992; March 1994.
Rolling Stone, September 6, 1990; April 15, 1993; March 10, 1994.
Spin, December 1991; March 1993; February 1994.
Village Voice, April 26, 1987; March 27, 1990.

—*Ondine E. Le Blanc*

Sly and Robbie

Drummer and bassist

Although drummer Sly Dunbar and bassist Robbie Shakespeare are primarily musicians who play backup on other artists' albums, they are nonetheless a significant force in the music business and are known as "Sly and Robbie," or sometimes the "riddim twins." Their bass and drum work has appeared on not just a remarkable number of reggae albums, but particularly on several of the genre's milestone productions. They have sometimes been credited with initiating several of reggae's most successful trends, including "dub" and, most recently, dancehall. In 1993, almost 20 years after Sly and Robbie began, Maureen Sheridan described them in *Billboard* as "the drum and bass duo who define Jamaican rhythm." In addition, rock legends outside of reggae, including Mick Jagger and Bob Dylan, have sought out the Sly and Robbie sound.

Lowell "Sly" Dunbar and Robbie Shakespeare were both born in Jamaica in the early 1950s. They came of age in Kingston, the island's major city, just as reggae was also coming of age. Like so many young musicians living in the ghetto, Sly and Robbie had no access to formal training or even to written music and were largely self-taught. Sly, whose first drum kit consisted of empty food cans, told Don Palmer of *Musician* that he "was all the time practicing ... in school and playing on the desk."

Sly played his first set of real drums at the age of 15, when he formed a group called the Yardbrooms. He made a brief try at a "legitimate" job—refrigeration mechanics—after dropping out of school; he soon decided to devote himself to music. Hanging around the Kingston music scene, he eventually became a regular with Dave and Ansell Collins, whose band had a good reputation in the city. The Collins brothers gave Sly his first opportunity to record, including his drums on their 1969 release, *Double Barrel*. Sly would also play with the Mighty Diamonds and I-Roy before meeting his musical soulmate.

Robbie Shakespeare sought out a mentor to guide his musical education. "I heard Family Man Barrett playing with the Hippy Boys one night," he recalled to Palmer, adding, "I liked the way he played bass—strong, simple, melodic lines with feeling—so I asked him to give me lessons." Family Man proved to be a demanding teacher: "When I practiced," Robbie told Palmer, "I'd cry and play. I had a six-string guitar, and I played it with my big finger till blood came from my finger. If I was looking for a note and my ears weren't at peak to find the note, I'd cry till I found it."

Impressed with his protégé, Family Man christened Robbie's career with his first bass and even allowed the young musician to replace him in occasional Hippy

Sly Dunbar (born Lowell Fillmore Dunbar, May 10, 1952, in Kingston, Jamaica), drums; **Robbie Shakespeare** (born September 27, 1953, in Kingston, Jamaica), bass.

First played together under the tutelage of Bunny Lee and began Taxi record label, mid-1970s; backup musicians for many reggae artists, including Bob Marley, Peter Tosh, Black Uhuru, Gregory Isaacs, Burning Spear, Mighty Diamonds, and Jimmy Cliff; Island Records took over Taxi distribution, 1980, and Sly and Robbie began playing backup for Island's non-reggae artists, including Grace Jones; played backup for other artists, including Bob Dylan, Mick Jagger, Joan Armatrading, and Herbie Hancock; focused primarily on solo work, mid-1980s—.

Addresses: *Record company*—Mango Records, 400 Lafayette St., New York, NY 10003.

Boys and Aggravators gigs. By 1970 Robbie had become the Hippy Boys regular bassist. Other opportunities filled out Robbie's apprenticeship, including recording two songs with Bob Marley, "Concrete Jungle" and the legendary "Stir It Up," on *Catch a Fire*.

The Ordained Meeting

Sly and Robbie finally encountered one another—"It was ordained to be," Robbie told Palmer—when they were playing at rival clubs in downtown Kingston. "Sly was playing at the Tit For Tat," Robbie recounted, "and I was playing next door at Evil People's with the Hippy Boys. At break we'd always check each other out. When I saw Sly, I said, 'Yes, whenever this drummer touch the recording scene, every drummer have to pack up.'" Sly, who first heard Robbie's bass on a single in 1972, shared a similar first impression of his future partner: "It was the whole body of the bass, the sound and the way it flowed against the drummer. At a certain part of a tune he'd play like three different lines, change the line on the bridge and the verses after that, and get four different lines."

Sly and Robbie didn't actually play together until Kingston producer Bunny Lee brought them both into the studio for a joint session in the mid-1970s. At first, the two tried forming a band with five other musicians. It quickly turned out, however, that only these two shared a real devotion to the music. Banking on the power of that shared enthusiasm, they created Taxi Records in

1974, one of the longest-living of Jamaica's homegrown labels, and began marketing themselves as producers and a professional rhythm section.

Sly and Robbie soon became regulars all over the reggae circuit, playing with more and more of Kingston's heavyweights, including Burning Spear, the Mighty Diamonds, Jimmy Cliff, Big Youth, and reggae's greatest legend, Bob Marley. *Musician's* Palmer declared of Sly and Robbie in 1983, "One or both their names appear on probably half the reggae albums in any record store." Robert Santelli wrote in *Modern Drummer* that Sly's "sparse yet crisp beats practically defined the Jamaican brand of drumming in the '70s and '80s."

Peter Tosh, second in stature only to Marley, offered Sly and Robbie their first real break in 1976 when he invited them to play rhythm on *Legalize It*. As Word, Sound and Power, the pair went on tour with Tosh in 1978, winning new fans wherever they played. "The Sly and Robbie thing started from there," Robbie told *Billboard's* Sheridan. By 1984 they were so important to the Jamaican music industry that their ten-year anniversary prompted a concert celebration at the National Arena that took over the city and featured most of the reggae greats of the day, including Black Uhuru, Gregory Isaacs, Jimmy Riley, and Yellowman.

Sly and Robbie launched Taxi Records with a single by Gregory Isaacs, "Soon Forward," which claimed the Number One spot on Jamaican music charts. Taxi gained a foothold outside of Jamaica with *Red,* a 1981 album by Black Uhuru; the LP has remained one of the landmark releases in reggae's history. While Sly and Robbie played backup for many of the artists who recorded at the Taxi studios, the pair also used the label to present their own music—recordings on which they headlined an ensemble of guest artists. As of 1980 Taxi's international distribution was prospering in the hands of London-based Island records, which managed Taxi through its Mango/Taxi subsidiary.

International Attention

Sly and Robbie's second album with disco diva Grace Jones, *Nightclubbing,* constituted the pair's first significant excursion into pop music. During the same year, 1981, they cut several more releases with British and American pop notables, consolidating their crossover from exclusive reggae celebrity to mainstream acclaim; not only Jamaica, but also Great Britain and the United States were in love with Sly and Robbie. By 1983 they had added Great Britain's Joan Armatrading and the United States' Bob Dylan to their list of international pop-star connections. When *Musician's* Palmer interviewed Sly and Robbie in 1983, they were "the Jamaican rhythm section whose rise to the brink of international stardom has been just the mortal side of meteoric."

Despite their fame and their tremendous currency, Sly and Robbie remained modest. They were known as highly effective musicians who loved their music and even felt it as a spiritual force, but who avoided all manner of music business drama. Writing for *Melody Maker* in 1981, Paolo Hewitt commented that Sly and Robbie "go in, create consistently high quality music, then go out again. No artistic traumas. No drug or record company problems. Almighty God provides the inspiration."

> *"People said whenever Sly and I played togedder, we di'nt need d'rest of d'band."*
> —Robbie Shakespeare

What made Sly and Robbie "great" wasn't just their love of music or their professionalism. Rather, listeners discovered an unparalleled artistry in their work. Alan di Perna identified "rapid-fire, one-take creativity" as a "Sly and Robbie trademark" in *Musician* in 1987. Di Perna focused in particular on Robbie's bass, noting that he "approaches it much as a jazz soloist would a familiar melody, producing infinite and subtle variations that transform, but never obscure, the riff."

"[People] said whenever Sly and I played togedder, we di'nt need d'rest of d'band," Robbie told Roy Trakin in a 1984 *Musician* interview. "Bass and drums are like a foundation for building a house," he continued. "Me and Sly each play melodies, though, on our individual instruments. If y'listen to Sly drummin' alone, y'could dance off dat. If y'listen to bass alone, y'can dance off dat. The secret is playin' somet'ing dat's locked in when you're both together, but, at de same time, de parts stand by demselves, too."

As early as 1983, Palmer described Sly and Robbie as "innovators and codifiers of rhythmic traditions." He summarized that innovation, listing their achievements: the pair has been "credited with popularizing a fleet, insistent cymbal style (*flyers*), founding the stepping, martial drum patterns of *rockers* (a deceptive rhythmic variation marked by an eight-to-the-bar bass drum that, coupled with Sly's cymbals, give the impression of acceleration while the tempo is actually slowed), and creating a languid, fluent bass style that is percussive and melodic."

Such innovation, and especially a willingness to play with non-Jamaican pop, was part of the Sly and Robbie magic and had been from the beginning, as Robbie told *Billboard's* Sheridan. "I can tell you one thing," he explained, "from the early part when Sly and myself used to share a room.... We wouldn't sleep at night. We would always talk music; arrange the songs we were going to play, and decide how we were going to do it, without rehearsing it, just by talking it.... We would buy dozens of cassettes to hear the difference between American music and Jamaican music, how it was mixed. And after being exposed to all that, we would experiment with our sound."

A shift in the reggae sound in the mid-1980s, however, initiated the end of British and American audiences' affair with reggae. As more and more Jamaican musicians, including Sly and Robbie, immersed themselves in the new "dub" trend, more and more white listeners lost interest, and reggae's overseas fashionability faded.

Frank-John Hadley, reviewing *Reggae Greats: Sly and Robbie* for *Down Beat* in 1985, described the new sound with typical disappointment. He argued that "their booming, uniform dub ... makes for a trying listening experience." While Sly and Robbie's work as two of the industry's most valuable back-up men suffered no setback, their efforts as solo artists and on the behalf of reggae in general did suffer. They had hoped to see reggae continue to expand as an international music force; instead, they saw its influence narrowing.

Dub Fade and Dancehall Fame

Mat Smith wrote in *Melody Maker* in 1987 that "working with Sly and Robbie has become the accepted seal of approval on any artist's career." Alan di Perna described them in *Musician* as "supporting players" who have "become as recognizable and popular as comic book superheroes." Despite their impact on milestone albums across musical genres, the pair had never yet had a hit with one of their own albums. Solo pieces released only in Jamaica fared well enough, but those marketed to a wider audience never traveled beyond reggae connoisseur circles.

Eventually Sly and Robbie's music gained more popularity, but only as general tastes changed. First, the pair had to discover a strong mentor in producer Bill Laswell, with whom they began working in the mid-1980s. The three first worked together on a Mick Jagger album, *She's the Boss,* and soon after, Laswell was recruited to help Sly and Robbie get more out of their solo efforts.

The first LP with Laswell, *Language Barrier,* encountered a lukewarm reception after its 1985 release. 1987's *Rhythm Killers,* however, produced a hit single in Great Britain, "Boops (Here to Go)." In an effort to draw in those listeners outside of reggae's consistent market, Sly and Robbie heightened their experimentation with non-reggae sounds, emphasizing funk in particular and tossing in some early hip-hop thoughts. "We're trying to get new fans," Sly told *Musician's* di Perna. "Once they come into the funk, they're going to have to come into the reggae, because that's where we're going to take them."

Rhythm Killers won the press attention that had eluded *Language Barrier.* "I listened to this on the fourth of July," wrote a reviewer for *High Fidelity,* "and ... didn't care that I missed the fireworks." *Melody Maker's* Smith described the album as "enthused and fused with a ... schizophrenic art of noise attack all lashed around a non-stop rhythm that bumps each track nose to tail tight."

Sly and Robbie followed *Rhythm Killers* with *The Summit,* in 1988, and earned a rave review from *Musician,* which called it "pure pulse." The real breakthrough, however, came with 1990's *Silent Assassin,* on which the pair solidified its collaboration with hip-hop. "Maybe *Silent Assassin* can bring some attention back to reggae again," Sly mused to *Modern Drummer's* Robert Santelli. "That is what we're hoping will happen: to bring reggae, modern reggae, back into people's ears."

To achieve this, the pair worked with a host of rap's most favored artists, including KRS-One from Boogie Down Productions, Queen Latifah, and Young M.C. "Dunbar and Shakespeare make the full plunge into rap and hip-hop," declared Santelli, "resulting in the duo's most exciting record in years."

Sly and Robbie were already paving the way for the next wave in reggae—the combination of American rap and Jamaican dub comprising the new "dancehall" sound. After breaking the barrier with *Silent Assassins,* the pair released *Sly and Robbie Present ... DJ Riot* in its wake, helping to kick off the dancehall frenzy that spread into the United States in the early 1990s. They filled out their own pioneering rhythm work with the vocals of nine dancehall deejays collected from clubs around Jamaica.

"Sly and Robbie," wrote *Down Beat's* Dan Ouellette, "bring alive the kinship of reggae and rap." Dancehall would, in fact, finally achieve what reggae artists had been seeking for years: an audience for Jamaican music among African-American listeners. When "Murder She Wrote" hit the American charts in 1992,

creating one of the first major dancehall hits in the states, Sly was credited not only as a producer, but also as the inventor of its "new reggae rhythm" known as "bam bam."

"Reggae will be mixed with every other rhythm of the world," Sly predicted at the end of the pair's interview with *Billboard's* Sheridan, "Japanese, Korean, African, Indian, all kinds of different musics, a mixture of everything so that everyone can dance. As long as there is a groove, that is the key."

Selected discography

Sly and Robbie Present Taxi, Mango/Taxi, 1981.
The Sixties, Seventies + Eighties = Taxi, Mango/Taxi, 1981.
Crucial Reggae Driven by Sly and Robbie, Mango/Taxi, 1982.
Raiders of the Lost Dub, Mango/Taxi, 1981.
A Dub Experience, Mango/Taxi, 1984.
Reggae Greats: Sly and Robbie, Mango/Taxi, 1985.
Language Barrier, Island, 1985.
Rhythm Killers (includes "Boops [Here to Go]"), Island, 1987.
Taxi Fare, Heartbeat, 1987.
The Summit, RAS, 1988.
Two Rhythms Clash, RAS, 1989.
Silent Assassin, Island, 1989.
Sly and Robbie Present ... DJ Riot, Mango/Taxi, 1990.
Sly and Robbie Hits, Sonic Sound, 1990.
Remember Precious Times, RAS, 1993.

With Peter Tosh

Legalize It, Columbia, 1976.
Equal Rights, Columbia, 1977.
Bush Doctor, Rolling Stones, 1978.
Mystic Man, Rolling Stones, 1979.

With Black Uhuru

Sensimillia, Mango/Taxi, 1980.
Black Sounds of Freedom, Shanachie, 1981.
Red, Mango/Taxi, 1981.
Tear It Up, Mango/Taxi, 1982.
Chill Out, Mango/Taxi, 1982.
The Dub Factor, Mango/Taxi, 1983.

With Grace Jones; on Island

Warm Leatherette, 1980.
Nightclubbing, 1981.
Living My Life, 1982.

With others

Bunny Wailer, *Bunny Wailer Sings the Wailers,* Mango/Taxi, 1980.

Ian Dury, *Lord Opminster,* Polydor, 1981.
Joe Cocker, *Sheffield Steel,* Island, 1982.
Rolling Stones, *Undercover,* Virgin, 1983.
Herbie Hancock, *Future Shock,* Columbia, 1983.
Bob Dylan, *Infidels,* Columbia, 1983.
Mick Jagger, *She's the Boss,* Atlantic, 1984.
Maxi Priest, *Maxi Priest,* Virgin, 1988.

Solo LPs by Sly Dunbar

Simply Sly Man, Front Line, 1976.
Sly, Wicked and Slick, Front Line, 1977, reissued, 1991.
Sly-Go-Ville, Mango/Taxi, 1982.

Sources

Billboard, April 11, 1992; June 26, 1993; July 10, 1993.
Down Beat, September 1983; July 1985; March 1991.
High Fidelity, September 1987.
Melody Maker, July 18, 1981; July 6, 1985; August 10, 1985; May 30, 1987; March 10, 1990.
Modern Drummer, April 1990.
Musician, August 1981; February 1982; August 1984; August 1987; October 1988.
Rolling Stone, October 24, 1985.
Village Voice, July 7, 1987.

—Ondine E. Le Blanc

Smashing Pumpkins

Rock band

Critics hear endless lists of influences in the songs of the Chicago-based Smashing Pumpkins—Black Sabbath, Queen, Boston, the Who, Jimi Hendrix, Led Zeppelin, David Bowie—and use countless hard-edged adjectives to describe the Smashing Pumpkins' sound. Murray Englehart in *RIP* observed, "The collage that makes up the Pumpkins—ranging from a Hüsker Dü guitar onslaught to a sometime Hendrix-like fret dynamism and flashes of dreamy ambience—also features slabs of Sabbath, the band Henry Rollins once called 'the ultimate lonely man's music.'" And lead singer-songwriter Billy Corgan, whose "lonely guy" persona has been much explored by the media, admitted to Englehart that he did indeed listen to Sabbath at a young age.

While many suspect that Corgan *is* the band—and no one denies that he is the major contributor of time, art, and effort—the other members do their share to bring this alternative rock and roll to full, impassioned life. Corgan got the band together in 1988 after warming up with a band in Florida called the Marked—so named because of Corgan's strawberry-colored birthmark on his arm and a similar mark on another band member's face. He and D'Arcy Wretzky, who usually goes without her last name, met in an argument in a parking lot outside of a concert; when he discovered she played the bass, they joined forces and brought in guitarist James Iha, who was a student at Chicago's Loyola University, and drummer Jimmy Chamberlin.

Functional Dysfunctionals

Though many critics spend their energy describing Corgan, the personalities—social and musical—of the other Smashing Pumpkins members has made its way into the press. Jim Greer offered this summary for *Spin:* "D'Arcy (thumbnail sketch: likes to wear sunglasses and act cool), Iha (shy, friendly, big fan of *Star Trek: The Next Generation*), and Chamberlin (madman)." Alluding to various personal problems, including the end of D'Arcy and Iha's long-term relationship, Chamberlin's drug problems, and Corgan's emotional problems, D'Arcy told Michael Azerrad of *Rolling Stone,* "It's really a dysfunctional band."

But their performances suggest otherwise. Michael C. Harris described one Chicago event for *Rolling Stone* at which the band "worked the crowd into a moshing, body-surfing frenzy, guitarists Corgan and James Iha urging each other on to spastic heights while the seemingly unmoved D'Arcy worked a bass groove deep enough to maintain the dueling guitarists. And drummer Jimmy Chamberlin forged an unwavering rhythm bed augmented by original, jazzed-up fills."

However, Billy Corgan's philosophies, personal and musical, give the band its shape and purpose. His angst pervades their full-length debut album, *Gish,* and follow-up, *Siamese Dream,* which was named for Corgan's longing for the perfect companionship of a siamese twin attached at the wrist. He describes his childhood as "terrible." After his parents' divorce, Corgan lived first with his great-grandmother, then his father, who was a musician often on the road, and his stepmother. He has always felt himself to be an outcast, he told *Request's* Bill Wyman. "People consistently make me feel that there's something wrong with me. That I'm an incorrect person.... Even today, the music community has not exactly opened its arms up to my ideology."

But these profound insecurities have in no way come between Corgan and his commitment to musical progress. To the contrary, he clarified, "The simplest thing I can say about it is that if I'd had a decent childhood, I definitely wouldn't do this. There's definitely something about that hole in my life that pushed me to need acceptance from a thousand people at a time."

Intense Lyrics, Innovative Guitar Work

While "acceptance" may be forefront in Corgan's thoughts, he does not cater to his audience. He challenges himself, his band, and his audience with consistent conviction and hard work. His lyrics are deeply intimate and revealing. "These are very personal songs.

I sing them because they mean something to me, and in that sense, I think they will signify things to other people," he told S. L. Duff of *RIP.* In addition, "a frightening amount of time was spent" in search of the right guitar sounds, Corgan told Brett Milano in *Pulse!* "Everybody's already heard every guitar sound ever, so we wanted to come up with something as new as it could possibly be when you're still using guitars, foot pedals and an amp."

For *Gish,* Corgan explained to Mike Mettler of *Guitar Player,* "I wanted the rideout to sound like World War I airplanes divebombing around your head." The band's ambitious goals can be summed up in Corgan's typically aggressive and simultaneously understated stance: "I've always thought we could do something that's basically stupid, which is playing rock music, but to take it to a level that's something of a higher art form, as daunting a task as that might be, and to do it with some intelligence and class." D'Arcy made clear how prevalent a philosophy that is for the band when she told Azerrad, "Perfection is not an easy thing to do. We're trying to do something that's great and beautiful and will last, that is a piece of *art.*"

Indie or Not Indie?

Smashing Pumpkins have inspired awe from critics since the release of *Gish.* Chris Mundy in *Rolling Stone* wrote that *Gish* "smacks ... of the opening of an alternative universe." But Smashing Pumpkins, its members have noted with a certain bitterness, were not received too warmly by the independent label music world: they were too successful at selling albums and booking shows; they simply did not suffer enough. For Billy Corgan, however, an indie label was the only way to go with their first album, even though they were actively pursued by major labels. The goal was to retain creative license, Corgan told Mundy. "What the band does is so specific that we couldn't dilute it in any way. We couldn't put ourselves in the position where we were powerless."

Smashing Pumpkins' adamant stance has paid off. Lorraine Ali of *Rolling Stone* wrote, "Even the most chaotic pileups of distortion are painstakingly orchestrated." *Entertainment Weekly's* David Browne remarked that the band's 1993 release, *Siamese Dream,* "represents the great lost link between alternative, pop, and metal." Mark J. Petracca, also of *Entertainment Weekly,* elaborated, "This psychedelic pop masterpiece is one of the most important rock records of the year. [They] probe emotional depths while pummeling you with grungy guitar riffs, then rescue you with a delicate acoustic-guitar arpeggio." And *Billboard* spotlighted the album as "a stupendous, brilliantly produced album that combines brute force with strong melodic sense."

Christopher John Farley of *Time* noted that the band's 1993 album *Siamese Dream* "relies heavily on Hendrix-era musical scores, but manages to transcend most of them and create a lush sound the Pumpkins call their own." In *Stereo Review,* one writer exclaimed, "Bombastic riffing—newly minted from the archives of Hendrix, Zeppelin, and others—gets reconfigured by this Chicago quartet into jagged shards and clumsy arpeggios. They've taken the beauty of heavy metal's obsessive hooking and messed with it." Praising *Siamese Dream,* the writer concluded that the album "kicks you in the solar plexus and leaves you gasping for more."

These "slackers with vision," as *Entertainment Weekly's* David Browne called Smashing Pumpkins, released a third album in late 1994 that was quite a departure for the group. *Pisces Iscariot* is a collection of B-sides and "songs never meant to come out," Corgan noted in the LP's liner notes, as quoted in *Entertainment Weekly.* "It's easy to see why these songs didn't make the cut for *Siamese Dream* or even *Gish,"* commented Jim Greer in *Spin.* Pointing out the element of humor in the eclectic blend of tunes on *Pisces Iscariot,* which includes a remake of Fleetwood Mac's "Landslide," Greer found that "Great Pumpkin Corgan rarely disappoints."

Change, experimentation, and irreverence are some of the qualities that have made the Smashing Pumpkins one of the most admired alternative bands even while they burst out from that rubric. As Kevin Kerslake, who filmed their video for "Cherub Rock," told Deborah Russell in *Billboard,* "I think of angels when I hear the Smashing Pumpkins music." And the band's many fans would agree that their music does seem transcendent.

Selected discography

"I Am One"/"Not Worth Asking," Limited Potential, 1989.
"Tristessa"/"La Dolly Vita," Sub Pop, 1990.
Gish, Caroline, 1991.
Lull (EP), Caroline, 1991.
"Drown," *Singles* soundtrack, Epic, 1992.
"Jackie Blue," *20 Explosive Hits of the '70s,* Pravda, 1992.
Siamese Dream, Virgin, 1993.
Pisces Iscariot, Virgin, 1994.

Sources

Billboard, August 7, 1993; August 21, 1993; September 25, 1993.
Details, December 1993.
Detroit Free Press, December 3, 1993.
Entertainment Weekly, August 6, 1993; September 20, 1993; October 7, 1994.
Guitar Player, March 1992; December 1993; September 1994.
Los Angeles Times, October 17, 1993.
Musician, September 1993; July 1994.
Pulse!, September 1993.
Request, September 1993; November 1993.
RIP, May 1993; August 1994.
Rolling Stone, August 8, 1991; September 16, 1993; September 30, 1993; October 14, 1993; December 23, 1993; April 21, 1994.
Spin, December 1991; August 1993; November 1993; January 1994; February 1994; November 1994.
Stereo Review, December 1993.
Time, August 16, 1993; January 3, 1994.

Additional information for this profile was obtained from a Virgin Records press release, 1993.

—*Diane Moroff*

Georg Solti

Conductor

Sir Georg Solti is perhaps the most famous living conductor in international music circles, and certainly the most sought after. His wide operatic and orchestral repertory—and his no-nonsense approach to music-making—have brought him respect and admiration onstage and off. In a career that has spanned more than 60 years, Solti has received accolades from around the world and continuous conducting engagements with the best orchestras and opera companies.

Solti was born on October 21, 1912, in Budapest, Hungary, and displayed an early affinity for music. When he was 13 years old, he saw conductor Erich Kleiber lead a performance of Beethoven's Fifth Symphony, and he knew then that he wanted to be a conductor. He studied piano, composition, and conducting at the renowned Franz Liszt Academy in Budapest, under the tutelage of eminent musicians Béla Bartók, Ernst von Dohnányi, and Zoltan Kodály. After graduating from the academy in 1930, he began work at the Budapest State Opera as a *répétiteur*—someone who assists backstage, coaches singers, and performs other miscellaneous duties.

In 1936 and 1937, Solti assisted world-famous conductor Arturo Toscanini at the Salzburg Festival in Austria, but he did not get his first conducting job until 1938, when he led a performance of Wolfgang Amadeus Mozart's *Marriage of Figaro* at the Budapest State Opera. His debut was unfortunately overshadowed by Nazi leader Adolf Hitler's invasion of Austria; Solti, who is Jewish, fled to Switzerland for the rest of World War II.

While in Switzerland, Solti turned his attention to the piano, coaching an operatic tenor and winning first prize at the Concours International piano competition in Geneva in 1942. After the war, the American forces occupying Germany began a search for musicians who could rekindle the country's musical life—but who did not have any Nazi associations. Solti was offered the post of music director of the Bavarian State Opera in Munich in 1946 and served in that capacity until 1952. He also appeared at the Salzburg Festival and conducted in Paris, Berlin, Rome, Vienna, Florence, and Buenos Aires.

Important to British Opera

With his reputation on the rise and his operatic repertory increasing, Solti next accepted a position as music director of the Frankfurt City Opera and remained there for nearly a decade. Then, from 1961 to 1971, he worked as music director at the Royal Opera House, Covent Garden, in England. His association with England and the English became a close one: he raised

Born György Solti (surname pronounced "*Shoal*-tee"), October 21, 1912, in Budapest, Hungary; son of Mores (a grain merchant) and Theres Solti; married Hedi Oeschli, 1946 (divorced, 1966); married Valerie Pitts; children: (second marriage) Gabrielle, Claudia. *Education:* Studied piano, composition, and conducting at Franz Liszt Academy, Budapest, under Béla Bartók, Ernst von Dohnányi, and Zoltan Kodály; graduated 1930.

Répétiteur at Budapest State Opera, 1930-38, and at Salzburg Festival, 1936 and 1937, where he assisted Arturo Toscanini; conducting debut at Budapest, March 11, 1938, with Mozart's *Marriage of Figaro;* went to Switzerland, 1939; appointments at Bavarian State Opera, Munich, Germany, 1946-52, Frankfurt City Opera, 1952-61, Royal Opera House, Covent Garden, 1961-71, Chicago Symphony Orchestra, 1969-91, l'Orchestre de Paris, 1970-75, and London Philharmonic Orchestra, 1979-84; co-founder of Solti Orchestral Project at Carnegie Hall, June 1994; recording artist with more than 250 releases, chiefly with Chicago Symphony Orchestra, London Philharmonic Orchestra, London Symphony Orchestra, and Vienna Philharmonic.

Selected awards: First prize in Concours International piano competition, Geneva, 1942; Gold Baton Award from ASCAP, 1970; dubbed Knight Commander of the British Empire by Queen Elizabeth II, 1972; Kennedy Center Honors, 1993; winner of more Grammy awards than any artist, including awards for recordings of Verdi's *Aïda,* Mahler's Symphonies Nos. 8 and 9, the complete Beethoven and Brahms symphonies, Schoenberg's *Moses und Aron,* Bach's *Mass in B Minor,* and Strauss's *Die Frau ohne Schatten;* numerous honorary degrees and international awards.

Addresses: *Management*—Colbert Artists Management, 111 West 57th St., New York, NY 10019.

later became its conductor emeritus. In 1992 he was made music director laureate at Covent Garden.

One of Solti's biggest career undertakings was the recording of Richard Wagner's monumental cycle, *Der Ring des Nibelungen,* which consists of four operas: *Das Rheingold, Die Walküre, Siegfried,* and *Götter-dämmerung.* Work on the legendary recording began in 1958 and took eight years to complete. Record producer John Culshaw wrote in *Ring Resounding,* his book about the project: "Nothing comparable in scope, cost, or artistic and technical challenge had been attempted in the history of the gramophone." The recording is still available and continues to serve as the definitive interpretation of the German composer's masterpiece.

Champion of Large Repertory

Many music specialists agree that Solti is at his best with German, Austrian, and Hungarian music from the late eighteenth to the early twentieth centuries—a repertory that includes the works of composers Franz Joseph Haydn, Wolfgang Amadeus Mozart, Ludwig van Beethoven, Franz Schubert, Robert Schumann, Johannes Brahms, Richard Wagner, Gustav Mahler, Anton Bruckner, and Richard Strauss. Yet Solti has also excelled in his performances of the music of Hungary's Béla Bartók, Italy's Giuseppe Verdi, and France's Hector Berlioz. In addition, Solti is notable for his willingness to program works that fall outside of the traditional orchestral and operatic repertory. In 1970, he won the Gold Baton Award from the American Society of Composers, Authors, and Publishers (ASCAP) for having programmed the greatest number of pieces written since 1940.

Solti's conducting style is clear and direct. Although he is one of the more acrobatic conductors, his movements are never superfluous. "The things that intrigue me," he was quoted as saying in *Time,* "are how to make forms clear. How to hold a movement together, or, if I am conducting opera, how to build an act or a scene." While he is commonly believed to be a commanding presence both on and off the podium, Solti is not tyrannical, and musicians respect his businesslike attitude.

Headed Chicago Symphony Orchestra

The pinnacle of Solti's career has been his association with the Chicago Symphony Orchestra (CSO). He began his post with the CSO in 1969, and, though he resigned formally in 1991, he holds the title of music

the visibility of both Covent Garden and British opera singers in general, and made a point of programming works by native composers such as Benjamin Britten. He also conducted the British premiere of Austrian composer Arnold Schoenberg's opera *Moses und Aron*—a production that won international acclaim. For his contribution to musical life in England, Solti was knighted by Queen Elizabeth II in 1972. From 1979 to 1984, he served as principal conductor and artistic director of the London Philharmonic Orchestra and director laureate and continues to work with the orchestra, though more sporadically than before. Solti brought the CSO to international prominence, increasing its repertory and its reputation. By the mid-1970s it had become one of the top five orchestras in North America. In an article in the *New Yorker* in 1974 Solti stated, "I have never found a group of musicians who take music so seriously. I think my Chicago Symphony is the finest in the world."

In 1992 Solti began an appointment as artistic director of the Salzburg Easter Festival, and the next year he recorded the festival's production of Strauss's opera *Die Frau ohne Schatten;* the recording won a Grammy Award in 1993. Solti has won more Grammy awards than any artist—31 as of 1994.

In June of 1994 Solti embarked upon the Solti Orchestral Project at Carnegie Hall, a two-week workshop during which 80 instrumentalists aged 18 to 30 worked with principal players from five U.S. orchestras. The purpose of the project—which was conceived by Solti and by Carnegie Hall executive director Judith Arron—was to give younger players an opportunity to perform with, and learn from, experienced orchestral musicians.

In a Carnegie Hall press release, Solti was quoted as saying: "Working with young musicians is one of the great joys of my life. For several years I have hoped to find a way in which I could pass on to tomorrow's generation of orchestral musicians the experience I have been fortunate to inherit from my teachers and from over 50 years of practical work with orchestras all over the world."

Selected discography

On London

(Chicago Symphony Orchestra and Chorus) Bach: *Mass in B Minor.*

(London Philharmonic Orchestra, with pianist Vladimir Ashkenazy) Bartók: *Piano Concertos 1-3; Sonata for Two Pianos and Percussion.*

(Chicago Symphony Orchestra and Chorus) Beethoven: *Symphony No. 9 ("Choral").*

(Chicago Symphony Orchestra) Brahms: *Symphonies 1-4; Tragic Overture; Academic Festival Overture.*

(Chicago Symphony Orchestra and Chorus) Haydn: *The Creation.*

(Chicago Symphony Orchestra, with Vienna Boys Choir, Vienna State Opera Chorus, and Vienna Singverein Chorus and Soloists) Mahler: *Symphony No. 8.*

(Chicago Symphony Orchestra) Mahler: *Symphony No. 9.*

(London Philharmonic Orchestra) Mozart: *The Marriage of Figaro.*

(Chicago Symphony Orchestra and Chorus, with Franz Mazura and Philip Langridge) Schoenberg: *Moses und Aron.*

(Vienna Philharmonic and State Opera Chorus, with Julia Varady, Hildegard Behrens, Placido Domingo, and Jose Van Dam) Strauss: *Die Frau ohne Schatten.*

(National Philharmonic Orchestra, with Luciano Pavarotti, Margaret Price, and Renato Bruson) Verdi: *Un Ballo in Maschera.*

(Vienna Philharmonic) Wagner: *Der Ring des Nibelungen* (complete).

Sources

Books

Culshaw, John, *Ring Resounding,* Viking Press, 1967.

Furlong, William Barry, *Season with Solti: A Year in the Life of the Chicago Symphony,* Macmillan, 1974.

Robinson, Paul, *Solti,* Lester & Orpen, 1979.

Periodicals

Chicago, October 1987.

Chicago Tribune, November 28, 1993.

Christian Science Monitor, December 3, 1993.

High Fidelity, January 1967.

Musician, March 1993.

New Yorker, May 27, 1974.

New York Times, April 25, 1971; December 10, 1972; June 5, 1994.

Opera News, January 12, 1974; September 1976.

Pulse!, October 1992.

Stereo Review, October 1987.

Time, May 5, 1973.

Washington Post, December 5, 1993.

Additional information for this profile was obtained from a press release for the Solti Orchestral Project at Carnegie Hall, February 17, 1993.

—*Joyce Harrison*

Sounds
of
Blackness

Gospel group

The gospel chorus that became the Grammy Award-winning ensemble Sounds of Blackness first took shape in the late 1960s—and began with no commercial aspirations whatsoever. Popularizing a new kind of sound, the experimental gospel chorus has been winning critical, market, and industry attention since the early 1990s. Sounds of Blackness boasts a dedicated membership of 40 artists: 30 vocalists, including a team of strong soloists, backed by a ten-piece orchestra. Ann Bennett-Nesby, their premier soloist, was able launch a solo career based on Sounds' success.

"For 20 long years," Britt Robson wrote in the Minneapolis-based periodical *City Pages* in 1994, "Sounds of Blackness persevered as an important but somewhat obscure component of the local music scene." That component began as the Macalester College Black Choir in St. Paul, Minnesota, in 1969. This early incarnation held until 1971, when Gary Hines became the group's director.

Hines took steps to shape a stronger character and purpose for the outfit, including changing the name to Sounds of Blackness. "In our repertoire we do the whole range of African American music," Hines told Leslie Tucker in *Rolling Stone*. "We wanted our name to reflect the scope of what we're doing." The change also spurred the choir's shift into a more experimental path, influenced by Hines's arrangements and visions.

Hines was responsible for expanding the ensemble's repertoire far beyond the usual gospel fare, experimenting with the influence of pop stars like Stevie Wonder and Marvin Gaye, as well as digging back into the roots of African and African American music. Sounds of Blackness began trying out more theatrical productions in the mid-1970s, beginning with a 1974 Christmas performance, *The Night Before Christmas ... A Musical Fantasy*. Other pieces included *The Soul of the '60s, Music for Martin,* and *Africa to America*. Their popularity on the local scene allowed for three albums

Photograph by Sandy May, courtesy of Perspective Records

over the years, all produced on small labels for their St. Paul market.

Years later, the group's producers would argue that this time of fermentation was necessary to create their Grammy-quality power. "Sounds of Blackness isn't something where a person can suddenly come along and say, "Hey, I've got this great concept,'" record producer Terry Lewis told Robson, "because it doesn't work that way. It almost had to come out of the inward search of that period.... Then it had to be nurtured and changed and rechanged and struggled with in terms of humility, strength, power, and faith."

The choir was also moving more regularly in the circles of the city's pop music scene. In the late 1980s and early 1990s, Sounds of Blackness provided backup vocals for a number of major recordings, including the soundtrack for *Batman* and various pop releases that were recorded in the Twin Cities. Furthermore, a powerful new asset came their way in the voice of Ann Bennett-Nesby, who first sang with the chorus on an invitation from her sister, Shirley Marie Graham. Jennifer Whitlock, another vocalist, noted in *City Pages* that those who happened to be in rehearsal that day "were

in shock" at the magnitude of Bennett-Nesby's voice. Bennett-Nesby not only became a new member of the choir, but overnight became their star soloist.

Discovered by Jam and Lewis

As the choir went about its musical business in the late 1980s, they came to the attention of Jimmy "Jam" Harris and Terry Lewis, the two successful young producers who turned Janet Jackson into a chart-topping megastar. Jam and Lewis decided to bring Sounds into the studio in the fall of 1988 to do some backup vocals for a Christmas album, *My Gift to You,* by Alexander O'Neal, a former vocalist with the choir.

Jam and Lewis were so enamored of the choir's sound that they decided to make Sounds of Blackness—hardly a sure bet in the pop market—the debut release on their new label, Perspective Records. Karen Kennedy, general manager at Perspective, explained to *Billboard's* David Nathan in 1991, "This album was picked as a first release [because] it reflects the tone for the label. It really gives honor to all aspects of black music and it's so different from what's on the radio today."

Perspective had the album, *The Evolution of Gospel,* ready for release in 1991. The public response was so positive that one single, "Optimistic," broke the Top Ten and became a Number One hit on the R&B airwaves; *Billboard* reported two more dance hits from the album. After more than 250,000 copies moved off the nation's record store shelves, *Evolution* was also honored with the industry praise of a Grammy Award.

Evolution's makers, however, measured its value not so much in terms of dollars, but in terms of mission. Lewis understood the release's success as fulfilling a certain need in the black community; as he explained to Robson: "It is timeless music; not what people wanted, but what people needed.... Sounds of Blackness is what we desire to achieve. We need somebody to provoke our spirituality, to calm us down and bring us back to reality."

In keeping with the group's history, *Evolution* was recognized as "one of the most adventurous projects released in years," according to Nathan. Hines expressed a sense of purpose for the album that eclipsed any commercial goals. "This album," he told the *Billboard* writer, "is meant to portray the essence of the African American experience through our music. It's an expression of where gospel music has been historically and where we're taking it." Where they were taking it apparently challenged traditional music genres. "With

Jam and Lewis contemporizing some of the songs and arrangements alongside Hines's ever-refining musical vision," Robson wrote, "*Evolution* was a jolting, joyous musical sprawl that synergized gospel with everything from African chants to hip-hop dance beats to a Sly Stone cover."

The choir maintained its usual pace of work in the year that followed, simply playing to a greatly expanded audience. The fall of 1992 took them on tour with singer Luther Vandross. That Christmas saw the release of *The Night Before Christmas ... A Musical Fantasy,* bringing one of Hines's mid-1970s theatrical productions to national attention. Writing for *Interview,* Joan Morgan announced that the album was "guaranteed to whisk your soul away from mere gift-buying and take you to a place where ... commercialism is displaced by pure hallelujah." Aside from their own albums, Sounds continued to lend their rich vocals to other productions, including albums by Vandross and John Mellencamp and soundtracks for the films *Mo' Money* and *Posse.*

Expanding Reputation Exerts Pressure

The growing circles of their reputation, and particularly their tour itinerary, did put a new kind of pressure on the members, all of whom still juggled full-time careers and pursued work in the choir with little or no monetary recompense. Because Sounds of Blackness is a non-profit corporation, none of its musicians had ever been able to live off of it—even when it functioned as a vital regular on the local music scene. Hines, for example, had earned his living for years with the Minnesota Department of Human Rights, where he was an investigator and mediator.

Other members were doctors and lawyers, engineers and designers; the 1994 lineup, as Robson documented, also included a horse trainer and a state trooper. "It was a labor of love for all the members," Robson wrote. "They have a love of the music," Hines explained to *Jet,* "and come in from all over and audition. They like the message of promoting Black pride through our music."

The choir continued to swell its commercial success with a third release in 1994, *Africa to America: The Journey of the Drum.* Like *The Night Before Christmas,* the album grew out of a production that Hines had originally penned in 1975—a work that Robson characterized as "an adventurous production spanning the entire spectrum of African American music." After Hines took the work on tour in 1992, Jam and Lewis decided they wanted to record it, although it required some downsizing. Comparing *Africa to America* with

Evolution, Robson felt that "it [didn't] hold together as well, primarily because its scope is simply too expansive for one CD to contain—the last third of the disc hopscotches from one style to the next. Hines," he concluded, "acknowledges that Sounds was trying to put a gallon of music in a quart jar."

The success of Sounds of Blackness brought certain success to some of its major players—not only soloist Bennett-Nesby, but also director Gary Hines. When Hines assumed the directorship of the Macalester College Black Choir in 1971, he was only 19 years old. The aspiring body-builder—he held the Mr. Minnesota title in 1981—had moved to Minneapolis with his family in 1964.

> *"We're here to reclaim ownership of African American music."*
> —Gary Hines

The Hines family started out in Yonkers, New York, where Gary and his five older siblings immersed themselves in music. "Sunday mornings," Hines related to Robson, "we had spirituals and gospel in church; out on the street corners we'd hear brothers singing doo-wop; and in an alley an old man singing the blues. The radio would play Frankie Valli and Nat King Cole. You didn't have any of the insane division the industry has today."

Hines's mother made her living as a professional jazz singer, and although his father was a furniture upholsterer, music was still an integral part of his work—he had a jukebox in his workshop. "It had everything on it," Hines told Robson. "We'd sneak down and listen to B. B. King, Oscar Peterson, jazz, blues, gospel, you name it." The Hines children also pursued musical experiences outside of their home, finding rich opportunity in the New York City streets. "When I was five," Hines recalled in the interview with Robson, "me and my brothers joined a fife and drum corps. The discipline of that has rubbed off to this day in terms of rehearsal and punctuality and work ethic, because we would practice ourselves into a sweat every day and just love it. The whole spirit, mind, and body thing—what is now called the holistic approach—came together for me."

The success of the choir changed Hines's career considerably, allowing him to devote his life to making music. He began working regularly for Jam and Lewis's Flyte Tyme studios as a writer, arranger, and producer, contributing to works beyond Sounds. Hines probably reached his most diverse, multinational audience with the theme song for the 1994 World Cup, on which he collaborated with Daryl Hall of the rock duo Hall and Oates.

Sounds of Blackness has come under fire in some circles, where it is perceived as "blackness lite, detailing the [centuries-long African American] struggle with a happy face," to quote Robson. Hines responded to such criticism by stating: "We sing about traditional strength, spiritual strength, not about anything passive or conciliatory, but active and militant. When we say, 'be optimistic,' it is said in the face of what we go through, that we are still able to keep faith in one's god and one's self."

In particular, Hines defined the ensemble's purpose as an effort to combat a history of racism in the music business. "We're aware that, historically, black music and musicians have been taken advantage of, excluded, underpromoted and pushed aside," Hines told Tucker in *Rolling Stone*. "We're here to reclaim ownership of African American music."

Selected discography

The Evolution of Gospel (includes "Optimistic"), Perspective/A&M, 1991.
The Night Before Christmas ... A Musical Fantasy, Perspective/A&M, 1992.
Africa to America: The Journey of the Drum, Perspective/A&M, 1994.

Sources

Billboard, June 1, 1991; February 26, 1994.
Cash Box, July 6, 1991; December 14, 1991.
City Pages (Minneapolis), April 20, 1994.
Interview, December 1992.
Jet, March 23, 1992.
Melody Maker, May 15, 1993.
Rolling Stone, August 22, 1991; July 14, 1994.

Additional information for this profile was obtained from Perspective Records press materials.

—*Ondine E. Le Blanc*

Mavis Staples

Singer

Mavis Staples told *USA Today* contributor James T. Jones that the Lord sent pop star Prince to her. It was in 1987 when her father, Roebuck "Pops" Staples, called to say that Prince wanted to talk to her. "What prince?," she asked. "That one they call purple," he answered. A longtime fan of the Staples Singers—Mavis Staples's family band, in which Mavis sang with Pops, sisters Yvonne and Cleo, and brother Pervis—Prince acted as a knight in shining armor to Staples, whose career had been static for a decade.

Troubled with taxes and unpaid bills, she had been reduced to selling her car for cash. Then Prince, who later changed his named to an unpronounceable symbol, offered her a seven-year contract on Paisley Park Records, and Staples's hometown of Chicago began to feel like a fairy-tale land.

Staples's musical life began when her father turned his family into a gospel band. They sang "message songs" throughout the southern United States, inspired by the words of civil rights activist Martin Luther King, Jr.; Pops is widely quoted as having said, "Listen, if this man can preach this, then we can sing it." As Amy Linden put it in *People,* Mavis Staples still "sings with a soaring, liberating power that can make you feel the intensity of a Sunday service."

Staples revealed to Leonard Pitts, Jr., in *Musician* that during her family's hardest times, she remained optimistic by repeating to herself: "Jesus, this is my gift, this voice you've given me. I don't even know what key I sing in.... And you're not keeping me to suffer. You're keeping me for a reason." Her father apparently agreed. When the family's career seemed to hit a dead end, Pops told her, "Mavis, you better go on and try to find a label. The Lord gifted you with your voice and if you don't use it he'll take it back."

Collaboration Caused Controversy

Prince's interest in Staples's career seemed like a godsend. But because of her deep religious convictions and political commitment, Staples's union with the controversial singer-songwriter miffed and confused a number of her listeners. Alf Billingham of *Melody Maker* reported Staples's amused response: "I was told that I shouldn't be doing stuff with Prince because of his reputation for writing suggestive lyrics. Who do they think I am? The Singing Nun?" Staples does not fear Prince's exhibitionist sexuality. She considers it a healthy sign of his youth and notes that he does not impose it on the music he writes for her. Prince has produced two albums for Staples: *Time Waits for No One* in 1989 and *The Voice* in 1993.

While Tom Moon, writing in *Details,* found that *Time Waits for No One* "failed to challenge [Staples's] sassy-to-scornful vocal range," other music critics found it an intriguing and remarkable blend of the pair's distinct talents. Simon Reynolds wrote in *Melody Maker,* "This record is a miniature triumph of futuristic R&B, old school meets techno-chic"; the title song, he commented, is "the killer: a 21st Century cathedral of a ballad, with an epic fade of soul mama throes and Hendrix squeals 'n' sobs." Phyl Garland, writing in *Stereo Review,* found Staples and Prince the perfect complements: "The result points up [Prince's] very real affinity for rhythm-and-blues while underscoring the close relationship between traditional and contemporary black popular music: the best of yesterday and today meet on the common ground of musical excellence."

Certainly Prince has been the major force in Staples's career's renaissance, and she is nothing but appreciative—but the singer also knows her own talents. According to Pitts, Staples is forever besieged by inquiries about "how it feels" to work with Prince; the music veteran is savvy enough to respond, "Well, how does Prince feel working with *me?*" Pitts pointed out that Staples "has been in music longer than Prince has

been alive," and that evidence of her talents comes not only from the success of the Staples Singers and from her own solo career, but also from the "raiding" of her "vocal arsenal" by such stars as Stevie Wonder, Michael Jackson, and Prince himself.

Garland assessed that although "[her] distinctive, heavy-throated voice and profound expressiveness became a hallmark of the Staples's sound as they fused elements of gospel with rhythm-and-blues to take their place on the cutting edge of the Sixties soul phenomenon, [her] interpretive strength was even more apparent in her occasional solo recordings." Staples has also appeared on albums with Ray Charles, Kenny Loggins, Marty Stuart, and others, and is featured on BeBe and CeCe Winans's hit remake of the Staples Singers' song "I'll Take You There."

Songs Come From the Heart

On the 1993 album *The Voice,* Staples's personality is wholly present, thanks in part to Prince's songs—he wrote or cowrote seven of the album's 12 songs—which Staples feels "are about my life," she told *Billboard'* s David Nathan. She found "Blood Is Thicker Than Time" particularly moving. "[It] is very special for me. I got so choked up when we were recording it that I had to stop. The song takes me back to my childhood, to those Sunday mornings when I couldn't wait to get to church.... The song's about family coming together, and love."

Prince listened very closely to Staples's stories and reminiscences and wrote songs that come as much from her heart as from his. "The Undertaker," ultimately about the effects of drugs on the African American community, was inspired by the singer's stories about her marriage to an undertaker. But again, Prince's main achievement is in spotlighting Staples. "Mavis's greatest marketing tool is herself," Kathy Busby, product manager at Paisley Park, told Nathan. "Wherever she goes, people love her." "Let's face it, " Michael Eric Dyson wrote in *Vibe,* "Mavis Staples—whose sensuous, sweet-husky gospel alto is one of pop's most distinctive voices—can blow away 95 percent of the competition just by showing up."

Blended Styles to Fit Unique Voice

With *The Voice,* Staples and Prince produced an album that, in Dyson's opinion, "makes clear that [Mavis] has finally found a musical and spiritual visionary [in Prince] quirky enough to suit both her demanding voice and her unique brand of message music." Dyson concluded, "She and Prince move the style forward by looking backward, raiding a cache of '70s forms from funk and contemporary gospel to jazzy, psychedelic soul. These sounds are wedded to house grooves and even new jack swing, updating her messages—brother- and sister-hood, self-respect, and mutual love—for the '90s." A *Village Voice* contributor noted that it is "the rare singer who can anchor Prince's often-flighty lyrics in the real world. At the same time, she makes his every call for other-worldly intervention sound justified—if not urgently necessary."

Mavis Staples, with help from the artist formerly known as Prince, is calling Jesus' name again—with the help of a little soul, a little gospel, and a little rap; by example, as she indicated to Billingham in *Melody Maker*, she wants to make sure that the world of younger musicians remembers to "put some humanity into their work."

Selected discography

With the Staples Singers; on Stax, except as noted

Soul Folk in Action, 1968.
"Heavy Makes You Happy (She-Na-Boom Boom)," 1970.
"Respect Yourself," 1970.
Bealtitude: Respect Yourself, 1972.
Be What You Are, 1973.
My Main Man, 1974.
Best of the Staples Singers, 1975.

Let's Do It Again, Curtom, 1975.
Pass It On, Warner Bros., 1976.
Hold on to Your Dream, 20th Century, 1981.
The Turning Point, Private I/CBS, 1984.

Solo recordings

"I Have Learned to Do Without You," Volt, 1970.
Only for the Lonely, Stax, 1970.
Time Waits for No One, Paisley Park, 1989.
The Voice, Paisley Park, 1993.

Sources

Billboard, September 8, 1984; September 4, 1993.
Details, October 1993.
Entertainment Weekly, August 27, 1993.
Melody Maker, June 10, 1989; July 22, 1989.
Musician, September 1989.
People, September 13, 1993.
Request, October 1993.
Stereo Review, October 1989.
USA Today, August 24, 1993.
Vibe, October 1993.
Village Voice, November 16, 1993.

Additional information for this sketch was obtained from Paisley Park Records press materials, 1993.

—Diane Moroff

The Story

Folk/pop duo

" I've always been obsessed with subjects and words that twist my heart, like a sob, and lose me in some way," singer-songwriter-guitarist Jonatha Brooke told *Billboard* magazine. She and vocalist Jennifer Kimball, who have been performing together since their college days, make up the Story, a duo that incorporates folk-music guitar traditions with melodic vocal harmonies. Their name is aptly chosen, according to Detroit *Metro Times* contributor Lisa Cramton, who suggested that the pair's lyrics sound "more like short fiction set to music than ordinary songs." Often compared to the early sound of Joni Mitchell and the all-female *a cappella* group the Roches, the Story combines a knowledge of literature with contemporary feminist themes in unexpected vocal blendings.

Music critics, however, have had a difficult time fitting the Story into rock, pop, folk, or even acoustic genres. *Billboard's* Timothy White called the ghostly tenor/soprano braid of Brooke and Kimball's voices "an intersecting hum," and "an airborne metaphor for heartache." In a review of their album *Angel in the*

Photograph by Melanie Acevedo, courtesy of Elektra Records

For the Record . . .

Members include **Jonatha Brooke** (born in 1964; daughter of Nancy and Robert Nelson; studied ballet in London; married Alain Mallet [a jazz pianist]), vocals, guitar, songwriter; and **Jennifer Kimball** (born in 1963; raised in New York City; daughter of Geoffry and Carol Kimball; married Dan Beard), vocals.

Brooke and Kimball met in 1982 at Amherst College; sang in college choir and doo-wop groups before debuting their own works under the name "Jonatha and Jennifer;" moved to Boston after college, where Brooke danced professionally and Kimball designed children's books; demo tape picked up by Green Linnet, 1988; duo renamed the Story, 1991; Green Linnet release *Grace in Gravity* reissued on Elektra; toured folk festivals.

Addresses: *Record company*—Elektra Records, 75 Rockefeller Plaza, New York, NY 10019. *Management*—Patrick Rains and Associates, 1543 Seventh St., 3rd floor, Santa Monica, CA 90401.

House, White elaborated: "If the strangely stirring music of the Story were overly spiritual or feminist in mood, it might be easier to qualify the issues of dignity and faith that it addresses.... But such simplifications fall short."

Vocally, the two singers play off each other, layering harmonies, creating echoes, and sometimes singing different lyrics at the same time. "That's our little signature," Brooke told *Rolling Stone.* In a 1994 press release issued by Elektra Records, Brooke added: "Our choices are our own—we found our 'thing' very naturally and nurtured it ourselves ... the singing style and the writing and the harmonies, the attraction to dissonance. We choose the notes no one else would choose."

Joint Effort as "Jonatha and Jennifer"

When Brooke was six years old, she lived with her family in London, England, and began studying ballet at an all-girls' school. She was very serious about dance until the end of high school, when she found herself having to choose between complete devotion to life as a ballet dancer or a traditional college education. Brooke had already spent summers as a part of the Joffrey Ballet's summer scholarship program; she loved dance but disliked the politics surrounding ballet. "I couldn't

stand it," she declared in the Elektra press release. "All of these obsessive, lithe-limbed talents, and few of them could even stay on the music."

In 1982, while majoring in English at Amherst College in Massachusetts, Brooke met up with Jennifer Kimball. Kimball was raised in Manhattan and considered herself first and foremost a visual artist, although singing had always been a big part of her family life. "We have these extended family reunions where someone invariably will break into a song and of course, everyone joins in. I learned to sing harmony that way," Kimball noted in the press release.

Kimball and Brooke became friends while performing together in a doo-wop *a cappella* group and the college choir. Throughout the 1983 school year, they experimented with harmonies and arrangements that incorporated Brooke's lyrics. Encouraged by a music professor, they began producing full-length concerts of their own under the humble signature of "Jonatha and Jennifer." These efforts resulted in the songs "Always" and "Over Oceans."

Local Release Leads to Label

After college, both women relocated to Boston to pursue their other interests—art and dance. Kimball worked as a graphic artist for Little, Brown publishers, designing children's books, while Brooke maintained a successful career as a professional dancer, joining three different modern dance companies. By 1988 Brooke had compiled a demo tape that was picked up by Green Linnet, an independent record label. The album, *Grace in Gravity,* was a hit in Boston, where the duo (now renamed the Story) was nominated for several Boston Phoenix and Boston Music Awards. In 1991 the Green Linnet release caught the attention of Elektra Records; the label signed the Story and re-released the album to a national audience.

Kimball's unmistakable alto vocals combine with Brooke's higher register and guitar on each of the *Grace in Gravity* cuts. The lyrics, all penned by Brooke, can easily be seen as a collection of narratives that skillfully intertwine humor and irony with more serious topics. "I'm an optimistic person, but I'm drawn to dark, urgent topics," Brooke noted in the Elektra press release. "My upbringing might be part of it—my [Christian Scientist] family was pretty religious, so I was always aware of the deeper connections."

The title track to *Grace in Gravity* tells the story of a black dancer/choreographer friend who was in a train wreck with his company while traveling through South

Africa. He sustained minor spinal chord damage but because he was refused treatment in the whites-only hospital, the injury eventually resulted in paralysis. Another song from the album, "Just One Word," describes a young girl's efforts to grapple with the emotional scars of sexual abuse. "It's what we do—create short stories, then leave," Brooke told Eliza Wing of *Rolling Stone* in a 1992 interview.

> *"I think I'm still messing with that stupid angel that says, 'Why don't you take care of your house before you write a song?'"*
> —Jonatha Brooke

Brooke's background in English literature informs many of the songs on *Angel in the House;* the album takes its title from a poem by Victorian poet Coventry Patmore. In the poem, Patmore extols the "virtues" of woman-hood: to stay at home by the hearth, take care of the husband and children, and always have a cheerful countenance.

Brooke found inspiration in English writer Virginia Woolf's response to the poem: "Woolf got a hold of the poem and used it as a metaphor for that particular phantom that tells us, as women, not to offend, not to do our work, but to flatter and coo. The song comes down to the struggle we still have with that notion of womanhood," Brooke explained in the Elektra release. In the *Billboard* interview, she added: "I think that I and my generation are still messing with this stupid angel that says, 'Why don't you take care of your house before you write a song!'"

Set up as a series of drawing room ballads, the first song on the album, "Mermaid," addresses the image of women portrayed in the Hans Christian Andersen fairy tale "The Little Mermaid." Referring to the difference between Andersen's version and the commercially popular, sugary-sweet, Walt Disney film version of the tale, Brooke wrote in the album's liner notes: "In the original story, she doesn't get the guy, she doesn't live happily ever after, she loses her voice, her tail, her family and turns into sea foam."

Cramton described "Mermaid" in the *Metro Times* as representative of the "multilayered meanings" present in many of the Story's songs. "They voice the frustrations of many women who want bustling lives but fear public reprisals for 'neglecting their feminine duties.'"

People magazine called *Angel in the House* "the year's most radiant folk record," while White, writing in *Billboard,* suggested that "fans of the fragile gleam of *Grace in Gravity* will find *Angel in the House* a darker prism."

The title track of *Angel in the House* was also inspired by a literary work—this time, a short story by Grace Paley about a middle-aged woman who is forced to re-examine her life: "My mother moved the furniture / When she no longer moved the man.... / She wanted to be a different person.... / And he walked away." "My mother is a big part of the song," Brooke told White in the *Billboard* interview. "It's about me and my mother, and ... any woman who's been torn between desires and what they're supposed to do as a female in this world."

Kimball added her own feelings about the song, which conjured up memories of her parents' divorce: "That was an awful time; they were very friendly, almost too friendly, and I wanted them to be more angry with each other and more separated."

In addition to its lyrical experimentation, *Angel in the House* differs from the Story's first release in musical arrangement: the duo added a band. "With the band, the sound still comes from Jonatha's guitar and the way she writes," Kimball related, "but there's all this room for other interpretation, other layers."

For example, Brooke's husband, jazz pianist Alain Mallet, produced the album and added his own Latin rhythms to "Fatso," a humorous treatment of the obsession with thinness and the larger, serious issue of eating disorders among women. In his assessment of the release for *People* magazine, Billy Altman wrote, "Though cellos and violins, the tools of mawkish song writing, filter through a few songs, this isn't the wispy, mopey chapter of folk."

The Story has been credited with the ability to transport listeners to different places or back to their own childhoods. While songs like "Fatso" have moved concert audiences to laughter, others like "So Much Mine" (about a teenage runaway) and "Just One Word" have moved them to tears. "We enter these characters," Brooke told *Billboard,* "and sometimes it's difficult when you see audiences being overcome by emotions. It's hard to know why we do it."

Selected discography

Grace in Gravity, Green Linnet, 1988; reissued, Elektra, 1992.
Angel in the House, Elektra, 1994.

Sources

Billboard, June 19, 1993.
Entertainment Weekly, August 13, 1993.
Metro Times (Detroit), October 6, 1993.
People, September 27, 1993.
Rolling Stone, August 6, 1992.

Additional information for this profile was obtained from Elektra Records press materials, 1994, and liner notes to *Angel in the House.*

—Sarah Messer

Billy Strayhorn

Composer, arranger, pianist

Billy Strayhorn spent his entire career writing music, but his name is unknown to many of those who love his work. As a composer, arranger, and sometime pianist with the Duke Ellington orchestra from 1939 until his death in 1967, he spent most of his life in Ellington's shadow, apparently content to remain behind the scenes.

Although Strayhorn composed many works for the Ellington band on his own, he never wanted his voice to be distinct. Instead, he strove for what he called the "Ellington Effect": to achieve the kind of sound that was right for the band. Ellington, for his part, did not let Strayhorn's efforts go unrecognized; in his autobiography, *Music Is My Mistress,* he wrote that Strayhorn "was not, as he was often referred to by many, my alter ego. Billy Strayhorn was my right arm, my left arm, and the eyes in the back of my head." Strayhorn was also credited on recordings, even though the appearance of his name did not bring him much notice among the band's many listeners.

William Strayhorn was born in Dayton, Ohio, in 1915; his family soon moved to Hillsborough, North Carolina, and then to Pittsburgh, where Strayhorn attended Westinghouse High School and studied at the Pittsburgh Musical Institute. His training in classical music is evident in his compositional style, which at times displays the influence of French composers Claude Debussy and Maurice Ravel.

Strayhorn played piano in small groups in the Pittsburgh area and wrote "Something to Live For" and "Lush Life," among other pieces, while still in his early twenties. Interested in having his work performed widely—at that time he was not considering a career as a composer—he showed some of his compositions to bandleader Duke Ellington when Ellington's orchestra played in Pittsburgh in 1938. As the story is generally related, Ellington was at first impressed primarily with Strayhorn's lyrics. A second meeting, this time in Newark, New Jersey, prompted Ellington to request Strayhorn's services as an arranger of some pieces for the band. In a retelling of the event, the *Village Voice* reported: "One detail remains consistent.... Ellington wrapped his arms around Strayhorn and announced, 'You are with me *for life.*'"

Wrote "Take the 'A' Train"

The next 29 years of Strayhorn's life were spent as part of the Ellington organization—writing, arranging, and sitting in on piano. A particularly notable period occurred during a strike by the American Society of

Composers, Authors and Publishers (ASCAP) in 1941. As an ASCAP member, Ellington was not allowed to have his own compositions performed on the radio. Strayhorn, not a member of ASCAP, was given the opportunity to write his own pieces. The most famous of these, "Take the 'A' Train," was inspired by two subway trains that went to Harlem: the "D" and the "A." The "A" went straight to Harlem, but the "D" veered off, ending up in the Bronx. As Strayhorn was quoted as saying in Stanley Dance's book, *The World of Duke Ellington:* "I said I was writing directions—take the 'A' Train to Sugar Hill. The 'D' Train was really messing up everybody."

Strayhorn composed many other pieces alone, but because they were recorded by the Ellington orchestra, they were often thought of as Ellington's own works. These include "Rain Check," "Passion Flower," and "Chelsea Bridge," all from 1941, and 1949's "A Flower Is a Lovesome Thing." Each of these compositions became standards in the band's repertory.

United with Ellington

Strayhorn's musical collaborations with Ellington from the 1950s and 1960s are numerous and include such classic compositions as *A Drum Is a Woman; Such Sweet Thunder;* adaptations of Russian composer Tchaikovsky's *Nutcracker Suite* and Norwegian composer Edvard Grieg's *Peer Gynt Suite;* and *The Far East Suite.* Jazz performers, critics, and scholars differ over whether it is possible to determine which portions of these pieces were written by Strayhorn and which by Ellington. In his book *The Swing Era: The Development of Jazz, 1930-1945,* Gunther Schuller points out four distinct characteristics that mark the music as Stray-

horn's, and some of Ellington's players have said that they could always tell what Strayhorn had written.

Others observers feel that it is impossible to determine whose writing is whose—and believe it worthless to try. The most important thing to remember is that both composers had the same end in mind. As Strayhorn told Bill Coss in an interview for *Down Beat* magazine in 1962: "I'm sure the fact that [Ellington and I are] both looking for a certain character, a certain way of presenting a composition, makes us write to the whole, toward the same feeling. That's why it comes together—for that reason."

Lived by Four Freedoms

Strayhorn was small and sedate—and a homosexual at a time in America's history when it was especially difficult to be a gay man, particularly in the very heterosexual jazz world. He was adored and protected by Ellington and by the members of the band, who had several affectionate nicknames for him, among them "Strays," "Weely," and "Swee' Pea." The last, by far the most widely used, was given him by alto saxophonist Toby Hardwick, who had picked up the name from the infant in the *Popeye* comics.

Strayhorn's death in 1967 from cancer of the esophagus affected Ellington deeply. As Hardwick told Dance in *The World of Duke Ellington,* it was "the one thing I know of that *really* touched Duke. The *one* thing ... that hit him *hard.*" Upon accepting the Medal of Freedom at the White House in 1969, Ellington recited the four freedoms by which Strayhorn lived. As recorded by Dance, they were: "Freedom from hate unconditionally; freedom from self-pity; freedom from the fear of doing something that would help someone else more than it would help me; and freedom from the kind of pride that makes me feel I am better than my brother."

In the 1970s and 1980s, Strayhorn's music became more familiar to listeners, thanks to performances and recordings of his compositions by individual artists. Tenor saxophonist Joe Henderson and trumpeter Art Farmer have each devoted albums to Strayhorn's work. After Strayhorn's death, Ellington released a tribute album to him, *And His Mother Called Him Bill.*

Selected compositions

"Something to Live For," 1938.
"Lush Life," 1938.
"I'm Checkin' Out, Goo'm Bye," 1939.
"Lost in Two Flats," 1939.

"Day Dream," 1940.
"Take the 'A' Train," 1941.
"Chelsea Bridge," 1941.
"Passion Flower," 1941.
"Rain Check," 1941.
"Johnny Come Lately," 1942.
"A Flower Is a Lovesome Thing," 1949.
"Lotus Blossom," 1962.
"Blood Count," 1967.

With Duke Ellington

The Perfume Suite, 1944.
The Newport Jazz Festival Suite, 1956.
A Drum Is a Woman, 1957.
Such Sweet Thunder, 1957.
Toot Suite, 1958.
The Nutcracker Suite, 1960.
The Peer Gynt Suite, 1960.
Paris Blues, 1960.
Suite Thursday, 1960.
Pousse Cafe, 1962.
Ishfahan, 1963.
The Far East Suite, 1964.
The Concert of Sacred Music, 1965.

Selected discography

With the Duke Ellington Orchestra

Duke Ellington: The Blanton-Webster Band, Bluebird, c. 1942, reissued, 1986.
Such Sweet Thunder, Columbia, 1957.
Billy Strayhorn: Cue for Saxophone, Master Jazz Recordings, 1959.
The Far East Suite, RCA, 1966, reissued, Bluebird, 1988.
Side by Side (recorded 1958-59), Verve, 1986.
Caravan (recorded 1947 and 1951), Prestige, 1992.

Lush Life (reissue), Red Baron, 1992.
A Drum Is a Woman, Columbia.
Duke Ellington: The Ellington Era, 1927-1940 (two volumes), Columbia/CBS.
Ella at Duke's Place, Verve.
Great Times!, Fantasy/OJC.

With others

Art Farmer, *Something to Live For: The Music of Billy Strayhorn*, Contemporary, 1987.
Joe Henderson, *Lush Life: The Music of Billy Strayhorn*, Red Baron, 1992.

Sources

Books

Collier, James Lincoln, *Duke Ellington*, Oxford University Press, 1987.
Dance, Stanley, *The World of Duke Ellington*, Scribner's, 1970.
The Duke Ellington Reader, edited by Mark Tucker, Oxford University Press, 1993.
Ellington, Duke, *Music Is My Mistress*, Doubleday, 1973.
Jewell, Derek, *Duke: A Portrait of Duke Ellington*, Norton, 1977.
Schuller, Gunther, *The Swing Era: The Development of Jazz, 1930-1945*, Oxford University Press, 1989.
Ulanov, Barry, *Duke Ellington*, Creative Age Press, 1946.

Periodicals

Down Beat, June 7, 1962; February 23, 1967; July 13, 1967.
Village Voice, June 23, 1992.

—Joyce Harrison

Al B. Sure!

Singer, songwriter

Photograph by Gerhard Yurkovic. ©1992 Warner Bros. Records

Self-confidence and style—even his name shows that Al B. Sure! possesses these qualities. Born Albert Joseph Brown, he moved with his parents from Boston, Massachusetts, to a comfortable New York City suburb, "money-earnin'" Mt. Vernon, while he was a student in grade school. By the age of ten, he had already worked as a singer in a video production for children called *Sesame Place Park.* After that, he never looked back: "I saved up a little bit of money, bought a 4-track [recorder] and some equipment, and started making music with my cousin Kyle West," Sure! told Bill Coleman in a *Billboard* magazine interview. (West is now a noted producer in his own right.)

After graduating from high school in 1986, Sure! moved to New York City and entered the Manhattan Center for the Performing Arts. He also started a collaboration with Heavy D and the Boyz, his old friends from Mt. Vernon, and was soon introduced to Andre Harrell of Uptown Records. Harrell sent Sure!'s demo tape to Warner Bros., and the label signed the young singer-songwriter in the summer of 1987.

Warner then entered Sure! in that year's Sony Innovator Talent Search. Music industry magnates Quincy Jones and Herbie Hancock were the judges of the competition and picked Sure! as the winner in a field of 51 aspiring artists. Their recognition left him "very surprised and very honored," he told Coleman. "To have Jones pick me is kind of amazing to me. It's kind of a dream."

Sure!'s first single, "Nite and Day," was released in January of 1988. By April it was on *Billboard's* Top Ten list, prompting Sure! to record French and Spanish versions as well. His first album, *In Effect Mode,* was released later that year and swiftly went platinum. By September of 1988, Davitt Sigerson of *Rolling Stone* was calling Al B. Sure! the best of the "hip-hop love men," describing him as a modern crossover artist who blends rap's pulsing beat with jazzy romantic crooning. "Nite and Day" won over even the toughest critics, like J. D. Considine of *Musician,* who allowed that the single had "insinuating appeal," but disparagingly called Sure! a "hip-hop Barry White."

In early 1989, Sure!'s career hit the kind of snag that could have ruined him: he was charged with rape in Los Angeles. Although he was cleared of the charges by April, Nelson George, writing in *Billboard,* wondered whether Sure! could recover his carefully wrought image: "Although the media worked during the last year to turn the 20-year-old vocalist into a sex symbol, it's not surprising that it loved the idea of connecting him to a sex scandal. That the story proved groundless, unfortunately, isn't as sexy."

Born Albert Joseph Brown, c. 1968, in Boston, MA; married wife, Jackie, 1993. *Education:* Attended Manhattan Center for the Performing Arts, 1986.

Began writing and mixing music with Kyle West; collaborated with Heavy D and the Boyz, 1986-87; signed with Warner Bros. Records, 1987. Co-writer and co-producer of numerous tracks for several other performers, including Tevin Campbell and Al Green.

Awards: Winner of Sony Innovator Talent Search, 1987; named best new artist by *Soul Train,* 1988; American Music Award for best new artist, 1988; New York Music Award for best male R&B vocalist, 1993.

Addresses: *Record company*—Warner Bros. Records, 3300 Warner Blvd., Burbank, CA 91505. *Management*—Phil Casey, International Creative Management, 8942 Wilshire Blvd., Beverly Hills, CA 90211.

By June of 1989, Sure!'s "If I'm Not Your Lover" had critics gushing with praise. Within 16 months, the single "Misunderstanding" (co-produced by Eddie F. of Heavy D and the Boyz), from Sure!'s second album, *Private Times ... and the Whole Nine,* was a Number One R&B hit. As the singer told Janine McAdams in *Billboard,* "I think when people hear the album they'll see that this is very much my growth process from album one [*In Effect Mode*] to album two.... It's nothing like album one and has nothing to do with album one."

Sure!'s second album clearly reflects his growing confidence as an artist, as in his duet with Diana Ross on "No Matter What You Do," a song he had written when he was a junior in high school. And his covers of the Eagles' "Hotel California," which begin and end the album, intrigued many listeners, including Amy Linden of *Rolling Stone.* In her review of *Private Times,* she called the "Hotel California" remake a "creepy combination of *Lifestyles of the Rich and Famous* and *Dark Shadows,*" that demonstrates "an element of risk absent from the rest of the LP."

By this time, however, Sure! was seriously developing his longstanding interest in producing music. He had already co-written and co-produced three tracks with DeVante Swing of the group Jodeci and by 1993 had done similar work with artists like Tevin Campbell, Chaka Khan, Robert Palmer, Michael McDonald, Rod Stewart, and Al Green.

Sure! was also planning to start his own label, Suretime Records. In late 1992, Sure! released his third album, *Sexy Versus,* another mixture of slow romantic cuts and high-speed hip-hop, featuring Grand Puba, Slick Rick, Rakim, and Chubb Rock (who had also appeared on *Private Times*). Sure! described the album to Jennifer Perry of the *Source* as "adult contemporary hip-hop" and told *EM* magazine that it "cover[s] every aspect of what love is, from promiscuity to shyness to anger to infatuation to teasing games. The whole thing." He even underscores the importance of safe sex in his romantic ballad "You and I," explaining to *EM:* "No matter how hot the moment of passion is, you still have to take care of your business."

Again, Sure!'s brand of bedroom hip-hop met with mixed critical response, though in January of 1993 he was voted best male R&B vocalist at the New York Music Awards. This honor confirmed Al B. Sure!, who planned to release a new album late in 1994, as a consummate "modern musician," equally skilled at his own craft and at bringing the best out of other artists. His fresh, sexy sound has popularized a new kind of hip-hop—one that is mellower, with as much emphasis on melody as beat. As Sure! told McAdams: "It was something that I've always kind of felt naturally. If you have [a] melody and you're really saying something in the song, you can't lose."

Selected discography

In Effect Mode, Warner Bros., 1988.
Private Times ... and the Whole Nine, Warner Bros., 1990.
Sexy Versus, Warner Bros., 1992.

Sources

Atlanta Journal and Constitution, January 2, 1993.
Billboard, March 26, 1988; April 30, 1988; April 1, 1989; December 1, 1990; September 21, 1991.
Call & Post (Cleveland, OH), March 4, 1993.
Cash Box, November 10, 1990.
Chicago Defender, February 28, 1994.
EM, January 1993.
Fresh, April 25, 1993.
Ledger-Enquirer (Columbus, GA), January 28, 1993.
Musician, July 1988.
Melody Maker, June 10, 1989.
Rolling Stone, September 22, 1988; January 24, 1991.
Source, December 1992.
Spin, January 1993.

Additional information for this profile was obtained from Warner Bros. Records publicity materials.

—*Daniel Passamaneck*

Joan Sutherland

Opera singer

Archive Photos

At her Italian debut in 1960, the audience dubbed her "La Stupenda," and throughout her 40-year career, few who heard Australian-born coloratura soprano Joan Sutherland sing would disagree with that assessment. With her husband, pianist/conductor Richard Bonynge, Sutherland expanded the common operatic repertoire, adding works that had not been heard for decades. She lent her artistry to some of the finest performances of opera in this century, and music critics agree that her gifts to the world of music are undeniable.

As a young child, Sutherland loved nothing better than to sit under the piano as her mother, a highly accomplished singer, practiced her craft. She also received more formal training from her mother, who very early instilled a proper understanding of the importance of breath support and vocal exercises. After graduating from high school, Sutherland went to work as a secretary by day and studied music by night.

When she was 18, Sutherland won a competition for a two-year scholarship to study voice with a locally renowned singer named John Dickens. In 1946, after her first two years with her new voice teacher, she made her public debut in German composer Johann Sebastian Bach's *Christmas Oratorio* at the Sydney Town Hall. Dickens extended her scholarship, and she began to think that her dream of singing at Covent Garden, the world-famous opera house in London, might be possible after all.

Sutherland soon joined the Affiliated Music Clubs of New South Wales, where she met a young pianist named Richard Bonynge. The pair began performing locally together, and she regularly entered—and won—many vocal competitions in her native country. Sutherland came in first in the "Mobile Quest" competition sponsored by Vacuum Oil, an Australian company, in 1950. In addition to the prize money, she received a year-long singing contract for performances all over the country. With her prize money and saved earnings, she left for England the following year.

Sang at Covent Garden

During her first year in England, Sutherland studied at the opera school of London's Royal College of Music. She met up with Bonynge again, who was also studying there. They began working together, and Bonynge proved to be an invaluable vocal coach. By 1952, she realized her dream and started singing at Covent Garden. For the first few years, she sang relatively small parts, taking virtually anything offered her; then, gradually, she began singing larger, more important

For the Record . . .

B orn November 7, 1926, in Sydney, Australia; daughter of William (a tailor) and Muriel (a singer; maiden name, Alston) Sutherland; married Richard Bonynge (a pianist and conductor) 1954; children: Adam. *Education:* Attended Royal College of Music in London.

Stage debut in Johann Sebastian Bach's *Christmas Oratorio,* Sydney Town Hall, 1946; operatic debut as Judith in Eugene Goossens's *Judith,* 1951; London debut as First Lady in Wolfgang Amadeus Mozart's *Die Zauberflöte* ("The Magic Flute"), Covent Garden, 1952; became international star as Lucia in Gaetano Donizetti's *Lucia di Lammermoor,* 1959; Italian debut in George Frideric Handel's *Alcina,* 1960; French debut in *Lucia di Lammermoor,* 1960; American debut in *Alcina,* 1960. Appeared in numerous other operas by Mozart, Handel, Donizetti, Bellini, Gioacchino Rossini, Giacomo Meyerbeer, Jules Massenet, Franz Lehár, Richard Strauss, Giuseppe Verdi, Giacomo Puccini, and Jacques Offenbach. Retired in 1990.

Awards: Australia's Quest Award, 1951; named Dame Commander of the Order of the British Empire, 1979; Grammy Award for best classical vocal soloist, 1981; named a fellow of the Royal College of Music, 1981; Order of Merit, England, 1991, and Sydney, Australia, 1992.

Addresses: c/o Ingpen and Williams, 14 Kensington Court, London W8, England.

roles. Meanwhile, she kept working with Bonynge, whom she married in 1954, and continued to expand her vocal range.

Sutherland's mother, a mezzo-soprano, had worked with Joan to develop her middle register. Dickens thought she might be a dramatic soprano, with a voice for the large, heavy roles of late nineteenth-century music. But Bonynge, an expert on the delicate "bel canto" repertoire of the early nineteenth century, realized that Sutherland's voice was lighter and more flexible than anyone had thought.

As her vocal coach, he encouraged her to sing in her highest register, and with his help, she became a coloratura soprano, a rarity at the time. After she received rave reviews for her first coloratura role in the Handel Opera Society's 1957 production of *Alcina,* Covent Garden's directors agreed to revive the gem of the bel canto repertoire, Donizetti's *Lucia di Lammermoor,* just for her.

During the first half of the twentieth century, the bel canto repertoire—eighteenth- and nineteenth-century Italian operas of Rossini, Bellini, and Donizetti, which stressed vocal precision and agility—received little performance; they were simply out of fashion. World-famous coloratura Maria Callas began reviving these works in the 1950s. Although they were still not the most popular operas, when Sutherland was ready to sing bel canto, the audience was ready to listen. As Norma Major wrote in her biography *Joan Sutherland,* the singer "opened up the whole field of bel canto, demonstrating a style of singing thought to have vanished beyond recall."

Sutherland's Covent Garden premiere as Lucia in 1959 was a smashing success. The following year she carried this success to international operatic circles, debuting in various roles in Italy, France, and the United States. Having achieved worldwide fame by 1960, the following year she was given the opportunity to sing with two of the most important opera companies in the world: La Scala in Milan and the Metropolitan Opera in New York. For the next three decades, Sutherland traveled all over the world, performing in the best and most famous opera houses as one of the most renowned and sought-after sopranos.

The Secret of Her Success

Sutherland's success was the product of hard work and common sense. She attributes her longevity as a singer to a sound technique resulting from a long and disciplined training. Always conscious of her health, she kept "social excesses at bay," wrote Major in *Joan Sutherland.* Sutherland carefully paced herself, accepted only those roles that were suited to her, conserved her voice before each performance, and tried not to exhaust herself with too many performances too close together.

Throughout her career, Sutherland was sometimes faulted by music critics for unconvincing acting and poor enunciation. Few, however, would deny her overall contributions to the world of music. As Rupert Christiansen wrote in *Opera,* "Sutherland's combination of precision in scales, runs and trills with control over dynamics and tone is, on the recorded evidence, unsurpassed." Her professionalism and hard work are legendary and have provided many budding singers with a realistic role model. As a singer, she was able to make more concrete contributions to the ephemeral world of music performance than many contemporary composers. She has enriched the lives of millions of music lovers and has left a large legacy of recordings for future generations.

Retired in 1990

In 1983 Sutherland told Christiansen, "I think I'll be stopping soon. I'm getting a bit doddery. I can still get those top E-flats, but they give me a terrible headache. The traveling exhausts me. I want to spend more time at home gardening." Seven years after making that statement, Sutherland finally did retire. Her last role was in the 1990 production of Giacomo Meyerbeer's *Les Huguenots* in Sydney.

Elizabeth Silsbury described Sutherland's final curtain call in *Opera:* "The last act over ... the curtain fell and formal bows were taken by [the six principal singers]. Then the full stage was shown, the whole company, minus one.... Then the curtain [fell] again and the whole house went dark and silent. Slowly the velvets parted, very slowly the lights came up, and there was the Great Dame, alone, center stage.... The house went berserk and exploded to attention, shouting wildly, pelting the Diva with daffodils and streamers until she was ankle deep in them. The whole company of the Australian Opera—artists, mechs and techs, wigs and wardrobes, management and make-up—joined her while we yelled and wept and beat our hands together."

In her introduction to Major's biography, Sutherland wrote: "I was the fortunate choice for this wonderful life—I have loved it and it has brought me rich rewards in every sense.... I am quite incredulous and profoundly grateful that I was able to accomplish such an amount of work."

Selected discography

On Decca, except where noted

Donizetti: *Lucia di Lammermoor,* 1962.
Wagner: *Siegfried,* 1962.
Bizet: *Carmen,* 1963.

Joan Sutherland and Luciano Pavarotti, 1975.
Verdi: *La Traviata,* 1983.
Verdi: *Requiem,* 1984.
Verdi: *Rigoletto,* 1985.
The Art of the Prima Donna, 1985.
Joan Sutherland: Bel Canto Arias, 1986.
Handel: *Athalia,* L'Oiseau-Lyre, 1986.
Sutherland, Horne, and Pavarotti: Live from Lincoln Center, 1987.
Mozart: *Don Giovanni,* EMI, 1987.
Rossini: *Semiramide,* Nuova Era, 1989.
Donizetti: *Lucrezia Borgia,* 1989.
Joan Sutherland's Greatest Hits, 1989.
Joan Sutherland: Command Performance, 1991.
Joan Sutherland: Grandi Voce, 1993.

Also appeared in video productions of Meyerbeer's *Les Huguenots,* Home Vision, 1990, and Strauss's *Die Fledermaus,* Virgin Classics Video, 1992.

Sources

Books

Eaton, Quaintance, *Sutherland and Bonynge: An Intimate Biography,* Dodd, Mead and Co., 1987.
International Dictionary of Opera, St. James Press, 1993.
Major, Norma, *Joan Sutherland,* Queen Anne Press, 1987.
The New Grove Dictionary of Opera, Volume 4, edited by Stanley Sadie, Macmillan, 1992.
Sutherland, Joan, *The Joan Sutherland Album,* Thames and Hudson, 1986.

Periodicals

Billboard, September 6, 1986; May 20, 1989.
Gramophone, December 1991.
New Yorker, December 15, 1986.
Opera, November 1990; February 1991.
Opera News, December 6, 1986; March 2, 1991; January 22, 1994.
Ovation, September 1984, p. 10.

—Robin Armstrong

Keith Sweat

Singer, songwriter, producer

As a child, Keith Sweat had a psychic intuition about his success as a singer. "I used to go to bed and dream I was on stage giving a concert," he told *Ebony*. "I could see myself singing and the people were screaming and the whole thing was so real to me, I used to wake up and really *believe* I had done a show. You couldn't tell me it didn't happen.... I would get up in the morning and start looking in my pockets for all the money I'd made from my shows. I don't know how to explain it, but those dreams seemed so real, I knew they were really premonitions."

Sweat not only took those dreams to heart, he made sure they came true, becoming one of the founders of the 1990s musical genre known as "new jack swing," a hybrid of contemporary street music and the traditional elements of R&B and pop. Born and raised the third of five children in New York City's Harlem, Sweat began performing at the age of 14. His own style of smooth vocals developed when he played in a band called Jamilah.

After he graduated from City College of the City University of New York with a communications degree, Sweat worked his way up from the mailroom to a position as a brokerage assistant in a Wall Street firm. Every spare minute and dollar went toward writing and recording his music. He spent the rest of his time trying to sell his songs to record companies for other artists to sing. But, for a time, every door he knocked on seemed to slam right back in his face. Determined to continue his musical pursuits, Sweat decided to sing and record his own songs. He submitted a demo tape to Vincent Davis, president of Vintertainment Recordings, who signed him to the label immediately.

From Wall Street to Street Music

In 1987 Sweat recorded his debut album, *Make It Last Forever*—but kept his Wall Street job as a safety net. Although his professional life was heading in the right direction, Sweat was experiencing trauma in his personal life, following a painful split with his longtime girlfriend. The recording sessions provided the artist with an outlet for his emotions. "It was a heartbreak relationship for me—the kind where you are hurting so much, you have to find someone to talk to or go crazy," Sweat told *Ebony*. "I didn't really have anyone to talk to, so what I did was talk to my album.... I was writing about my life. And I really think that's why people responded to it so strongly. They knew it was real."

Sweat reached out and grabbed the hearts of millions of fans with *Make It Last Forever*. Co-produced by longtime friend Teddy Riley, the 1987 release sold

For the Record . . .

Born in New York City; children: Keia (daughter). Education: Received degree in communications from City College of the City University of New York.

Began performing in clubs in New York City when he was 14 years old. Signed with Vintertainment Recordings, 1987, and released first album, *Make It Last Forever*; signed with Elektra Records, 1991; formed his own record label, Keia Records, with distribution through Elektra.

Addresses: *Record company*—Elektra Entertainment, 345 North Maple Dr., Suite 123, Beverly Hills, CA 90210.

more than three million copies and later won an American Music Award nomination for best R&B album.

Sweat and Riley collaborated on the single "I Want Her," which eventually reached Number One on *Billboard*'s R&B chart and Number Three on their pop chart. *Soul Train* nominated the single for their "best song of the year" honors, and Sweat became the first artist in ten years to have the Number One R&B single and the Number One R&B album at the same time. Having accomplished that, he finally quit his day job and devoted all of his energy to making music. He went on tour with his own live band, playing in 6,000- to 20,000-seat arenas worldwide, with sold-out shows dominating the tour—including two at London's Hammersmith Odeon.

Pressure-Cooked Multiplatinum Success

In 1990 Sweat returned with a vengeance on his second effort, *I'll Give All My Love to You,* featuring the hit single "Make You Sweat." He produced the album himself and wrote or co-wrote each one of its songs. *I'll Give All My Love to You* sold a million copies in less than two months and ultimately went multiplatinum. "On the first album, I felt completely relaxed," Sweat explained in his press biography. "Working on the *I'll Give All My Love to You* album felt like being in a pressure cooker. I felt pressure not only from the expectations of my fans, but also from myself to produce an album that was just as good or better than the first one."

Sweat kept on working without slowing down. In 1991 he split with Vintertainment to sign with their distributor, Elektra Records. Around the same time, he discovered Silk, a band from Atlanta, Georgia, that would later become the first act to sign on his own label, Keia Records—named after his daughter. Sweat first saw Silk at a picnic singing Boyz II Men songs and soon enlisted them to sing background vocals on his album.

That same year, Sweat released his third offering, *Keep It Comin',* with the title track as the first single. Both the album and the single quickly jumped to the Number One slots on the *Billboard* R&B charts. On the second single, "Why Me Baby?," Sweat collaborated with Teddy Riley and hit rap artist L.L. Cool J.

Sweat joined the "Triple Threat Tour" to support *Keep It Comin',* which featured New Edition spinoffs Bell Biv DeVoe and Johnny Gill in what *Rolling Stone* called the "New Jack all-star package." Then, he moved on to his own "For Ladies Only" tour. By 1992, Silk had recorded and released their debut album, *Lose Control,* produced by Sweat. The following year, they topped *Billboard*'s R&B and Hot 100 charts with their hit "Freak Me." Sweat soon began working with other artists for Keia Records, including hardcore rappers Triflin' Pack and the female singing group About Face.

Returned to Earlier Style in the "Sweat Shop"

The singer released his next album, *Get Up on It,* with its first single, "How Do You Like It?," in 1994. Collaborating with Fitzgerald Scott and working with engineer Michael Ffrench, Sweat recorded the album in the "Sweat Shop," his own home basement studio in Atlanta, Georgia. Several critics have noted that on *Get Up on It,* the singer reached back to the style of his first release, *Make It Last Forever.* "My first album is like I was another person, and I [needed] to get back in touch with who that person was," Sweat told *Vibe.* "I didn't get tired. I'd work all night if I had to. That was the feeling that I had working with Silk.... I just had a vibe, and it felt good. It was like energy flowing that I wanted to get off my chest. It was like doing my first album again." Having made his childhood premonitions of a career as a singing sensation come true, Sweat now believes his job is to keep making music-lovers happy.

Selected discography

Make It Last Forever (includes "I Want Her"), Vintertainment/Elektra, 1987.
I'll Give All My Love to You (includes "Make You Sweat"), Vintertainment/Elektra, 1990.
Keep It Comin' (includes title track and "Why Me Baby?"), Elektra, 1991.
Get Up on It (includes "How Do You Like It?"), Elektra, 1994.

Sources

Billboard, January 9, 1988; July 23, 1988; July 21, 1990; January 19, 1991; January 26, 1991; February 8, 1992; October 24, 1992; November 28, 1992; June 12, 1993.

Ebony, September 1992.

Entertainment Weekly, July 15, 1994.

Keyboard, March 1992.

Musician, May 1988; March 1992.

New York Times, January 14, 1991; December 11, 1991.

People, July 9, 1990; July 11, 1994.

Rolling Stone, September 22, 1988; August 9, 1990; November 15, 1990; February 21, 1991.

Variety, March 4, 1991.

Vibe, May 1994.

Additional information for this profile was obtained from Elektra Records press materials, 1994.

—Sonya Shelton

Billy Taylor

Pianist, composer, arranger, writer, educator

Courtesy of GRP Records

Billy Taylor is one of the foremost disseminators of jazz music and knowledge, working to promote a wider appreciation for what he calls "America's classical music." From his performances, lectures, and workshops since the 1950s to his appointment as artistic advisor on jazz at the Kennedy Center for the Performing Arts in 1994, Taylor's life has been filled with activites on behalf of his chosen musical genre. An accomplished performer, educator, media figure, composer, and author, Taylor's indefatigable energy as a jazz ambassador has not only won him admiration and acclaim, but, probably more important to Taylor, has resulted in an audience of jazz fans that might not exist if not for his efforts.

Billy Taylor was born in Greenville, North Carolina, in 1921; his family moved shortly after his birth to Washington, D.C. Taylor's father was a dentist who directed the church choir on Sundays. Young Billy started piano lessons at age 7, and one of his uncles, a jazz pianist, was his informal tutor in jazz piano style. As Taylor remarked in an interview in *Down Beat* magazine in 1985: "I used to bug him: 'Show me how to do that.' And he'd say, 'Oh, I just do it.' Finally in desperation he gave me a Fats Waller record." Taylor listened to and imitated the style of the great master of the stride piano. Later, his uncle gave him another record—this one by Art Tatum. Taylor continued, "It was a record called *The Shout.* I had never in my life heard the piano played like that, and I just went nuts.... Tatum was probably the biggest and most lasting influence on my solo piano playing of any single mentor that I had."

Taylor continued his formal music training, attending the historically black Virginia State College, first majoring in sociology and then in music and playing jazz on the side. "As in most black colleges at that time," Taylor was quoted as saying in a *New York Times* article in 1971, "playing jazz was frowned on; so I played in Richmond as much as I could." He graduated with a bachelor's degree in 1942.

Played in New York Jazz Clubs

In 1944 Taylor arrived in New York City determined to make his way as a jazz pianist. What happened is a milestone in jazz history. As he explained in the liner notes to his 1994 recording *It's a Matter of Pride:* "I arrived in New York on a Friday night, went to Minton's Playhouse in Harlem, was heard by one of my idols, tenor saxophonist Ben Webster, who auditioned me and hired me to replace Johnny Guarnieri in his quartet at the Three Deuces on Sunday. I was in town three days, and I had a job playing the piano on 52nd Street with Ben Webster, [drummer] Big Sid Catlett and [bassist] Charlie Drayton opposite the Art Tatum Trio! I was in heaven!"

Fate continued to smile upon Taylor. In 1949 he began a two-year engagement as house pianist at Birdland, at that time the greatest jazz club in the world, in the greatest jazz center in the world—New York's 52nd Street. He performed with the best musicians in the business, including saxophonists Charlie Parker, Lee Konitz, and Zoot Sims, trumpeters Dizzy Gillespie and Miles Davis, bassist Oscar Pettiford, vibraphonist Milt

Jackson, drummers Roy Haynes and Art Blakey, and other luminaries. "The years 1944 through 1951 were unbelievable when I was living through them," Taylor recalled in his liner notes to *It's a Matter of Pride.* "Now when I reflect on the great artists I was privileged to meet, work with and learn from I realize what unique opportunities I was given."

Formed the Billy Taylor Trio

Since 1952 Taylor has led the Billy Taylor Trio. Over the years, his sidemen have included some of the giants of jazz, including bassists Charles Mingus and Oscar Pettiford and drummers Billy Cobham, Jo Jones, and Ed Thigpen. Taylor's own playing is uniquely his own. Primarily playing in a style he calls "prebop"—between swing and bebop—he also displays a keen understanding of the styles of his predecessors at the keyboard, including Art Tatum, Duke Ellington, Earl Hines, Fats Waller, and Erroll Garner. As Jim Roberts noted in *Down Beat* in 1985: "His style is strong and deeply rooted, but even the most powerful passages are marked by the unmistakable elegance of the Taylor touch."

In addition to his performing activities, Taylor has composed dozens of pieces for various ensembles and over 300 songs, including the often-performed "I Wish I Knew How It Would Feel to Be Free." Many of the larger works were commissioned by universities and performing ensembles. Some of Taylor's best pieces can be heard on the 1994 recording *It's a Matter of Pride.*

Jazz Spokesperson

Taylor is the author of a history of jazz piano as well as many jazz instruction books, but he is perhpas best known for his activities as a public spokesperson for jazz. In 1958 he hosted a program on the pioneering Educational Television network (ETV) titled *The Subject Is Jazz.* He also hosted radio programs on WLIB and WNEW in New York City and was musical director for Tony Brown's *Black Journal Tonight* in the 1960s. His widest exposure on television came in 1969 when he was appointed musical director and bandleader for the *David Frost Show*—a post he held for three years. Frost, then at the height of his popularity, had a weekly talk show; Taylor, the first African American to lead a television studio orchestra, became familiar to millions of viewers.

Taylor's most important contribution in the 1960s was his founding of Jazzmobile, which began in 1965 as part of the Harlem Cultural Council's summer programs. It started out on a parade float borrowed from a beer company and blossomed into a unique outreach organization that brings jazz to underprivileged urban areas and features performances by major jazz artists. Jazzmobile's free concerts attract over 400,000 people every season.

Hosted Popular Jazz Radio Show

In 1975 Taylor received a doctorate of music education from the University of Massachusetts at Amherst, where he now holds a teaching position. From 1977 to 1982 he hosted a weekly program on National Public Radio (NPR) called *Jazz Alive!* The program, which combined Taylor's engaging and informative commentary with the playing of recorded music, became the most popular jazz show in NPR's history. Since 1980 he has profiled jazz musicians on the television program *CBS Sunday Morning;* his segment on Quincy Jones won him an Emmy Award in 1983. Taylor's appointment in 1994 as artistic advisor for jazz at the Kennedy Center for the Performing Arts in Washington, D.C., led to a series of 26 jazz programs released to NPR member stations in 1995.

Taylor's accomplishments have been recognized with a Lifetime Achievement Award from *Down Beat* magazine; Peabody, Emmy, and Tiffany awards; and numerous other honors. A respected jazz pianist and spokesperson, Taylor's efforts have been most instrumental in the popularity and appreciation of that unique musical form.

Selected writings

Jazz Piano: History and Development, W. C. Brown, 1982.
A Touch of Taylor, Duane Music, Inc.
Combo Arranging, Duane Music, Inc.
Billy Taylor Sketches for Jazz Trio, Duane Music, Inc.
Ragtime Piano Solos and How to Play Them, Duane Music, Inc.
Billy Taylor's Bebop for Piano, Duane Music, Inc.

Selected compositions

"I Wish I Knew How It Would Feel to Be Free."
Suite for Jazz Piano and Orchestra.
Step Into My Dream.
Peaceful Warrior (a tribute to Martin Luther King, Jr.).
For Art Tatum.
It's a Matter of Pride.

Selected discography

A Touch of Taylor, Prestige, 1955.
One for Fun, Atlantic, 1959.
Sleeping Bee, MPS, 1969.
Where've You Been?, Concord, 1980.
We Meet Again, CBS Masterworks, 1989.
Jazzmobile All-Stars, Taylor-Made, 1989.
My Fair Lady Loves Jazz (reissue of 1957 recording), GRP, 1993.
Dr. T, GRP, 1993.
Customed Taylored, Fresh Sound, 1994.
It's a Matter of Pride, GRP, 1994.
Taylor Made Jazz, Argo, resissued on Fresh Sound.
The Billy Taylor Trio, Vols. I and II, Prestige.
Billy Taylor at Town Hall, Prestige.

Sources

Books

Conversations With Jazz Musicians, Gale, 1977.
Lyons, Len, *The Great Jazz Pianists: Speaking of Their Lives and Music*, Morrow, 1983.

Periodicals

Down Beat, May 1980; March 1985; February 1991; March 1994; May 1994; June 1994.
New York Times, January 3, 1971.

Additional information for this profile was obtained from the liner notes to *It's a Matter of Pride*, GRP, 1994.

—Joyce Harrison

Teenage Fanclub

Rock band

"Rarely has a pop group come equipped with a more perfect name than Teenage Fanclub," opined *Los Angeles Times* critic Steve Hochman, "not so much because it has teen fans, but because the group's members are fans of teens. Few bands have ever written with so much affection for the teen-age condition—especially the role that rock plays in it." The Glasgow, Scotland, natives mix the melodic, stylistically complex approach of classic British pop with punk's irony and distorted guitars. The result is at once earnest and distanced, sugary and hard.

Their major-label debut, *Bandwagonesque,* made Teenage Fanclub alternative-rock heroes and critical darlings. *Spin* deemed the record the year's best rock album and proclaimed, "This music makes your spine shiver." The Fanclub's 1993 follow-up, *Thirteen,* marked the band's further explorations into power-pop formalism, and though it elicited less enthusiastic reviews than had its predecessor, it displayed a band clearly growing into its powers.

Photograph by Neil Cooper, © 1993 Geffen Records

Members include **Norman Blake,** guitar, vocals; **Gerry Love** (studied urban and regional planning at University of Strathclyde), bass, vocals; **Raymond McGinley** (received engineering degree from University of Glasgow), guitar, vocals; and **Brendan O'Hare** (born c. 1969), drums, vocals.

Blake (a music store employee) and McGinley performed with Glasgow band Boy Hairdressers, mid-1980s-1989; formed Teenage Fanclub with Love and O'Hare (a cancer research assistant), 1990; released debut album, *A Catholic Education,* Matador, 1990; signed with David Geffen Company (DGC) and released *Bandwagonesque,* 1991.

Addresses: *Record company*—David Geffen Company, 9130 Sunset Blvd., Los Angeles, CA 90069. *Fanclub*—P.O. Box 41, Stretford, Manchester, M32 8AT England.

Norman Blake and Raymond McGinley, both singer-songwriter-guitarists, played together in a Glasgow band called Boy Hairdressers during the mid- to late 1980s. When that band dissolved in 1989, Blake took a job in a music store, and McGinley pursued an engineering degree. Before long, however, they teamed up with bassist-vocalist Gerry Love—himself in the process of completing his university education—and Brendan O'Hare, a research assistant, longtime Hairdressers fan, and aspiring drummer, to form Teenage Fanclub. Their independently released debut, *A Catholic Education,* appeared on the Matador label in 1990 and was described by *Rolling Stone's* Chris Mundy as "a stunning genuflection to American indie strum and grunge." After generating a buzz with *Education,* the band made a splash at New York City's yearly New Music Seminar. Shortly thereafter, Geffen Records subsidiary DGC—one of the most adventuresome of the major labels—signed them up.

Bandwagonesque Acclaimed

Nonetheless, Teenage Fanclub released another Matador album, an instrumental collection titled *The King,* in order to meet their contractual obligation, despite having nearly completed *Bandwagonesque* for DGC. The hastily recorded *King* sold poorly; Matador head Gerard Cosloy was measured when asked for comment by Mundy: "I respect their desire to move to a major label," he insisted. "I just believe they should have fulfilled their contractual obligations." The band, meanwhile, asserted that they could not have survived any longer making independent records. "Gerard did a lot for us, but we did a lot for him, too," Blake said. "Most indie labels have major-label mentalities anyway. It was kind of a Catch-22 situation. We weren't going to be paid, but because of the record, we weren't entitled to unemployment benefits. What were we supposed to do?" Ultimately, the band and Cosloy were amply compensated by Geffen, and *Bandwagonesque* would improve Teenage Fanclub's fortunes even further.

Released late in 1991, *Bandwagonesque* scored on college and alternative radio. Demonstrating the influence of pop's master tunesmiths, notably the Beatles, Badfinger, the Beach Boys, Neil Young, and Big Star, the group indulged a penchant for songcraft when rage and bombast dominated the alternative scene. Mundy observed that while other alt-rock bands explored heavy metal, "Teenage Fanclub has actually peeled off its topcoat to reveal a Beach Boy-ish heart lurking beneath the flannel." *Spin* reviewer Jim Greer called the band "God's gift to college radio," adding the backhanded compliment, "*Bandwagonesque* pulls the kinds of moves you'd expect from a much smarter, more ambitious group of guys." The album earned the band a positive critical reputation and an enlarged fan base. Still, it spent only four weeks on the Billboard 200 chart, never moving past the 137th position.

"Nothing Too Satanic"

A quote from McGinley in a 1993 DGC publicity release summarized the Fanclub's aim: "We're never intentionally indie or left-field. We always say it's really easy to make a record that's hard to listen to; we just want to make good pop records, whatever they might be classified as. We don't want to limit it or appeal to any specific market." Part of the band's renowned irreverence grew out of an unwillingness to adopt the rebellious, fiercely self-serious demeanor of many of their fellow rock bands. "To me, that whole thing of making a big ugly noise is a very middle-class thing," Blake noted to Shane Danielson of *Melody Maker.* "All that angst. I mean, working-class people generally don't bother with all that." Instead, the band's sound emphasized melody and structure, and its attitude has been playful and unpretentious. Thus, the backward-masked "message" on *Bandwagonesque's* "Satan" says merely, "God bless my cotton socks. I am wearing a blue shirt." As Blake averred to *Rolling Stone's* Mundy, "I guess it's nothing too Satanic." O'Hare evinced a similarly unfashionable niceness when he told Hochman of the *Los Angeles Times,* "None of us have any message for young people.... Um, look both ways before you cross [the street], don't be cheeky to your parents." The drummer went on to practically apologize, "We're not a very rock 'n' roll band. We don't take drugs and we don't try to corrupt young people. Sad, really, but true."

A highlight of the band's career came when they were afforded an opportunity to work with one of their idols, Big Star cofounder and songwriter *extraordinaire* Alex Chilton, with whom they recorded a single to benefit the victims of the war in Bosnia-Herzegovina. "We got on well with him," remarked Blake in the group's press release. "I think he genuinely likes us, because he's the sort of guy who if he didn't like you, wouldn't pretend that he did." The Fanclub enjoyed a collaboration of a different sort when they backed up rap group De La Soul for a track on the *Judgment Night* film soundtrack. "We'd never met them before," Blake said of the rappers in a *Billboard* interview. "We met up in the studio; we put down some drum tracks and guitar tracks, and they sort of rapped on it."

Hoped for Luck With *Thirteen*

Perhaps the biggest challenge the group has faced was following up *Bandwagonesque.* Indeed, they found the task daunting; after its release, Love told *Melody Maker's* Danielson that he found the new album less "honest," mostly "because of the time involved: it took eight months, and we kept revising it, re-recording it, and just generally trying to improve it. We were getting paranoid, trying to outdo the last album. Producing it ourselves was probably a mistake: we really missed having someone around to say, 'That's okay—leave it.' To me it's a much more self-conscious, indulgent album." Blake agreed that perfectionism may have made their playing seem more mannered but insisted, "The songs definitely stand up." *Thirteen* was re-leased in late 1993. "There's a Big Star song called 'Thirteen,' you know," McGinley reminded *Billboard.*

Reviews were mixed; *Spin* this time denounced the band for making "a fetish of smothering emotion under a blanket of stoic formalism." *Rolling Stone,* however, called the release "even sweeter than its predecessor" and lauded the group as "among the best recyclers [of power pop and bubblegum rock] around." *Musician* reviewer Rob O'Connor deemed *Thirteen* "great ear candy that we may one day learn is also nutritious." No longer the flavor of the month, Teenage Fanclub had distinguished itself as a maverick pop band more interested in melodic hooks and boyish harmonies than clamorous sound and fury. "It's funny," McGinley noted to *Melody Maker,* "just about the most radical thing you can do these days is write a song."

Selected discography

A Catholic Education, Matador, 1990.
The King, Matador, 1990.
Bandwagonesque (includes "Satan"), DGC, 1991.
(Contributors, with De La Soul) "Fallin'," *Judgment Night* (soundtrack), Immortal/Epic, 1993.
Thirteen, DGC, 1993.

Sources

Billboard, November 27, 1993.
Los Angeles Times, April 24, 1992.
Melody Maker, August 28, 1993; September 25, 1993.
Musician, December 1993.
Rolling Stone, May 14, 1992; November 11, 1993; April 7, 1994.
Spin, December 1991; December 1993.

Additional information for this profile was obtained from DGC publicity materials, 1993.

—*Simon Glickman*

Toots Thielemans

Harmonica player, guitarist, composer

Toots Thielemans is the undisputed master of the harmonica. "The instrument is so small. It's so close to your person, so close to the tone. You blow here and the tone comes out two inches away so it's really a part of your body. It's such a close friend. It's so essential, it's like being a part of your very soul," he told Jan Holland in an interview for *Venice* magazine. Further revealing how deeply devoted he is to his music, he explained to Michael Bourne in *Down Beat:* "It's fate that I became a musician. I studied math. I was supposed to become an engineer or professor. If it hadn't been for jazz, I'd still be in Belgium."

Toots was born Jean-Baptiste Thielemans in Brussels, Belgium, on April 29, 1922, and was playing the accordion by the age of three. While in his teens, before he even knew what jazz was, he bought his first harmonica. Prior to World War II, Thielemans had seen movies with legendary harmonica player Larry Adler "playing light classical things." He listened to American swing records with his friends, who later named him "Toots" because they felt that "Jean just didn't swing." They encouraged him to play his harmonica with their band, and when they saw how gifted he was they suggested that he try a *real* instrument, like the guitar.

Thielemans told Bourne that he came to learn the guitar by chance. He had been sick, and a friend came to visit him, bringing along a black-market guitar. "We were listening to Fats Waller records like 'Hold Tight.' There's the quintessence of the jazz scale and everything you need in the blues in that song. I knew the song but I'd never touched a guitar. I said that if he'd give me five minutes, I'd play 'Hold Tight' on one string. I played it, and he gave me the guitar."

A natural in his field, Thielemans never really studied music. He had been raised on the Swing Era stylings of Gypsy guitar genius Django Reinhardt. Jamming with other Belgian jazzers like saxophonist Bobby Jasper and guitarist Rene Thomas, he learned his craft "on the job." Thielemans gravitated to the American bebop sound in the 1940s. After World War II ended, he worked as an accompanist to headliners like Edith Piaf and Charles Trenet in Brussels. By the 1950s he was playing all over Europe with Benny Goodman, Roy Eldridge, and Zoot Sims.

In 1951 Thielemans immigrated to the United States. He had jammed with Charlie Parker while in Sweden, and for one memorable week in 1952 he joined Bird's All-Stars at the Earle Theatre in Philadelphia. "I had met Bird in Europe before coming to the United States," he told Holland in *Venice.* "When I got here, I played a little with him. I really wasn't ready for that. Miles Davis was with him. He teased me, had fun with me. Here I was,

Born Jean-Baptiste Thielemans, April 29, 1922, in Brussels, Belgium; changed first name to "Toots" as a teenager; immigrated to United States, 1951; married wife, Huguette.

Began playing the accordion at the age of three; bought first harmonica when he was in his teens. Self-taught guitarist, working as an accompanist to headliners like Edith Piaf and Charles Trenet in Brussels after World War II; became well-known composer and self-accompanist, whistling and playing guitar on his international hit "Bluesette." Played with jazz greats Charlie Parker, Benny Goodman, Miles Davis, and George Shearing; recorded two-volume *Brasil Project*, 1992-93. Appeared as a featured soloist on albums, commercials, and motion picture soundtracks; played harmonica solo for PBS-TV's *Sesame Street* theme.

Awards: Hohner (harmonica manufacturer) created a special chromatic harmonica named for Thielemans.

Addresses: *Record company*—Private Music, 9014 Melrose Ave., Los Angeles, CA 90069.

just come to this country, and was sharing a dressing room with Bird."

From the latter part of 1952 to mid-1959, Thielemans played with pianist George Shearing. It was the only steady job he ever had. It was during this time that he became friends with Bill Evans and Quincy Jones, recording some of his favorite tunes with them.

By the early 1960s, Thielemans had become increasingly popular in the studios as a harmonica player and whistler. A big fan of Slam Stewart, who hummed with the bow on the bass, Thielemans thought it might be fun to do something like that with his guitar. So he whistled a note and paralleled it one octave lower on the guitar. Before long, he was whistling for companies like Firestone, Singer, Dogburgers, and Old Spice, with its memorable "fresh as a breeze" theme. Over the years, his harmonica playing has been featured on many movie soundtracks including *Midnight Cowboy, The Getaway, Sugarland Express,* and *Intersection;* he also played the featured solo in the theme for PBS-TV's classic children's show *Sesame Street.*

In 1963 Thielemans broke though to a worldwide audience with his composition "Bluesette." He told Bourne in *Down Beat* about how the tune was written: "I was playing a concert with [violinist] Stephane Grappelli in Brussels in 1962. I was in the same dressing room as Stephane and I was tuning my guitar and somehow this little song came out. I was humming it and Stephane said, 'That's nice. What is it?' I just said he inspired me, but he said 'Ecrivez tout de suite! Write it down right away!' I called it 'Bluette' for this little blue flower in Belgium, but when I played it on a show in Sweden, the producer said 'Isn't that a blues? Why don't you put the 's' in there?' I owe the 's' to him." Another popular—but not as frequently recorded—composition of his is "Ladyfingers," which was featured on Herb Alpert's hit album *Whipped Cream and Other Delights.*

Thielemans's interest in international music expanded over the next decade. He had first been introduced to Brazilian music in the early 1960s through Stan Getz and was given the chance to participate in a Brazilian music session in 1972. When the opportunity arose to do an album with singer Elis Regina—she is often dubbed "Brazil's Billie Holiday"—Thielemans was ready to immerse himself in the undertaking.

Working on the album paved the way for his entry onto the Brazilian music scene; since then, the music of the country has been his passion. "It's more than a flirt what I feel for Brazilian music. This idea [for the *Brasil Project* albums] came from Miles Goodman and Oscar Castro Neves. They said all these Brazilian guys love me. They all know [the] album I did in 1972 with Elis Regina." So together with the Brazilian players, the dream session was realized with two consecutive releases, volumes one and two of *The Brasil Project* in 1992 and 1993, respectively.

Toots Thielemans has been featured on recordings with contemporary artists such as Billy Joel, Paul Simon, Quincy Jones, Pat Metheny, and Ella Fitzgerald. And although he is an adept guitarist and an exceptional whistler, his harmonica playing is unrivaled. As he told Jim Macnie of *Musician* magazine, "Some people will agree that a harmonica player can be a good musician. But many will also tell you that they just don't like the way it sounds. Anybody who listens closely should appreciate it, however, because music transcends the instrument it's played on—whether it's a harmonica or a broomstick."

Selected discography

Man Bites Harmonica, Original Jazz Classics, 1958.
(With Elis Regina) *Aquarela de Brasil,* Phonogram, 1972.
Do Not Leave Me (live in Belgium), Milan, 1988.
Only Trust Your Heart, Concord Jazz, 1988.
Do Not Leave Me (American version), Stash, 1989.

Footprints, Polygram, 1991.
(With the Shirley Horn Trio) *For My Lady,* Polygram, 1991.
The Brasil Project: Volume 1, Private Music, 1992.
The Brasil Project: Volume 2, Private Music, 1993.
Apple Dimple, Denon.
Compact Jazz, Verve.
In Tokyo (live), Denon.
Live in the Netherlands, Pablo Records.
The Soul of Toots, Columbia.
Yesterday and Today, Gazell.

Sources

Billboard, September 25, 1993.
Crescendo, March 1978; April 1978.
Down Beat, November 1971; August 1993.
Entertainment Weekly, August 27, 1993.

Jazz Hot, May 1972.
Jazziz, August/September 1993.
Jazz Times, December 1990.
LA Jazz Scene, September 1993.
LA Weekly, November 12, 1993.
Los Angeles Times, November 15, 1993.
Musician, March 1992.
New York Times, September 24, 1993.
Philadelphia Daily News, August 24, 1993.
Public News Houston, September 15, 1993.
Pulse!, May 1993.
Variety, December 6, 1972.
Venice, January 1994.

Additional material for this profile was obtained from Private Records publicity materials, 1994.

—Charlie Katagiri

Thin Lizzy

Rock band

Phil Lynott, described in the *Encyclopedia of Pop, Rock & Soul* as a "brash black musician-poet from Dublin," founded Thin Lizzy in 1969 along with drummer and childhood buddy Brian Downey. The label "poet" stems from Lynott's early attempts at verse, which received some serious attention in Ireland. (Readers also found poetic sensibility in books of Lynott's lyrics that were published later.) As for Lynott's band, it would have to wait six years to chart an album—a record aptly named *Fighting,* given Thin Lizzy's struggles to find stable personnel and success.

Growing up black in Dublin proved relatively free of racist difficulties, according to Lynott, though presumably life in a Catholic working-class neighborhood raised by a single mother—Lynott's Brazilian father deserted his son at age four—provided trials enough. Although he was for a time a fairly serious boxer, Lynott soon found, as he told *Rolling Stone* in 1978, that "the tough guy with the thick ear wasn't getting the chicks, while your man up on stage seemed to be doing okay." The observation was not misleading. That same year

MICHAEL OCHS ARCHIVES / Venice, CA

the British tabloid the *Sun* crowned Lynott "the superstud of rock."

Rejecting the ring for a musical career brought Lynott to London in the early 1970s, where he did encounter some prejudice because of his skin color. In 1973 Thin Lizzy secured a Number Six hit with a rock version of the traditional Irish tune "Whiskey in the Jar." The band, wishing to avoid being pegged as a folk-rock cover group, did not allow this song to be included in *Vagabonds of the Western World,* an album that came out later that year.

Three Strikes Almost Knocked Them Out

Thin Lizzy had already endured the record-buying public's apathy toward two earlier albums, their 1971 debut effort *Thin Lizzy,* and the following year's *Tales from a Blue Orphanage. Vagabonds* unfortunately followed suit, despite a more traditional "rock" sound. These mediocre sales strained the band's willingness to stay together. After guitarist Eric Bell collapsed on stage during a New Year's Eve show and quit the band, a series of guitarists took a swing at the job. No one seemed to work out, and for a time even Lynott's childhood friend Downey quit Thin Lizzy.

Finally Lynott settled down with Scotland's Brian Robertson and a Yank, Scott Gorham, from Los Angeles, thinking that perhaps two guitarists could equal the departed Bell. Downey returned and Thin Lizzy entered its most successful period. Robertson would stay with Thin Lizzy until 1978—although he was forced to miss a 1977 U.S. tour after suffering a cut hand in a London club brawl.

Thin Lizzy scored big with their 1976 album *Jailbreak.* The record did well on both sides of the Atlantic, going gold. A single from this album, "The Boys Are Back in Town," received much airplay and hit Number 12 on the U.S. charts and Number Eight in the U.K. The following year saw the release of *Johnny the Fox,* an album that was well received in Britain but fared poorly in the States. A follow-up U.S. concert tour folded early after Lynott contracted hepatitis. Thin Lizzy's constant touring of Britain had helped to establish a loyal fan base there—something which, perhaps from difficulties like Lynott's illness, the band could never quite do stateside.

Macho Music

Lynott's lyrics, as suggested by the title of Thin Lizzy's biggest hit "The Boys Are Back in Town," often concerned male bonding. As one *Rolling Stone* writer noted, some of the band's songs were "replete ... with comic book heroism." Aggression and violence interested Lynott, and his songs reflected that. He claimed the music and raucous concerts were a release from violence that young men, including himself, might otherwise wreak on society.

Part of that anger came from the limited economic opportunities that England offered to working-class kids. Later, hard rock as a protest vehicle gave way to punk rock. Lynott's interest in this new music found expression in his participation in a side band called Greedy Bastards, which dabbled in less commercial waters. Gary Moore of Colosseum played guitar in Greedy Bastards and also wound up playing with Lizzy on concert tours.

But internal dissension plagued Thin Lizzy. Spats with guitarist Brian Robertson caused him to depart for a solo project. He did not return for months. The insufficiently attended 1977 U.S. concert tour stressed the band. Lynott realized that Thin Lizzy was too good to open for someone else but not a big enough name in the States to draw a crowd on its own. He told *Rolling Stone* that Americans weren't happy unless they could pigeonhole a band; perhaps, as some critics have suggested, Thin Lizzy simply failed to develop a sufficiently distinctive sound for U.S. ears.

Lynott also expressed some dissatisfaction with Thin Lizzy's longtime record label, Mercury, feeling the company partly to blame for spotty American showings. The band's final Mercury product was the 1977 album *Bad Reputation.* Thin Lizzy then signed with Warner Bros. and quickly turned out the 1978 concert album *Live and Dangerous,* which struck English gold within two weeks of its release, hitting Number Two. The following year yielded a studio effort, *Black Rose—A Rock Legend.* A U.S. tour was again somewhat jinxed when band management fired new guitarist Gary Moore. Midge Ure was flown in from London to act as a temporary replacement.

On the Loose

Subsequent Thin Lizzy releases on the Warner Bros. label included 1980's *Chinatown* and 1981's *Renegade. Chinatown's* "Killer on the Loose" caused a British stir following the Yorkshire Ripper killings. However, Warner had come in on a fading comet—U.S. popularity seemed to have peaked with the band's mid-'70s albums *Jailbreak* and *Johnny the Fox,* although subsequent efforts continued to sell well in the U.K. During this time, Lynott struck out on his own, releasing the 1980 album *Solo in Soho.* It reached Number 28 in Britain.

Thin Lizzy disbanded in 1983, 14 years after its inception; Lynott felt the group's music had grown predictable. *Thunder and Lightning* from that year was the band's final studio effort. Lynott then tried to form a new band, again with his childhood friend Brian Downey, but the two failed to secure a recording deal. Lynott also attempted another solo effort, but that too was unsuccessful. On Christmas Day, 1985, he fell into a drug- and alcohol-induced coma. After ten days, he died of liver, kidney, and heart failure complicated by pneumonia and acute blood poisoning.

Various Thin Lizzy compilation albums continue to appear in Britain, where a taste for the band was always strong. In 1991 a "best of" album reached Number Eight there. Despite this lingering interest, Thin Lizzy never attempted to re-form and hit the road in self-tribute, although they did play a single concert in 1986. This one-time performance was a tribute to the recently deceased Lynott, who was clearly the band's inspiration.

Selected discography

Thin Lizzy, Decca, 1971.
Tales From a Blue Orphanage, 1972.
Vagabonds of the Western World, Decca, 1973.
Night Life, Polydor, 1974.
Fighting, Mercury, 1975.
Jailbreak, Mercury, 1976.
Johnny the Fox, Mercury, 1977.
Bad Reputation, Warner Metal Blade, 1977.
Live and Dangerous, Warner Metal Blade, 1978.
Black Rose—A Rock Legend, Warner Metal Blade, 1979.
Chinatown, Warner Metal Blade, 1980.
Renegade, Warner Metal Blade, 1981.
Thunder and Lightning, Warner Metal Blade, 1983.
Life—Live, Warner Metal Blade, 1984 (recorded pre-break-up).
Dedication: The Very Best of Thin Lizzy, Mercury, 1991.

Sources

Books

Rees, Dafydd, and Luke Crampton, *Rock Movers & Shakers,* Billboard Books, 1991.
Stambler, Irwin, *The Encyclopedia of Pop, Rock & Soul,* St. Martin's, 1989.

Periodicals

Audio, December 1991.
Billboard, May 29, 1976.
Rolling Stone, June 17, 1976; January 27, 1977; September 21, 1978; February 27, 1986.

—*Joseph M. Reiner*

Third World

Reggae band

hird World is widely recognized as one of the legendary bands of reggae history. When Janine McAdams spoke with the band for *Billboard* in July of 1992, Michael "Ibo" Cooper, one of the founding members, declared: "Third World is now the longest-existing unit ever in Jamaican music history." While a few other reggae bands approach their mark of longevity, Third World is distinctive by virtue of their crossover skill: a great deal of their success grew from their ability to blend reggae music with other sounds, particularly those coming out of black American culture.

Although most of the band's members over the years have been Kingston, Jamaica-born, their musical roots are unusually diverse. Many reggae bands are spawned from the ambitions of Jamaican teenagers who have taught themselves to play their instruments, but Third World was the brainchild of two young men with classical training. Cooper, the son of a police officer, trained on a variety of keyboard instruments at the Royal School of Music in Kingston until 1969.

© Bobby Holland / MICHAEL OCHS ARCHIVES / Venice, CA

For the Record . . .

Members include **Michael Cooper** (born January 14, 1955, in Kingston, Jamaica; son of a police officer; educated at Kingston's Royal School of Music), vocals and keyboards; **Stephen Coore** (born April 6, 1959, in Kingston; son of a deputy prime minister and a music teacher; trained at Forster Davis School of Music), vocals and guitar; **Richard Daley** (born July 4, 1953), bass; **Milton Hamilton** (bandmember 1973-79; replaced by **William Clarke**), vocals; **Irwin Jarrett** (born c. 1952), percussion; **Cornel Marshal** (bandmember 1973-75; replaced by **William Stewart** [born February 15, 1956]), drums.

Cooper and Coore formed band in 1973 with Hamilton, Daley, and Marshal in Kingston, Jamaica. Self-produced first single, "Railroad Track," released in England only, c. 1973; moved to England soon after and signed record deal with Island Records; first album, *Third World,* released to critical acclaim, 1975; stayed with Island until 1980; signed with Columbia, 1981, then Mercury, 1989. Crossover hits include "Now That We Found Love," 1978, "Try Jah Love," 1982, and "Sense of Purpose," 1985.

Awards: Medal of peace from United Nations for contributions to African causes; invited guests at tribute to Nelson Mandela, Atlanta, GA, 1990.

Addresses: *Record company*—Mercury Records, 825 Eighth Ave., New York, NY 10019.

Stephen "Cat" Coore, whose father had served as deputy prime minister of Jamaica, first learned to play a range of stringed instruments from his mother, a music teacher with a sterling reputation throughout the Caribbean. His studies led to training at Forster Davis School of Music, where he gained a reputation as a child prodigy for his talent on the cello. By the time they decided to join forces in a reggae band, the young men had studied jazz as well as classical music, and they shared a taste for stateside rock.

Before Cooper and Coore decided to launch their own band, both had experience on the reggae circuit in Kingston, playing separately and together. Cooper formed his first reggae band, the Rhythms, in 1970. He went on to play with other outfits, including the Dynamic Visions and the Alley Cats; he first worked with Coore when the two played with a moderately successful Kingston group known as Inner Circle.

Reggae Vets Joined Forces

By 1973 Coore, Cooper, and Inner Circle vocalist Milton "Prilly" Hamilton decided to strike out on their own; they completed the band with self-taught bassist Richie Daley and Cornel Marshal on drums. Irwin "Carrot" Jarrett provided further percussion, including occasional conga playing; Jarrett also brought the band considerable professional experience on both the musical stage and in television production. These ingredients alone seemed likely to set them apart from the many new bands springing up in Kingston at the time.

The group officially began their career as Third World with a performance at the Jamaican Independence Celebration in the summer of 1973. After playing the Jamaican club circuit for a while, they relocated to England, where mainstream audiences were just beginning to discover the reggae sound. The budding band undertook their first release themselves, without the patronage of a label, offering a single called "Railroad Track" exclusively in England.

The fortuity of Third World's timing landed them a contract with Island Records, a strong label in the process of creating a market for reggae music. Island released Third World's self-titled debut album in 1975. In another timing coup, a positive critical response to the album won the band the opportunity to open for Bob Marley, the most acclaimed reggae musician of the time, on his summer tour of the United Kingdom.

Journey Through Genres

But Third World's potential wasn't quite realized for another three years. Although a second album, *96 Degrees in the Shade,* was released in 1977, it was 1978's *Journey to Addis* that caught the attention of record buyers and established the group's sound. In particular, *Journey to Addis* offered listeners a chance to hear "Now That We Found Love"—the single that demonstrated Third World's ability to blend reggae sound with other musical genres then burgeoning in England and the United States. The single was a crossover hit that grabbed listeners who didn't normally buy reggae albums.

In an article for *Melody Maker,* Paolo Hewitt described "Now That We Found Love" as "a song that by encompassing reggae, funk and pop bypasses any kind of recognized categorization." *Billboard* reported in 1993 that the single made Top Ten charts "worldwide," including the Number Nine spot on *Billboard's* R&B chart.

Third World completed three more albums with Island—*The Story's Been Told, Prisoner in the Street,* and *Arise in Harmony*—before deciding to find another label. Maureen Sheridan reported in *Down Beat* that they felt they would earn more attention if they didn't have to compete with the company's commitment to Marley.

Columbia soon picked up their contract and produced five Third World albums over the next seven years: *Rock the World* in 1981, *You've Got the Power* in 1982, *All the Way Strong* in 1983, *Sense of Purpose* in 1985, and *Hold On to My Love* in 1987. The first four releases all had significant success on U.S. and British music charts—"Hooked on Love," from *Rock the World,* broke into the British Top Ten as a single release.

Around the same time as their move to Columbia, the band began collaborating with American pop star Stevie Wonder, developing their hybrid sound still further and finding a niche with both white and black American audiences. Specifically, Wonder wrote and recorded "Try Jah Love" with the band, creating another R&B chart hit for them in 1982.

Since reggae was then largely embraced by white audiences in England and America, it took Wonder's support and the band's experimental style to capture the ear of black listeners. This was an important goal for the band; as Clarke told Sheridan, they believe that "reggae is a spiritual force ..., a positive force for black people."

Accused of "Selling Out"

Third World's particular aptitude for crossover hits has earned them a somewhat double-edged place in the landscape of reggae music. On the one hand, they are recognized as innovators, willing to take risks that challenge the limitations of the genre; on the other hand, however, their particular ability to combine the distinctive sound of Jamaican music with the commercial polish of English and American pop has prompted some critics to charge them with "selling out."

As Jim Bessman wrote in *Billboard,* Third World has been "criticized by reggae purists for being too commercial." Sheridan noted that "to the downtowner, Third World plays uptown reggae, a variant that has traveled too far from the ghetto to be roots." The harshest criticism, as Hewitt noted in *Melody Maker,* came from those quarters that discerned a financial motivation behind crossover experiments. "This of course," Hewitt commented, "opens them up to that age-old accusation of being sell-out merchants, peo-

ple diluting tunes to the shadows of flashing dollar signs."

Third World has taken time over the years to explain where their experimentation fits into their views on music. "Roots reggae is a good foundation," Cooper explained to Sheridan, "but we get impatient with the static form. What we do is add to it and stretch it further." He added: "No one ever says we can't play roots; they just say we don't. If roots is basic rhythm, then you must be able to move on from that to communicate to a wider audience. Music is energy and comes from the ultimate source, and how can you limit that? That would limit the ultimate possibilities of the music."

> "Third World represents the voice of the people internationally, not just in our own country. It's music of all forms."
> —William Clarke

Clarke presented a similar argument to *Melody Maker* contributor Alan Jackson, stating, "Third World represents the voice of the people internationally, not just in our own country. It's music of all forms, be it African or Latin, reggae or funk, R&B or whatever." Ben Mapp concurred in a 1992 *Vibe* article, asserting that "the music is about inclusion—a little bit of reggae, a little bit of R&B, topped with some ska, and just enough 'message' to add some weight."

Whatever the reasons behind the band's experimentation, even detractors can't deny that Third World has contributed to new developments in reggae. Deeming them "the first band to funk up the reggae beat," Sheridan noted that they were also "the first reggae group to add synthesizer" and pioneers in popularizing "the poetry-read-to-reggae art form known as dub poetry."

The dub sound, which originally seemed to abandon the "roots" sound, eventually came to dominate the reggae scene in the 1980s. By the end of the decade, it was mutating into dancehall—the "reggae-hip-hop" combination that breathed new life into the musical form both in Jamaica and abroad.

The 1985 release *Sense of Purpose* was identified by Sheridan as "an album that reinforces the group's reputation as innovators." It demonstrated Third World's crossover strength by appearing on a variety of charts, including pop and dance music.

Clarke explained the hybrid strength of the album's title cut to Jackson in the *Melody Maker* interview: "It's dance music," he conceded, "but the lyric is deep. It could be to a woman or it could be to the world. I love you with a sense of purpose—a lot of people love as a simple reaction to the way they feel about someone, because there's that spark, but with no sense of purpose. And that's the important thing, whatever you are doing, that it should be with a sense of purpose.... We aimed to make the message danceable. It's as simple as that."

Sense of Purpose also demonstrated the band's willingness to take a risk with the sounds of American rap music. By 1989 they were indulging heavily in hip-hop on *Serious Business,* their first release for Mercury. As with their earlier experiments with American music, Third World saw this as an opportunity to unite Afro-Caribbean and African American listeners, as Clarke explained to McAdams in *Billboard:* "We brought a lot of black Americans to the reggae table through our forum, and we wanted to pursue that direction."

Without abandoning the band's spectrum of styles, 1992's *Committed* featured a stronger dancehall rhythm. The title track spent several weeks on *Billboard's* R&B charts. Mapp in particular felt that Third World had brought to the album an entirely new musical dimension, arguing that they "seem more at home with the dancehall tracks, which generate all of the album's creative tension and its most compelling songcraft."

Such aptitude is remarkable for a band that came to life at least a decade before the inception of dancehall—and demonstrates that Third World's longevity is based on musical vitality. Lisa Cortes, a representative of the Mercury label, explained in *Billboard:* "They're not 'forefathers' because they continue to evolve and build musical bridges."

Selected discography

Third World, Island, 1975.
96 Degrees in the Shade, Island, 1977.
Journey to Addis (includes "Now That We Found Love"), Island, 1978.
The Story's Been Told, Island, 1979.
Prisoner in the Street, Island, 1979.
Arise in Harmony, Island, 1980.
Rock the World (includes "Hooked on Love"), Columbia, 1981.
You've Got the Power (includes "Try Jah Love"), Columbia, 1982.
All the Way Strong, Columbia, 1983.
Sense of Purpose, Columbia, 1985.
Hold On to My Love, Columbia, 1987.
Serious Business, Mercury, 1989.
Committed, Mercury, 1989.
Reggae Ambassadors: 20th Anniversary Collection, Mercury, 1993.
(Contributors) *The Little Mermaid* (soundtrack).

Sources

Books

The Encyclopedia of Pop, Rock & Soul, edited by Irwin Stambler, St. Martin's, 1989.

Periodicals

Billboard, July 25, 1992; October 2, 1993.
Down Beat, January 1986.
Melody Maker, May 22, 1982; March 23, 1985.
Record, January 1984.
Reggae Report, issue 7, 1991; issue 8, 1992; issue 5, 1993.
Vibe, fall 1992.
Village Voice, April 27, 1982.

Additional information for this profile was obtained from Mercury Records publicity materials.

—*Ondine E. Le Blanc*

Toad the Wet Sprocket

Rock band

" I'm not deaf but I / Can't hear everything," warns Toad the Wet Sprocket's lead singer-lyricist Glen Phillips in his song "Unquiet." The band—which supposedly took its name from an obscure Monty Python skit that mocked rock news reports—have "a certain flair for the absurd," according to Josef Woodward in *Musician*. Guitarist Todd Nichols, bassist Dean Dinning, drummer Randy Guss, and Phillips often gloss their traditional rock tunes with equally unusual titles, such as "Sounds Like Teen-age Mutant Ninja Turtles," and lyrics that depict barbecues gone bad because of hallucinatory potato salad.

Although their roots are in the eclectic music scene of Santa Barbara, California, Toad found most of their success as a college band. James Hunter of *Musician* described their music as "a rich autumnal flow of steely strumming" with "variations on 3/4 time, suspended or extended folk chords [and] swirling vocal harmonies" that are "clearer with textures than words." This indirectness has become part of the band's strategy: in a 1989 interview with *Rolling Stone*, Phillips remarked, "If

Photograph by Michael Wilson, © 1994 Sony Music

a song is ambiguous, you can bring out a feeling in somebody else.... They'll get a lot more out of it than if you give them everything."

Yet unlike most alternative bands that shy away from hype and publicity, Toad seems to give everything to their fans, at least materially. In 1994 their free grassroots mailing list boasted 50,000 names of people who were sent a yearly Christmas card, concert information, and photos. "We made a concerted effort to make sure that everyone who ever came to our gigs got a mail-in card," the band's manager, Chris Blake, told *Billboard.*

Hopped Onto the Santa Barbara Scene

Although Toad credits the mailing list for their touring success, the list can't be held entirely responsible for their rapid rise in popularity. For example, after being signed by Columbia in 1988, they were paid $25,000 for a music video that originally cost them only $100 to record. "[Toad's] act is unique," commented Steve Tipp, vice-president for alternative music at Columbia, in *Billboard.* "They're real Santa Barbara kids who stick around for hours after sets just to talk with their fans, and their audience has grown because of this."

Yet however homegrown they may initially seem, the band with the unforgettable name undoubtedly blossomed because of their commercial ventures: appearing on the *Tonight Show* and *Late Night With David Letterman;* recording tracks for the *Buffy the Vampire Slayer* film soundtrack; and releasing four albums on Columbia, one of them, *Fear,* reaching gold sales status in 1991.

Former schoolmates with no specific musical aspirations in mind, Toad the Wet Sprocket got together to combat boredom and first rehearsed in a storage unit complex 15 miles north of the University of California-Santa Barbara campus. The units were owned by 70-year-old Sid Goren, whom *Billboard* called "the Godfather of the Santa Barbara scene." Goren rented almost entirely to bands—including Overdrive and Ugly Kid Joe—and asked dirt-cheap prices. Santa Barbara has never been known for its music scene; in the 1960s, Strawberry Alarm Clock came out with the pop hit "Incense and Peppermints," but the area—unlike Seattle for example—has yet to earn fame for producing a particular sound.

Leapfrogged to Stardom

Originally calling themselves Three Young Studs and Glenn, Toad began to play for free at a local club called the Shack. "The owner would sometimes give us free beer and peanuts," Randy Guss told *Rolling Stone* in 1989, "so we played for peanuts because we weren't old enough to drink." Yet when they changed their name to Toad the Wet Sprocket in 1986, they caught the attention of Brad Nack, former lead singer and founder of the early 1980s band and local flop Tan. After catching a Toad gig at the Shack, Nack introduced the band to his former manager, Chris Blake.

Although they had plenty of original material, Toad had never set foot in a recording studio. Nack and Blake agreed to manage the band, and together the six of them produced a recording in a garage studio for $650. In 1988 this recording made its way onto a cassette titled *Bread and Circus* that was sold at cash registers in local music stores. The cassettes quickly began to sell out, and news of the new band made its way down to Los Angeles, where major labels began to show interest. At Toad shows in early 1988, as many as five record company representatives at a time were in attendance.

The money Toad made selling cassettes was used to finance their next recording, *Pale.* This second album cost considerably more to record ($6,500) than *Bread and Circus,* yet when the band finally signed with Columbia, the LPs were licensed for $50,000 each. Toad chose Columbia not because it offered them the most money up front but because the label agreed to re-release *Bread and Circus* and *Pale* without any new production. By 1989 the band had developed a following.

Soon after *Bread and Circus* was nationally distributed, Toad began touring as the opening band for acts like the B-52's, Deborah Harry, and Michael Penn. In the meantime, Brad Nack, who had renewed interest in his formerly defunct band Brad is Sex, relinquished his role as manager to Chris Black so that he could spend more time touring. Over the course of two years, Toad developed a slow but steady cult following, continuing to play what Josef Woodard of *Musician* called "evocative folk-tinged rock."

Yet in 1992, the unpredictable happened: Toad found itself jumping into the popularity pool with a Top 40 hit titled "All I Want," a song off their third album, *Fear,* released in 1991. More commonly known for their ironic, bittersweet sound, the band neither planned nor wanted a pop hit. "It's strange to have 'All I Want' be *the* song because it's kind of a fluke," Glenn Phillips told *Musician.* "Normally, if anything sounded half that poppy, we wouldn't even finish it." In the interview, other band members stated that the song was almost left off the album 12 times, partly, Phillips added, because it "sounds like a Toyota commercial."

Jumped "Weird Band Name" Hurdle

In 1992, when Toad the Wet Sprocket toured England, the British press picked up on some of the band's own criticism of their new pop sound. Writing for *Melody Maker,* Peter Paphides quipped that the band had so much jangle that he was "convinced Santa's started his rounds early." In a November issue of the same magazine, review columnist Stephen Trousse called the band "a fifth-form retard Monty Python's obsessive excuse for a name," praising the jangley sound but stating that "sadly, whenever singer Glenn Phillips bleats lines like 'He nudged the moth to make it fly away/But moths are fragile things' it all come crashing back to earth with a pathetic thump. It's a small pleasure," he continued, "rather like watching someone trip over the pavement." And of Toad's onstage persona, Paphides commented that Phillips is a singer who plucked "[rock group] the Waterboys' 'Spirit' from the heavens and smear[ed] it with cat-sick."

In the United States, however, Toad received the opposite response. By 1992 *Fear* had sold approximately 750,000 copies, and "All I Want," which had climbed to Number 15 on the *Billboard* Hot 100 charts, was followed by another hit at Number 23, "Walk on the Ocean." Columbia originally worried that *Fear* would fare poorly; the original single, "It's for Me," flopped on modern rock radio. Yet the band continued to sell as many records as they always had, due in part to heavy touring—a total of 275 dates in support of *Fear.* Columbia sent "All I Want" to alternative rock, album rock, and Top 40 format radio stations. "Top 40 went

bonkers," manager Chris Blake told *Billboard,* and to the pop market, Toad the Wet Sprocket essentially became a brand new band.

The third single off *Fear,* "Hold Her Down," created some controversy that ultimately earned the band more fame than negative press. Originally misinterpreted as pro-rape, the song was pulled from alternative radio, creating much discussion. "In the process of the moderate discussion about the song, people got over their problems with the band's name," Blake told *Billboard.* "They used it enough times so it became acceptable. To a general extent that had been a real hurdle for us."

> *"If a song is ambiguous, you can bring out a feeling in somebody else. They'll get a lot more out of it than if you give them everything."*
> —Glenn Phillips

Although *Fear* was eventually certified gold, it was the result of three solid months in the studio and exhibited a recording style that, according to Jim Bessman of *Billboard,* "cut against the essence of a band that had structured a loyal core following on constant touring." While *Fear* was layered in production, *Dulcinea,* released in May of 1994, had a more stripped-down quality closer to Toad's live touring sound.

Diarmuid Quinn, West Coast vice-president for marketing at Columbia, told *Billboard,* Toad "built [themselves up] to where they became a viable radio band by touring incessantly and creating demand." Yet the success of *Fear* did not seem to change the band's original vision. "If anything," wrote Jim Bessman in *Billboard,* "Toad the Wet Sprocket's commercial breakthrough has returned the band to its original ethos: live sound."

Primarily a concept album, *Dulcinea* dealt primarily with the theme of idealized love. Four songs, "Woodburing," "Windmills," "Listen," and "Something Always Wrong," allude to the story of fictional character Don Quixote and his somewhat misguided love interest. Phillips related in *Billboard* that the album stemmed from "kind of a weird year" during which he got married and travelled to India. Because *Dulcinea* is a concept album, it lacks the slick definition of the singles present on *Fear.* Although the songs may not be as radio-friendly as those on the band's previous LP, the tracks appeal first and foremost to fans. "Hey, sometimes you get it right. And when you don't, two years down the road, maybe you will," Dean Dinning told *Musician* in a 1992 interview. "When you're a live band you have a thousand second chances. That's a great luxury."

In the summer of 1994, Toad the Wet Sprocket was on the road again headlining with British alternative rock band the Cranberries and promoting *Dulcinea*.

Selected discography

Bread and Circus, 1987, reissued, Columbia, 1989.
Pale, 1988, reissued, Columbia, 1990.
Fear, Columbia, 1991.
Dulcinea, Columbia, 1994.

Contributed to *Buffy the Vampire Slayer* soundtrack, 1992.

Sources

Billboard, September 19, 1992; February 13, 1993; April 7, 1990; April 4, 1994.
Melody Maker, October 31, 1992; November 7, 1992.
Metro Times (Detroit), July 27, 1994.
Musician, November 1989; October 1992.
People, February 10, 1992; August 1, 1994.
Rolling Stone, October 5, 1989.

—*Sarah Messer*

Big Joe Turner

Singer

Blues and jazz singer Big Joe Turner began his career as a teenager, singing in the beer joints and nightclubs of Kansas City. In the late 1930s he moved to New York City, where he sang in society cafes and helped to spark a nationwide boogie-woogie craze. After recording a long-running series of boogie-woogie hits, he became one of the few singers of his generation to cross over into rock and roll in the 1950s. In the later years of his career, he released a series of critically acclaimed jazz albums and continued to perform regularly until his death in 1985.

As a singer, Turner was an "original who could sing urbane jazz or down-and-dirty blues," according to Mark Rowland in *Musician*. "His voice," critic Benny Green wrote in the notes to Turner's album *Nobody in Mind,* "had a body to it, a certain aural succulence, which makes its impact very nearly a physical sensation."

Joseph Vernon Turner was born in Kansas City, Missouri, on May 18, 1911. Like many black entertainers of his era, he began his career as a boy, working the streets for tips. When he was in his early teens, his father died and Turner left school for a series of jobs in Kansas City nightspots, working variously as a bartender, cook, and bouncer.

Learned From the Pros

Turner would occasionally sing at after hours jam sessions and get pointers from more experienced performers. "I got acquainted with a lot of musicians," he told *Living Blues*. "They used to help me a lot you know, teach me all the gimmicks and things. I got so I was pretty good at it. So from then on I just took it up for a profession." With the help of his musician friends, Turner began singing around Kansas City. In the late 1920s and early 1930s he occasionally toured with the regional bands led by Bennie Moten, George E. Lee, Andy Kirk, and Count Basie, but his most common partner was childhood friend and boogie-woogie pianist Pete Johnson.

At the time, Kansas City musicians like Basie and Kirk were combining big-band jazz and rural blues to create what Rowland in *Musician* called a "driving, danceable R&B." Turner and Johnson participated in this innovation by taking "the traditionally laconic 12-bar blues ... upbeat and uptown," according to Rowland.

In 1936 Turner tried to make it in New York City but failed. Two years later he got another chance. Famed jazz promoter John Hammond was traveling through Kansas City when he caught Turner and Johnson's live

Born Joseph Vernon Turner in Kansas City, MO, May 18, 1911; died in Los Angeles, CA, November 24, 1985; married, 1954; wife's name, Lou Willie (died, 1972).

Toured regionally with Kansas City bands led by George E. Lee, Bennie Motein, Count Basie, and others, late 1920s to early 1930s; appeared with pianist Pete Johnson in the "Spirituals to Swing" concert at Carnegie Hall and on Benny Goodman's *Camel Caravan* radio program, 1938; appeared at Cafe Society, New York City, 1939-44; recorded extensively for Vocalion, 1938-40, and Decca, 1940-44; recorded hit "Roll Em Pete" with the Boogie Woogie Boys; signed to Atlantic Records, 1951; recorded rock and roll and R&B hits in the 1950s, including "Shake Rattle and Roll," 1954, and "Teenage Letter," 1957; left Atlantic to play Los Angeles clubs, 1962; recorded a series of jazz albums on the Pablo label, 1970s.

Awards: Silver Award for Male Vocalist in All-American Jazz Band, *Esquire* magazine, 1945; named Best New Male Singer, *Down Beat* magazine critics' poll, 1956; named Top Male Singer, *Melody Maker* magazine critics poll, 1965; Best Blues Record, *Jazz Journal* poll, 1965; Outstanding Achievement Award from Los Angeles Mayor Tom Bradley.

act. Hammond was impressed and booked the duo to play at his Christmas Eve "Spirituals to Swing" concert at New York's Carnegie Hall.

Spread Boogie-Woogie Fever

"Spirituals to Swing" was a huge success, and with Hammond behind him Turner soon became a successful performing and recording artist. He and Johnson appeared on Benny Goodman's *Camel Caravan* radio broadcasts. He was booked into what became a five-year engagement at New York City's Cafe Society, and he recorded frequently with Johnson as well as pianists Art Tatum and Joe Sullivan.

Perhaps most significantly, his recording of "Roll Em Pete" with the Boogie Woogie Boys—Johnson, Albert Ammons and Meade Lux Lewis—"ignited the boogie-woogie fever that subsequently swept the nation," according to *Blackwell's Guide to Recorded Blues.* Through the late l930s and early 1940s Turner record-

ed often and successfully with the Vocalion, Varsity, Okeh, and Decca labels. He displayed himself as a line jazz singer, a blues shouter, and a master of boogie-woogie. His themes were "wine, women and song ... and [he] sang them in a way that let you know he'd researched his subjects well," according to *Musician's* Rowland.

In the late 1940s Turner, like many jazz singers, experienced a decline in popularity. He returned to Kansas City, and given the general direction of popular music, it seemed likely that he would fade into obscurity. But in 1951 he was approached by a young record producer named Ahmet Ertegun. Ertegun had recently started Atlantic Records and had a plan to make Turner a renewed success. Ertegun coupled Turner with a relatively unknown pianist and songwriter named Harry Van Walls. Over the next few years the duo knocked out one hit disc after the next, including "I'll Never Stop Loving You," "Bump Miss Suzie," and "Still in Love."

On a Roll With Rock in the '50s

In 1954 Turner travelled to Chicago and New Orleans where he recorded some protean rock and roll. Rock proved fertile ground for Turner, and he became one of the few jazz/blues singers of his generation to regain healthy record sales in the teenage rock and roll market. He hit the charts repeatedly with songs like "Morning, Noon, & Night," and "Lipstick, Powder and Paint." His biggest hit—"Shake, Rattle & Roll"— became a teen anthem, though most kids heard versions of the song recorded by white artists Bill Haley and Elvis Presley.

While the 1950s were commercially successful years for Turner, some argue that they marked a deterioration in the quality of his material. David Penny in *Blackwell's Guide to Recorded Blues* commented that Turner's songs of adolescent love were "unworthy of his talent," and that it was only when he reverted to "such standards as 'Trouble in Mind' or 'Tomorrow Nights'... that the old Joe Turner shone through."

In the early 1960s Atlantic producers began saddling Turner's records with vocal choirs and symphonic string sections. Dissatisfied with this approach, Turner left Atlantic in 1962 and spent a decade playing clubs in Los Angeles, making an occasional film appearance, and releasing singles on the Coral and Kent labels.

In 1970 Turner was reintroduced to a national audience by the enterprising Bluesway label, and in 1971 he was signed by the Pablo label. Until his death in 1985 Turner remained a vibrant presence, recording a series of fine albums often surrounded by old colleagues such as Count Basie, Eddie Vinson, Pee Wee Crayton, Jay McShann, Lloyd Glenn, and Jimmy Witherspoon. Writing in *Musician,* Rowland recalled a 1981 appearance in which Turner was backed by the rock and roll group the Blasters. "Big Joe had just turned 70 and needed crutches to maneuver his ample frame and a stool on the bandstand," wrote Rowland. "But ... an amazing transformation took place: Swinging the mike in his mighty paw, Turner began to belt out rich swinging boogie woogie blues.... For two hours the room had exploded, and by the end it was the kids who were staggering."

Selected discography

Boss of the Blues, Atlantic, 1956, reissued, 1976.
Big Joe Rides Again, Atlantic, 1959, reissued, 1988.
Texas Style, Evidence, 1971, reissued, 1992.
(With the Count Basie Orchestra) *Flip, Flop & Fly,* Pablo, 1975, reissued, 1989.
Things That Used to Do, Pablo, 1975.
Midnight Special, Pablo, 1976.
(With Pete Johnson) *Jumpin' Blues,* Arhoolie, 1981.
The Best of "Big" Joe Turner, Pablo, 1982.
Have No Fear, Joe Turner Is Here, Pablo, 1982.
In the Evening, Pablo, 1982.
(With Jimmy Witherspoon) *Nobody in Mind,* Pablo, 1982.
(With Dizzy Gillespie, Roy Eldridge, and others) *Trumpet Kings Meet Joe Turner,* Fantasy/Original Jazz Classics, 1982, reissued, 1991.
Life Ain't Easy, Pablo, 1983.
Kansas City Here I Come, Fantasy/Original Jazz Classics, 1984, reissued, 1992.
Rock This Joint, Intermedia, 1984.

(With Roomful of Blues and Doctor John) *Blues Train,* Muse, 1986.
(With Jimmy Witherspoon) *Patcha, Patcha All Night Long,* Pablo, 1986.
Memorial Album: The Rhythm & Blues Years, Atlantic, 1986.
Greatest Hits, Atlantic, 1987.
I've Been to Kansas City, Volume 1, Decca Jazz, 1990.
Singing the Blues, Mobile Fidelity, 1990.
Stormy Monday, Pablo, 1991.
Everyday I Have the Blues, Fantasy, Inc., 1991.
1938-1941, L'art Vocal, 1992.
Joe Turner with Milt Jackson, Roy Eldridge, Fantasy, 1992.
(With Pete Johnson's Orchestra) *Tell Me Pretty Baby,* Arhoolie, 1992.
(With Milt Buckner, Slam Stewart, and Jo Jones) *Texas Style,* Evidence, 1992.
Stride by Stride, Solo Art, 1993.
Big Bad and Blue: The Big Joe Turner Anthology, Rhino, 1994.

Sources

Books

The Blackwell Guide to Recorded Blues, Blackwell, 1991.
Blues Who's Who: A Biographical Dictionary of Blues Singers, edited by Sheldon Harris, Arlington House, 1979.

Periodicals

Living Blues, autumn 1972.
Musician, May 1994.

Additional information for this profile was obtained from the liner notes to *Everyday I Have the Blues,* Fantasy, Inc., 1991.

—*Jordan Wankoff*

James Blood Ulmer

Guitarist, flutist, singer

Guitarist, flutist, and vocalist James Blood Ulmer once joked that he cannot find where his music is located in record stores. Having worked and recorded with Ornette Coleman, Art Blakey, Joe Henderson, Arthur Blythe, David Murray, Ronald Shannon Jackson, and George Adams as bandleader and sideman, Ulmer is recognized as a central figure in the post-fusion movements of 1970s and 1980s jazz. Yet within this experimental framework, his guitar playing and songwriting incorporate blues, funk, and rock idioms, making it difficult to categorize his innovative musical forms. A 1981 *Newsweek* profile hailed him as "the most original guitarist since Jimi Hendrix and Wes Montgomery," comparisons that also suggest the different rock and jazz worlds in which his music has moved.

Ulmer has, on occasion, called his music "black rock"— a term later popularized by admirer Vernon Reid of Living Color—and "harmolodic diatonic funk." Critics over the years have tried to pin it down: *Musician's* Chip Stern labeled the sound "punk jazz," *Guitar Player's* Bill Milkowski named it "avant gutbucket," and Greg Tate, author of *Flyboy in the Buttermilk: Essays on Contemporary America,* claimed it possessed an "urbane primitivism." Whatever its name, Ulmer's hybrid vision helped define the role of electric guitar in contemporary free jazz; and, when working with volume, distortion, blues phrasings, and conventional song structures, his dissonant music has periodically crossed over to rock audiences.

From South Carolina to Detroit

Ulmer was born in St. Matthews, South Carolina, on February 2, 1942. Gospel and the blues—spiritual hymns and worldly tales—were formative influences during Ulmer's youth. At the age of seven, he joined his father's gospel quartet, the Southern Sons, where he learned to play guitar and sing baritone. He performed with the group until he was 13. His interest in the blues occasionally led to trouble on the homefront. "Down South," he told *Guitar Player* magazine in 1990, "we had two kinds of blues: one that was forbidden, and one that wasn't."

The sexual frankness of the former style, as practiced by a local named Johnny Wilson, did not appeal to the guitarist's mother. "I used to love to hear [Wilson] play the blues," Ulmer reported, "and I used to go up there and try to listen to him. But every time I'd tell Mama, I'd get my ass beat just for listening to Johnny Wilson." A high school group organized around chapel meetings provided the teenaged Ulmer with an outlet for his musical energies.

Born James Ulmer, February 2, 1942, in St. Matthews, SC; also uses Muslim name, Adamu (or Damu) Mustafa Abdul Musawwir.

Began playing guitar and singing with gospel quartet the Southern Sons, 1949-55; moved to Pittsburgh, PA, and began performing professionally, 1959; formed Blood and the Bloodbrothers, Columbus, OH, 1963; wrote and played original jazz compositions in the James Ulmer Trio and Focus Novii, Detroit, MI, 1967-71; studied and toured with Ornette Coleman, New York City, 1972-77; released debut solo record, 1979; signed by Columbia Records, 1981; released solo records and toured with three-piece rock band; toured and recorded with Phalanx, 1984-88; recorded with Music Revelation Ensemble, 1980, 1988, and 1990; led blues trio, beginning in 1989.

Awards: Named Talent Deserving Wider Recognition in guitar category, *Down Beat* Critics' Poll, 1980; *Odyssey* named Album of the Year, *Village Voice* Critics' Poll, 1983.

Addresses: *Home*—New York, NY. *Record company*—Columbia Records, 550 Madison Ave., 26th Floor, New York, NY 10022.

Ulmer moved to Pittsburgh in 1959 to begin his professional career. He played rhythm guitar with pop R&B groups like the Savoys and doo-wop outfits like the Del-Vikings. His encounters with Chuck Edwards and a 15-year-old George Benson introduced Ulmer to straight-ahead jazz guitar playing; indeed, Edwards taught Ulmer that music-making could be generated from feelings other than the blues.

In a 1980 interview with *Down Beat*'s Clifford Safane, Ulmer explained: "Edwards showed me that it was all right to play from a happy frame of mind.... I've never felt bad enough physically to deal with the blues. Rather, I think of myself as being in a funk bag, which comes from either mental repression, which I've experienced, or happy feelings." Benson directed Ulmer to strum and pick with his thumb, following the jazz guitar innovator Wes Montgomery. Gigs with organ-based combos led by Jimmy Smith and Richard "Groove" Holmes further refined Ulmer's jazz technique. Finally, Pittsburgh was the breeding ground for Ulmer's famous moniker: nicknamed "Youngblood," he was soon just called "Blood."

Ulmer's first band, Blood and the Bloodbrothers, was formed in 1963. Now based in Columbus, Ohio, the guitarist sought opportunities to express himself creatively; but the Bloodbrothers, who backed visiting acts like Dionne Warwick with their steady gig at Columbus's 502 Club, couldn't meet his aspirations. He played with organist Hank Marr, whom Ulmer appreciated for not, as the guitarist told *Down Beat* in 1980, "just pumpin' the blues."

After touring Europe with Marr's quartet and recording with the group, Ulmer relocated to Detroit in 1967. There he learned how to read and write music, and he taught guitar at the Metropolitan Art Complex; he also formed two bands, the James Ulmer Trio and Focus Novii. Featuring drums, bass, alto sax, trombone, and guitar, Focus Novii was a free jazz forum for Ulmer's original compositions. During this time Ulmer also experimented with "unison tuning"—this method, which tunes a number of the guitar strings to the same note, was to become a hallmark of Ulmer's sound.

Studied With Ornette Coleman

Frustrated with the limited role of the guitar in traditional jazz combos and inspired by his original work in Detroit, Ulmer left for New York in 1971. A friend who worked at the Bluebird club in Detroit where Ulmer performed had spurred on the guitarist. Ulmer told Howard Mandel of *Down Beat* that his friend said, "'I want you to take this month and go to New York and find Miles Davis. Tell him I sent you to play with him.' I said, 'Good, give me the money, I'm ready to go.' He did, and I came to New York. I never found Miles. But I found Coleman!"

Influential jazz composer and alto saxophonist Ornette Coleman proved a vital collaborator for Ulmer throughout the 1970s. While Ulmer briefly gigged with Art Blakey as the first guitarist for the Jazz Messengers in 1973 and did session work with Joe Henderson, it was Coleman who truly pushed Ulmer. After a nine-month stint in 1971 at Minton's Playhouse in Harlem—where Ulmer was hired to play the blues but instead performed his originals—the two met through Rashied Ali, a drummer the musicians shared during this time.

Ulmer soon moved into Coleman's loft and studied "harmolodic" theory. Harmolodics is Coleman's term for an ensemble style that combines harmony, movement, and melody. As *Down Beat*'s Safane put it, "Each instrument ... is both a melody *and* a rhythm instrument; players abandon their traditional role and, for example, instruments such as bass and drums that ordinarily accompany now share as lead voices in musical creation."

Questioning how innovative this was, Gary Giddins, author of *Rhythm-a-ning: Jazz Tradition and Innovation in the '80s,* soberly reminded audiences of the theory's "primary significance for jazz": he maintained that in harmolodic music, "melody dictates harmony rather than vice-versa" and a new *sound* is developed by the music's emphasis on "coloration and rhythm." Affirming harmolodics' refusal of conventional harmonic patterns, Ulmer told the *Chicago Tribune* that "you don't really have to play chord changes if your melody is strong enough."

"Down South, we had two kinds of blues: one that was forbidden, and one that wasn't."

Harmolodics jibed with Ulmer's atonal explorations in Detroit, where he was seeking a new expressive range for the jazz guitar. Indeed, Ulmer was integral to Coleman's harmolodic theory, as he taught the saxophonist the potential for guitar in an electrified, free jazz setting. Their work in the decade was marked by appearances at the Ann Arbor Jazz and Blues Festival in 1974, at New York's Five Spot in 1975, and at the Newport Jazz Festival in 1977. Ulmer also spent time in the studio with Coleman's band Prime Time, recording a set of then-unreleased performances.

Coleman's tutelage bore fruit in Ulmer's solo career, inaugurated for a wider public with the guitarist's first studio release. Ulmer's 1979 LP, *Tales of Captain Black,* was a record of instrumentals, featuring Coleman as a sideman on sax, Denardo Coleman on drums, and Jamaaladeen Tacuma on bass. In 1990 Walter Hetfield of *Guitar Player* called *Tales* "a landmark jazz guitar LP that showcased Ulmer's aggressive, open-ended approach and his inspired polyrhythmic interaction with a superb band."

Ulmer followed *Tales* with 1980's *Are You Glad to Be in America?,* a record that featured David Murray, Oliver Lake, Olu Daru, and a rhythm section of Amin Ali and G. Calvin Weston, who would support Ulmer off and on through the 1980s. The album also introduced the sweet and hoarse roar of Ulmer's singing. In 1982 Stanley Crouch of the *Village Voice* praised the record's eclecticism, particularly the guitarist's "combination of Eastern drones and quick be-bop like passages, held together by his knowledge of shuffles, funk beats, and march rhythms."

And as Coleman influenced 1960s avant rockers like the Velvet Underground, so too Ulmer began to hold sway in New York City's punk/new wave scene of the late 1970s. His band often played New York's legendary punk club, CBGB, and in 1980 opened for Public Image Ltd., formed and fronted by ex-Sex Pistols singer John Lydon. But 1980 also saw Ulmer recording with the Music Revelation Ensemble, a new jazz group whose album title—*"No Wave"*—drolly commented on trends in pop music. *Down Beat* critics honored Ulmer that year with the Talent Deserving Wider Recognition award in the guitar category. Then, in what was a singular lineup of blues surrealists, Ulmer and Captain Beefheart took the stage together in 1981.

On the heels of Ulmer's independent-label releases, Columbia Records signed the artist. With wider distribution and critical praise, the three records he made for Columbia—*Freelancing, Black Rock,* and *Odyssey*—aimed to create a larger market for Ulmer's unique methods. The records featured him primarily in a three- to four-piece rock format, with horns relegated to individual tracks. For author Greg Tate, Ulmer's distinctive guitar style delivered "shrill, disjointed fragments, nervous bits and rickety pieces tied together by a staggered but wryly swinging thematic sensibility." He performed live during this period with a power-blues group consisting of himself, Weston, Amin Ali, and occasionally second guitarist Ronnie Drayton; this outfit, coupled with Ulmer's embrace of distortion and wide acceptance of the guitarist by white rock fans, inevitably led to comparisons with Jimi Hendrix.

On *Odyssey,* Ulmer worked with an unusual trio of drums, guitar, and violin. Howard Mandel of *Guitar Player* called the record "a rocking blues raga hoedown," while *Coda's* Ben Ratliff itemized its many effects: "It's music that can simultaneously bring to mind the [Rolling] Stones' choppy groove, the cyclical rhythmic and melodic vamps from Jajouka or Nigeria, Georgia Sea Islands call-and-response gospel, and most definitely the high lonesome jigs of early southwestern country music." Both jazz and pop critics for the *Village Voice* voted *Odyssey* album of the year in 1983.

Separated Jazz Playing From Blues Preaching

Nonetheless, Columbia dropped Ulmer after *Odyssey,* and Ulmer himself abandoned the "harmolodic pop songs" of the Columbia efforts, as he termed them in a 1990 *Guitar Player* interview. Ulmer-led trios and quartets existed through the 1980s, but the guitarist also turned his attention to two improvisational outfits, Phalanx and the Music Revelation Ensemble. These were on-again, off-again combos that sought a less systematic vision of free jazz than the Coleman method; Ulmer contributed to the bands as accompanist and, occasionally, chief songwriter. Phalanx reunited Ulmer with one of Hank Marr's horn players, George Adams. The quintet first played publicly in 1984, when the *Village Voice* called the music "melancholy and rowdy, but almost always coherent and persuasive.... Phalanx could become a key band of the '80s."

A different quartet of musicians featuring Ulmer was mistakenly called Phalanx by a record company on a 1986 release, *Got Something Good for You*. A 1987 album with Sirone and Rashied Ali—members from 1984—was thus called *Original Phalanx*, but, in fact, this version of the band lacked violinist Billy Bang from the 1984 gigs. Without violin, the interaction of Ulmer and Adams as soloists defined the Phalanx sound. *In Touch* showcased Ulmer on flute as well as guitar.

Ben Ratliff wrote in *Coda* that Ulmer's other improv group, Music Revelation Ensemble, was a shifting entourage whose "only requirements are for a backbeat and that [Ulmer] and David Murray be the principal soloists." A *Cadence* writer called *Elec. Jazz* primarily "a James Blood Ulmer date with Murray being deputized as star soloist," while the *Washington Post* thought it "funkier and generally more accessible" than Phalanx. In 1992 Ulmer told *Jazz Journal International,* however, that neither of the groups was his central concern.

By this time Ulmer returned his creative energies to blues music. His solo efforts in the late 1980s and early 1990s led him to work within the very boundaries his earlier music dissolved, and this sound met with mixed reviews. The jazzier *America—Do You Remember the Love?* brought Ulmer together with producer/bassist Bill Laswell. A *Musician* reviewer called the album "a likable country-blues synthesis, but in trying to make an 'important' statement it succeeds only at being ordinary," but *Down Beat* thought its "rhythmic support, catchy hooks, [and] fuller production values" made it his "best album since ... *Freelancing*."

The blues-identified music of *Blues Allnight, Black and Blues,* and *Blues Preacher* gave Ronnie Drayton a larger role as second guitarist. Simon Adams of *Jazz Journal International* considered Ulmer's "blues playing ... an unsubtle thrash" compared to his work with Phalanx and MRE, while Bob McCullough of the *Boston Globe* found that *Blues Preacher*'s "slower tempos ... [left] Ulmer plenty of room for his sonic explorations and gritty vocals." By 1994 Ulmer had made a decisive break from the eclectic style of earlier years, telling *Down Beat,* "I want to separate the styles of my music, I don't want to play all mixed-up." He introduced *Blues*

Preacher by saying, "In this way, we can perfect each style by itself and make it a more satisfying experience for the listener."

Selected discography

(With Joe Henderson) *Multiple,* Milestone, 1973.
(With Arthur Blythe) *Lenox Avenue Breakdown,* Columbia, 1979.
Tales of Captain Black, Artists House, 1979.
Are You Glad to Be in America?, Rough Trade, 1980.
Freelancing, Columbia, 1981.
Black Rock, Columbia, 1982.
Odyssey, Columbia, 1983.
Part Time, Rough Trade, 1984.
Live at the Caravan of Dreams, Caravan of Dreams, 1986.
America—Do You Remember the Love?, Blue Note, 1987.
Blues Allnight, In + Out, 1989.
Black and Blues, DIW, 1990.
Blues Preacher, DIW/Columbia, 1994.
Revealing, In + Out (recorded 1977).
(With Hank Marr) *Hank Marr in the Marketplace,* King.

With Music Revelation Ensemble

"No Wave," Moers Music, 1980.
Music Revelation Ensemble, DIW, 1988.
Elec. Jazz, DIW, 1990.

With Phalanx

Got Something Good for You, Moers Music, 1986.
Original Phalanx, DIW, 1987.
In Touch, DIW, 1988.

Sources

Books

Giddins, Gary, *Rhythm-a-ning: Jazz Tradition and Innovation in the 80's,* Oxford, 1985.
Tate, Greg, *Flyboy in the Buttermilk: Essays on Contemporary America,* Simon & Schuster, 1992.

Periodicals

Boston Globe, March 24, 1994.
Cadence, July 1991.
Chicago Tribune, March 21, 1990.
Coda: The Journal of Jazz and Improvised Music, May 1993.
Down Beat, October 1980; April 1981; June 1987; April 1994.
Guitar Player, May 1990; April 1994.
Jazz Journal International, December 1991; September 1992.

Musician, September 1979; June 1982; January 1983; December 1987.

Newsweek, December 7, 1981.

Rolling Stone, June 12, 1980; April 1, 1982; October 28, 1982.

San Francisco Chronicle, December 10, 1989.

Village Voice, November 9, 1982; February 28, 1984; May 22, 1984.

Washington Post, April 12, 1991.

Additional information for this profile was obtained from liner notes to *Blues Preacher,* DIW/Columbia Records, 1994.

—*Matthew Brown*

Townes Van Zandt

Singer, songwriter

Photograph by Peter Figen, courtesy of Keith Case & Associates

Townes Van Zandt is one of a handful of Texas born singer-songwriters who can only be described as modern day troubadours. While Van Zandt has written country hits for others, he has remained largely an obscure figure, endlessly traveling the coffeehouse/juke joint circuit. He declared in the *New York Times* in 1989, "It looks like I'm forever going to be a folk singer." Van Zandt's compositions include such hits as "Poncho & Lefty" for Willie Nelson and "If I Needed You" for Emmylou Harris. Although he remains unknown to a mainstream audience, he has had an enormous influence on other songwriters. Critical praise is equally fawning; the word "legend" pops up often in regard to Van Zandt.

Van Zandt was born in Fort Worth, Texas, in 1945, the son of a prominent oil man. He described his nomadic childhood in an interview with *Contemporary Musicians* (*CM*) in 1992, "I lived in Fort Worth till I was 8, Midland till 9, Billings, Montana, till 12, Boulder, Colorado till 14, Chicago till 15 ... Houston till I was 21. And *then* I started traveling."

Van Zandt began playing guitar at age 15, turned on by the blues and early records by folk great Bob Dylan. The young musician began pursuing songwriting more seriously while attending the University of Colorado; by 1968 he was signed to the small Poppy label. The first artists to record his songs were Doc and Steve Watson, both of whom were attracted by the plaintive quality in Van Zandt's work.

Van Zandt came to be considered one of Texas's best kept secrets, playing the Old Quarter coffeehouse in Houston. In 1968 he released his first album, *For the Sake of the Song,* which was followed by a record each year for the next five years: *Our Mother the Mountain* (1969), *Townes Van Zandt* (1970), *Delta Man Blues* (1971), *High, Low and in Between* (1972), and *The Late, Great Townes Van Zandt* (1973). A double performance album, *Live at the Old Quarter,* was released in 1977. All are now considered cult classics.

Van Zandt met his wife, Jeanene, on December 9, 1980, and she took on responsibility for much of his booking and publishing business. As the 1980s faded and acoustic music again became valued, Van Zandt was cited by several new acts as a seminal influence. After releasing *At My Window* in 1987 and *Live and Obscure* in 1990, Van Zandt was asked to open up for the Cowboy Junkies on their 1991 U.S. tour.

As critic Robert Palmer wrote in the *New York Times,* "Figures like Townes Van Zandt remind us that the wandering bard, that American archetype, is still very

For the Record . . .

Born in 1945 in Fort Worth, TX; married; wife's name, Jeanene. *Education:* Attended University of Colorado, 1966-67.

Released first album, *For the Sake of the Song,* Poppy, 1968; began playing coffeehouse circuit, 1970; song "Poncho & Lefty" recorded by Willie Nelson and Merle Haggard, 1977; moved to Nashville, 1985; signed with Sugar Hill records, 1986; toured with Guy Clark, 1988.

Addresses: *Record company*—Sugar Hill, P. O. Box 55300, Durham, NC 27717.

much with us—and his music will live long after the voices that declare it in or out of fashion have been stilled or forgotten." Or, as Van Zandt's friend Guy Clark simply stated, "Townes was the biggest single influence on my writing. Working around a poet like him, you learn not to throw away a phrase for a rhyme or a word for a pattern. You learn to keep your work clean."

Van Zandt was possibly the first Texas songwriter to embody the qualities that came to be attributed to anyone in the city of Austin with a guitar. He was the first folk artist to put forth a tough existential attitude, although it was softened by the wry sentimentality of his songs.

Van Zandt is aware of the praise he has received from younger artists such as Earle and Lyle Lovett, yet he remains modest. "It's very flattering, very nice," he told the *Detroit Free Press* in 1992. "The fact that I decided to do this, and made a little mark, is very nice. It's not something I think of day to day or minute to minute. It's mostly B.S. [bull shit], but very pleasant B.S."

West Texas has produced a great number of valued musicians: Buddy Holly, Joe Ely, Butch Hancock, Michelle Shocked, Guy Clark, Jimmie Dale Gilmore, Earle, Lyle Lovett, Waylon Jennings, and Nanci Griffith. Van Zandt offered *CM* an explanation for the wealth of Texas talent: "There is a freer attitude in Texas. And there is not a lot to do. You can work in a gas station, herd cows or play guitar. A lot of people would play guitar. Guy Clark says there is something in the water; I think a meteor hit Lubbock [Texas] in the Paleolithic Age."

Influenced by the extemporaneous style of bluesman Lightnin' Hopkins, Van Zandt writes lengthy songs rife with cinematic storytelling. He sings in a dry, cracked voice, a voice as lived in as his jeans. His "image," if such a show business buzzword can even be applied to Van Zandt, is that of the frail drifter tossed around by life. Van Zandt's most respected songs—"Poncho and Lefty" and "To Live Is to Fly"—deal with the bittersweet grip of love or the temporal nature of life. His simple voice and unassuming song style also suggests a comparison with Woody Guthrie or Hank Williams—songwriters who used detailed stories and country/folk song forms to humorously reach large truths.

"I'm trying to define the relationship between man and the universe," Van Zandt told *CM,* describing the purpose behind his songwriting. "Often it's between man and man, or man and woman, or man and the cosmos. Whatever song comes through the door I'm happy with.... I'm lucky just to play the guitar and sing."

Van Zandt does not just like to travel, he *needs* to move. He often travels with his wife and two children. "I love the hum of the wheels," Van Zandt told *CM.* "I really consider myself very fortunate. I started when I didn't have a family. It was easier then—we could play for $20 a night and still have enough left for the week. We could audition in a club on Wednesday and play on Friday. Now it seems guys go to a garage or basement and then send tapes to record companies and MTV. We used to pick up our guitar and suitcase, hit the highway and go to Oklahoma City."

The figures who people Van Zandt's songs—a woman in a wind-blown calico dress, dust bowl ranchers, pugilists, drunks, and outlaws—are straight out of real life, although usually from a less sophisticated time. Yet the famous West Texas mysticism is there, deep in Van Zandt's songs and stories. For every moment of realism, such as the elegant "Loretta," there is the ring of imagination, the rush of the West Texas wind.

In 1994 Van Zandt released *Roadsongs,* a collection of cover tunes, on the Sugar Hill label. The songs were recorded "over a number of years in joints all over America," the singer observed, according to Robert Palmer in *Rolling Stone.* "Van Zandt's blues are so casually authentic," noted Palmer, "the issue of authenticity doesn't even come up." The reviewer further declared in his critique of *Roadsongs,* "Whatever [Van Zandt's] singing, there's a singular vision, an indelible individuality."

As the godfather of the early 1990s songwriter boom, Van Zandt, in his interview with *CM,* offered daunting advice for young artists. "You've got to get a guitar, or harmonica, or piano—a guitar and harmonica are easiest to carry—and blow *everything* off. I mean everything. Blow off family, love, security, comfort, money, food—everything, and see what happens. Certain truths will become self-evident ... or you'll starve to death. It deters a lot of people. But that's the only way to do it."

Selected discography

For the Sake of the Song, Poppy, 1968, reissued, Tomato 1989.
Our Mother the Mountain, Poppy, 1969, reissued, Tomato 1989.
The Great Tomato Blues Package, Tomato, 1989.
At My Window, Sugar Hill, 1986.
Roadsongs, Sugar Hill, 1994.
The Nashville Sessions, Tomato/Rhino, 1994.
First Album, Tomato/Rhino, 1994.
High, Low and in Between, Rhino, 1994.
Flyin' Shoes, Rhino, 1994.

Sources

Books
Rolling Stone Album Guide, edited by Anthony DeCurtis and James Henke, Straight Arrow, 1992.

Periodicals
Billboard, June 16, 1990.
Boston Rock, June 1993.
Detroit Free Press, December 11, 1992.
Folk Roots, October 1989.
LaCasagram, December 1992.
Nashville Scene, October 12, 1988.
New York Times, June 7, 1987.
Rolling Stone, June 30, 1994.

CM interviewed Van Zandt on December 7, 1992.

—Stewart Francke

Porter Wagoner

Singer, songwriter, guitarist

Courtesy of Porter Wagoner Enterprises

Legendary country music performer Porter Wagoner is noted for his long-standing commitment to his craft. Randy Travis, Alison Krauss, Kitty Wells, George Jones, Bill Monroe: the photographs on the walls of his dressing room backstage at Nashville's famed Grand Ole Opry reflect both country music's past and future. And the name "Porter Wagoner" does as well, conjuring up an image of this tall, blond man with the engaging smile and the flashy, sequined suits.

But behind the smile and the sequins is a gifted individual whose deep love for country music is matched by his gift for songwriting, singing, and, most of all, entertaining. "Porter Wagoner is a country music star in the truest sense of the word," noted the *Official Opry Picture-History Book.* "As a showman on stage, he is without equal, for he is not merely a singer, but an entertainer par excellence."

Wagoner's story is the quintessential rags-to-riches tale. He was raised in South Fork, Missouri, the fifth child of farming couple Charley and Bertha Wagoner. As a boy, young Porter stood alongside his father, tending to the cattle and hogs and working the crops the family depended on for food and income.

Wagoner's musical roots were like those of many rural Americans during the Depression era. He listened to radio shows like the Chicago-based *National Barn Dance* and WSM-Nashville's *Grand Ole Opry.* On the family Victrola, he was introduced to the new "bluegrass-style" sounds of Bill and Charlie Monroe—Bill Monroe would become Wagoner's first musical idol.

In his biography *A Satisfied Mind: The Country Music Life of Porter Wagoner,* author Steve Eng quoted a recollection of Wagoner's sister, Lola: after playing a Monroe recording, "[Porter] would ask, 'Isn't that the purtiest thing you ever heard?' [Recalled] Lola, 'It *was* pretty, but he was obviously getting something out of it I was not.'"

Country Boy, City Boy

During the lean years of the Depression, the Wagoner family was visited by both personal tragedy and the dire economic downturn common to many in the rural Midwest. Porter's older brother, Glenn—who had drawn Porter on stage to play for local barn dances and had helped him choose his first guitar—succumbed to myocarditis, an inflammation of the heart, in August of 1942. As Wagoner told Eng, "I felt like after he [Glenn] died, that I should carry on his music ... because it meant so much to him."

Born Porter Wayne Wagoner, August 12, 1930, in South Fork, MO; son of Charles E. (a farmer) and Bertha May (Bridges) Wagoner; married Velma Johnson, 1944 (marriage ended); married Ruth Olive Williams, 1946 (divorced, 1986); children: (second marriage) Richard, Denise, Debra.

Radio performer, KWTO, Springfield, MO, beginning in 1951; featured singer on *Ozark Jubilee,* 1954-55; signed with RCA Records, 1952-81; joined Grand Ole Opry, 1957; host of *The Porter Wagoner Show* (syndicated television series), 1961-80; established Fireside Studio (recording studio), 1972; signed with Warner/Viva, 1982-83; Opryland, USA, Nashville, TN, goodwill ambassador and full-time performer on Grand Ole Opry Stage, 1984—.

Awards: Grammy awards for best gospel performance (with the Blackwood Brothers Quartet), 1966, for *Grand Old Gospel,* 1967, for *More Grand Old Gospel,* and 1969, for *In Gospel Country;* Country Music Association (CMA) awards (with Dolly Parton), 1968, for vocal group of the year, and 1970 and 1971, for vocal duo of the year; TNN/*Music City News* award (with Parton), 1968, 1969, and 1970, for vocal duo.

Addresses: *Office*—P.O. Box 290785, Nashville, TN 37229.

Early the next spring, Charley Wagoner was forced to auction off the family farm: horses, cows, hogs, and other livestock, as well as Pete, the family mule, were all sold at the auctioneer's block. The Wagoners moved to West Plains, Missouri, in search of jobs; the move from the country to the city brought Porter closer to the public—and to the recognition that would someday take him all the way to Nashville.

In 1944 14-year-old Wagoner got a job as a grocery store clerk, where he idled away slow periods by strumming his guitar and singing the songs of his musical idols Monroe, Ernest Tubb, and the legendary Hank Williams, Sr. The storeowner was so impressed by the young man's vocal ability that he shrewdly put the teenager on an early morning local radio show to help promote his business.

From there Wagoner moved to radio station KWTO in nearby Springfield, where he performed a 15-minute spot on a weekly series in 1951. When popular country star Red Foley asked him to join the cast of his *Ozark Jubilee* in 1954, Wagoner was quick to accept. Foley, a veteran Opry star, schooled his protege in many facets of entertaining; with the dawn of a new media format called television, Wagoner's career as a TV personality was born.

From his role as a featured artist on *Jubilee,* he went on to host *The Porter Wagoner Show*—the longest-running country music television show in history—from 1961 to 1980. Downplaying his part in the show's success, Wagoner noted in an interview with *Contemporary Musicians (CM),* "I think the show is always the star. I've always been a team player, tried to make the show and the band—especially something that I was responsible for, like *The Porter Wagoner Show* or my show on the Grand Ole Opry—successful."

The program did prove to be a success. Featuring the talented Wagonmasters band and a variety of guest stars, many of whom went on to fame in Nashville, *The Porter Wagoner Show* was syndicated to over 100 stations across the United States and Canada. Its viewing audience of over 45 million people boosted Wagoner's popularity as a touring act far beyond the borders of Music City.

A Satisfied Mind

Wagoner had signed a recording contract with the RCA label in August of 1952, but his first few albums were released to indifferent critical response. "For the first couple of records that I made I just tried to sing like Hank Williams, you know, because I liked his things so much," Wagoner recalled in the *CM* interview. "But I realized early that you have to be your own person, and you can't be like someone else or pattern your career after them. So I just said, 'Hey, I need to be my own self, you know, sing like I do at home, and like I would want to sing myself.'"

Wagoner's new approach struck gold; his 1955 single "A Satisfied Mind" jumped to the Top Ten on the *Billboard* charts. This success was the first of many: two years later, he was asked to join the Grand Ole Opry, and for the next 27 years, it was rare when Wagoner's name wasn't on the country music countdown. Among his other Top Ten hits were 1956's "What Would You Do (If Jesus Came to Your House)," 1961's "Your Old Love Letters," the following year's "I've Enjoyed as Much of This as I Can Stand," 1964's "Green, Green Grass of Home," 1968's "Carroll County Accident," and "Big Wind," released in 1969.

In addition, the gospel music that played a big role in Wagoner's musical upbringing continued to influence him. In the mid-1960s, he recorded several albums with the Blackwood Brothers Quartet: *Grand Ole Gospel, More Grand Old Gospel,* and *In Gospel Country.* This series of albums netted Wagoner and the Blackwoods three Grammy awards for their work.

"I think some of the records that were made during my career—and, well, let's say from the '60s up to the '80s—were some of the greatest records in history because they reflected reality," Wagoner told *CM,* describing a period when pop-minded Nashville producers like RCA's Chet Atkins reigned supreme on the country music charts. "We are humans in a studio playing music and singing so that you will feel it when you get it into your home. It came more from the heart than ... from all this digital material that's there today. All the records today are basically perfect; but they don't have that deep inner feeling that some of the music did back then."

> *"I think when you just kind of turn your mind loose and let it just wander wherever it will wander, some different things come out of it. I wrote some real different songs by doing that."*

Reminiscing about country music's past, Wagoner admitted: "There's a part of the heart of the business that I truly miss. And I'm talking about songs like Patsy Cline recorded, songs like Hank Williams [Sr.] did. Man, they breathed so much life into 'em. You could feel it in your heart. And now I think it's why fans love one performer today, and somebody else tomorrow, and somebody else the next day and so on down the line, because it's a lot more plastic now than it was in those days."

Throughout the late 1960s, *The Porter Wagoner Show* remained as popular as ever. Wagoner's leading lady, Miss Norma Jean, whose lovely voice had harmonized on such hits as "I'll Take a Chance on Loving You," left the show in 1967, and he signed a new female accompanist, a young woman who had traveled from her native Tennessee to make it big in Nashville.

That woman was Dolly Parton; together the two would become well known as a duet act, garnering major

awards and a number of hits, including 1971's "Burning the Midnight Oil" and 1974's "Please Don't Stop Loving Me." Wagoner and Parton's individual flamboyance blended perfectly: her bouffant hairdos and revealing gowns were a perfect match to his characteristic pompadour and collection of rhinestone-laden Nudie suits—intricately fashioned to the tune of up to $10,000 per ensemble and weighing in at an average 35 pounds each.

The couple's successful partnership lasted until 1974, when Parton made a break from the show to go in her own musical direction. Wagoner went on to record and produce other artists in his Fireside Studio and experimented with non-country influences like soul, pop, and disco. After ending his recording career in 1981, he devoted himself to what he does best: spreading the word on country music. He became the official "goodwill ambassador" for Nashville's Opryland Theme Park and has continued to perform regularly on the Opry stage. During the Opry's off-season, he tours the country, playing an additional ten concerts each year.

From Stage to Sanctuary

In addition to being a consummate entertainer, Wagoner has a distinctive talent for songwriting. Remarking on the contrast between his upbeat public image and the introspective nature of many of his compositions, he explained to *CM:* "I love to write but it lays real heavy on your mind. Because I'd have to get so involved in ideas, I'd get lost in them, you know.... Whenever I wrote songs, a lot of the times I was in sort of a down mood, an off-time. But I did that to have a *contrast,* because you can't run wide open all the time, you know."

Wagoner described the writing process that led to the songs he penned for albums like *Skid Row Joe:* "I had a room in my home that I had designed myself. It was made out of a tent inside of a room. There was no furniture in it. I could go in that room and go almost anyplace I wanted to go in my mind. I had stayed in so many motel and hotel rooms that were all the same thing and I wanted something different when I got home. I think when you just kind of turn your mind loose and let it just wander wherever it will wander, some different things come out of it. I wrote some real different songs by doing that."

Wagoner elaborated on his unique method of songwriting: "One of the first songs that I wrote in this room was called 'The Rubber Room'—a real far-out song about a guy who went crazy. And it was probably the most unique song of that time that I've written. I started working on some other songs along that line—of insanity and so forth. I worked on it a couple of days and I said, 'Wow, I'm gonna have to stop this.' Because it was really puttin' me in such a frame of mind I began to worry about myself, you know."

An Eye on Country's Future

From a viewpoint that embraces so much of country music's recent past, Wagoner has begun to look ahead at the future of both the music and its institutions. "I really hate to see people like Bill Monroe, and, well, like myself—the artists that's been around the business so long—move on. You always hate to give up those things, but that's a part of reality. And I hope that the people that follow in Bill Monroe's footsteps and in my footsteps, and the other people I've known like Roy Acuff and so on back down the line, will not stray so far away that it just becomes music, just becomes sound—with no history or no heart."

Porter continued, "I hope that a lot of the new people in the industry will look at [country music] as though it's an art form. I hope that they won't just try to be the world's greatest singer, but be an entertainer and a contributor too." In the minds of many fans of country music, Wagoner has been and will continue to be exactly that: an entertainer and a contributor to this uniquely American, much-loved part of our musical inheritance.

Selected discography

A Slice of Life—Songs Happy 'n' Sad, RCA, 1962.
A Satisfied Mind, RCA, 1963.
The Porter Wagoner Show, RCA, 1963.
The Thin Man From West Plains, RCA, 1965.
(With the Blackwood Brothers Quartet) *Grand Ole Gospel,* RCA, 1966.
The Cold, Hard Facts of Life, RCA, 1967.
(With the Blackwoods) *More Grand Ole Gospel,* RCA, 1967.
Soul of a Convict, and Other Great Prison Songs, RCA, 1967.
Green, Green Grass of Home, Camden, 1968.
(With the Blackwoods) *In Gospel Country,* RCA, 1968.
(With Dolly Parton) *Always, Always,* RCA, 1969.
Carroll County Accident, RCA, 1969.
Skid Row Joe—Down in the Alley, RCA, 1970.
Blue Moon of Kentucky, Camden, 1971.
Highway Headin' South, RCA, 1974.
Porter Wagoner Today, RCA, 1979.
(With Parton) *Porter & Dolly,* RCA, 1980.
Porter Wagoner, Dot, 1986.

Sources

Books

Eng, Steve, *A Satisfied Mind: The Country Music Life of Porter Wagoner,* Rutledge Hill Press, 1994.
Official Opry Picture-History Book, Volume 8, edited by Jerry Strobel, Opryland USA, 1992.
Stambler, Irwin, and Gredlun Landon, *Encyclopedia of Folk, Country & Western,* St. Martin's, 1983.

Periodicals

Country Weekly, volume 1, number 9.

Other

Shelton, Pamela, interview with Porter Wagoner, Nashville, TN, June 10, 1994.

—Pamela L. Shelton

Jerry Jeff Walker

Singer, songwriter, guitarist

With his whiskey-and-cigarette voice, Jerry Jeff Walker embodied the era during the mid-1960s when pop, folk, and country music collided. His companions in those days were the "outlaws" of Nashville, Willie Nelson and Waylon Jennings, and other singer-songwriters such as Jimmy Buffet. Walker was a mainstay of the Austin sound, or progressive country, which became a worldwide commercial success in the 1980s. In the 1990s the gravelly voiced singer could still slide a ballad across a country dance hall or college auditorium. Walker's most popular song was the semisweet "Mr. Bojangles," a fable about a brief stay in a New Orleans jail.

Walker has estimated that at one time there were more than 60 versions of "Mr. Bojangles" on the market. Artists as dissimilar as Tom T. Hall and Harry Belafonte interpreted the song; George Burns, Sammy Davis, Jr., and Harry Nilsson also covered it. In 1971 the Nitty Gritty Dirt Band had a Top Ten hit with a folk-oriented version. Ironically, when Walker himself recorded "Mr. Bojangles," it barely reached the charts. However, the ballad made him known to a national audience and sustained a lifelong "adventure with a guitar," as Walker observed to Rebecca Bailey of the *Valley News* in White River Junction, Vermont. Walker's exploits took him from folk venues in New York City to honkytonks in Key West, Florida, but most importantly, to Austin, Texas, where he wrote such tunes as "Gettin' By" and "Up Against the Wall (Redneck Mothers)." He also recorded memorable renditions of "L.A. Freeway," by Guy Clark, and Gary P. Dunn's "London Homesick Blues."

Walker was born Ronald Clyde Crosby in the Catskill Mountains on March 16, 1942. He grew up in Oneonta, New York, in a suburban, middle-class family that enjoyed participating in numerous community activities. His grandparents were members of a square dance band, and his mother and sister sang in a local harmony group. As a teenager, Walker played guitar in several local bands around town, including the Pizzarinos, the Chymes, the Tones, and the Townies. He started at forward on the high school basketball team and wanted to become an astronaut. Later, the post-World War II subterranean restlessness bit him, and he quit high school to look for America, which for him turned out to be bars where he could sing for drinks and pass the hat. He returned to finish high school and graduated in 1960.

Hit the Road

The taste for the road stayed with Walker. After high school, he did a stint in the National Guard; upon

Born Ronald Clyde Crosby, March 16, 1942, in Oneonta, NY; son of Melvin and Alma Crosby; married Susan Streit, 1974; children: Jessie Jane, Django Cody.

Hitchhiked cross-country, singing on the street and in clubs, early 1960s; adopted the name Jerry Jeff Walker, 1966; formed the group Lost Sea Dreamers (name later changed to Circus Maximus), 1966; Circus Maximus signed with Vanguard Records, 1967; signed with Atco (Atlantic) Records as a solo performer and released *Mr. Bojangles,* 1968; relocated to Key West, FL, and released *Bein' Free,* 1970; moved to Austin, TX; moved to MCA label and recorded *Jerry Jeff Walker,* 1972; recorded with and produced albums for Lost Gonzo Band, 1970s; formed production company Tried and True Music, 1986; hosted *The Texas Connection* television show for The Nashville Network, 1991; played at the inauguration of Texas Governor Ann Richards, 1991; toured England and Europe and played at the inauguration of U.S. President Bill Clinton, 1993.

Addresses: *Office*—Tried and True Music, P.O. Box 39, Austin, TX 78767.

returning home, he hitchhiked to Florida, where he participated in the first Spring Break festivities. Walker's first appearances singing and playing guitar were at venues in the burgeoning Greenwich Village folk scene, which later spawned performers Bob Dylan and Joan Baez. Eventually, his travels took him to the French Quarter in New Orleans, where he sang on the street for spare change. Throughout his decades of performing, Walker would often play 280 nights out of the year.

One day, Walker was arrested for public intoxication during a police sweep, along with a number of other street musicians and dancers. They all had nicknames: Walker was "The Kid," while "Bojangles" was a white street dancer who paid tribute to the great soft-shoe artist Bill Robinson by stealing his moniker. Mr. Bojangles told his cellmates the tale of his late, lamented dog. Three years later, in 1968, Walker would recount the story in song. As Walker mentioned to Roger Kay of the Fort Worth, Texas *Star Telegram,* "Because 'Bojangles' had a kind of jazz/waltz beat, it meant more established people could do the song, which still had a very contemporary feel."

The performer adopted the name Jerry Jeff Walker in

1966. While in Texas, he met songwriter Bob Bruno. They formed a band called Lost Sea Dreamers, which later became Circus Maximus. The group relocated to New York in 1967 and won a contract with Vanguard Records. Walker lived on a shoestring. He told Kay in the *Star Telegram,* "We were based out of Austin, but we had gone to New York to try to make it. After we were there only about a week, all of our equipment was stolen. That left us in a financial bind. We decided to go where each member of the band knew how to make money quickly." He spent six months on the Austin bar circuit until the band could buy new gear and return to play gigs at clubs in New York.

Introduced "Mr. Bojangles"

"Mr. Bojangles" came out in the first flush of the counterculture rock wave. The popularity of the song enabled Walker to sign as a solo artist with Atco Records. He built a house in the hills near Austin and embarked on an odyssey that took a toll on his body but left an indelible imprint on country music with the "Austin sound," a fusion of country, rock, folk, and hot salsa. In 1973 Walker again dominated the pop charts with the single "L.A. Freeway," the apotheosis of the new country mix. The song expresses the hope that the singer will make it back to his country home, if he can just get off the city's expressway without getting killed or caught.

Walker signed a contract with MCA in the early 1970s and recorded a self-titled album originally cut on a portable tape recorder with some friends. His next album, *Viva Terlingua,* was a cornerstone of the country-western revival of the 1970s and 1980s. His mature style influenced many other artists, such as Nanci Griffith, Lyle Lovett, and Steve Earle. *Viva Terlingua* was recorded in Luckenbach, Texas, a ghost town owned by a man named Hondo Crouch and later commemorated by Waylon Jennings in a 1977 hit song. Walker began to celebrate his birthday in Luckenbach—an occasion that grew annually to Texas-sized proportions.

Walker's "outlaw" persona became legendary. His wife, Susan, who took on the prodigious task of managing her husband in 1984, recalled his early eccentricities for *People:* "Maybe he'd throw a coffee table through a hotel window, or sweep his hat through an aquarium to catch fish." Walker himself has developed a wry but unapologetic attitude toward his past. He told the *Birmingham News,* "I think you have to have a little sense of humor about yourself as you get older. The harder it is for me to bend over, the more I drop things on the floor. I have to make more trips now because I forget the things that I went to get."

Formed Production Company

Through the 1970s, Walker produced and appeared on albums with a group called the Lost Gonzo Band, who were known for their tight backup instrumentation. When Walker changed labels from MCA to Elektra/Asylum in 1978, the band launched a career of their own. Walker was never entirely happy with the procedures of corporate album making. He returned to MCA in 1981 but finally left to form his own production company. As he explained to Gene Harbrecht of the *Orange County Register*, "I did one (album) every six months for over ten years and it was just a lot of pumping out. Now, I spend a whole year, year and a half, two years on each project." By 1992 Walker had released his 23rd album, *Hill Country Rain*.

Walker has always been an outstanding live performer. His shows draw audience members onstage for bawdy numbers like "Trashy Women" and "Pick Up the Tempo" and hush them with contemplations like "Hands on the Wheel." The latter is a typical Walker effort, a late 1980s prayer that looks back on his youthful days and proclaims a new serenity: "I looked to the stars, busted up a few bars/My life nearly went up in smoke/With my hands on the wheel of something so real/I feel like I'm heading home."

Connected With Nashville Network

In 1991 Walker landed a job as host of the television program *The Texas Connection* on the Nashville Network (TNN) cable channel. The success of that show brought him new, enthusiastic fans. Describing his audience of college students and older followers, Walker told the *Birmingham News*, "We call 'em flatbellies and roundbellies. [The younger fans] whoop and hoot and do that little I'm-not-worthy bow. They call me 'The Man.' It's kind of neat. They first heard me while riding around with their dads in old pickup trucks with eight-track players." Walker's renown as a performer filled auditoriums past his 50th birthday. In 1994 he returned to Luckenbach once more to record a tribute to his 30 years on the road, *Viva Luckenbach*.

Walker is bemused about his continued appeal and told Claudia Perry, pop music critic for the *Houston Post*, "Young people are interested in how people survive by not playing by all the rules. They're trying to check out their own theories to see if someone is happy who's done things his own way. I've done that, and I'm kind of happy.... Some of it is luck, some was good fortune and little was common sense."

Selected discography

Circus Maximus, Vanguard, 1967.
Neverland Revisited, Vanguard, 1968.
Mr. Bojangles, Atco/Rhino, 1968.
Driftin' Way of Life, Vanguard, 1969.
Five Years Gone, Atco/Linea, 1970.
Bein' Free, Atco/Linea, 1970.
Jerry Jeff Walker (includes "L.A. Freeway"), MCA, 1972.
Viva Terlingua, MCA, 1973.
Walker's Collectibles, MCA, 1974.
Ridin' High, MCA, 1975.
It's a Good Night for Singing, MCA, 1976.
A Man Must Carry On, MCA, 1977.
Contrary to Ordinary, MCA, 1978.
Jerry Jeff, Elektra/Asylum, 1978.
Too Old to Change, Elektra/Asylum, 1979.
The Best of Jerry Jeff Walker, MCA, 1980.
Reunion, MCA, 1981.
Cowjazz, MCA, 1982.
Gypsy Songman (includes "Mr. Bojangles" and "Railroad Lady"), Tried and True/Rykodisc, 1986.
Live at Gruene Hall (includes "Man in the Big Hat," "Pickup Truck Song," and "Trashy Women"), Tried and True/Rykodisc, 1989.
Navajo Rug, Tried and True/Rykodisc, 1991.
Great Gonzos (includes "Sangria Wine," "Desperadoes Waiting for a Train," and "London Homesick Blues"), MCA, 1991.
Hill Country Rain (includes "Last Night I Fell in Love Again"), Tried and True/Rykodisc, 1992.
Viva Luckenbach! (includes "Gettin' By" and "Keep Texas Beautiful"), Tried and True/Rykodisc, 1994.

Sources

Books

The Encyclopedia of Folk, Country and Western Music, edited by Irwin Stambler and Grelun Landon, St. Martin's, 1983.

Periodicals

Austin American-Statesman, March 8, 1992.
Austin Chronicle, October 22, 1993.
Houston Post, March 9, 1992.
Music Row (Nashville, TN), April 8, 1994.
Orange County Register (Santa Ana, CA), November 6, 1989.
People, August 31, 1987.
Richmond Times-Dispatch (VA), February 27, 1994; March 4, 1994.

Rolling Stone, June 2, 1994.
San Jose Mercury News (CA), September 28, 1992.
Seattle Times (WA), July 3, 1992.
Star Telegram (Fort Worth, TX), January 24, 1988.
Texas Monthly, December 1993.
Valley News (White River Junction, VT), May 2, 1988.

—*Paul E. Anderson*

Lawrence Welk

Bandleader

UPI / Bettmann

Adored by loyal fans, ridiculed by the younger set, bandleader Lawrence Welk still managed to lead one of the longest-running shows in television history. From 1951 to 1982 this camera-shy bandleader stiffly conducted his orchestra's trademark "champagne music," while good-looking, clean-faced young men and women danced, sang, and smiled their way across the television screen. With his signature phrases "ah-one an ah-two" and "wunnerful, wunnerful," Welk either thrilled or bored hundreds of thousands of people every Saturday night for years, and in reruns after the show ceased production.

Born on March 11, 1903, in a sod farmhouse near the village of Strasburg, North Dakota, Welk was one of eight children. To avoid religious persecution, his parents, Christine and Ludwig Welk, had fled their home in the Alsace-Lorraine region of France. The mixed heritage of this area—it was once part of Germany—helps explain Welk's unusual accent. Although his polka-playing accordion talents led people to believe that Welk was Polish, his parents actually emigrated from France to Russia and then to the United States, resulting in a mixed German and middle European twang.

Although Welk was born in the United States, his second-generation accent was thick. He lived in a rural German-speaking town and dropped out of school in the fourth grade in order to farm full time. In the *New York Times,* Welk credited his incredible success in part to his hard youth; he did not speak English until he was 21. He remarked, "There's something you learn by hardship, by a little fear."

The Early Accordion Bands

At night, blacksmith-turned-farmer Ludwig Welk taught his son to play the accordion. By the time Lawrence was 13, he was playing at barn dances, weddings, and other social events. Although he regularly performed with local bands, his extremely loud and sometimes off-key playing often prompted his removal from the group. At age 17 Welk decided to form his own band. Lack of funds prevented him from hiring other musicians, but he eventually found a drummer to accompany him. Local radio stations let the Biggest Little Band in America, as they were called, play for free in exchange for publicizing upcoming dance engagements.

At age 21 Welk left home, and by 24 he had formed the Hotsy-Totsy Boys. At the same time he began investing in a series of small businesses. Although original, an accordion-shaped grill that served "squeezeburgers" failed to charm the customers. Not even his Lawrence Welk's Fruit Gum Orchestra succeeded—free gum at dance engagements only made for a sticky dance floor. He kept at it, though, and soon the popularity of his ever-growing band led to a slew of engagements in ballrooms, hotels, and on the radio across the Midwest.

It was during this time that the term "champagne music" was coined to describe Welk's style. During a 1938 live radio broadcast from Pittsburgh's William Penn Hotel, a radio announcer read a fan letter over the air: "They say that dancing to your music is like sipping champagne." *Band Leaders* magazine called the music "lilting, danceable music," and a *Variety* writer liked the band's enthusiasm. *Newsweek's* David Gates called it "a sedate blend of woodwinds, strings and muted brass, tripping through familiar melodies above ripples of accordion and Hammond organ." Welk had suggested several origins for this "champagne" sound. "You have to play good to hold a note," Gates quoted Welk as saying. "We decided to play short notes so nobody would notice we weren't that good. The audience wrote letters that our music was bubbly like champagne." Gates commented, "One problem with this story: Welk didn't hire bad musicians."

The Television Debut

The decline in big band popularity prompted Welk's move to Los Angeles in the late 1940s. In 1951 the band landed an engagement in the Aragon Ballroom on the Ocean Park pier in Los Angeles. KTLA-TV broadcast that night and for four weeks from the Aragon. The flood of calls to KTLA on that May 2 evening was so overwhelming that KTLA extended Welk's contract for four years. In 1955 the show, which had been in the Top Ten in Southern California ratings, was hired by Chrysler Corporation for a weekly broadcast on ABC. On July 2, 1955, the *Lawrence Welk Show* had its nationwide premiere.

Through long-term contracts, Welk was able to retain the relatively unknown group of performers he'd hired. Audiences grew to love ballroom dancers Bobby Burgess and Elaine Niverson in their cowboy outfits; toothy singers Guy and Ralna; the elegant dancing, singing "Champagne Lady"; booming bass Larry Hooper; and even Big Tiny Little always playing "Mairzy Doats" on the piano. But the most applause erupted when Lawrence Welk was heard to say, "Here dey are, dah luffley Lennon Sisters," although even they never made it much beyond the state fair circuit.

Welk Kept It Pure

Throughout the years on television, Welk's pathological shyness, due in large part to his thick Alsatian accent, caused him to keep his eyes glued to the TelePrompTer for even the briefest announcement. He was known to be as bashful and wholesome off the camera as well. There could never be cigarette or beer advertising on his show, nor would Welk ever hire comedians, because he feared off-color jokes. The orchestra's material was combed for suggestive lyrics, and a female performer was once fired for wearing a miniskirt. No matter how high the hemlines rose everywhere else, it was always the idyllic 1950s to Lawrence Welk.

Every Saturday night for years brought the lilting strains of Welk's theme song, "Bubbles and Wine," over the ABC airwaves. But by 1971 sponsors felt, in the words of the *New York Times,* that the show's audience was "too old, too rural and too sedate." Welk was sure there were still enough folks at home who loved his music. He launched a heavy campaign for himself, signing up more than 250 independent television stations in the United States and Canada and keeping the show alive until 1982. In 1987 the Public Broadcasting System began running reruns of the show as *Memories with Lawrence Welk*.

Welk's Riches

Although many of Welk's early businesses failed, he could still be shrewd off the dance floor. Throughout the 1960s and 1970s his entrepreneurial skills were at work in real estate and publishing. Some of his investments included the Lawrence Welk Village, a 1,000-acre resort and retirement complex in Escondido, California; the 1960s folk revival label Vanguard Records; a huge music library; and the rights to 20,000 songs, including all of composer Jerome Kern's work. Welk's 1971 best-selling biography, *Wunnerful, Wunnerful,* simply added to his riches.

In time Lawrence Welk became the second wealthiest performer in show business, just behind comedian Bob Hope. His band and production company became the second-biggest tourist draw of Los Angeles, following Disneyland. Welk continued to make appearances until his advanced age ended his career in 1989. On May 17, 1992, Lawrence Welk succumbed to pneumonia and died at age 89.

"You have to play what the people understand," Welk had always said. "Keep it simple so the audience can feel like they can do it too." Lennon Sister Katy told *People,* "If we would want to try out a song, [Welk] would always say it would only work if the woman in Minnesota doing dishes could hum it afterward." That simple sweet image is what remained after his death, overriding Welk's reputation for thrift—he gave out penknives with his name on them instead of tipping—and for sometimes being very strict with his performers.

Welk's many recognitions included honorary doctorates, numerous awards for his orchestra, and the distinction of playing at President Dwight D. Eisenhower's inaugural ball. In 1990 Congress approved a $500,000 grant to build a German-Russian museum at Welk's birthplace as a tribute, but when critics later cried "pork-barrel politics," the grant was rescinded. Private sponsors eventually paid for refurbishing the North Dakota farm.

A 1992 musical anthology of Welk's work spanning the years from 1957 to 1981 was well received. Although detractors called Welk's music corny, critics such as Jeff Tamarkin in *Pulse!* reminded, "Welk hired fine musicians and led them well." And the bandleader represented the idea that romance and luxury should be within everyone's reach, even if only for the short time each week when his show was on the air. *Newsweek's* Gates quoted Welk as saying, "Where I lived on a farm by a small town, poor, I always felt the other folks were—oh, maybe a little better." Gates wrote, "His core audience, rural people of modest means who weren't getting any younger, sure knew that feeling. He was there to say, Don't you believe it." Because of Lawrence Welk, everybody and everything was wunnerful on a dance floor full of bubbles and champagne music.

Selected writings

(With Bernice McGeehan) *Wunnerful, Wunnerful,* Prentice-Hall, 1971.
Ah-One, Ah-Two: Life With My Musical Family, Prentice-Hall, 1974.
My America, Your America, Prentice-Hall, 1977.
This I Believe, G.K. Hall, 1979.
You're Never Too Young, G.K. Hall, 1981.

Selected discography

On Ranwood, except where noted

Polka & Waltz Time, MCA, 1961.
Celebrates 25 Years on Television, c. 1980.
Plays for a Dance Party, 1985.
Dance to the Big Band Sounds, 1987.
Best Of, 1987.
16 Most Requested Songs, Columbia/Legacy, 1989.
Salutes the Big Bands, 1990.
A Musical Anthology, 1992.
Calcutta.
Champagne Music.
Hymns We Love.

Sources

Books

Coakley, Mary Lewis, *Mister Music Maker, Lawrence Welk,* 1958.
Welk, Lawrence, and Bernice McGeehan, *Wunnerful, Wunnerful!,* Prentice-Hall, 1971.
Welk, *Ah-One, Ah-Two: Life With My Musical Family,* Prentice-Hall, 1974.
Welk, *My America, Your America,* Prentice-Hall, 1977.
Welk, *This I Believe,* G.K. Hall, 1979.
Welk, *You're Never Too Young,* G.K. Hall, 1981.

Periodicals

Chicago Tribune, May 19, 1992.
Detroit Free Press, May 19, 1992; May 24, 1992.
Entertainment Weekly, May 29, 1992.

Forbes, September 26, 1983.
Los Angeles Times, May 19, 1992.
Maclean's, December 21, 1992.
Newsweek, June 1, 1992.
New York Times, May 19, 1992.
People, November 19, 1990; June 1, 1992; June 22, 1992.
Pulse!, November 1992.
Time, June 1, 1992.
Times (London), May, 20 1992.
U.S. News & World Report, June 11, 1992.
Variety, May 25, 1992.
Wall Street Journal, May 20, 1992.
Washington Post, May 19, 1992.

—Joanna Rubiner

Cumulative Indexes

Cumulative Subject Index

Volume numbers appear in **bold**.

Berlin, Irving **8**
Bernstein, Leonard **2**
Bley, Carla **8**
Braxton, Anthony **12**
Brubeck, Dave **8**
Burrell, Kenny **11**
Byrne, David **8**
  Also see Talking Heads
Cage, John **8**
Cale, John **9**
Casals, Pablo **9**
Clarke, Stanley **3**
Coleman, Ornette **5**
Cooder, Ry **2**
Cooney, Rory **6**
Copland, Aaron **2**
Crouch, Andraé **9**
Davis, Chip **4**
Davis, Miles **1**
de Grassi, Alex **6**
Dorsey, Thomas A. **11**
Elfman, Danny **9**
Ellington, Duke **2**
Eno, Brian **8**
Enya **6**
Foster, David **13**
Gillespie, Dizzy **6**
Glass, Philip **1**
Gould, Glenn **9**
Grusin, Dave **7**
Guaraldi, Vince **3**
Hamlisch, Marvin **1**
Hancock, Herbie **8**
Handy, W. C. **7**
Hartke, Stephen **5**
Hunter, Alberta **7**
Jarre, Jean-Michel **2**
Jarrett, Keith **1**
Jones, Quincy **2**
Joplin, Scott **10**
Jordan, Stanley **1**
Kern, Jerome **13**
Kitaro **1**
Kottke, Leo **13**
Lee, Peggy **8**
Lincoln, Abbey **9**
Lloyd Webber, Andrew **6**
Loewe, Frederick
  See Lerner and Loewe
Mancini, Henry **1**
Marsalis, Branford **10**
Marsalis, Ellis **13**
Masekela, Hugh **7**
Menken, Alan **10**
Metheny, Pat **2**
Mingus, Charles **9**
Monk, Meredith **1**
Monk, Thelonious **6**
Morton, Jelly Roll **7**
Nascimento, Milton **6**
Newman, Randy **4**
Ott, David **2**
Parker, Charlie **5**
Peterson, Oscar **11**
Ponty, Jean-Luc **8**

Porter, Cole **10**
Reich, Steve **8**
Reinhardt, Django **7**
Ritenour, Lee **7**
Roach, Max **12**
Rollins, Sonny **7**
Rota, Nino **13**
Satriani, Joe **4**
Schickele, Peter **5**
Schuman, William **10**
Shankar, Ravi **9**
Shaw, Artie **8**
Shorter, Wayne **5**
Solal, Martial **4**
Sondheim, Stephen **8**
Sousa, John Philip **10**
Story, Liz **2**
Strayhorn, Billy **13**
Summers, Andy **3**
Sun Ra **5**
Takemitsu, Toru **6**
Talbot, John Michael **6**
Taylor, Billy **13**
Taylor, Cecil **9**
Thielemans, Toots **13**
Threadgill, Henry **9**
Tyner, McCoy **7**
Washington, Grover, Jr. **5**
Weill, Kurt **12**
Williams, John **9**
Wilson, Cassandra **12**
Winston, George
Winter, Paul **10**
Worrell, Bernie **11**
Yanni **11**
Zimmerman, Udo **5**

Conductors
Bacharach, Burt **1**
Bernstein, Leonard **2**
Casals, Pablo **9**
Copland, Aaron **2**
Domingo, Placido **1**
Fiedler, Arthur **6**
Jarrett, Keith **1**
Levine, James **8**
Mancini, Henry **1**
Marriner, Neville **7**
Masur, Kurt **11**
Mehta, Zubin **11**
Menuhin, Yehudi **11**
Rampal, Jean-Pierre **6**
Schickele, Peter **5**
Solti, Georg **13**
von Karajan, Herbert **1**
Welk, Lawrence **13**
Williams, John **9**
Zukerman, Pinchas **4**

Contemporary Dance Music
Abdul, Paula **3**
B-52's, The **4**
Bee Gees, The **3**
Brown, Bobby **4**
Brown, James **2**

Cherry, Neneh **4**
Clinton, George **7**
Deee-lite **9**
De La Soul **7**
Depeche Mode **5**
Earth, Wind and Fire **12**
English Beat, The **9**
En Vogue **10**
Erasure **11**
Eurythmics **6**
Exposé **4**
Fox, Samantha **3**
Gang of Four **8**
Hammer, M.C. **5**
Harry, Deborah **4**
Ice-T **7**
Idol, Billy **3**
Jackson, Janet **3**
Jackson, Michael **1**
James, Rick **2**
Jones, Grace **9**
Madonna **4**
New Order **11**
Pet Shop Boys **5**
Prince **1**
Queen Latifah **6**
Rodgers, Nile **8**
Salt-N-Pepa **6**
Simmons, Russell **7**
Summer, Donna **12**
Technotronic **5**
Village People, The **7**
Was (Not Was) **6**
Young M.C. **4**

Contemporary Instrumental/New Age
Ackerman, Will **3**
Clinton, George **7**
Collins, Bootsy **8**
Davis, Chip **4**
de Grassi, Alex **6**
Enya **6**
Hedges, Michael **3**
Jarre, Jean-Michel **2**
Kitaro **1**
Kronos Quartet **5**
Story, Liz **2**
Summers, Andy **3**
Tangerine Dream **12**
Winston, George **9**
Winter, Paul **10**
Yanni **11**

Cornet
Cherry, Don **10**
Handy, W. C. **7**

Country
Acuff, Roy **2**
Alabama **1**
Anderson, John **5**
Arnold, Eddy **10**
Asleep at the Wheel **5**
Atkins, Chet **5**
Auldridge, Mike **4**

McCartney, Paul **4**
   Also see Beatles, The
Menken, Alan **10**
Mercer, Johnny **13**
Metheny, Pat **2**
Nascimento, Milton **6**
Nilsson **10**
Peterson, Oscar **11**
Porter, Cole **10**
Reznor, Trent **13**
Richie, Lionel **2**
Robertson, Robbie **2**
Rollins, Sonny **7**
Rota, Nino **13**
Sager, Carole Bayer **5**
Schickele, Peter **5**
Shankar, Ravi **9**
Taj Mahal **6**
Waits, Tom **12**
   Earlier sketch in CM **1**
Weill, Kurt **12**
Williams, John **9**
Williams, Paul **5**
Willner, Hal **10**
Young, Neil **2**

Flute
Anderson, Ian
   See Jethro Tull
Galway, James **3**
Rampal, Jean-Pierre **6**
Ulmer, James Blood **13**
Wilson, Ransom **5**

Folk/Traditional
Arnaz, Desi **8**
Baez, Joan **1**
Belafonte, Harry **8**
Blades, Ruben **2**
Brady, Paul **8**
Bragg, Billy **7**
Bulgarian State Female Vocal Choir, The **10**
Byrds, The **8**
Carter Family, The **3**
Chapin, Harry **6**
Chapman, Tracy **4**
Cherry, Don **10**
Chieftains, The **7**
Childs, Toni **2**
Clegg, Johnny **8**
Cockburn, Bruce **8**
Cohen, Leonard **3**
Collins, Judy **4**
Colvin, Shawn **11**
Crosby, David **3**
   Also see Byrds, The
Cruz, Celia **10**
de Lucia, Paco **1**
DeMent, Iris **13**
Donovan **9**
Dr. John **7**
Dylan, Bob **3**
Elliot, Cass **5**
Enya **6**

Estefan, Gloria **2**
Feliciano, José **10**
Galway, James **3**
Gilmore, Jimmie Dale **11**
Gipsy Kings, The **8**
Griffith, Nanci **3**
Guthrie, Arlo **6**
Guthrie, Woodie **2**
Harding, John Wesley **6**
Hartford, John **1**
Havens, Richie **11**
Hinojosa, Tish **13**
Iglesias, Julio **2**
Indigo Girls **3**
Ives, Burl **12**
Khan, Nusrat Fateh Ali **13**
Kingston Trio, The **9**
Kottke, Leo **13**
Kuti, Fela **7**
Ladysmith Black Mambazo **1**
Larkin, Patty **9**
Lavin, Christine **6**
Leadbelly **6**
Lightfoot, Gordon **3**
Los Lobos **2**
Makeba, Miriam **8**
Masekela, Hugh **7**
McLean, Don **7**
Melanie **12**
Mitchell, Joni **2**
Morrison, Van **3**
Morrissey, Bill **12**
Nascimento, Milton **6**
N'Dour, Youssou **6**
Near, Holly **1**
Ochs, Phil **7**
O'Connor, Sinead **3**
Odetta **7**
Parsons, Gram **7**
   Also see Byrds, The
Paxton, Tom **5**
Peter, Paul & Mary **4**
Pogues, The **6**
Prine, John **7**
Proclaimers, The **13**
Redpath, Jean **1**
Ritchie, Jean, **4**
Rodgers, Jimmie **3**
Sainte-Marie, Buffy **11**
Santana, Carlos **1**
Seeger, Pete **4**
   Also see Weavers, The
Shankar, Ravi **9**
Simon, Paul **1**
Snow, Pheobe **4**
Story, The **13**
Sweet Honey in the Rock **1**
Taj Mahal **6**
Thompson, Richard **7**
Tikaram, Tanita **9**
Van Ronk, Dave **12**
Van Zandt, Townes **13**
Vega, Suzanne **3**
Wainwright III, Loudon **11**
Walker, Jerry Jeff **13**

Watson, Doc **2**
Weavers, The **8**

French Horn
Ohanian, David
   See Canadian Brass, The

Funk
Bambaataa, Afrika **13**
Brown, James **2**
Clinton, George **7**
Collins, Bootsy **8**
Fishbone **7**
Gang of Four **8**
Jackson, Janet **3**
Khan, Chaka **9**
Mayfield, Curtis **8**
Parker, Maceo **7**
Prince **1**
Red Hot Chili Peppers, The **7**
Stone, Sly **8**
Toussaint, Allen **11**
Worrell, Bernie **11**

Fusion
Anderson, Ray **7**
Beck, Jeff **4**
   Also see Yardbirds, The
Clarke, Stanley **3**
Coleman, Ornette **5**
Corea, Chick **6**
Davis, Miles **1**
Fishbone **7**
Hancock, Herbie **8**
McLaughlin, John **12**
Metheny, Pat **2**
O'Connor, Mark **1**
Ponty, Jean-Luc **8**
Reid, Vernon **2**
Ritenour, Lee **7**
Shorter, Wayne **5**
Summers, Andy **3**
Washington, Grover, Jr. **5**

Gospel
Anderson, Marian **8**
Boone, Pat **13**
Brown, James **2**
Carter Family, The **3**
Charles, Ray **1**
Cleveland, James **1**
Cooke, Sam **1**
   Also see Soul Stirrers, The
Crouch, Andraé **9**
Dorsey, Thomas A. **11**
Five Blind Boys of Alabama **12**
Ford, Tennessee Ernie **3**
Franklin, Aretha **2**
Green, Al **9**
Houston, Cissy **6**
Jackson, Mahalia **8**
Knight, Gladys **1**
Little Richard **1**
Louvin Brothers, The **12**
Oak Ridge Boys, The **7**

Pickett, Wilson **10**
Presley, Elvis **1**
Redding, Otis **5**
Reese, Della **13**
Robbins, Marty **9**
Smith, Michael W. **11**
Soul Stirrers, The **11**
Sounds of Blackness **13**
Staples, Mavis **13**
Staples, Pops **11**
Take 6 **6**
Waters, Ethel **11**
Watson, Doc **2**
Williams, Deniece **1**
Winans, The **12**
Womack, Bobby **5**

Guitar
Ackerman, Will **3**
Allman, Duane
　See Allman Brothers, The
Atkins, Chet **5**
Autry, Gene **12**
Baxter, Jeff
　See Doobie Brothers, The
Beck, Jeff **4**
　Also see Yardbirds, The
Belew, Adrian **5**
Benson, George **9**
Berry, Chuck **1**
Bettencourt, Nuno
　See Extreme
Betts, Dicky
　See Allman Brothers, The
Boyd, Liona **7**
Bream, Julian **9**
Buck, Peter
　See R.E.M.
Buckingham, Lindsey **8**
　Also see Fleetwood Mac
Burrell, Kenny **11**
Campbell, Glen **2**
Chesnutt, Mark **13**
Christian, Charlie **11**
Clapton, Eric **11**
　Earlier sketch in CM **1**
　Also see Cream
　Also see Yardbirds, The
Clark, Roy **1**
Cockburn, Bruce **8**
Collins, Albert **4**
Cooder, Ry **2**
Cray, Robert **8**
Cropper, Steve **12**
Dale, Dick **13**
Daniels, Charlie **6**
de Grassi, Alex **6**
de Lucia, Paco **1**
Dickens, Little Jimmy **7**
Diddley, Bo **3**
Di Meola, Al **12**
Earl, Ronnie **5**
　Also see Roomful of Blues
Eddy, Duane **9**
Edge, The
　See U2

Feliciano, José **10**
Fender, Leo **10**
Flatt, Lester **3**
Ford, Lita **9**
Frampton, Peter **3**
Frehley, Ace
　See Kiss
Fripp, Robert **9**
Garcia, Jerry **4**
George, Lowell
　See Little Feat
Gibbons, Billy
　See ZZ Top
Gill, Vince **7**
Gilmour, David
　See Pink Floyd
Green, Peter
　See Fleetwood Mac
Guy, Buddy **4**
Haley, Bill **6**
Harrison, George **2**
Hatfield, Juliana **12**
　Also see Lemonheads, The
Havens, Richie **11**
Healey, Jeff **4**
Hedges, Michael **3**
Hendrix, Jimi **2**
Hillman, Chris
　See Byrds, The
　Also see Desert Rose Band, The
Hitchcock, Robyn **9**
Holly, Buddy **1**
Hooker, John Lee **1**
Hopkins, Lightnin' **13**
Howlin' Wolf **6**
Iommi, Tony
　See Black Sabbath
Ives, Burl **12**
James, Elmore **8**
Jardine, Al
　See Beach Boys, The
Johnson, Robert **6**
Jones, Brian
　See Rolling Stones, The
Jordan, Stanley **1**
Kantner, Paul
　See Jefferson Airplane
King, Albert **2**
King, B. B. **1**
Klugh, Earl **10**
Knopfler, Mark **3**
Kottke, Leo **13**
Larkin, Patty **9**
Leadbelly **6**
Lennon, John **9**
　Also see Beatles, The
Lindley, David **2**
Lockwood, Robert, Jr. **10**
Marr, Johnny
　See Smiths, The
May, Brian
　See Queen
Mayfield, Curtis **8**
McGuinn, Roger
　See Byrds, The

McLachlan, Sarah **12**
McLaughlin, John **12**
McReynolds, Jim
　See McReynolds, Jim and Jesse
Metheny, Pat **2**
Montgomery, Wes **3**
Morrissey, Bill **12**
Nugent, Ted **2**
Owens, Buck **2**
Page, Jimmy **4**
　Also see Led Zeppelin
　Also see Yardbirds, The
Parkening, Christopher **7**
Patton, Charley **11**
Perkins, Carl **9**
Perry, Joe
　See Aerosmith
Petty, Tom **9**
Phillips, Sam **12**
Prince **1**
Raitt, Bonnie **3**
Ray, Amy
　See Indigo Girls
Reid, Vernon **2**
　Also see Living Colour
Reinhardt, Django **7**
Richards, Keith **11**
　Also see Rolling Stones, The
Richman, Jonathan **12**
Ritenour, Lee **7**
Robbins, Marty **9**
Robertson, Robbie **2**
Robillard, Duke **2**
Rodgers, Nile **8**
Rush, Otis **12**
Santana, Carlos **1**
Saliers, Emily
　See Indigo Girls
Satriani, Joe **4**
Scofield, John **7**
Segovia, Andres **6**
Skaggs, Ricky **5**
Slash
　See Guns n' Roses
Springsteen, Bruce **6**
Stewart, Dave
　See Eurythmics
Stills, Stephen **5**
Stuart, Marty **9**
Summers, Andy **3**
Taylor, Mick
　See Rolling Stones, The
Thielemans, Toots **13**
Thompson, Richard **7**
Tippin, Aaron **12**
Townshend, Pete **1**
Tubb, Ernest **4**
Ulmer, James Blood **13**
Vai, Steve **5**
Van Halen, Edward
　See Van Halen
Van Ronk, Dave **12**
Vaughan, Jimmie
　See Fabulous Thunderbirds, The
Vaughan, Stevie Ray **1**
Wagoner, Porter **13**

Waits, Tom **12**
  Earlier sketch in CM **1**
Walker, Jerry Jeff **13**
Walker, T-Bone **5**
Walsh, Joe **5**
  Also see Eagles, The
Watson, Doc **2**
Weir, Bob
  See Grateful Dead, The
Wilson, Nancy
  See Heart
Winston, George **9**
Winter, Johnny **5**
Yamashita, Kazuhito **4**
Yarrow, Peter
  See Peter, Paul & Mary
Young, Angus
  See AC/DC
Young, Malcolm
  See AC/DC
Young, Neil **2**
Zappa, Frank **1**

Harmonica
Dylan, Bob **3**
Guthrie, Woodie **2**
Lewis, Huey **9**
Musselwhite, Charlie **13**
Thielemans, Toots **13**
Waters, Muddy **4**
Williamson, Sonny Boy **9**
Wilson, Kim
  See Fabulous Thunderbirds, The

Heavy Metal
AC/DC **4**
Aerosmith **3**
Alice in Chains **10**
Anthrax **11**
Black Sabbath **9**
Danzig **7**
Deep Purple **11**
Def Leppard **3**
Faith No More **7**
Fishbone **7**
Ford, Lita **9**
Guns n' Roses **2**
Iron Maiden **10**
Judas Priest **10**
King's X **7**
L7 **12**
Led Zeppelin **1**
Megadeth **9**
Metallica **7**
Mötley Crüe **1**
Motörhead **10**
Nugent, Ted **2**
Osbourne, Ozzy **3**
Pantera **13**
Petra **3**
Queensryche **8**
Reid, Vernon **2**
  Also see Living Colour
Reznor, Trent **13**
Roth, David Lee **1**
  Also see Van Halen

Sepultura **12**
Slayer **10**
Soundgarden **6**
Spinal Tap **8**
Stryper **2**
Whitesnake **5**

Humor
Coasters, The **5**
Jones, Spike **5**
Lehrer, Tom **7**
Pearl, Minnie **3**
Russell, Mark **6**
Schickele, Peter **5**
Shaffer, Paul **13**
Spinal Tap **8**
Stevens, Ray **7**
Yankovic, "Weird Al" **7**

Inventors
Fender, Leo **10**
Paul, Les **2**
Scholz, Tom
  See Boston
Teagarden, Jack **10**

Jazz
Allen, Geri **10**
Anderson, Ray **7**
Armstrong, Louis **4**
Bailey, Mildred **13**
Bailey, Pearl **5**
Baker, Anita **9**
Baker, Chet **13**
Basie, Count **2**
Belle, Regina **6**
Benson, George **9**
Berigan, Bunny **2**
Blakey, Art **11**
Blanchard, Terence **13**
Bley, Carla **8**
Blood, Sweat and Tears **7**
Braxton, Anthony **12**
Brown, Ruth **13**
Brubeck, Dave **8**
Burrell, Kenny **11**
Burton, Gary **10**
Calloway, Cab **6**
Canadian Brass, The **4**
Carter, Benny **3**
Carter, Betty **6**
Charles, Ray **1**
Cherry, Don **10**
Christian, Charlie **11**
Clarke, Stanley **3**
Clooney, Rosemary **9**
Cole, Nat King **3**
Coleman, Ornette **5**
Coltrane, John **4**
Connick, Harry, Jr. **4**
Corea, Chick **6**
Davis, Miles **1**
DeJohnette, Jack **7**
Di Meola, Al **12**
Eckstine, Billy **1**

Eldridge, Roy **9**
Ellington, Duke **2**
Ferguson, Maynard **7**
Fitzgerald, Ella **1**
Fleck, Bela **8**
  Also see New Grass Revival, The
Fountain, Pete **7**
Galway, James **3**
Getz, Stan **12**
Gillespie, Dizzy **6**
Goodman, Benny **4**
Gordon, Dexter **10**
Grappelli, Stephane **10**
Guaraldi, Vince **3**
Haden, Charlie **12**
Hampton, Lionel **6**
Hancock, Herbie **8**
Hawkins, Coleman **11**
Hedges, Michael **3**
Herman, Woody **12**
Hines, Earl "Fatha" **12**
Hirt, Al **5**
Holiday, Billie **6**
Horn, Shirley **7**
Horne, Lena **11**
Hunter, Alberta **7**
James, Harry **11**
Jarreau, Al **1**
Jarrett, Keith **1**
Jones, Elvin
Jones, Quincy **2**
Jordan, Stanley **1**
Kennedy, Nigel **8**
Kirk, Rahsaan Roland **6**
Kitt, Eartha **9**
Klugh, Earl **10**
Kronos Quartet **5**
Krupa, Gene **13**
Laine, Cleo **10**
Lee, Peggy **8**
Lincoln, Abbey **9**
Lovano, Joe **13**
Mancini, Henry **1**
Manhattan Transfer, The **8**
Marsalis, Branford **10**
Marsalis, Ellis **13**
Marsalis, Wynton **6**
Masekela, Hugh **7**
McFerrin, Bobby **3**
McLaughlin, John **12**
McRae, Carmen **9**
Metheny, Pat **2**
Mingus, Charles **9**
Monk, Thelonious **6**
Montgomery, Wes **3**
Morgan, Frank **9**
Morton, Jelly Roll **7**
Nascimento, Milton **6**
Norvo, Red **12**
Parker, Charlie **5**
Parker, Maceo **7**
Paul, Les **2**
Peterson, Oscar **11**
Ponty, Jean-Luc **8**
Professor Longhair **6**

Rampal, Jean-Pierre **6**
Redman, Joshua **12**
Reid, Vernon **2**
    Also see Living Colour
Reinhardt, Django **7**
Rich, Buddy **13**
Roach, Max **12**
Roberts, Marcus **6**
Robillard, Duke **2**
Rollins, Sonny **7**
Sanborn, David **1**
Santana, Carlos **1**
Schuur, Diane **6**
Scofield, John **7**
Scott-Heron, Gil **13**
Severinsen, Doc **1**
Shaw, Artie **8**
Shorter, Wayne **5**
Simone, Nina **11**
Solal, Martial **4**
Strayhorn, Billy **13**
Summers, Andy **3**
Sun Ra **5**
Take 6 **6**
Taylor, Billy **13**
Taylor, Cecil **9**
Teagarden, Jack **10**
Thielemans, Toots **13**
Threadgill, Henry **9**
Torme, Mel **4**
Tucker, Sophie **12**
Turner, Big Joe **13**
Turtle Island String Quartet **9**
Tyner, McCoy **7**
Ulmer, James Blood **13**
Vaughan, Sarah **2**
Walker, T-Bone **5**
Washington, Dinah **5**
Washington, Grover, Jr. **5**
Williams, Joe **11**
Wilson, Cassandra **12**
Winter, Paul **10**

Keyboards, Electric
Corea, Chick **6**
Davis, Chip **4**
Dolby, Thomas **10**
Emerson, Keith
    See Emerson, Lake & Palmer/Powell
Eno, Brian **8**
Foster, David **13**
Hancock, Herbie **8**
Jackson, Joe **4**
Jarre, Jean-Michel **2**
Jones, Booker T. **8**
Kitaro **1**
Manzarek, Ray
    See Doors, The
McDonald, Michael
    See Doobie Brothers, The
McVie, Christine
    See Fleetwood Mac
Pierson, Kate
    See B-52's, The
Shaffer, Paul **13**

Sun Ra **5**
Waller, Fats **7**
Wilson, Brian
    See Beach Boys, The
Winwood, Steve **2**
Wonder, Stevie **2**
Worrell, Bernie **11**
Yanni **11**

Liturgical Music
Cooney, Rory **6**
Talbot, John Michael **6**

Mandolin
Bush, Sam
    See New Grass Revival, The
Duffey, John
    See Seldom Scene, The
Hartford, John **1**
Lindley, David **2**
McReynolds, Jesse
    See McReynolds, Jim and Jesse
Monroe, Bill **1**
Rosas, Cesar
    See Los Lobos
Skaggs, Ricky **5**
Stuart, Marty **9**

Musicals
Allen, Debbie **8**
Allen, Peter **11**
Andrews, Julie **4**
Andrews Sisters, The **9**
Bacharach, Burt **1**
Bailey, Pearl **5**
Baker, Josephine **10**
Berlin, Irving **8**
Brown, Ruth **13**
Buckley, Betty **1**
Burnett, Carol **6**
Carter, Nell **7**
Channing, Carol **6**
Chevalier, Maurice **6**
Crawford, Michael **4**
Crosby, Bing **6**
Curry, Tim **3**
Davis, Sammy, Jr. **4**
Garland, Judy **6**
Gershwin, George and Ira **11**
Hamlisch, Marvin **1**
Horne, Lena **11**
Jolson, Al **10**
Kern, Jerome **13**
Laine, Cleo **10**
Lerner and Loewe **13**
Lloyd Webber, Andrew **6**
LuPone, Patti **8**
Masekela, Hugh **7**
Menken, Alan **10**
Mercer, Johnny **13**
Moore, Melba **7**
Patinkin, Mandy **3**
Peters, Bernadette **7**
Porter, Cole **10**
Robeson, Paul **8**

Rodgers, Richard **9**
Sager, Carole Bayer **5**
Shaffer, Paul **13**
Sondheim, Stephen **8**
Waters, Ethel **11**
Weill, Kurt **12**

Opera
Adams, John **8**
Anderson, Marian **8**
Bartoli, Cecilia **12**
Battle, Kathleen **6**
Bumbry, Grace **13**
Callas, Maria **11**
Carreras, José **8**
Caruso, Enrico **10**
Cotrubas, Ileana **1**
Domingo, Placido **1**
Gershwin, George and Ira **11**
Hampson, Thomas **12**
Hendricks, Barbara **10**
Horne, Marilyn **9**
Norman, Jessye **7**
Pavarotti, Luciano **1**
Price, Leontyne **6**
Sills, Beverly **5**
Solti, Georg **13**
Sutherland, Joan **13**
Te Kanawa, Kiri **2**
Upshaw, Dawn **9**
von Karajan, Herbert **1**
Weill, Kurt **12**
Zimmerman, Udo **5**

Percussion
Baker, Ginger
    See Cream
Blakey, Art **11**
Bonham, John
    See Led Zeppelin
Burton, Gary **10**
Collins, Phil **2**
    Also see Genesis
DeJohnette, Jack **7**
Densmore, John
    See Doors, The
Dunbar, Aynsley
    See Jefferson Starship
    Also See Whitesnake
Dunbar, Sly
    See Sly and Robbie
Fleetwood, Mick
    See Fleetwood Mac
Hampton, Lionel **6**
Hart, Mickey
    See Grateful Dead, The
Henley, Don **3**
Jones, Elvin
Jones, Kenny
    See Who, The
Jones, Spike **5**
Kreutzman, Bill
    See Grateful Dead, The
Krupa, Gene **13**
Mason, Nick
    See Pink Floyd

Moon, Keith
  See Who, The
N'Dour, Youssou 6
Palmer, Carl
  See Emerson, Lake & Palmer/Powell
Peart, Neil
  See Rush
Powell, Cozy
  See Emerson, Lake & Palmer/Powell
Rich, Buddy 13
Roach, Max 12
Sheila E. 3
Starr, Ringo 10
  Also see Beatles, The
Watts, Charlie
  See Rolling Stones, The

Piano

Allen, Gerri 10
Amos, Tori 12
Arrau, Claudio 1
Bacharach, Burt 1
Basie, Count 2
Berlin, Irving 8
Bley, Carla 8
Bronfman, Yefim 6
Brubeck, Dave 8
Bush, Kate 4
Charles, Ray 1
Clayderman, Richard 1
Cleveland, James 1
Cliburn, Van 13
Cole, Nat King 3
Collins, Judy 4
Collins, Phil 2
  Also see Genesis
Connick, Harry, Jr. 4
Crouch, Andraé 9
DeJohnette, Jack 7
Domino, Fats 2
Dr. John 7
Dupree, Champion Jack 12
Ellington, Duke 2
Feinstein, Michael 6
Flack, Roberta 5
Frey, Glenn 3
Glass, Philip 1
Gould, Glenn 9
Grusin, Dave 7
Guaraldi, Vince 3
Hamlisch, Marvin 1
Hancock, Herbie 8
Hinderas, Natalie 12
Hines, Earl "Fatha" 12
Horn, Shirley 7
Hornsby, Bruce 3
Horowitz, Vladimir 1
Jackson, Joe 4
Jarrett, Keith 1
Joel, Billy 12
  Earlier sketch in CM 2
John, Elton 3
Joplin, Scott 10
Kissin, Evgeny 6
Levine, James 8

Lewis, Jerry Lee 2
Liberace 9
Little Richard 1
Manilow, Barry 2
Marsalis, Ellis 13
McDonald, Michael
  See Doobie Brothers, The
McRae, Carmen 9
McVie, Christine
  See Fleetwood Mac
Milsap, Ronnie 2
Mingus, Charles 9
Monk, Thelonious 6
Morton, Jelly Roll 7
Newman, Randy 4
Perahia, Murray 10
Peterson, Oscar 11
Professor Longhair 6
Rich, Charlie 3
Roberts, Marcus 6
Rubinstein, Arthur 11
Russell, Mark 6
Schickele, Peter 5
Sedaka, Neil 4
Shaffer, Paul 13
Solal, Martial 4
Solti, Georg 13
Story, Liz 2
Strayhorn, Billy 13
Taylor, Billy 13
Taylor, Cecil 9
Tyner, McCoy 7
Waits, Tom 12
  Earlier sketch in 1
Waller, Fats 7
Wilson, Cassandra 12
Winston, George 9
Winwood, Steve 2
Wonder, Stevie 2
Wright, Rick
  See Pink Floyd

Piccolo

Galway, James 3

Pop

Abba 12
Abdul, Paula 3
Adam Ant 13
Adams, Bryan 2
Alpert, Herb 11
Amos, Tori 12
Andrews Sisters, The 9
Armatrading, Joan 4
Arnold, Eddy 10
Astley, Rick 5
Atkins, Chet 5
Avalon, Frankie 5
B-52's, The 4
Bacharach, Burt 1
Bailey, Pearl 5
Basia 5
Beach Boys, The 1
Beatles, The 2
Beaver Brown Band, The 3

Bee Gees, The 3
Bennett, Tony 2
Benson, George 9
Benton, Brook 7
Blood, Sweat and Tears 7
BoDeans, The 3
Bolton, Michael 4
Boone, Pat 13
Boston 11
Bowie, David 1
Bragg, Billy 7
Branigan, Laura 2
Brickell, Edie 3
Brooks, Garth 8
Brown, Bobby 4
Browne, Jackson 3
Bryson, Peabo 11
Buckingham, Lindsey 8
  Also see Fleetwood Mac
Buffett, Jimmy 4
Campbell, Glen 2
Campbell, Tevin 13
Carey, Mariah 6
Carlisle, Belinda 8
Carnes, Kim 4
Carpenters, The 13
Case, Peter 13
Chapin, Harry 6
Chapman, Tracy 4
Charlatans, The 13
Charles, Ray 1
Checker, Chubby 7
Cher 1
Cherry, Neneh 4
Chicago 3
Chilton, Alex 10
Clapton, Eric 11
  Earlier sketch in CM 1
  Also see Cream
  Also see Yardbirds, The
Clayderman, Richard 1
Clooney, Rosemary 9
Coasters, The 5
Cocker, Joe 4
Cocteau Twins, The 12
Cole, Lloyd 9
Cole, Natalie 1
Cole, Nat King 3
Collins, Judy 4
Collins, Phil 2
Colvin, Shawn 11
Connick, Harry, Jr. 4
Cooke, Sam 1
  Also see Soul Stirrers, The
Costello, Elvis 12
  Earlier sketch in CM 2
Crenshaw, Marshall 5
Croce, Jim 3
Crosby, David 3
  Also see Byrds, The
Crowded House 12
Daltrey, Roger 3
  Also see Who, The
D'Arby, Terence Trent 3
Darin, Bobby 4

Queen **6**
Rabbitt, Eddie **5**
Raitt, Bonnie **3**
Rea, Chris **12**
Redding, Otis **5**
Reddy, Helen **9**
Reeves, Martha **4**
R.E.M. **5**
Richie, Lionel **2**
Robbins, Marty **9**
Robinson, Smokey **1**
Rogers, Kenny **1**
Rolling Stones **3**
Ronstadt, Linda **2**
Ross, Diana **1**
Roth, David Lee **1**
    Also see Van Halen
Ruffin, David **6**
Sade **2**
Sager, Carole Bayer **5**
Sainte-Marie, Buffy **11**
Sanborn, David **1**
Seals, Dan **9**
Seals & Crofts **3**
Secada, Jon **13**
Sedaka, Neil **4**
Shaffer, Paul **13**
Sheila E. **3**
Shirelles, The **11**
Shonen Knife **13**
Siberry, Jane **6**
Simon, Carly **4**
Simon, Paul **1**
Sinatra, Frank **1**
Smiths, The **3**
Snow, Pheobe **4**
Spector, Phil **4**
Springfield, Rick **9**
Springsteen, Bruce **6**
Squeeze **5**
Stansfield, Lisa **9**
Starr, Ringo **10**
Steely Dan **5**
Stevens, Cat **3**
Stewart, Rod **2**
Stills, Stephen **5**
Sting **2**
Story, The **13**
Streisand, Barbra **2**
Summer, Donna **12**
Supremes, The **6**
Sweat, Keith **13**
Sweet, Matthew **9**
Talking Heads **1**
Taylor, James **2**
Tears for Fears **6**
Teenage Fanclub **13**
Temptations, The **3**
10,000 Maniacs **3**
They Might Be Giants **7**
Three Dog Night **5**
Tiffany **4**
Tikaram, Tanita **9**
Timbuk 3 **3**
Toad the Wet Sprocket **13**

Tony! Toni! Toné! **12**
Torme, Mel **4**
Townshend, Pete **1**
    Also see Who, The
Turner, Tina **1**
Valli, Frankie **10**
Vandross, Luther **2**
Vega, Suzanne **3**
Vinton, Bobby **12**
Walsh, Joe **5**
Warnes, Jennifer **3**
Warwick, Dionne **2**
Was (Not Was) **6**
Washington, Dinah **5**
Watley, Jody **9**
Webb, Jimmy **12**
"Weird Al" Yankovic **7**
Who, The **3**
Williams, Andy **2**
Williams, Deniece **1**
Williams, Joe **11**
Williams, Lucinda **10**
Williams, Paul **5**
Williams, Vanessa **10**
Wilson, Jackie **3**
Wilson Phillips **5**
Winwood, Steve **2**
Womack, Bobby **5**
Wonder, Stevie **2**
XTC **10**
Young, Neil **2**
Young M.C. **4**

Producers
Ackerman, Will **3**
Alpert, Herb **11**
Baker, Anita **9**
Bogaert, Jo
    See Technotronic
Browne, Jackson **3**
Burnett, T Bone **13**
Cale, John **9**
Clarke, Stanley **3**
Clinton, George **7**
Collins, Phil **2**
Costello, Elvis **2**
Cropper, Steve **12**
Crowell, Rodney **8**
Dixon, Willie **10**
DJ Premier
    See Gang Starr
Dolby, Thomas **10**
Dozier, Lamont
    See Holland-Dozier-Holland
Edmonds, Kenneth "Babyface" **12**
Eno, Brian **8**
Ertegun, Ahmet **10**
Foster, David **13**
Fripp, Robert **9**
Grusin, Dave **7**
Holland, Brian
    See Holland-Dozier-Holland
Holland, Eddie
    See Holland-Dozier-Holland
Jam, Jimmy, and Terry Lewis **11**

Jones, Booker T. **8**
Jones, Quincy **2**
Jourgensen, Al
    See Ministry
Lanois, Daniel **8**
Lillywhite, Steve **13**
Lynne, Jeff **5**
Marley, Rita **10**
Martin, George **6**
Mayfield, Curtis **8**
Miller, Mitch **11**
Parsons, Alan **12**
Prince **1**
Robertson, Robbie **2**
Rodgers, Nile **8**
Rubin, Rick **9**
Rundgren, Todd **11**
Simmons, Russell **7**
Skaggs, Ricky **5**
Spector, Phil **4**
Sure!, Al B. **13**
Sweat, Keith **13**
Swing, DeVante
    See Jodeci
Toussaint, Allen **11**
Vandross, Luther **2**
Willner, Hal **10**
Wilson, Brian
    See Beach Boys, The

Promoters
Clark, Dick **2**
Geldof, Bob **9**
Graham, Bill **10**
Hay, George D. **3**
Simmons, Russell **7**

Ragtime
Joplin, Scott **10**

Rap
Bambaataa, Afrika **13**
Basehead **11**
Beastie Boys, The **8**
Biz Markie **10**
Campbell, Luther **10**
Cherry, Neneh **4**
Cypress Hill **11**
De La Soul **7**
Digital Underground **9**
DJ Jazzy Jeff and the Fresh Prince **5**
Eazy-E **13**
    Also see N.W.A.
EPMD **10**
Eric B. and Rakim **9**
Gang Starr **13**
Geto Boys, The **11**
Hammer, M.C. **5**
Heavy D **10**
Ice Cube **10**
Ice-T **7**
Kane, Big Daddy **7**
Kid 'n Play **5**
Kool Moe Dee **9**
Kris Kross **11**

KRS-One **8**
L.L. Cool J. **5**
MC Lyte **8**
MC Serch **10**
Naughty by Nature **11**
N.W.A. **6**
P.M. Dawn **11**
Public Enemy **4**
Queen Latifah **6**
Rubin, Rick **9**
Run-D.M.C. **4**
Salt-N-Pepa **6**
Scott-Heron, Gil **13**
Shanté **10**
Simmons, Russell **7**
Sure!, Al B. **13**
Tone-Loc **3**
Tribe Called Quest, A **8**
Vanilla Ice **6**
Young M.C. **4**
Yo Yo **9**

Record Company Executives
Ackerman, Will **3**
Alpert, Herb **11**
Busby, Jheryl **9**
Davis, Chip **4**
Ertegun, Ahmet **10**
Foster, David **13**
Geffen, David **8**
Gordy, Berry, Jr. **6**
Hammond, John **6**
Harley, Bill **7**
Jam, Jimmy, and Terry Lewis **11**
Marley, Rita **10**
Martin, George **6**
Mayfield, Curtis **8**
Mercer, Johnny **13**
Miller, Mitch **11**
Mingus, Charles **9**
Near, Holly **1**
Penner, Fred **10**
Phillips, Sam **5**
Reznor, Trent **13**
Rhone, Sylvia **13**
Robinson, Smokey **1**
Rubin, Rick **9**
Simmons, Russell **7**
Spector, Phil **4**

Reggae
Black Uhuru **12**
Cliff, Jimmy **8**
Marley, Bob **3**
Marley, Rita **10**
Marley, Ziggy **3**
Sly and Robbie **13**
Third World **13**
Tosh, Peter **3**
UB40 **4**
Wailer, Bunny **11**

Rhythm and Blues/Soul
Abdul, Paula **3**
Baker, Anita **9**

Basehead **11**
Belle, Regina **6**
Berry, Chuck **1**
Bland, Bobby "Blue" **12**
Blues Brothers, The **3**
Bolton, Michael **4**
Brown, James **2**
Brown, Ruth **13**
Bryson, Peabo **11**
Busby, Jheryl **9**
Campbell, Tevin **13**
Carey, Mariah **6**
Charles, Ray **1**
Cole, Natalie **1**
Cooke, Sam **1**
    Also see Soul Stirrers, The
Cropper, Steve **12**
D'Arby, Terence Trent **3**
Diddley, Bo **3**
Domino, Fats **2**
Dr. John **7**
Earth, Wind and Fire **12**
Edmonds, Kenneth "Babyface" **12**
En Vogue **10**
Fabulous Thunderbirds, The **1**
Four Tops, The **11**
Fox, Samantha **3**
Franklin, Aretha **2**
Gaye, Marvin **4**
Gordy, Berry, Jr. **6**
Green, Al **9**
Hall & Oates **6**
Hayes, Isaac **10**
Holland-Dozier-Holland **5**
Ingram, James **11**
Isley Brothers, The **8**
Jackson, Freddie **3**
Jackson, Janet **3**
Jackson, Michael **1**
Jacksons, The **7**
Jam, Jimmy, and Terry Lewis **11**
James, Etta **6**
Jodeci **13**
Jones, Booker T. **8**
Jones, Grace **9**
Jones, Quincy **2**
Jordan, Louis **11**
Khan, Chaka **9**
King, Ben E. **7**
Knight, Gladys **1**
Kool & the Gang **13**
LaBelle, Patti **8**
Los Lobos **2**
Mayfield, Curtis **8**
Medley, Bill **3**
Milli Vanilli **4**
Moore, Melba **7**
Morrison, Van **3**
Neville, Aaron **5**
    Also see Neville Brothers, The
Neville Brothers, The **4**
Ocean, Billy **4**
O'Jays, The **13**
Pendergrass, Teddy **3**
Pickett, Wilson **10**

Pointer Sisters, The **9**
Prince **1**
Redding, Otis **5**
Reese, Della **13**
Reeves, Martha **4**
Richie, Lionel **2**
Robinson, Smokey **1**
Ross, Diana **6**
    Also see Supremes, The
Ruffin, David **6**
    Also see Temptations, The
Sam and Dave **8**
Scaggs, Boz **12**
Secada, Jon **13**
Shirelles, The **11**
Stansfield, Lisa **9**
Staples, Mavis **13**
Staples, Pops **11**
Stewart, Rod **2**
Stone, Sly **8**
Supremes, The **6**
    Also see Ross, Diana
Sure!, Al B. **13**
Sweat, Keith **13**
Temptations, The **3**
Third World **13**
Tony! Toni! Toné! **12**
Toussaint, Allen **11**
Turner, Tina **1**
Vandross, Luther **2**
Was (Not Was) **6**
Watley, Jody **9**
Williams, Deniece **1**
Williams, Vanessa **10**
Wilson, Jackie **3**
Winans, The **12**
Womack, Bobby **5**
Wonder, Stevie **2**

Rock
AC/DC **4**
Adam Ant **13**
Adams, Bryan **2**
Aerosmith **3**
Alice in Chains **10**
Allman Brothers, The **6**
Anthrax **11**
Band, The **9**
Basehead **11**
Beach Boys, The **1**
Beastie Boys, The **8**
Beatles, The **2**
Beaver Brown Band, The **3**
Beck, Jeff **4**
    Also see Yardbirds, The
Belew, Adrian **5**
Benatar, Pat **8**
Berry, Chuck **1**
Black Crowes, The **7**
Black Sabbath **9**
Blood, Sweat and Tears **7**
BoDeans, The **3**
Bon Jovi **10**
Boston **11**
Bowie, David **1**

Bragg, Billy **7**
Brickell, Edie **3**
Browne, Jackson **3**
Buckingham, Lindsey **8**
  Also see Fleetwood Mac
Burnett, T Bone **13**
Buzzcocks, The **9**
Byrds, The **8**
Byrne, David **8**
  Also see Talking Heads
Cale, John **9**
Captain Beefheart **10**
Cave, Nick **10**
Charlatans, The **13**
Cheap Trick **12**
Cher **1**
Chicago **3**
Clapton, Eric **11**
  Earlier sketch in CM **1**
  Also see Cream
  Also see Yardbirds, The
Clash, The **4**
Clemons, Clarence **7**
Clinton, George **7**
Coasters, The **5**
Cocker, Joe **4**
Collins, Phil **2**
Cooder, Ry **2**
Cooke, Sam **1**
  Also see Soul Stirrers, The
Cooper, Alice **8**
Costello, Elvis **12**
  Earlier sketch in CM **2**
Cougar, John(ny)
  See Mellencamp, John "Cougar"
Cracker **12**
Cream **9**
Crenshaw, Marshall **5**
Crosby, David **3**
  Also see Byrds, The
Crowded House **12**
Cure, The **3**
Curry, Tim **3**
Curve **13**
Dale, Dick **13**
Daltrey, Roger **3**
  Also see Who, The
Daniels, Charlie **6**
Danzig **7**
D'Arby, Terence Trent **3**
Dave Clark Five, The **12**
Davies, Ray **5**
Deep Purple **11**
Def Leppard **3**
Depeche Mode **5**
Devo **13**
Diddley, Bo **3**
Dinosaur Jr. **10**
Doobie Brothers, The **3**
Doors, The **4**
Duran Duran **4**
Dylan, Bob **3**
Eagles, The **3**
Eddy, Duane **9**
Einstürzende Neubauten **13**

Electric Light Orchestra **7**
Elliot, Cass **5**
Emerson, Lake & Palmer/Powell **5**
English Beat, The **9**
Eno, Brian **8**
Etheridge, Melissa **4**
Eurythmics **6**
Extreme **10**
Faith No More **7**
Fall, The **12**
Ferry, Bryan **1**
fIREHOSE **11**
Fishbone **7**
Fleetwood Mac **5**
Fogelberg, Dan **4**
Fogerty, John **2**
Ford, Lita **9**
Fox, Samantha **3**
Frampton, Peter **3**
Frey, Glenn **3**
  Also see Eagles, The
Fugazi **13**
Gabriel, Peter **2**
Gang of Four **8**
Garcia, Jerry **4**
Genesis **4**
Gift, Roland **3**
Graham, Bill **10**
Grateful Dead **5**
Grebenshikov, Boris **3**
Guns n' Roses **2**
Gwar **13**
Hall & Oates **6**
Harrison, George **2**
  Also see Beatles, The
Harry, Deborah **4**
Harvey, Polly Jean **11**
Hatfield, Juliana **12**
  Also see Lemonheads, The
Healey, Jeff **4**
Hendrix, Jimi **2**
Henley, Don **3**
  Also see Eagles, The
Hiatt, John **8**
Holland-Dozier-Holland **5**
Idol, Billy **3**
INXS **2**
Iron Maiden **10**
Isaak, Chris **6**
Jackson, Joe **4**
Jagger, Mick **7**
  Also see Rolling Stones, The
Jane's Addiction **6**
Jefferson Airplane **5**
Jesus and Mary Chain, The **10**
Jethro Tull **8**
Jett, Joan **3**
Joel, Billy **2**
Johansen, David **7**
John, Elton **3**
Joplin, Janis **3**
Judas Priest **10**
Kennedy, Nigel **8**
Kiss **5**
Knopfler, Mark **3**

Kravitz, Lenny **5**
L7 **12**
Led Zeppelin **1**
Lemonheads, The **12**
Lennon, John **9**
  Also see Beatles, The
Lennon, Julian **2**
Lindley, Dave **2**
Little Feat **4**
Living Colour **7**
Loggins, Kenny **3**
Los Lobos **2**
Lush **13**
Lydon, John **9**
  Also see Sex Pistols, The
Lynne, Jeff **5**
Lynyrd Skynyrd **9**
Martin, George **6**
Marx, Richard **3**
McCartney, Paul **4**
  Also see Beatles, The
MC5, The **9**
McKee, Maria **11**
McMurtry, James **10**
Meat Loaf **12**
Meat Puppets, The **13**
Megadeth **9**
Mellencamp, John "Cougar" **2**
Metallica **7**
Midnight Oil **11**
Miller, Steve **2**
Ministry **10**
Moby Grape **12**
Morrison, Jim **3**
  Also see Doors, The
Morrison, Van **3**
Mötley Crüe **1**
Motörhead **10**
Mould, Bob **10**
Myles, Alannah **4**
Nelson, Rick **2**
Newman, Randy **4**
Nicks, Stevie **2**
Nirvana **8**
NRBQ **12**
Nugent, Ted **2**
Ocasek, Ric **5**
O'Connor, Sinead **3**
Ono, Yoko **11**
Orbison, Roy **2**
Osbourne, Ozzy **3**
Page, Jimmy **4**
  Also see Led Zeppelin
  Also see Yardbirds, The
Palmer, Robert **2**
Pantera **8**
Parker, Graham **10**
Parker, Maceo **7**
Parsons, Alan **12**
Parsons, Gram **7**
  Also see Byrds, The
Pearl Jam **12**
Petty, Tom **9**
Perkins, Carl **9**
Phillips, Sam **5**

Black, Clint **5**
Blades, Ruben **2**
Bono
    See U2
Brady, Paul **8**
Bragg, Billy **7**
Brickell, Edie **3**
Brooke, Jonatha
    See Story, The
Brooks, Garth **8**
Brown, Bobby **4**
Brown, James **2**
Browne, Jackson **3**
Buck, Peter
    See R.E.M.
Buck, Robert
    See 10,000 Maniacs
Buckingham, Lindsey **8**
    Also see Fleetwood Mac
Buffett, Jimmy **4**
Burnett, T Bone **13**
Bush, Kate **4**
Byrne, David **8**
    Also see Talking Heads
Cahn, Sammy **11**
Cale, John **9**
Calloway, Cab **6**
Captain Beefheart **10**
Carpenter, Mary-Chapin **6**
Carter, Carlene **8**
Cash, Johnny **1**
Cash, Rosanne **2**
Cetera, Peter
    See Chicago
Chapin, Harry **6**
Chapman, Tracy **4**
Charles, Ray **1**
Childs, Toni **2**
Chilton, Alex **10**
Clapton, Eric **11**
    Earlier sketch in CM **1**
    Also see Cream
    Also see Yardbirds, The
Cleveland, James **1**
Clinton, George **7**
Cockburn, Bruce **8**
Cohen, Leonard **3**
Cole, Lloyd **9**
Cole, Nat King **3**
Collins, Albert **4**
Collins, Judy **4**
Collins, Phil **2**
Cooder, Ry **2**
Cooke, Sam **1**
    Also see Soul Stirrers, The
Cooper, Alice **8**
Corgan, Billy
    See Smashing Pumpkins
Costello, Elvis **12**
    Earlier sketch in CM **2**
Crenshaw, Marshall **5**
Croce, Jim **3**
Crofts, Dash
    See Seals & Crofts
Cropper, Steve **12**

Crosby, David **3**
    Also see Byrds, The
Crowe, J. D. **5**
Crowell, Rodney **8**
Daniels, Charlie **6**
Davies, Ray **5**
DeMent, Iris **13**
Denver, John **1**
Diamond, Neil **1**
Diddley, Bo **3**
Difford, Chris
    See Squeeze
Dion **4**
Dixon, Willie **10**
Domino, Fats **2**
Donovan **9**
Dorsey, Thomas A. **11**
Doucet, Michael **8**
Dozier, Lamont
    See Holland-Dozier-Holland
Dylan, Bob **3**
Edge, The
    See U2
Edmonds, Kenneth "Babyface" **12**
Elfman, Danny **9**
Ellington, Duke **2**
Emerson, Keith
    See Emerson, Lake & Palmer/Powell
Ertegun, Ahmet **10**
Etheridge, Melissa **4**
Everly, Don
    See Everly Brothers, The
Everly, Phil
    See Everly Brothers, The
Fagen, Don
    See Steely Dan
Ferry, Bryan **1**
Flack, Roberta **5**
Flatt, Lester **3**
Fogelberg, Dan **4**
Fogerty, John **2**
Foster, David **13**
Frampton, Peter **3**
Frey, Glenn **3**
    Also see Eagles, The
Fripp, Robert **9**
Frizzell, Lefty **10**
Gabriel, Peter **2**
Garcia, Jerry **4**
Gaye, Marvin **4**
Geldof, Bob **9**
George, Lowell
    See Little Feat
Gershwin, George and Ira **11**
Gibb, Barry
    See Bee Gees, The
Gibb, Maurice
    See Bee Gees, The
Gibb, Robin
    See Bee Gees, The
Gibbons, Billy
    See ZZ Top
Gibson, Debbie **1**
Gift, Roland **3**
Gill, Vince **7**

Gilley, Mickey **7**
Gilmour, David
    See Pink Floyd
Goodman, Benny **4**
Gordy, Berry, Jr. **6**
Grant, Amy **7**
Green, Al **9**
Greenwood, Lee **12**
Griffith, Nanci **3**
Guthrie, Arlo **6**
Guthrie, Woodie **2**
Guy, Buddy **4**
Haggard, Merle **2**
Hall, Daryl
    See Hall & Oates
Hall, Tom T. **4**
Hamlisch, Marvin **1**
Hammer, M.C. **5**
Hammerstein, Oscar
    See Rodgers, Richard
Harding, John Wesley **6**
Harley, Bill **7**
Harris, Emmylou **4**
Harrison, George **2**
    Also see Beatles, The
Harry, Deborah **4**
Hart, Lorenz
    See Rodgers, Richard
Hartford, John **1**
Hatfield, Juliana **12**
    Also see Lemonheads, The
Hawkins, Screamin' Jay **8**
Hayes, Isaac **10**
Healey, Jeff **4**
Hedges, Michael **3**
Hendrix, Jimi **2**
Henley, Don **3**
    Also see Eagles, The
Hiatt, John **8**
Hidalgo, David
    See Los Lobos
Hillman, Chris
    See Byrds, The
    Also see Desert Rose Band, The
Hinojosa, Tish **13**
Hitchcock, Robyn **9**
Holland, Brian
    See Holland-Dozier-Holland
Holland, Eddie
    See Holland-Dozier-Holland
Holly, Buddy **1**
Hornsby, Bruce **3**
Hutchence, Michael
    See INXS
Hynde, Chrissie
    See Pretenders, The
Ian, Janis **5**
Ice Cube **10**
Ice-T **7**
Idol, Billy **3**
Isaak, Chris **6**
Jackson, Alan **7**
Jackson, Joe **4**
Jackson, Michael **1**
Jagger, Mick **7**
    Also see Rolling Stones, The

Sager, Carole Bayer **5**
Saliers, Emily
  See Indigo Girls
Satriani, Joe **4**
Scaggs, Boz **12**
Schneider, Fred III
  See B-52's, The
Scott-Heron, Gil **13**
Scruggs, Earl **3**
Seals, Dan **9**
Seals, Jim
  See Seals & Crofts
Secada, Jon **13**
Sedaka, Neil **4**
Seeger, Pete **4**
  Also see Weavers, The
Shannon, Del **10**
Sheila E. **3**
Shocked, Michelle **4**
Siberry, Jane **6**
Simmons, Gene
  See Kiss
Simmons, Patrick
  See Doobie Brothers, The
Simon, Carly **4**
Simon, Paul **1**
Skaggs, Ricky **5**
Slick, Grace
  See Jefferson Airplane
Smith, Patti **1**
Smith, Robert
  See Cure, The
  Also see Siouxsie and the Banshees
Sondheim, Stephen **8**
Spector, Phil **4**
Springsteen, Bruce **6**
Stanley, Paul
  See Kiss
Stanley, Ralph **5**
Starr, Ringo **10**
  Also see Beatles, The
Stevens, Cat **3**
Stevens, Ray **7**
Stewart, Dave
  See Eurythmics
Stewart, Rod **2**
Stills, Stephen **5**
Sting **2**
Stipe, Michael
  See R.E.M.
Strait, George **5**
Streisand, Barbra **2**
Strickland, Keith
  See B-52's, The
Strummer, Joe
  See Clash, The
Stuart, Marty **9**
Summer, Donna **12**
Summers, Andy **3**
Sure!, Al B. **13**
Sweat, Keith **13**
Sweet, Matthew **9**
Swing, DeVante
  See Jodeci
Taj Mahal **6**

Taylor, James **2**
Taylor, Koko **10**
Thompson, Richard **7**
Tikaram, Tanita **9**
Tilbrook, Glenn
  See Squeeze
Tillis, Mel **7**
Tillis, Pam **8**
Timmins, Margo
  See Cowboy Junkies, The
Timmins, Michael
  See Cowboy Junkies, The
Tippin, Aaron **12**
Tone-Loc **3**
Torme, Mel **4**
Tosh, Peter **3**
Toussaint, Allen **11**
Townshend, Pete **1**
  Also see Who, The
Travis, Randy **9**
Tritt, Travis **7**
Tubb, Ernest **4**
Twitty, Conway **6**
Tyler, Steve
  See Aerosmith
Vai, Steve **5**
  Also see Whitesnake
Vandross, Luther **2**
Van Halen, Edward
  See Van Halen
Van Ronk, Dave **12**
Van Shelton, Ricky **5**
Van Zandt, Townes **13**
Vedder, Eddie
  See Pearl Jam
Vega, Suzanne **3**
Wagoner, Porter **13**
Waits, Tom **12**
  Earlier sketch in CM **1**
Walker, Jerry Jeff **13**
Walker, T-Bone **5**
Waller, Fats **7**
Walsh, Joe **5**
  Also see Eagles, The
Waters, Muddy **4**
Waters, Roger
  See Pink Floyd
Webb, Jimmy **12**
Weill, Kurt **12**
Weir, Bob
  See Grateful Dead, The
Welch, Bob
  See Grateful Dead, The
West, Dottie **8**
Whitley, Keith **7**
Williams, Deniece **1**
Williams, Don **4**
Williams, Hank, Jr. **1**
Williams, Hank, Sr. **4**
Williams, Lucinda **10**
Williams, Paul **5**
Wills, Bob **6**
Wilson, Brian
  See Beach Boys, The
Wilson, Cindy
  See B-52's, The

Wilson, Ricky
  See B-52's, The
Winter, Johnny **5**
Winwood, Steve **2**
Womack, Bobby **5**
Wonder, Stevie **2**
Wynette, Tammy **2**
Yoakam, Dwight **1**
Young, Angus
  See AC/DC
Young, Neil **2**
Zappa, Frank **1**
Zevon, Warren **9**

Trombone
Anderson, Ray **7**
Dorsey, Tommy
  See Dorsey Brothers, The
Miller, Glenn **6**
Teagarden, Jack **10**
Watts, Eugene
  See Canadian Brass, The

Trumpet
Alpert, Herb **11**
Armstrong, Louis **4**
Baker, Chet **13**
Berigan, Bunny **2**
Blanchard, Terence **13**
Cherry, Don **10**
Coleman, Ornette **5**
Davis, Miles **1**
Eldridge, Roy **9**
Ferguson, Maynard **7**
Gillespie, Dizzy **6**
Hirt, Al **5**
James, Harry **11**
Jones, Quincy **2**
Loughnane, Lee **3**
Marsalis, Wynton **6**
Masekela, Hugh **7**
Mills, Fred
  See Canadian Brass, The
Romm, Ronald
  See Canadian Brass, The
Severinsen, Doc **1**

Tuba
Daellenbach, Charles
  See Canadian Brass, The
Phillips, Harvey **3**

Vibraphone
Burton, Gary **10**
Hampton, Lionel **6**
Norvo, Red **12**

Viola
Dutt, Hank
  See Kronos Quartet
Jones, Michael
  See Kronos Quartet
Killian, Tim
  See Kronos Quartet
Menuhin, Yehudi **11**

Cumulative Musicians Index

Volume numbers appear in **bold**.

Blues, "Joliet" Jake
  See Blues Brothers, The
Blues Brothers, The **3**
Blunt, Martin
  See Charlatans, The
BoDeans, The **3**
Bogaert, Jo
  See Technotronic
Bogguss, Suzy **11**
Bolade, Nitanju
  See Sweet Honey in the Rock
Bolan, Marc
  See T. Rex
Bolton, Michael **4**
Bon Jovi **10**
Bon Jovi, Jon
  See Bon Jovi
Bonebrake, D. J.
  See X
Bonham, John
  See Led Zeppelin
Bono
  See U2
Bonsall, Joe
  See Oak Ridge Boys, The
Boone, Pat **13**
Booth, Tim
  See James
Bordin, Mike
  See Faith No More
Bostaph, Paul
  See Slayer
Boston **11**
Bostrom, Derrick
  See Meat Puppets, The
Bottum, Roddy
  See Faith No More
Bouchikhi, Chico
  See Gipsy Kings, The
Bowen, Jimmy
  See Country Gentlemen, The
Bowens, Sir Harry
  See Was (Not Was)
Bowie, David **1**
Boyd, Liona **7**
Brady, Paul **8**
Bragg, Billy **7**
Bramah, Martin
  See Fall, The
Branigan, Laura **2**
Brantley, Junior
  See Roomful of Blues
Braxton, Anthony **12**
B-Real
  See Cypress Hill
Bream, Julian **9**
Brickell, Edie **3**
Bright, Ronnie
  See Coasters, The
Briley, Alex
  See Village People, The
Brix
  See Fall, The
Brockie, Dave
  See Gwar

Bronfman, Yefim **6**
Brooke, Jonatha
  See Story, The
Brookes, Jon
  See Charlatans, The
Brooks, Garth **8**
Brooks, Leon Eric "Kix"
  See Brooks & Dunn
Brooks & Dunn **12**
Broonzy, Big Bill **13**
Brown, Bobby **4**
Brown, Clarence "Gatemouth" **11**
Brown, George
  See Kool & the Gang
Brown, James **2**
Brown, Jimmy
  See UB40
Brown, Ruth **13**
Browne, Jackson **3**
  Also see Nitty Gritty Dirt Band, The
Brubeck, Dave **8**
Bruce, Jack
  See Cream
Bruford, Bill
  See Yes
Bruster, Thomas
  See Soul Stirrers, The
Bryan, David
  See Bon Jovi
Bryant, Elbridge
  See Temptations, The
Bryson, Bill
  See Desert Rose Band, The
Bryson, Peabo **11**
Buchholz, Francis
  See Scorpions, The
Buck, Mike
  See Fabulous Thunderbirds, The
Buck, Peter
  See R.E.M.
Buck, Robert
  See 10,000 Maniacs
Buckingham, Lindsey **8**
  Also see Fleetwood Mac
Buckley, Betty **1**
Buckwheat Zydeco **6**
Budgie
  See Siouxsie and the Banshees
Buffett, Jimmy **4**
Bulgarian State Female Vocal Choir,
  The **10**
Bulgarian State Radio and Television
  Female Vocal Choir, The
  See Bulgarian State Female Vocal
  Choir, The
Bumbry, Grace **13**
Bumpus, Cornelius
  See Doobie Brothers, The
Bunker, Clive
  See Jethro Tull
Burch, Curtis
  See New Grass Revival, The
Burgess, Tim
  See Charlatans, The
Burnett, Carol **6**
Burnett, T Bone **13**

Burnette, Billy
  See Fleetwood Mac
Burnham, Hugo
  See Gang of Four
Burns, Bob
  See Lynyrd Skynyrd
Burns, Karl
  See Fall, The
Burr, Clive
  See Iron Maiden
Burrell, Kenny **11**
Burton, Cliff
  See Metallica
Burton, Gary **10**
Busby, Jheryl **9**
Bush, Dave
  See Fall, The
Bush, John
  See Anthrax
Bush, Kate **4**
Bush, Sam
  See New Grass Revival, The
Bushwick Bill
  See Geto Boys, The
Butler, Terry "Geezer"
  See Black Sabbath
Buzzcocks, The **9**
Byrds, The **8**
Byrne, David **8**
  Also see Talking Heads
Cafferty, John
  See Beaver Brown Band, The
Cage, John **8**
Cahn, Sammy **11**
Cale, John **9**
  Also see Velvet Underground, The
Calhoun, Will
  See Living Colour
Callas, Maria **11**
Calloway Cab **6**
Cameron, Duncan
  See Sawyer Brown
Cameron, Matt
  See Soundgarden
Campbell, Ali
  See UB40
Campbell, Glen **2**
Campbell, Luther **10**
Campbell, Phil
  See Motörhead
Campbell, Robin
  See UB40
Campbell, Tevin **13**
Canadian Brass, The **4**
Cantrell, Jerry
  See Alice in Chains
Canty, Brendan
  See Fugazi
Captain Beefheart **10**
Carey, Mariah **6**
Carlisle, Belinda **8**
Carlos, Bun E.
  See Cheap Trick
Carlos, Don
  See Black Uhuru

Colt, Johnny
　　See Black Crowes, The
Coltrane, John **4**
Colvin, Shawn **11**
Conneff, Kevin
　　See Chieftains, The
Connick, Harry, Jr. **4**
Cooder, Ry **2**
Cook, Jeff
　　See Alabama
Cook, Paul
　　See Sex Pistols, The
Cooke, Sam **1**
　　Also see Soul Stirrers, The
Cooney, Rory **6**
Cooper, Alice **8**
Cooper, Michael
　　See Third World
Coore, Stephen
　　See Third World
Copland, Aaron **2**
Copley, Al
　　See Roomful of Blues
Corea, Chick **6**
Corgan, Billy
　　See Smashing Pumpkins
Cornell, Chris
　　See Soundgarden
Cornick, Glenn
　　See Jethro Tull
Costello, Elvis **12**
　　Earlier sketch in CM **2**
Cotoia, Robert
　　See Beaver Brown Band, The
Cotrubas, Ileana **1**
Cotton, Caré
　　See Sounds of Blackness
Cougar, John(ny)
　　See Mellencamp, John "Cougar"
Country Gentlemen, The **7**
Coverdale, David
　　See Whitesnake **5**
Cowan, John
　　See New Grass Revival, The
Cowboy Junkies, The **4**
Cox, Andy
　　See English Beat, The
Cracker **12**
Crain, S. R.
　　See Soul Stirrers, The
Crawford, Ed
　　See fIREHOSE
Crawford, Michael **4**
Cray, Robert **8**
Creach, Papa John
　　See Jefferson Starship
Cream **9**
Crenshaw, Marshall **5**
Criss, Peter
　　See Kiss
Croce, Jim **3**
Crofts, Dash
　　See Seals & Crofts
Cropper, Steve **12**
Crosby, Bing **6**

Crosby, David **3**
　　Also see Byrds, The
Crouch, Andraé **9**
Crowded House **12**
Crowe, J. D. **5**
Crowell, Rodney **8**
Cruz, Celia **10**
Cure, The **3**
Curless, Ann
　　See Exposé
Currie, Steve
　　See T. Rex
Curry, Tim **3**
Curve **13**
Cypress Hill **11**
Cyrus, Billy Ray **11**
Dacus, Donnie
　　See Chicago
Dacus, Johnny
　　See Osborne Brothers, The
Daddy Mack
　　See Kris Kross
Daellenbach, Charles
　　See Canadian Brass, The
Daisley, Bob
　　See Black Sabbath
Dale, Dick **13**
Daley, Richard
　　See Third World
Dall, Bobby
　　See Poison
Dalton, Nic
　　See Lemonheads, The
Daltrey, Roger **3**
　　Also see Who, The
Dando, Evan
　　See Lemonheads, The
D'Angelo, Greg
　　See Anthrax
Daniels, Charlie **6**
Daniels, Jack
　　See Highway 101
Danko, Rick
　　See Band, The
Danzig **7**
Danzig, Glenn
　　See Danzig
D'Arby, Terence Trent **3**
Darin, Bobby **4**
Darling, Eric
　　See Weavers, The
Dave Clark Five, The **12**
Davidson, Lenny
　　See Dave Clark Five, The
Davies, Ray **5**
Davies, Saul
　　See James
Davis, Chip **4**
Davis, Michael
　　See MC5, The
Davis, Miles **1**
Davis, Sammy, Jr. **4**
Dayne, Taylor **4**
Deacon, John
　　See Queen

de Albuquerque, Michael
　　See Electric Light Orchestra
Dee, Mikkey
　　See Motörhead
Deee-lite **9**
Deep Purple **11**
Def Leppard **3**
DeGarmo, Chris
　　See Queensryche
de Grassi, Alex **6**
Deily, Ben
　　See Lemonheads, The
DeJohnette, Jack **7**
De La Soul **7**
DeLorenzo, Victor
　　See Violent Femmes
Delp, Brad
　　See Boston
de Lucia, Paco **1**
DeMent, Iris **13**
Dempsey, Michael
　　See Cure, The
Dennis, Garth
　　See Black Uhuru
Densmore, John
　　See Doors, The
Dent, Cedric
　　See Take 6
Denton, Sandy
　　See Salt-N-Pepa
Denver, John **1**
De Oliveria, Laudir
　　See Chicago
Depeche Mode **5**
Derosier, Michael
　　See Heart
Desert Rose Band, The **4**
DeVille, C. C.
　　See Poison
Devo **13**
Devoto, Howard
　　See Buzzcocks, The
DeWitt, Lew C.
　　See Statler Brothers, The
de Young, Joyce
　　See Andrews Sisters, The
Diagram, Andy
　　See James
Diamond, Mike
　　See Beastie Boys, The
Diamond, Neil **1**
Diamond "Dimebag" Darrell
　　See Pantera
Diamond Rio **11**
Di'anno, Paul
　　See Iron Maiden
Dickens, Little Jimmy **7**
Dickinson, Paul Bruce
　　See Iron Maiden
Diddley, Bo **3**
Diffie, Joe **10**
Difford, Chris
　　See Squeeze
Diggle, Steve
　　See Buzzcocks, The

Farrell, Perry
　　See Jane's Addiction
Farriss, Andrew
　　See INXS
Farriss, Jon
　　See INXS
Farriss, Tim
　　See INXS
Fay, Martin
　　See Chieftains, The
Fearnley, James
　　See Pogues, The
Feinstein, Michael **6**
Fela
　　See Kuti, Fela
Felder, Don
　　See Eagles, The
Feliciano, José **10**
Fender, Freddy
　　See Texas Tornados, The
Fender, Leo **10**
Ferguson, Keith
　　See Fabulous Thunderbirds, The
Ferguson, Maynard **7**
Ferguson, Steve
　　See NRBQ
Ferry, Bryan **1**
Fiedler, Arthur **6**
Fielder, Jim
　　See Blood, Sweat and Tears
Fields, Johnny
　　See Five Blind Boys of Alabama
Finch, Jennifer
　　See L7
Finer, Jem
　　See Pogues, The
Finn, Micky
　　See T. Rex
Finn, Neil
　　See Crowded House
Finn, Tim
　　See Crowded House
fIREHOSE **11**
Fishbone **7**
Fisher, Eddie **12**
Fisher, Jerry
　　See Blood, Sweat and Tears
Fisher, John "Norwood"
　　See Fishbone
Fisher, Phillip "Fish"
　　See Fishbone
Fisher, Roger
　　See Heart
Fishman, Jon
　　See Phish
Fitzgerald, Ella **1**
Five Blind Boys of Alabama **12**
Flack, Roberta **5**
Flansburgh, John
　　See They Might Be Giants
Flatt, Lester **3**
Flavor Flav
　　See Public Enemy
Flea
　　See Red Hot Chili Peppers, The

Fleck, Bela **8**
　　Also see New Grass Revival, The
Fleetwood, Mick
　　See Fleetwood Mac
Fleetwood Mac **5**
Flemons, Wade
　　See Earth, Wind and Fire
Fletcher, Andy
　　See Depeche Mode
Flür, Wolfgang
　　See Kraftwerk
Flynn, Pat
　　See New Grass Revival, The
Fogelberg, Dan **4**
Fogerty, John **2**
Ford, Lita **9**
Ford, Mark
　　See Black Crowes, The
Ford, Tennessee Ernie **3**
Fortune, Jimmy
　　See Statler Brothers, The
Fossen, Steve
　　See Heart
Foster, David **13**
Foster, Malcolm
　　See Pretenders, The
Foster, Paul
　　See Soul Stirrers, The
Fountain, Clarence
　　See Five Blind Boys of Alabama
Fountain, Pete **7**
Four Tops, The **11**
Fox, Lucas
　　See Motörhead
Fox, Oz
　　See Stryper
Fox, Samantha **3**
Frampton, Peter **3**
Francis, Connie **10**
Francis, Mike
　　See Asleep at the Wheel
Franke, Chris
　　See Tangerine Dream
Franklin, Aretha **2**
Franklin, Larry
　　See Asleep at the Wheel
Franklin, Melvin
　　See Temptations, The
Frantz, Chris
　　See Talking Heads
Fraser, Elizabeth
　　See Cocteau Twins, The
Frehley, Ace
　　See Kiss
Freiberg, David
　　See Jefferson Starship
Frey, Glenn **3**
　　Also see Eagles, The
Friedman, Marty
　　See Megadeth
Friel, Tony
　　See Fall, The
Fripp, Robert **9**
Frizzell, Lefty **10**
Froese, Edgar
　　See Tangerine Dream

Frusciante, John
　　See Red Hot Chili Peppers, The
Fugazi **13**
Gabriel, Peter **2**
　　Also see Genesis
Gadler, Frank
　　See NRBQ
Gahan, Dave
　　See Depeche Mode
Gaines, Steve
　　See Lynyrd Skynyrd
Gaines, Timothy
　　See Stryper
Gale, Melvyn
　　See Electric Light Orchestra
Gallup, Simon
　　See Cure, The
Galway, James **3**
Gambill, Roger
　　See Kingston Trio, The
Gang of Four **8**
Gang Starr **13**
Gano, Gordon
　　See Violent Femmes
Garcia, Dean
　　See Curve
Garcia, Jerry **4**
　　Also see Grateful Dead, The
Gardner, Carl
　　See Coasters, The
Gardner, Suzi
　　See L7
Garfunkel, Art **4**
Garland, Judy **6**
Garrett, Peter
　　See Midnight Oil
Garvey, Steve
　　See Buzzcocks, The
Gaskill, Jerry
　　See King's X
Gaudreau, Jimmy
　　See Country Gentlemen, The
Gaye, Marvin **4**
Gayle, Crystal **1**
Geary, Paul
　　See Extreme
Geffen, David **8**
Geldof, Bob **9**
Genesis **4**
Gentry, Teddy
　　See Alabama
George, Lowell
　　See Little Feat
Gershwin, George
　　See Gershwin, George and Ira
Gershwin, George and Ira **11**
Gershwin, Ira
　　See Gershwin, George and Ira
Geto Boys, The **11**
Getz, Stan **12**
Gibb, Barry
　　See Bee Gees, The
Gibb, Maurice
　　See Bee Gees, The
Gibb, Robin
　　See Bee Gees, The

Harding, John Wesley **6**
Harley, Bill **7**
Harrell, Lynn **3**
Harrington, Carrie
 See Sounds of Blackness
Harrington, David
 See Kronos Quartet
Harris, Addie "Micki"
 See Shirelles, The
Harris, Damon Otis
 See Temptations, The
Harris, Emmylou **4**
Harris, Evelyn
 See Sweet Honey in the Rock
Harris, Gerard
 See Kool & the Gang
Harris, R. H.
 See Soul Stirrers, The
Harris, Steve
 See Iron Maiden
Harrison, George **2**
 Also see Beatles, The
Harrison, Jerry
 See Talking Heads
Harry, Deborah **4**
Hart, Lorenz
 See Rodgers, Richard
Hart, Mark
 See Crowded House
Hart, Mickey
 See Grateful Dead, The
Hartford, John **1**
Hartke, Stephen **5**
Hartman, Bob
 See Petra
Hartman, John
 See Doobie Brothers, The
Harvey, Polly Jean **11**
Hashian
 See Boston
Haslinger, Paul
 See Tangerine Dream
Hassan, Norman
 See UB40
Hatfield, Juliana **12**
 Also see Lemonheads, The
Hauser, Tim
 See Manhattan Transfer, The
Havens, Richie **11**
Hawkins, Coleman **11**
Hawkins, Screamin' Jay **8**
Hay, George D. **3**
Hayes, Isaac **10**
Hayes, Roland **13**
Haynes, Warren
 See Allman Brothers, The
Hays, Lee
 See Weavers, The
Hayward, Richard
 See Little Feat
Headon, Topper
 See Clash, The
Healey, Jeff **4**
Heart **1**
Heavy D **10**

Hedges, Michael **3**
Heggie, Will
 See Cocteau Twins, The
Hellerman, Fred
 See Weavers, The
Helm, Levon
 See Band, The
  Also see Nitty Gritty Dirt Band, The
Hendricks, Barbara **10**
Hendrix, Jimi **2**
Henley, Don **3**
 Also see Eagles, The
Herman, Woody **12**
Herman's Hermits **5**
Herndon, Mark
 See Alabama
Herron, Cindy
 See En Vogue
Hester, Paul
 See Crowded House
Hetfield, James
 See Metallica
Hewson, Paul
 See U2
Hiatt, John **8**
Hickman, Johnny
 See Cracker
Hicks, Chris
 See Restless Heart
Hidalgo, David
 See Los Lobos
Highway 101 **4**
Hijbert, Fritz
 See Kraftwerk
Hill, Dusty
 See ZZ Top
Hill, Ian
 See Judas Priest
Hillman, Bones
 See Midnight Oil
Hillman, Chris
 See Byrds, The
  Also see Desert Rose Band, The
Hinderas, Natalie **12**
Hines, Earl "Fatha" **12**
Hines, Gary
 See Sounds of Blackness
Hinojosa, Tish **13**
Hirst, Rob
 See Midnight Oil
Hirt, Al **5**
Hitchcock, Robyn **9**
Hodo, David
 See Village People, The
Hoenig, Michael
 See Tangerine Dream
Hoffman, Guy
 See BoDeans, The
  Also see Violent Femmes
Hoke, Jim
 See NRBQ
Holiday, Billie **6**
Holland, Brian
 See Holland-Dozier-Holland
Holland, Dave
 See Judas Priest

Holland, Eddie
 See Holland-Dozier-Holland
Holland, Julian "Jools"
 See Squeeze
Holland-Dozier-Holland **5**
Holly, Buddy **1**
Honeyman-Scott, James
 See Pretenders, The
Hook, Peter
 See New Order
Hooker, John Lee **1**
Hopkins, Lightnin' **13**
Hopwood, Keith
 See Herman's Hermits
Horn, Shirley **7**
Horn, Trevor
 See Yes
Horne, Lena **11**
Horne, Marilyn **9**
Hornsby, Bruce **3**
Horovitz, Adam
 See Beastie Boys, The
Horowitz, Vladimir **1**
Hossack, Michael
 See Doobie Brothers, The
House, Son **11**
Houston, Cissy **6**
Houston, Whitney **8**
Howe, Steve
 See Yes
Howlin' Wolf **6**
Hubbard, Greg "Hobie"
 See Sawyer Brown
Hubbard, Preston
 See Fabulous Thunderbirds, The
  Also see Roomful of Blues
Hudson, Garth
 See Band, The
Huffman, Doug
 See Boston
Hughes, Bruce
 See Cracker
Hughes, Glenn
 See Black Sabbath
Hughes, Glenn
 See Village People, The
Hughes, Leon
 See Coasters, The
Hunt, Darryl
 See Pogues, The
Hunter, Alberta **7**
Hunter, Mark
 See James
Hunter, Shepherd "Ben"
 See Soundgarden
Hurley, George
 See fIREHOSE
Hutchence, Michael
 See INXS
Huth, Todd
 See Primus
Hütter, Ralf
 See Kraftwerk
Hutton, Danny
 See Three Dog Night

Joyce, Mike
    See Buzzcocks, The
    Also see Smiths, The
Judas Priest 10
Judd, Naomi
    See Judds, The
Judd, Wynonna
    See Judds, The
    Also see Wynonna
Judds, The 2
Jukebox
    See Geto Boys, The
Jungle DJ "Towa" Towa
    See Deee-lite
Jurado, Jeanette
    See Exposé
Kahlil, Aisha
    See Sweet Honey in the Rock
Kakoulli, Harry
    See Squeeze
Kalligan, Dick
    See Blood, Sweat and Tears
Kaminski, Mik
    See Electric Light Orchestra
Kanawa, Kiri Te
    See Te Kanawa, Kiri
Kane, Big Daddy 7
Kanter, Paul
    See Jefferson Airplane
Karajan, Herbert von
    See von Karajan, Herbert
Kath, Terry
    See Chicago
Katz, Steve
    See Blood, Sweat and Tears
Kaukonen, Jorma
    See Jefferson Airplane
Kaye, Tony
    See Yes
Kay Gee
    See Naughty by Nature
K-Ci
    See Jodeci
Keane, Sean
    See Chieftains, The
Kelly, Kevin
    See Byrds, The
Kendrick, David
    See Devo
Kendricks, Eddie
    See Temptations, The
Kennedy, Nigel 8
Kenner, Doris
    See Shirelles, The
Kentucky Headhunters, The 5
Kern, Jerome 13
Khan, Chaka 9
Khan, Nusrat Fateh Ali 13
Kibble, Mark
    See Take 6
Kibby, Walter
    See Fishbone
Kid 'n Play 5
Kiedis, Anthony
    See Red Hot Chili Peppers, The

Killian, Tim
    See Kronos Quartet
Kimball, Jennifer
    See Story, The
King, Albert 2
King, B. B. 1
King, Ben E. 7
King, Bob
    See Soul Stirrers, The
King, Carole 6
King, Ed
    See Lynyrd Skynyrd
King, Jon
    See Gang of Four
King, Kerry
    See Slayer
King, Philip
    See Lush
King Ad-Rock
    See Horovitz, Adam
Kingston Trio, The 9
King's X 7
Kinney, Sean
    See Alice in Chains
Kirk, Rahsaan Roland 6
Kirkwood, Cris
    See Meat Puppets, The
Kirkwood, Curt
    See Meat Puppets, The
Kirwan, Danny
    See Fleetwood Mac
Kiss 5
Kisser, Andreas
    See Sepultura
Kissin, Evgeny 6
Kitaro 1
Kitt, Eartha 9
Klein, Jon
    See Siouxsie and the Banshees
Klugh, Earl 10
Knight, Gladys 1
Knight, Jon
    See New Kids on the Block
Knight, Jordan
    See New Kids on the Block
Knopfler, Mark 3
Knudsen, Keith
    See Doobie Brothers, The
Konto, Skip
    See Three Dog Night
Kool & the Gang 13
Kool Moe Dee 9
Kooper, Al
    See Blood, Sweat and Tears
Kottke, Leo 13
Kotzen, Richie
    See Poison
Kraftwerk 9
Kramer, Joey
    See Aerosmith
Kramer, Wayne
    See MC5, The
Krause, Bernie
    See Weavers, The
Krauss, Alison 10

Kravitz, Lenny 5
Kreutzman, Bill
    See Grateful Dead, The
Krieger, Robert
    See Doors, The
Kris Kross 11
Kristofferson, Kris 4
Kronos Quartet 5
KRS-One 8
Krupa, Gene 13
Krusen, Dave
    See Pearl Jam
Kulick, Bruce
    See Kiss
Kunkel, Bruce
    See Nitty Gritty Dirt Band, The
Kuti, Fela 7
L7 12
LaBelle, Patti 8
Lady Miss Kier
    See Deee-lite
Ladysmith Black Mambazo 1
Laine, Cleo 10
Lake, Greg
    See Emerson, Lake & Palmer/Powell
LaLonde, Larry "Ler"
    See Primus
Lally, Joe
    See Fugazi
Lamm, Robert
    See Chicago
Lane, Jay
    See Primus
Lang, K. D. 4
Lanois, Daniel 8
Larkin, Patty 9
Lataille, Rich
    See Roomful of Blues
Lauper, Cyndi 11
Laurence, Lynda
    See Supremes, The
Lavin, Christine 6
Lavis, Gilson
    See Squeeze
Lawrence, Tracy 11
Lawry, John
    See Petra
Laws, Roland
    See Earth, Wind and Fire
Lawson, Doyle
    See Country Gentlemen, The
Leadbelly 6
Leadon, Bernie
    See Eagles, The
    Also see Nitty Gritty Dirt Band, The
Leavell, Chuck
    See Allman Brothers, The
LeBon, Simon
    See Duran Duran
Leckenby, Derek "Lek"
    See Herman's Hermits
Ledbetter, Huddie
    See Leadbelly
LeDoux, Chris 12
Led Zeppelin 1

Masdea, Jim
  See Boston
Masekela, Hugh **7**
Maseo, Baby Huey
  See De La Soul
Mason, Nick
  See Pink Floyd
Masse, Laurel
  See Manhattan Transfer, The
Massey, Bobby
  See O'Jays, The
Masur, Kurt **11**
Mathis, Johnny **2**
Matlock, Glen
  See Sex Pistols, The
Mattea, Kathy **5**
May, Brian
  See Queen
Mayall, John **7**
Mayfield, Curtis **8**
Mays, Odeen, Jr.
  See Kool & the Gang
Mazibuko, Abednigo
  See Ladysmith Black Mambazo
Mazibuko, Albert
  See Ladysmith Black Mambazo
MCA
  See Yauch, Adam
McBrain, Nicko
  See Iron Maiden
McCall, Renee
  See Sounds of Blackness
McCarrick, Martin
  See Siouxsie and the Banshees
McCartney, Paul **4**
  Also see Beatles, The
McCarty, Jim
  See Yardbirds, The
MC Clever
  See Digital Underground
McConnell, Page
  See Phish
McCracken, Chet
  See Doobie Brothers, The
McCready, Mike
  See Pearl Jam
McDaniels, Darryl "D"
  See Run-D.M.C.
McDonald, Barbara Kooyman
  See Timbuk 3
McDonald, Michael
  See Doobie Brothers, The
McDonald, Pat
  See Timbuk 3
McDorman, Joe
  See Statler Brothers, The
McDowell, Hugh
  See Electric Light Orchestra
McEntire, Reba **11**
MC Eric
  See Technotronic
McEuen, John
  See Nitty Gritty Dirt Band, The
McFee, John
  See Doobie Brothers, The

McFerrin, Bobby **3**
MC5, The **9**
McGeoch, John
  See Siouxsie and the Banshees
McGinley, Raymond
  See Teenage Fanclub
McGuinn, Jim
  See McGuinn, Roger
McGuinn, Roger
  See Byrds, The
McIntosh, Robbie
  See Pretenders, The
McIntyre, Joe
  See New Kids on the Block
McKagan, Duff
  See Guns n' Roses
McKay, Al
  See Earth, Wind and Fire
McKay, John
  See Siouxsie and the Banshees
McKean, Michael
  See St. Hubbins, David
McKee, Maria **11**
McKernan, Ron "Pigpen"
  See Grateful Dead, The
McKnight, Claude V. III
  See Take 6
McLachlan, Sarah **12**
McLaughlin, John **12**
McLean, Don **7**
McLeod, Rory
  See Roomful of Blues
MC Lyte **8**
McMeel, Mickey
  See Three Dog Night
McMurtry, James **10**
McQuillar, Shawn
  See Kool & the Gang
McRae, Carmen **9**
M.C. Ren
  See N.W.A.
McReynolds, Jesse
  See McReynolds, Jim and Jesse
McReynolds, Jim
  See McReynolds, Jim and Jesse
McReynolds, Jim and Jesse **12**
MC Serch **10**
McShane, Ronnie
  See Chieftains, The
McVie, Christine
  See Fleetwood Mac
McVie, John
  See Fleetwood Mac
Mdletshe, Geophrey
  See Ladysmith Black Mambazo
Meat Loaf **12**
Meat Puppets, The **13**
Medley, Bill **3**
Medlock, James
  See Soul Stirrers, The
Megadeth **9**
Mehta, Zubin **11**
Meine, Klaus
  See Scorpions, The
Meisner, Randy
  See Eagles, The

Melanie **12**
Melax, Einar
  See Sugarcubes, The
Mellencamp, John "Cougar" **2**
Menken, Alan **10**
Menuhin, Yehudi **11**
Menza, Nick
  See Megadeth
Mercer, Johnny **13**
Merchant, Natalie
  See 10,000 Maniacs
Mercier, Peadar
  See Chieftains, The
Mercury, Freddie
  See Queen
Metallica **7**
Methembu, Russel
  See Ladysmith Black Mambazo
Metheny, Pat **2**
Meyers, Augie
  See Texas Tornados, The
Michael, George **9**
Michaels, Bret
  See Poison
Midler, Bette **8**
Midnight Oil **11**
Midori **7**
Mike D
  See Diamond, Mike
Mikens, Robert
  See Kool & the Gang
Miles, Richard
  See Soul Stirrers, The
Miller, Glenn **6**
Miller, Jerry
  See Moby Grape
Miller, Mark
  See Sawyer Brown
Miller, Mitch **11**
Miller, Rice
  See Williamson, Sonny Boy
Miller, Roger **4**
Miller, Steve **2**
Milli Vanilli **4**
Mills, Fred
  See Canadian Brass, The
Milsap, Ronnie **2**
Mingus, Charles **9**
Ministry **10**
Miss Kier Kirby
  See Lady Miss Kier
Mitchell, Alex
  See Curve
Mitchell, John
  See Asleep at the Wheel
Mitchell, Joni **2**
Mizell, Jay
  See Run-D.M.C.
Moby Grape **12**
Moginie, Jim
  See Midnight Oil
Molloy, Matt
  See Chieftains, The
Moloney, Paddy
  See Chieftains, The

Örn, Einar
    See Sugarcubes, The
Örnolfsdottir, Margret
    See Sugarcubes, The
Orr, Casey
    See Gwar
Orzabal, Roland
    See Tears for Fears
Osborne, Bob
    See Osborne Brothers, The
Osborne, Sonny
    See Osborne Brothers, The
Osborne Brothers, The 8
Osbourne, Ozzy 3
    Also see Black Sabbath
Oslin, K. T. 3
Osmond, Donny 3
Ott, David 2
Outler, Jimmy
    See Soul Stirrers, The
Owen, Randy
    See Alabama
Owens, Buck 2
Owens, Ricky
    See Temptations, The
Page, Jimmy 4
    Also see Led Zeppelin
    Also see Yardbirds, The
Page, Patti 11
Paice, Ian
    See Deep Purple
Palmer, Carl
    See Emerson, Lake & Palmer/Powell
Palmer, David
    See Jethro Tull
Palmer, Robert 2
Pankow, James
    See Chicago
Pantera 13
Parazaider, Walter
    See Chicago
Parkening, Christopher 7
Parker, Charlie 5
Parker, Graham 10
Parker, Kris
    See KRS-One
Parker, Maceo 7
Parsons, Alan 12
Parsons, Gene
    See Byrds, The
Parsons, Gram 7
    Also see Byrds, The
Parsons, Tony
    See Iron Maiden
Parton, Dolly 2
Partridge, Andy
    See XTC
Pasemaster, Mase
    See De La Soul
Patinkin, Mandy 3
Patti, Sandi 7
Patton, Charley 11
Patton, Mike
    See Faith No More
Paul, Alan
    See Manhattan Transfer, The

Paul, Les 2
Paul, Vinnie
    See Pantera
Paulo, Jr.
    See Sepultura
Pavarotti, Luciano 1
Paxton, Tom 5
Payne, Bill
    See Little Feat
Payne, Scherrie
    See Supremes, The
Payton, Denis
    See Dave Clark Five, The
Payton, Lawrence
    See Four Tops, The
Pearl, Minnie 3
Pearl Jam 12
Peart, Neil
    See Rush
Pedersen, Herb
    See Desert Rose Band, The
Peduzzi, Larry
    See Roomful of Blues
Pegg, Dave
    See Jethro Tull
Pendergrass, Teddy 3
Pengilly, Kirk
    See INXS
Penn, Michael 4
Penner, Fred 10
Perahia, Murray 10
Peretz, Jesse
    See Lemonheads, The
Perez, Louie
    See Los Lobos
Perkins, Carl 9
Perkins, John
    See XTC
Perkins, Percell
    See Five Blind Boys of Alabama
Perkins, Steve
    See Jane's Addiction
Perlman, Itzhak 2
Perry, Doane
    See Jethro Tull
Perry, Joe
    See Aerosmith
Peter, Paul & Mary 4
Peters, Bernadette 7
Peterson, Oscar 11
Petersson, Tom
    See Cheap Trick
Petra 3
Pet Shop Boys 5
Petty, Tom 9
Phantom, Slim Jim
    See Stray Cats, The
Phelps, Doug
    See Kentucky Headhunters, The
Phelps, Ricky Lee
    See Kentucky Headhunters, The
Phife
    See Tribe Called Quest, A
Phil, Gary
    See Boston

Philips, Anthony
    See Genesis
Phillips, Chynna
    See Wilson Phillips
Phillips, Glenn
    See Toad the Wet Sprocket
Phillips, Harvey 3
Phillips, Sam 5
Phillips, Sam 12
Phillips, Simon
    See Judas Priest
Phish 13
Phungula, Inos
    See Ladysmith Black Mambazo
Piaf, Edith 8
Picciotto, Joe
    See Fugazi
Piccolo, Greg
    See Roomful of Blues
Pickett, Wilson 10
Pierson, Kate
    See B-52's, The
Pilatus, Rob
    See Milli Vanilli
Pink Floyd 2
Pinnick, Doug
    See King's X
Pirner, Dave
    See Soul Asylum
Pirroni, Marco
    See Siouxsie and the Banshees
Plakas, Dee
    See L7
Plant, Robert 2
    Also see Led Zeppelin
P.M. Dawn 11
Pogues, The 6
Poindexter, Buster
    See Johansen, David
Pointer, Anita
    See Pointer Sisters, The
Pointer, Bonnie
    See Pointer Sisters, The
Pointer, June
    See Pointer Sisters, The
Pointer, Ruth
    See Pointer Sisters, The
Pointer Sisters, The 9
Poison 11
Poland, Chris
    See Megadeth
Ponty, Jean-Luc 8
Pop, Iggy 1
Porter, Cole 10
Porter, Tiran
    See Doobie Brothers, The
Posdnuos
    See De La Soul
Potts, Sean
    See Chieftains, The
Powell, Billy
    See Lynyrd Skynyrd
Powell, Cozy
    See Emerson, Lake & Palmer/Powell

Romm, Ronald
   See Canadian Brass, The
Ronstadt, Linda **2**
Roomful of Blues **7**
Roper, De De
   See Salt-N-Pepa
Rosas, Cesar
   See Los Lobos
Rose, Axl
   See Guns n' Roses
Rose, Michael
   See Black Uhuru
Rosen, Gary
   See Rosenshontz
Rosenshontz **9**
Rosenthal, Jurgen
   See Scorpions, The
Rosenthal, Phil
   See Seldom Scene, The
Ross, Diana **1**
   Also see Supremes, The
Rossi, John
   See Roomful of Blues
Rossington, Gary
   See Lynyrd Skynyrd
Rota, Nino **13**
Roth, David Lee **1**
   Also see Van Halen
Roth, Ulrich
   See Scorpions, The
Rotsey, Martin
   See Midnight Oil
Rotten, Johnny
   See Lydon, John
   Also see Sex Pistols, The
Rourke, Andy
   See Smiths, The
Rowe, Dwain
   See Restless Heart
Rubin, Rick **9**
Rubinstein, Arthur **11**
Rudd, Phillip
   See AC/DC
Ruffin, David **6**
   Also see Temptations, The
Rundgren, Todd **11**
Run-D.M.C. **4**
Rush **8**
Rush, Otis **12**
Russell, Alecia
   See Sounds of Blackness
Russell, Mark **6**
Rutherford, Mike
   See Genesis
Rutsey, John
   See Rush
Ryan, David
   See Lemonheads, The
Ryan, Mick
   See Dave Clark Five, The
Ryder, Mitch **11**
Ryland, Jack
   See Three Dog Night
Sabo, Dave
   See Bon Jovi

Sade **2**
Sager, Carole Bayer **5**
Sahm, Doug
   See Texas Tornados, The
St. Hubbins, David
   See Spinal Tap
St. John, Mark
   See Kiss
St. Marie, Buffy
   See Sainte-Marie, Buffy
Sainte-Marie, Buffy **11**
Salerno-Sonnenberg, Nadja **3**
Saliers, Emily
   See Indigo Girls
Salt-N-Pepa **6**
Sam and Dave **8**
Sambora, Richie
   See Bon Jovi
Sampson, Doug
   See Iron Maiden
Samuelson, Gar
   See Megadeth
Samwell-Smith, Paul
   See Yardbirds, The
Sanborn, David **1**
Sanders, Steve
   See Oak Ridge Boys, The
Sanger, David
   See Asleep at the Wheel
Santana, Carlos **1**
Saraceno, Blues
   See Poison
Satriani, Joe **4**
Savage, Rick
   See Def Leppard
Sawyer Brown **13**
Saxa
   See English Beat, The
Saxon, Stan
   See Dave Clark Five, The
Scaccia, Mike
   See Ministry
Scaggs, Boz **12**
Scanlon, Craig
   See Fall, The
Scarface
   See Geto Boys, The
Schenker, Michael
   See Scorpions, The
Schenker, Rudolf
   See Scorpions, The
Schermie, Joe
   See Three Dog Night
Schickele, Peter **5**
Schlitt, John
   See Petra
Schmelling, Johannes
   See Tangerine Dream
Schmit, Timothy B.
   See Eagles, The
Schmoovy Schmoove
   See Digital Underground
Schneider, Florian
   See Kraftwerk
Schneider, Fred III
   See B-52's, The

Schnitzler, Conrad
   See Tangerine Dream
Scholten, Jim
   See Sawyer Brown
Scholz, Tom
   See Boston
Schroyder, Steve
   See Tangerine Dream
Schulze, Klaus
   See Tangerine Dream
Schuman, William **10**
Schuur, Diane **6**
Scofield, John **7**
Scorpions, The **12**
Scott, Bon (Ronald Belford)
   See AC/DC
Scott, George
   See Five Blind Boys of Alabama
Scott, Sherry
   See Earth, Wind and Fire
Scott-Heron, Gil **13**
Scruggs, Earl **3**
Seals, Dan **9**
Seals, Jim
   See Seals & Crofts
Seals & Crofts **3**
Sears, Pete
   See Jefferson Starship
Secada, Jon **13**
Sedaka, Neil **4**
   Seeger, Pete **4**
   Also see Weavers, The
Segovia, Andres **6**
Seldom Scene, The **4**
Sen Dog
   See Cypress Hill
Sepultura **12**
Seraphine, Daniel
   See Chicago
Sermon, Erick
   See EPMD
Setzer, Brian
   See Stray Cats, The
Severin, Steven
   See Siouxsie and the Banshees
Severinsen, Doc **1**
Sex Pistols, The **5**
Seymour, Neil
   See Crowded House
Shabalala, Ben
   See Ladysmith Black Mambazo
Shabalala, Headman
   See Ladysmith Black Mambazo
Shabalala, Jockey
   See Ladysmith Black Mambazo
Shabalala, Joseph
   See Ladysmith Black Mambazo
Shaffer, Paul **13**
Shakespeare, Robbie
   See Sly and Robbie
Shallenberger, James
   See Kronos Quartet
Shane, Bob
   See Kingston Trio, The
Shankar, Ravi **9**

Stevenson, Don
    See Moby Grape
Stewart, Dave
    See Eurythmics
Stewart, Ian
    See Rolling Stones, The
Stewart, John
    See Kingston Trio, The
Stewart, Larry
    See Restless Heart
Stewart, Rod 2
Stewart, William
    See Third World
Stills, Stephen 5
Sting 2
Stinson, Bob
    See Replacements, The
Stinson, Tommy
    See Replacements, The
Stipe, Michael
    See R.E.M.
Stoltz, Brian
    See Neville Brothers, The
Stone, Curtis
    See Highway 101
Stone, Doug 10
Stone, Sly 8
Stookey, Paul
    See Peter, Paul & Mary
Story, Liz 2
Story, The 13
Stradlin, Izzy
    See Guns n' Roses
Strain, Sammy
    See O'Jays, The
Strait, George 5
Stratton, Dennis
    See Iron Maiden
Stray Cats, The 11
Strayhorn, Billy 13
Street, Richard
    See Temptations, The
Streisand, Barbra 2
Strickland, Keith
    See B-52's, The
Strummer, Joe
    See Clash, The
Stryper 2
Stuart, Marty 9
Stubbs, Levi
    See Four Tops, The
Such, Alec Jon
    See Bon Jovi
Sugarcubes, The 10
Summer, Donna 12
Summer, Mark
    See Turtle Island String Quartet
Summers, Andy 3
Sumner, Bernard
    See New Order
Sun Ra 5
Super DJ Dmitry
    See Deee-lite
Supremes, The 6
Sure!, Al B. 13

Sutcliffe, Stu
    See Beatles, The
Sutherland, Joan 13
Sweat, Keith 13
Sweet, Matthew 9
Sweet, Michael
    See Stryper
Sweet, Robert
    See Stryper
Sweethearts of the Rodeo 12
Sweet Honey in the Rock 1
Swing, DeVante
    See Jodeci
Sykes, John
    See Whitesnake
Tabor, Ty
    See King's X
Taj Mahal 6
Take 6 6
Takemitsu, Toru 6
Talbot, John Michael 6
Talking Heads 1
Tandy, Richard
    See Electric Light Orchestra
Tangerine Dream 12
Tate, Geoff
    See Queensryche
Taylor, Andy
    See Duran Duran
Taylor, Billy 13
Taylor, Cecil 9
Taylor, Dick
    See Rolling Stones, The
Taylor, Earl
    See Country Gentlemen, The
Taylor, James 2
Taylor, James "J.T."
    See Kool & the Gang
Taylor, John
    See Duran Duran
Taylor, Johnnie
    See Soul Stirrers, The
Taylor, Koko 10
Taylor, Leroy
    See Soul Stirrers, The
Taylor, Mick
    See Rolling Stones, The
Taylor, Philip "Philthy Animal"
    See Motörhead
Taylor, Roger
    See Duran Duran
Taylor, Roger (Meadows)
    See Queen
Teagarden, Jack 10
Tears for Fears 6
Technotronic 5
Teenage Fanclub 13
Te Kanawa, Kiri 2
Temptations, The 3
Tennant, Neil
    See Pet Shop Boys
10,000 Maniacs 3
Terminator X
    See Public Enemy
Terrell, Jean
    See Supremes, The

Texas Tornados, The 8
Thayil, Kim
    See Soundgarden
They Might Be Giants 7
Thielemans, Toots 13
Thin Lizzy 13
Third World 13
Thomas, Alex
    See Earth, Wind and Fire
Thomas, David
    See Take 6
Thomas, David Clayton
    See Clayton-Thomas, David
Thomas, Dennis "D.T."
    See Kool & the Gang
Thomas, Mickey
    See Jefferson Starship
Thomas, Olice
    See Five Blind Boys of Alabama
Thompson, Dennis
    See MC5, The
Thompson, Les
    See Nitty Gritty Dirt Band, The
Thompson, Porl
    See Cure, The
Thompson, Richard 7
Threadgill, Henry 9
Three Dog Night 5
Tiffany 4
Tikaram, Tanita 9
Tilbrook, Glenn
    See Squeeze
Tillis, Mel 7
Tillis, Pam 8
Timbuk 3 3
Timmins, Margo
    See Cowboy Junkies, The
Timmins, Michael
    See Cowboy Junkies, The
Timmins, Peter
    See Cowboy Junkies, The
Tippin, Aaron 12
Tipton, Glenn
    See Judas Priest
Toad the Wet Sprocket 13
Tolhurst, Laurence
    See Cure, The
Toller, Dan
    See Allman Brothers, The
Tone-Loc 3
Tony K
    See Roomful of Blues
Tony! Toni! Toné! 12
Took, Steve Peregrine
    See T. Rex
Topham, Anthony "Top"
    See Yardbirds, The
Tork, Peter
    See Monkees, The
Torme, Mel 4
Torres, Hector "Tico"
    See Bon Jovi
Tosh, Peter 3
Toussaint, Allen 11
Townes, Jeffery
    See DJ Jazzy Jeff and the Fresh Prince

Whelan, Gavan
    See James
White, Alan
    See Yes
White, Barry **6**
White, Clarence
    See Byrds, The
White, Freddie
    See Earth, Wind and Fire
White, Maurice
    See Earth, Wind and Fire
White, Verdine
    See Earth, Wind and Fire
Whitehead, Donald
    See Earth, Wind and Fire
Whitesnake **5**
Whitford, Brad
    See Aerosmith
Whitley, Keith **7**
Whitwam, Barry
    See Herman's Hermits
Who, The **3**
Wiggins, Dwayne
    See Tony! Toni! Toné!
Wiggins, Raphael
    See Tony! Toni! Toné!
Wilder, Alan
    See Depeche Mode
Wilkeson, Leon
    See Lynyrd Skynyrd
Wilkinson, Keith
    See Squeeze
Williams, Andy **2**
Williams, Boris
    See Cure, The
Williams, Cliff
    See AC/DC
Williams, Dana
    See Diamond Rio
Williams, Deniece **1**
Williams, Don **4**
Williams, Hank, Jr. **1**
Williams, Hank, Sr. **4**
Williams, Joe **11**
Williams, John **9**
Williams, Lamar
    See Allman Brothers, The
Williams, Lucinda **10**
Williams, Otis
    See Temptations, The
Williams, Paul
    See Temptations, The
Williams, Paul **5**
Williams, Phillard
    See Earth, Wind and Fire
Williams, Vanessa **10**
Williams, Walter
    See O'Jays, The
Williamson, Sonny Boy **9**
Willie D.
    See Geto Boys, The
Willis, Kelly **12**
Willis, Larry
    See Blood, Sweat and Tears
Willis, Pete
    See Def Leppard

Willis, Victor
    See Village People, The
Willner, Hal **10**
Wills, Bob **6**
Wilson, Anne
    See Heart
Wilson, Brian
    See Beach Boys, The
Wilson, Carl
    See Beach Boys, The
Wilson, Carnie
    See Wilson Phillips
Wilson, Cassandra **12**
Wilson, Cindy
    See B-52's, The
Wilson, Dennis
    See Beach Boys, The
Wilson, Jackie **3**
Wilson, Kim
    See Fabulous Thunderbirds, The
Wilson, Mary
    See Supremes, The
Wilson, Nancy
    See Heart
Wilson, Ransom **5**
Wilson, Ricky
    See B-52's, The
Wilson, Wendy
    See Wilson Phillips
Wilson Phillips **5**
Wilton, Michael
    See Queensryche
Wimpfheimer, Jimmy
    See Roomful of Blues
Winans, Carvin
    See Winans, The
Winans, Marvin
    See Winans, The
Winans, Michael
    See Winans, The
Winans, Ronald
    See Winans, The
Winans, The **12**
Winfield, Chuck
    See Blood, Sweat and Tears
Winston, George **9**
Winter, Johnny **5**
Winter, Paul **10**
Winwood, Steve **2**
Wolstencraft, Simon
    See Fall, The
Womack, Bobby **5**
Wonder, Stevie **2**
Wood, Danny
    See New Kids on the Block
Wood, Ron
    See Rolling Stones, The
Wood, Roy
    See Electric Light Orchestra
Woods, Terry
    See Pogues, The
Woodson, Ollie
    See Temptations, The
Woody, Allen
    See Allman Brothers, The

Woolfolk, Andrew
    See Earth, Wind and Fire
Worrell, Bernie **11**
Wreede, Katrina
    See Turtle Island String Quartet
Wretzky, D'Arcy
    See Smashing Pumpkins
Wright, David "Blockhead"
    See English Beat, The
Wright, Jimmy
    See Sounds of Blackness
Wright, Norman
    See Country Gentlemen, The
Wright, Rick
    See Pink Floyd
Wright, Simon
    See AC/DC
Wurzel
    See Motörhead
Wyman, Bill
    See Rolling Stones, The
Wynette, Tammy **2**
Wynonna **11**
    Also see Judds, The
X **11**
XTC **10**
Ya Kid K
    See Technotronic
Yamamoto, Hiro
    See Soundgarden
Yamano, Atsuko
    See Shonen Knife
Yamano, Naoko
    See Shonen Knife
Yamashita, Kazuhito **4**
Yankovic, "Weird Al" **7**
Yanni **11**
Yardbirds, The **10**
Yarrow, Peter
    See Peter, Paul & Mary
Yates, Bill
    See Country Gentlemen, The
Yauch, Adam
    See Beastie Boys, The
Yearwood, Trisha **10**
Yella
    See N.W.A.
Yes **8**
Yoakam, Dwight **1**
York, John
    See Byrds, The
Young, Angus
    See AC/DC
Young, Faron **7**
Young, Fred
    See Kentucky Headhunters, The
Young, Grant
    See Soul Asylum
Young, Jeff
    See Megadeth
Young, Malcolm
    See AC/DC
Young, Neil **2**
Young, Richard
    See Kentucky Headhunters, The